Faulkner

Faulkner

Essays by
Warren Beck

The University of Wisconsin Press

Published 1976

The University of Wisconsin Press
Box 1379, Madison, Wisconsin 53701

The University of Wisconsin Press, Ltd.
70 Great Russell Street, London

First printing

Printed in the United States of America

DESIGNED BY GARY GORE
COMPOSED BY FOX VALLEY TYPESETTING, MENASHA, WISCONSIN
MANUFACTURED BY CUSHING MALLOY, INC., ANN ARBOR, MICHIGAN
TEXT AND DISPLAY LINES ARE SET IN BASKERVILLE

Library of Congress Cataloging in Publication Data
Beck, Warren.
Faulkner: essays.
1. Faulkner, William, 1897-1962 — Criticism and
interpretation — Addresses, essays, lectures. I. Title.
PS3511.A86Z625   813'.5'2   73-15258
ISBN 0-299-06500-6

To my dear sister, Marjorie
and her husband, Robert Kehlenbrink

Contents

ESSAYS AS OF 1941

1 Faulkner's Point of View   3
2 Faulkner and the South   18
3 William Faulkner's Style   34

FURTHER CONSIDERATIONS

4 Faulkner after 1940   55
5 Fictional Entities and the Artist's *Oeuvre*   103
6 Good and Evil   122
7 Realist and Regionalist   144
8 Short Stories into Novels   275
9 *Go Down, Moses*   334
    "Was"   347
    "The Fire and the Hearth"   351
    "Pantaloon in Black"   370

    The Story of Isaac McCaslin   374
    "The Old People"   377
    "The Bear"   382
    "Delta Autumn"   478
    Epilogue   537

    "Go Down, Moses"   571
10 *Requiem for a Nun*   583

ACHIEVEMENT AND CELEBRATION:
FAULKNER'S LAST TWO NOVELS

11 Faulkner in *The Mansion*   639
12 Told with Gusto   660

Essays as of 1941

1

Faulkner's Point of View

CRITICISM of William Faulkner's novels has diverged conspicuously between two tendencies. Some of the most discerning have praised Faulkner highly; for instance, six years ago Mark Van Doren spoke of his possessing "one of the greatest natural gifts to be found anywhere in America," and Conrad Aiken's recent article in the *Atlantic* was on the whole constructively appreciative. Even Henry Seidel Canby, after having written of *Sanctuary* that it showed "no concern for significance," "no predilection for 'ought,'" came around two years later to say of *Light in August,* "It is a novel of extraordinary force and insight . . . and filled with that spirit of compassion which saves those who look at life too closely from hardness and despair. . . . I think that no one can deny it the praise of life caught in its intensities both good and bad." Yet much journalistic criticism of Faulkner has continued to be detractory, sometimes even abusive; and such is almost always the tone toward him in those volumes on contemporary fiction which American professors write for their students and for one another.

This failure of much American criticism properly to evaluate and support the novels of William Faulkner seems based chiefly on two erroneous propositions — first, that Faulkner has no ideas, no point of view, and, second, that consequently

This essay first appeared in *College English,* May 1941, pp. 736-49.

3

he is melodramatic, a mere sensationalist. One academic critic has called his work the *reductio ad absurdum* of American naturalism and complains that there is "no cosmic echo . . . behind his atrocities"; another calls Faulkner's profound masterpiece *Absalom, Absalom!* disappointing, in that it presents "an experience of limited value"; another says Faulkner "is not a novelist of ideas but of mood and action, physical and psychic" — as though mood and action were antithetical to ideas, instead of their legitimate artistic media in fiction. Of Faulkner's whole work a dogmatic sectarian critic (who within three pages makes four mistakes of fact about the stories) says that "to read these books is to cross a desert of terrifying nihilism" and accuses Faulkner of almost mathematically computing a maximum of shock. Another, characterizing *Light in August* as "murder and rape turning on the spit over the flames of arson," says that in this book "nothing is omitted, except virtue."

One of the most recent insults to Faulkner's artistic integrity is Burton Rascoe's suggestion that he plays with his material and his readers, that he writes with his tongue in his cheek. Following the vogue of denying Faulkner any philosophic outlook and purpose, another academician accuses him of "the calculated manufacture of superfluous horrors." "He is a belated literary descendent of Edgar Allen Poe," writes one of the professors, in a favorite and utterly false correlation. "He works like Poe," says another, "to freeze the reader's blood"; still another says, "He stresses the grotesque and horrible to the point where they become simply ludicrous." Taking up where the pedagogues leave off, one leading periodical reviewer hurls the epithet "Mississippi Frankenstein"; another, in a title, sums up Faulkner's achievement as "witchcraft."

Perhaps the most obvious of these errors is the comparison to Poe. The association of ideas is typical of these critics' superficiality; Poe deals in horror, Faulkner presents horror — therefore Faulkner is like Poe. Horror is of different kinds, however. The essence of Poe's frightful fiction is unreality, product of a morbid taste for prearranged nightmares and self-induced hallucinations, that narcissism of the imagination which is the seamy side of romanticism. Faulkner, on the other hand, is a brilliant realist. In Poe's most typical stories there is little evidence that he studied other human beings, but it seems certain that Faulkner, like his character Gavin Stevens the attorney, might have been seen "squatting among the overalls on the porches of country stores for a whole summer afternoon, talking to them in their own idiom about nothing at all."

Indeed, if Faulkner in all his work does not have his eye studiously on the object, a locale and its *dramatis personae,* his has been a very foresighted piece of fabrication, for *The Hamlet,* published in 1940 but telling a story of the 1890's, is glanced back at in its details in *As I Lay Dying* (1930) and in *Sanctuary* (1931), and there are many other systematic connections back and forth between the novels, especially in reference to the tribes of Sartoris, Compson, Sutpen, and Snopes. On the map of Yoknapatawpha County appended to *Absalom, Absalom!* Faulkner writes himself down as "sole owner and proprietor," but this community centering in Jefferson either has more than a coincidental resemblance, however synthetic, to real Mississippians white, black, and brown, or else William Faulkner is running both God and the devil a close second as a creator and confounder of human beings. Unmistakably, whatever horror there is in Faulkner — and there is a great deal — is out of life.

It may be the very brilliance of Faulkner's realism that has confused others of the critics; details may have so startled them that they have missed the subtle implications of idea in the novels. Certainly the implications are there. While Faulkner differs radically from Poe in being a close observer and realistic reporter of the human tragedy, he departs just as radically from the naturalistic school's baldly objective, documentary method. He is constantly interpretive; he sees his subjects in the light of humane predilections, and thus his realism always intends signification. This lifts his most extreme passages above sensationalism; and striking as his scenes are, his conception of novels as meaningful wholes is still more impressive, at least for qualified attentive readers.

Faulkner's interpretive bent has also led him to transcend the modern realists' cult of a simply factual diction and colloquial construction and to employ instead a full, varied, and individual style. Perhaps, too, some of the unappreciative critics may have evaded the challenge of this style, with its overtone, ellipsis, and suspension, and so may have missed Faulkner's themes in somewhat the way of a high-school student reading *Hamlet* only as a melodramatic series of murders. However, the widely proclaimed frustrations over Faulkner's style, like the revulsions against his realism, will be dispelled once his point of view is grasped, for this style is a powerful instrument handled for the most part with great skill for the realization of his ideas.

William Faulkner's view of human life is one of the most pessimistic ever voiced in fiction, and his writing, like Mr. Compson's "sloped whimsical ironic hand out of Mississippi attenuated," is of a predominantly melancholy tone. "All breath," he says in *The Wild Palms,* has as its only immortality, "its infinite capacity for folly and pain." Not often, however, does Faulkner speak in his own right, out of the omniscience of third-person narrative, for he is devoted to dramatic form and to the perspective it supplies, and most of his stories are told largely through the consciousness of participant characters. And even when Faulkner himself speaks, through third-person narrative, he usually keys his utterance to the mood of the scene and makes himself the lyrical mouthpiece of his characters' experiences. Consequently, it is not possible to comprehend Faulkner's point of view from separate quotations but only from implications in his novels as wholes and from the positions of his various characters in relation to these implied themes.

His critics have sometimes failed to make the necessary distinction between the statements of his dramatic characters and his own ideas. The words of Mr. Compson, "history is an illusion of philosophers and fools," are shoved back into

Faulkner's own mouth by one recent critic and are made basis for asserting that Faulkner never transcends the level of bare perception but sees the universe as "bereft of authentic proprieties and the accents of logic," when certainly his keen sense of authentic proprieties and the accents of logic is part of Faulkner's artistic inspiration — a central part of that superhuman unrest in him which has produced so prolifically and so passionately.

Undoubtedly Faulkner, like any other novelist or dramatist, stands behind some of his characters, but which are his spokesmen cannot be decided except in terms of the preponderance and system of his ideas. Therefore it should be noted, for example, that in *Mosquitoes* it is not Faulkner but the flippant Semitic who declares that man's tendency to follow illusions to his death must be "some grand cosmic scheme for fertilizing the earth"; it is an ignorant, bitter man crazed by greed for supposed treasure — Armstid in *The Hamlet* — whom the author describes as digging himself "back into that earth which had produced him to be its born and fated thrall forever until he died"; and it is a man heartbroken by his wife's death — Houston in *The Hamlet* — who felt himself "victim of a useless and elaborate practical joke at the hands of the prime maniacal Risibility."

Even Faulkner's dramatization of such negative characters need not mislead the critic if he contemplates such portraits in their entirety — Houston's disenchantment, for instance, does not include a surrender to apathy, for he not only viewed the idiot Ike Snopes at his worst with "furious exasperation which was not rage but savage contempt and pity for all blind flesh capable of hope and grief," but he gave the poor fellow what help he could. Thus the reporter in *Pylon* says you "walk the earth with your arm crooked over your head to dodge until you finally get the old blackjack at last and can lay back down again," but in spite of that despairing view he is sympathetic and aggressively philanthropic.

Pity is significantly a common emotion among Faulkner's characters. The old justice who appears incidentally but vividly in the closing pages of *The Hamlet* looks at Mrs. Armstid, the victim of her husband's stubborn folly and Flem Snopes's rapacity, "with pity and grief." Hightower, in *Light in August,* murmurs "Poor man. Poor mankind," and his words encompass not only the negro murderer but his victim and the people who now pursue him. Such humane sensitivity is epitomized when Faulkner calls the reporter in *Pylon* "patron (even if no guardian) saint of all waifs, all the homeless the desperate and the starved," and describes him as manifesting "that air of worn and dreamy fury which Don Quixote must have had."

In many of Faulkner's stories there is the compassionate troubled observer — Quentin Compson in *The Sound and the Fury* and in *Absalom, Absalom!,* a whole chorus of country folk one by one in *As I Lay Dying,* Benbow in *Sanctuary,* Hightower in *Light in August,* the reporter in *Pylon,* and Ratliff in *The Hamlet.* In *The Unvanquished,* Bayard Sartoris, while closely involved in the action, also evolves into a typical Faulknerian observer as he matures. It is no doubt significant of Faulkner's own attitude that these compassionate observers so largely provide the reflective point of view from which the story is told and thereby determine its moral atmosphere. This typical technique is in itself refutation of the charge that Faulkner is nihilistic and merely sensational. Indeed, it shows that the intention of Faulkner's temperament is idealistic, while its awareness of the preponderant realities of human behavior is pessimistic, and hence its conviction is a melancholy which recoils in protest. This protest is, of course, not didactic but rather inheres in an implicative tone, which the imaginative reader will not miss and will respect for its art as well as its idealism.

The skeptical may test this thesis fairly by re-reading *Sanctuary* (not the most skilful or organic of Faulkner's narratives) with attention fixed primarily on Horace Benbow. His unrest amid hypocrisies and viciousness and his fanatical resistance suffice to throw the events of the book into their true ethical perspective. Faulkner's exuberant and as yet undisciplined realism at times carried him into digression, as with Virgil and Fonzo at Madame Reba's house, or Red's riotous funeral, or the unassimilated and hence anticlimatic documentary chapter on Popeye's youth; however, behind the main events of the plot is the brooding corrective spirit of the perfectionist Benbow, bringing the rich imagery and profusion of fact into harmony with the dire theme. And what Faulkner achieves not without extravagances in *Sanctuary* can be found done better in *Light in August* and done to perfection in *Absalom, Absalom!*

Naturally revulsion often carries these compassionate observers into aloofness. The clergyman Hightower, perhaps the most broadly sympathetic of all, is also the most detached. Deprived of his pulpit because of his wife's scandalous behavior, he has lived alone and inactive for years; and when he hears that the posse is about to catch Joe Christmas, he refuses to be involved, saying to himself, "I won't! I won't! I have bought immunity. I have paid." Later when Byron Bunch comes to him with Lena's troubles and those of Mrs. Hines and Joe, the tears run down his cheeks like sweat as he says, "But it is not right to bother me, to worry me, when I have—when I have taught myself to stay—have been taught by them to stay— That this should come to me, taking me after I am old." Quentin Compson's revulsion is still more acute, for he is more severely involved through his sister's disgrace, and he retreats all the way into self-annihilation. Even the quizzical self-possessed Ratliff, in *The Hamlet,* pauses somewhere between despair and defiance to thank God "men have done learned how to forget quick what they ain't brave enough to try to cure." Benbow makes a more direct and moodier self-accusation—"I lack courage: that was left out of me. The machinery is all here, but it won't run." And Ratliff, after stepping in several times on the side of the angels, cries out to a companion, "'I could do more, but I won't. I won't, I tell you!'"

These retreats are not repudiations of principle; they are simply a natural human weakness and weariness, which Faulkner represents dramatically for purposes of characterization, and which serve also the artistic method of vicissitude. It is significant that the pendulum of mood usually swings back to positive assertion; Hightower and Benbow and the reporter, for instance, return again and again to the struggle. Even the crazed Quentin Compson realizes that beyond despair is something still more intolerable — indifference; he says, "It's not when you realize that nothing can help you — religion, pride, anything — it's when you realize that you don't need any aid." Benbow, oppressed by "the evil, the injustice, the tears," lets himself think it might be better if Goodwin, the woman and her child, Popeye, and he himself too were all dead, "cauterized out of the old and tragic flank of the world," and goes on to imagine "perhaps it is upon the instant that we realize, admit that there is a logical pattern to evil, that we die"; but he does not cease to postulate and appeal to a logical pattern of good in his efforts to save a falsely accused man and to befriend that man's family. Quentin Compson is obsessed by his father's teaching that "all men are just accumulations, dolls stuffed with sawdust swept up from the trash heaps where all previous dolls had been thrown away the sawdust flowing from what wound in what side that not for me died not," but nevertheless he cannot accept his father's argument that virginity is just words.

These characters' refusal to surrender principle even when they seem overmatched by circumstance not only intensifies their melancholy, and Faulkner's, but enhances it with human dignity. Indeed, in the darkest pages of these novels Faulkner and his compassionate spectators often exemplify Carlyle's dictum that a man's sorrow is the inverted image of his nobility. The reporter in *Pylon* tells his editor that he tried to let the fliers alone but couldn't — couldn't refrain, that is, from the impulse to help them, in spite of their desperate state beyond his help, and his own acknowledged awkwardness. Benbow says he "cannot stand idly by and see injustice," and when Miss Jenny suggests Pilate's cynical query, Benbow declares himself still moved to oppose what he identifies as "that irony which lurks in events." When Goodwin's woman assumes that she must give herself to Benbow in lieu of cash payment for his legal services, he says, "Can't you see that perhaps a man might do something just because he knew it was right, necessary to the harmony of things that it be done?" Ratliff similarly asserts that in opposing the Snopes clan he was "protecting something that don't want nothing but to walk and feel the sun and wouldn't know how to hurt no man even if it would and wouldn't want to even if it could, just like I wouldn't stand by and see you steal a meat-bone from a dog."

Even the skeptical Mr. Compson often shows awareness that the moral issue is not fragmentary. He sees human virtue manifested sometimes in acts of apparent evil—"Have you noticed," he asks Quentin, "how so often when we try to reconstruct the causes which lead up to the actions of men and women, how with a sort of astonishment we find ourselves now and then reduced to the belief, the only possible belief, that they stemmed from some of the old virtues? the thief who steals not for greed but for love, the murderer who kills not out of lust but pity?" Thus the man whose motives the Compsons try to reconstruct—Thomas Sutpen—is driven on in his acquisitiveness, they find, by a boyhood complex of honor; and even in his materialistic pride he holds himself to a code which will not let him traduce the wife who deceived him. The persistence of such moral resolution in Faulkner's beset and melancholy characters is typified in Judith Sutpen's feeling that "it can't matter . . . and yet it must matter because you keep on trying."

Closely related to this attitude, and furnishing another fixed point in the ethics of Faulkner's characters, is an idealization of honesty. The aristocratic Rosa Millard, in *The Unvanquished,* never whipped her grandson for anything but lying and prayed for pardon for herself after she had lied to a Yankee officer to protect her family; later, having obtained mules by forged requisitions upon Union troops and having sold them back to other Union troops for gold, she confesses before the congregation, asks their prayers, and then distributes the money among them as she had intended. When at last she is murdered by carpet-baggers, the negro boy Ringo says discerningly of her, "It wasn't him or Ab Snopes either that kilt her. It was them mules. That first batch of mules we got for nothing." Nor is this integrity represented as limited to the aristocrats of the Old South. Addie Bundren, the country woman, believed "deceit was such that, in a world where it was, nothing else could be very bad or very important." Her carpenter son Cash holds to what he calls "the olden right teaching that says to drive the nails down and trim the edges well always like it was for your own use and comfort you were making it," and so great is his passion for rightness that when asked how far he fell when he broke his leg, he answers, "Twenty-eight foot, four and a half inches, about." Relevantly, honest Cash is the Bundren who judges most fairly the erratic brother Darl, crediting his motives even while condemning his acts. Byron Bunch is another honest workman; he keeps his own time strictly when he works alone at the mill, and he says, "It beats all how some folks think that making or getting money is a kind of game where there are not any rules at all." No wonder that, when Hightower hears Byron's class disdainfully called "hillbillies," he says, "They are fine people, though. Fine men and women." Another example is in *The Wild Palms;* the lost convict has the woman wash his prison suit, while he goes barebacked in the blistering sun; then he wraps up the clean suit, saving it for his return; and Faulkner himself remarks that the woman said nothing, "since she too doubtless knew what his reason was, . . . she too had stemmed at some point from the same dim hill-bred Abraham."

Often the unassuming virtue of simple people provides the foil to evil and furnishes the atmospheric tension in Faulkner's scenes, as, for instance, an incidental character in *The Hamlet,* a farmer whose gentility is symbolized by the spray of peach blossoms he holds in his teeth, who plows the Armstid field so that Mrs. Armstid won't be forced to do it but who will not answer when Ratliff asks how many hours he has put in for his neighbor, this detail pointing up Henry Armstid's brutality to his wife and Flem Snopes's ruthless seizure of the five dollars she had earned weaving. In the same way the professional integrity and chivalry of the flier Roger Shumann, in *Pylon,* contrasts with the commercial trickery and inhumanity of the airport promoters. Thus Faulkner furnishes frames of moral reference, not only by suggesting ideals through his repellent pictures of their opposites but by showing protagonists of them among all sorts of men and women.

And thus Faulkner's deep pessimism does not proceed from a denial of values but from a melancholy recognition of the great weight of evil opposition to very real values. Not much can be done for the Mrs. Armstids in a community overrun by rapacious Snopeses, nor can Benbow effectually help Goodwin and his woman against Popeye's viciousness, Temple's treachery, and the mob's intolerance and brutality. Thus when Faulkner's compassionate observers actually intervene, they are quite often defeated. Byron Bunch is the most successful of them all, and that perhaps because he largely shifts to Hightower the paralyzing contemplative function and himself seeks simply to protect and cherish the abandoned Lena and her child. Lena is a still simpler character, representing the will to life in an elementary human form, and she passes through Jefferson at the time of Miss Burden's murder and the mobbing of Joe Christmas as untouched and unperturbed as Eck Snopes's little boy among the wild horses that injured grown men. Most of Faulkner's characters are more complex and less stable than Lena; they are far gone in all sorts of involvements, either with others or with their own fantasies. Hence conflict and impasse in lives where suffering prevails and succor is difficult.

Under the resultant emotional strain Faulkner's characters sometimes attribute malevolence to the cosmos, but they more often see men themselves as the direct agents of evil. The whole theme of Faulkner's early work, *Mosquitoes,* seems to be that humans pester one another insufferably by passionate encroachments of one egotism upon another. Seeing these aggressive tendencies accumulated in social pressures, Wilbourne, the lover in *The Wild Palms,* who attempts with

Charlotte to escape out of the world, thinks "you are born submerged in anonymous lockstep with the teeming anonymous myriads of your time and generation; you get out of step once, falter once, and you are trampled to death." And the ironic repercussions of consequence are inevitable. In *Sanctuary* young Gowan Stevens says he has injured no one but himself by his folly, whereas his drunken blundering had actually set into motion the whole chain of events that brought, besides Temple's debauchment, the deaths of Tommy, Red, and Goodwin. Hightower thinks "it is any man's privilege to destroy himself, so long as he does not injure any one else," but then almost at once he realizes that his ego had been the instrument of his wife's despair and shame.

When the parachute jumper in *Pylon* tells the reporter goodbye, he thanks him for "trying to help," but he advises, "Stick to the kind of people you are used to after this." That, however, is difficult counsel, not only for the reporter, but for most of Faulkner's characters. They are not used to one another, never become used to one another; they are as Addie Bundren sees human beings, "each with his and her secret and selfish thought, and blood strange to each other blood." A key to the enigma of this separation may be found in a bit of omniscient narrative where Faulkner says, "Man knows so little about his fellows. In his eyes all men or women act upon what he believes would motivate him if he were mad enough to do what that other man or woman is doing." *If he were mad enough.* To the spectator, mankind seems predominantly irrational. This does not mean that Faulkner himself repudiates rationality; he seems rather to hold with the judge, in the short story "Beyond," who says he cannot divorce himself from reason enough to accept the pleasant and labor-saving theory of nihilism.

Faulkner's own inclination is shown by his endowing his most positive characters, his observers, with two primary elements of rationality — inquiry and disinterestedness — and with the reasonable man's idealization of justice. Yet in the whole body of Faulkner's work the results thus far of man's struggles toward rational self-control and social adjustment are not shown to be encouraging. The rector in *Soldiers' Pay* is convinced that man learns scarcely anything as he goes through this world and nothing whatever of help or benefit. The open conflict between human passions and rationality, and, alternatively, the unsatisfactory compromises of that conflict in woodenly conventional restraints, create the paradoxes so poignantly dramatized in Faulkner's most abstractly symbolic story, *The Wild Palms*. Wilbourne repudiates man's self-imposed systems and tries to live all for love; the convict, swept away on the flooded river, laboriously returns himself, the woman he had been told to rescue, and even the boat he was sent in; both men get prison sentences. The ironic dissonances of this somber novel, its dilemmas of escape and surrender, love and suffering, freedom and fate, and basically of reason and passion, give an incomparable suggestion of the confused and turbulent life of man in his present stage of imperfect mental and moral development.

Tull, in *As I Lay Dying*, suggests a severe functional limitation of the human brain: "It's like a piece of machinery: it won't stand a whole lot of racking." Perhaps Faulkner's frequent inclusion of feeble-minded characters is the result not only of their horrid fascination for his own acutely sensitive and subtle consciousness, but also to emphasize the precariousness and difficulty of rationality, the resemblance of the supposedly sane and the insane, and the short distance thus far traveled in the evolution of mind. The idiot, in the cow-stealing episode in *The Hamlet,* is described as one who "is learning fast now, who has learned success and then precaution and secrecy and how to steal and even providence; who has only lust and greed and bloodthirst and a moral conscience to keep him awake at night, yet to acquire." Thus far human rationality is not strong enough to rule out lust, greed, and bloodthirst; it can only recoil at them, usually after indulging them. And Cash suggests that there is little distinction between the various stages of supposed rationality in man: "I ain't so sho that ere a man has the right to say what is crazy and what aint. It's like there was a fellow in every man that's done a-past the sanity or the insanity, that watches the sane and the insane doings of that man with the same horror and the same astonishment."

There may be no such detached and perceptive fellow in every man, or even in most men; but there is such a fellow in William Faulkner, and all his works show his horror and astonishment, proceeding from an exacting and outraged idealism. Faulkner's integrity is all the more obvious in that his is an advanced outpost's stand against odds, the odds of the predominance of base passions over supposed rationality and their resultant confusions in the average man. The desperateness of the issue, as he pictures it, is what gives his books their startling intensity, unequaled in our contemporary fiction. Faulkner's own extreme mood, growing out of his absolute demands, has been so powerfully communicated that reading him is like an actual experience of catastrophe — not only the "lightning and tempest, battle, murder, and sudden death" from which all men would be delivered, but, what is still more terrifying, "all inordinate and sinful affections."

His is, indeed, an apocalyptic vision of sin and of its complex consequences. He is unsurpassed in recording those spasms of greed and lustfulness and animosity that eclipse human qualities and saddle men with fixations which are not so much ideas as appetites. He has epitomized such crises in his record of Jiggs, the mechanic in *Pylon,* as he goes on drinking: "He could have heard sounds, even voices, from the alley beneath the window if he had been listening. But he was not. All he heard now was that thunderous silence and solitude in which man's spirit crosses the eternal repetitive rubicon of his vice in the instant after the terror and before the triumph becomes dismay — the moral and spiritual waif shrieking his feeble I-am-I into the desert of chance and disaster." Faulkner can picture as well the despair of the rational and well-intentioned when they contemplate uncontrollable suffusions of passion in others and oppose their results. Such, on a broad narrative scale, is Ratliff confronting Snopes, Benbow maneuvering against Popeye and the townspeople, Bayard Sartoris resisting his father and Drusilla, and Quentin Compson viewing his family in *The Sound and the Fury* and the South's evil genius in *Absalom, Absalom!*

Those who lack Faulkner's knowledge of good and evil, or lack his courage in facing knowledge, may shut their eyes and put their hands over their ears while they gibber about Frankenstein or nihilism. Such ostrich tactics become increasingly ridiculous in a world where a recrudescense of irrationality and brutal passions have pointed up for even the most impercipient those melancholy facts about human nature and progress which Faulkner has confronted all along and has unequivocally attacked. A virile critical approach will first recognize the coherent rationality and humanity of Faulkner's point of view, and might then profitably go on to its particular sources, in Faulkner's own experience and in his contemplation of his native South, past and present, and so might finally come to a reappraisal of his narrative techniques, so brilliantly adapted to his profound artistic visions.

2

Faulkner and the South

ALTHOUGH for more than a decade William Faulkner's successive novels have made a conspicuous contribution to American literature, their extraordinary values, both artistic and sociological, have yet to be recognized. Faulkner's searching view of life has not always been rightly and fully understood; furthermore, the novel's wide base in Southern history and present-day society, and the author's profoundly philosophical interpretation of that history and society, have not been appreciated.

William Faulkner grew up in the South, and of the South. He was born in Mississippi, of a distinguished family which had included governors and generals and one man of letters. After two years at the University of Mississippi, Faulkner joined the Canadian Flying Corps in July 1918 as "cadet for pilot," was transferred to the Royal Air Force, and was in preliminary stages of training at the University of Toronto when the war ended. After the war he traveled in Europe and sojourned briefly in New Orleans, but he returned to Oxford, Mississippi, where he has lived ever since. He has not cut himself off from his roots; instead he has attempted to penetrate and utilize those aspects of life presented him by heritage and circumstance.

Faulkner's conspicuous melancholy seems to have been con-

This essay first appeared in *The Antioch Review*, Spring 1941, pp. 82-94.

tributed to by two wars—not only the first World War, but the American Civil War. His disillusionment was indicated in his first novel, *Soldiers' Pay,* with its ghastly portrait of the disfigured flier's return and his frivolous sweetheart's revulsion and infidelity. Intensification of melancholy by World War experiences may be traced also in a short story, "Ad Astra." Herein the concept attributed by Hemingway to Gertrude Stein—"You are all a lost generation"—recurs in a still more somber form; Faulkner's character remarks, "All this generation which fought in the war are dead tonight. But we do not yet know it." And in another story, "All the Dead Pilots," Faulkner himself says that

all the old pilots dead on the eleventh of November . . . swaggered hard and drank hard because they had found that being dead was not as quiet as they had heard it would be.

In their composite experience, Faulkner says, "there stood into sight the portent and the threat of what the race could bear and become."

The most profound generalization of this war-born melancholy is in the description in *Sartoris* of Narcissa Benbow contemplating the boyhood miniature of John Sartoris, her husband Bayard's twin brother, shot down over the western front in 1918:

And as Narcissa held the small oval in her hand while the steady blue eyes looked quietly back at her and from the whole face among its tawny curls, with its smooth skin and child's mouth, there shone like a warm radiance something sweet and merry and wild, she realized as she never had before the blind tragedy of human events. And while she sat motionless with the medallion in her hand and Miss Jenny thought she was looking at it, she was cherishing the child under her own heart with all the aroused constancy of her nature: it was as though already she could discern the dark shape of that doom which she had incurred, standing beside her chair, waiting and biding its time.

In all Faulkner's novels this "dark shape of doom" is recognized as eternal and omnipresent. Faulkner is chronologically of that generation which went to the first World War when they were barely out of their teens, but he rapidly transcended the view which narrowed and paralyzed some of them, that this catastrophe was unique, a special fate victimizing them as no other men before them had been victimized. In *Sartoris* Faulkner makes Horace Benbow say, on his return from France, that within ten years individual ex-soldiers will "realize that the A. E. F. didn't invent disillusion." Faulkner's own reflective temperament seems to have risen almost at once above the special outlook of the "lost generation" and its attendant limitations.

To the sense of man's fate, sharpened by personal knowledge of war's violence, is added in Faulkner's make-up the consciousness of his native South's tragic history, with the interruption and wastage of its original culture, and its inheritance of economic and moral dilemmas. The real and complete Faulkner first stands out in his third novel, *Sartoris,* where the theme of the soldier's return from France is linked to the theme of the decay of an old Southern family, and of all the traditions which once supported it. As the South's dilemmas are apparently insoluble, so is memory of their precipitation in the Civil War inescapable. In Faulkner's novels the post-bellum South seems to stand like Lot's wife, petrified in a morbid backward glance at the holocaust consuming a damned people. Considering this, the Canadian Shreve describes Quentin Compson's land as "a kind of vacuum filled with wraithlike and indomitable anger and pride and glory at and in happenings that occurred and ceased fifty years ago."

This view of the South, and the mood of his return to it, is one thing which sets off Faulkner from the rest of the literary lost generation. The man who had known war's horrors in his youth seems to have brought back an enlarged perspective which discerned the decadence of his native region while still holding to his associations with it. That confrontation, with its unavoidable demands both on sympathy and on judgment, must have created the dynamic tension so obvious in Faulkner's temperament — a tension productive, in the whole body of his work, of the reflectiveness which raises him so far above

the inverted aestheticism of the post-war school of Hemingway. Faulkner is a Mississippian who has transcended pro-
vincialism without losing artistic devotion to a locale; he is a
Southerner who has become disinterested without losing interest. No wonder he is melancholy; his is the excruciation of a
Hamlet, forced to chide his own mother, on the grounds of
his realistic discernment of fact and the demands of his indomitable idealism. And thus in the midst of his melancholy
he has been able to grasp themes larger than those of his
contemporaries.

Faulkner's detachment and judiciousness concerning the
South are not completely shared by any of his characters, save
perhaps Bayard at the close of *The Unvanquished*. Even Mr.
Compson sees those of Civil War times as "people too as we
are, and victims too as we are, but victims of a different circumstance, simpler and therefore, integer for integer, larger,
more heroic and the figures therefore more heroic too, not
dwarfed and involved but distinct, uncomplex," which leads
him to call them "shadowy paragons," "possessing now heroic
proportions." The most striking instance of ancestor-worship
is in the significant character of Hightower, in *Light in
August*. In the "final copper light of afternoon," the "lam-
bent suspension of August," his life renews itself in recollections of his grandfather, a Confederate cavalryman killed in a
raid at Jefferson. Hightower's boyhood had been meager of
experience and his later life had been ruined by the scandalous failure of his marriage and his resultant ostracism, and so in
the imaginative reconstruction of his grandfather's exploit he
seeks intimations of the heroic, as redemption from the sordidness around him. His addiction to this dream is a vice, however; he is ensnared in an habitual nostalgia which has helped
shut him off from reality and constructive activity. Hightower's story suggests a stultification of Southern psychology, a
self-insulation from issues presently confronting it.

As Faulkner shows it, this preoccupation with a cult existed
before the Civil War and continued in a variety of degenera-
tive imitations. An early effect of the South's immersion in its

provincial illusions was the conferring of military command, says Faulkner, "by an absolute caste system" upon "generals who should not have been generals," who were without training or aptitude for learning, and who contributed to the loss of many battles by what old Bayard Sartoris calls, for its combination of valor and folly, "the goddamnedest army the world ever saw." In a post-bellum stage Southern complacency moves Mrs. Compson to declare that God would not permit certain things to happen to her, because she is a lady. In its secondary form of snobbery, the hallucination leads Temple Drake to assert again and again, as a demand for privilege and as talisman against evil, "My father's a judge"; and the tradition of gentility and gallantry reaches its final perversion in her drunken escort Gowan Stevens, who takes Temple into Goodwin's sinister farmhouse, gets himself knocked down in a quarrel over her "honor," and then deserts her, after which he can still write Narcissa Benbow a Byronic note (which shrewd Miss Jenny calls "a delicate operation on the human heart without anaesthetic") sentimentally consoling himself that he alone has suffered.

Certain other Faulkner characters, however, cannot flatter themselves with the unction of a decayed legend. Their consciousness of the South's real history and position is painfully acute; they have come individually to what Mr. Coldfield, in *Absalom, Absalom!,* foresaw as

that day when the South would realize that it was now paying the price for having erected its economic edifice not on the rock of stern morality but on the shifting sands of opportunism and moral brigandage.

Hence what Rosa Coldfield feels as "fatality and curse on the South." Yet no matter how detached and judiciously critical Faulkner's Southerners become, most of them are still bound by their instinctive and habitual filial piety, and are not inclined to disown their infirm, corrupt mother. The hypersensitive Quentin Compson, conceiving of "the South, the deep South dead since 1865 and peopled with garrulous out-

raged baffled ghosts," thinks of himself as two separate Quen-
tins, the one preparing for Harvard, and the one "still too
young to deserve yet to be a ghost, but nevertheless having to
be one for all that, since he was born and bred in the deep
South." Thus, Faulkner says that

he was not a being, an entity, he was a commonwealth. He was a barracks
filled with stubborn back-looking ghosts still recovering, even forty-three
years afterward, from the fever which had cured the disease, waking from
the fever without even knowing that it had been the fever itself which they
had fought against and not the sickness, looking with stubborn recalcitrance backward beyond the fever and into the disease with actual regret,
weak from the fever yet free of the disease and not even aware that the
freedom was that of impotence.

Quentin's Canadian-born Harvard roommate Shreve caus-
tically remarks, "The South. Jesus. No wonder you folks all
outlive yourselves by years and years and years." "Why do they
live there?" asks Shreve. "Why do they live at all?" And on
another occasion, "Jesus, the South is fine, isn't it. It's better
than the theatre, isn't it. It's better than Ben Hur, isn't it. No
wonder you have to come away now and then, isn't it." This
collegiate jesting ironically emphasizes the mental torture of
Quentin, who in *Absalom, Absalom!* has been witness in
imagination, and the philosophical expositor, of Thomas
Sutpen's overthrow by the South, and who sees in his own
family, in *The Sound and the Fury,* the irredeemable products
of a cycle of degeneration. Along with Benbow and Hightower
and the Bayard Sartoris of *The Unvanquished,* Quentin
Compson is undoubtedly one of his creator's chief representa-
tives, and it is perhaps an echo of Faulkner himself at the close
of *Absalom, Absalom!* when Quentin must cry out to himself
the repeated assurance that he does not hate the South. Quentin's suicide is the escape of a fastidious mind from the horror
and shame of life as his own family leads it. Significantly the
Compson who best endures is the thirty-three year old idiot
Ben; he bellows when the carriage takes an unaccustomed
turn which presents an unfamiliar scene, but when the cus-

tomary route is resumed, he sits quiet. Thus the final rut of
decadent formality and tradition is symbolized in the closing
sentence of *The Sound and the Fury:*

The broken flower drooped over Ben's fist and his eyes were empty and
blue and serene again as cornice and facade flowed smoothly once more
from left to right; post and tree, window and doorway, and signboard,
each in its ordered place.

Faulkner's most comprehensive view of the South's history is
contained in the magnificently executed *Absalom, Absalom!*.
Not only Thomas Sutpen's whole life is represented, from his
boyhood in the 1820s to his death on his Mississippi plantation
in 1869, but his story and subsequent events in the life of his
family are reconstructed from observation and hearsay in
1910, so that the novel sketches almost a century, with the
Civil War as its crisis, and with the dramatic arc of Sutpen's
rise and fall as a graph of slavery's evil and the furious fatality
of retribution.

Sutpen's original trouble, Quentin discovers through his
father and grandfather, was innocence; as a poor white moun-
taineer he

didn't even know there was a country all divided and fixed and neat with a
people living on it all divided and fixed and neat because of what color
their skins happened to be and what they happened to own.

(The irony is Quentin's, but certainly it is Faulkner's also,
since no author can create an irony of a higher order than he
himself shares.) At first the young Sutpen thinks that the
luckier white men would be "slower and loather" than the unlucky to take advantage of their fortune of birth or to take
credit for it, but he is disillusioned. When he is turned away
from the front door of the big house where he has been sent on
an errand, to his backwoods mind it is

like he might have been sent with a lump of lead or even a few molded
bullets so that the man who owned the fine rifle could shoot it, and the

man came to the door and told him to leave the bullets on a stump at the edge of the woods, not even letting him come close enough to look at the rifle.

He knows that "something would have to be done about it; he would have to do something about it in order to live with himself for the rest of his life." At first he thinks of shooting the owner of the house (just as his father and other poor whites had relieved themselves by beating up a man simply because he was "that goddam son of a bitch Pettibone's nigger"). But young Sutpen is shrewd enough to make a tactical compromise; he tells himself "this ain't a question of rifles. So to combat them you have got to have what they have that made them do what the man did." In that thought is born Sutpen's lifelong and fatal complex, that he must have "land and niggers and a fine house," that he must found a family and leave behind a son of his name. The Civil War ruins him as a landowner, and miscegenation wrecks his hopes for family; but his error, his "initial mistake" for which he patiently searches (and unsuccessfully, "he not calling it retribution, no sins of the father come home to roost") is obviously his unprincipled surrender to and fanatical participation in the unrighteous caste system at which he had at first taken affront.

Thus Quentin's grandfather sees him trying to hold "his code of logic and morality . . . whose balanced sum and product declined, refused to swim or even float." Faulkner seems to imply that for all its rationalization into a code, the South's system, as imitated by Sutpen, was untenable and productive of aberration because in victimizing the Negro the South lost its integrity. Hightower's father had been "an abolitionist almost before the sentiment had become a word to percolate down from the North," and his disapproval of slavery, Hightower realizes, lay in a throwback to the "austerity" of pioneer times when a man had to do for himself "by means of a sheer fortitude." Here again, as in Faulkner's frequent idealizations of honesty, is an index to a fixed value and the resurgent virtue it elicits.

Picturing the post-bellum fate of the South and Southerners, Faulkner seems to adumbrate what Rosa Coldfield
calls

that justice which presides over human events which, incept in the individual, runs smooth, less claw than velvet: but which, by man or woman
flouted, drives on like fiery steel and overrides both weakly just and unjust
strong, both vanquisher and innocent victimized, ruthless for appointed
right and truth.

It is a justice sometimes working for redress through man's
destructive violence. In Sutpen's story of the West Indian slave
riots, the smell of the burning sugar is as if intensified by the
"secret dark years which had created the hatred and implacability." Faulkner does not attribute implacability, however, to
the typical Negroes in his Mississippi scenes. He more often
shows them resigned in that state of life to which it has pleased
generations of white folks to call them. "It rests with the
servant to lend dignity to an unnatural proceeding," he writes
in *Mosquitoes,* and frequently he shows the black man making
that contibution. The Negro's unnatural, paradoxical status is
keenly felt by Faulkner, as in his description of overalls, "that
harsh and shapeless denim cut to an iron pattern and sold by
the millions — that burlesque uniform and regalia of the tragic
burlesque of the sons of Ham." Quentin Compson realizes that
"a nigger is not a person so much as a form of behavior: a sort
of obverse reflection of the white people he lives among." He
credits that behavior as having a quality of "shabby and
timeless patience, of static serenity: that blending of childlike
and ready incompetence and paradoxical reliability that tends
and protects them it loves out of all reason and robs them
steadily and evades responsibility and obligations by means
too barefaced to be called subterfuge," yet showing "a fond
and unflagging tolerance for whitefolks' vagaries like that of a
grandparent for unpredictable and troublesome children."
Caspey, the family factotum in *Sartoris,* is a full-length
picture and something of a caricature of such a Negro. A
more profoundly conceived and more symbolic Negro
character, perhaps the finest in all of Faulkner, is in *The*

Sound and the Fury, the servant Dilsey, who is crucified by work and worry, who speaks with open bitterness to her employers and her own family, but whose fidelity, beneficence, and endurance are unending. There is an unforgettable glimpse of her in the Negro church, when "two tears slid down her fallen cheeks, in and out of the myriad coruscations of immolation and abnegation and time."

Significantly, Faulkner's most implacable characters are not pure Negroes, but those in whom is a mixture of black and white bloods. These characters — most notably Joe Christmas in *Light in August,* Charles Bon and his son in *Absalom, Absalom!* — seem to bear forever in their hearts the sharp dilemma of an ancient inexpiable wrong. All Joe Christmas craved was peace, an escape from fury and despair, but peace was the one thing denied him, by the compulsions of his own mixed teperament and by social pressures upon the half-caste. Both he and Charles Etienne St. Valery Bon are shown in raging acts of provocation and violence against Negroes, at moments when their bitterness grows unbearably strong. Faulkner himself views Joe Christmas' dilemma with pitying detachment as "that stain either on his white blood or his black blood, whichever you will." Miss Burden, in *Light in August,* says more bluntly that the Negroes are "a race doomed and cursed to be forever and ever a part of the white race's doom and curse for its sins." The intolerable burden of forefathers' offence is indicated in the cynical resignation of Charles Bon, the wealthy, cultivated New Orleans gentleman with the imperceptible taint of Negro blood, who by forcing his half brother Henry Sutpen to shoot him really commits suicide, no other course of action being left to him but a fatal affront to the social order that has damned him for the wrong it has done him.

This implacability of the half-caste, driving on to self-destruction, is complemented by the implacability of those Southern whites who rationalize the irritations of an unsound social order into a cult of race prejudice and terrorism. Faulkner is painfully conscious of this streak of sadism in his people, and has rendered his revulsion to it most powerfully in that great and almost unbearable short story, "Dry September," as well as in scenes throughout the novels. When Miss Burden is found murdered, Faulkner shows the gathering mob of those

who believed aloud that it was by an anonymous negro crime committed not by a negro but by Negro . . . and some of them with pistols already in their pockets began to canvass about for someone to crucify.

Such race prejudice diffuses into ruthlessness both within and outside the law. In *The Wild Palms* Faulkner shows a man

with the indelible mark of ten thousand Southern deputy sheriffs, urban and suburban — the snapped hatbrim, the sadist's eyes, the slightly and unmistakably bulged coat, the air not swaggering exactly but of a formally preabsolved brutality.

The frenzied Jason Compson, in *The Sound and the Fury*, imagines himself stealing a country church-goer's team, and himself striking the man down:

"I'm Jason Compson. See if you can stop me. See if you can elect a man to office that can stop me," he said, thinking of himself entering the courthouse with a file of soldiers and dragging the sheriff out.

Then each little country church seems

a picket-post where the rear guards of Circumstance peeped fleetingly back at him. "And damn You, too," he said, "See if You can stop me," thinking of himself, his file of soldiers with the manacled sheriff in the rear, dragging Omnipotence down from His throne, if necessary.

That violent spirit in the South is seen in various degrees and contemplated in various moods by Faulkner's more philosophic characters. Doc Peabody feels it simply as an influence of climate and country — weather, land, and rivers are "opaque, slow, violent; shaping and creating the life of man in its implacable and brooding image." Benbow (declaring that either he needs a change, or Mississippi, one) accuses Southern society, what he ironically calls the "free Democratic-Protestant atmosphere." Hightower, as the most detached and speculative of Faulkner's characters, feels even in sectarian church music "the apotheosis of his own history, his own land, his own environed blood: that people . . . who can never take either pleasure or catastrophe or escape from either, without brawling over it"; "their escape from it is in violence," their very religion driving them "to crucifixion of themselves and one another." Thus even the perpetrators of the fatal mobbing and mutilation of Joe Christmas see in him at last their own inescapable and unforgettable fate, as he

lay there, with his eyes open and empty of everything save consciousness, and with something, a shadow, about his mouth. For a long moment he looked up at them with peaceful and unfathomable and unbearable eyes. Then his face, body, all, seemed to collapse, to fall in upon itself, and from out the slashed garments about his hips and loins the pent black blood seemed to rush like a released breath. It seemed to rush out of his pale body like a rush of sparks from a rising rocket; upon that black blast the moon seemed to rise soaring into their memories forever and ever. They are not to lose it, in whatever peaceful valleys, beside whatever placid and reassuring streams of old age, in the mirroring faces of whatever children they will contemplate old disasters and newer hopes. It will be there, musing, quiet, steadfast, not fading and not particularly threatful, but of itself alone serene, of itself alone triumphant.

Whether inherent in blood or environment, this doom of the South abides. After the Civil War Bayard Sartoris, in *The Unvanquished,* tried to repudiate the code of so-called honor and violence, but that violence reasserts itself disastrously in his grandson Bayard, in *Sartoris,* and leads to the violent death of both men. Young Bayard, the returned war pilot, is an end product of the Southern legend of privilege, expressing in a traditional physical arrogance his wild and inconsolable nature. At the close of *Sartoris* Faulkner makes the name of that tribe of Southern gentlemen representative of "glamorous fatality," and suggests that perhaps Sartoris is not just the Player's name for his pawns, but "the game itself—a game outmoded and played with pawns shaped too late and to an old dead pattern, and of which the Player Himself is a little wearied."

A correct estimate of Faulkner's penetration into these aspects of the South will not mistake his view for mere nostalgia and ancestor-worship. His scarcely seems to be the old Southern-mansion, old-massa type of pseudo-humanism with which the Mississippian George O'Donnell recently attempted to saddle him in an article, "Faulkner's Mythology." Faulkner is never seen "looking with stubborn recalcitrance backward beyond the fever and into the disease with actual regret," like the ghosts in Quentin Compson's mind. Indeed, the whole of Faulkner's work, far from idealizing the old South and its lingering legend, seems to suggest the thesis that the sin of human slavery was so great as to require for its expiation nothing less than a wiping the slate clean, by a complete reversal to primitivism among a people who, whatever their pretensions to a culture, were never really just and sound enough to bequeath a working tradition. What they did bequeath, besides degeneration or disillusion, was ruthlessness (resurgent in the Snopes tribe, typical practitioners of amoral exploitation) with the hypocritical mask of aristocracy finally fallen away. The ultimate expression of this pessimistic view of the South's doom Faulkner puts into the mouth of Shreve, the totally detached, sarcastic observer, who thinks that "in time the Jim Bonds [the one nigger Sutpen left] are going to conquer the western hemisphere."

Perhaps nowhere has Faulkner written more feelingly of the South, with a more filial sympathy for it, yet with so much of a Hamlet's grieving disillusionment, as in *The Unvanquished;* and young Bayard Sartoris in narrating this story seems to speak most directly for his author. An early passage in the book epitomizes the Old South's excruciating insoluble dilemmas precipitated by the Civil War, when the slave Loosh shows the raiding Yankees the buried Sartoris silver, follows them, and is disconsolately followed by his wife Philadelphy. He says:

"I going. I done been freed; God's own angel proclamated me free and gonter general me to Jordan. I don't belong to John Sartoris now; I belongs to me and God."

"But the silver belongs to John Sartoris," Granny said, "Who are you to give it away?"

"You ax me that?" Loosh said. "Where John Sartoris? Whyn't he come and ax me that? Let God ax John Sartoris who the man name that give me to him. Let the man that buried me in the black dark ax that of the man what dug me free."

And just as there is no rebuttal to this, so there is no hopeful answer for Granny's question to Philadelphy—"Don't you know he's leading you into misery and starvation?"

In the book's last section, "An Odor of Verbena," comes what seems to be Faulkner's own cutting of the Gordian knot, as Bayard withdraws to aloofness from the South's cult still perpetuated by men like his father who "have killed too much," and by the abetting women like his sweetheart Drusilla, "priestess of a succinct and formal violence." Nine years after the war, when Bayard, then twenty-three, is studying law, his father is shot by his badgered political and financial rival, Redmond. As he rides home, the only surviving Sartoris male, Bayard knows Drusilla and his servant Ringo and all the family's friends will expect him to take conventional vengeance; yet he realizes he has become different from them, "despite my raising and background (or maybe because of them)." Consequently he rejects the loaded pistols Drusilla offers him, and unarmed confronts Redmond, who fires twice without aiming and leaves Jefferson at once, forever. A friend and fellow-soldier of Colonel Sartoris tells Bayard, "Maybe you're right, maybe there has been enough killing in your family"; but Bayard returns home to find that Drusilla has gone, Drusilla to whom "the dream" is worth more than human life, who had summarized the fatal ideal of the unvanquished when she told him:

"There are worse things than killing men, Bayard. There are worse things than being killed. Sometimes I think the finest thing that can happen to a man is to love something, a woman preferably, well, hard hard hard, then to die young because he believed what he could not help but believe and was what he could not (could not? would not) help but be."

It seems probable that William Faulkner, not only refusing to try to revenge the South but even refusing to condone its sins, feels himself like Bayard equally bereaved and alone. Such a personal feeling about himself as a Southerner added to the fundamentally melancholy bent of Faulkner's temperament could account in no small degree for the dark tinge of his stories.

Faulkner, however, while consistently a Southerner of his own kind and a novelist of the South, is no mere sociological regionalist. He is a literary genius who has painted what he has seen in the light of a temperament sensitive, comprehensive, and profound. From his contemplation of a region vexed with problems of peculiar complexity and difficulty he has developed a view of human life that is psychologically representative, and in books which depend least on the Southern locale, such as *The Wild Palms* and *Pylon*, he has generalized the theme that man, when passion-ridden and irrationally seeking privilege or sensation or escape, plunges on toward stultification and tragedy. Fundamentally Faulkner is as right as Swift, and he seems equally to cherish the ideal of man as a creature capable of rationality or he would not be so inconsolably affronted by the evils he contemplates, nor would he so diligently search out their historical and psychological roots, nor would he create his humane protagonists like Benbow and Hightower, Quentin Compson and the reporter in *Pylon*, Ratliff in *The Hamlet* and young Bayard Sartoris in *The Unvanquished*, in systematic protest against those evils, as well as in expression of his personal disenchantment.

Faulkner's pessimism is perhaps morbid, but it is impossible to reject the essential veracity of the tragic graph he traces through from Colonel John Sartoris to Sutpen to the postbellum Sartorises and Compsons and finally to the Snopses and to that howling primitive Jim Bond. Perhaps Faulkner's melancholy is excessive, and certainly it is within the function of philosophical criticism to chide any such excess. Before that is attempted in Faulkner's case, however, a preliminary issue in criticism of him should be faced. Is he merely riding on the momentum of a waning, vitiated romance that lends his narratives a scandalous interest, or do the evils pictured conform fundamentally to observable and characteristic acts of men, and do these evils pictured stand proportionately silhouetted against an implied background of enduring ideals? If Faulkner were only the sensationalist he is so often accused of being, then he would be a most vicious pander, procurer of his own kin. However, an unprejudiced and careful reading of his entire work may be expected to reveal his deep knowledge of his subject, his rationality and detachment, his moral awareness and his uncompromising opposition to evil. A reader whose sensitivity and courage approach Faulkner's own can scarcely find anything melodramatic or titillating in such books as *Light in August* or *Absalom, Absalom!* but will rather experience that catharsis of pity and terror which comes only of great literature, and which can be conveyed only by a temperament of genius, proceeding from a humane point of view, and employing a comprehensive grasp of a significant section of life.

3

William Faulkner's Style

NO OTHER contemporary American novelist of comparable stature has been as frequently or as severely criticized for his style as has William Faulkner. Yet he is a brilliantly original and versatile stylist. The condemnations of his way of writing have been in part just; all but the most idolatrous of Faulkner's admirers must have wished he had blotted a thousand infelicities. However, an enumeration of his faults in style would leave still unsaid the most important things about his style. There is need here for a reapportionment of negative and positive criticism.

It is true that the preponderant excellences of Faulkner's prose, when recognized, make his faults all the more conspicuous and irritating. And under criticism Faulkner has not only remained guilty of occasional carelessness, especially in sentence construction, but seems to have persisted in mannerisms. On the other hand, his progress as a stylist has been steady and rapid; his third novel, *Sartoris,* while still experimenting toward a technique, was a notable advance over his first two in style as well as in theme and narrative structure, and in his fourth novel, *The Sound and the Fury,* style is what it has continued to be in all his subsequent work, a significant factor, masterfully controlled. This growth has been made largely without the aid of appreciative criticism,

This essay first appeared in *American Prefaces,* University of Iowa, Spring 1941, pp. 195-211.

and in the face of some misunderstanding and abuse of the most dynamic qualities in his writing. It is quite possible that Faulkner would have paid more attention to the critics' valid objections if these had not been so frequently interlarded with misconceptions of his stylistic method, or indeed complete insensitivity to it.

Repetition of words, for instance, has often seemed an obvious fault. At times, however, Faulkner's repetitions may be a not unjustifiable by-product of his thematic composition. Some of his favorites in *Absalom, Absalom!* — not just Miss Rosa's "demon," which may be charged off to her own mania, nor "indolent" applied to Bon, but such recurrent terms as effluvium, outrage, grim, indomitable, ruthless, fury, fatality — seem to intend adumbration of the tale's whole significance and tone. Nor is the reiteration as frequent or as obvious here as in earlier books; perhaps Faulkner has been making an experiment over which he is increasingly gaining control.

Faulkner often piles up words in a way that brings the charge of prolixity. He has Wilbourne say of his life with Charlotte in Chicago,

"it was the mausoleum of love, it was the stinking catafalque of the dead corpse borne between the olfactoryless walking shapes of the immortal unsentient demanding ancient meat."

However, these word-series, while conspicuous at times, may have a place in a style as minutely analytical as Faulkner's. In their typical form they are not redundant, however elaborate, and sometimes their cumulative effect is undeniable — for example, the "long still hot weary dead September afternoon" when Quentin listens to Miss Rosa's story. Colonel Feinman, the wealthy exploiter of impecunious aviators, had as secretary "a young man, sleek, in horn rim glasses," who spoke "with a kind of silken insolence, like the pampered intelligent hateridden eunuchmountebank of an eastern despot," and here the amplification redounds to the significance of the whole scene. Quite often too these series of words, while seemingly extravagant, are a remarkably compressed rendering, as in the phrase "passionate tragic ephemeral loves of adolescence."

In fairness it must be noted too that Faulkner's later work never drops to the level of fantastic verbosity found in the thematic paragraph introducing his second novel, *Mosquitoes.* Nor does he any longer break the continuum of his narrative with rhapsodies like the notable description of the mule in *Sartoris,* a sort of cadenza obviously done out of exuberance. In the later books profuseness of language is always knit into the thematic structure. Thus the elaborate lyrical descriptions of the sunrise and of a spring rain in book three of *The Hamlet* furnish by their imagery and mood a sharp, artistically serviceable contrast to the perversion of the idiot Ike Snopes, and as such they deepen the melancholy perspective from which this episode is observed.

Faulkner's studied use of a full style and his sense of its place in the architectonics of an extended and affecting narrative is well displayed in the last chapters of *Light in August,* chapter nineteen closing with the first climax, of Joe Christmas' death, poetically expressed; chapter twenty closing similarly in the second and more comprehensive climax of Hightower's final vision; and then chapter twenty-one, which completes the book, furnishing a modulation to detached calm through the simply prosaic, somewhat humorous account, by a new and neutral spokesman, of the exodus of Lena and Byron into Tennessee. Indeed, one of the best indexes to the degree of Faulkner's control of eloquence is in a comparison of the novels' conclusions — some of them in a full descriptive style, as in *Soldiers' Pay, Sartoris, Sanctuary,* and to a degree in *The Sound and the Fury* and *The Unvanquished;* more of the novels closing with a meaningful but plainly stated utterance or gesture of a character, as in *Mosquitoes, As I Lay Dying, Pylon, Absalom, Absalom!, The Wild Palms,* and *The Hamlet* — (the last that wonderful "Snopes turned his head and spat over the wagon wheel. He jerked the reins slightly. 'Come up,' he said.") This ratio suggests that while Faulkner does not avoid elaboration, neither is he its slave.

Faulkner's diction, charged and proliferate though it may be, usually displays a nice precision, and this is especially evident in its direct imagery. An example is in the glimpse of Cash, after he has worked all night in the rain, finishing his mother's coffin:

In the lantern light his face calm, musing; slowly he strokes his hands on his raincoated thighs in a gesture deliberate, final and composed.

Frequently, however, Faulkner proceeds in descriptive style beyond epithet and abstract definition to figurative language. Having written,

It is just dawn, daylight: that gray and lonely suspension filled with the peaceful and tentative waking of birds.

he goes on in the next sentence to a simile:

The air, inbreathed, is like spring water.

The novels abound in examples of his talent for imaginative comparisons; for instance, the hard-boiled flier Shumann, dressed up:

He wore a new gray homburg hat, not raked like in the department store cuts but set square on the back of his head so that (not tall, with blue eyes in a square thin profoundly sober face) he looked out not from beneath it but from within it with open and fatal humorlessness, like an early Briton who has been assured that the Roman governor will not receive him unless he wear the borrowed centurion's helmet.

There is nothing unique, however, in Faulkner's use of direct and forceful diction or fine figurative image. What is most individual in his style is its persistent lyrical embroidery and coloring, in extended passages, of the narrative theme. In this sense Faulkner is one of the most subjective of writers, his brooding temperament constantly probing and interpreting his subject matter. Thus his full style is comprehensive in its intention. He may often be unfashionably rhapsodic, but he seldom falls into the preciosity that lingers over a passage for its own sweet sake. Definition of his story as a whole and the enhancement of its immediate appeals to the imagination are his constant aims.

The latest of Faulkner's novels demonstrates the grasp he has developed upon all the devices of his style. *The Hamlet* is a sort of prose fantasia; the various episodes employ colloquial tall stories, poetic description, folk humor, deliberate reflective narration, swift cryptic drama, and even a grotesque allegory, of Snopes in hell. Differing in tone from the elegaic brooding of *Light in August,* or the exasperated volubility of *Pylon,* the modulant intricacy and fusion of *Absalom, Absalom!,* the tender directness of *The Unvanquished,* or the eloquent turbulence of *The Wild Palms, The Hamlet* seems an extravaganza improvised more freely in a more detached mood, the author apparently delighting in the realizations of varied subject matters through the flexibilities of his multiform style.

A number of passages in *The Hamlet* give precise indications of Faulkner's purpose as a stylist, inasmuch as they are reworkings of material released as short stories in magazines from four to nine years before the novel's publication. "Spotted Horses," which appeared in *Scribner's* for June, 1931, contains in germ Flem Snopes' whole career in *The Hamlet.* The story is in first person; Ratliff is the reciter, but he is not quite the shrewd and benevolent spectator he becomes under the touches of Faulkner's own descriptions in the third-person narrative of the novel. The short story moves faster, of course, sketching the drama more broadly and making no pause for brooding lyrical interpretation. Faulkner's omniscient narration of the episode is almost twice as long as Ratliff's simple monologue, and rises to an altogether different plane of conception and diction. The contrast is almost like that between a ballad and a tone poem.

This difference, which certainly must indicate Faulkner's free and considered choice and his fundamental aesthetic inclination, can be defined by a comparison of parallel passages from the horse-auction scene, when the Texan tries to hold one of the animals and continue his salestalk. The Scribner short story read as follows:

"Look it over," he says, with his heels dug too and that white pistol sticking outen his pocket and his neck swole up like a spreading adder's until you could just tell what he was saying, cussing the horse and talking to us all at once: "Look him over, the fiddle-headed son of fourteen fathers. Try him, buy him, you will get the best—" Then it was all dust again, and we couldn't see nothing but spotted hide and mane, and that ere Texas man's boot-heels like a couple of walnuts on two strings, and after a while that two-gallon hat come sailing out like a fat old hen crossing a fence. When the dust settled again, he was just getting outen the far fence corner, brushing himself off. He come and got his hat and brushed it off and come and clumb onto the gate post again.

In the novel the parallel passage has been recast thus:

"Look him over, boys," the Texan panted, turning his own suffused face and the protuberant glare of his eyes toward the fence. "Look him over quick. Them shoulders and—" He had relaxed for an instant apparently. The animal exploded again; again for an instant the Texan was free of the earth, though he was still talking: "—and legs you whoa I'll tear your face right look him over quick boys worth fifteen dollars of let me get a holt of who'll make me a bid whoa you blare-eyed jack rabbit, whoa!" They were moving now—a kaleidoscope of inextricable and incredible violence on the periphery of which the metal clasps of the Texan's suspenders sun-glinted in ceaseless orbit, with terrific slowness across the lot. Then the broad clay-colored hat soared deliberately outward; an instant later the Texan followed it, though still on his feet, and the pony shot free in mad, stag-like bounds. The Texan picked up the hat and struck the dust from it against his leg, and returned to the fence and mounted the post again.

Obviously the difference is not only quantitative but qualitative. Instead of Ratliff's "that old two-gallon hat come sailing out like a fat old hen crossing a fence" there is Faulkner's "the broad clay-colored hat soared deliberately outward"; Ratliff sees "that ere Texas man's bootheels like a couple of walnuts on two strings," but Faulkner shows a "kaleidoscope of inextricable and incredible violence on the periphery of which the metal clasps of the Texan's suspenders sun-glinted in ceaseless orbit with terrific slowness across the lot." This latter represents the style Faulkner has chosen to develop; he can do the simpler and more objective narration, but when given such an opportunity as in the amalgamating of these magazine stories into a novel, he insists on transmuting the factual-objective into the descriptive-definitive colored by his imagination and elaborated by his resourcefulness in language.

In its typical exercise this style gives image only incidentally and exists primarily to enhance and sustain mood. Thus Wilbourne's first approach to the house where his meeting with Charlotte is to begin their passionate and disastrous love story is set in this key:

. . . they entered: a court paved with the same soft, quietly rotting brick. There was a stagnant pool with a terra-cotta figure, a mass of lantana, the single palm, the thick rich leaves and the heavy white stars of the jasmine bush where light fell upon it through open French doors, the court balcony—overhung too on three sides, the walls of that same annealing brick lifting a rampart broken and nowhere level against the glare of the city on the low eternally overcast sky, and over all, brittle, dissonant and ephemeral, the spurious sophistication of the piano like symbols scrawled by adolescent boys upon an ancient decayed rodent-scavengered tomb.

The reporter's mood of anxious inquiry and the frustration which is thematic in *Pylon* are both represented as he telephones:

Now he too heard only dead wirehum, as if the other end of it extended beyond atmosphere, into cold space; as though he listened now to the profound sound of infinity, of void itself filled with the cold unceasing murmur of aeonweary and unflagging stars.

This organic quality of Faulkner's style, sustaining through essentially poetic devices an orchestration of meaning, makes it impossible to judge him adequately by brief quotation. In the description of Temple's first hours in Madame Reba's brothel, for instance, the thematic recurrence from page to page of subjectively interpreted imagery builds up in a time continuum the mood of the girl's trance-like state of shock and also the larger fact of her isolation in the sordid. First,

The drawn shades, cracked into a myriad pattern like old skin, blew faintly on the bright air, breathing into the room on waning surges the sound of Sabbath traffic, festive, steady, evanescent . . .

and then, three pages further,

The shades blew steadily in the windows, with faint rasping sounds. Temple began to hear a clock. It sat on the mantel above a grate filled with fluted green paper. The clock was of flowered china, supported by four china nymphs. It had only one hand, scrolled and gilded, halfway between ten and eleven, lending to the otherwise blank face a quality of unequivocal assertion, as though it had nothing whatever to do with time . . .

and then, two pages further,

In the window the cracked shade, yawning now and then with a faint rasp against the frame, let twilight into the room in fainting surges. From beneath the shade the smoke-colored twilight emerged in slow puffs like signal smoke from a blanket, thickening in the room. The china figures which supported the clock gleamed in hushed smooth flexions: knee, elbow, flank, arm, and breast in attitudes of voluptuous lassitude. The glass face, become mirror-like, appeared to hold all reluctant light, holding in its tranquil depths a quiet gesture of moribund time, one-armed like a veteran from the wars. Half past ten oclock. Temple lay in the bed, looking at the clock, thinking about half-past-ten-oclock.

Yet side by side with this richly interpretative style there exists in almost all of Faulkner's work a realistic colloquialism, expressing lively dialogue that any playwright might envy, and even carrying over into sustained first-person narrative the flavor of regionalism and the idiosyncrasies of character. In the colloquial vein Faulkner's brilliance is unsurpassed in contemporary American fiction. He has fully mastered the central difficulty, to retain verisimilitude while subjecting the prolix and monotonous raw material of most natural speech to an artistic pruning and pointing up. *Sanctuary,* for an example, is full of excellent dialogue, sharply individualized. And Faulkner's latest book not only contains some of his most poetic writing but has one of his best talkers, Ratliff, both in extended anecdote in monologue and in dramatic conversations. Ratliff's reflective, humorous, humane, but skeptical nature, a triumph in characterization, is silhouetted largely out of his talk about the hamlet's affairs.

Faulkner also can weave colloquial bits into the matrix of a more literary passage, with the enlarging effect of a controlled dissonance. Thus Quentin imagines Henry Sutpen and Charles Bon, at the end of the war, Charles determined to marry Juidth, Henry forbidding; and then into Quentin's elaboration of the scene breaks the voice of his father, continuing the story, giving its denouement in the words vulgarly uttered by Wash Jones:

(It seemed to Quentin that he could actually see them. . . . They faced one another on the two gaunt horses, two men, young, not yet in the world, not yet breathed over long enough, to be old but with old eyes, with unkempt hair and faces gaunt and weathered as if cast by some spartan and even niggard hand from bronze, in worn and patched gray weathered now to the color of dead leaves, the one with the tarnished braid of an officer, the other plain of cuff, the pistol lying yet across the saddle bow unaimed, the two faces calm, the voices not even raised: *Don't you pass the shadow of this post, this branch, Charles;* and *I am going to pass it, Henry*)—and then Wash Jones sitting that saddleless mule before Miss Rosa's gate, shouting her name into the sunny and peaceful quiet of the street, saying, "Air you Rosie Coldfield? The you better come on out yon. Henry has done shot that durn French feller. Kilt him dead as a beef."

Master of colloquialism in dramatic scene though he is, Faulkner sometimes lays aside this power in order to put into a character's mouth the fullest expression of the narrative's meaning. The mature Bayard Sartoris, looking back to Civil War times, telling the story of his boyhood and youth in *The Unvanquished,* opens what is Faulkner's most straightforward narrative, and his only novel related throughout by one character in first person, in this strain:

Behind the smokehouse that summer, Ringo and I had a living map. Although Vicksburg was just a handful of chips from the woodpile and the River a trench scraped into the packed earth with the point of a hoe, it (river, city, and terrain) lived, possessing even in miniature that ponderable though passive recalcitrance of topography which outweighs artillery, against which the most brilliant of victories and the most tragic of defeats are but the loud noises of a moment.

At times it seems as though the author, after having created an unsophisticated character, is elbowing him off the stage, as when the rustic Darl Bundren sees "the square squat shape of the coffin on the sawhorses like a cubistic bug," or as when in the short story, "All The Dead Pilots," the World War flier John Sartoris is characterized as having a vocabulary of "perhaps two hundred words" and then is made to say,

> . . . I knew that if I busted in and dragged him out and bashed his head off, I'd not only be cashiered, I'd be clinked for life for having infringed the articles of alliance by invading foreign property without warrant or something.

For the most part, however, the transcending of colloquial verisimilitude in the novels is a fairly controlled and consistent technique, the characters Faulkner most often endows with penetration and eloquence being his philosophical spectators. Undoubtedly his chief concern, though, is with a lyric encompassment of his narrative's whole meaning rather than with the reticences of objective dramatic representation.

Thus many of his characters speak with the tongues of themselves and of William Faulkner. As Quentin and his Harvard roommate Shreve evolve the reconstruction of Thomas Sutpen's story which constitutes the second half of *Absalom, Absalom!,* Quentin thinks when Shreve talks, "He sounds just like his father," and later, when Quentin has the floor, Shreve interrupts with "Don't say it's just me that sounds like your old man," which certainly shows that Faulkner realizes what he is doing. Actually he does make some differences among these voices: Miss Rosa rambles and ejaculates with erratic spinsterish emotion, Mr. Compson is elaborately and sometimes parenthetically ironic, Quentin is most sensitively imaginative and melancholy, Shreve most detached and humorous. What they have in common is the scope and pitch of an almost lyrical style which Faulkner has arbitrarily fixed upon for an artistic instrument. The justification of all such practices is empirical; imaginative writing must not be judged by its minute correspondence to fact but by its total effect; and to object against Faulkner's style that men and women don't really talk in such long sentences, with so full a vocabulary so fancifully employed, is as narrowly dogmatic as was Sinclair Lewis, in *Main Street,* insisting that Sir Launcelot didn't actually speak in "honeyed pentameters."

Typical instances of Faulkner's endowing his characters with precise diction and fluency may show that on the whole it is not an unacceptable convention. Thus Wilbourne's full and finished sentence.

> "We lived in an apartment that wasn't bohemian, it wasn't even a tabloid love-nest, it wasn't even in that part of town but in a neighborhood dedicated by both city ordinance and architecture to the second year of wedlock among the five-thousand-a-year bracket . . ."

though it is not stylistically rooted in his manner as characterized up to this point, is not inconsistent with his personality and sensibilities, and it does get on with the story. Equally acceptable is Ratliff's remark about the platitudinous family-fleeing I. O. Snopes,

> "What's his name? that quick-fatherer, the Moses with his mouth full of mottoes and his coat-tail full of them already half-grown retroactive sons?"

Its keen diction and nice rhythm are not essentially false to Ratliff, but only an idealization in language of the percipient humorous sewing-machine salesman the reader already knows. The same is true of those tumbling floods of phrases, too prolonged for human breath to utter, with which the reporter in *Pylon* assaults the sympathies of editor Hagood; they are not so much a part of dialogue as an intense symbol of the pace of racing aviation and the reporter's frantic concern for his proteges among the fliers.

It is interesting to note that Faulkner's full style somewhat resembles older literary uses, such as the dramatic chorus, the prologue and epilogue, and the *dramatis personae* themselves in soliloquy and extended speech. The aim of any such device is not objective realism but revelation of theme, a revelation raised by the unstinted resourcefulness and power of its language to the highest ranges of imaginative outlook. No wonder that with such a purpose Faulkner often comes closer than is common in these times to Shakespeare's imperial and opulent use of words. If unfortunately his ambition has sometimes led Faulkner to perpetrate some rather clotted prose, perhaps these lapses may be judged charitably in the light of the great endeavor they but infrequently flaw.

More particularly Faulkner's full sentence structure springs from the elaborateness of his fancies ramifying in descriptive imagery. Thus editor Hagood, perpetually beset by small annoyances and chronically irritated by them, drops himself wearily into his roadster's low seat,

> . . . whereupon without sound or warning the golfbag struck him across the head and shoulder with an apparently calculated and lurking viciousness, emitting a series of dry clicks as though produced by the jaws of a beast domesticated though not tamed, half in fun and half in deadly seriousness, like a pet shark.

Another typical source of fullness in Faulkner's sentences is a tendency to musing speculation, sometimes proceeding to the statement of alternative suggestions. Thus Miss Rosa speaks of wearing garments left behind by the eloping aunt in "kindness or haste or oversight," that doing its bit in a sentence well over three hundred words long. Such characteristic theorizing may run to the length of this postscript to a description of Flem Snopes:

> . . . a thick squat soft man of no establishable age between twenty and thirty, with a broad still face containing a tight seam of mouth stained slightly at the corners with tobacco, and eyes the color of stagnant water, and projecting from among the other features in startling and sudden paradox, a tiny predatory nose like the beak of a small hawk. It was as though the original nose had been left off by the original designer or craftsman and the unfinished job taken over by someone of a radically different school or perhaps by some viciously maniacal humorist or perhaps by one who had only time to clap into the center of the face a frantic and desperate warning.

Even the most elaborate and esoteric of these speculations are not limited to third-person narrative; Faulkner's pervasive subjectivity injects such abstractions too, as well as extended imagery, into the reflections and speech of many of his characters, again most typically those who contemplate and interpret the action of the stories, who act as chorus or soliloquize. Here too the device proves itself in practice. When such characters brood over the events, painstakingly rehearsing details, piling one hypothesis upon another, their very tentativeness creates for the reader the clouded enigmatic perspective of reality itself. Thus Miss Rosa's account, with reinterpretation imposed upon memory, of Sutpen's driving in to church with his family:

It was as though the sister whom I had never laid eyes on, who before I was born had vanished into the stronghold of an ogre or a djinn, was now to return through a dispensation of one day only, to the world which she had quitted, and I a child of three, waked early for the occasion, dressed and curled as if for Christmas, for an occasion more serious than Christmas even, since now and at last this ogre of djinn had agreed for the sake of the wife and the children to come to church, to permit them at least to approach the vicinity of salvation, to at least give Ellen one chance to struggle with him for those children's souls on a battleground where she could be supported not only by Heaven but by her own family and people of her own kind; yes, even for the moment submitting himself to redemption, or lacking that, at least chivalrous for the instant even though still unregenerate.

The foregoing examples, however, do not illustrate Faulkner's style at its most involved, as in this passage from Quentin's consciousness, while he listens to Miss Rosa's reconstruction of the Sutpen family history:

It should have been later than it was; it should have been late, yet the yellow slashes of mote-palpitant sunlight were latticed no higher up the impalpable wall of gloom which separated them; the sun seemed hardly to have moved. It (the talking, the telling) seemed (to him, to Quentin) to partake of that logic- and reason-flouting quality of a dream which the sleeper knows must have occurred, still-born and complete, in a second, yet the very quality upon which it must depend to move the dreamer (verisimilitude) to credulity—horror or pleasure or amazement—depends as completely upon a formal recognition of and acceptance of elapsed and yet-elapsing time as music or a printed tale.

By its parentheses and involution and fullness this last sentence illustrates that occasionally extreme eccentricity most often and most rightfully objected to in its author's style. At the same time this sentence may give a key to Faulkner's entire method and typify its artistic purposefulness — to create "that logic- and reason-flouting quality of a dream," yet to depend upon the recognized verisimilitude of "elapsed and yet-elapsing time." Such a product is not necessarily mere nightmare; it is often a real quality of experience at its greatest intensity and acuteness. In his most characteristic writing Faulkner is trying to render the transcendent life of the mind, the crowded composite of associative and analytical consciousness which expands the vibrant moment into the reaches of all time, simultaneously observing, remembering, interpreting, and modifying the object of its awareness. To this end the sentence as a rhetorical unit (however strained) is made to hold diverse yet related elements in a sort of saturated solution, which is perhaps the nearest that language as the instrument of fiction can come to the instantaneous complexities of consciousness itself. Faulkner really seems to be trying to give narrative prose another dimension.

To speak of Faulkner's fiction as dream-like (using Quentin's notion as a key) does not imply that his style is phantasmagoric, deranged, or incoherent. Dreams are not always delirium; and association, sometimes the supplanter of pattern, can also be its agent. The dreaming mind, while envisaging experience strangely, may find in that strangeness a fresh revelation, all the more profound in that the conventional and adventitious are pierced through. Similarly inhibitions and apathies must be transcended in any really imaginative inquiry, and thus do Faulkner's speculative characters ponder over the whole story, and project into cumulative drama its underlying significations. Behind all of them, of course, is their master-dreamer; Faulkner's own dominating temperament, constantly interpreting, is in the air of all these narratives, reverberant. Hence no matter how psychological the story's material, Faulkner never falls into the mere enumeration which in much stream-of-consciousness writing dissolves all drama and reduces the narrative to a case history without the shaping framework of analysis, or even to an un-mapped anachronistic chaos of raw consciousness. Faulkner is always a dynamic story-teller, never just a reporter of unorganized phenomena. His most drastic, most dream-like use of stream-of-consciousness, for instance, in *The Sound and the Fury,* is not only limited to the first two sections of the book, but it sketches a plot which in the lucid sections that follow gradually emerges clear-cut.

As clear-cut, at least, as Faulkner's stories can be. Here again is illustrated the close relation of his style to his whole point of view. If Faulkner's sentence sometimes soar and circle involved and prolonged, if his scenes become halls of mirrors repeating tableaux in a progressive magnification, if echoes multiply into the dissonance of infinite overtones, it is because the meanings his stories unfold are complex, mysterious, obscure, and incomplete. There is no absolute, no eternal pure white radiance in such presentations, but rather the stain of many colors, refracted and shifting in kaleidoscopic suspension, about the center of man's enigmatic behavior and fate, within the drastic orbit of mortality. Such being Faulkner's view of life, such is his style.

To this view the very rhythm of Faulkner's prose is nicely adjusted. It is not emphatic; rather it is a slow prolonged movement, nothing dashing, even at its fullest flood, but surging with an irresistible momentum. His effects insofar as they depend on prose rhythms are never staccato, they are cumulative rather than abrupt. Such a prose rhythm supplements the contributions of full vocabulary and lengthy sentence toward suspension rather than impact, and consequently toward deep realization rather than quick surprise. And the prolonged even murmur of Faulkner's voice throughout his pages is an almost hypnotic induction into those detailed and darkly-colored visions of life which drift across the horizons of his imagination like clouds — great yet vaporous, changing yet enduring, unearthly yet of common substance. It might be supposed that his occasionally crowded and circumlocutory style would destroy narrative pace and consequence. Actually this hovering of active imagination, while employing the sustained lyricism and solid abstraction which differentiate Faulkner from the objective realist, furnishes the epitome of drama. The whole aim is at perspective, through the multiple dimensions of experience, upon a subject in that suspension which allows reflection. The accomplishment is the gradual, sustained, and enriched revelation of meaning; in Faulkner's novels drama is of that highest form which awaits the unfolding of composite action, characterization, mood, and idea, through the medium of style.

Faulkner himself probably would admit the relative inadequacy of instrument to purpose, would agree with Mr. Compson in calling language "that meager and fragile thread by which the little surface corners and edges of men's secret and solitary lives may be joined for an instant." Faulkner perhaps has no greater faith in the word than have his contemporaries who have partially repudiated it, but instead of joining that somewhat paradoxical literary trend, he seems determined to exploit an imperfect device to the uttermost within the limits of artistic illusion. Thus although in certain passages he has demonstrated his command of a simplified objective method, he has not made it his invariable device, nor does he allow its contemporary vogue to prevent his using words in the old-fashioned way for whatever they are worth descriptively and definitively.

Faulkner's whole narrative method, as described, may seem to be a retrogression in technique. Two main tendencies in modern fiction have been toward a more and more material dramatic presentation, depending simply upon the naming of objects and acts and the reporting of speech, and on the other hand, toward an ostensibly complete and unbroken reproduction of the free flow of consciousness. These methods have produced books as radically different as *The Sun Also Rises* and *Ulysses,* yet they have elements in common. In both types the author attempts to conceal himself completely behind his materials, to give them the quality of integral phenomena, and in line with this purpose the style aims at pure reproduction, never allowing definition and interpretation from any detached point of view. These have been honest attempts, a great deal of fine craftsmanship has gone into them, and some of the products have been excellent in their kind. Yet at their most extreme these have been movements in the one direction toward bareness, impoverishment, and in the other toward incoherence. Confronted by the imperfections and confusions of the present scene, and made hyper-skeptical by deference to scientific method, the writers who have attempted absolute objectivity (whether dramatic or psychological, whether in overt event or stream of association) have sometimes produced what looks like an anti-intellectual aesthetic of futility and inconsequence. So in another sense Faulkner's narrative technique, particularly as implemented by his full style, instead of being a retrogression may represent one kind of progression through the danger of impasse created by too great submission to vogues of photographic or psychographic reproduction.

Yet Faulkner's is not altogether a return to an older expressiveness, not a complete departure from the modern schools of Hemingway and Joyce. In his colloquial passages he is quite as objectively dramatic as the one, in his rehearsal of the fantasies of acute consciousness he follows the other — and it should be remembered that he is superlatively skillful at both, so that it cannot be said that he puts these objective methods aside because he cannot use them. Furthermore, Faulkner is fond of employing in extended passages one of the favorite modern means of objectivity in fiction, the first-person narrator, using the device toward its most honored modern purpose, the attainment of detached perspective and the creation of realistic illusion concerning large vistas of the story. In short, there is no method in modern fiction which Faulkner does not comprehend and use on occasion. Fundamentally Faulkner's only heterodoxy by present standards of style is his fullness, especially as it takes the form of descriptive eloquence or abstraction and definitiveness. What is stylistically most remarkable in his work is the synthesis he has effected between the subtleties of modern narrative techniques and the resources of language employed in the traditionally poetic or interpretative vein. That such a synthesis is feasible is demonstrated in the dynamic forms of his novels, and it may be prelude to significant new developments in the methods of fiction.

Further Considerations

4

Faulkner after 1940

*"there would always be a next time, since
there is only one truth"*

ON ARRIVAL at *The Hamlet,* published in 1940,
Faulkner had already created one of the great domains in
modern fiction, a brilliant as well as formidably energetic display of range, conceptual and delineative power, and artistic
originality. Besides *Sartoris* and *The Sound and the Fury*
(1929), the issuance within eleven years included *As I Lay
Dying* (1930), *Sanctuary* (1931), *Light in August* (1932),
Pylon (1935), *Absalom, Absalom!* (1936), *The Unvanquished*
(1938), and *The Wild Palms* (1939). Any fictionist's production in little more than a decade of ten published novels, with
a number of short stories besides, would be remarkable — and
the more so if, as with Faulkner, their author had
concurrently put in distracting stints as a Hollywood screen-
writer, to supplement scanty income from his vocation. What
is even more noteworthy in Faulkner is that this prolific era
included novels which still rank high in the whole body of his
accomplishment and are preeminent in his country's and century's fiction. From this period some might select their favorite
Faulkner novel, and even nominate it as his masterpiece —
Absalom, Absalom! perhaps, or *Light in August* or *The
Hamlet?* Near his true beginnings, by that spurt within one
year beyond his third novel, *Sartoris,* into *The Sound and the
Fury* and then the following year on a modified but related
trajectory of composition in *As I Lay Dying,* serious readers
should have been alerted to the presence of genius and

55

prepared for the separate further achievements, in the next two years, in *Sanctuary* and *Light in August*. Never in American literature had there been such a thunderous illuminated dawning. What in retrospect is most astonishing, therefore, is that Faulkner's significant and scintillant output up to 1940 had fared so ill with most reviewers and the reading public, while also going largely neglected or no more than suspiciously regarded by American scholars and critics and many other serious readers. Thus Faulkner's position in 1940 was classic, but only as instance of genius abundantly demonstrated, yet scantily recognized and sometimes ignorantly ridiculed.

Unfortunately a negative attitude toward Faulkner's work spread and persisted among those who read fiction only occasionally and casually. Such scanted attention is not a unique phenomenon, but it is always a waste when a dynamic cultural influence is neglected or prejudicially evaded, and especially one such as Faulkner's, which while rooted in locale reaches wide in its socioethical and psychological implications. It is necessary that continuing account be taken of the peculiarly stubborn disinclination to hear what Faulkner was saying. This occurred most explicitly but negligibly among recusant Confederate flag-wavers, who found him a traitor, writing slanderous stuff about his own folk, past and present. More generally felt, though obscurely, in a disregarding of Faulkner may be that endemic sectional antipathy, with historical and political sources, which festers in a national life so cumbersome, culturally fragmented, and uneasy in its necessitous interactions. Illustratively seen from the opposite side, at one point in *Intruder in the Dust* a lively twentieth-century Mississippi youth, who is coming courageously into manhood on the wave of hard and generous assertions, resentfully envisages the North as a multitude of faces looking down on him with "amazement and outrage and frustration and most curious of all, gullibility: a volitionless, almost helpless capacity and eagerness to believe anything about the South not even provided it be derogatory but merely bizarre enough and strange enough." Fantastic as this is, it answers to the regionally biased attitude of some of Faulkner's Northern detractors. Most broadly, Faulkner met with the habitual resistance to realism; also, as a highly sophisticated artist, he suffered from the quite common obstacle between writer and reader, a superficial reading. Often the two were combined, in a failure to recognize Faulkner's penetration into the never fully scrutable struggles between good and evil, with his implication that the resisters of evil, even if defeated, have secured an intangible victory beyond private advantage, as principled men whose disinterestedness implies an honorable and compassionate affiliation with others of their kind and commitment.

Even by 1940 what general attention Faulkner had received was preponderantly disapproving. Considered shocking, his works acquired that persistent wider disrepute the public can impose on books it hasn't read. Such an animosity at large was exacerbated by the immoderation of certain journalists, some of them perhaps annoyed over these powerful novels not amenable to a reviewer's skimming glance. And derogation of Faulkner was augmented when *Sanctuary* was reissued in 1932 in a Modern Library edition with a preface by its author. This like so much else from him was carelessly read. Phrases isolated from context there were bruited about to prove Faulkner had expediently fabricated sensational effects, and this view was widely taken on faith as index to the man in all his works. At a safe aseptic distance *Sanctuary* became well known to rumor as a book containing wanton murder, a rape by an impotent gangster with a corncob, and the girl's abduction to a Memphis brothel where the gangster was voyeur to his henchman's couplings with her. Such isolate naming of details slandered the work of art — a dark account of certain human beings' grossness, brutalities, and crimes, yet also of others' despairing but sustained resistance. Moreover, Temple Drake's story is so subtly contained and implicatively rendered

that fanciers of present-day explicitness in designedly erotic
fiction, blind to Faulkner's superb art as well as his discriminating ethic, might consider him afraid to come out with it.

Those who had registered what that preface to *Sanctuary*
said in its entirety could approach this novel knowing it was
not an opportunistic first draft but a seriously intended revision, to subordinate the senastional while admitting sordidness
of event and showing consequent human defects and desolation. Superficial readers, whatever the level of their expectations, probably failed to grasp the weighted relations of
characters and interplay of opposing forces in the novel's
structure, or to sense the perspectives, not only aesthetic but
moral, from which Faulkner had treated corruption for what
it was, whether in the menage at Frenchman's Bend or in Miss
Reba's brothel, whether in Popeye's stunted, vicious mind or
in a privileged Southern gentility gone soft and corrupt in
both Gowan and Temple. And the coin has another side, as is
typical in Faulkner's mintings. Even the faintest understanding of *Sanctuary* must note two characters as proponents of
decency, compassion, and fair play. One is the half-witted
Tommy, in his instinctive attempts to protect Temple from
being "pestered" by "them durn fellers." The other is the
rational ironic Benbow, demoralized in his personal life and
by his melancholy view of existence, but persistently well-
intentioned, trying to the last to save the falsely accused
Goodwin. That both Tommy and Benbow are defeated does
not cancel out but sets into dramatic perspective the ethical
assertions they have enacted, under the aegis of the artist's
outlook. Yet while *Sanctuary* is not overtly sensational, neither
does it moralize. A refined work of art, it vividly bodies forth;
nothing is defined, all is realized, and in a skilful rush of narrative momentum. Intelligently appreciated, it could have
furnished a number of keys to Faulkner's scope, intent, and
art.

Nevertheless, adverse reaction to *Sanctuary,* prolonged in
ripples of uninformed rumor that widened under journalistic
exploitation, spread into a more general distaste for

Faulkner's works through the thirties. Strangely complementary to this was disapproval by that conservative but
entrenched minority of the academic world which on principle
resisted candid contemporary realism and also its often unconventional artistic embodiments, both extreme in Faulkner's
novels. What is hardest to understand is how scholars professionally acquainted with earlier literary representations of
foolish, grotesque, and evil human behavior could have overlooked Faulkner's profound and in a sense traditional humanism, manifested by peopling his stories with some of its virtues'
committed and intent protagonists, drawn out of all ranks,
from the lowly to the most sophisticated and cultured. Even in
the face of this some academicians based a rejection of Faulkner most positively on the notion that he was more than merely
random, he was nihilistic. And with Faulkner's nihilism
assumed, some were the more inclined to see his work as a
series of wild assaults on the supposed form of the novel and
the classroom properties of English sentence structure.

Though there continues some fallout from this period of
Faulkner's disrepute (as it was given focus early in the 1930s
through scandalous misinterpretations, maintained through
sectional antipathies, then further inflamed by some
chronically antagonistic reviewers at all levels of journalism,
and irritably supplemented by academic conservatives) that is
not the whole story nor indeed the heart of the issue. When all
these insubstantially based carpings had begun to decline in
volume or at least were less attended to, an undeniable reality
remained, and remains, as obstacle to wide acceptance of
Faulkner. Briefly it is put that he is "difficult." But opinion
cannot be left at that. Nor is it enough to describe his fiction
in general terms, indicating merely that his narrative structures are complicated and his style intricate, but thereby
implying that these characteristics are faults, either as temperamental indulgence or an outright failure of control.
Surely to criticize the artist for creating difficulties yet without
specific allusions to his uses of the medium he works in would
be as impertinent as if one chided an athlete for unnatural

contortions without taking account of his purpose within the ways of his game, wherein achievement of the end in view can claim the spectators' most intense response.

For instance, Faulkner's frequently sneered-at sentence structuring: sometimes (not often) his constructions do lose syntactical flow, they swerve tangentially, they stammer or grow prolix. Yet how can these be judged without taking into account that this is not necessarily Faulkner nodding but often the representation of a character's consciousness in turmoil, as it wrestles and feints under immediate circumstance? Nor can affectation be charged against Faulkner's occasional use of something like the steps of a chemical analysis, proceeding through a naming of not this and not even that but rather this. Thereby attentive reading is brought to a deliberate pace so that in passing through a series of reductive exclusions it may come to a point of sharpest delineation, in a heightening of the sense of particularity. Most importantly this again is conveyed as if within a character's ongoing attempt to gauge what he confronts. Such a sophisticated practice, formally rhetorical, is kept fully fictional by its grounding in subjective existence; in the actor's consciousness, however secretive, is the very essence of drama, the mirror of motive and reaction. Nor should Faulkner be indiscriminately condemned under the simplistic doctrine that adjectives and adverbs are mere ornaments. Generally his modifiers, even in a multiple use, will make distinctions and add shades of meaning which otherwise would require a phrase of even a complete clause, in a spelling-out which would obtrude and delay. Complexities in Faulkner's prose are inherent in what he is representing, and his created effects in all their richness and depth are made more intense by conveyance at an accelerated pace, through economical concentrations, rewardingly intriguing to the attentive reader.

Judgment of Faulkner's fiction must rest on recognition that he developed rapidly into a highly sophisticated artist in his genre, sensitive to modern tendencies in the craft, yet no imitator but quite idiosyncratic and amazingly originative, gifted with both conceptualizing and evocative powers at a notable level of imagination, and dynamic in their uses. Difficulty is felt in his fiction because tremendous force emanates from its substance and intricacies, its minutely precise detail and its modulations all the way from lyrical suspension to accelerant compression, its structural proportionings and orderings beyond chronology for climactic closures, and its richly implicative diction and supportive prose rhythms. Such recognized means of literary effect, given aesthetic response, can convey subtleties and verities about the human beings who move through Faulkner's tales; and always to suggest their living immediate reality is what the art is for. To experience this in its essence and continuity requires unremitting, close, responsive attention, and that is demanding, but concurrently rewarding. Given some capacity (Faulkner's are not books for boys) only the indolent or uneasy reader who has begrudged full attention will turn "difficult" into a pejorative term against such humanely communicative fictional art at the level of dynamism Faulkner achieves.

With the whole of Faulkner now at hand, and with accumulating recognition of pertinence in its sociological and other thematic components, there may now be special need to emphasize his pure creative accomplishments as a superlative fictionist. Fame having followed slowly after defamation or impercipient neglect, most retrospection may settle upon Faulkner's amassed subject matter and his abstractable points of view, while his art as such (especially in its ingenious narrative patternings and its fluid penetration of the subjective) has not even yet been given proportionate scrutiny. Before his high achievements are more or less silted over with a residue of thematic abridgment (or suffer the pseudoprofessional symbol-snatching and the other fragmenting procedures that conventionally follow upon reputation) and while a reckoning of the balance between his technical merits and faults remains still somewhat in question, perhaps furthered awareness of his mastery of fictional procedures might naturally poise readers closer also to his most profound concepts and their bases. By illuminating the substance of his works in making the means of its effects more steadily apparent to readers'imaginations, criticism might prevent a reductive disjunction between his matter and his art and thus spare Faulkner a demotion to the rank of novelist of the twentieth-century social-consciousness school. What "school" Faulkner the artist most significantly appertains to is that of explored individual experience itself, both overt and subjective. In this he is the one American novelist of his times comparable with James and Joyce, while also being both more natively worldly and naturally intense than the one, and more sustainedly dramatic than the other through the positioning and motion he gives auxiliary characters. Conversely, what the social-consciousness novelist is conscious of is an attitude to society, often a genuine empathy but sometimes made rather too obvious in a presiding over his characters; Faulkner, with a most alert and concerned awareness of the total situations he represents, nevertheless submerges his own consciousness into the existence of his characters as they move through their experiences. His artistic trend was anything but introvertive. Autobiographic traces of the man himself and his connections fade and dissolve, or cross upon trails in another direction, but inconclusively. His interests, though deeply centered in temperament, are widely inquiring.

To this end, his art rests chiefly in a peculiarly close yet concealed subjective control of narration, by covert entry into characters' awareness, yet it sets that central fictional reality of conscious states and processes at a distance to elicit the reader's intuitive apprehension of it. In the hands of genius this has been a further refinement of inherent point of view, such as in first-person narratives, or as more easily and aptly but subtly modulated in third-person narration, through the implied continuum of a comprising intelligence, as with the tutor in "The Pupil," Maria in "Clay," or Isaac McCaslin in "The Bear," or most recently by Eudora Welty through the protagonist in "The Optimist's Daughter." The method, at least as it is masterfully used in these instances, is definitely not an art for its own sake, but for a more telling penetration into the human matter of the fiction. It proves its validity by the hold it lays on the reader's attention and intuitions, with immediacy and sustained effect. At its height such a mode can give fictional works an almost poetic resonance, as of a pure metal rightly cast. And this covert subjective centering in a deployment of the story can enfranchise the imagination for what Coleridge defined as "reconcilement . . . of the general with the concrete; the idea with the image; the individual with the representative." Though the general and representative substance of fiction is the human condition, its particulars to be imaged are of individual lives, and the truth of that (beyond the physical and factual) is in the continuum of their reality as beings "breathing thoughtful breath," self-aware even if in self-deceptiveness, and subject even at their most secretive to the intuitions of others who sense some recognizable traits and motion in them. In Faulkner's subjective control of narration, whether through a first-person voice like the successive three in *The Town,* or in third person with the intensely conscious lad in "Barn Burning," or in some dilution of the method to accommodate sheer eventfulness, there is always that one soundless step by the artist himself into the story's human realities, deploying awareness in his characters not just as to their part in it, but in some accretive perceiving of it, from a concerned and thereby a more discerning view.

Along the line of modern fiction's most penetrating techniques, and for the sake of projecting verisimilitude into the largest representativeness, Faulkner's fiction is pervaded by individualization which in great part is authenticated and vitalized by its strong tincture of the recurrently subjective. Because one of the characters not only acts but observes, thinks, and feels, therefore and thereupon each and all exist. Technically this holds whether the operative consciousness is that of a protagonist, as with Chick Mallison in *Intruder in the Dust,* or whether the affective tones are filtered chiefly through an adjunctive character, such as Lawyer Stevens in "Go Down, Moses," where old Mollie Beauchamp is at the center of concern, though her being is known here only through her demands that cast the shadow of her grief, to be mollified by an appeased sense of the amenities, in the proper burial of her grandson, the executed murderer. These two examples also point to the tenuous nuances in Faulkner's technique, in that Chick's consciousness may be felt (but not obtrusively) in the presence of such overtly assertive but objectively rendered characters as Lucas and Gavin, and while among the ministrants to Mollie, Gavin Stevens is only one, along with Miss Worsham and the newspaper editor. In Faulkner's narratives there is no fixed degree for permeation of the action by the reactive consciousness of some character, there is no one type to whom this evaluating function is given, and no set ratio but only modulations within any story between a character's most comprehensively enhancing moments of awareness and his subsidence into his own perhaps even minor but observant participation in event. The practice seems to have no rules but rather has sprung up instinctively through the artist's engagement with characters in ongoing actions, yet the consciousness borrowed out of the midst of all that action sets its tone and is the canny servant of emerging theme. And this is true as well, perhaps even the more so, if in an intricately patterned novel such as *Light in August* consciousness as operant in several characters is heard, to give proportionate depth to interrelated themes, while continuity is maintained by brief passages of omniscient narration which still may include suggestions of characters' active consciousness.

Considering the number and variety of actors in almost any Faulkner story, when steadily pervasive centrality is given the consciousness of any one, such as Isaac McCaslin or Chick Mallison, the devotee of fiction might wonder why, only to arrive at the closed Byzantine doors behind which the artist's imagination celebrates its rites, yet the intoning is heard, with its portents that transcend the singer. This much seems discernible, though, that out of all the swirl of observed and pondered reality the artist has found in each instance a nucleus in the reactive consciousness of some one or more of the characters, and it is around this that the story could constitute itself, tonally and conceptually. Thus Lucas Beauchamp in "The Fire and the Hearth" must be there, an expressly living presence, not the imperturable old schemer, but more closely and earlier in his agonized reclaiming of his young wife from his patron Zack McCaslin. Thus in *Intruder* though Lucas's life is in jeopardy, it is primarily the youthful Chick's consciousness (and not the creek, the country store, the jail, the cemetery) that is the area of the essential action, his inner struggle between evasion and assertion. Behind these (and the myriad similar instances of the artist's locating a psychological pivot which his story is to turn on) there lies the hieratic mystery of what large idea, derived from the artist's widest experience and observation and distilled into a tentative generality, might have precipitated a notion of a story to bring the abstraction down to earth, perhaps to give it over to a clearer rediscovery in the consciousness of a fictitious character.

Such creative processes are beyond definition, even by the fictionist himself. Yet he knows and his reader can come to sense something of them through their fulfillment, as of the wind in a swaying tree. Conrad could tell how the sight of a melancholy English girl in an orchestra traveling to out-of-the-way places in the Far East suggested a predicament like Lena's, but not how that unfolded into the whole of *Victory*—though it might be hazarded that in the incident itself he had felt a challenge to his own aloofness, and confessed it through Heyst, who then illustrated the fate of disenchanted souls in the world of Schombergs and that unholy trinity of the subhuman, the violently passionate, and the coldly vicious, all of whose prototypes Conrad reports actually encountering. James can tell how a companion's description of an American family, exploring the European marriage market and carrying along their incongruously superior and sensitive young son on their shabby adventures, impressed the writer with the boy's plight, but he could scarcely define the sympathies that brought him to the tutor as not just actor and factor in the events but as the consciousness through which they were to be conveyed with a chosen effect. Yet to identify what seems the precipitant of a fiction's conception, to point out retrospectively the possibly primary stimulus which James termed the *donnée,* naturally falls far short of the whole history of a creative act. And whether some comparatively minute instance has imperatively called for more extended realization with thematic implications, or whether a cloudy concept has found itself precipitated by instance into a more immediate bodying forth—to attempt such a distinction is perhaps to analyze too finely the always operative reciprocities in the humane commonalty of the creative imagination, at a high level of psychological organicism. In a wide variety of works Faulkner's genius appears in remarkable syntheses of fiction's basic components. He seems never at a lack or a loss, but inexhaustibly charged with concern and caught up in delineation, nor does vivid particularity impede movement or diminish scope, and the interfusion of occurrence and concept becomes a constitutive reality, fully as organic aesthetically as a melody and its harmony. For the fictionist, however, this cannot be an isolated exercise in pure form within the terms of a technique; it bears responsibility to whatever awareness of the human situation the artist possesses, as experience and observation, and as intuitive empathic response. With Faulkner this was an immense complex endowment: the valid, profuse, viable Yoknapatawpha matter and his engaged, tempered imaginative grasp upon it.

Genius itself is not always symmetrical, even in its most genuine manifestations, and readers of literature may accept a preponderance of substance over its means of conveyance or their reverse, may range along the shelf admiring one writer's grasp, another's finesse, and may even incline their interest more one way than the other. A hazard here to art is in the neglect of a work's intrinsic total worth, by a reductive disjunction, a partial relishing, whether in a preciosity or a subordinating of the work's autonomous reality to extractable generalizations. The second is more questionable, as it may come to be taken for an artist's history and a summary estimate of him, whereas the first will have the ephemerality of fashion, whether the vogue is the impressionable aesthete's or that of superficial imitators. Faulkner has already suffered some from both, and the present need is an even-handed view of what is not always a case of simple balance between art and scope as equal factors. While diligent consideration of substance in Faulkner's works continues, it could be much assisted at present by increased attention to all aspects of his techniques, from the comprising designs which massively silhouette themes to the subtleties in an often slight, unobtrusive touch upon details which can become crucially determinant of meaning and tone. Awareness of these latter, more particular and evanescent effects may be sharpened by recognizing as their frequent medium the conveyed sense of characters' consciousness, in whatever presence and degree, linking such effects contributively into narrative procedure.

A minor artist, conserving his limited means, may tend to substantiate his claim by consistency of method, and its familiarity may become a large part of his stock in trade, and a measure of his reach. Faulkner is the very opposite of a man with one method; he never uses the same inclusive story pattern twice, and he does not refract all his narratives in every part through the lens of a character's temperamental presence. In a work with extended tincturings of the subjective, as in *Light in August*, he will nevertheless temporarily assume openly omniscient command. Even where there is a fictionally controlling center of awareness, as with Isaac in "The Bear," there is necessarily a variableness of subjective intensity, which will often give primacy to overt events, as in the last great hunt. Here the rush of what he is witnessing and doing leaves little time for what he is feeling, yet even so his consciousness deepens the effect, as when at their closing-in on the bear, "the woods . . . and the rain-heavy air were one uproar . . . until it seemed to the boy that all the hounds which had ever bayed game in this land were yelling." Even so slight an

example is essentially of a piece with Faulkner's typical practice in its greater extensions and deeper intensities. In his narratives with all their varieties of actors and multiple incidents
the total import rests for its dynamic conveyance upon individual awareness and often a completely private subjective response. This is of course nothing new in essence and intent; for
instance, as soliloquy it was once much practiced in drama, and
in modern fiction its many refinements have been conspicuous.
What is to be remarked in Faulkner is how purposeful and
with what explicit originative sense of means to a total compositional effect is his apt and subtle use of his characters'
awareness, their momentary existential actuality constituting
both substance and the medium of its aesthetic evocation. Not
that Faulkner is anything as simple as a stream-of-consciousness writer, and (as *The Sound and the Fury* or *As I Lay
Dying* variously suggest) he would not commit himself through
his characters to the strictest confinements of pure *monologue
interieur*. Yet his instinct as fictionist that here was where the
truth of the matter lay is shown even in those *personae* he
treats with narrative objectivity but with something like a
dramatist's projection of what they are thinking and feeling,
through nuances of gesture and bearing, and of speech that
partially discloses momentary attitude as well as more constant personal traits. To this end his excellent dialogue, given
all the acuteness that strategies of composition and diction can
achieve, is never mere characterization but part of the narrative texture, wherein it abets a fundamentally subjective tone,
giving an immediate and maximum reality as of interactive
human beings in living motion.

Faulkner's is an extension and extreme refinement of the
classic concept of an action, a plot. Beyond curiosity as to a
specific outcome he creates those more basic tensions, a
constant of human existence, between overt action and the
actors' consciousness of themselves in its process, contributors
to it, and to some degree in the grip of its consequences. In his
own practice this high intent is carried forward in many ways,
by design and detail, and through tonalities, proportionings,

and culminations. What is perhaps most steadily revealing of all this is Faulkner's style, truly and vitally impressionistic in its flow, connecting external actualities and individually attuned encounterings, through which object and response become realities as of the fictional world, wherein to behold is to know. As readers progressed through Faulkner's successive works, seeing in each its unique elucidation of a weighty theme, there was also this something more immediate and dynamic to be realized — the artist's adaptation of refined fictional techniques to a disclosure of his characters as real beings, in those motions of their natures out of which the story arose, not only in its form but with its tone and deepest appeal to imaginative response.

A deplorable aspect of the lag in appreciating Faulkner was that among the tardy were so many who while imposing a totally negative judgment gave no evidence of having noticed, even occasionally and if only to a degree, his sheer technical achievements. Though the question remains indeterminable, cultural historians of American literature may come to wonder whether it was Faulkner's sometimes grim realism which so troubled critics that they were readier to mete out denunciation of his style and narrative structuring, or whether it was over these techniques in themselves that their distaste was at once aroused and so they came down the more harshly upon subject matter as it emerged. What is plainly on the record is that the spate of negative opinion about Faulkner was almost altogether undiscriminating; impercipient of a significant content given potent artistic thrust, it made no distinctions. Therefore any disputing of such nonjudiciousness seems to require matter-of-fact, even pedestrian repetition of what is obvious in the aesthetics of modern fiction — including at least not only matters of connotative language and thematic composition, but the situating of point of view, maintenance of subjective-objective interpermeation, and every enhancement of the implicative mode and supportive patternings which may convey representative concepts to an intuitive reading.

It is of course anomalous and a waste all around if anyone approaches a Faulkner work without desire to view it attentively and imaginatively as literature, whether considered good or bad, yet at least an ambitious creation in its genre. But beyond anomaly it would be absurd to complain because Faulkner will never be widely read. Obviously close attention and active imagination, which genuine art can serve and reward so highly, are not cultivated in an era of mass communication, with its commercially beamed ministrations to an only nominally educated majority, polyglot and lost in alienations except in their gregarious cravings for shallow sensationalism or tranquilizing banalities. These as dispensed not only in television drama and popular fiction, but in politics and mass-production evangelism converted into vulgarized art forms, collectively affect the climate of human alertness and awareness, by their allure toward passive acceptance, under vague assurances, with muted evasion of issue. Much of this is perhaps data for the cultural historian; some present responsibility falls on those educators who in doctrinaire permissiveness neglect the need to cultivate a more precise and extensive perception of realities. The problem within the world of letters is not so much a recruitment of readers for Faulkner and other intricately profound artists, it is the defensive rebuttal of those who having read great literature, criticize it imperceptively, and even with a morbid hostility to excellence. Here allegations of "difficulty" carry an odor of anxiety, not just in irritation at demands made upon attention by the subtleties of highly original art, but by its responsible projection of human realities, often harsh or pathetic, as a challenge to value judgments. With Faulkner, to flinch and pass by the issue is to fail completely. That he is the complete fictionist of first rank is clear too in this—he is not to be relished for his ingenuities alone, since they will not even be perceived rightly except through an experiencing of all they shadow forth of the human condition, and with an answering to it.

It is such response to realities that can liberate and enfranchise the reader, as it has the writer of fiction, each in his voluntary role and his conditional dependence on the other. In that tentatively expanding acquaintance there are mutual civilties looking toward understanding but projecting no demands. The fictionist schemes to captivate attention by an artful setting-forth, but all his craft cannot create life, can only transmute something of its realities into perceptible representations and suggest their essences. Such a specialized enterprise can fall short by its own insufficiencies or excesses, but it is also vulnerable to readers' impercipience. That may occur from lack of experience as basis for recognitions or too short a reach of intuition. But even given such potentialities in some degree, the reader's attention may remain too flaccid to enter upon a sustained imaginative projection, or may reflexively evade appeals to empathy and concern. Against either indolence or obduracy the sophisticated and serious fictionist's intimative art cannot operate, and under any such begrudging scrutiny it will be falsely judged. While men's aversion from recognizing human wrongs and woes may be itself a subject for fiction, its obstructive presence in a reader is a problem beyond aesthetics. Even so, quite as large and perhaps a larger obstacle to appreciation of Faulkner has been a scanting of close sustained attention to his pages as fiction at a high level of that art. While to remind either antagonistic reviewers or even more casual readers of the vitalizing reciprocities between a fiction's conception and its implicative ways of conveyance is not to prescribe solemn ponderings on theory, it is to assert that until a reading becomes imaginatively responsive to how the fictionist is saying it, what is being said will scarcely be heard, or may be heard all wrong. Nor need receptive attention mean minute technical analysis but rather the contrary, a sustained reading with that quickening absorption in detailed narrative flow, emerging patterns, and thematic interrelations which can liberate empathic response moment by moment.

It remains of practical importance in estimating any literary artist that basic factors in communication, commonplace in themselves and of widest applicability but sometimes disre-

garded, be kept in view. Pointing out the obvious sometimes
becomes necessary, to establish that what (for instance in
Faulkner) is called obscurity and prolixity is instead comparable, at the literary level, to what in utilitarian expository
modes is recognizable as precision, economy, and lucidity. In
all uses of language, whether in literary art, abstract
discourse, or explicit definition, there is an operative ratio between degree of the subject's intrinsic complexity and the
achievement of its conveyance. "Difficulty" for readers (especially that arising from syntax and vocabulary) cannot be
faulted in itself but only if it is in a disarrangement of this
quid pro quo. The language of philosophy and the language
of the law, for instance, are often difficult, and require close
attentive reading, yet typically the complexities arise not from
the writer's prolixity or vagueness but from his aim at precision and inclusion. Philosophy must set aside alternative views
in a defining of its own, the law must mark out whole ranges of
contingencies, and these statements must be definitively expressed in a logical order. Similarly, criteria for language in
any literary form include an equilibrium between substance
and expression. Thus as with philosophy or the law, no charge
of undue "difficulty" can be substantiated except through a
simplifying paraphrase which loses no refinement of meaning,
no relative ordering by subordination, nor any definition or
shade of effect which either an expositor had found necessary
or the artist had chosen to include. Beyond that, and more
particularly with the artist, if inclusion itself is questioned it
becomes less a problem of language than of structure, as to
continuity and design in their furthest reach. In this aspect of
literary art rhetoric becomes most subtle and poetic reaches its
purest manifestations through apt and intense function, while
still resting on a kind of logic in silhouette, through the
literary work's detectable and felt form. It is the literary
artist's privilege, with its risks, to fix upon his subject, to
regard it from where he stands, and to come at it creatively in
his own way. He is following his vocation when he proceeds according to his own envisionings and mood, with intent to

evoke readers' corresponding recognitions. This is a touchy matter, since even the most attentive and congenially imaginative reader will only approximate the artist's thrust of cumulative realization in an ambitiously self-determined composition. Yet gifted creation however bold and idiosyncratic has a way of finding its audience, of whatever number and to whatever degree of responsiveness, and such a tentative but ideally personal meeting of minds has its unique qualitative rewards. No kind or measure of success, however, can give the artist outright claim upon attention or grant an immunity from criticism. The fictionist takes the whole imaginative venture upon himself, only hoping to be heard and credited; his reader accords a merely conditional hearing which he may choose to break off midway; and by common consent this is not subject to dispute, being a matter of gusto. However, rejection of a literary work raises complementary questions: is it not worthy of this reader's attention, or does it lie beyond his capacities? In the latter case the reader is entitled to go his way in peace, but quietly; obviously he does not qualify as a judge, and any honest man will admit it. Some of Faulkner's relentlessly disapproving critics anomalously stood on no such footing. There is scarcely any evidence that they found his fiction worthy of that close sustained attention which literature at its most sophisticated must have for conveyance; and the more severe their judgments the less penetratingly were these defined, with their references to content, form, and style merely as catch-words propped up by pejorative adjectives. From any such journalistic malfeasance there spreads a fog of stupid misapprehension about all communication but especially literary art, in its voluntary and self-determinant nature as an exercise of imagination, for both the writer and the reader.

While the degree to which the genius of Faulkner's creations could be obscured by indifference and impercipience posing as critical expertise is a disreputable episode of prejudice against emergent creativity of a high order, and large amends have been made by appreciative critics, this does not prove

Faulkner faultless. Artists who aspire greatly will sometimes fall short, like the ambitious vaulter who brings the bar down with him, or the well-intentioned friend who speaks inadequately or inordinately at a crucial moment. Admittedly Faulkner may be charged with occasional extravagances, but these were the overreachings of an intense creativity, they were never an indifferent looseness, and certainly not affectation. Moreover, any momentary nimiety weighs but little against the more characteristic succinctness which gives his narratives their absorbing celerity, and for every somewhat awkward passage there can be found many quite similar and even characteristic procedures where the intended effect is neatly brought off. As a fictional narrator Faulkner is both fluent and economical. His intensities are not a lingering; instead, they accelerate by their aptness. His involutions engage closely attentive imagination. And Faulkner is superlative in a blending of plenitude and dispatch.

Certainly few fictionists have asked more of readers than Faulkner does, by the complexities of his tempermentally tinged art, with its demand upon concentrated attention, cumulative remembering of interrelated detail and grasp of emerging pattern, sensitivity to connotative language and the nuances of prose rhythms, and an empathic envisioning of sharply individualized characters and the particularities of situation. For access to what is most significant in Faulkner's novels, this all needs to be comprised in the reader's view, with a high degree of that sustained imaginative responsiveness which the fictional mode when purely employed solicits and rewards. Yet some fairly experienced and seriously attentive readers have turned away from the narrative tensions and prodigalities of stylistic effects in the master's works and are still inclined to consider these as hyperromantic excesses. Possibly to such sensibilities Faulkner may appear wilful, yet unquestionably his complexities are purposeful, intent on evolving a dynamism never to be had by mere extravagance. And his fictions are furnished, structured, and styled for sustained artistic effects in support of impelling concepts, not in any such lack. The demands he makes are therefore no more than commensurate with how much he does for the reader to sustain him in an intent imaginative experience. So Faulkner is not to be skimmed, yet neither is he to be fragmented under analysis. He is to be approached without preconception; he is to be met with eager intelligence and wakeful imagination; his works merit being heard out as music should be, in detail, continuity, pattern, and resolution.

Blindly negative criticism or merely scant attention, whether from aversion to Faulkner's realism or in misapprehension of his fictional mode, were not the only forces bearing against Faulkner's great works in the thirties. Like any fictionist Faulkner was not just heir but thrall to his sources as of his times, and he liberated himself into artistic autonomy only through penetrating discernments and humanely judicious responses, conveyed with originative genius. But because his effects are often such fleet touches in the intricate progression of his narratives, and may be threaded in allusively with subtle shades of diction, he was the less accessible or acceptable to readers in a period when increasingly commercialized communication was debasing style and blurring definition, when "simplified" or "basic" English was raised beyond it limited utility into a cult, egalitarian and implicitly anti-intellectual, and when in public education the disciplines of language were being eroded—all this to the point where it was widely believed that anyone with anything to say was obliged to say it so that everyone could understand it. Literary artists of course gave no credence to such outright cultural nihilism. Conversely twentieth-century poetry in English was resounding in Faulkner's time with strong voices as various as Frost and Cummings, Auden and Yeats, and many others sufficiently relevant, original, and vigorous to be heard along with them, nor did the pedantic cult of Eliot submerge, much less eclipse them. In the art of the novel a conventional superfigure, the presiding and expository author, had been reduced from his nineteenth-century preeminence; point of view was assimilated into subtlest fictional practice, for the evoking of a more immediate and sustained illusion and freer imaginative response. The intrinsic aesthetic advances in fiction as well as those in poetry drew an enlarging and increasingly knowing adherance, yet the gap between literary or subliterary and simply utilitarian communication continued to widen, and the culture's decline in ability to make distinctions, particularly under the increase and wider spread of raw data, bred more of the kinds of animosity Faulkner suffered from.

In these same decades, however, one talent in the American novel had arisen to stand between the extremes. Hemingway, working carefully and ably at the level of a serious and genuine art, showed how in fiction simplicity could operate as something more than just that, a lucidity beyond the literal, subtly implicative. (Glories as of the sun and the moon, each integral and consummate, can be found for instance by contrasting the prose of the opening paragraphs in *A Farewell to Arms* and *Absalom, Absalom!*). Hemingway was not closely apprehended either, yet the difference from Faulkner in their own times was most perceptible in the early acceptance Hemingway won, partly as type of the "lost generation," but also as an allegedly simple writer. There was a consequent degree of overestimation. Despite his wide rangings over countries and continents, his are the more limited themes compared to Faulkner's; and a subjectivity of a morbidly introverted sort frequently tinges his narratives, whereas Faulkner's absorption, projected impersonally through his more comprehensive and distancing art, is with the inner lives of his various personae. Some show traits he seems to sanction, but none is a semblable, much less an *alter ego* such as moves lightly masked through Hemingway's works. These distinctions (though they measure scope and a certain significance in fictional art) were not the concern of Hemingway's most avid followers. In his idiosyncrasies (utterly different from Faulkner's own but as pronounced) Hemingway was elevated willing or not as guru for a vogue of simple fictional style, which his imitators naively reduced to parodies that lacked Hemingway's elemental vigor and subtle overtones but persisted as a fashion.

What more broadly eclipsed Faulkner's novels during the thirties was a predominance in fiction of doctrinaire "social consciousness," working in a naturalistic vein, its embodiments for the most part cumbersomely factual and weighed upon by currently improvised sociopolitical ideologies. Some of this fiction was intelligent and honest and carried a certain authenticity and perceptive compassion, as in the work of James Farrell. However, it had a most conspicuous and commercially successful pretender in Sinclair Lewis, whose attempted social satire became such a grotesque caricature of its substance as to suggest a transference of self-loathing. Other fiction more realistically oriented to contemporary American sociopolitical problems during the depression was widely valued for distinctive qualities, especially an immediate relevance narratively made explicit. Preeminent in that period were works of Dos Passos and Steinbeck, especially *The Grapes of Wrath* and the trilogy *USA*. These were found impressive in their ample representations and also their ingenuities of structure and style. Wide focusing upon contemporaneous subject matter of current concern and overt ideological treatment gave these novelists (and others like them in this regard) a kind of claim not to be made by Faulkner's great work in the thirties, with its wider chronological scope and penetration and more sustaining art. Moreover, nothing in American fiction of that period went as deep psychologically and sociologically as did *Light in August* or looked as far into societal-individual sources of human tragedy as did *Absalom, Absalom!* And these both were completely sustained and powerfully evocative fictions, finished works of art, whereas in Steinbeck and more drastically in Dos Passos there were elements of journalism, case history, and direct exhortation, sooner heard but less acutely, and sooner forgotten, as structure fell short of form, having made less than a complete claim upon imagination.

In the nation's years of a great depression, involvement in

World War II, and postwar reaction Faulkner's uniquely brilliant and demanding art was not the only factor against perception of him as a socioethically oriented novelist. As of his times, but well in advance of a "social consciousness" as promulgated in simplistic terms to an apathetic public, Faulker discerned that the deepest problems of modern American life, like those in the past, were not to be got rid of by patchwork legislation, its blueprints drawn in the dim ink of self-appeasing sentimentality. Though his Yoknapatawphan stories, with their homely close-ups of relatively small communities and focusings on unique individuals, could not comprise the most obviously disruptive elements in the society as a whole, Faulkner did see more profoundly than most fictionists engaged in wider scrutinies that, considering the scarcely definable complexity of human beings, not all social problems are solvable, but are only perhaps amenable to some control, judiciously exercised at a humane level. It was in this light, and with intuitive searchings into varieties of human behavior that he devoted years to an ironic trilogy revealing an endemic human rapaciousness at its core, shockingly potent yet positively countered to a degree. In the Snopes trilogy he had begun and continued with more regard for the factor of heredity than social reformers would have acknowledged. Yet he does not rest on stereotypes; the cousins Flem and Mink move into the complementary opposites of an accomplished poetic justice, and among his portrayals of unique individualities the volunteers on the angels' side are made fully credible by their human fallibilities.

Faulkner's sober ponderings of human affairs were measured in his fiction; they did not descend to propaganda nor lose themselves in naturalistic data, nor were they allowed to dilute and cloud in any way the artistry which was his essential means of profoundest imaginative effect. Yet his judgments of society were independent and acute. Out of his personal experience and observation, joined by heritage with a historically oriented view, Faulkner conceived of the biracial factor sectionally and in general as a melancholy fate for all

concerned — inhumanly brutal in its inceptions and uses, catastrophic in its past results, and presently a distressing confusion, potentially calamitous. He did not live to see the full-
blown successive flowerings from school integration ideology,
but how he might have regarded it all can be imagined from
his own theory of segregation, not by color but in one school
for those who could and would learn, another for those who
couldn't or wouldn't. (This opinion, which he voiced not fictionally but *in propria persona,* no doubt would have called
for some refinements, especially as between those who couldn't
and those who wouldn't, but such separate schools in each
locality could have largely replaced color with a more deeply
relevant criterion, while maintaining local community as
grounds for cultural roots, and to Faulkner this principle was
not sentimentally fanciful but humanly integral. In this light
it might even be speculated that Faulkner — with an understanding regard for the Negro which he delegates credibly to
many of his major white characters — would have felt at the
undefined center of the surge toward "black power" and the
declared beauty of blackness something deeper than political
revolutionism, an instinctive resistance to an even faceless con-
formism that might lie ahead on a legislated road to integration.) Faulkner's sense of American history, given his psychologically intuitive bent, is made to haunt variously his postbellum characters, most notably Quentin Compson, Hightower, and Isaac McCaslin. Primarily regional in its detail,
and turning upon the Civil War even into the second and third
generations, its facts as an abiding influence are given their
particularly somber local shadings as they play upon individuals and yet are made humanly representative, suggesting
as of any large flow of events a turbulence of interrupted high
purposes and expedient improvisations, shot through with
personal contentions, and altogether too wasteful and often
brutal. In this context a worldly wisdom, as Faulkner shows it
operant in many for gain, evasion, or mere survival, is anything but reassuring; this makes credible as well as com-
mendable a reactive idealism with its guarded resoluteness,

which is confirmed through confrontations with astounding disorderliness at every level from cunning to obsession. Faulkner's camera eye comes in closer than on panoramas of sectional war or tides of racial antagonisms. Yet inordinateness in man as a diversely social animal, amply shown in Faulkner's fiction with sometimes harsh detail, nevertheless is particularized beyond sensationalism, chiefly in an art transcending melodrama's simplistic antitheses. It also penetrates by dramatic individuation into realities beyond those sociological generalizations that had left much fiction of the social-consciousness school short of empathic persuasiveness.

Such aesthetic deficiency, with its insulating of content itself, continued into later decades, when the nation's fiction grew more tangential and introspective, and less energetically concerned with the sociopolitical, perhaps instinctively shrinking from it as society's ongoing disintegrations reduced the phrase "the great American novel" from a cliché to a tired joke. Still there were pretensions to comprehensiveness, as in such a book as *Herzog,* which (if not to be taken as elephantine satire) was a prime example of failure for lack of compellingly progressive characterization. The protagonist remains nondescript to the imagination, arrested in spite of a frantic activity, throughout which his sensations and very emotions drift off into detached intellectual cadenzas like wind-blown scraps from an undergraduate's notes on Western Civ. I, II, and yet this curious facultative dichotomy in the novel's matter does not appear to be its proposed theme, and if it were, a mere sketch would have exhausted it. Conversely Faulkner not only knew as everyone did the special path to realization opened up in modern fictional narrative with its closer approach to the individual, he had the genius, the requisite imagination to follow through in a deep enough penetration of the protagonist's unique ongoing inner life yet with ample sense of environmental involvement. Joyce had done it with Stephen across a whole spectrum in the "Telemachia" of *Ulysses;* Hemingway had done it with Jake

Barnes in *The Sun Also Rises,* where most subtly the trau-
matized narrator-protagonist is made to begin his tale with an
account of a subordinate character, thus intimating his own
need to keep his mind turned outward, a course he continues
to attempt.

The mode of suspending a fictional action in a vital continuum of awareness was nothing new, of course; with the
ingenuous appeal of first-person narrative it is simply but
engagingly basic in *Robinson Crusoe,* and with greater penetration and inclusiveness in third-person containment it purely
becomes more than ever the real story, as in the multiple-
facted *Mrs. Dalloway.* James and Conrad had similarly refined
the narrative mode, through such intensifications of effect as by
the narrator's detached conveyance in "Four Meetings" of Miss
Caroline Spencer's whole life, essentially, under its sequence of
determinants, or in Marlow's roles in his own initiatory experience in "Heart of Darkness" and through the wider grasp,
both objective and empathic, in *Lord Jim.* As to fictional technique, Quentin Anderson's statement concerning James —
"We can never separate the question, What has he done in this
story? from the question, How has he done it?" — can be as
truly propounded about Faulkner. Moreover, the questions
are not only inseparable but their answers exist in each other:
the art is not an end in itself but exists for what it elicits, and
what the story tells is dependently relative to readers' imaginative responses. Each reader in the privacies of his own experience is not only acknowledging the largesse of unique genius,
he is also verifying by his assent a wide human commonalty of
recognitions and evaluations. Thus fictional characterization
through entry into the actor's consciousness is not merely an
engaging but isolable aspect of technique. A further dramatizing of issue, it bases significance and fictional credibility upon
creating the illusion of reality in the characters not just as
named and described but as they live and move in their
existential being. And the reader must perceive and find
persuasive what passes in the minds of fictional characters in

order for that element to contribute to validation of the narrative as an action, in the dramatic sense, evolving a significant theme.

Beyond Faulkner's structural and stylistic traits as a fictionist and his temperamentally tinged view of a localized subject matter, readers' receptiveness to him also turns with peculiar acuteness on their entering imaginatively into societal considerations, psychologically dimensioned and adroitly implied. The demand upon empathy as well as intuitiveness is immense; there is imperative need for concerned awareness of other men's ongoing individual existence in the unceasing current of their lives as variously beset within a fabric of circumstance and the motions of their own natures. Perhaps a clear estimate of the lingering indifference or antipathy to Faulkner must await supplement by an American social historian with a view (not unlike some of Faulkner's intimations) of paradoxical leveling effects in an increasingly mechanized society, confusingly diversified in its continental and cultural sprawl, with stratifications which alienate rather than reciprocally influence, yet where desperation broadens down into mere inquietude. With personal aims eroded and fragmented, there is a diminished alertness to the sequential, compensated for by preoccupation with "happenings" made transiently portentous. (A plenitude of these have already been seen not only as the norm of the mass media but in puerile innovations, preposterously *avant-garde,* in drama, fiction, and music. Any sharing here, beyond their coterie's claque, is perhaps chiefly of noncommitment, the artists themselves intransitively stranded, lost beyond the assurances and achievements of a spontaneously intentional impressionism. Conversely, any paradoxical trend toward noncommitment and unphilosophical absurdity became at least a cloudy and crooked mirror of a disoriented era, and that small potency must be allowed it. But a commanding transcendence in a looking before and after and directly at the matter in question is what has constituted cultural utility and contained an effective aesthetic order in great fictional works, and this is to be found in Faulkner, recognizably the preeminent American novelist of his times.

At points in the perspectives of his works Faulkner might be envisaged as if at an eminence commanding the South's history as it turned upon the Civil War, and thereby (in subsequence to all that confusion of mores, catastrophic devastation and disorientation, and a legacy of aggravated human problems) Faulkner looms as if apprehending the later fate of a whole society bemused by illusions of the nation's strength, cohesion, and stability—this though it could be moving into socioeconomic disorder and conflict essentially as great (even at a semiguerrilla stage) as the outright sectional confrontation several generations earlier, when at least issues were more explicit, the antagonists more identifiable, with clearer assumptions, and definite goals. In such aspects Faulkner maintained lengthy historical perspective in some of his novels (notably in *Absalom, Absalom!* and the prose interludes in *Requiem for a Nun*) but in others he came close to his own time—in *The Town* (1957) and *The Mansion* (1959) he arrives at the years of World War II, with Flem meeting his end in 1945, and "Delta Autumn," published in 1942 in *Story* as well as in *Go Down, Moses,* reaches to the verge of entry into that war already begun, and touches on the state of the nation at that juncture. In *Intruder in the Dust,* with its setting shortly after World War I, Faulkner shows (through Gavin Stevens' ironic outlook) the Yoknapatawphan populace attached almost erotically to their automobiles and filled with cravings for army goods surpluses and other newly manufactured products out of the first of those industrial spasms a war induces in an increasingly mechanized economy, for purveyance to a materialistically seduced society. (From Faulkner's treatment of this it seems fairly clear that he shared Gavin's ironic view.)

While portions of Faulkner's fiction might be turned to in pondering whether there can be a *modus vivendi* between idealism and appetite, verities and expediency, what he treats more comprehensively (and with greater profundity than his contemporaries) is not just those socially disintegrative and culturally demeaning trends he so acutely detected, but also their human implications, shown with individuation and shades of distinction all the way from the amorality of Flem Snopes to the probity of Isaac McCaslin. It is in this aspect that American literature's most distinguished regionalist becomes not only its most acute explorer of individualities but its most philosophical twentieth-century fictionist. Faulkner's conceptions and his empathic intuitions were not bounded by Yoknapatawpha County; his inquiries, in their humanistic dimensions, were a far venture from his hereditary grounds, and his discoveries, as it would seem from his disposition of his characters, were approximations of the human condition, in a complex of grave forebodings, endurance, and hope.

In the forties, having published *The Hamlet* and while largely occupied in projecting *A Fable,* Faulkner completed and published two major works, *Go Down, Moses* and *Intruder in the Dust,* as well as the collection of detective stories capped by the Gavin Stevens novella, *Knight's Gambit. Go Down, Moses* was largely retrospective, dominated at the heart and in half the book by the figure of Isaac McCaslin, who while refusing his inheritance accepted his heritage, in austere confrontation of the South's past from his pivotal point in the 1880s with its continuing racial dilemma. Though *Go Down, Moses* (through "Delta Autumn") comes up from antebellum days to the verge of World War II, as to more general states of mind then *Intruder in the Dust* is closer to its times, representing the 1920s as in Jefferson and Yokapatawpha County through ironic sociological vignettes, glimpses of the untamed Gowries and other rough countrymen of Beat Four, and also more reassuring persons, especially Miss Habersham and Sheriff Hampton. The novel's events, turning upon the saving of a falsely accused Negro from a lynch mob, project from past into future socioeconomic and political problems of race and also interregional relations together with the chronic uneasiness and occasional ambivalence of the twentieth-century

Southerner's responses, which have their implications beyond that place and decade. Both *Go Down, Moses* and *Intruder* are regionally representative through the acute involvement of their protagonists with their history and its ongoing demands; each in its way is deeply rooted societally and yet turns most pointedly on personal ordeal, in the characterizations of Isaac McCaslin and Charles Mallison. In this same decade in American fiction more attention was being given to war novels, centering on ordeals of combat and personal disorientations. This was succeeded by a vogue for metropolitan-based and ethnic-centered works, which manifested a recurring expression of social malaise but were of limited representativeness and morbidly self-conscious, yet such fiction had its considerable coteries and expedient commercial support. Meanwhile in the early 1940s Faulkner's great works of the preceding decade were mostly out of print, the plates of some of his books had been melted down, and certain reviewers were proving their consistency by continued growls at him.

Those who had become acquainted admirers in the thirties, however, could take special delight in what disturbed the less convinced and less literary-minded. With every new Faulkner novel, readers were invited to begin all over again, in an unparalleled excursion, until the marvel grew that one artist, indubitable genius though he was, could father so many shapes each with its own vital symmetry and aptness. Though some who made slow going of it were inclined to write off this unique, purposefully sustained complexity of design as nothing but a random wildness, here too, as with style, complexities and involutions were to be recognized as a penetrating searching-out of human experience and humane concerns. It was absorbed regard for individuals in their natures, as circumstantially situated and in their responses to consequence, that carried Faulkner on to the particular devising of each autonomous novel. There is no dividing of plot and character; in a sense it is all character, but conceived alive and hence in motion, and human and hence moving through consciousness with its constant flicker of thoughtful feeling. Given Faulkner's dimensioned acquaintance with persons, his intuition of the individual life within the type, and his close but detached view of their conditioning enclosure within period and place, he could trust characters to spin out a story; yet the tale remained his in a profound perception of what was at the heart of that whole and proportioned matter, and his characters were franchised and deployed for that enactment. With each work, reading can sense that this and no other is how the tale came to Faulkner, of this shape and so garbed and with these tidings, and what he proffers is a composition tempered to voice the hold this apprehension had laid on the artist, and a share in his imaginative commitment to it. That being so, no matter how eccentric the characters or outlandish the situations, there can inhere in the fictional illusion that affecting validity which emerges when crucial issues elicit typically human responses, and the artist's presence as creator is transmuted into a sense of his submission to a vision he would share.

That Faulkner was not working from superficially conventionalized notions of the genre but rather was making his own adaptations of the novel's newly vitalized modes and means is shown in his disregarding even his own previous works as patterns. He returned often to certain of his strategies and devices, but always in a fresh adaptation to the new context. His achievement of a vital autonomy in each work shows as something greater than mere inventive craft and virtuosity; it comes of a genius totally committed to the matter in hand, and in being possessed by it, possessing it. The reader as beneficiary of another's commitment is privileged to devote attention and intuition in commensurate measure, being an imaginatively responsive witness to the work in its continuities, resonances, and evolving realizations. Faulkner is accessible, given as close reading as generally would be accorded serious literary works of any kind, and few could be more intriguing than he is in the movement of his masterfully structured narratives. Faulkner is neither mysterious nor monstrous, he is not arcane or remote, he is merely prodigious in every sense. He strove to give containment to ranging and penetrating recognitions, and thus to let something complete and potent become and be, to be proffered out of the artist's restlessly inquiring solitude as a feeling communication with his fellow-beings. For the reader to sense this also as he too goes along where this novelist has gone is not only an engrossing aesthetic experience but one of the strongest assurances of a humane solidarity that modern art can offer. In this aspect Faulkner's preeminence loomed monumentally plain before the nations in 1950, not so much through the award of the Novel Prize in itself but by what his acceptance speech defined in large and lasting terms as the artist's role in the modern world, according to the august concepts upon which he based a dedication to his calling, and which he urged upon younger writers everywhere.

Though Faulkner put it in 1941 that he had written "too fast, too much," his beneficiaries cannot regret the release of that daemonic power which in all its extremes had produced in the preceding decade so many works of such integrity, variety, and persuasive power. Nor did production cease, and the novels which followed *The Hamlet* were no less dynamic, each in its own surprisingly original way. If the units of *Go Down, Moses* (1942) are fully perceived as a subtly composed totality, he will be seen continuing with particularized subjects, yet with interfusing themes that were to give not just unity to each novel but a large consistency to his whole career. Supreme originative power in the structuring of fictions still showed itself in the adapted singularity of each work, with such variety as between *Intruder in the Dust* (1948) and *Requiem for a Nun* (1951). Then in his connectedly rounding out the long-meditated Snopes trilogy with *The Town* (1957) and *The Mansion* (1959) Faulkner not only sustained a massive totality as thematic composition following upon *The Hamlet,* but gave each of the three volumes a distinctive tone as if echoing a certain imperative *now* in the ongoing life of the artist's protean imagination. It remains the resonant, modulated dramatic and lyrical voice of Faulkner even in those two most widely different works from his later years, *A*

Fable (1954), epical in concept, stupendously elaborated, aesthetically distanced, and grandly allegorical; and then finally *The Reivers* (1962), unpretentious, lively, and benign, with its engaging immediacy, indigenous humor, and natural sentiment.

Within little more than a month after publication of *The Reivers* Faulkner was suddenly dead, just short of his sixty-fifth birthday, and his readers were left to regret what further works his still vigorously originative mind and intense spirit might have given them, but most of all to wonder over the prodigality of his genius and his acuteness of insights, conveyed with such versatile and brilliant art, in its many superbly integrated originations.

While *The Hamlet* had bounded an eleven-year period of almost superhuman productivity, 1940 scarcely marked a great divide or the beginnings of any essential variation in Faulkner's work. His career is not open to description as a rise and a falling-off, nor can his novels be grouped within periods or as to modes. In his grasp on the immediate and his conceptual range he was able to contain the paradox of consistency and variety, and even to make such factors complementary in service to his art. He continued to represent the human typicality of local characters through regionally centered and conditioned events, most often within the confines of a fictitious but credibly realized Mississippi county, of which Faulkner as its cartographer wryly wrote himself down as "sole owner and proprietor," yet in the artist's hospitable way, with no areas marked restricted. Within the transcendentally expanding *oeuvre* there are links with earlier novels through recurrence of major characters, and not just as to the *Snopes* trilogy. Lucas Beauchamp of *Go Down, Moses* reappears importantly in *Intruder;* Temple Drake comes all the way from *Sanctuary* into a still more enigmatic role in *Requiem for a Nun;* and most pervasive is Gavin Stevens, who proceeds from "Go Down, Moses" into *Intruder, Knight's Gambit,* and *Requiem,* and thence, with his nephew Charles of *Intruder* now a grown man in his own right, to join Ratliff in *The Town* and *The Mansion*. Yet these reappearances do not entail repetition, even with the consistently idiosyncratic Gavin; new circumstances in their singularity evoke responses that turn upon other facets of personality and illustrate recurrently the theme of man in motion. Faulkner's novels continued to be that run of amazing fictional surprises, each an unparalleled origination within the genre. More profoundly, from within their provincial limits (excepting *A Fable*) and through their unique forms they increasingly shadowed forth the temperament of a creative genius who envisioned his realm philosophically, finding in its past and present and sensing in the seeming trends of its ongoing life certain validly admonitory and reassuring instances illustrative of the human condition. In the two decades between publication of *Go Down, Moses* and Faulkner's death, he sometimes spoke out directly rather than in fictional mode, yet such public utterances, whether soberly sociopolitical or wryly humorous or in measured explication of his work, did not reduce or blur a profile, that of the wholly committed artist. His successive works continued to show a native concern deepened by ever close acquaintance, bespoken reflectively yet with a high sense of drama, through a dynamic and inventive craft, undersigned by a value-oriented view of life, expressed not didactically but through a highly imaginative art.

Such an integration, consistently manifested through sheer creative power with major thematic significations, could not go forever unnoticed. Greater numbers of seriously committed critics indicated in one way or another that this was the century's most remarkable American novelist, and there began to accumulate that body of studies which has accorded Faulkner's achievements a close appreciative regard. Meanwhile in the unreadable future there lay an event which would place his name and himself in an eminence before the literate world and would evoke from him a brief but dynamic public utterance declaring what his fiction had implied throughout, his position as committed humanistic realist. Yet within the decade preceding this august hour Faulkner was still receiving comparatively little attention from sophisticated readers or even in the academic community, and in a reciprocity of in-difference most of his novels had been allowed to go out of print. Faulkner himself, while trying to get on with his hercu-lean labors in constructing *A Fable,* was still necessitously sell-ing off sizable portions of precious time to Hollywood. Mean-while, certain habitual detractors (among whom Clifton Fadi-man continued to occupy the deplorable position of *primus inter pares*) were still at it, whether out of sheer impercipience or incorrigible stubbornness. But in the latter half of the decade Faulkner was gradually and then abruptly brought to wider and more responsive attention. *The Portable Faulkner,* devotedly edited by Malcolm Cowley, appeared in 1946, allowing timorous initiates a sampling, and furnishing occa-sional readers of Faulkner some perspective on the master's scope to that date. (However, Cowley's attempted general view, leaning toward a chronology extractable from details in the separate works, focused more attention on Faulkner's regionalism in its epical, mythic, legendary perspectives than on the larger elements these were ancillary to—the artist's humanism, his penetrations into his characters' subjectivity, and the sheer genius of a totally enabling structural and stylis-tic art.) In 1948 came *Intruder in the Dust,* a more accessible story than the bemusingly intricated, incomparably great *Go Down, Moses,* yet with its own profundities and subtleties of rendition. Energetic and well focused, as its matter required, *Intruder in the Dust* had a substantial sale, and it gained further attention the following year when it was made into a film, in Faulkner's own Oxford. *The Collected Stories of Wil-liam Faulkner,* including forty-two selected titles, was issued in August of 1950. Then on November tenth the award of the Nobel Prize was announced, and one month later Faulkner received it in Stockholm from King Gustave.

The acceptance speech, often reprinted and quoted, was more than an occasional utterance, and other than a formality in rhetorical vein. Its idealism, entirely sincere, is directly to a point. Its profound abstractions, though summoned up in prolonged series, are not redundant; neither are they amorphous, but rather meant as axioms to guide human augury and endeavor. More particularly Faulkner, as he said, was "using this moment as a pinnacle" from which he "might be listened to" by younger writers, the selected audience he addressed throughout that speech. He did so without condescension to neophytes and with concern not just for literature's future in itself but for its ongoing service, not merely by diverting and beguiling readers, and certainly not by denigrating humanity, but by warning and heartening, linking courage and compassion as proved human values in a formidably restive world. And he spoke not only out of his gathered convictions and invincible stamina, but to the young as of their own time, admitting the mid-century crisis of the spirit, in fear of the atom, endured under that sense of impasse which in its despair may discount "problems of the spirit." Yet only "the problems of the human heart in conflict with itself," said Faulkner, were "worth writing about." Such phrasing echoes his lifelong fictional attempt to present the subjective existential reality of human beings in their struggling toward self-possession and integrity, still tempted to indifference, slackening into ambivalence, yet rousing themselves to moral assertion based on "the old verities." It is, Faulkner told his younger colleagues, "the writer's duty to write about these things . . . his privilege to help man endure by lifting his heart, by reminding him of the courage and honor and hope and pride and compassion and pity and sacrifice which have been the glory of his past."

All mankind's past was what Faulkner referred to, primarily in its development of personal and communal criteria. In man's history he found demonstrated those positive qualities of character and conduct he so earnestly enumerated; he saw too their vulnerability, yet found witness of their endurance through certain men's drive to reassert them in adapted forms against other men's destructive impulses. Faulkner believed human aspiration to be general and perennial; he would have assented in spirit to Santayana's profound aphorism: "The ideal is a function of reality." At Stockholm Faulkner was speaking of what he had known and deeply learned of too in his native South. Yet neither as man nor as novelist was he uncritically provincial or sentimentally nostalgic; beyond such escapism he chose that resolute facing of circumstance which comprehends both continuance and change in the flow of a people's life. And both good and bad, often with an appearance of more bad than good, as his novels variously had showed, yet always in the presence of stoutly asserted ideals, whatever the relative effectuality of their champions. If in his most public moment Faulkner acknowledged so lofty an imperative, it was in all candor, for as his followers from the thirties on could assert, that was what he had been projecting fictionally all the time, and with enough variety of character and circumstance to support its generalizations.

Not for Faulkner nor for his soundest characters was there the "fear" of "those big words which make us so unhappy," in apprehensions such as Joyce bequeathed to the alienated and melancholy Stephen Dedalus—though at the moment merely for his warding off of Mr. Deasy's all-purpose axioms. Some of Faulkner's untutored commoners couldn't have found language for definition of their experientially earned sense of principle, but they feel it no less, and sometimes are moved to avow it in quaintly figurative folk parlance, a real gift of tongues. Faulkner's informed realism hearteningly shows even the unlettered sometimes putting it right to the point, yet not just out of a readiness with homely correspondences but because the principle involved is what they have come to stand on in good faith. And neither to Faulkner nor to his more knowing protagonists was history "a nightmare" out of which they were "trying to awake." Though to postbellum Southerners their region's past remained haunting, many found it all too palpable, a stressful reality to be wakened into out of its own antecedent hallucinations; and for such as Quentin Compson and Isaac McCaslin the issues were multifaceted and also more agonizingly personal than were

Stephen's in the cunning of his aloofness. Faulkner conveys to chosen protagonists his broader sense of history, not set down as a petit point of subjective allusions, but conceptual of the past as operationally relevant to the present, the bygone a once daylight external reality men are obliged to remember and make engagement with, to know its admonitions even at the cost of some despair, and also for possible assurances, hard come by and perhaps even harder to retain, yet source of enduring faith and measured hope.

Bestowal of the Nobel Prize did not scotch the Faulkner scandal nor dissuade his journalistic detractors. At the moment one view was that this award resembled the earlier one to Sinclair Lewis, for his exposures of life's seamier aspects in the United States. An editorial in the *New York Times* seemed to detect such European condescension in this choice "by a Swedish jury" and expressed a hope that Faulkner's "picture of American life" would not be taken as "typical and true." Showing no awareness of the acute literary judgments voiced earlier in French appreciations of Faulkner, the editorial writer countered all such foreign interest with a sentence that proved his ignorance of the literature he was deploring: "Incest and rape may be common pastimes in Faulkner's 'Jefferson, Miss.' but they are not elsewhere in the United States." And this in the face of Faulkner's profound humanistic declaration only the day before in the Stockholm address, an artist's credo that could have stood as preface to any of his novels, but superfluously, in view of the ubiquitous type there who "endures" as proponent of a civil morality, with concern for individual rights and dignity. He or she may be an aristocrat, a tenant farmer, a Negro, a woman, a boy. Nor are these protagonists always as nearly isolate and disheartened as Benbow in *Sanctuary* or the reporter in *Pylon.* Most become aware of others of like mind and adhere to them, improvising undefined consensus and at least making do, like the townsmen and country folk quietly resistant to the upsurge of Snopesism, or those first settlers told of in *Requiem for a*

Nun, who in "ramshackle confederation" and through "simple
fortuity" turn a trading post into a town named Jefferson.
Such agents in fictional advocacy of a common good are not
paragons; the Roth Edmonds who in "The Fire and the
Hearth" humanely and patiently assists toward a reconciliation
when old Molly threatens to divorce Lucas Beauchamp is the
same Roth whose indifference to his mulatto mistress and his
child by her adds so sharply to old Isaac McCaslin's further
disenchantment in "Delta Autumn." Neither are such actors
made into simplistic evangels. One of the most admirable
among them, the generally consistent Ratliff, is unpretentious, a moderate man, with enough discretion to keep himself
closely positioned for further fencing against forces he assesses
realistically, scarcely hoping to defeat but only to obstruct
them in some degree. And when Gavin Stevens declaims, he
can be read not as Faulkner's instrument for amplification nor
as self-ordained pulpiteer but as a recognizably human type,
the beset idealistic intellectual, exasperated into prolixity by
stress, which he, being both more sophisticated and less
steadily realistic than Ratliff, cannot endure with such
equanimity.

Faulkner does not depend alone on fully deployed characters like Gavin and Ratliff; sometimes only an incidental
glimpse and on the most elementary scale suffices for representation of principled behavior. For instance, in *Intruder
in the Dust* there is Legate, an excellent woodsman and a
farmer, sitting at the jail's unlocked door with a breech-
loading shotgun to discourage any lynch mob that might try to
make away with Lucas, awaiting trial. And as usual, Faulkner
dramatizes the issue of responsibility, and shows the
ambivalence of some men's answering to it. The jailor, Tubbs,
"a snuffy untidy potbellied man with a harried concerned
outraged face," armed with pistol and cartridge belt, cries
out, "Me? Me get in the way of them Gowries and Ingrums for
seventy-five dollars a month? Just for one nigger? And if you
ain't a fool, you wont neither," to which Legate, "in his easy
pleasant voice," says, "Oh, I got to. I got to resist. Mr [Sheriff]

Hampton's paying me five dollars for it." This by implication passes beyond the mercenary, and can tell readers something other and more than that some men will do anything for a few dollars. Legate has not been bought, he has enlisted on the side of order, and he operates unequivocally under a woodsman's explicit code (and a farmer's), drawing support for his ethic, as does Isaac McCaslin, from the disciplines of natural realities. So Legate's easy minimizing reply to the demoralized jailer veils what he will not try to voice, especially in those circumstances, where any real emergency will call for action not words.

What then follows is brilliant example of Faulkner's power to develop intrinsically tense situations into sustained narrative, through which the enactors are given further dimensions as issue is fully defined. The vignette of fear versus courage typified in a few lines of dialogue immediately leads into another somewhat more complex exchange which makes the harried jailer other than a flat character and shows close up something central about Lawyer Stevens. Having come to the jail at Lucas's request, Gavin has heard the exchange between Tubbs and Legate, and the jailer has turned his irritation on Gavin also — "So you got to get mixed up in it too. Yo cant let well enough alone neither." Yet as they climb the stairs to Lucas's cell, Tubbs suddenly turns apologetic and confessional. "Don't mind me. I'm going to do the best I can. I taken an oath of office too." Then with rising voice, but "still calm," he mentions wife and children and asks, "What good am I going to be to them if I get myself killed protecting a goddamn stinking nigger?" But with a voice "not calm now" he goes on to ask how he is to live with himself if he lets "a passel of nogood sonabitches take a prisoner away from me." Finally, "his face once more harried and frantic, his voice frantic and outraged," (the reiterative diction here matching face and voice in one man and a further moment) he exclaims, "Better for everybody if them folks [at the scene and time of the shooting] had took him as soon as they laid hands on him yesterday." Stevens tries to steady the jailer with logic and by summoning up a sense of community: "They either will or they wont and if they dont it will be all right and if they do we will do the best we can, you and Mr Hampton and Legate and the rest of us, what we have to do, what we can do. So we dont need to worry about it. You see?"

The jailer answers in one word, yes, but as he takes Stevens along to Lucas's cell there is no sign that the implied commitment will hold. Yet Faulkner has already proceeded to show Tubbs as more than a mere pot-bellied coward, expediently shirking what he has sworn to perform. This jailer becomes one with many Faulkner characters (and as of a common human trait) in the dilemma he has described to Stevens. Legate's calm resoluteness, stated with such laconic wryness, has not just irked Tubbs, it has challenged him by its implied reproof, and his perverse human response has been irascibility at having a hard choice made clear. Consequently, as is typical of all but the most resolute, he has arrived at a wish to have been excused, not that evil should not be done but that it might occur beyond his domain and he be spared the call to resist it. In such a shabby pseudostoicism, with recourse to passivity as a social being, the avoider may even rail at whoever or whatever would suggest an imperative need for confrontation and response. It is a trait Faulkner frequently represents, in telling revelations of human volatility and an individual variableness of resolve. The maturing Chick Mallison, perplexed for years between local conventions and a dawning sense of more humane interrelations, was for a while of two minds about Lucas. But it is also typical that men who balk may then rally, as did Chick, and Faulkner has shown many such instances, throughout his novels. And in their rallying men may find themselves joined to each other, not as mobs, and intent not on destruction but preservation, whether of property or life or principle itself. Sometimes there will be a coalescence of individual tendencies into a positive communal attitude and action, with an interplay of attitudes reinforcing a concept of some general value. That this can rise to the fixed transcendent status of a verity is at the heart of Faulkner's faith and practice. He saw in the history of mankind and in Yoknapatawpha County's immediate spectacles not just a gregarious huddling nor an unrelieved rapacity but also some natural persistent motivation toward an ethos. This is his humanism, secular, tentative, and relativistic, yet conservative in the highest sense, looking toward fixed yet vital referents beyond transient opportunism or apathy. In those brief jail scenes a positive societal force is seen operant with apparently constructive effect on the jailer, through Legate's ironic mention of five dollars and Gavin Steven's patient, tactically low-keyed explanation to Tubbs that he will not be alone, with implication that he need never be isolate in the arid solitude of the noncommitted, since there are always others who are resolving the heart's conflict with itself on the side of what comes to be seen as the better part. With Faulkner, though, there remains the ultimate realism, never promising ease in Zion, and forgoing any sentimental doctrine of conversion, such as in Hamlet's suggestion that "the worser part" can be simply thrown away. As Faulkner shows it, the heart while whole and living will always have its conflicts, of various aspects, in the succession of encounters implicit under ongoing existence. Therefore after Charles Mallison's subduing of his contradictory feelings and his fixed courage in helping to save the falsely accused Lucas, Stevens tells his nephew, "Just dont stop."

At Stockholm in 1950 Faulkner counseled young writers abstractly; the matter of that advocacy is made richly implicit in his fictions, and can be found at heights of artistic perfection in numerous sustained continuities comparable to those pages bearing the exchange between the jailer and Legate and the jailer and Stevens. For readers such passages illuminate to the full Faulkner's power in recounting an action and deploying those from whose natures it stems, whom it thus progressively expresses. Legate the naturally integrated man is as fixed as the constellations this farmer and notable hunter can find his sure way by. The jailer epitomizes encounter with personal dilemma and the unrest of irresolution, as does the youthful Chick more extensively in his growth throughout the novel. Though Stevens responds with unusual moderation, as usual he is being drawn to a person's need at the moment and in the long run. For the fictionist or critic any such passage in Faulkner can be exemplary, showing that in serious narrative art the plot is not a prime mover as precise and internally sufficient as a clockwork, nor are characters the fixed subordinate reagents of its process. Rather, a narrative action is progressive interaction, its springs are vital beyond fabrication and fixity, plot's motion is energized by human motivations, and overt action fictionally respresented should be a steadily implicative translation of existential being and becoming, on which scale rather than that of any contributory but lesser reality the worth of a novel or short story should be judged. Understanding this, the attentive reader will know that everything depends on how clearly and intuitively an artist can perceive his fellow beings and how rationally and compassionately he can conceive of setting them forth, while recognizing that they like himself and his readers are in motion and process, intent on arrivals and beset by alternatives. Such an operative attitude told Faulkner how to employ Legate, the jailer, and Stevens each in character, out of which came speech and actions separately tinged by their different temperaments, yet working upon each other and through each other. Within itself, that episode of less than three pages sketches cogent illustrations of diversity and interrelation among men, chronicles each in his unique motion and mode, and projects a concept of how animate yet precariously improvisatory is human society, constituted of separate and variable members.

The passage is a telling epitome of Faulkner's dynamic and scrupulous art; it is an immediate, economical realism, narrated with vigor and dispatch, vividly tinted yet subtly implicative, and at its limits there is to be discerned how inconspicuously yet firmly it is articulated into the larger continuities. These in all Faulkner's works are sustained and predominant in their effect. Though both critic and practicing fictionist can find broad exemplification of Faulkner's merits contained in brief passages, his synthesizing and symphonic power exercises its sway on much larger scales throughout each unique work as compositional entity, and reading can proceed absorbedly under an expanding sense of the presence of conceptual and instrumental control. Beyond this, what remains to be recognized is that here creativity has totally given itself over to what it projects. So doing, it shows that genuine works of art, each in its communicative kind and specific ways, are clearest instances of idealization. The self fully exercised conceives of formulations transcending itself, yet expressing it most truly because an inmost awareness has found realization in the representative. Indeed, Faulkner at Stockholm and in other discoursings implied a timeless universality in the "verities" he named. However, in his particular fictions they were not defined, merely silhouetted, and only in transient situational confrontations, wherein Faulkner's realism acknowledged his characters' human liability to defeat and the long odds that any victory would be only an approximation and a temporary foothold. Yet for them then, as with Faulkner the writer, concerning himself, "there would always be a next time, since there is only one truth and endurance and pity and courage."

Lengthening perspectives on Faulkner's fiction make still more plain the speciousness of terming it melodramatic. Indeed, qualities central to all his conceivings and creations may be elucidated by noting their antitheses to melodrama, with its fabricated sensationalism to provide the *frisson* craved by those who seek escape into feigned experiences. Contrasted with modernity's commercialized purveying of exaggerated violence and sensualism, Faulkner's stories are measured; he is almost oblique in narrating what is shocking, and he was no huckster of titillation. However, no one has ventured to call him timorous in his undertakings of subject matter, while what he had in view always went beyond melodrama's dead ends. In its basic mode melodrama deals with open conflict between villains and heroes, as constant exemplars of outright evil and resolute goodness, and with a happy issue foreordained; to Faulkner evil is of many shapes, degrees, and involutions, and so too are the contrary responses of those who elect to resist it, not without misgiving, and never with complete and final success. A further element which Faulkner significantly adds to his representations is what melodrama, whether sensational or sentimental, never reckons with — the presence between extremes of good- and evildoing of a vast human inertia, whether in chronic apathy or avoidance of an immediate ethical confrontation. Faulkner senses the relation of this trait to modern society's increased complexities and confusions; still, he wrote nothing as shocking as the true and widely reported story of a young woman's repeatedly crying for help while being sadistically stabbed to death in a doubly dark New York City street, with a number of her neighbors listening behind their double-locked doors. Faulkner's protagonists engaged against whatever forays by the wicked are aware too that their average fellow citizens will not rally as "all one body we" when issue arises. That this deplorable certainty enters into the finesse of designing malefactors is made apparent, especially in Flem Snopes, whose craftiness runs one step ahead of the community's tardy and futile outrage.

Faulkner show even his stoutest resisters of Snopesism visited by a natural human dread of that invading horde, apprehending them almost as a reptilian subspecies out of one of evolution's disastrous quirks. Yet reason rallies and recognizes variants, which range from the arch-Snopes Flem to the ridiculously incompetent I. O. Snopes, bigamist and petty conniver, who moves behind a glib barrage of banalities. In the resumption and rounding out of the Snopes trilogy Faulkner not only continued to show that within this clan evil had many degrees and faces, his protagonists' attitudes as they ride out their encounters with Snopesism invite readers to share an awareness of many shades of culpability. Minor offenses, especially when they miscarry (as with I. O. in his pretensions as blacksmith or mule drover) become more ludicrous than outrageous in their grotesquerie, so that there hangs over the Snopesian mode a drifting aura of the elementally comic, in the sensing of those departures from the desired norm as more of life's ironies. At another extreme Faulkner increasingly accorded a pathos to Mink, as that much-beset man moves under impetus of a sense of honor to enact a tribal punishment against Flem, in a ritual of primitive justice that becomes a kind of expiation of his own earlier "meanness" and of his relatives' multifarious offenses against society. Mink becomes thereby an instance of the living fluidity of typical Faulkner characters, whatever their status. In itself his shooting Flem, a direct lawless action such as neither Gavin nor Ratliff could allow himself, is of the order of melodrama, but it rises above that into the full psychological dimensions given Mink in his ordeal and enterprise, and supports the trilogy's emotion-racked yet finally elegaic closure, which he and Linda and Gavin convey in character, under Ratliff's stabilizing auspices.

The most telling factor in Faulkner's representations of evil, however, is not the mere naturalistic picturing of its varieties nor a tracing to its roots, though he does often point to sociopsychological influences. Evil figures prominently in his narratives because it is endemic in the world of men, and therefore Faulkner's concern (in the classic epical and dramatic tradition) is with those who resist evil. It is in this nexus that his fictions are most fully removed from melodrama, with its simplistic absolutes of good and evil and the destined triumph of faultless heroes. Instead there is at the heart of Faulkner's realism the plain fact that verities by which both society and the individual life are to be constituted do persist, but fluctuantly in their vulnerability. In *The Reivers: A Reminiscence,* sometimes carelessly dismissed as of minor import, there is not only a picturesque robustness and sustained *élan,* but a running parable of good and evil, full of drolleries in a bizarre lawlessness whimsically pursued, encountering real evil and genuine grief, and reaching to expiation and restitution. It is all couched as Lucius Priest's recol-

5

Fictional Entities and the Artist's *Oeuvre*

ANY great artist's death, while widely felt as a bereavement, magnifies him by evoking a sustained look at the sum of his endeavors. The pathos of cessation, its august finality, in stimulating renewals of awareness also extends beyond a reverencing of the man himself to an inclusively abstracted view of the many admirable completions which, without loss to any one in its own relative right, are now gathered into the total estimable achievement. The sense of this plenitude becomes itself a transcendent and immanent reality, unobtrusively an affective increment at every point in further experience of the works, especially if (as with Faulkner) the artist had been assuredly intent in certain directions. A passage epitomizing some known aspect of his genius may project a generalization which then may find further illustration elsewhere, and in other works of that artist; yet in such detailed complementary instances there is the uniqueness of each in its adaptation to particular context, while behind it all is the sensed presence of a certain creative imagination. Genius in literature is thus perceived not just as origination and ingenuity but in largeness of effects, and in a strong consistency not only of outlook but of modes and even manner. In Faulkner there is narrative procedure made not merely tactical but proportionate and engaging, the colloquial exactly caught and accented, images elaborately suspended until they exercise almost hpnotic persuasion, the sustained objective-subjective reality in its modulations, the intent celerity, the or-chestrated closures, and the lingering resonance of total effect.

It is with a sense of luck that a reader, on first looking into the work of an artist hitherto unknown to him, feels a master-ful presence, an ardent outlook conveyed through an enabling intelligence, a committed concern, and accomplishment of a high order. The natural course is to seek further disclosures from the same source, with the hope that such dynamism would continue to show its admirable gifts in the creative paradoxes of an ever-fresh consistency. Such expectations are disappointed more often than not. With Faulkner, though, for those of humanistic inclination and temperamental affinity there were always surprises yet reassuringly from the same welling source; the colorful extravagances were safely this side of disarray, enigmas intrigued without impeding, and however dynamic the intention, its artistic containment was complete. With Faulkner's work all done and at hand, new readers can come upon him at any point and then going further this way and that can confirm in each story and throughout its flow the same versatile presence. With growing acquaintance any great artist's novelties begin to carry an appearance of typicality—as when in an increasing friendship one might think the person never did anything quite like that before, yet how like him it is. As to Faulkner, it is thus that intimations gather into a conception of his genius. The works' successive revelations also bear recurrent marks of his imaginative nature in the trend of his concerns. The reader's expectations grow more alert, and being confirmed are trans-formed into deeper perceptions, not only of the just-dis-covered but retrospectively of those likenesses preceding it which may have prompted its recognition.

With Faulkner, as with other indubitably great fictionists such as James or Conrad, a reader's aesthetic intimation of the artist as a ghostly presence in his *oeuvre* may be scarcely more palpable than a cloud volatilized in the genial climate of increasing acquaintance. Yet while it remains ethereal even as it grows and shapes itself, it can seem as close, too, as a known step or voice in the next room. Something of this achieved and expanding awareness, operating unobtrusively but with felt assurances, can permeate a reader's imaginative responses to added experiences of Faulkner's works, and to rereadings in them, with echoes between the open page and the sense of colossal genius as silhouetted throughout his known works. However, in any penetrating consideration of the arts the thing in itself, the singular work, is preeminent, an immediate, composed, and autonomous entity, not just in its mode but intrinsically. It is as such that a work of whatever position within its creator's *oeuvre* can be returned to for familiar and enlarged delights. Yet while any great work can enhance its claim in repeated encounters, every such composition can exist more strikingly as part of a distinguished company, that artist's various productions, each being reflectively illuminated by that totality while uniquely augmenting it. Out of such a felt reciprocation a deepened aesthetic awareness is come upon when paradoxically a certain work presently reconsidered becomes more vividly *sui generis,* as a whole and in its details, even as its consistencies within the *oeuvre* are sensed as emanating from that artist's temperament in its recognizable thrusts and tones. Thus for Keats, "once again" burning through *King Lear* (though he already knew its theme of "fierce dispute/Betwixt damnation and impassion'd clay") there must have been added discoveries on many pages, with intensified recognition of something less definable but of a magnitude — the Shakespearian essence which so moved him that he came back to its intensities to be revitalized. The works of a master in any art can take on a transcendent reality, a domain of experience, to be known in its extent and features by much travel in its provinces, and repeated readings in Faulkner's fictional representations may lead into an abiding sense of his realm's entity and its variable climate, its air as felt throughout all the details and implications it comprises.

While such an alerted and familiar sense of the body of Faulkner's work gives the studious reader some opportunities for further understanding, this is to be followed out with

circumspection. An inclusive as well as appreciative knowledge of an artist's *oeuvre* can lead on into broad estimations
and may even give some support to a literary historian's defined critical judgments. It is a less sure basis, however, for
predicating an aesthetic epitome. Encompassment should be
attempted only as far as certainty and some acuteness may extend, finding its sufficiently fixed points of reference within
certain of the artist's most strikingly representative works.
Here the largest possible sense of his whole accomplishment
can be helpful, yet only suggestively, this side of definition.
With Faulkner, however, this distinction is no insuperable bar
to some generalization. The uniqueness of any single composition is illustrated in the particular shading it gives, in its
own interest, to the attitudes and modes more widely pervasive
throughout the *oeuvre*. Faulkner's quite various originations
thus still bear a certain warranty. One factor making for such
complementary relations between Faulkner's works and work
is that his genius (like that seen in the most eminent masters) is
put into motion under what is literary art's most enduring
convention, assumption of values. His narrative "actions," like
those in drama and as in a lyric's progression, are thus related
conceptually to men's enterprises and fates. Faulkner's varieties
reiterate a steady perspective upon the human condition as he
has concernedly observed it at first hand, but under auspices
of something enduringly valid, as mankind's multifarious
strugglings turn again and again, pro and con or in confusion
yet somehow upon the same premises and polarities.

Studious readers of Faulkner will often be intrigued by the
recurrences, from novel to novel, of similar thematic
elements, and by his aptly empowering narrative techniques
too, that are found not quite repetitively but in suggestively
comparable ways. As with other great artists, in Faulkner a
uniqueness of separate autonomous forms has counterpart in a
pervasiveness of outlook and tone which creates the most
vibrant sense of unity and most clearly voices genius. Recognition of traits comparably recurrent but with wide variability in
their specific adaptations can put the artist's total achieve-

ment into a clearer light while giving some sharper focus upon each work. Specifically as to Faulkner's traits displayed in themes and techniques, readers can find increasing understanding through each such instance in its adapted containment by its unique context. As with the testings of a law, not only are its limits defined but unanticipated applicabilities are discovered. Conversely, recognition of genius revealed in its identifiable traits will often rescue some such instances from oversight or misunderstanding, by a noting of their resemblance to other such usages where either the import or its conveyance is less subtilized. All such artistically contributive interrelations become clearly appreciable in the several areas of Faulkner's thematic motifs, functional stylistic devices, and strategic patternings.

The further a reader goes into Faulkner, the greater may be the discovered intricacies; they are not altogether impenetrable, though, and to a degree they may be found complementary. Consistencies made manifest and a spontaneously originative variety can create perspectives in their many-angled and intersecting beams. Consequently any discussion which attempts responsibility as well as responsiveness to Faulkner's genius will strive to be both widely referential and closely analytical. Yet by nature the two critical procedures can be combined only in alternation, which must serve but is never enough. Still the reader like the artist tries to say what he thinks he sees and how he feels about it, and as to Faulkner's work neither any sum of abstractions nor the most minute explication can lay hold on the composed thing in itself or relay its operant effects and its consummated effect, all of which exists through the work's total complexity held suspended in its commingled elements, as with a saturated solution. In this direction, even a barely adequate statement of Faulkner's potency and skill as conceiver and creator has scarcely been approached, nor is it likely to be approximated soon. For one thing, serious misapprehensions about Faulkner still have some currency; in his having become notorious before his genius had been expressed in varieties of works (and

years before commensurate current recognition) he attracted
the attention of opportunistic journalists, whose keeping
slander alive discouraged consideration by more serious
readers. For another thing, the rounding out of his work so
suddenly in a still vigorous life is too close in its finality for
many of his readers to have moved beyond their favorite works
toward a comprehensive appreciation of the *oeuvre* in its parts
and aspects and as a whole. And most of all, Faulkner's
plenitude is of a munificence and variety that does not abide
question so soon. Thus most formal consideration has confined
itself with becoming reserve to facets of the matter, in quiet
respect for the felt mysteries of his art.

One perhaps useful approach for further study might be in
an examination of Faulkner's conveyance of interactive
antitheses. On the representational level, and with special pertinence to his fictional art, there is the ongoing dialectic of human consciousness, with its objective orientations subjectively
contained and construed. In their fluidity, inflections, and
penetrations, Faulkner's fictional uses of this modern mode,
with his measured adaptation of it to compelling narrative
continuity, are impressive. On the substantive level of conveyed interactive antitheses there is, amidst the vagaries of
persons and variable circumstance, the persistence of concept,
according to that imperative by which Faulkner brings his
characters' behavior under consideration as conduct. The
poles of reality upon which Faulkner's creative imagination
turned were the antipodes of good and evil, concerning which
he sought out a worldly knowledge in many forms, so that he
might diagram not impossible courses, against whatever opposite currents, toward magnetic constants as directives. His
commitment to verities pervades everything he wrote, and his
power to embody it fictionally unites him to literature in its
most august and enduring aspects. In a restive era of opposing
dogmas from which some manner of nihilism was a popular
route of escape, Faulkner's incidental but weighty contribution to a flexible secular humanism was chiefly by his bringing
ethical issue authentically into representations of the ongoing

current of workaday existence. Given a recognizable milieu typically peopled by a variety of individuals and pervaded by some major tensions, his fiction treated of human virtues as not wholly attainable and difficult to maintain in whatever degree, it confronted human indifference whether fatalistic or simply passive, it revealed beneath such apathy the dearth of understanding, and it admitted the fluctuant nature of highest resolves, yet it stressed men's and societal mankind's natural, almost instinctive orientation toward values and the fostering of them within an order.

Was it perhaps a large apprehension of this potential by which the young Faulkner, putative lyric poet and writer of descriptive sketches, was turned toward the novel as a field with sufficient scope and recently enlivened conventions for deployment of those narrative actions he so soon learned to lift to heights of substantive significance and in a consummate literary art? However, the impressive thematic consistencies apparent in the Faulkner *oeuvre* cannot suffice in themselves as basis for comprehensive judgment of his genius. In his fictions Faulkner was the complete artist; he never posed himself as didactic spokesman for any system of thought. It is one of his accomplishments that opinions, even when extending into sustained attitudes, are dramatized credibly as one fictitious person's motivated outlook, and indeed its often passionate, ironic, or even extravagant expression serves to characterize that actor and, by disclosing him in its context, enhances the scene. Whatever concepts may be abstracted from Faulkner's fiction, and whatever such extractions may illustrate to sociologist, psychologist, cultural historian, or philosopher, these have come by way of an artist's representations and after the manner of art's largesse, which proceeds out of its creator's intuitions and toward the projection of concretely realized and conceptually implicative forms. To these the world is welcome, yet under the artist's hope that attention will not be selective but will answer to the whole in all its parts, finding in these equilibrated tensions the sustained and consummate imaginative experience art can offer.

Yet with Faulkner, artistically the most sophisticated American fictionist of his times, a reader's readiness to respond must be acquired through some general acquaintance with contemporary modes in the novel, and also by sufficient knowledge of several writers' output to be alert to relations between autonomous works and the resemblances and consistencies in the artist's work as a whole. Any significant writer will have liberally allied himself with the tendencies of his craft while preserving a personal integrity and zest as a creator, and in this currency the reader too must deal. By its concreteness and fluency fiction requires that attention be immediate and response be conjunctively cumulative. The intent exercise of recognition, association, memory, and surmise, a complex process at any level, is made more so in that fiction elicits it at the full extent of consciousness, in a total mentation beyond such facultative divisions as reason and emotion. Moreover, and most vitally, since fiction's subject is some representation of human existence, it must be accorded a human response, receptive, intuitive, and empathic. Out of such fully exercised intelligent imagination the reader of a Faulkner novel can achieve in some degree realizations complementary to the artist's own, and can sense a work of art, whether the entity is as distinctively unique as *Go Down, Moses, Requiem For a Nun,* or *As I Lay Dying,* or any others from that hand.

Beyond all these but not separate, with its reality rooted in their instances, the essence of Faulkner's genius volatilizes in a large concept of the *oeuvre;* and if it be known, wisps of its substantiating and illuminating intimations will drift reciprocally into the experiencing of any Faulkner novel. Thus an inclusive estimating of the master's genius is not of a different order from perceptively reading one page of his; response is of the same aesthetic nature, yet on different scales, ranging from the microscopically close to the panoramic, from the ingeniously concrete to the evolved disclosure of outlook. It is this disposition of potent elements and effects which leads the happily persistent reader of Faulkner to range imaginatively from the minute to the aggregate, while seeking a substantiated comprehension, and also remembering the obvious — that Faulkner did not set out to create this *oeuvre* but let each work become as it might befall, as he let even the Snopes trilogy take on distinctive patterns in each of three novels, while welding them congruently into a tragicomic regional epic.

For too long, including years that had seen the production of some of Faulkner's most remarkable work, he had borne contumely from imperceptive reviewers and inadequate financial return from his novels, yet he had the reward of his measured but sustained faith and his private satisfactions in what he was accomplishing. He depreciated some of his short stories as "pot-boilers," and he begrudged time spent as a script writer out of economic necessity, but although he was not a boastful man he had the quiet pride that comes with commitment. As his biographer Professor Joseph Blotner tells of it, he showed the just-completed manuscript of *Absalom, Absalom!* to an intelligent young Hollywood colleague and companion, and when asked what it was, Faulkner said, "I think it's the best novel yet written by an American." There must be those who even now would concur — and would be glad for Faulkner that he had had his venture and joy in it as of his time. Certainly the work's convoluted intensities, thematic antiphonies, and paradoxically fantastic realism, taken with Professor Blotner's running account of the artist's prolonged absorption in its painstaking composition, would suggest not a fluttering visitation by the divine afflatus, but an exercise of powerful intellectual control in an immense imaginative realization, and by an artist who having troubled to determine what he was about, would have a reasonable estimation of what he had done. Though *Absalom, Absalom!* was shamefully derogated by Clifton Fadiman et alii, as eighteen years later *A Fable* was to be by Brendan Gill and a cloud of other blind witnesses, meanwhile Faulkner had been accorded a high place in the Western World, and most importantly for himself, continued in a splendid rounding out of his creative life. What is said now of that can be of no account to him, who anyhow had never been deflected by perfunctory or antagonistic reviewers or the generally impercipient. And now this his *oeuvre* "survives,/ A way of happening, a mouth," to be and to become a matter of possible perplexity and consequent pique, or of enlivenment and humane reassurance to potential, relatively perceptive readers hereafter.

They too must be realistic, seeing the idiosyncratic Faulkner as of the company of the eminent in a proved vocation. It is bluntly obvious that judiciously appreciative reading of any fictional work calls for some experientially acquired notion of literature as a particular way of communication, a creation intended, under its genre's conventions, to evoke its semblance in a corresponding response of an imaginative kind. (This means, for one thing, that even those who look for sermons in stones shouldn't seek out homilies in novels. Ethical implications, yes, almost certainly, but neither exhortation nor demonstration is *comme il faut* in the serious fiction of these times. Obviously too the effective weight of any reader's concept and consequent expectations of fiction as a literary genre will be relative to the extent of his acquaintance with such compositions known at first hand, since only they can communicate themselves in their kind. It is out of such encounterings that a reader of works in any mode comes to project a composite idea of this or that type of literary creation, and growing acquaintance with its potentials and their viable modulations continues to extend and sharpen the working sense of such critical abstraction. Although under this auspices preferences will develop, some as special as for a certain author and even for one of his works, yet this is not often a completely exclusive favoritism. A major art's rich variety and the cravings of avid readers prevent that, as interest in one artist leads to others of similar bent, or conversely (and at a more eclectic level of taste) a vital idiosyncrasy relished in one artist may stir appreciation of another for his opposite uniqueness of temperament, while more acutely the perceived distinctiveness in any one of a favored artist's works may illuminate the autonomy and singular worth of his others.

These aesthetic interrelations are obvious enough to be called elementary, but though patent in themselves they may need to be reasserted as points of reference in critical opinions of fiction. It is especially so with Faulkner. They will serve in identifying and crediting achievement, and for regulation of judicious comparison — for instance, the distinct manifestation of inscrutably private bent in Hemingway and in Faulkner, when truly differentiated, may serve a closer view of unique skills in each, in a less superficial relative evaluation of their work than generally was made in the thirties. Of most importance, however, because in its immediacy it can penetrate more deeply into artistic values, there is the estimating of any artist's single autonomous works as separately realized within the larger but less defined contours of his *oeuvre*. No major and voluminous novelist (or poet) can be adequately appreciated except through such an inclusive approach, yet those particulars of fictional art on which its very makeup and functioning depend sometimes enter too little into the reader's responses, in which they should be of primary influence, being constituent to the work as thing in itself. As is typical with literary geniuses, what is most consistent in Faulkner is a vigorous and varied creativity, with all its products marked by an intent dynamic temperament. In exercising this he shows greater virtuosity by far than it seems is recognized even by some of his most consistent advocates, and apparently his sheer skills at their subtlest are passed over by reviewers and other casual readers, who even if they read every word do not sense the organic reciprocities of parts and their containments or recognize by its results the artist's enacting presence and unremitting grasp. Some influential critics, such as the perceptive and judicious Michael Millgate, have sufficiently noted the careful structuring of aesthetically affective forms in Faulkner's novels to contradict the superficial notion of him as a haphazard narrator. For every desirous reader, however, form as total implementation of concept is to be vitally realized only by sustained aesthetic awareness of particulars in their most telling contextual relations. In their artistry

Faulkner's novels warrant readings almost as scrupulously attentive as that solicited by the most compactly implicative poetry. (To Coleridge's suggestive generalization that the language of poetry has "the property of exciting a more continuous and equal attention than that of prose" it might be added that this depends upon which poem, whose prose, for certainly the distinction cannot stand as between Southey's verse and Lamb's essays.) In viewing any period's literary works there is some profit in giving primary attention to the writer's language itself and noting the mode it is being employed in, if only as those special conventions limit and liberate expression. With literary prose quite as rightly as with poetry, language can be estimated for its evocations, and as for perplexes, it is generally more productive to approach them in either form through the language in its immediate context than from possible substantive resemblances elsewhere in the writer's *oeuvre*, or by still more tangential references to established characterizations of the artist and of his work. Yet as to fiction, because of greater structural span, dramatic movement, and multiplicity of sheer narrative detail as well as imagery, there is much temptation to interpret by parallels drawn from the fictionist's other works; moreover, from the greater bulk of fiction and of journalistic attention given it, clichés about the writer more frequently develop. By way of alleged analogies serious misconception may be set going, such as were imposed upon the *Dubliners* stories in discovering them esoterically revealed through Joyce's later works; and much of Hemingway's accomplishment was denigrated by hasty superficial generalizations about the man himself, as it was also minimized by inept imitation. There have not been conspicuous attempts to imitate Faulkner except in parody (as likewise with Shakespeare) but though he has scarcely suffered as much as Joyce from cross-reference within his *oeuvre,* that operated to breed generalizations which obscure the essence of his achievements.

For more just judgments and richer appreciation, the essential means is a constant attention to the word, sentence, page in its immediacy and yet not for itself alone but as it merges into that accretive process by which the work of art is organically realizing itself. Imaginative grasp of such a consummation in Faulkner's works and others' is as close as a reader can come to the artist himself at the heart and in the heat of his accomplishment. For appreciative insights (which is all art proposes to provide) one story rightly read can outweigh numerous bits of biographical data. As for style, properly it cannot be a flourish or adornment, nor the liberties of looseness, but simply the impressment of language as bearer of the sense of a conceptualized aesthetic reality in its imaginative emergence and consummation. Most of the allegations against Faulkner's style and all of any uneasiness about it could be put aside by such a recognition. And form, which in modern criticism's pantheon is companioned by style, enters in here, as it should be in its preeminence. In a Faulkner novel, form is more than the compostions's skeletal frame. Such supportive structuring is only instrumental to form as an accomplished realization, the concept organically rendered as a total appearance, an imaginatively constituted autonomy. Structure can be diagramed, to illustrate the connection of elements as interdependent parts; aesthetic form as Faulkner's genius achieves it is only to be sensed as what that arrangement in those relations has imaginatively metamorphized into something more, transcendingly constituting concept and all its substantive factors in the organismic unity of a work of art. In this respect Faulkner is a purer artist than some of his contemporaries, not only the opportunistically topical and episodic novelists but certain composers, sculptors, and architects, who do not see or hear form as an aesthetic transformation into an entity beyond structure, and who even under the rubric that form follows function have not got as far as aesthetically functional form, stopping short at structure as a final assertion. If such bones live, it can only be as a pretension, out of a laboring without passion or pleasure, and such an *oeuvre* as Faulkner's with all its accomplished entities is a rebuke to such lapses.

While the literary historian and the literary critic are not of separate guilds, nor does either have a monopoly exclusive of the other's visits, yet there is a perceptible although not strict division, which relates closely in considerations of Faulkner. As with weather and crops, "there are roughly zones," which can be approximated as between consideration of a writer's body of work or of his works in their individually distinguishing aspects. Obviously either history or criticism which centers upon literature must draw upon the whole field, yet eclectically in line with particular purpose, whether for textual explication or for widely comprehensive definition and description. Either historian or critic may make excursions, but the literary historian will feel primarily obliged to weigh any artist's total achievement in its relation to that of comparable writers and perhaps even as to cultural history beyond its specifically artistic aspects, while the literary critic might well make it his chief function to suggest insights into particular works, each in its aesthetically formed autonomy. These procedures, specialized to a degree, are invigorated in the common way by tensions between the general and the particular, and thus become reciprocal to each other. For the critic or any other avid reader, one of the chief such aids from a comprehensive view of an artist's *oeuvre* may be that his pervasively recurrent traits, if closely understood as they stand at certain points, will so illuminate aspects of composition and style, for instance, that elsewhere subtleties otherwise passed over imperceptively or even questioned would be found to be brilliantly effective.

In this area of evaluations often a buildup of negative assumptions needs to be critically combatted. For instance, as with any artist already excessively faulted for idiosyncrasies, one of Faulkner's closely wrought passages may be discounted as more of the same instead of being grasped as a typical feat yet uniquely pertinent in its place. Such recurrences are not monotonous in Faulkner; and to recognize a characteristic trait, a tone, a motif as one reads is the fruit of acquaintance, while to discover it anew as it exists in a further context is to find and hold its essence. Such perceptions answer to the artist's sustained craft and particular aptness at that point, but also and more largely there is an evolving grasp upon composition and the increasingly sensed presence of concept given aesthetic form, in the containing work's organismic unity. Since some such operative fictional effect is aimed at by all genuinely committed novelists, in their reliance not on exposition but on evocation, a criticism of fiction can serve by substantiating the special workings of artists' techniques, through illustrative references to details and also by review of the context in which these function relevantly. Literature has not been created to make criticism possible, but careful assessment has its function in promulgating a humanistic culture by distinguishing the characteristics and relative worth of imaginative creations. Since a literary work becomes communicative only through responses in kind to its creator's exercise of postulating mentation, conceptive and empathic, a commentator's central task and opportunity is to formalize such experience of the creation in itself, as he has come to know it, not as an abstract but by touching upon what specifically and in a continuum has given the composition its consistency and implicative power.

Genius lies beyond critical definition, but it may be apprehended through the experience of reading, and identified in aspects of a narrative art which, by modulatedly projecting an autonomous work's major implications and its variable tones, silhouettes a temperament in its creativity. An enduring *oeuvre* signifies genius, yet as with the laws of nature in their derivation from phenomena, vital understanding requires a maintained grasp upon instances. In taking account of a work's dominant literary effects, commentary may need to cite passages, and may even summarize their contextual containment, not because this matter might not be known but to turn scrutiny toward aesthetic function within it. Such close attention within a continuity has been assumed by the artist; it is one part of his social contract with the reader, yet not a presumption, since its implied corollary is that if the reader will look and listen as intently as he can, then he is privileged to make what he will of it, with no indemnities on either side. The reader may even be asked to note a detail repeatedly, recalling it from earlier context as it now takes on new shadings in contributing to a further instance. In Faulkner's art recurrence with a difference is a lively kind of emphasis and enhancement; as it concerns persons it may round out characterization, and in its connections with overt action it may add intensifying substance with no imbalance of narrative momentum. When a reader notes the means which functionally underlie cumulative effect, this need not detain or preoccupy attention but can enhance perception of the larger ends they serve. This in effect is quite opposite to the application of critical formulae and stereotyped criteria, such as in the not too recent surge of zeal for identifying symbols, the likes of which sometimes were seized upon in disregard or outright contradiction of their context — a sort of false arrest on mere appearance, with a confusion and fragmenting of narrative or lyric movement. Such malpractice conversely indicates the certain rewards of attentive, recollective, and imaginatively responsive reading; it may also suggest that fruitful studies in the vein of comparative literature, but usually with closer explication, could be made within the substantial *oeuvre* of any writer in whom genius manifested its imaginative power through remarkable craft.

Such studies of Faulkner are still to be made, but if literature remains a humanistic concern, a genius so notable will probably attract such attention to his *oeuvre,* a comprehensive view of which will still depend upon incidence. In such fictional art as Faulkner's, structure though only a factor becomes a detectable paradigm of a work's organic unity, while texture is the living evidence, supporting the aesthetic illusion of an existential reality. Transcendent imagination (in the artist and of necessity with some correspondence in his readers) holds this ideation at a substantiated moving point between memory and expectation; event is immediate, but bears marks and influences out of its past, while it carries intimations which materialize as consequences. This is not just fiction, it is natural human consciousness in its continuous motion, which even men's dreams strive madly to emulate, and for Faulkner it is the firm main stage for his narrative actions. Consequently with him, as to degrees with those other modern writers who have scrupulously attempted to make their fictional works completely sustained and self-sustaining compositions, one discrimination which Coleridge made between poetry and literary prose does not now stand: novels in Faulkner's imaginative vein do indeed also propose to convey "such delight from the *whole,* as in compatible with a distinct gratification from each component *part.*" To see this in Faulkner, not just as consolidation or even compatibility but as the total organic truth of the matter in any of his works, is to hold each most closely in terms of its elements as factors in a continuity, where they constitute as well as are constituted into more than the sum of themselves, the sustainedly living creation, in which they move with vital force.

Faulkner's considerable demands upon a reader are nevertheless not immoderate; they hold and extend commensurate rewards. Each work deserves its kind and measure of attention, and out of all these variables a sense of the *oeuvre* is most worth having got for what it leads back to, the adapted uniqueness of works, yet all of them recognizably in the bent of one powerfully creative imagination. This idiosyncratic Faulkner is best heard out in the midst of his calling and its full practice, and his genius is seen in right perspective and proportion only in recognition of his place among his true peers, not as classed with his most tangential contemporaries, and certainly not as related to the American novel in one of its present extremes, such as what might be termed the metropolitan-catatonic. Faulkner is in fiction's mainstream, and was *en avant* only in developing some of the great potentials that were to be evolved out of established conventions and newly demonstrated techniques. That he proceeded with real understanding of his accomplished predecessors and yet advanced on his own chosen way with such self-assurance evinces the alertness and spontaneous originality and the claimed inner poise essential to the complete artist.

Each of Faulkner's fictional works was a unique envisioning and devising to its own particular end and effect, a reification out of his stirred imagination at a point in the secret calendar of his creative life. Even the three Snopes novels (1940, 1957, 1959) are variables, yet held within that trilogy, and the closest estimation throughout will not depend upon a remarking of minor factual inconsistencies among them but upon an awareness of each in its fulfilled autonomy as at the same time it takes a related place in the trilogy as a great polyhedral structure. Those of Faulkner's contemporaries who were eagerly reading his novels as they appeared, and who grew more and more certain of his genius during the thirties, perhaps cannot hope, lacking a *tabula rasa* innocence, to envisage the Snopes trilogy as sheer composition, contrapuntally inventive and richly orchestrated; probably neither can those more lately but only haphazardly come to his work. Possibly some young critic who will read the three volumes straight through at a first encounter may provide a comprehensive response to the patterns of refracted crosslights from the various planes as juxtaposed from volume to volume and within each. Such criticism might even reach to an apprehension of the creator's control of a strenuous virtuosity which never rests in itself but constantly forwards the existential realities of the tales, and so affectingly as to suggest the expansive growth of the artist as such, at all points in the actualizing of his visions.

Two effective factors, intensity and fluency, are found in all Faulkner's fiction, and in his greatest works they are at a height. The intensity arises primarily from close substantive and artistic integration of the work as thematic-aesthetic entity. This trait might be called density, in the physical sense, as in atomic weight or the specific gravity of a compound, or as in an electrical current. Yet in fiction such intensity is not to be got by addition, which on the contrary may tend to dilute; in Faulkner above all fictionists a potent "density" results from the particularly apt rendering of the thing in itself yet as of its context and in its subjective mode through insight conveyed by form and style, controlled, but unreservedly infused with imagination. As remarkable in Faulkner's fiction as this intensity is the trait of fluency, a continuum as of music, measured without lapse, and its tempo modulated to the substance of the passage. There is a simple but subtly applied reciprocity in regulating this fluency; Faulkner does not tread ahead monotonously in route march; in the less dense passages action is narrated more speedily, with an intentness of its own, whereas at points of extreme realization for the enactors the narrative may flow slow and deep with the intensity of its suspended subjective matter. Most inclusively, beyond their ratios as gathered up through form and style, concentration and momentum merge into the reality of that existential motion which is both the substance of Faulkner's works and the manner of their imaginatively projected being, a remarkable fusion of matter and expression, achieving organicism and autonomy in each total composition.

Because of significant content, the variety of its embodiments, and the interactive intensity and fluency of its artistic representations, there is no more rewarding twentieth-century fictionist than Faulkner to know in his *oeuvre,* the better to read and relish page after page of his works. Here substance in its humane import is made immediate in a myriad of fictional instancings, which illustrate themselves the more fully by their relative measure and pertinence along the way of an unfolding revelation through a consummated work. The *oeuvre* has no such perfected unity and completion, nor should it be expected to stand and deliver such effects, but it does cast a large shadow of more than itself, and of more than a man; the *oeuvre* can conjure up an intimation of genius, as almost a sensed presence, in an air resonant with the intonations of a recognized voice.

6

Good and Evil

FAULKNER'S insistent dramatizings of varieties of wrong-doing, ranging from folly to outright evil, was a chief cause of outcry against him from the first, to be continued by some in blindness to the ethical advocacy inherent in all his fictional representations. That his alleged offenses against conventional taste and morality itself were seen as aberrations of a morbidly introverted personality was a deeper error. Faulkner's vital imagination turned outward with intuitive empathy, projecting a humane interest in his fellow beings and a troubled concern for a more sound and certain commonalty, as the area of honorable self-realization under the aspect of proved verities. And human values, implicit beyond resort to definition or need of it, are at the center of those personal struggles and more extended conflicts which run and sometimes rage through Faulkner's perfectedly fictional narratives. Here too was no malpractice, no seeking out of trouble for its direct sensational effects. It is never a question of whether any story involves conflict; all dramatic and fictional "actions" do, and the issue is, at what level of human significance? That matter recently enough came into sight in a popular mode, through attempts at the so-called "adult Western" movie. Basically this aspired to look beyond melodrama, with its confrontations between outright good and absolute evil, each simplistically (or cynically) assumed by the concocters and expected by its naive and habituated audience. What a more genuine and ambitious art attempted was some recognition of relativism, especially as to both the "Western" protagonist and the villain, disclosing beyond the longest chase or the law's remedies those subjective ambiguities which Faulkner indicated as of "the human heart in conflict with itself."

It is by interpersonal relations turning upon what is humanly veritable and crucial that beings come into closest awareness, with the potential of a maximum mutuality or severest opposition. These ventures of uncertain but assertive hearts constitute the matter of drama and fiction, and in such projections the strife between individuals which gives vitality to the composition can involve the whole subjective being of the enactor. Beyond conflicting ideas and intentions there even may lie the melancholy of a regret that it must be so. All this ensues when Isaac McCaslin, having renounced his inheritance at twenty-one and removed himself next day from the plantation to a cramped little room in a Jefferson boarding house, is visited by his still solicitously disputatious elder cousin McCaslin Edmonds. Now McCaslin has pressed money upon Isaac for his needs, and finally "tossed the folded banknotes onto the bed," and Isaac has specified "As a loan. From you. This one," meanwhile "looking peacefully at McCaslin, his kinsman, his father almost yet no kin now as, at the last, even fathers and sons are no kin." Later, listening peacefully to his landlady's scolding him for trustfully leaving money in his unlocked room, he is to recur to that theme and extend it prophetically: "no kin at all yet more than kin as those who serve you even for pay are your kin and those who injure you are more than brother or wife." In that same rented room Isaac is to come into most severe contest, not in overt struggle, but in the ambiguous stresses of marital love. When his wife, having accepted or pretended to accept Isaac as he had candidly presented himself to her, then specifies his repossession of the plantation as the price of her body and his hope of having a son, she is making a conventional value judgment that many might have concurred with, but she is also repudiating the principled man she had married after well knowing his intent.

These crises in the great fourth section of "The Bear" are at a high pitch even for Faulkner, yet they are not inconsistent with a pervading implication in his works that ethos is what substantiates drama. Action becomes urgent in the actor and arresting to the beholder when its locale is genuinely the realm of conduct. Good and evil are constant alternatives in the cosmology of a humane existence, but in that subjective region the voyager's compass trembles, deflected by currents of relativism, and amid external confusions and contradictions the pole of truth is known to lie beyond human vision. Furthermore, whatever apprehension of verities is arrived at may only show that not all societal criteria are valid and indeed some may be directly productive of evil. By their rigid fanaticisms those true believers Hines and McEachern harass Joe Christmas from childhood on, and set him upon the road toward his execution by another defender of the faith, Percy Grimm. Even those who are not without gentleness may be driven to violence by convention, as is Henry Sutpen, fatally shooting his dearest friend and thereby nullifying his own life as well as widowing his sister before the event of bridehood. On a lesser scale but still to a depth of personal grief are the cousins Isaac McCaslin and McCaslin Edmonds, both humanely principled and congenial in many ways, who come to a parting, while beneath all their societally oriented contention is the private stress of each ambivalent human heart, denied assured repose. It is also in *Go Down, Moses,* in the "Delta Autumn" section, that Faulkner lets his actors deal explicitly, but all the more dramatically, with the question of human behavior, as the deer-hunters' supper-table conversation drifts into larger problems than protecting does. Now nearly eighty, Isaac McCaslin nevertheless is on this hunt, and so is the middle-aged Roth, McCaslin Edmonds' grandson. Isaac believes there are "good men everywhere, at all times" and asserts that "most men are a little better than their circumstances give them a chance to be." Roth considers all men to be "animals" and roughly suggests Isaac has been dead not to have learned that, but Isaac seems "untroubled and merely

grave" as he declares he's "satisfied" with what he's learned to
believe.

In the continuing talk, Roth says men behave only when
watched, as by a man with a badge, and Henry Wyatt retorts
that he's "glad" he doesn't hold such an "opinion of folks,"
adding pointedly, "I take it you include yourself." Roth
neither admits nor denies inclination to lawlessness and
animality, but he suggests a fatalism (perhaps exacerbated by
bad conscience) by returning to the factor of circumstances.
These Isaac had said "most men" may transcend, can be "a
little better than," but now Roth asks, "Who makes the circumstances?" Wyatt admits the incidence of "Luck, Chance,
Happen-so," but in continuing to identify himself with "what
Uncle Ike said" he tentatively sharpens the point, putting it
that "now and then, maybe most of the time, man is a little
better than the net result of his and his neighbors' doings,
when he gets a chance to be." Isaac had spoken of knowing
"some" men "that even the circumstances couldn't stop";
Wyatt's remark properly assesses this not as a triumphant reversal of fate, but a willed extension beyond the happen-so,
into which conduct may enter as action constructively amend-
ing circumstances themselves. Wyatt is not naive; he again
admits "luck," in that a man can cope with men's "doings"
only "when he gets a chance." But Wyatt believes that given
such, man can be "a little better" than the circumstances he is
immersed in, which are in part at least the "net result of his
and his neighbor's doings." Such implication of society's man-
made contribution to man's fate, an intrication which is enig-
matically a complement to the heart's conflict with itself, also
implies what may be achieved by individual adherence to the
something "better," presumably conceived of as a representative and not inaccessible human value.

This supper-table episode showing unsophisticated but
canny practical men wrestling with large abstractions about
human behavior considered as conduct is parabolic, but it is
also a lively enactment, a scene that plays itself sustainedly.
Their colloquial talk is fluent and pointed — the vast concept

of behavior is brought down to provincial dimensions by Wyatt's phrase, "the net result of his and his neighbors' doings," yet "net result" is a neat equivalent for even the most immense of consequences. As men may do in pauses from their main intent, these hunters become intrigued by speculation, except for Legate, who extends the spectrum of the *dramatis personae* (and advances the plot) by staying apart from the theoretical debate and regaling himself with insinuating jibes about Roth's affair with a mulatto woman, cryptically referred to as the doe Roth hunts each season. (That factor certainly has to do with his surliness and his offensive remark to old Uncle Ike. But the protagonist of "Delta Autumn" remains quietly self-possessed; he has stood on his convictions too long and consistently to be perturbed by Roth's mood, and he is yet to learn of that scandal which for him will take on the appearance of a family doom repeating itself.) And for the moment the other hunters have become so genuinely engaged in their philosophical weighing of circumstances and good, bad, or better personal conduct that they are not to be diverted by Legate.

Now in the moment of pause after Wyatt has made his striking paraphrase supporting "what Uncle Ike said," Legate can break in upon the sober talk with an almost uninterrupted speech: "Well, I wouldn't say that Roth Edmonds can hunt one doe every day and night for two weeks and was a poor hunter or a unlucky one neither. A man that still have the same doe left to hunt on again next year — ." The man next to Legate says, "Have some meat," and offers him the dish, and when Legate says, "I got some," Wyatt suggests, "Have some more. You and Roth Edmonds both. . . . Clapping your jaws together with nothing to break the shock." The men laugh, tension is eased, the weighty and brilliantly executed scene is left intact but vitally conjoined within the story's continuity. Perhaps the hunters were trying to shield the old man; it had been apparent on the way to camp, when Legate had begun to jest about the "doe" Roth hunts, that Uncle Ike knew nothing of it and seemed bewildered by the cryptic talk. But now Isaac has not been listening to Legate; he is reaching back to the source of his faith in goodness. Speaking "even into" the men's laughter over the offer to Legate and Roth of something to chew on, Isaac asserts "in that peaceful and still untroubled voice" that he believes and sees proof everywhere, though he grants "that man made a heap of his circumstances, him and his living neighbors between them," and "even inherited some of them." Isaac declares the creative providence of God, and God's immanence in man through love, but the older hunter's phrasing is quaintly immediate; his is scarcely a theological discourse but rather a seasoned woodsman's mysticism. This still wears the mark of his novitiate under Sam Fathers, as told in "The Old People" and "The Bear," which when capped by "Delta Autumn" make up the epic of an aspiringly idealistic life in its resoluteness and its doom to deprivation and successive disenchantments.

The close interpersonal and broad societal involvements in Faulkner's fictional narratives project an implication that virtue is not manifest *in vacuo,* while evil is most obvious and deplorable in its impact upon the guiltless and merely fortuitously involved—worst in the destruction of life but also and more commonly in the attrition of communal faith and hope, with the subjective threat of despair. The graph of Isaac's life demonstrates this interplay of good and evil, and displays his constancy under stress. Even in what awaits him next morning at the hunters' camp, the last episode in his provided history, he pauses this side of indifference, and though in his own mind he cannot fend off a large vision of worse to come, he continues to incline to kindness, in this case toward the mulatto woman and child whom Roth has abandoned. But shocks are nothing new to Isaac, whether from the mere miscarriage of events or from men's wrongdoing. In section 3 of "The Bear" he witnesses in the last of the great hunts not merely the death of Old Ben the incomparable bear and the fearless dog Lion but also the fatal collapse of Sam Fathers. In section 4, on arrival at his majority, he rejects inheritance of the McCaslin plantation, specifically because of his discoveries in the ledgers of his grandfather's sins against his female slaves, and in general because he cannot affiliate himself with a system stranded in the backwash of an exploitation not only of land but of a still partially shackled race. Then in the central personal event of his life the idealistic young carpenter is denied hope for a son by his wife because he will not reclaim the plantation. Section 5 of "The Bear," in an arranged effect of manipulated chronology, turns back from this crisis to the youth who, already knowing what the McCaslin plantation ledgers contain and having experienced the finale of the great hunt, is returning for a valedictory visit to the great woods which lumbering is beginning to destroy. Thus later when he must endure the painful division of opinion between himself and his valued cousin McCaslin and thereafter when his wife turned against him, he was already experienced in loss and had learned the discipline of relinquishment, as long as it was not a surrender of principle.

Virtue, in its ancient masculine sense as Faulkner writes of it, is individual, seated in the ideal of honor, but manifest as ethos, a societally applicable concept, to be enacted unequivocally in whatever confrontation. In this key, from the first line of "The Old People" to the last line of "Delta Autumn" Isaac's life story is all of a piece. In Faulkner's works it is central and complete as the most consistent and relevantly detailed fable of ethical conduct. The boy had been formed by his elder cousin McCaslin's oversight and reassuring kindness and by the woodsman Sam Fathers' native wisdom and scrupulousness; early in his novitiate Isaac had elected to range the big woods alone, till finally without interposition of gun or compass he sighted Old Ben and in turn was glanced at by the great legendary creature; later in a close encounter he had not fired his gun at the bear but had rushed in to hold back his fearless little dog; his cousin McCaslin, learning of the incident, tried to help Isaac understand a sense of something ideal that the bear embodied for him. Those formative ventures solitarily undertaken before Isaac was old enough to ride at the fore of the great final hunt have prepared him to confront evil in his ancestry and a peculiarly cruel betrayal in his marriage. By their interpersonal and societal nature these stresses suggest hazards of another order than those of the big woods. Woodsmanship as craft and ethos can sustain the hunter bodily and in clear conscience, but Isaac's forthrightness and good will cannot protect him from a punishing deprivation by his wife for holding consistently to his principles, and Isaac's inborn humane regard for his fellow beings had made him the more vulnerable to early disillusionment by what he pieced together about his ruthless grandfather out of the commissary ledgers. "Delta Autumn" rounds out Isaac's history consistently and with no evasion of the reality of human impasse versus recurrent evil in circumstances that are the work of other human beings. With the hunters the old man had been still assertive of principled conduct as an imperative, but he is all the more to be subject to further shock. This latest is to bear a bitter irony in that the family patriarch's offense which had influenced Isaac's major decisions is now repeated in old Lucius McCaslin's desendant, Roth, by his unfeeling use of the mulatto woman. Racked again by revulsion from the offense and pity for the victimized, old Isaac can find his only settlement in a resignation that with its residue of grief is still this side of the easy apathy some procure through a noncommital passing by on the other side.

In that Faulkner's narratives turn closely on matters of conduct humanistically considered, moral shock to his protagonists is of frequent occurrence. To some, like Isaac — or like Quentin Compson, who feelingly confronts in the Sutpen story some of the same basic regional issues even if at a further distance — the perturbation is as great as at a stir of the earth itself in a tectonic faulting that leaves the known surface forever altered. Horace Benbow of *Sanctuary* is so deeply, literally disconcerted by Popeye and Temple Bailey in their separate styles of iniquity and by the resultant fate of Goodwin, whom he couldn't save from her perjury or the lynch mob, that beyond tears his despair extends to the cosmos, and the season's "snow of the locust blossoms" moves him to cold irony: "It does last. Spring does. You'd almost think there was some purpose to it." In *The Hamlet*, where evil appears chiefly though not exclusively through the Snopes incurison with Flem its archetype of villainy, Faulkner's champions of equity show less extreme reactions to wickedness than Quentin Compson's or Benbow's. Nevertheless two incidents seem purposefully juxtaposed near the novel's end, with thematic effect from their similar examples of recoil by patient benevolent men whose will to resist miscreance temporarily flags. In the first instance Bookwright and Ratliff ar talking over Flem's latest maneuverings, and when Bookwright touches on Ratliff's earlier remedial interventions between Flem and his victims, Ratliff cries out, "I could do more, but I wont. I wont, I tell you!" and Bookwright has to soothe him with a wagon-driver's metaphor: "All right. Hook your drag up. It aint nothing but a hill." The second episode, which follows immediately, is of two damage suits against Flem Snopes, by Armstid and by Tull, both victims of accidents with the wild ponies Flem brought back from Texas after his extended honeymoon, along with Eula and the incredibly mature baby. The case is tried by an old Justice of the Peace, "resembling a tender caricature of all grandfathers," and the action is not only a brilliant bit of Faulknerian regionalism but a telling example of his tragicomic mode in its combination of rustic grotesqueness, recurrent pathos, and outrage over the obstruction of justice by perjury. In neither case can the scrupulous old Justice make a satisfactory finding because in each a Snopes henchman swears that Flem had nothing to do with the horses the Texan had auctioned off. The scene ends in an uproar, with the Justice crying out, "I cant stand no more! I wont! This court's adjourned! Adjourned!"

Yet beyond doubt this court will be called to order again by that same scrupulous and humane old Justice, as he takes up once more his duties in repairing the local fabric of the social order as best he can. He will well remember how covert malefaction can shield itself through the frightening anarchism of perjury, but he will steady himself with the jurist's faith in verities that men have known for themselves and have approximated into the law, as communally generated concepts of equity among themselves and for their children. Such a moral rallying this side of despair may be assumed as almost a certainty in the old Justice, who with long experience and strong convictions may be staggered but will not be overset; Ratliff will be shown by Faulkner to have got himself in hand, to become a chief equilibrator in the whole Snopes story, as between the quixotism of the susceptible Gavin Stevens and Flem's coldly calculated exploitations, together with the grotesque disorderliness of lesser members of that tribe.

What has been shown in *The Hamlet* through the similar refusals by the Justice and Ratliff to struggle any further against Snopesism, at least for the moment, illustrates what is seen variously in Faulkner's fiction: that not all conflicts of the heart with itself are deeply subjective, in an uneasy private ambivalence. Many passive victims of others' wrongdoing can bear it out stoically, sure at least that the guilt is not theirs, and able to make endurance their virtue; wrongdoers, whether like the amoral Snopes or the obsessed Sutpen, seem not to conceive of what those they injure are suffering; between them are the societally right-minded and actively well-intentioned, but peculiarly susceptible because extremely tensed by issue. On occasion these last can be tempted to give it all up in the face of Non-virtue's advantage through the greater ease of its self-accorded laxities. The champions of human values may even approach a state such as Wordsworth confessed in *The Prelude* when "wearied out with contrarieties," he "Yielded up moral questions in despair," but Faulkner shows that most men once committed to ethical principles then rally, as did Wordsworth, as did Ratliff, and that there are some "even the circumstances couldn't stop."

For Faulkner such men as Ratliff, Bayard Sartoris of "An Odor of Verbena," Gavin Stevens, or Chick Mallison when he shakes off Yoknapawphan prejudice and determines to help Lucas, are favored protagonists, and their fluctuant but ardent sensibilities become the clearest conveyors of narratives. Neither Flem Snopes nor Thomas Sutpen could have given his own story adequate socioethical or even psychological realization. That becomes evident in the pretentious, somewhat labored, and still naive accounts Sutpen had given to explain it all to Quentin's grandfather; while to depend for conveyance of Snopes's story on whatever could be imagined as passing through his mind and yet to give it the ethical perspective Faulkner intended would make greater demand on an intuitive sense of irony than readers of fiction might care to exercise, and still would have supplied only a sluggish tale. The intensity and momentum, the tone of urgency in Faulkner's narratives, is not a calculated expedient, not something technically laid on by a craftsman nor any makeshift to invigorate a fictional matter beyond its intrinsic significance. Indeed, it can scarcely be considered a device at all; it is rather an aspect of the artist's close representation of ethically concerned men's sensibilities in the midst of issue, where the stress between better and worse is of a wracking severity. Hence deepest realism in the narrating of such a fictional action is to be come at in the subjectivity of protagonists, not as the artist's *alter ego* or with his voice from behind a mask but, out of whatever identity, yet as attuned to the humanistic vision that has determined the work's whole thrust. Thereby not only are the narrative's immediate moments and its turns most closely realized, but the total continuity is pervaded and a thematic unity is imaginatively established. This is neither by the author's intrusive definition nor exclusively through any one character, and not by the events alone but in a field of force generated by the artist's conception furnished forth with unremitting commitment and inexhaustible inventiveness. It extends through texture and sustains the opalescence that comprises modulations of tone and pace and variability of mood in the characters' engagement with circumstance. This sustained keying of a whole narrative action to the concerned consciousness of protagonists is a perfected subtlety, made so not to mystify but to attain to a central reality; recognition of it may serve to convert certain readers from indifference or even distrust to an entrancement that elicits the close constant imaginative attention which is the only door to a genuine experiencing of Faulkner's potent art.

Faulkner's treatment of evil, not sensationally or exaggeratedly but as pervasive fact, widely fateful in its impingements upon the lives of men and women, and as an issue to be strenuously confronted in the light of postulated human values, is a theme made so pervasive that some readers' general recollection of his works may take on a peculiarly sombre tinge. In the novels separately this grave tone may be felt in proportion to the artist's degree of dependence upon the consciousness of troubled characters for communicating the narrative. This basic practice Faulkner employed in ways as various as between its almost purely musing form in *As I Lay Dying* or its enhancing containment of an urgent eventfulness in *Intruder in the Dust;* yet with both their subjective illumination casts intersecting shadows. Wherever it is feasible, and especially at acute points in his protagonists' struggles upon the premises of evil and good, Faulkner's instinct is for a presentation at some distance from any possible clouding of experiential realities by protrusion of bare sensationalism. Quite an opposite prejudicial opinion is still held by many about Faulkner's intentions and how he implements them fictionally. An opportunity for further service by critical studies may lie in closer analysis of his techniques under a clearer view of his temperament and of his commitment to the maximizing of a primary fictional reality by penetration to its center in the characters' often melancholy, sometimes dire experience at those moments when issue is joined and behavior as conduct becomes crucial.

It is not that Faulkner hesitated to take narrative fully into his own hands; he frequently does so, intermittently, but masterfully by every criterion, especially with an expedite pace and the realization of scene through motion and dialogue. Moreover, in the most sophisticated reaches of his art, beyond verbal similitude Faulkner will lend a measure of language to enhance the reader's intuition of a protagonist's state of mind, not for fixed characterization but in responsive encounter with issue. Such a centering upon the action's existential core solicits intuitive response, subtle degrees of the figurative bring the matter home to the reader's imagination beyond the merely overt, and under such enhancement the event more readily merges into its widest relations, tonal as well as thematic, within the whole work. In even the simplest fiction, what has preceded then progressively supports ongoing event and intimates or at least makes ready for what may come in the logic of plot; if in Faulkner such continuity is felt to run with peculiarly intriguing effect, it may be credited to sheer artistic devising as well, in that the veritable issues of right and wrong emerge commandingly through the private as well as interpersonal responses of those involved.

Although in Faulkner's preference for focus upon issue through his characters' individual and subjectively tinged confrontation of it narrative often centers there rather than upon overt circumstance, even when action is forcefully narrated it will still be given strong overtones of humane evaluations. Though the death of Joe Christmas is directly described, it is put in an elegaic mode that eclipses the sensational. Fatally shot and horribly mutilated, he lay motionless on the floor, "with his eyes open and empty of everything save consciousness, and with something, a shadow, about his mouth" and "looked up at them with peaceful and unfathomable and unbearable eyes. Then his face, body, all seemed to collapse, to fall in upon itself, and from out the slashed garments about his hips and loins the pent black blood seemed to rush like a released breath," upon which "the man seemed to rise soaring into their memories forever and ever." That projection becomes prophecy, a narrative abstract of what they "are not to lose," this vision of the sum of what has been done to Christmas, a martyrdom become "of itself alone serene," and their unforgettable recollection of responsibility for it. A more typical avoidance of focus on what might be deemed merely sensational is the instance of the shot which terminated Bon's and Henry's confrontation at the gate to Sutpen's Hundred. The whole episode is disclosed through Quentin's intense enhancing envisioning as Mr. Compson tells what is known of it — the two devoted friends returning from the lost war, Bon determined to marry Judith Sutpen now that they "both are doomed to live," and Henry Sutpen, now knowing from his father that Bon is his half-brother and of mixed blood, determined to prevent miscegenation though he would have allowed the incest. Quentin, whose consciousness is the chief medium, among many, in communicating the novel's essences, imagines the two men right up to the fatal moment — "the two faces calm, the voices not even raised: *Don't you pass the shadow of this post, this branch, Charles; and I am going to pass it, Henry,*" but here the curtain falls on the impending act, and as Mr. Compson continues the account the shot has its reverberation distanced in time and space and distorted to another level of feeling, with Wash Jones on a mule before Miss Rosa's gate in Jefferson, twelve miles away, "shouting her name into the sunny and peaceful quiet of the street, saying, 'Air you Miss Rosie Coldfield? Then you better come on out yon. Henry has done shot that durn French feller. Kilt him dead as a beef.'" In *Sanctuary*, in an explicit reservation of effect for intensified conveyance through a major character's sensibilities, there is the matter of the burning of Goodwin after he had been mistakenly found guilty of Popeye's crimes. The mob's seizure of the victim and his death are not narrated directly, and the only witnessing is of its immediate aftermath, as Horace Benbow, Goodwin's lawyer, hurries in the wake of the running crowd's clamor and comes upon nothing but the not yet subsiding fire, he bearing his already seared consciousness of the recent subversion of justice by Temple's perjury and now faced with this outbreak of the malevolence latent in many men and all too easily ignited.

Faulkner's delegation of episodic narrative conveyance to an involved reactive consciousness is never an avoidance but a choice, for focus upon ethical issue come to its ultimate tribunal in a humane conscience, as well as for enhancement of various fictional effects ranging from the immediate to the structural. *Scènes à faire* are always done, but in their own place and way as the artist sees it, in his concern with men's relative awareness of good or evil intent. There may be more that a reader would like to know about some character, either before or after, but such an interest scarcely establishes that something essential to the work is lacking. By his spareness for the sake of momentum and his measured touch for modulation Faulkner took more than ordinary fictional risks, and it has cost him — for instance, with readers who insufficiently weigh Isaac McCaslin's major obstruction and restraint from a full life, not just his youthful disillusionment out of the commissary ledgers but rather the impasse in early manhood with a wife who tried to make him over and punished his refusal to revise his principles by denying him a son. Yet while Faulkner capably conducted many stories or parts of them as a recognizable though not identified third-person narrator, he did not forget that fictional art is not expository but presentational, especially as it finds for its pivot something as abstract yet humanly centered as individual awareness of good and evil. Faulkner's temperament not only inclined but swept him toward the more than ordinarily intense and immediate conveyance of that imaginative matter through the deeply plumbed reactions of involved characters. Beyond his fictionally potent imagism in itself he calls up its realization, not just a visualizing but as relevant response within that very fictional world, and not just incidentally but relatively, as of those fictional times and participants' crucial personal involvement. In another aspect of his practice, chronology runs beyond clock and calendar for a subtler progression into a further measuring of character, in which another kind of suspense is felt, together with thematically proportionate emphasis, and the fuller climax in consummate resoluton of felt issue rather than mere eventful surprise. In these ways Faulkner was well to the fore, and some readings have yet to catch up with him, but as with much else in his work, alertness to his primary concern with ethical verities will give more ready access to his fictional creations, both in their substance and its enabling art.

Still Faulkner was not a theoretical practitioner of an abstractly conceived art; he had read widely and perceptively enough to know the lay of the land and its viable conventions, yet he was himself, too, a genius caught up by acute visions of arresting individuals in meaningful narrative actions. Fired though he was, on the whole he had commensurate control over a prolific and ingenious inventiveness, through which his work lays its unique claim upon imagination. There is little abatement from a remarkably engendered and sustained aesthetic awareness, becoming almost one of intrigue consented to by the intent expeditious artist himself, even when matters of some magnitude are being treated of. This no doubt is made possible because Faulkner's craft in all its intensities of style and structure maintains a sort of symbiotic relationship to humane concern and evaluation. No modern writer of fiction has come closer than Faulkner to a full evocation of one of art's immense paradoxes, an intimation of fulfillment through realization of the tragic. Mysterious as this apprehension is, in Faulkner it is not inscrutible; his asserted humanism and fictional illustrations of operant verities suggest that a reassuring sense of selfhood and reality-oriented self-realization are to be approached through an experiencing of compassionate commonalty.

In this connection it is well to note the nature of melancholy as it occurs in a number of Faulkner characters, and as its tone recurs in the novels' total effects. It is not typically a Byronic melancholy, not introspectively self-pitying, but the opposite. Faulkner's protagonists are twentieth century figures, even those who lived earlier; theirs is not the elected lassitude of *Weltschmerz* but the wide scannings in an alerted *Angst*. Quentin Compson of *Absalom, Absalom!* and Isaac McCaslin of *Go Down, Moses* are notably among many others of this order; consequently those stories draw their fullest force from the continuum of those protagonists' subjective responsiveness.

Even as Isaac at twenty-one and his elder cousin McCaslin debate the widest socioethical relevances of Isaac's determination to renounce inheritance, along with the emotionally augmented talk itself there run recurrent obbligatos of Isaac's unspoken reflection, extending complementary motifs, sometimes momentarily even suspending the immediate continuity. And whether it is Quentin's father or his Harvard roommate Shreve who for the moment is speculatively reconstructing the Sutpen saga, Quentin's mind is moving one step closer in his own intuitions of what must have been its realities. For him their immense scope is overwhelming, constraining him into ambivalence as he envisions in the Sutpen debacle a paradigm of the South's fate as enclosing his own inescapably. Isaac's earlier encounter with a regionally related family history was a closer thing, and his reaction no less severe, but his attempt to escape from the system might have succeeded had not heritage in its lingering societal trends touched him through his wife, and the defeat of his main hope leaves him the more vulnerable to melancholy in old age, as he sees old inhumanities repeated by his younger kinsman Roth Edmonds.

Though some of the most somber tones in Faulkner's novels are primarily of such a Southern derivation, this is not exclusively so. The artist's accepted subjects were primarily regional, often with deep historical roots and in extended societal contexts, but he did not follow Miss Rosa Coldfield in supposing his neighbors were collectively cursed and doomed beyond other men, and he found in the best of them certain special merits. Perhaps his most morbidly melancholy character is Hightower, of *Light in August;* his fate has been an enslavement by nostalgia, which others suffer too, in the natural human way, but less than abjectly. A more despairing man than Hightower, and even cynical, is Horace Benbow of *Sanctuary,* whose griefs are over present offenses and whose outlook reaches beyond the regional. There is in Faulkner's works much of evil that postdates slavery and the Civil War and has little or no relation to that defeat or to a continuing racial issue; the acquisitive Flem Snopes epitomizes this in his depredations. As if everything human were foreign to him, making unresponsiveness his only pose, and deaf except to the clink of money, he moves with that coldly relentless predatory zest which is the uglier side of competitive materialism. Faulkner was conscious of how rapacity had violated the good land itself, and that ecological fact comes into his fiction as moral concern, especially through Isaac McCaslin, for whom it was an article of faith derived from Sam Fathers' native piety, to become a noteworthy though scarcely stressed factor in his renunciation of the McCaslin inheritance. Furthermore, among offenses there is intemperance compounded into a lust for indulgence itself, such as burns defiantly in Temple Drake both in *Sanctuary* and in *Requiem for a Nun,* and enters, though with less specific regional connection, into *The Wild Palms.* And enmity against societal requirements makes Ab Snopes, as in "Barn Burning" and elsewhere, a savage relisher of his own nihilism. On a wider scale, as young Chick Mallison sees, evil can erupt in the frightful paradox enacted when community itself becomes deadly, and the saving conventions of orderliness are overset by dehumanized composite mankind. To him the coalesced mob that would have lynched old Lucas Beauchamp takes on the monstrousness of a nightmare:

not faces but a face, not a mass or even a mosaic of them but a Face . . . insensate, vacant of thought or even passion . . . without dignity . . . just neckless slack-muscled and asleep . . . yet in the same instant rushing and monstrous down at him.

Here was such conventionalized brutality as had pursued Joe Christmas to his death.

Byron Bunch, though not unaware of evil, is incredulous over men's consciously inclining toward it. In *Light in August,* working alone at the sawmill on Saturday afternoon, he "keeps his own time" and docks himself for the five minutes he took off to answer Lena's questions in her search for the father of her unborn child; at another point he says, "It beats all how some folks think that making or getting money is a kind of game where there are not any rules at all." But Byron, a realist, is a profound moral economist too. He has remarked to Hightower that "there is a price for being good the same as for being bad; a cost to pay. And it's the good men that cant deny the bill when it comes around. . . . The bad men can deny it; that's why dont anybody expect them to pay on sight or any other time. But the good cant. Maybe it takes longer to pay for being good than for being bad." A profound aspect of Faulkner's realism is in its representation, in various characters major and minor, of the oppressive melancholy following upon what must be borne beyond choosing because of others' offenses, and these not just against him but in denial of the human verities through which one may feel the common life of man to be regulated, conserved in its beneficial effects, and possibly advanced. A wry quatrain points out that the rain falls mainly on the just because the unjust have appropriated the just's umbrellas; it is no joke, though, but a harsh central fact in mankind's knowledge of good and evil. It engenders melancholy and even despair, and it imposes a tragic sense of life; the world's sorrow is seen as larger than any man's, and not just a sum of items beyond counting but a dark abstraction, and yet an inescapable aspect of reality. And because of evil's random monstrousness as well as its inscrutability to rational assessment it may impose an almost superstitious apprehension of recurrently devastating fate.

In his biography of Virginia Woolf, Quentin Bell reports that in the 1930s she had asked him why, in his opinion, "things had gone so very wrong with the world during the last few years." He gave, he says, "what I suppose was the stock answer of any young socialist: the world economic crisis," which had bred "unemployment, revolution, counter-revolution, economic and political nationalism, hence Communism, Fascism, and war . . . all these things were but the effects of an economic cause. She was frankly amazed," his account continues, and "neither agreed nor disagreed, but thought it a very strange explanation. To her, I think, it appeared that the horrible side of the universe, the forces of madness, which were never far from her consciousness, had got the upper hand again." Something "horrible" in the nature of things had been glimpsed by Chick Mallison as the faces of the mob melded into a "Face," impersonal, slack, and vacant, yet inexorable. Such a force is figured more subtly in *Sanctuary* when Benbow reaches the vacant lot where a mob has just burned Goodwin, the innocent client he could not save from Temple's perjured evidence. There is "a blazing mass in the middle of the lot" but its center is "indistinguishable" and from it "there came no sound at all"; the unspeakable deed has been carried out. Yet as if in omen of inextinguishable evil the fire "still swirled upward unabated, as though it were living upon itself."

The fear Virginia Woolf expressed in 1930s that of late "things had gone so very wrong" was no hallucination. Though she did not analyze its causes, she deeply sensed the time's realities as to human situation; and while she had pledged herself to the primacy of that centrally subjective existence in a merely glimpsed Mrs. Brown which Arnold Bennett might never reach to with his enumeration of externalities, she also answered to her characters' milieu as a determinant, though as subjectively factored by the individual. The comprehensive social, psychological, and historical insights in such works as *Mrs. Dalloway, To the Lighthouse, Orlando,* and *Between the Acts* cannot be depreciated, nor, despite the artist's occasional ironic aloofness, can her humane empathy be doubted. And her melancholy apprehensions over the state of the world were shared by many; H. G. Wells had acutely prefaced World War I in *Tono Bongay,* Auden had told the story twice over, in "Spain, 1937" and in "September 1, 1939," and repeatedly in other poems. Nor was it left to literary artists; a statesman's frequently recalled remark, that lights were going out and their rekindling would not be easy, seemed to epitomize an age of more than anxiety, indeed of apocalyptic vision. As these dire forebodings have fulfilled and exceeded themselves in a rash of disorientations and increasingly cataclysmic major wars, the sense of evil as being inherent in reality deepened in many minds, and entered into a suppressed fatalism that has been exposed by the superficiality of remedial schemes and pretenses of optimism. As humanistic realist, Faulkner at Stockholm cited the pall that had descended upon twentieth-century man's spirit, from the bomb's psychological fallout in advance. His advocacy against such passive despair, especially to younger artists, was for a reassertion of human verities, even out of the undependable human heart in conflict with itself. Virginia Woolf, seeing an impending ascendancy of "the horrible side of the universe" as "largely independent" of the world's economic and political "mechanics," felt (as Bell put it) that "the true answer to all this horror and violence lay in an improvement of one's own moral state." It may seem a simplistic prescription, as Faulkner's may seem naive, yet this essential coincidence of outlook between two such different artists, and persons so differently situated, merits some attention as it unites them on grounds of ethical principle that may claim the validity of a categorical imperative. Moreover, it appears that between them—this sophisticated and culturally experienced woman and this provincial man, more nearly a "natural" than he was any kind of sophisticate, and absorbed in his imaginative art's autonomy and deep privacy—there was in common the special intuitiveness of artistic genius together with the ready empathies of genuinely humane beings.

In a way that hearteningly suggests the great common grounds and liberties of literature. The traits of intuitive apprehension and ethical affirmation comparably yet individually manifested by Virginia Woolf and Faulkner may lead on to perception of a common denominator in their fictional art, the searching-out even though so differently of the buried inner life as the central reality of human existence to which above all else the serious fictionist is devoted. In that vital context the culmination of any era's variously compounded disorders in the multiple calamities of war is evil emergent in a most monstrous form. For the humanist in particular it must seem indubitably the worst evil, not just as it indiscriminately deals out death but in that it distorts whole societies to that dispensation. The title of Virginia Woolf's last novel, *Between the Acts,* suggests World Wars I and II as the frame of her productive life; and the novel itself, with its fantastically expressed yet penetrating sense of history and its realization of an experienced people shrinking from the repetition of what they know too well, shows the artist appalled yet creatively aroused, and is her real epitaph over the sad gesture of laying her life aside.

For Faulkner in his time and place it was not just a matter of rumored wars but of an actuality, bygone yet recurrent in the history and legends of its local incursion. Like every informed and humanely concerned twentieth-century Southerner he was under a special necessity to look before and after, back as well as forward. When in 1918, not yet twenty-one, he enlisted for pilot training in the Canadian R.A.F., he must have carried with him something of what he was to suggest through Chick Mallison as every Southern boy's heritage, an ambivalent retrospection upon the Civil War. This awareness the developing novelist was to extend, modify, and deepen in a process of maturation sufficiently extensive and penetrating to embrace the existential progression of a variety of characters. Increasing knowledge (intensifying the heart's fated struggle within itself) was to weigh heavily upon Bayard Sartoris and Chick Mallison, and heavier still upon Quentin Compson and Isaac McCaslin. Then the novelist himself, always humanely concerned over the riddle of good and evil, and having repeatedly recognized the emergence of issue in its largest dimensions and most brutal aspects in war, was to go beyond treating it in certain regional terms and as to the peculiar aftermath of that war in racial strain between black and white. In *A Fable* he was still to address himself to the problem of evil within a historical context, that of World War I, but in more nearly universal terms, while at the same time orchestrating in the veritable mural of his largest composition some of the main motifs in his whole body of work.

7

Realist and Regionalist

AS A fictionist Faulkner was not of any school, nor would he
have abetted or blessed the recruitment of one. A conspicuous
mark of his rectitude is that he kept himself unspotted from
the literary world's camps and coteries. In each work, and
throughout each, he is his own man; and at his truest and best
he has not yet been proved imitable. In various ways at many
points he brilliantly intensified and refined effective fictional
practices, by apt extensions of known artistic techniques; and
since some of these are fundamentally applicable, his fresh de-
ployments of them no doubt have been of considerable
influence on certain younger writers. In the large, however,
his accomplishments remain unparalleled; and with the
conspicuous tangentiality and cultural dispersions in more
recent American fiction, it becomes plain that no one since
him draws any such strong bow so closely aimed. What is still
to be fully appreciated (in the most weighty sense of the word)
is that despite some extravagances and excursions into the
baroque, Faulkner stands as the central and preeminent
American novelist, and if that fabulous entity the great
American novel has already loomed above the horizon, it must
be one of his major displays of mastery, such as *Absalom,
Absalom!*, *Light in August*, *Go Down, Moses*, or the Snopes
trilogy.

An intensely imaginative writer, with corresponding demands upon readers, and at times as inclined to the fanciful

144

or the grotesque as a purposeful fictionist dare be, Faulkner is nevertheless fundamentally a realist. He is also a regionalist, and as such perhaps the most dynamic and significant in American literature. Realistic regionalist, regional realist— the factors are reciprocal in the substantive and artistic unity of a Faulknerian work. This will be felt if the thrust of his realism and the focus of his regionalism are closely discerned. Their interrelations are complex yet harmonized. Faulkner cannot be given two discrete faces, even though sharply drawn, as a kind of realist and conversely a kind of regionalist. To see these separately would be like failing to perceive the identity comprised in some of Picasso's singularly superimposed profiles. Faulkner's realism and regionalism are most distinctly recognizable in their complementary aspects, the local matter broadly conceptualized in a sustained artistic unity. For Faulkner realism is something more than naturalism, and quite the opposite of its extreme forms. His narratives do not move at an automated pace along determinism's constricted path, nor are his protagonists wholly indentured to milieu, no matter how weighty its impingements. Faulkner well knew that his creations, like other aspiring fictional projections, ventured into frontier country of the mind and often pressed close to that *terra incognita,* human behavior at its most intensely personal. So confronted by realities as he intimately sensed them in actors and locale, he did not turn to any of the two-dimensional, selectively detailed maps proffered by the current social sciences. As an extraordinarily observant and intuitive amateur, he acknowledged through his narratives what he apprehended of heredity and environment operating as related factors, whether among Sartorises or Snopeses, Compsons or McCaslins; however, he made such matter supportive to a central concern with individuals, such as Mink Snopes, Quentin Compson, Isaac McCaslin, and a large company of more or less typically situated but uniquely reactive persons. Faulkner feels too nearly and concernedly for his major characters to consider any of them wholly explicable, and yet he ventures to represent them in their conscious active lives as discernibly motivated, and suggests in each some bent toward congruence, so that through successive actions there aggregates the suggestion of a personal trend in which character becomes the more defined to others as also more deeply committed to its intentional self. And this realism is grounded upon observed human lives, as circumstanced and in their traits, tendencies, and relative progressions.

In Faulkner's vision there is no felt dichotomy between plot and character, since character as he treats it is cognizant being and becoming. His people are what they do and feel in an ongoing existence, and thus they constitute the action in the extended interweaving of its substantive and subjective threads. If any preeminence is given, it is to character; in Faulkner's dramaturgy the effect sought in free movement forward and back through the plot's chronology is not just a quickening of momentum and curiosity, it is so that earlier events withheld can take on fuller dimensions through what they are seen to have meant and now mean to a previously and presently involved character. Faulkner's rangings through a narrative's chronology are most often cast within someone's recollections and forward returns; these major figures have their existence in the midst of things, looking before and after; this communicated distilling of the matter's essence reveals the individual most clearly; it also creates a true dramatic intensity, since a narrative action takes on potency only in ratio to its evocation of empathic regard for a represented human opportunity and hazard. Yet while character is fundamental to Faulkner's fictional realism, lives must be given their localized and conditioning habitat, for he knows that realistic fiction or drama has its responsibility to a milieu. The serious artist will not only come upon and recognize all this but can then approach it most creatively under temperamental impetus, in the light of his achieved outlook and convictions.

It is one measure of a considerable literary artist that he has looked upon the human condition thoughtfully as well as feelingly and has developed relevant attitudes of certain import. The undergraduate Joyce, delivering his lecture on Mangan to the literary society of University College, Dublin, in 1902, had asserted this principle, with balanced regard for substance and art:

> Finally, it must be asked concerning every artist how he is in relation to the highest knowledge and to those laws which do not take holiday because men and times forget them. This is not to look for a message but to approach the temper which has made the work . . . and to see what is there well done and how much it signifies.

Joyce delegated the extension of such views to Stephen in his several embodiments; James and Conrad more specifically described artistic outlook and implemental processes in prefaces to their works, and Conrad's to *The Nigger of the 'Narcissus'* is a profound, acute, and moving *credo* and *apologia* resting on more than a sailor's world view. Faulkner's formal statement of a writer's faith was made at Stockholm in 1950 in acknowledging the award of the Nobel Prize. His relatively simple and brief address was in no way technical; he did not directly identify himself as either realist or regionalist, nor as Southerner or even a native of the States. He alluded to the present in terms of world-wide fear of the bomb, but only to dismiss being afraid as "the basest of all things," adding that "I decline to accept the end of man," and asserting that "man will not merely endure: he will prevail." In a paradoxical terminology implying the objective-subjective nexus which his fictions rest upon, he defined the writer's proper subject matter as "the materials of the human spirit." Hence the writer's "duty" and "privilege" is "to help man endure by . . . reminding him of the courage and honor and hope and pride and compassion and pity and sacrifice which have been the glory of his past." With fear set aside, the writer is to find "no room in his workshop for anything but the old verities and truths of the heart, the old universal truths."

Faulkner's generalizations may bring to mind a statement in Conrad's Familiar Preface to *A Personal Record:* "Those who read me know my conviction that the world, the temporal world, rests on a few very simple ideas; so simple that they must be as old as the hills. It rests notably, among others, on the idea of Fidelity." Certainly those "old universal truths," which at Stockholm Faulkner indicated simply by large abstractions, would seem to relate to that "highest knowledge" the young Joyce had stipulated as a criterion for judging any artist. Faulkner's urging upon fellow artists their duty to remind readers of such virtues as honor, courage, and compassion may have struck strangely upon those who knew of his fiction only by hearsay as being rife with sensational representation of vices and monstrous evil. And some of Faulkner's casual and still disgruntled readers, hearing his profession from that eminence, may have wondered uneasily whether they'd missed something, or might more readily have suspected him of adding a perfunctory pretentiousness to his earlier offenses. However, Joyce as the still putative but prescient artist speaking in advocacy of Mangan and soon to endow characters of his choosing with illustrative act and utterance and reverie, had also mentioned absolutes which remain veritable even when "men and times forget them." And when Faulkner spoke of *man's* virtues "which have been the glory of his past," he was not elegizing the lost perfection of a golden age, he was pointing more closely to what persists and endures in those who do not "forget" what he called "truths of the heart." That these truths have had proof in the past is instructively a factor in certain men's maturation and commitment, and the likes of such men, as of recent times and contemporaneously, assert themselves in Faulkner's narratives, frequently with good effect. Indeed, Faulkner's fiction turns quite realistically as well as centrally upon representations that "universal truths" do not become inoperative just because they are not universally recognized and observed.

At Stockholm in 1950, after passing reference to fear of the bomb as a debilitating influence upon men and art, Faulkner spoke of man generically and in historical perspective, positing the persistence of certain ideals having to do with conduct. In Faulkner's stories a moving force operates through some major characters in their disinterested and magnanimous advocacy of these values, overtly in a socioethical context but also at deep subjective levels of their private realizations. Recognized in this aspect, Faulkner's realism can be termed humanistic. This would be of course at the purely secular level, and improvisatory rather than systematic, with unillusioned acknowledgment that evil is endemic, and not always and never easily put down, nor can the mass of men be as readily aroused to resist it as to abet or at least suffer it, while even the well-intentioned may succumb to irresolution and momentary despair. It was in this light that the Nobel laureate mentioned "the problems of the human heart in conflict with itself" as the only subject "worth writing about." While Faulkner's fictional proponents of humanistic values resolutely combat unprincipled men, they cannot always prevail, nor can they stave off further offenses by such as Flem Snopes and lesser villains; therefore a weighty element in many of the stories is at a subjective level, in the protagonists' frustration, somber doubt, and sometimes outrage under the stress of a resisted temptation to give up. Through their uncertainties, disenchantment, and exacerbations in the struggle against socioethical offenses and incorrigible disorderliness there comes to be heard as a recurrent undertone the artist's own melancholy apprehensions. By some this has been felt as morbidity, but these readers may not have fully assessed Faulkner's realism, with its humanistic imperatives. Those who had read him attentively and receptively could not have been surprised by his resolute assertions at Stockholm, for they had seen these attitudes embodied in the immense ideograms of his most dynamic novels. Their promulgations had not been didactic, nor did they spring from an unrealistic sentimental optimism; they were idealistic, however, in representing that whenever certain men have stepped forward as the courageous and unequivocal proponents of "verities and truths of the heart," they have at least proved man's humane potential, and often have achieved ameliorations in a human situation. His recognition in his fiction that the well-intentioned are often deflected and even defeated and the innocent may be basely betrayed, while moral victories are transient in the flux of ever-changing circumstances only proves the honest percipience of Faulner's realism and makes more exemplary the persistence of his agents of justice and mercy.

HUMANISTIC REALIST

It remains an oddity and a wry intimation of the fate of genius in a multicultural society that during the thirties, when "social consciousness" took a certain admissible priority in the matter of American fiction, the profound socioethical import of Faulkner's works was not duly weighed. Nor has that lack been fully offset in later judgments, perhaps in part because social concern itself has been diverted by the vaguely mechanistic amateur sociology which fosters supposedly remedial legislation, token of the nation's transfer of conscience. Faulkner, however, was not schematical; his focus on human problems was at the living center, the trends of individual conduct, the degrees of personal awareness, and the intuition of verities through the heart's conflict with itself in the entanglements of circumstance. His societally relevant realism, being humanistic, was in fact the most radical of its times. Though his themes are abstract, they are not insisted upon but are to be sensed as vast shadows cast on the distanced permanent backdrop of the veritable by the actors' dynamic gestures in the momentum of their intent existence. Herein his fictions are indeed of a certain magnitude. Though most, and the most characteristic, are set in one Mississippi county, even there the characters are various and the measured narrative grasp upon them is firm, while the time range is unusually wide, not by means of chronicled historical minutiae or cradle-to-grave accounts, but by evocation of the crises and resolutions that shape individual assertions within society's drifts and arrests.

It is with primary reference to character that humanistic-realistic aspects merge in Faulkner's art, through works rising to an enhanced organicism and authenticity beyond the inconsistencies of average behavior and the transient improvi-

sations of expedient men in societal contexts. Readers of a
novel may extrapolate from it a defined abstraction of man's
fate, but literature in its essences lies closer home than that.
Faulkner does not purport to deal comprehensively with the
human race but with certain men and women whose destinies
are private despite all involvements, and are played out within
temporal and circumstantial confinements, by each within
his or her separate and unstable yet evolving composite of
individuality and situation. Faulkner is objectively-subjectively aware of his characters not only as individual but
intrinsically solitary beyond any conforming or gregariousness
or even the remedies of love; his narratives comprehend such
isolation, yet treat of it not with that autographic mock-
pathetic solipsism often exhibited in modern novels, but as
under the genuine ordeal of onerous, frustrating, sometimes
disastrous human involvement. For Faulkner as oriented artist
the existential being always is of primary interest and importance; yet this humanistic realist constantly remembers that
society, while only instrumental and often clumsily and inadequately so, has at its heart "one of the old universal truths,"
the folk wisdom that senses *de facto* a social contract out of
which socioethical concepts have been evolved, for getting
done and saving what none could do or save alone. That a
necessitously summoned sense of community can be inspiriting
is shown in many ways, whether as in the opening section of
Requiem for a Nun or in the hunting of Old Ben; and the
strenuousness it can rise to shows in the effectively concerted
efforts of Gavin Stevens and Sheriff Hampton, assisted by Will
Legate, and implemented by that broadly representative
team, Chick Mallison and Miss Habersham and Alec Sander in
Intruder in the Dust.

Such a societal instinct rooted in man's nature is conversely
implied by Faulkner's fictions not only as to its constructive
advances but in its aberrations, ranging from systematized
material exploitation and gang-up civic corruption to lynch
mobs and war. For good or evil, alone or in concert, men
become movers and shapers; it is through vitally realized com-

plex individuals that Faulkner shows the resultant intricacies and confusions of society, and the daily difficulties of its infrequent and inadequate accomplishments. Since it seems a reality, however sad, that humans encounter each other more tellingly and passionately in their differences than in any stable consensus, the fictionist or dramatist can best represent characteristic actions and suggest the involved values through conflicts. Melodrama does this continuously but under a simplistic antithesis of right or wrong, good or bad. In Faulkner's fiction, actions however strenuous and extreme are made not only realistic but significant because they spring from individuated characters, figured in their processes or realization and nuances of emotional response, all of it part of that reactive motion, in adaptation or resistance, which is a necessitous trend in imperfect societies and an innate factor in the operative conscious life of less than satisfied and far from perfect human beings. The shadings in men's conflicts between good and evil, the fluctuations of individual awareness and assertion, and the closely communicated subjective stresses in certain beset protagonists all give Faulkner's accounts of human conflict a far greater tension and deeper human meaning than can be found in the simplified commotion of any melodrama, or are derivable from the attenuated abstractions of "socially conscious" fiction.

There is no inconsistency in Faulkner's speaking *in propria persona* of "old universal truths" and identifying them in such "verities" as courage, hope, compassion, and sacrifice, but then in his writing fictionally of their opposites as they enter into the ordeals and disasters of many men and women. Like Swift, Faulkner saw man not as innately virtuous, but as capable of virtues; beyond Swift, Faulkner realistically conceives of mankind in a vast gradation from virtue to vice, playing out under changing circumstance their separate private motives and the resultant mutations in themselves, as in any mortal existence. At Stockholm Faulkner had acknowledged some men's tendency to surrender under odds which other men tended to impose, and had mentioned the contemporary prevalence of fear and despair, yet he had claimed for mankind the durability of those positive traits on which his novels' dramas turn in a humanistic realism. What validates his fiction in this aspect is a relativism, in recognition of endemic evil often having its insidious or brutal way, or only barely overcome and incorrigibly recurrent, imperfectly resisted with fluctuant resolution by a few among the many apathetic or intimidated, yet with reasserted grasp upon proved human verities. In these complications and movements of persons and circumstance a constant factor is mutability; human values ascertained by experience, approximated by society, and uniquely absorbed into the lives of individuals must be reassessed situationally and their further use amended as new requirements arise and new opportunities are discovered. Concerning this reality, Carlyle passed byond his flaming metaphor of a Phoenix rebirth to a closer figure, the constant weaving-in of "organic filaments" for the repair and strengthening of society as an old but still useable garment. A similarly modified analogy would hold for the individual life, where total rebirth by conversion, despite its vulgar advocacy and boasted successes, is perhaps as fabulous as the Phoenix, whereas a gradual modification of temperament and character is the human norm. This process, in various degrees and stages of consciousness, is everyman's drama, the unique story implicit in any life, and Faulkner's fiction is strongly invigorated and in part shaped by his unusual sensitivity to this common human denominator—the one thing inclusively and at all times describable as man's fate, and also uniquely each man's sense of a living selfhood. With the dynamism of his narrative actions deriving from the represented individuals' consciousness of being and becoming, it is this central reality as his mode which secondarily requires attention to interpersonal and societal influences upon his protagonists as persons. Yet this does not minimize social awareness in Faulkner's novels, but comparatively strengthens it. Milieu takes on deeper perspectives through the characters' involvements with it, and they in their specifically dimensioned existences within a less scrutable general order bring into clearer light human "verities," under which aspect societal matters acquire relative degrees of significance.

A vitalizing factor in the flow of Faulkner's subjectively realistic narratives enters through recurrence in some characters of recollected awareness, whether out of earlier acts or observations or information, and now returned to in a not merely extended but experientially modified perception and evaluation of them. This strategic use of repetition is acutely illustrative of Faulkner's constant basic concern with existential motion and change; in the worlds of his creation not only is it impossible for a man to step into the same river twice but at that next step it will not be the same man, even if only in a modified mood. The complex changes which living has wrought in him make each subjective return into his own past experience a new thing with a more than ordinary claim upon his attention. And on the reader's, for some of Faulkner's most penetrating effects are to be found in such repetitions, where substance previously communicated, especially as a character's subjective experience, is transposed by further instance into another mode and reorchestrated with a fuller significance. Under the aspects of mutability and relativism a character's conditioned recall and fuller awareness of an earlier experience is a particularly effective way of intensifying the fictional illusion of certain beings in the stresses of ongoing struggle, with its interwoven elements not of victory or defeat but of a prevalence or a thwarting as transient experience. Faulkner as humanistic realist maintains his positive characters in motion that thrusts beyond any finalities short of the work's closure. Situations make way for others, which they have had a part in shaping and animating, and other circumstance will alter memory's living awareness of what has gone before. Into such a fluidity the reader may enter with lively empathy. When read with response to this mode of a ranging subjectivity, Faulkner becomes a most absorbing storyteller, paradoxically the more so by his repetitions, in which matter is modified within the character's further realizations under changed circumstances, and this is to be valued not only in itself for its honestly realistic relativism, but in the artist's tactical use of it in the total narrative structure. Such a basic progressional-consequential setting-forth is of course the plain main way of all fiction; Faulkner's unique, dynamically objective-subjective use of it show genius at its height.

It might appear that Faulkner, though so scrupulously detached in his dedication to the artistic autonomy of each of his fictional works, did adroitly risk introducing into his last novel a figuration of his aesthetics, through the fully awakened consciousness of a rapidly maturing boy, as told of by that character in his old age. *The Reivers* may seem to some a mere *jeu d'esprit,* but it is intriguingly subtitled *A Reminiscence,* and beginning with the words *"Grandfather said:"* it takes on narrative scope and depth in that Lucius Priest's experiences when he was eleven—a brief but gaudy, unguarded, random, and exacting first encounter with the world at large—are an ordeal in maturation. While remembered truly and so reported by the old man, these events are allowed a wider stage and more picturesque production given all the relish of a ripened mind. Thus the grandfather coverts a series of boyhood escapades into a prismatically dimensioned story of a story. It becomes an examplar of fiction's transmuting art, almost a celebration of how experience may be recalled in augmented form through earned wisdom, a process the boy himself had begun to understand toward the close of that one wild week. What had repeatedly impinged on young Lucius was a growing awareness of good and evil in their forebodingly unequal ratio; Grandfather Priest now ironically verbalizes what as a boy he had acutely sensed. In this essentially picaresque novel, as moving through worlds undreamed of by its young protagonist, with ventures reconstituted from first to last by that boy now a reminiscent old man, the novelist lifts matters of fact to the level of insights, in the objective-subjective nucleus that is pivotal to a humanistic realism. *The Reviers* is a robust tale and more. In its transcendence it corresponds to unwritten stories a man may tell himself long after the fact; by its complex subjectivity, with the boy's actual experience running as a constant stream in the old man's literally translating yet interpretatively modulating memory, this in its entirety, engagingly lucid, is yet a subtly affecting imaginative treatment.

When it comes to central issues, Grandfather Priest's fanciful-ironic tone somehow conveys the fluid sense of boyhood's drifting intimations. To begin with, "Virtue does not — possibly cannot — take care of its own as Non-virtue does," the latter having "matchless capacity for invention and imagination," as when the boy realized that being smarter than the man Boon, he could be leader, boss, master in their adventure with the surreptitiously borrowed family automobile, and accordingly Lucius had taken over. Then too Non-virtue was found to have the advantage of operating by chance while Virtue dallies, and Non-virtue is aided when people "refuse quick and hard to think about next Monday," as the "spellbound" but also dimly appalled boy felt he had done by telling "more lies than I had believed myself capable of inventing," and found them accepted, and himself saddled with them. (The whole passage is a trenchant grotesque of human capacity for leading the self into temptation.) As the boy's adventure continued and misdemeanors multiplied, it became apparent to him that (as the reminiscent old man puts it) "who serves Virtue works alone, unaided . . . where, pledge yourself to Non-virtue and the whole countryside boils with volunteers to help you," and moreover, even in what Non-virtue knows nothing about, it succeeds. Yet when the challenge came in more explicit human terms and the boy championed the beset Miss Corrie, he sensed that "maybe there are after all other things besides Poverty and Non-virtue that look after their own."

In the eleven-year-old's six-day introduction to the ways of vagabondage and the mores of whorehouse-racetrack circles, he encountered no archvillain comparable to Flem, and no such begetter of dooms as Sutpen; the worst is a juvenile delinquent who seems to exemplify the "bad seed" theory.

More widely there are samples of wrongdoing in the common-place, endemic fashion, together with instances of human goodness quietly assertive even against odds, as by the wily Negro Ned, inscrutibly devious in a good cause, and bringing it off notably. In the midst of all this as the boy is hurried toward maturation, what his wakened sense of good and evil turned upon is a rudimentary but genuinely emergent sense for conduct, on which he begins to act. Not until he is brought back home does he arrive at certain consolations, and only through the assistance of his grandfather, who intervenes when the boy's father is about to punish him by a strapping. This grandfather, "Grandfather's" own, had talked it out with young Lucius, to make him realize that only he himself can "do something about it," as a "gentleman"—a word which (as variously used in the narrative and as the boy already understands) indicates not social status but a sense of honor in all contexts. Under this rubric, a gentleman does not seek to forget his mistake, he lives with it; "A gentleman can live through anything. He faces anything . . . accepts the responsibility of his actions and bears the burden of their consequences." Lucius acknowledges that Boon would have returned earlier "if I had said so," and remembering that, he knows "what grandfather meant: that your outside is just what you live in, sleep in, and has little connection with who you are and even less with what you do." It is a child's definition but an adequate one of the actuated realization of selfhood, the consciousness of one's subjective existence as a central reality of being, behaving, and becoming, and thus the arena of responsibility to others as well as to self. Given that knowledge, young Lucius understands what his grandfather had said when the boy wanted "something" done about his having lied, and the grandfather answered "I cant . . . you can," but the boy wants to know how to "forget it," and is told "You cant. Nothing is ever forgotten. Nothing is ever lost. It's too valuable," and in that aspect it is to be lived with, for admonition and support.

While *The Reivers* is genuinely a picaresque novel, its

action headlong through multiple scenes with a stream of *outré* characters, incisively materialized at the top of Faulkner's bent, what makes it most representative of his realism is its predominantly subjective conveyance through an old man's first-person reminiscence, an experience not just reexperienced but assessed. Like *Huckleberry Finn,* like *The Shadow Line* it shows more strongly than many novels in the *Bildungsroman* mode that what best serves the sought effect is the protagonist's consciousness, narratively recollective in fiction's way, but transcendently selective for the essence of past experience. In *The Reiver* this in enhanced by the old man's fondly ironic reconstruction, a judicious distancing and a humorous distilling of verities out of his boyhood adventure. Here, as with many of Faulkner's most typical and significant protagonists, consciousness does not flinch from remembering; instead a human responsiveness, within the full extent of personal knowledge and for its situationally applicable points of reference, is a sort of life function. As Conrad has Captain Giles declare, "a man should stand up to his bad luck, to his mistakes, to his conscience," and learn "how not to be fainthearted"; indeed, "A man has got to learn everything." Certainly this weathered realist is not prescribing omniscience, nor infallibility, as is shown by his reference to a man's mistakes; moreover, his mentioning "bad luck" recognizes possible intrusion of the incalculable and uncontrollable, as did the "Delta Autumn" hunters, widely debating ethics. Such relativism is not compromise nor is it incompatible with a humanistic realism, which poses principled exertions by the not always totally competent in the face of the never entirely remediable. Actually a proper relativism, such as in Conrad or Faulkner, stands on the side of realism in both art and life, in its avoidance of a deceptive optimism or an equally flabby nihilism. And it is precisely through its unequivocal commitment to verities that a humanistic realism must allow for relativism. In the disputed area of "situational" ethics the real issue turns on a sufficiently comprehensive and responsible estimate of what constitutes "situation." One respondent individual may perceive it only on the scale of his present impulse and immediate personal convenience; conversely, another may feel it calls for strongest possible assertion in accord with the highest attainable human values, supportive of honorable self-realization within just and rewarding interpersonal relations, extending beyond individuals to the whole social order. An always assumed priority for immediate promptings and private convenience may be of the present inclination to escape from mankind's history and, as must follow, from one's own. In the arts certain cliques have drifted in this direction, with a characteristic blend of indulgence and opportunism. An ephemeral but telling instance was the vogue of a fragmentary pseudodrama in the "happening." This has had its like in other arts, especially painting and music, by proffers of noncommunication unconditionally turned over to hearer or viewer, and sensational at least in their capacity to astound by a pretentiousness not always detected — though it does allow a real response in kind. Less sensational but similarly incidental as literature is the fragmented line-up of "happenings" in the dreary natualism of that semicommercialized modern fiction devoted to esoteric types distinguished only as spin-offs from a whole society's discontent, often in an urban accentuation of isolated yet far from self-directed individual existence.

The estimating of any modern American fictionist's work needs to take account of calculated approaches to outright sensationalism. In fiction (as in drama) this may be defined as excitingly striking, morbidly tinged incident without provision of conceptual and subjective depth. Lacking close representation of characters as conscious beings in their uniquely personal responses to experience, and evading relativism in a simplistic implication or denial of values, sensationalism can evoke little more empathic response than that depending upon the clichés which must suffice for bemused unexamined lives, or upon paradoxical formulations of the absurd. Considered under this aspect, Faulkner the humanistic realist is never sensational. He does not embroider events for their separately arresting effects, and while aspects of his stories are startling and in some degree shocking, yet the more intense this is, the more pervading is the created sense, in a many-toned, subjectively-attuned composition, that the issue is one of basic values. Concurrently there is always Faulkner's strategic narrative momentum, which does not dwell unduly upon event in itself, much less exploit it, but draws action into the modulations of consequence as realized and ethically evaluated by at least some of its enactors. His practice seems a careful avoidance of preoccupation with mere incidents, lest they overshadow the realities of a continuum in which "situation," through human concern, can wear the larger temporal and logical dimensions of cause and effect, and thus impinge upon the actors in the aspect of hazards and values. Through their subtle and passionate enactment Faulkner's stories progressively show that a situation is an emergence, and it too like what led to it will pass, contributing and yielding to another, all this in the ongoing extensions of human experiences, as a complex of societal and uniquely personal realizations, the weight and pathos of which a reader can intuitively enter into, with expanded knowledge of his own. Not just plotted event, however serviceable, but conception and embodiment of such a deepening fluidity of experience, conveyed primarily through a directly represented awareness in his characters, is at the heart of Faulkner's humanistic realism, and is what his dramaturgically apt composition is designed to undergird.

It is only as seen in the unified functioning of such complementary factors that Faulkner's realism can be adequately estimated. Within the conceptualized and imaginatively rendered unity of a Faulkner novel the abstracting of verities increasingly apprehended by the working consciousness of protagonists is in an intuitive and responsive relationship with reality. Here the subjective and the societal are interactive and indeed symbiotic. Recognition of humane principles at issue is a human function, and it is out of men's most fully realized experiences in extensive contexts that viable procedures are validated, in everything from the law to a community's mores. The process, as Faulkner's fictions show, is arduous, and its achievements are maintained only precariously, since men are not always sufficiently alert and sometimes waver, and circumstance as often as not is contradictive. Thus relativism, in itself a reality, becomes dynamic in narrative "actions," since it sharpens delineation of any human life in the endured fluxions that are its cumulative lot, and in particular makes fully veritable a conveyance of the matter through the turbulent counterpoint of a protagonist's objective-subjective experience. Herein Faulkner's searching realism is unflinching in its admission that grave threats to humanistic values persist, since mankind, diversely inclined and fated to mutability, hardly arrives at stable consensus, while "the human heart," citadel of the verities, is also "in conflict with itself," out of the world's lack and its own, while evil, though driven into corners, is still hydra-headed and inscrutable.

Even so, ideals remain functional, and the notion of a best of all possible worlds becomes a sentimentality only if it considers possibility in more than relativistic terms and sinks into dreams of absolute perfection, whether in a golden past or a misty future. Significantly such dreams, in striving toward a plateau of fixed societal perfection, tend to minimize the human individual and the unique aspects of his behavior as conduct whether for good or ill, and depend instead on a to-be-established conformity, with its institutionalized guarantees. Conversely, for Faulkner as humanistic realist, men individually are the undependable but essential and not impossible agents of melioration and can most fully realize themselves within such orientations. This is of course not unique in Faulkner, but he stands supreme in modern American fiction through the primacy and potency he gives this fundamental view.

As for social consiousness in fiction, though major tensions in Faulkner's stories are represented as individually experienced and often at deep levels of subjectivity, the embodying action is always in a fully depicted and variously populated societal context, as it reflexively implies that community depends upon approximated mores resting on individual fidelities. Faulkner as fictionist concerns himself with stresses, frustrations, and miscarriages even under the law and more often under the looser rule of custom, yet he postulates that while implemental conventions and institutions as well as personal attitudes ask for reassessment situationally, certain value-concepts though pragmatically arrived at have proved abidingly applicable and hence imperative whatever the pains. Faulkner discovers this again and again as an active kind of folk knowledge among common people tempered in the brunt of their beset lives, and he finds it equally operative among men and women whose good fortune imposes a strict sense of obligation. For these as for uncounted generations of men truth has been found the necessary mode of reliable inter-relationship, both personal and societal, and consequently honor holds men to apprehended verities so that a supportive ethos may be kept going.

However, while Faulkner's favored protagonists do not equivocate about recognized principles, they are not rigidly ideological but tentative in their endeavors as advocates, being fairly aware of their own possible bias and natural human fallibility, and with painful worldly knowledge of many men's apathy and others' incorrigible opportunism. To compensate his heroes for their not infrequent setbacks he arms most of them with an irony that staves off despair and saves them for the challenges of another day, while most of those who are incurably hurt in spirit are allowed their grief and also the dignifying cloak of resignation. Faulkner's humanistic realism, embracing many sorts of beings and behavior, can bear the confinements and denials of relativism because this may be made to contain with searching fictional veracity the dynamic actions that move not only through time and change but in characters' sustained enlarging responsiveness. This transcends chronology and gathers disparate incidents and separate realizations into a new function in representing an always deepening experience; this animates realistic narration, with a profound evocation of empathy, through the dynamism of the human condition, conceived of and given enaction as predicament and inspirited venture.

In Faulkner's body of work the pervasiveness of an outlook, given artistic variety in a succession of unique fictional originations, derives from engagement with predominantly regional material. This is viewed in the light of a native and lifelong involvement, with its actualities distilled into concepts and patterns by the artist's clarifying discernments and the heat of his genius. It may appear that in this propinquity Faulkner had greatness thrust upon him; clearly it was with a gifted writer's innate imaginativeness and a cultivated virtue rising above opportunism that he embraced this destiny. The declared "Sole Owner & Proprietor" of that variously peopled and fabled "Yoknapatawpha Co., Mississippi" is one of the greatest of regionalists and irresistibly solicits consideration as such, yet as a rigorous realist. Moreover, in the light of his relativistic humanism and his corresponding attention to his characters' subjectivity as the way of close approach to theme and a medium of the matter's full imaginative realization his regionalism may be termed romantic in the most central and persistent sense of the term.

Faulkner's Yoknapatawpha map (inserted in *Absalom, Absalom!*, 1936) seems a symbolic declaration of artistic autonomy and of fidelity as a witness, as well as that total possession the novelist aspires to, in terms of his substance, concepts, and the temperamental bent of his art. He was indeed sole owner of that metamorphosed county, yet how could he bequeath it except with an artist's largesse, as an area left in trust, open to all who care to sojourn there. How acutely he sensed the realm of his endeavors as a transcendent reality was suggested in an interview given his friend Jean Stein and published in the *Paris Review*. Without formalizing it, Faulkner implied a description of the literary imagination when he said,

"Beginning with *Sartoris* I discovered that my own little postage stamp of native soil was worth writing about and that I would never live long enough to exhaust it, and by sublimating the actual into apocryphal I would have complete liberty to use whatever talent I might have to its absolute top." Faulkner's term apocryphal asks to be understood in its context with "sublimating." In such fictional creation the apocryphal is not spurious, though it is only a simulation of actualities in the fabled lives of hypothetical individuals; reality in a fictional work inheres fundamentally in its conception, a sublimation out of humanly typical instances into a sufficient refinement and concentration to achieve a degree of representativeness. Faulkner's word is pointed enough in a matter where definition may stumble between two worlds, the palpably physical as in a crystalline sublimate, or the imaginative verity of a great novel's achieved organicism. Faulkner's mention of "complete liberty" is not a capricious presumption but relates to his confidence that his regional and indeed localized material was both "worth writing about" and inexhaustible in a lifetime. The "postage stamp" was room enough for conceptualizing with broad humanistic implications what he knew so closely and with such acute intuitions. To one of his temperament that abundance of regional material in all its human "worth" called for sublimation, and elbowroom for what was the liberty he seized upon. It would be erroneous to characterize Faulkner as self-indulgent in any aspect of his art. He claimed no license in its name; his profession was an allegiance to something given, that vastly inclusive *donnée* which compelled him to render imaginatively interpretive accounts. What remains to be more fully recognized by some readers of Faulkner is that at the top of his bent his selectivity, coherent composition, and celerity are major factors in a high artistic achievement. Even when his style is copious it is to a point and of a calculated weight; and his narrative structures however complex are not loosely rambling but of proportionate and effective design, entirely to serve his brooding reflectiveness even in proximity to a throng of characters in a flood of events.

Faulkner not only illustrated as transcendental reality that one can go venturing in one's own back yard, he showed that what a fictionist has seen most of he may be able to see into most deeply, evolving from close acquaintance the insights that call up imaginative embodiments. Given, of course, an inventiveness compatible with resolute scrutiny of realities, a genial curiosity and empathic intuitions about his fellow beings, and some concepts by which to assess behavior as conduct, in that pointing-up of issue needful for drama. All this Faulkner grew into. Native to a many-faceted locale, offspring of a lineage that bound him to a significant past, inheritor of a veritable library of lore, he was held to all that as boy and man, and he held to it as an artist, with necessary detachment but if anything with increased concern in a focused quest.

Writing evocatively of "Mississippi" in the April 1954 issue of *Holiday* magazine, Faulkner autobiographically alluded to "the boy himself" as "knowing about Vicksburg and Corinth and exactly where his grandfather's regiment had been at First Manassas before he remembered hearing very much about Santa Claus." (Much about that grandfather went into *Sartoris* and *The Unvanquished.*) In *Intruder in the Dust* Faulkner represents a twentieth-century, sixteen-year-old Chick Mallison as remembering he had found true what his Uncle Gavin Stevens had said earlier, that for "every Southern boy fourteen years old . . . there is the instant when it's still not yet two o'clock on that July afternoon in 1863 [at Gettysburg] . . . and it's all in the balance . . . and that moment doesn't need even a fourteen-year-old boy to think *This time. Maybe this time* with all this much to lose and all this much to gain." It is significant in the strategy of this novel that young Mallison has just seen a mindless lynch mob scattered after he and others, with much hazard and in the nick of time, have proved the innocence of old Lucas Beauchamp, a Negro accused of shooting a white man in the back. Thus thematic consideration widens to represent a society still pervaded by ambivalences in the wake of a military defeat which many a Southerner beyond the age of fourteen cannot forget nor look back on dispassionately, under the continuing strains of a stratified society, regionally isolated yet increasingly sharing the pressures of unresloved and enigmatic racial tensions with the twentieth century North—which Chick at another point has pictured as condescending, from a scarcely tenable assumption of superiority. In *The Reivers,* Grandfather Priest touches on that more detachedly, not with an unreconstructed rebel's bitter nostalgia, but seeing it presciently in its latter-day national context, and alluding to "that Cause which, the longer I live the more convinced I am, your spinster aunts to the contrary, that whoever lost it, it wasn't us." Slavery, war, emancipation and reconstruction, and still in the twentieth century the grievous racial issue, rooted in ancient wrongs and exacerbated into modern dilemmas of socioeconomic adjustment which have spilled over into the whole nation—this many-faceted perplexity, changeable but enduring, is thematically recurrent (with reference to its roots and with deep understanding of its human elements) in Faulkner's regionally based stories. Three of them treat, as in different periods, of maturing young men's ethical grapplings with these difficulties. In *The Unvanquished* Bayard Sartoris is at first too young to ride to war with his impetuous father, but he and his Negro companion Ringo trace its course on a rough map scratched into the ground, and they themselves react with precocious violence after the murder of Granny Millard, yet after the war's end Bayard, grown and with more perspective, refuses to be drawn into a typical act of vengeance under what he considers an outworn code; unarmed he confronts his father's provoked murderer, facing him down. *Intruder in the Dust* tells more extendedly and with more psychological penetration of adolescent Chick Mallison's maturation, first resenting old Lucas Beauchamp for presuming equality and refusing to "act like a nigger," but finally becoming his champion against the lynch mob, though he had been tempted to ride out of town until it was all over. In *Go Down, Moses* there is instanced a most profound crisis of conscience in Isaac's postbellum discovery of what had been an inhuman use of female slaves, mother and daughter, by his grandfather, the family's founder in Mississippi. This, in the youth's idealistic mind, so taints the McCaslin inheritance that he refuses to accept it; yet even that abstention does not exempt him in old age from family shame and compassionate grief over further effects of racial aloofness. The chasm between white and black is shown in twentieth-century terms in *Light in August* through Joe Christmas, orphaned early and unsure whether he has Negro blood or is merely darkskinned; being so stigmatized, he is unable to create an identity for himself in stable societal context. The most extensive and impressive deployment of the racial theme in detail and through an elaborate regional narrative is in *Absalom, Absalom!*, reaching as it does from antebellum ruthlessness, deceptions, and abuses into the twentieth century, with melancholy Quentin Compson's augmented disenchantment and ambivalence toward the South because of what he learned of even worse familial disasters than in his own through the Sutpen saga, in desolation and deaths triggered by stresses over miscegenation, out of Supen's obsessive drive for power and prestige as slave-holding plantation owner.

The broad dimensions of Faulkner's genius are to be estimated both from the magnitude and substantiality of his conceivings of regional subjects and from his commensurate imaginative penetration into a continuum of events given their coloration through characters involved by their awareness as well as in their actions. Thus his regionalism, humanistically realistic, goes deeper than the data of naturalism; thus his representations of subjectivity, going beyond that of an isolate introverted life, show involvement in matters of wide relevance and personal interrelation, and more than single import. Not that the narrative may not include characters' states of mind concealed from all but the reader, but those transpire in a context of circumstances; these are contributively particularized by the subjective responses to them, an interaction that epitomizes Faulkner's basic idiosyncratic fictional mode. In this fusion of scope and subjectivity his fictional art achieves an equilibrium and a steadily operative reciprocation, with a suggested symmetry, a uniquely potent aesthetic effect. It is indefinable, and its factors are scarcely to be analyzed, but it is there, the characteristic Faulknerian tone, an extraordinary achievement in the craft of fiction, that distinctive resonance which in some novels and in portions of others may seem comparable to the sostenuto of a perfected lyric poem or an unintermitted musical composition. Like an remarkable aesthetic effect, this does not exist abstractly in itself but as of its substance, imaginatively grasped and controlled. There at first hand in Yoknapatawpha was an abundance of life, discernible in full consequential flow, and in it were to be seen posited values upon which typical issues of conduct are found to turn in men's attentive consciousness and situationally challenged consciences. What constitutes Faulkner's romanticism as an informed and concerned regionalist is such an insight closely brought to bear upon such a profusion of uniquely intriguing and humanly representative matters, weighed according to that penetrating and unequivocal realism by which human lives in process maintain their humanity.

Not that Faulkner's close, sustained focusing on human consciousness in process was currently unique, or even *en avant*. This mode, though not new and never dominant, showed a growing trend contemporary with Faulkner's emergence, and gained discriminating recognition in English and American fiction. Among several perceptible influences were the variously formulated advances in psychology, together with an increasingly analytical sociology under stresses of rapidly changing times; but perhaps the most radical force propelling much fiction toward focus upon individual consciousness was as of its own traditional and inherent right, by a return to human realities in extensions beyond the clichés of a shallow popular fiction grown even more superficial with the rise of large-circulation, mass-oriented magazines, themselves the entrepreneurs of increasingly materialistic and sentimental conventions. Though some fictional experimentation in representing subjectivity was tainted by vogue and became grotesquely tangential, much instead was a genuine deepening of literary art. The tendency was substantially realized in part by a flowering of the open-ended, epiphanal short story, under the Chekhovian aegis and following upon Joyce's *Dubliners*. This mode prevailed in the distinguished work of Katherine Mansfield, Virginia Woolf, and others in England, and was notably displayed in the United States by Katherine Anne Porter, Eudora Welty, Faulkner, Hemingway, Sherwood Anderson, and a number of others. In such writers' best works the penetration into subjective realities is neither sentimental nor esoteric; the artists were intent upon a more finely discerning realism, recognizing that drama is compact of its members' realizations arising within an experienced, societally situated action but related through associative consciousness to the unique individual venture of being and becoming. Hence the open-ended short story is often centered in the awareness of one character—though that does not necessarily preclude a certain objectivity in the structuring of the narrative and the fictionist's unobtrusive provision of substantiating and conditioning detail. At this level in fiction, however, subjectivity is a twofold factor. There is consciousness in the protagonist, to be intuitively discerned as it is implicatively traced in a narrative; but primarily there is temperament in the artist, which has conditioned his recognition of his subject in the guise his imagination is consequently inclined to give it. The integrity and worth of the creation will depend not upon a writer's preoccupation with his own feelings (though they are essential to the enterprise) but upon a vision earned by the attentiveness and empathy of his outward gaze upon his fellow beings, and the glimpsing of something representative in a portrayable segment of their mortal journey. This is a central reality in literature, through approach to the essences of human experience, and its worth is

to be judged not only by the enlivening stimulus of its necessary aesthetic demands upon the reader for a corresponding
discernment and response, but by the verity and profundity of
what is shadowed forth. Requirements upon the artist are
greater still, not only for care with whatever is the found truth
and for utmost ingenuity in disclosing it, but for a
scrupulousness stemming from the remembered fact that what
he deals with is other than himself and of larger reference,
though for himself it had naturally and honestly come to
mind. Here the makeup and conscience of the professedly serious fictionist are challenged and measured. With stream-of-
consciousness seized upon as a vogue, indulgence in pretentiousness may occur, offering nothing more than a sample of
self-preoccupation, its insignificance made apparent not just in
itself but because of the paucity of represented milieu and circumstance. A truly engaged writer, while centering his presentation in his characters' lives as conscious beings, cannot see
deeply into them except as they are situated and are relevantly
reactive. In this respect, though Faulkner was one of the most
diversely and extremely experimental fictionists, he was
soundly oriented, and his commitment of himself to his
subject was not only ardent but in the nature of an act of
piety. Thereby, even with his idiosyncrasies, as a romantic
regionalist he is notable in the main stream of subjectively
tinged and attuned fiction, in which his work increasingly
validated itself by generous extension of empathic concerns, as
well as by its more searching view of consciousness as process,
the better to identify and communicate the human predicament, in its tensions between individual will and circumstance, under the relativistic aspect of time, change, and
conditioned identity.

The Yoknapatawphan matter, which constitutes the heart of
Faulkner's *oeuvre* and represents to the full the range of his
art in its sweep across recovered generations and centuries,
shows one great eminence, a divide and yet a juncture, the
War Between the States. Yet Faulkner never produced one of
those literary hybrids, an "historical novel." (Obtuse critics

who fancied he had attempted that in *A Fable* missed the point entirely.) Wherever this country's civil conflict comes to the fore, military aspects are treated only incidentally, even in *The Unvanquished,* and not through spectacular or panoramic scenes but as to the characters' consequent personal crises and fates. The Civil War is important to his fiction as it extends beyond the battlefields, back down to the roots and proliferations of its causative socioeconomic tensions, and forward into its residue of stubborn enigmas that breed personal ambivalences in a reconstructed racial stratification. Although throughout the nation the nineteenth century and the first part of the twentieth saw immense changes, such as a continuing westward movement and a mushrooming industrial development—in perceptible ways the South, until the war, was less affected than other sections; no other region, however, has yet suffered anything as drastic and as lingering in its disconcerting effects as has the South from its defeat. Besides the trauma of that itself and of its myriad instancings, there were the basic disruptions and continuing anomalies after legal emancipation of the slaves on whom the plantation system depended; and all this was exacerbated by the near-anarchy of an official but lawless "reconstruction," which loosed human predators, whether immigrant or native, upon a collapsed society.

Out of this there continued even into the twentieth century something the North too was required to learn a great deal about (though so far scarcely enough)—the material and psychological problems of a biracial coexistence in which neither party is yet wholly freed, whether from want, fear, or chronic unrest. Among Faulkner's characters there are those who (like their creator) recognize the complexity of the racial problem, with some reflection upon its original elements and secondary forms, and acknowledge the unrest of a heart in conflict with itself even as it accepts the call to compensate for indifference and to oppose the heartless. As Faulkner pondered it and wrote of it, not only in fiction but notably in the 1955 letters to the *Memphis Commercial Appeal* and in the 1956 articles in

Life and *Harper's Magazine,* the Civil War in itself was acute crisis and speedy catastrophe, but the South's defeat and fate, with its violent reversal from one long-standing economic order and its ingrained mores into an opposite situation, extended beyond the disorder and exploitation and the desperate counter-violence of "reconstruction," continuing through mutations of stresses into his own times in another century, with still the minimizing and masking of real issues by inadequate remedial measures. The racial factor in the aspect of issue and enigma, with its chronological extent and protean manifestations, was enough to startle and even dismay an intuitive and humane twentieth-century Mississippian; its chains of consequences, decades long and yet borne under the shadow of impasse, and its rigorous personal involvement for all sorts of individuals, naturally could intrigue a virile artistic imagination, especially that of one to whom the matter was native and more than heritage, the kind of largesse a great artist's "dedicated spirit" dare not turn away from.

Under survey therefore Faulkner' regionalism seems of most weight and significance in its embracing the multifaceted subject of slavery and war and the related variables emergent in the postbellum South. Whether it is Lucius Carothers McCaslin's use of his female slaves or his grandson Isaac's crisis of sensibility and a disclaimer that seems almost an attempted propitiation for that earlier offense, whether it is youthful Chick Mallison's painfully learning to live and let live along with old Lucas and finally to risk his white skin in saving Lucas from a mob, whether it be what Joe Christmas knows as his world in total and such brutal rejection of him that he can never know himself, or whether at war's end the bequeathed undying darkness of mind that makes Henry Sutpen consider miscegenation more repugnant than fatalistic incest and turn fratricide to prevent it, these various instances are all credible, having had their counterparts in essence in a past and a present that Faulkner conceived of comprehensively. He brought the racial issue up to the verge of his own century less overtly but with full implications in Dilsey of *The Sound and the Fury,* legally emancipated servant to the disoriented

Compson family; by necessity and under her ingrained sense of others' need to be cared for she is more pitiably enslaved than many Negroes had been in antebellum times. Further on, into the era of the "motion pictures," Faulkner sets forth in the short story "Dry September" two profiles of evil-doing under the promptings of warped minds—that of McLendon, leader of a gang that without waiting for evidence or even any clear account, lynched the Negro night watchman whom the neurotic middle-aged Miss Minnie Cooper had accused of assaulting her. Several such summary, almost reflexively performed executions are represented in Faulkner's fiction, with clear indication of latent racial hysteria in certain whites which can erupt into mass psychosis and ritualized murder. Professor Joseph Blotner's recently issued biography sets forth at their various chronological points Faulkner's open, rational, and consistent assertions on the side of moderation and civil conciliation between the two races in the South, yet no man's personal word could enforce the terrible fatality of a lack of such a principle as strongly as does "Dry September" in its starkness, or could look more deeply than *Light in August* does into the vicious madness that may be loosed by a mere suspicion of mixed blood. As with all fictionists, so with this artist in his dealings with what remains the ongoing problem or race relations in the postbellum South, it is best to let him rest his case on his explicit autonomous works of art, especially those as powerfully consummate and humanistically realistic as Faulkner's.

Though racial interrelations constituted a major and in some ways central theme in Faulkner's regionally focused fiction, that was not his whole story. Tensions arising from racial antipathies and anxieties may have widest societal significance, and he seems to be probing most deeply when it comes to that, but there are other kinds of conflict on less extended grounds to which he gives as much intensity, and race itself can be treated fictionally only as of persons and individual attitudes, to which he properly holds. The socio-economic and psychological stratifications in the South as typified in Yoknapatawpha County are not only a matter of race but of antecedents and ongoing tendencies and consequent distinctions in the whole society, within the perspectives of regional history. Yet quite possibly an adequate appreciation of Faulkner's *oeuvre* was retarded, perhaps even impeded for a while by the emphasis some critics put upon considering it a kind of epic in many episodes and books, even a saga of the South. Misapprehensions stemming from this could be multiplied by the imposition of a total ordering or by selective rearrangement, as if to imply a sort of *tragi-comédie humaine*. The great plenty and reality of Faulkner's closely localized regionalism does not depend upon seriality in the separate works, except in the trilogy *Snopes,* and even here the episodic and tonal variety which had been established and brilliantly exploited in *The Hamlet* was extended further in *The Town* and *The Mansion.* More markedly throughout the *oeuvre* from novel to novel there are great differences in magnitude, narrative structure, and mode; and this may well be noted not only as evidence of a profuse imagination but also as a passion at that particular point for its own focus and concentration of effect. It seems especially the characteristic of his artistic temperament to be susceptible to absorbing commitments. With each work the artist appears to have given himself completely during the process of its creation, bent upon the most intense realization of its potentials. No doubt such absorption in the singular task and its opportunities was made easier by a continuing familiarity with regional materials, but the perfected autonomy in each novel as a work of art is closer to the essence of the Faulknerian achievement than the sense of locale or of recurring racial tensions, and a proof of the matter is that when an already known character enters into yet another narrative action he or she is absorbed into it, depending on no credentials from another country, and manifesting a fresh aspect in his new surroundings. This, however, is not by subordination of identity, but in fresh instancing of the subjective element as the pervading factor imaginatively uniting a humanistic reality and a romantic regionalism.

Faulkner's accomplishment, though for the most part so

closely centered in Yoknapatawpha County and especially in Jefferson as its seat, is of a breadth and significance which regionalism did not reach in other parts of the United States. Beyond the *sine qua non* of this artist's genius, there is a vital societal basis for this. Paradoxically the South, which through defeat in a civil war suffered the most convulsive upheaval and disruption as yet visited upon any region in these disparate and only adventitiously united states, had retained into Faulkner's time a sense of identity and a continuity, in a sort of mystique distilled from its history. Herein Faulkner's characters do not find an easy state of being, and for them their society at every level seems crisscrossed by tensions that erupt into conflicts or are answered to extravagantly, for the artist found no operative consensus in the South he wrote of, though he did show its strong sense of regional identity. Yet whatever their status and intelligence, it is in representing his characters' constant even if clouded awareness of private situation and of self in a society that Faulkner finds the medium for conveying his regionally based stories with a clearly pitched representativeness. To some readers it may even seem that when Faulkner did move beyond the regional in locale and its conditioning factors, his art lost some of its dynamism. Conversely, others may blame a morbid preoccupation with locale for what they identify in his fiction as bizarre, fantastic, or sensational — which would disclose a failure to recognize that Faulkner's regionalism is also a realism concerned with humanistic verities deeply rooted in men's experience. In the large, Faulkner's *donnée* as regionalist was the history-conscious, history-haunted South. Beyond that, however, his still wider approach as realist was representative of mankind, and even in his most particularized narratives the ultimate reference is to "the human heart," assertive of values even "in conflict with itself."

MATTER AND ART: VARIETY AND DEVELOPMENT

Thorough readers of Faulkner have given careful attention to *Sartoris,* his third novel, for its development of a regional theme in historical and familial terms and its firm situation in that mythical Mississippi county he was later to claim with a sojourner's and explorer's map affixed as endpaper in *Absalom, Absalom!* By that time he could include on it not only the spot "where old Bayard [Sartoris] died in young Bayard's car" but "Compson's, where they sold the pasture to the golf club so Quentin could go to Harvard," and "Bundren's" south of the Yoknapatawpha River, across which Addie's body was perilously borne for burial in Jefferson, and nearby the "Old Frenchman place . . . where Popeye killed Tommy" and the Jefferson "courthouse where Temple Drake testified," perjuring herself, and "Miss Joanna Burden's where Christmas killed Miss Burden and where Lena Grove's child was born," and of course "Sutpen's Hundred" and "Miss Rosa Coldfield's" house in Jefferson. These represent six more or less closely localized novels inclusively between *Sartoris* and *Absalom, Absalom!,* and the only other in that span was *Pylon,* concerning the desperate lives of stunt pilots, and this, Faulkner said, had been written "to get away from *Absalom, Absalom!*" for a while, which he did after flying his recently acquired Waco to an airport dedication at New Orleans. Now *Sartoris* is to be seen in a further light as only diligent Faulkner scholars have known it hitherto, as a retailoring, with the issuance of its recently exhumed Ur-form, the five-versioned, repeatedly rejected *Flags in the Dust.* Here is what *Sartoris* was cut down from, at publisher Alfred Harcourt's insistence, and by another hand—that of Ben Wasson, Faulkner's diligent literary agent and trusted friend. After the immediate curiosity and first interest in this expanded look at Faulkner, perhaps the chief effect will be a clearer realization of the extraordinary rapidity with which this artist matured, and the assurance with which he extended his virtuosity in all its directions.

A proportionate as well as penetrating comprehension of Faulkner's achievement might be approached to begin with by noting the accelerated development of several different aspects to be seen variously in those seven consecutive novels, from the barely achieved *Sartoris* in 1929 to his masterpiece *Absalom, Absalom!* in 1936. In them Faulkner projected himself as realist and regionalist, humanist and romanticist, across a broad spectrum of actions and enactors, yet with a preponderance of localized subject matter, a wide reach of historical perspective, a consideration of various sorts of human beings, and a developing commitment to the consciousness of his characters as the inner stage and veritable center of the dramatic action. Not that much of this is in *Sartoris;* perhaps little of it can be discerned there or in its earlier form, except in relation to these further works to which Faulkner so rapidly advanced. *Flags in the Dust* shows one thing clearly, that Faulkner already had in mind (if not wholly in hand) his heritage as an artist, though still with scanty intimation of how it was to be best projected fictionally. And his had been the gifted neophyte's typical error, in that he tried to seize at once upon the whole of his opportunity, to let none of it escape, though he had not taken full command of any of it. *Flags in the Dust* (like *Sartoris*) enters into his own time, with the return of young Bayard Sartoris from World War I; it is resonant of the South's past and filled with ongoing family affairs, not just Sartoris but Benbow, to the regionally tinged theme of tradition and disintegration; Snopeses have appeared in their grotesque odiousness, with Flem up from the fleeced Varner domain and installed as restaurateur in Jefferson; there are Negroes, chiefly house servants, and poor whites, casually sketched; there is the locale, its weather, its ghosts, and the deliberateness of scarcely purposeful existence. As Professor Michael Millgate penetratingly set forth a decade ago, there was an inherent juxtaposition and counterpoint in the structure of *Flags in the Dust* which was lost when Wasson's revision reduced the Benbow factor in favor of the Sartoris story. Nevertheless it may be questioned whether a more proportioned narrative structure would have greatly improved *Sartoris,* and it may be seen increasingly that the novel's chief effects are not truly Faulknerian; *Sartoris* is labored rather than dynamic, and with more of lassitude than

of motion, an effect inherent not so much in the characters as
in their characterization. It is as if Faulkner realized that a
mode for this essential effect was the thing now most needful
for him and that he must find it not imitatively but to accord
with his own visions and temperament. However this came
about, whether by chance or in a heroic thrust of creative
imagination, he fell upon it and rapidly made himself its
master.

It is not difficult to imagine what must have been the young
artist's frustration in his obstructed attempt to set it all down
at once and in both its intrications and ramifications. Though
after eleven rejections Faulkner agreed to Alfred Harcourt's
demands for a shortened version of *Flags in the Dust,* in his
farther work Faulkner did not turn from the regional claim he
had already staked out in its contemporary variety and historical depth, nor did he deny his temperamental bent. More
Yoknapatawphan novels followed quickly, and the first of
these, *The Sound and the Fury,* scarcely suggests a struggling
artist's timid attempts to appease publishers. In it and in the
next, *As I Lay Dying,* he centered events close and closer still
not only in a local context but again in a familial containment; and even more crucially for his developing art, he
evolved a sustained use of his characters' consciousness as
means of narrative conveyance and sonority — almost as if to
prove doubly the potent fitness of this preempted mode and
make more sure his command of its adapted uses. Besides, as
it may be in any art that a particular devising can diffuse an
enhancing effect beyond its integral function, it was so in
Faulkner's turn to a more subjective mode. Not only was the
matter more strongly highlighted but narration was lifted into
a further celerity through this refraction of immediate realities
within characters' processes of consciousness. Most importantly, though, as Faulkner does it, this not only makes the
story more intensely theirs, but creates them totally as in and
of it, through characterizations that are integrated, relevant,
and economical, giving the consummate work of art a
sustained shimmer of import as well as ongoing life. It is

another of Faulkner's achieved fictional paradoxes that such a penetration beyond types into the uniqueness of individual make-up and conscious existence can lay such representative claims upon readers' collaborative intuitions.

Any notion that after frustrations over *Flags in the Dust* Faulkner performed a calculated act of defiance in *The Sound and the Fury* might claim some evidence from his having opened the novel with the Benjy section. However, this immediate entry into the elected narrative mode at its utmost pitch deserves a more considerate estimation, both for the artist and the work. From the first Faulkner had taken his writing too seriously to make it a vehicle for pique, and given his intention in *The Sound and the Fury* as well as the onset of its *donnée,* it was sound strategy to carry the reader to its extremities at once. What there is to be understood about Benjy must be seen in itself, his arrest and isolation in the discontinuities of his associative processes. That much is soon apparent, and if it is accepted this elementary but attentive consciousness in a full-grown, mentally retarded member will serve well enough to lead into the story of the other more sophisticatedly disconcerted and all too expressively morbid Compsons in their familial situation. At the same time Benjy's idiot innocence, his invincible naiveté beyond that of a child's in his utter lack of an ongoing sense of the temporal and consequential, can indicate by contrast that such preoccupied subjectivity as Quentin's or Jason's is far from disinterested and may be self-serving, self-deceptively. Faulkner's representations of consciousness simply proffer something immediate and unique about the individual; what is nearer the truth of the matter is to be seen in the situational interrelations of persons; the vital organicism of his fictions depends upon the reciprocity of these two factors, and in *The Sound and the Fury* this function is extremely subtle but most intriguing to the imagination. Beyond *Flags in the Dust/Sartoris* it stands as a sudden amazing demonstration of his genius at its most idiosyncratic. In the flickering kaleidoscope that is Benjy's awareness adrift among its immediate stimuli, he can be seen only as static and irretrievable among the other Compsons as they weave complications out of their own more intent yet erratic sensibilities. Together they may alert readers to that furthest empathic extension of dramatic irony, the use of nothing more than a situated character knows himself to understand more about him than he will ever know. With this response undeniably required toward Benjy, its relevance to the others may be made clearer. In that sense *The Sound and the Fury* is a tale not only begun but told throughout by an idiot.

Benjy sees and hears the others and directly registers enough physical phenomena to constitute the scene even though he has no understanding except through fragments of simple memories adventitiously associated with previous overt experience, and his consciousness is not so much a stream as a succession of momentary apprehensions even less cumulative than in the most idle reverie. Nevertheless Benjy's scarcely intelligible glimpses of reality communicate not just detailed knowledge of the other Compsons and their servants but suggest the unease beneath the tiresome plod of events in their fretful household, while something of what his own bounded consciousness might have been like is represented in perhaps the only possible way, through the almost spastic narrative with its fragmented continuity and minute obscurities. Hinted matters are brought into a clearer but still oblique light through the second and third sections, in the more coherent but beset and obsessed speaking consciousness of Quentin, (who absorbs others' lives peculiarly and agonizingly into his own loneliness), and then less subtly through the defensively aloof and sardonic mind of the much-provoked Jason. Finally the omniscient narrative of the fourth section, though direct and sustained, remains under the burden and hazy gloom of what has gone before, while presenting as thematic counterpoint and tonal balance the notable character of the postbellum Negro servant Dilsey, who though emancipated is still enslaved by compassionate fidelity to a decaying family she could not heal with her own virtue. Among them she must

carry on commandingly; and only in the Negro church, during the hypnotic sermon, can she release her tears. But among
the self-tortured Compsons, nothing is to be set right beyond a
mere resumption of the carriage's accustomed route, which at
least allays Benjy's bellowing over the interruption of a
routine. In such a story the fragmentary, only feebly or
morbidly associated, becomes conclusively thematic.

Faulkner himself disparged this novel, professing to care for
it only because it had cost him so many pains, though it then
left him feeling he had failed four times, (in each part with the
same story retold), and on one occasion he evaded the awkward question of which was his favorite among his works by
citing *The Sound and the Fury* under the metaphor of a
parent's special care for the child who has not turned out well.
Obviously an artist as much as any man is entitled to privacy,
nor is he obliged to explain his practice; the reader of fiction
must take on the equally personal enterprise of responsive
understanding, along with the privilege — which artists have
too, and sometimes exercise — of abandoning an unfinished attempt. But *The Sound and the Fury,* a surprising departure
and advance over his first three novels, became one of
Faulkner's most widely noticed works, and not merely as an
experiment in a narrative technique then much discussed and
sometimes attempted but seldom so well brought off. It was
also more directly regarded for its uncanny power in the
partial yet cumulative disclosures under its fluctuantly
clouded light, and through the sense of familial stress and
personal fate which emerges with intense effect from the
objective-subjective nexus of even the most cryptic passages of
individual consciousness. As for the novel's four parts being the
same story reattempted, that is an illuminating concept, to
which many readers may be inclined to add that each part not
only succeeds in itself but excellently complements the others.
In any case, whatever Faulkner's difficulties in creating this
novel and whatever his doubts after it was done, he did not
abandon his quest for an ultimate fictional reality to be
conveyed through his characters' subjectivity, while he con-

tinued to structure each of his novels uniquely, with that envisioned organicism of substance and mode which is an indubitable mark of his genius.

The Compson family shown in *The Sound and the Fury* has traits variously detectable as *fin de siècle* effects of a regional history and its impact upon a class within it. In the Compson parents this is a manifest decadence of a more than regional kind, but its Yoknapatawphan form is particular and extreme. The Compsons, as their creator wrote in an appendix to *The Portable Faulkner,* were "that long line of men who had something in them of decency and pride, even after they had begun to fail at the integrity and the pride had become mostly vanity and selfpity." Mrs. Compson is of less notable descent but more inclined to claim its merit, as she and her sponging brother Maury meet change and misfortune with neither fortitude nor grace but with pretentions and self-indulgent dependence. By all their behavior they illustrate in detailed regional terms the debilitation which their kind anywhere are liable to when ample security and supposed privilege once enjoyed are severely reduced; more particularly they suggest the shallowness of certain presumptions which change had undercut in the postbellum South. Mr. Compson is given to drink and reading classical Latin and expressing a lofty fine-edged cynicism that comprises not just his family's situation or the South's but all humanity and the cosmos itself. He comes into focus most often in the novel's second section, through Quentin's recalling as a freshman at Harvard, the very phrasings of his father's elegantly uttered abstractions deprecating the whole scheme of things. The remembering runs back into Quentin's childhood and troubled adolescence, along with his unforgettable fixation upon his sexually restless and incautious sister Caddy, and all such melancholy details enter chillingly into the flow of Quentin's reveries as he fatalistically prepared for suicide. Jason, whose stream of consciousness and actions constitute the novel's third section, is as embittered as his father, but unlike the more sensitively attuned Quentin, he has not subsided into melancholy. Intent on advancing himself materially and meanwhile freeing himself from encumbrance by his relatives, he gives the practical man's two-dimensional and opportunistic view of all the others, yet he too shows in his own way their commn trait of inordinateness when at the novel's end he intervenes brutally in all directions during the contretemps in the public square. His mother's son, and Mr. Compson's and Quentin's opposite, he is still a Compson, spoiled in yet a different way, in a family's deterioration which is also disintegrative. In Jason, a bachelor cotton merchant with a weekend mistress from Memphis according to the note in the *Portable Faulkner,* the Compson line ends.

Quentin's brief tortured existence spans the last decade of the nineteenth century and first of the twentieth; the narrative as a whole comes up to 1928, and the three sections other than Quentin's look back from that Good Friday-Easter weekend. From Quentin's birth in the 1890s to 1928 is roughly the period of Faulkner's observant boyhood and youth and his early manhood's turn to his vocation. While the Falkners were not a demoralized and disintegrating family, they too had forebears more distinguished, including a daring Confederate general and man of affairs and property, and biography seems to show in Faulkner himself a certain Southern *amour-propre,* but in his transmuting of observation and hearsay into Yoknapawphan fiction he was judiciously detached though fully empathic, the complete artist impeccable in attitude as well as potent in his craft. He shaped *The Sound and the Fury* out of alerted awareness of life in a Mississippi town and county where the past still lived as influence, and not just as vague sentiment emanating from sight of the statue in the town square, where "the Confederate soldier gazed with empty eyes beneath his marble hand into wind and weather." In a society devastated by a still-remembered lost war with its reversal of a whole order of things, memory itself is a more recurrent and insistently conditioning function than on a frontier or among a long-settled people; under this aspect the fusion of sociohistorical fact and the privately felt weight of the past is a reality deserving representation; *The Sound and the Fury* with all its extremities is not tangential, but tends toward the imaginative center of his regional subject as Faulkner knew it; out of such knowledge he found the subjective approach a means of giving these realities the articulation and accents of fiction. The application of this novel's drastically experimental techniques to matter so broadly grounded in the region's transitions was a daring risk, but the results suggest the sure instinct of genius in dealing with the Compsons as conditioned by place, time, and a complicated personal-societal heritage. It is an almost incredible creative advance beyond Faulkner's first attempt with the Yoknapatawphan matter; and it is not his infatuation with detailing the events and types of *Flags in the Dust* that marks him as a truly romantic regionalist but the assurance and aptness with which the heart of his story was to be sensed in *The Sound and the Fury* through the modulations of his characters' subjectivity.

Yet within his wide comprehensiveness the classic regional Faulknerian figure in *The Sound and the Fury* is none of the uneasy Compsons, not even Quentin, but their Negro servant Dilsey. She too is of course native to that place, inheritor of its history and bearer of its burdensome ongoing processes, but she has "endured" in the way that Faulkner attributes to Negroes. This is not a mere brute survival but a morale of self-possession and a barely scrutable philosophic-mystical fortitude. It is Dilsey, with the limited assistance of her husband and her adolescent son, Benjy's attendant, who must sustain the Compsons in what passes for custom and ceremony in their deranged and disconcerted existence. Present in the others' awareness, she pervades the whole story, a critical but constant guardian whose every glance and act is a just evaluation. She is not called upon to account for herself as Benjy, then Quentin, then Jason have been cast to do; throughout those three sections her appearances, acts, and direct utterances show her veritably even through such different eyes—a token of her wholeness—and in the last section she is set forth in an omniscient narrative which deploys the remaining family as of this time, after Quentin's suicide eighteen years earlier, and then his father's death and Caddy's defection, and now the flight of Caddy's daughter Quentin after stealing Jason's cash box.

In this climactic fourth part Dilsey is seen at two extremes — first in the midst of her continuing trials, with the uproar this Easter morning over the theft of Jason's money, and then in her only respite, with her only anodyne, her simple religion, as she listens in the Negro church to a stirring sermon on the theme, "I got the recollection and the blood of the Lamb." Dilsey, who always outspoken had often been as stern with her dependent white folks as with anyone else who made it necessary, now lets her store of grief overflow, and there is a memorable image of tears running down her time- and tribulation-wrinkled cheeks as she listens to the sermon. She continues to weep as she walks from the church, and when a companion tells her to quit because they'll be passing white folks soon, Dilsey only says, "I've seed de first en de last. . . . I seed de beginnin, en now I sees de endin." Thereby she measures a family's history, and hers intricated with it, but she does not utter what it seems her instinct for the truth must have told her all along, that for all of them so situated it had been a fate, an irreversible doom. Perhaps this illuminates her stoic endurance, in that she has never deceived and wasted herself by any hope except through her religion, which was not of this world and saw no remedies here and now.

Unique as Dilsey was, to Quentin she had become a point of reference in his haunted and appalled sense of the South with its postbellum life still turning in many ways upon a disorienting defeat and a heritage of scarcely tractable biracial questions. On this Faulkner was to give Quentin fullest scope and exercise as a predominant central intelligence concerning the Sutpens in *Absalom, Absalom!*, but in *The Sound and the Fury,* where he is more involved in the rigors and griefs of his own unfolding life, he has at least begun to generalize about the curious ambiguities of relationship between white folks and their Negro servants. From childhood he remembers as an

example that when mental deficiency became evident in the
Compson son whom his mother had named after her brother
Maury, she changed the name to Benjamin, with allusion to
Jacob's son held hostage in Egypt, and Dilsey had said it was
done "because Mother was too proud for him." This recollection leads the maturing youth to credit the Negroes' acuteness
in dealing with their white employees:

> They come into white people's lives like that in sudden sharp black trickles
> that isolate white facts for an instant in unarguable truth like under a
> microscope.

In the same context Quentin acknowledges their inscrutibility
—"voices that laugh when you see nothing to laugh at, tears
when no reason for tears"—and wonders at their passion for
gambling, their proneness to religious trance. On Quentin's
first trip to the North he had looked out the train's window at
a stop in Virginia and threw a quarter to an old Negro man
whose presence there seemed to say "You are home again." It
leaves him thinking of

> that quality about them of shabby and timeless patience, of static serenity:
> that blending of childlike and ready incompetence and paradoxical reli-
> ability that tends and protects them it loves out of all reason and robs them
> steadily and evades responsibility and obligations by means too barefaced
> to be called subterfuge even and is taken in theft or evasion with only that
> frank and spontaneous admiration for the victor which a gentleman feels
> for anyone who beats him in a fair contest, and withal a fond and un-
> flagging tolerance for whitefokds' vagaries like that of a grandparent for
> unpredictable and troublesome children.

Later he comes to think that

> the best way to take all people, black or white, is to take them for what they
> think they are, then leave them alone. That was when I realized that a
> nigger is not a person so much as a form of behaviour; a sort of obverse
> reflection of the white people he lives among.

Here are a troubled young Yoknapatawphan's expanding
intuitions about interpersonal contacts in general, together
with his more particular realization of the closely reciprocal
though still enigmatic and uneasily self-conscious relations

between the races in the South during the twentieth century's first decade. Faulkner's further and more nearly current instancing of appreciated elements in the Negro temperament are to be seen in such portrayals as that of Lucas Beauchamp in *Intruder in the Dust* (as of about 1940) where characterization centers on the conception of himself that Lucas holds vis-à-vis the white folks' world. The maturing Quentin, in approximating the concept that differences between races, groups, or individual human beings may be made constructively complementary, was not the first Faulkner character to ponder such matters humanely, nor the last, though it is the more impressive in him in that he does so under the compounded disadvantage of a susceptible temperament darkly conditioned by familial influences. Probably it was this conceived worth and vulnerability in Quentin which led Faulkner to return to him and secure him shortly before untimely death for his hypersensitively subjective role in *Absalom, Absalom!* There he is to ponder race itself as fate in the Sutpen-begotten extremes of Clytie and Bon, going on hearsay but probing deeper than in his boyhood's perception that Dilsey was not swayed by his mother's pretensions. In *The Sound and the Fury,* however, the presence of Dilsey is contributive to theme not so much by her racial traits and talents as in the more nearly universal terms of her grimly principled character and behavior among the unnerved volatile Compsons. Dilsey's endurance in the midst of the action and throughout its course certifies the novel's interrelated regionalism and realism, implying human verities in the face of contradictory actualities. Concurrently the local is evoked under trailing vapors of an erosive past; that history is disastrously compounded by inscrutible heredity, and, for all the characters, situation is given arrest in a secondary, reflexive period of a region's and a family's life. Yet with all this local and contemporary veracity *The Sound and the Fury* stands out in the Faulkner *oeuvre* primarily for a mode of representation which even at its most experimentally subjective could penetrate realistically into the diverse existences of three brothers, to give a sense of Benjy's automatically associative nonsequential consciousness, Jason's volcanic bitterness, and Quentin's fixations and his fevered turning away from all the life he knew, including his own. In hazarding this projection of fictional technique Faulkner did not surrender any claimed ground or minimize his elected responsibility as realist and regionalist.

Consolidating what he had made sure of in his craft, the artist then applied it with further specialization to a more strictly and indeed narrowly regional subject which, while of less general sociohistorical import, allowed sharply etched effects in delineation of characters and of representative human involvements. *As I Lay Dying* (1930) was another novel focused upon a family, and this story was conveyed not just largely but totally through passages in the consciousness of its members and a few neighbors. The subjective narrative moves from one mind to another, and recurrently, in relatively brief sections each with the speaker's name for title. It is a comparatively short novel, and a more accessible and uniformly surfaced fiction than *The Sound and the Fury,* yet full of event made vivid despite its diversely implemented presentation and the abrupt rather than transitional shifts from one mind to another. In contrast to the Compsons, the Bundrens are hill-country farm folk, with no pretensions to keep up and no intimations of decline to haunt them: however, they have the ruggedness and personal independence of their kind, and an enlivening habit of speaking their minds, often to others but more sustainedly to themselves. The mother, Addie, is eccentric among them, a town-bred woman come to teach country school, and to supply Anse with phrases to court her. She has a melancholy view of human personality and heredity—"each with his and her secret and selfish thought, and blood strange to each other blood"—but she has an acute sense of the integrity of individual being and the comparative insufficiency of words, such as love and motherhood; when her son Cash is born it is that "aloneness had been violated and then made whole again by the violation: time, Anse, love, what you will, outside the circle." The novel's circumstantial thread is Addie's dying and death and, at her long-standing request, her transportation (by wagon and mule team) for burial not with Bundrens but in Jefferson with her long-dead kinfolk. The journey is arduous, full of delay and mishaps, glimpsed in one consciousness or another; separate views of the same event not only overlap but take on coloration from private awareness and supposition. As Addie had discovered, not only do words fall short of equivalence with experienced realities but the object is open to any ruling which any mind inclines to lay upon it. This is obvious and a commonplace, but it marks the area where discourse may enter into the realm of literature — even unknowingly, as with the personae of this novel compiling among themselves a fragmented Bundren epic. Whatever wholeness it has is as of a crystalline polyhedron, its planes their speaking minds, each with its own timbre, out of a shared pilgrimage but from their inner centers of unique being.

These private streams of responsive consciousness do not lapse into languid reverie or isolated self-preoccupation; they relate to what makes up a quite substantial action, in which each character takes part overtly and as to his or her separate sense of the involvement. Therein this curiously constructed and deceptively simple work becomes a paradigm of objective-subjective fusion into full yet subtle imaginative effect. Addie Bundren's dying is a stimulus to recollection, her own and in those around her, and in this mode a quantity of familial and personal history emerges. Yet while whole scenes, including dialogue heard and engaged in, are set forth substantially, each is shaped by the range and tinged by the trend of the registering mind it is being filtered through. This intensification of event in a personal impression of it is practiced even with the novel's central catastrophe, the overturning of the funereal wagon during the attempt to cross the Yoknapatawpha river at the flood-swollen ford, as this registers variously upon the bystander Tull and the Bundrens. Details are repeated but always as modified and even transmuted by the individual response. There is even a rearrangement of chronology to make possible a deeper subjective treatment, when after Addie's death and the accident at the river in which her coffined body is nearly lost, her voice is heard — not as of a ghost but in a transcendence — through a recital antedating all that had preceded, going back to her as a Jefferson-born melancholy-minded country schoolteacher who consents to marry Anse Bundren, and including too her adultery with the preacher Whitfield which produced her favored son Jewel — a flashback which intensifies the pathos of her known fate in its private ratio to the person she had been to herself. In this sense that voice from her living past epitomizes the deepened reality given fiction through the motions of a character's consciousness.

As I Lay Dying, by its restricted structure and specialized mode, yet with its material grasp, and with characters each given an uninterrupted, colloquially flavored private say at intervals, might be cited as the purest exemplification, and one of the most sustained and subtlest of Faulkner's bent toward the subjective mode for penetrating access to fictional matter and its most engrossing conveyance. Yet the magnitude and complexity of a fictional subject is a relative determinant of the effectiveness (or even the feasibility) of dominantly subjective narration, and especially in the extreme form of *monologue interieur.* In *Ulysses,* with its full, sometimes turgid streams of consciousness accompanying a generally thin line of event, Joyce had found it needful to vary the factors of subjective immediacy and intensity. In the "Telemachia," for Stephen at the tower and then in the schoolroom and finally walking along the beach there is a progressive increase and deepening; Bloom at the funeral is drawn outward to observe and listen as well as reflect, but more often he is the complete thrall of his random and fanciful associations; Molly in her curiously crowded bed has it all to herself but rallies the whole external world for supporting cast to her continuous performance. To set *As I Lay Dying* beside *Ulysses* is like contrasting a series of etchings with an immense mural or a frieze as lengthy and peopled (even though not as elevated) as the Elgin Marbles, but it may suggest how remarkably contained and consistent was Faulkner's experiment, in which the deployment of events by witnessings is adequate, while the separate voices become recognizable and alive. Only so closely bounded and casually episodic a story as that doled out in *As I Lay Dying* could be set forth in such a series of comparatively brief monologues entirely private in their point of view, each a specializing of mode that allowed a sparse selectivity to highlight character while projecting throughout the one abstract unifying overtone, in the stresses from the synergistic-separatist ambivalences of that intimate collective life of isolated beings. (It is perhaps to strengthen such a theme that Faulkner lets Addie Bundren speak from her body rotting in the homemade coffin to tell her whole story from her young womanhood and marriage to the point where she "knew at last" the meaning of her father's saying, that "the reason for living is getting ready to stay dead.") Thus paradoxically has the novel made it vitally apparent that "These our actors . . . were all spirits."

THE TRANSFORMATION OF *SANCTUARY*

Sanctuary (1931) suffered from an unfortunately concocted scandal which the prejudiced continued to propagate, branding Faulkner as one who dealt in calculated sensationalism, whereas the novel confirmed what Professor Blotner reports was said by Faulkner's mother: "Billy looks around him and he is heartsick at what he sees." *Sanctuary* is pervaded by the artist's strong natural aversion and revulsion from evil; and, as he would repeatedly do in his fiction, he placed in this work a melancholy advocate of ethical principles, putting him in a sufficiently forward though the more exposed position. Here Faulkner is emergent as the humanistic realist, though with the least assured of his protagonists. *Sanctuary* also is characteristic in its regionalism; going beyond the somewhat limited setting in *The Sound and the Fury* and *As I Lay Dying,* it occupies a wider stage, Memphis as well as Jefferson, and presents a greater variety of characters and their actions, as will be done still further in *Light in August, Absalom, Absalom!,* and the Snopes trilogy. Yet *Sanctuary* not only makes such excursion beyond the two novels preceding it, in strange ways it overlaps as well as complements them, in that like *Sartoris* it too is a novel reconstituted, and its writing and rewriting were closely of the same period as that of *The Sound and the Fury* and *As I Lay Dying.* This time, however, it was not just an expedient shortening and supposed simplifying, as with the rejected *Flags in the Dust,* by deletions made by his literary agent; it was a painstaking recasting and revising by the artist himself, and not so much with intent to modify what might be taken for sensationalism but more importantly to heighten the novel's effects as a work of art. *The Sound and the Fury,* finished in October 1928, had been dallied over by one publisher and then taken up Harrison Smith and contracted for on February 28, 1929, and published the following October. Meanwhile Faulkner had written *Sanctuary* in its first version, starting it in January of that year, according to a note on the manuscript; and Harrison Smith, agreeing with his readers that it was too shocking to be issued, had rejected it. Then some time later Smith changed his mind and had the novel set up—though that process was interrupted to let the printers work on *As I Lay Dying,* which was to appear in October 1930. When Smith finally (and apparently without earlier notice) sent Faulkner the galley proofs of *Sanctuary,* the situation was reversed. Now the author, having his rather desperately performed and previously rejected work thus freshly thrust upon his attention, found it "badly written," and it was he who declared it could not be printed "like this." He reshaped and revised it carefully, trying (as he wrote later) to make it "something which would not shame *The Sound and the Fury* and *As I Lay Dying* too much," and he could honestly say he felt he had "made a fair job" of it.

This revision did not, however, depend upon an eliminating of violence and shockingly crude occurrences but rather upon their assimilation into a more carefully conducted narrative, in which with truly classic effect overt incidents are volatilized into their significance under humanistic perspectives. The structural recasting of *Sanctuary,* chiefly by rearrangements of chronology and some reapportioning of detail, did indeed "make a fair job" technically of what had been a more sprawling narrative, while at the same time preserving the episodic quality required by this broadly focused and variously peopled tale. As for excisions from the earlier attempt, the most significant are those which reduce details about Horace Benbow in his personal and familial relationships (matter which might seem to have drifted into *Sanctuary* all the way from *Flags in the Dust*) but this simplifying of Benbow's role is significant for what it thereby emphasizes, the deeper complexity of his troubled quixotic reaction to evil as he encounters it in wider contexts. As Goodwin's lawyer he becomes more than professionally concerned in attempting to clear him of the contrived false charge of having murdered Tommy, whom the gangster Popeye had shot to make way for his horrible attack on Temple. Horace visits Goodwin in the jail; he learns Temple is being hidden in a Memphis brothel and seeks her out as a witness against Popeye; he does what he can to provide for Goodwin's wife with her small child as she awaits her husband's trial. In the course of this, like others among Faulkner's proponents of humane verities, Horace Benbow reveals himself as a melancholy moral philosopher.

Events beat him down. He is aghast to find that Goodwin's wife has assumed she must give herself to him in lieu of the money they do not have for lawyer's fees. Wondering what kind of life, what unfeeling use by men she must have known, he asks "cant you see that perhaps a man might do something just because he knew it was right, necessary to the harmony of things that it be done?" But as for such an ideal, after he had visited the by now debauched Temple at Miss Reba's and got her whole sordid story along with her promise to testify against Popeye as the murderer, he himself thinks "perhaps it is upon the instant that we realize, admit that there is a logical pattern to evil, that we die." Presumably it is the death of the heart he speaks of, acknowledging it in himself. Earlier he had felt his existence as "a dream filled with all the nightmare shapes it had taken him forty-three years to invent"; now he faces the reality that lies beyond invention, and beyond control, as he is to find. Later, after Temple's false testimony has condemned Goodwin, Benbow's widowed sister Narcissa takes him out to the Sartoris home near Jefferson, and as the car mounts the slope of driveway that has "still a little snow of locust blooms on it" he voices his despair in a reduction to quiet irony: "It does last. Spring does. You'd almost think there was some purpose to it." He stays for supper but then compulsively wanders back to town; resting at the hotel, he hears disorder in the middle of the night, and comes upon the mob and the blazing timbers in which they have immolated Goodwin. Benbow is wordless as he looks into "the central mass of the fire," from which "there came no sound at all," though it still swirled upward unabated, as though it were living upon itself," and it is as if he confronts beyond any power to challenge it the disintegrative, destructive force which in the very order of nature is always ready to be loosed and to augment itself from its own energies.

That squander of another spring's locust blossoms and that fire's killing fury deriving from the men who kindled it are set forth in the novel's Chapter XXIX; significantly this was part of what Faulkner added in his reworking of *Sanctuary,* which in its original draft did not mention this particularly brutal lynching. Nothing could point more clearly to Faulkner's matured intention in revising this novel. He did not remove those earlier harsh and sordid instances upon which of necessity the narrative itself turned (derived as it was from a story Faulkner heard of such a rape), and indeed by rearranging portions of the galley proof he brought over many other details essentially unchanged from their original form; then he added this whole chapter with its ultimate melancholy and the horrifying climax of Goodwin's fate despite all Benbow's efforts. Yet the artist's treatment of that outcome is at one remove from anything grossly sensational; there is the sound in the night of running feet, the event is uncertainly rumored, the murmur of the crowd is heard nearby, but when Benbow comes directly upon the scene, although there is one of the mob running and screaming after having set himself afire accidentally while carrying gasoline, now from the central blaze there is no human sound and nothing to be seen except the timbers in those consuming flames that seem self-sustaining, self-promulgating. By such treatment Faulkner plainly had carried the matter far beyond sensationalism with its *frisson* which may pander to a dark atavistic residue in humans that is always ready to be inflamed. Instead, by bringing the disconcerted Horace Benbow forward as a significant character in his blend of resoluteness and uneasy sensibility, the artist has dealt with the terrible and the pitiable in a humanistically realistic way. Nevertheless that theme as an abstraction is aesthetically contained within its own dramatic right in a much wider sweep of fictional narration, which is crowded with a succession of diverse events, played out by a variety of regional characters grotesquely juxtaposed in their erratic and often headlong behavior, in a world Horace Benbow was scarcely made for.

What would have been a fit place for him and he for it is hard to say. He is a flawed man and admits it, and it is significant that this is developed in the novel's opening pages, when he stumbles into the sordidness and incipient viciousness at Frenchman's Bend and complusively dilates on his flight not only from his wife Belle but from ambiguous feelings about his stepdaughter Little Belle. Goodwin's woman, Ruby Lamar, formerly a Memphis prostitute, considers Benbow a fool and thinks, "He better get on to where he's going, where his women folks can take care of him." Then listening to his stream of elaborate talk to the men on the porch, she tells herself, "He's crazy," but his natural compassion toward her is to evoke a touching womanly response. Then Popeye, though threateningly holding him captive at the spring, listens to him and brings the "professor" to the house to be fed and sends him to Jefferson on the truck bound for Memphis with

Popeye's load of bootleg liquor. Benbow has drawn two persons, an abnormal man conditioned to ruthlessness and a much-beset woman become grimly stoical, to respond in ways beyond their sadly habituated lives; and despite his own crisis of griefs that has set him adrift he has shown a certain self-possession and humane interest in others. Nevertheless he has wrought no lasting changes among those at Frenchman's Bend, much less given anyone a talisman against the evils that are about to occur with the arrival several days later of the drunken Gowan Stevens and the frantic Temple Drake. Neither has Benbow taken a new hold on his own life, but has charged himself with an inherent lack of that driving force which he names as courage.

Not only in the characterization of Horace Benbow but throughout *Sanctuary* there are nuances and shadings of complexities which place the novel far beyond the psychological and ethical black-and-white of sensational fictions. A romantic regionalist, Faulkner is intent on penetrating into his characters' natures and subjective lives as these are restricted and exacerbated by milieu, but he pursues this effect realistically, beyond simplistic sensationalism or sentimentality. Specifically Faulkner does not make his advocates of humane verities infallible champions and place them beyond reproach, nor is Horace Benbow the only one of such protagonists defeated in the end and to some degree demoralized by that. And among those he represents as victims there is only one pure innocent, Tommy.

Certainly among fictional figures destined to take a role as ethical advocate there could scarcely be at first sight a less impressive one than Horace Benbow in *Sanctuary*. The brilliantly narrated Chapter II, succinct and richly tonal, shows him detained at the spring by a sinister Popeye, then at the Goodwin supper table, and thereafter talking confessionally of himself to the group of rough men on the porch of the old house at Frenchman's Bend, and later more sympathetically and concernedly to Goodwin's woman, before he leaves on the bootlegger's truck to be dropped off in Jefferson; all this is conveyed with such immediacy and implicative overtones that Faulkner's intention to disclose Benbow's present private disconcertion and basic instability cannot be doubted. It is a complex characterization. In his compulsively voluble and fanciful talk to the men of his reasons for running from wife and stepdaughter in Kinston in the flat Delta country and heading for his home town, Jefferson, he characteristically reduces his half-repressed domestic frustrations and incestuous desires to an obsession with a compensatory image of just "a hill to lie on," while to Goodwin's woman when she asks why he had left his wife he confesses seeing his life as spelled out on a Mississippi sidewalk by spots dripped from the box of shrimp he had carried home to his wife every Friday for ten years. Yet Benbow's self-deprecation—"I lack courage: that was left out of me. The machinery is all here, but it wont run"—does not accord with his persistent, exhausting efforts later to prove Goodwin innocent of Tommy's murder. Nor does Faulkner seem to reach too far in one character; the fluctuating extremes of despair and assertion may be complementary, especially in one so painfully conscious of evil's many visages and also of the felt need to "do something just because he knew it was right, necessary to the harmony of things that it be done."

However, as Faulkner's protagonists are fated to discover, events too often are not to be brought into an order for which there is a felt need, whether in religion, law, the arts and sciences, interpersonal relations, or a conduct of life that privately aspires to ethical integration. As history and drama typically show, even with the best of intentions and endeavor by some of the most humanely inclined, a harmony conceived of and desired falls away into components which paradoxically become its negation. In the matter of *Sanctuary,* what remains as gist and atmosphere transcends the novel's most cruel and shocking occurrences; it is the pervasive suggestion of insensitivity and wilfulness in all sorts of men and women, a climate conducive to abuses, deceits, inordinate desires, and outright violence, and consequently oppressive and even relatively demoralizing to persons of good will. Yet knowledge of

good and evil remains most abstruse, veiled beyond proof and
definition, for in phiosophical considerations relativity may
inject its demurrers, and among the mass of men whose limited and necessitous lives do not allow for the systematic consideration of human conduct there can be little advance beyond the accustomed religious dogmas and secular propositions they have found it expedient to stop short at.

Faulkner seems to enter upon this very real and extensive
ground of mankind's natural uncertainties and erroneous approximations (considered as man's fate this side of death) in
the triple closures of *Sanctuary*. These follow that climactic
Chapter XXIX (inserted in the course of Faulkner's revisions)
which ends with Benbow's coming upon the still-flaming fire
where the mob had burned Goodwin. Thereafter the brief
Chapter XXX, (opening transitionally with a vignette of the
Kinston taxi driver) shows Horace Benbow returning from his
defeat in Jefferson to his Kinston house and finding his wife
already in bed, reading a magazine. He telephones his stepdaughter Little Belle, who is at a "house party," and they have
a fragmented conversation, with mutual assurances that he
and her mother are "all right" and that she is "having a good
time" and will write her mother tomorrow. Except for the
initial confusion and, for Benbow, the disappointing neutrality of this interchange, there is a bare flatness about the
five-page chapter. As he "put the receiver back" he saw "light
from his wife's room" falling "across the hall" and heard Belle
tell him for the second time to lock the back door, though he
had already done so and said so in answer to her first words to
him when he returned after those several days of absence.

The episode's full implications must be assumed intuitively
from this cryptic closure wherein Benbow's thoughts do not
surface nor does the context imply them. His first answer to his
wife about locking the back door suggests that it is often left
open for Little Belle and he knows she is away tonight, and
this asks to be connected with matter in Chapter II, when at
the far point of his flight from domestic confustions he is pour-

ing out his wild talk to the men on the porch at Frenchman's Bend, and tells them that "From my window I could see the grape arbor" and "in the twilight her—Little Belle's—voice would be like the murmur of the wild grape itself." Before that he had mentioned Little Belle "in a little white dress in the twilight," not introducing "Louis or Paul or Whoever but it's just Horace," and "the two of them all demure and quite alert and a little impatient," with the grape arbor so near at hand. From this he passes to a particular happening before he left home five days ago (to him it still seems like "this morning") when he had humorously chided Little Belle for bringing home a young man she had met on the train. She had said, "'What business is it of yours who comes to see me? You're not my father. You're just—just—'" and he challenged her— "'What?' I said. 'Just what?'"—and she had avoided that hovering question by taunting him in return over the shipment he regularly brings home for Belle from the train, crying "Shrimp! Shrimp!" But, as he tells the men, "Then she was saying 'No! No!' and me holding her and she clinging to me. 'I didn't mean that! Horace! Horace!'" This seems almost an answer to his hazarded questioning as to "just what" he is to her if not her father, yet as he held her he could see in the mirror her watching the back of his head "with pure dissimulation." From this shabby and perilous ambiguity there precipitates his realization that what lies at the bottom of his unrest is Belle, and he puts it to his strange captive audience that "When you marry somebody else's wife, you start off maybe ten years behind." All this about Benbow is known to the reader from the beginning, and the artist who was perfecting techniques for significantly compounding even remote and slight connections may have relied on its recall, (along with a later instance, Horace Benbow's severe solitary crisis of consciousness passing associatively from Little Belle and Temple into an onset of retching sexual nausea). These support a closure in his return to Kinston and his wife, which by its starkness epitomizes his unnerved, stunned private fate, and almost

autonomic arrest beyond speech or thought, there where the
back door can be locked because Little Belle will not be coming in later.

Chapter XXXI, ending the novel, completes a tripartite
closure by dealing with Popeye and Temple, the one at length,
the other in only a brief impressionistic glance suggesting the
sullen stagnation of her life in exile in Paris with her father.
First is the account of Popeye's exit, and it begins with another
irony: on his way to visit his mother in Florida he was arrested
and charged with having murdered a policeman in a small
Alabama town where he had never been. He was not even in
Alabama at the time of that murder; he was in Memphis,
murdering someone else, for which he had never been apprehended — that shooting of his henchman Red, for having con-
spired to make love secretly to the now besotted Temple without Popeye's presence as voyeur. The chapter's second paragraph tells in two sentences that it was Popeye's custom each
summer to visit his mother, whom he supports and has led to
believe that he is night clerk in a Memphis hotel. Then, in
what is to be a major interpolation, the next paragraph drops
back into her life story: she had married a strikebreaker who
left her pregnant and with "the legacy" of a "disease." Popeye
was born a weakling who "did not learn to walk and talk until
he was about four years old," and as he grows into his stunted
self he shows incorrigible cruelty as well as sickliness and con-
genital impotence. In the development of these matters and of
his mother's emotionally deranging distress, his grandmother's
pyromania, and the efforts of a wealthy woman to help these
irredeemable ones, Faulkner is at his least effective: his lapse
into naturalism to explain Popeye as a sociobiological phenomenon seems more imitative of a current determinism in fiction than spontaneous, some of its illustrative detail is not only
digressive but incongruous, with a kind of gray humor, and
style grows stumbling. The almost incredible fact is that this
drearily prolonged flashback is not what Faulkner might well
have struck out of the galleys, it is entirely something he added

in his painstaking revision of the novel. It could be speculated that at this point the artist's developing selectivity and control were superseded by accumulating anxieties. One might have been in misdirected eagerness not to fall short of the import, momentum, and adapted tones of the two preceding chapters, also newly inserted, and so finely centered on Benbow. Yet their brilliance makes the inserted case history of Popeye seem the more inept and indeed contradictorily tangential from the novel's main direction. Perhaps Faulkner thought that to bring in the nature-nurture enigma concerning its villain might give further dimension to the theme of evil, yet there is only a kind of sociologic murk over the whole grotesque passage. And at the least some readers may doubt that such a stunted, retarded child, however morbidly cruel, could become a successful domineering gangster, for as Faulkner showed elsewhere and as Popeye demonstrates, evil has its own animal intelligence as well as ruthlessness, so that to have left his origins inscrutable would have made his whole appearance and effect in *Sanctuary* more credible and finally more forceful thematically. Beyond the murderer Popeye's execution for a murder he did not commit, the greatest irony in the chapter is that through laboring for improvement Faulkner the developing artist sank into a swamp of narrative, leaving it as roiled as some of Sherwood Anderson's, such as that great-heartedly imagined, clumsily embodied story "Brother Death."

When beyond this unfortunate insertion the narrative returns to the false Alabama murder charge and Popeye's arrest it becomes more sure in its detail and momentum and the theme of fatalism. His indifference about legal defense, together with his repeatedly exclaiming "For Christ's sake," suggest a hopeless incredulity at this complication of errors; his inertness marks the detachment of one on whom life itself has played tricks from the first. (It suggests too that evil is finally made vulnerable by imperviousness to human verities.) The District Attorney, assuming arrangements have been made for a Memphis lawyer to initiate an appeal, says that Popeye took the death sentence "like he might be listening to a song he was too lazy to either like or dislike, and the Court telling him on what day they were going to break his neck." Popeye, having given the turnkey a hundred dollar bill to bring him a shaving kit and Pinaud's lotion and to keep him supplied with cigarettes, lies all day on his cot, smoking—the gleam of his shined shoes growing duller, his tight high-waisted black suit more wrinkled—and though the turnkey brings him daily papers he leaves them untouched.

When a Memphis lawyer does come, evidently an acquaintance, and his help is refused there is only the slightest halt in Popeye's feigned indifference and a quick recovery in his reply to what the lawyer says:

"You, to have it hung on you by a small-time j.p.! When I go back to Memphis and tell them, they won't believe it."

"Don't tell them, then." He lay for a time while the lawyer looked at him in baffled and raging unbelief. "Them durn hicks," Popeye said. "Jesus Christ. . . . Beat it now," he said. "I told you. I'm all right."

A minister had visited him the night before the execution and asked him, "Will you let me pray with you?" and Popeye, lying on his cot, had said, "Sure. Go ahead. Dont mind me." When the man returns early next morning Popeye is still lying there, but now it is he who speaks first.

"Ready to go?" he said.

"Not yet," the minister said. "Try to pray," he said. "Try."

"Sure," Popeye said; "go ahead."

Then the turnkey brings forty-eight dollars "change from that hundred you never—" and Popeye, without moving, coolly answers the turnkey's awkwardly broken-off accounting, in the lingo of the day: "Keep it. Buy yourself a hoop." At the scaffold, while the minister prayed and others stood with bowed heads, the sheriff and his deputy adjusted the rope, "dragging it over Popeye's sleek, oiled head, breaking his hair loose," and intent on his stance in the face of the world, he at last allows himself to show a concern.

Popeye began to jerk his neck forward in little jerks. "Psssst!" he said, the sound cutting sharp into the drone of the minister's voice; "psssst!" The sheriff looked at him; he quit jerking his neck and stood rigid, as though he had an egg balanced on his head. "Fix my hair, Jack," he said.

"Sure," the sheriff said. "I'll fix it for you"; springing the trap.

Sic transit Popeye in this second closure to the novel, and although the excursion into his antecedents is dilatory and poorly written, the pages thereafter brilliantly effect a sort of pathos and a sustained portrait of irremediable alienation, in "that man who made money and had nothing he could do with it," since "alcohol would kill him like poison" and he "had no friends and had never known a woman and knew he could never," and had been described by Tommy as "the skeeriest durn *white* man I ever see" — this in picturing the old dog at Frenchman's Bend "sniff his heels, like ere a dog will" and Popeye "flinch off like it was a moccasin and him barefoot" and shoot the dog with "that little artermatic pistol," the one which will be turned on Tommy when he tries to protect Temple from being "pestered" by this misbegotten human derelict whose only compensation has been ruthless violence, and who faces execution with the paradoxical defiance of an almost complete passivity.

This quality joins, despite their uniqueness, the three closures of *Sanctuary*. For Benbow and Temple too their roles play out into a relapse from his strenuous championing of Goodwin and her inordinateness and perjury into an enforced cessation, an arrest and suspension in their living personal dooms. In the less than two pages which conclude the novel Temple and her father, toward the end of what "had been a gray day, a gray summer, a gray year," come into the Luxembourg Gardens and sit there, refugees from turmoil and scandal, but weighted with melancholy. Temple's face in miniature in her compact is "sullen and discontented and sad," a telling admixture of a complex mood, which may suggest what was to draw Faulkner back to this character in *Requiem for a Nun*. The imagery of a desolation, concluding with "the sky lying prone and vanquished in the season of rain and death," is strongly effective of closure on this note, except for one strained and awkward simile, of band music, "Massenet and Scriabine, and Berlioz like a thin coating of tortured Tschai-kovsky on a slice of stale bread," yet in the same sentence the mood is recaptured — "while the twilight dissolved in wet gleams from the branches [one of Faulkner's acute visualizations of natural light], onto the pavilion and the sombre toadstools of umbrellas." Three times Faulkner has sounded this tone of a separate passivity masking despair, and except for dispropor-tionate material too loosely set forth concerning Popeye's early life, it is a remarkable employment of closures as a developing technique in his narrative art.

The issuance of that *Ur-Sartoris, Flags in the Dust,* together with the inclusive documenting of Faulkner's entire endeavor by Professor Joseph Blotner's biography, may stimulate fur-ther considerations, from various points within the *oeuvre,* of the artist's extraordinary dynamism. This in a career so full of surprises is not to be defined as systematic development and symmetrical rounding out but rather a series of distinct consoli-dations, each contributive to a work that is autonomous and *sui generis,* in an ongoing discovery of aptitudes that support as-surance in writer and reader but so particularly serve the moment that they never cool and harden into a fixed manner. Basic to Faulkner's eminence in the art of fiction is a sturdily idiosyncratic temperament inexhaustible in its devisings yet not tangential but steadily centered. Every work is unlike any other, all are new yet none is eccentric, and beginning with *The Sound and the Fury* in 1929 no novel from then on lacks its discriminatingly admiring advocates, nor were there any in which practices that were to become recognized characteristics of Faulkner's art did not appear with fresh effects. In this aspect of his work *Sanctuary,* through its particularly inspired and dedicated act of revision, becomes a primary affirmation which was to hold throughout the long career, with all those richly and substantially individuated creations that lay ahead.

As Faulkner stated in the famous introductory note to *Sanctuary,* he was anxious not to shame his concurrent achievements in *The Sound and the Fury* and *As I Lay Dying*, with their direct and sustained fictional representations of subjectivity — an approach which would recur variously as a major factor in subsequent works. Obviously, however, his concern went beyond that. *Sanctuary* was a matter of another kind; in its story's concentrations of evil more widely and sharply manifest it was a weightier subject, and its fictional techniques, while more nearly conventional, were of greater variety. In its apportioning between extended episodes and a bare, sometimes even elliptical economy, its advanced structural and stylistic effects, shifts and bridgings, incisive characterization through brisk colloquial scenes, and its modulations of both pace and point of view, *Sanctuary* reveals an artist who is extending an already demonstrated control, and who with his head full of substantially dimensioned and lively local matters could do no other than make this somewhat *outré* but well-substantiated novel as nearly right as he could at the moment and also make way through it for works to come. Here was a point at which he consolidated some assertions transcending the correction and improvement of *Sanctuary* itself, a point from which he could sense he need not look back to know the road he was taking, and a prelude to two monumental achievements, *Light in August* (1932) and his masterwork *Absalom, Absalom!* (1936), together with his respite from that, the not inconsiderable *Pylon* (1935). With the addition of *The Hamlet* (1940) and *Go Down, Moses* (1942) Faulkner the romantic regionalist had fully and realistically declared himself before he had reached mid-career, and his experiments thereafter showed the commanding artist forever commanded to tell some new thing in its own unparalleled way — even when it came to the volumes in 1957 and 1959 which, in rounding out the Snopes trilogy, gave it a continuing variety.

Sanctuary has its juncture with Snopesism seen as moral obtuseness in the midst of community, through State Senator Clarence Snopes; in his peregrinations among his constituents he has discovered that Temple is at Miss Reba's establishment and he peddles this information to Benbow; generically Snopes represents evil in an insidious form, as Popeye does its virulence. Through the pretentious and cowardly Gowan Stevens and the presumptuous, self-indulgent Temple Drake *Sanctuary* updates beyond World War I and into the era of gangsterism the motif of the deterioration of "first families" which had been made thematic through the Compsons in *The Sound and the Fury.* The tripartite closure in *Sanctuary,* with its repetition in different voices of the tone of despair in Benbow, Popeye, and Temple, is a simpler model for the trio of extended closures in *Light in August,* with its wide differentiations among Hightower, Christmas, and Lena, not only in their outlooks but fates. The portrayal of Tommy as a simpleton more memorably human than a mere bit-player and the flatly objective, subtly subjective characterization of Goodwin's woman Ruby Lamar are instances of a skilled etching which Faulkner will practice again and again, and with his special aptness for amalgamating secondary characters into the narrative's episodic flow. The almost cinematic flexibility of shiftings back and forth among scenes of interrelated and nearly coincidental but differently pitched events is a skill Faulkner typically consolidated in *Sanctuary,* along with his resourceful maintenence of a character such as Benbow to move with a complex consistency of being through several disparate worlds within the one milieu. Such related techniqueness of arresting characterization and expedite narration make for strong yet subtle fictional composition in which Faulkner modulates between rapidity and amplitude, with a remarkable control that creates some of his most typical effects.

Another subtlety in *Sanctuary* that may go unrecognized (and so may even lead to unappreciative discountings) is the infusion of irony into the grotesque. Of grotesquerie there is perhaps more than enough, and not just in the scenes in Miss Reba's brothel and at Red's funeral. But even there the burlesque is laced with sordid substance; Clarence Snopes quickly orients his country cousins to the iniquitous opportunities of Memphis night-life, and the brawl which upsets Red's coffin and dislodges the corpse is followed by the brief solemnity of the cortege to the edge of town (which will have its parallel in "Go Down, Moses") and by the whores' self-sustaining and gin-lubricated sentimentalities after the event. This is not mere caricature, however, and it moves in too close to ingrained coarseness and callousness to allow any of satire's hopeful intention to correct. Instead it is the fully colored exposure of deviation and a corresponding absence of sufficient congruity with operative human values. Its irony becomes the language in which a humanistic realism addresses with a special precision "those who care to attend," neither to laugh nor to wring their hands but to confront and intuitively ponder. The inordinate grown ludicrous descends so far into the unseemly as to become deplorable, and in Faulkner the irony latent in the grotesque is other and more than supercilious art for its own sake. It expresses a troublingly complex human response to disorderliness, as such instances expose the hazards when liberties are preempted through those human traits unreckonable to the rational observer as well as to the unconcerned aberrant one himself. Here at a degree beyond simple drollery Faulkner was probing the grotesque to touch upon an insidiousness at its core, even beyond that point where the clown becomes merely fatuous yet suggests a voiceless malancholy too privately intricated to be analyzed as the tragicomic. There are vigorous yet subtilized excursions into this enigma in *Sanctuary,* and such penetrations of the grotesque are to recur variously in later works.

As a story explosive with startling actions *Sanctuary* commensurately involved acute states of mind in its enactors, and here Faulkner found he could adapt into a variety of modified effects what he had masterfully grasped for artistic use in its pure form in *The Sound and the Fury* and *As I Lay Dying,* the subjective element and its potential narrative modes. In *Sanctuary* Faulkner confronted a range of fictional realities, both overt and psychological, with the alluring extent of their possible representations, but witnessed under some deference to the total account. To begin with, this story as he conceived of it did not grant him an unabated access to any characters' streams of consciousness, such as he had projected concerning Benjy and had freely enjoyed throughout his account of the Bundrens. Yet these experiences apparently taught the artist that sustained stream-of-consciousness narration, if it is to be anything more than solipsistic associative reverie, must be sustained by circumstance and unique personal involvements therein. Faulkner's brilliant achievement in *As I Lay Dying*, that more than merely ingenious *tour de force*, depended not only upon its familial containment but upon their transitory common preoccupation, Addie's death and burial, while at the same time marking the solitariness of each soul. Conversely in *Sanctuary* Faulkner recognized, notably with Popeye, that some fictional figures in certain stories will be unamenable to evocation through instancings of their consciouness in progress and must be realized at some remove, by what they do and say and by others' overt and subjective response to them. Such another one is Flem Snopes; in the evenings when the banker sits solitary with his feet propped on the unpainted ledge nailed for that purpose to the fine mantelpiece of the fireplace, what may be passing through his mind is not even hinted, and he remains an unrealizable being, the quintessential Snopes, beyond that reach of fictional imagination which requires a degree of empathic intuition or at least some shrewd guesswork. Ratliff employed the latter when he estimated Flem's living in the mansion, though in only two rooms, as something deemed to befit his "being a banker now and having to deal not jest in simple usury but in respectability too." This need also explained the automobile Flem bought though he could not drive it, and Ratliff ironically notes as a ploy for respectability "the motto that Flem his-self had picked" for the monument to Eula:

> A Virtuous Wife Is a Crown to Her Husband
> Her Children Rise and Call Her Blessed

—this wife he had acquired in what was essentially a chattel transaction with Will Varner, with the Old Frenchman's Bend property as settlement for the impotent man's marriage to the already pregnant daughter. Yet even the alert and canny Ratliff can make nothing more of Flem than such two-dimensional projections. That this is a sufficiency, however, and may mark proper limits for the effective presentation of certain characters may seem suggested by those weakest pages of *Sanctuary,* in which Faulkner felt impelled to provide a sociological case history and sort of epitaph for Popeye as the stunted offspring of venereally infected parents and graduate of a school for incorrigible children. But this is not the disturbingly grotesque, it is mere naturalism. Popeye's abnormalities both physical and psychical are evident, and if his degree of ascendancy as a Memphis gangster is taken as read, as it must be for the main narrative's credibility, that could have been enough. Indeed, without the final chapter's first pages the story could have moved more bluntly and inexorably into that sharper presentation, his fatalistic inertia as Tommy's murderer, who having escaped through Temple's perjury now awaits execution for a murder he did not commit. Here is the stark mystery of one man's fate, and no tracing of formative influences in this perverted, unhappy, and deadly life can penetrate his opaqueness and reach to what it may have been to walk about in Popeye's skin, or define what beyond physical threat makes his grotesqueness seem so ominous.

At the opposite extreme is Faulkner's multidimensioned presentation of Horace Benbow. He is seen widely vagrant all the way to Frenchman's Bend, from his Kinston home and his vexatious wife, his tantalizing stepdaughter, but then strenuously and more intently to Memphis searching out evidence from Temple at Miss Reba's to clear Goodwin of the concocted murder charge. He is heard here and there by a variety of persons in much talk, often elaborately reflective, with a wryness sometimes masking the extent of a melancholy that is both privately and cosmically conditioned. Most of all, he is revealed in his meditations and other more immediate sujective responses to externalities—not only a sophisticated but a strangely complicated man, suspended between his almost complete disenchantment and his refusal to "cease from mental fight" and open efforts against encountered evils. In his sensibility, animation, and wit, his susceptibility to grief over others as well as himself, his bleak resignation to ultimate inscrutabilites, and his recurrent rallyings, he shadows forth not so much a life as a temperament and a projective imagination that may intrigue conjecture, suggesting a semblable of its begetter. Yet Benbow lives and moves in his own right, so volatile a character that there could be but one stabilizing fictional closure, the flat narration of his return to his Kinston house and his wife there, and the inconclusive telephone call to Little Belle, in all of which what passes through his mind is not of record, though its tenor can now be imagined of this man *Sanctuary* has brought so intensely into being.

Variations in the fictional setting-forth of Horace Benbow have ranged through shadings from such distanced objective narration as closes his story to portions of the secret drift of his consciousness. Such detailings are loosely comparable to cinematic techniques in that the camera too, like fiction, not only may make instant transitions as to place and time but may move its focus repeatedly from the panoramic to close-up, yet fiction, admittedly more demanding upon the receiving imagination, is in its other ways more intricate and penetrative, which Faulkner constantly sought to maximize. The camera is only an eye, which must serve human gesture and voice, and though the cinema can well show a masklike face across which emotions may pass like cloud shadows, it hesitates to ventriloquize the thoughts that lie behind (a narrative device largely neglected, perhaps lest this too strongly contradict the ascendancy of the visual). Fiction, though, with that fuller collaboration the reader must give the printed page, can do what it pleases with its players' bodies, voices, and thoughts, and sometimes its techniques have become too plainly gamesome, in uses of the stream of consciousness that for lack of interpersonal and situational connections invert into merely random inconclusive association.

In such matters of fictional art Faulkner, for all his adapted uses of his characters' subjectivity to come to the heart of the story, is sturdily conventional and even exemplary, in that he draws upon still viable and indeed essential principles as old as the beginnings of fiction and drama. During his novitiate as a writer Faulkner had learned from a great deal of reading in literature that these modes rest upon a represented "action," a series of connected, related, and cumulative events, in which the overt and subjective responses of the participants become an intricacy of operative and determining factors. This fictional or dramatic composite can be pondered (and has been, over the centuries) in terms of plot and character, but in the realized work of art itself the two are to be made vitally symbiotic, and for Faulkner the final determinant of that is characterization. Crises in the relations of human beings and within the larger contexts of community recur with some degree of typicality, and plots may become archetypal, perhaps even gaining thereby a certain assurance of verity, yet this is to be made fictionally or dramatically viable only through dimensioned, revealing, and engaging personae. Trite stereotyped characters will unavoidably impose mediocrity on any fictional or dramatic matter, reducing it to shallowness. Such plot as that in *As I Lay Dying* is at once recognizable and can even, without derogation, be termed commonplace: the mother of a farm family dies and is carried on what becomes a hazardous journey for burial in her home town. This could have been made into a stock piece of sentimentalized melodrama; instead, while the novel in no way minimizes unusual hardship or natural grief, it rises beyond its spare dimensions and rustic tonalities to something representative of the nature of families and the impact of death. Such significations, however, are not intrinsic to the plot or supplied by it; they are evoked by the artist's unique individuation and subtle psychological penetration of characters, through direct recordings of consciousness in each. Faulkner's treatment of this "plot" was a specialized work of art, and in its confinement to a particular patterning and technique it could not be a model for the fictional treatment of more extended, complicated, and eventful subject matter, but for Faulkner it was an explicit demonstration of aesthetic principle, confirming the centrality in his art of his characters' subjectivity, according to their situational involvements but in the privacy of their intuitions and evaluations, each under his own impetus and outlook.

The two novels immediately preceding the revision and issuance of *Sanctuary* were conspicuously and, to many eyes, recklessly experimental, yet they were not carelessly done, but rather with a rapidly deepening responsibility to the elements and potentialities of fictional art, already tentatively explored in his first works, including in goodly number his most carefully developed short stories. In *The Sound and the Fury,* having committed his tale at once and outright to the stream of a consciousness in Benjy Compson, Faulkner followed through with the same method the somewhat more accessible though often cryptic subjective processes in Quentin, and then quite transparently in Jason; only in the fourth part does the artist turn to omniscient narration, giving special prominence to Dilsey and Jason but chiefly dramatizing the complication of events for that melancholy household's various members, on that grievously tumultuous Easter Day. Then in *As I Lay Dying* Faulkner rested the entire composition on an ultimate device, a series of witnessings and experiencings in which the various interior monologues, uniquely keyed, are each self-contained as point of view. Indeed, here the experimental mode is carried further; while the Bundrens are more steadily and closely together, they have less extended interchange. These two novels, richly regional at different levels of Yoknapatawphan society, both continue to express beyond *Sartoris* and with closer focus the localized Faulknerian theme of existence within the family as a world to itself, but in the very way of nature no resting place for the selves comprising it. Yet even with all such potent regional matter realistically viewed it may seem that the artist's working concern was primarily with technique, though without neglect of substance, under the self-imposed stringencies of an ardent novitiate. Then, having laid a certain hold on subjectivity at its extremes and in its sustained operations as an element in his chosen art, he was called upon to pass on to a less obvious test of powers but a subtler one — the modulations of subjectivity and objectivity necessary in the conducting of fictional narrations that were larger in range and scope than anything he had yet done. In an approach to this, the rapidly developing artist's self-impelled revision of *Sanctuary* may be seen as an act of vocational piety in a consolidation of ongoing discoveries, and the curious sequence of events which brought the issue to Faulkner just when and as it did seems one of those fortunate precipitating intrusions to which creativity sometimes may be indebted. Behind his simple prefatory statement that he had "made a fair job" of revising this novel must have lain a quiet confidence that he had declared himself as an artist and was about to proceed under full sail.

CONVENTION AND ENHANCEMENT

As Faulkner's work rapidly emerged between 1929 and 1940 and reached some of its highest levels during that period, an obstacle to an adequately appreciative estimation of it was the notion that he was an immoderate, undisciplined extremist whose innovations were calculated for their sensational effects, and also an untutored nihilist whose art was anarchistic. Conversely, among those who came to recognize his genius there was some disposition to exaggerate the prodigious uniqueness of his creations. Indubitably Faulkner himself was one of nature's rarest constructs, yet though each of his works was a self-fulfilled aesthetic entity, his voice grew recognizable, his thrust was increasingly defined, and it became evident that he was more than a warbler of native wood-notes wild. Though he did choose to tarry at home, somewhat apart not only from academia but from the gregariousness of the Left Bank and New York's literary coteries, he was not an uncultivated man. A factor in this was his great good fortune in having the patronage and friendship of the brilliant, literary-minded Phil Stone, who provided Faulkner in his formative young manhood with a flood of books and companionable talk about them. Stone, of an old and affluent Oxford family, and four years Faulkner's senior, must have been a better mentor for the latent artist than any university professor could have been. Grounded in the classics at the University of Mississippi, he had gone on to Yale for a second *cum laude* B.A., and while there had bought and read much current fiction and poetry, with a lively interest which he continued to follow when he returned to Oxford to practice law. It was he who brought *Ulysses* to Faulkner's attention (in its fourth printing, of January 1924) with the remark that "This fellow is trying something new . . . something you should know about," but that sprang out of a discriminating as well as catholic taste, not a superficial enthusiasm for the latest vogue or the *avant-garde* as such. Actually as to fiction Phil Stone and Faulkner in those days agreed that Balzac stood at the top.

It was Faulkner's mother, however, who first abetted his natural appetite for books, and Balzac was one of the writers she put into the hands of the precociously observant, reflective, and imaginative boy—along with Shakespeare, Victor Hugo, Fielding, Dickens, and Conrad. Late in life Faulkner was still reading in these authores: when he settled for a period in Virginia he wanted complete sets of Dickens and Conrad for his library there; meanwhile throughout his most strenuous years he was reading such American contemporaries as Wolfe, Willa Cather, Dos Passos, Hemingway, Steinbeck. What may well be kept in mind is not only Faulkner's wide and sustained acquaintance with European and American fiction, past and present, but his insider's attention to various fictionists' chosen means of embodying their visions. His regional centering of his work made him note particularly the same trait in other novelists, but it was Balzac rather than Zola whom he resembled in spirit; his localized scrutiny did not decline into naturalism nor was he diverted from his intent humanistic regarding of behavior as conduct. It is relevant to his whole practice that from the beginning techniques of characterization were of special interest to Faulkner; he and Phil Stone had particularly regarded Balzac's progressive revelation of individual natures and motives. In his informal but intense education as fictionist he would have singled out adaptations in others' methods that answered to his temperament and could serve the interests wakened by his acute watching and listening to the people around him. Faulkner showed that an artist's maturation must be fundamentally self-directed, but its perfect freedom should serve ends beyond itself, and these are to be pursued in a potent mood of ardor and stringency. In the main this, and not laxity or self-indulgence, was Faulkner's way, and particular scrutiny of his developed techniques can show that in his intensity and occasional denseness of texture he had ends in view which he meticulously and dynamically accomplished.

In *Sanctuary* Faulkner is to be found plainly commited to the principle that characterization is at the living center of illusional reality in fiction. Beyond that, he knew from reading and was learning by practice that characters are not to be given life by description, which falls short at one remove from the apparition of personae as conscious beings in living motion. While formal portraiture is not utterly without fictional effect, it leaves realization too largely to the reader's supplementing imagination. This may be assisted by a first-person narrator, through the infusion of his sustained evaluative point of view, and there can be the closer access and further refinement by use of a "central intelligence" told of in third-person narrative but made to enclose as well as color the matter of the story, by presence, observation, and some participation. Whatever his course, the serious modern fictionist appears to have determined that pure description is no longer a licensed major rhetorical mode, such as either narration or exposition, but is merely an adjunct. Given primary place in fiction, even in passing, description may lapse into naturalistic enumeration or static portraiture. Attempting to vivify characterization, fiction may describe not just appearance but an individual's qualities of temperament, yet this may settle into an inert abstract of what is typical of him. It has been to reach beyond such limits that fiction has attempted to merge characterization and action by entry into a stream of consciousness, not descriptively summarized or merely pantomimed in overt aspect alone, but sustainedly set forth as personal experience verbally realized in its situational context. There have been roughly three main degrees of such use of the subjective: the teller of the tale, the delegated I, given his first-person say from first to last; the selected him or her used as the "central intelligence" from whose ongoing experience and responses the story is to derive its reverberating tones and its shades of coloration; the *monologue interieur,* by a consciousness examining itself, the teller preoccupied with his or her own situation. The vogue of this last mode in its ultimate forms has been brief; it offered complete access to a consciousness, yet thereby lost extended outlook and involvement; and as practiced by close representation of random associative process, it lacked the significance that rises out of purposeful situational engagement and thus not only evokes setting but supports narrative structure, which further has depended upon economical selectivity for proportion and climax. First-person narrative, by contrast, is older than written language and will endure as long as there is utterance and listening, and Faulkner often used it with great liveliness. Third-person narration, in which a central intelligence operates perceptively as in a field of force, is a more recent preference, as already demonstrated to perfection by Henry James, and Faulkner brilliantly followed in this tradition, adapting it fluently into stories that also conveyed a remarkably large measure of externalized overt action.

It is possible for a first-person narrator to project a peopled, eventful, and consequential narrative action, supplying a focusing control and a permeating sense of interpretively responsive temperament without eclipsing the other actors in the tale. (This is shown in *The Town,* through repeatedly alternating and always idiosyncratic testimonies by Charles Mallison, V. K. Ratliff, and Gavin Stevens in their Snopes-watching; the method in its more nearly primary form carries throughout *The Unvanquished,* with its sole conveyor, Bayard Sartoris, following out his arduous maturation to arrive at a climax of some weight.) In the related but more flexible and subtler conveyance through third-person narration supportive of a "central intelligence," the communicating consciousness is personified and significant but less insistently present than a constantly direct speaker, and therefore not so closely bound to the limits of credible oral discourse. Either of these narrative methods which heighten realism through the lens of a character's subjectivity can convey more of external event and its colorations, and present other characters in fuller dimensions, than can pure stream-of-consciousness narrative— which is to be seen in the way the Bundrens separately sink into private and introverted musings despite the present grip of their common familial duties and preoccupation. But in this novel that reality was in itself made thematic, and there was quite enough overt action and mishap, with its demands upon all of them, to keep a narrative thread intact. *As I Lay Dying* is a splendid fictional accomplishment and was no doubt a great assurance to its creator, but neither its method nor that of *The Sound and the Fury,* with its masterfully composed four-sectional structure supporting predominantly subjective procedure, was widely applicable fictionally, even with subject matter in which characters' private passages of consciousness were major factors. And while the scale and diversities of *Sanctuary* required frequent resort to omniscient narration, the novel takes on Faulknerian vibrancy most intensely in those parts and to the degrees that Horace Benbow's awareness is the conductor.

From such accomplished exercises in technique way led on to way for Faulkner. In his intent responsive reading of fiction apparently its ways of saying had been laid upon him ideally as influences, not to the point of definition but as something experienced subliminally in their functioning modes. Then in the period when he was coming into his own full practice as fictionist, these conventions were being so notably modified and specialized that they could not be disregarded by serious writers. Some of this novelty was tangentially experimental; more of the changes were by extensions and refinements of potentialities latent in long-established fictional practice. Their chief consolidators for English and American fictionists had been James and Conrad, especially in the use of the perceptive narrator or, more subtly, the involved central intelligence, and in the rearrangement of events beyond chronology, for narrative economy and the preeminence of psychological penetration over dramatic disclosure. (Pursuing this potentiality, Faulkner tried several orderings of unitary passages before he hit upon his choice for the revised *Sanctuary*.) The influence of Flaubert, Joyce, and Chekhov also had filtered into American fiction, largely through the examples of adaptation by English writers; and others as idiosyncratic as Virginia Woolf and Sherwood Anderson were creating more nearly open-ended narratives to strike a new balance in favor of subjective particularity and depth rather then simplistic finalities. Of course then as now, and despite a period of remarkable innovations and refinements, the bulk of current writing, fictional and dramatic, directed its ventures chiefly as a cyclically stereotyped commercial expediency suggested. Faulkner knew this world also, and to support his family he would enter temporarily into it with certain short stories he called potboilers, and with stints of script-writing in what he named the salt mines of Hollywood. But his aspiration as an artist never flagged, and with no surrender of a fundamental freedom of imaginative choice he sought to adapt his craft's most effective techniques to his zealous purposes as realist and regionalist, using his liberties for the veracious and affecting conveyance of his visions.

Faulkner's works are each so particularly formed, colored, and consummated that he continues to defy the sort of imitation which can produce a school, of littler fish trying to swim in the same direction. What was characteristic that could be an influence (in addition to a brilliant example of the regional transmuted into dynamically representative art) was his alertness to the forceful centrality of the subjective element, as he had found it in the strongest fiction of his times, and as he had gone along with this trend but to his own ends, with rapidly acquired skills, through adaptations less conspicuously technical than in *The Sound and the Fury* and *As I Lay Dying*. Therein he became more various, with a greater tonal range even if in less extensive subject matter and with less sophistication than James, from whom most significant fiction then recognizably stemmed, and whom serious fictionists can never forget, though some may sometimes try. Faulkner was also more originative than Conrad, whom nevertheless he resembles greatly as a spirit, a temperament that must have some place in the work, though Faulkner's felt infiltrations, while more forceful, are less frankly personal. While a plain mark of genuineness in any artist is an often achieved autonomy in his separate works, there is also the more surely known voice with its recognizable timbre, and a certain personal artistic consistency, in which techniques acquire typicality and emerge as the artist's productive reaction to aesthetic conventions. Faulkner is as conspicuously *sui generis* in his art as was Hopkins or Joyce, and he too worked in reaction to the yielding resistance and propulsion of literary tradition, as if on a trampoline. If a point is to be supposed from which Faulkner projected himself into the full practice of his art (though as yet without its superlative successes) it might be when he unfolded those galley proofs of *Sanctuary* in its first desperate draft and himself pronounced the verdict, out of his gathered surety, that this would never do. What possible remedies he imagined and turned to at least silhouette what was to be characteristic and central in his works to come, even in all their variety.

Most conspicuous in a surveying of the *oeuvre* will be his further advances in structurings and excursions in style, obviously intended to represent behavior both overtly and at its psychological roots, in the situational realities of individual experience. Inherent in such practice by Faulkner is a principle of modulation as it operates to admit variety of discourse, at shifting levels of momentary penetration into the subjective essence of the matter, with an accommodating fluctuation of weightiness and pace, and a transcending of time-bound chronology for the sake of some higher order of realizations. It was to become a calculated and immensely complex art, and already in the revised *Sanctuary* there is to some degree the hazard of an immediate brilliance which almost but not quite dazzles a clear vision of the proffered regionalism and its thematic import. Yet Faulkner as fictionist was not in rebellion against current conventions; his originations were no more than an all-out exercise of aesthetic options, for humane communication with the concerned and attentive at potent levels of fictional art. He was in the main stream and remains there, no tangential experimenter but a consolidator in a purposefully selective adaptation of techniques to his unique needs as humanistic realist and romantic regionalist. It was surprising that many readers took so long not only to recognize the positive significance of his point of view but to see his originations as legitimately independent tactics under the then current strategies of contemporary fiction.

In Faulkner's narrative art a progressive modulation operates regulatively within the mingled flow of objective-subjective matter. Such gradations result in a more complex texture than that in pure stream-of-consciousness narration or in the typical uses of a central intelligence, whether first or third-person. Both these modes, as well as overt omniscient narration, enter into Faulkner's practice; the difference is that often they are refracted from a formal, sustained employment of one or the other into transitory uses in a complexity that fluctuantly combines modifications, sometimes of them all, always with variances between objective-subjective extremes. Faulkner is not unique in this, but he was an independent pioneer in such synthesizing of representational modes within a unitary fictional narrative, and what is extraordinary is the intensity of his achieved effects, combining a fluidity of subjective penetration and an enhanced momentum. Going beyond such unbroken consistency of narrative mode as in the *monologues intérieurs* of *As I Lay Dying* or such containment by a narrating central intelligence as in either *The Unvanquished* or that of *The Reivers,* Faulkner in his most characteristic bent left still further behind the easiness of a preempted and constantly presiding authorial omniscience, to achieve instead an almost Flaubertian aloofness. Even when narration is in first person it is the verified player speaking; and the widely proved advantage of such distancing in modern fictional art is that the characters, left on their own whatever the mode of expression given them, are made to stand forth and represent themselves in deeds, words, and states of inner being, as these are the immediate passing aspects of their roles. The artist's touch may be most surely felt in his regulation of their movements into and out of the situation's center, including most importantly what is played upon the inner stage of some crucially responsive consciousness amid all the existenial movement. So deployed, even minor figures may be sensed in their quiddities, but it is from major characters' subjectivity that Faulknerian narrative draws its chief thrusts. These come to accord with the pure energies of the imaginative life and art itself, as Shelley put it in *A Defence of Poetry:* "The mind in creation is as a fading coal, which some invisible influence, like an inconstant wind, awakens to transitory brightness; the power arises from within. . . ." By their involved, responsive, and projective imaginations Faulkner's protagonists become impressionistic poets of situation and involvement, and the artist himself, with his innovative modulations of the story's mingled objective-subjective flow, was knowing enough to provide that some ascendancy over the narrative's events was conserved for what resembled in its own part an ulterior central intelligence, the imaginative source, determinant of import and tone, as well as of proportioned structuring and regulated pace and emphasis, yet deferential to others' imaginative assent and asseveration.

The "fair job" which is the revised *Sanctuary* suggests that Faulkner had confirmed what for himself was to be a cardinal rule supportive of many of his strongest effects—the positing that given some suggestion of a fictional figure's inner nature through access to his experiential way of being, readers can answer more readily and imaginatively in their further encounters with him than with a comparatively objectified character, wholly dependent upon overt behavior and formal description for recognition. Moreover, with a fictional being known to some degree in the subjective aspects of his nature, outlook, and intention, a reader's empathic understanding will proceed with a kind of geometric acceleration, as in an expanding actual acquaintance in which intuitive response to another temperament has operated from the first. Key characters upon whose inner natures Faulkner bases thematic presentation and appropriate compositional tone can move quickly into dimensioned entity and rapidly take on stature through self-disclosure, verifying a consistent veiw in the subtleties of a reader's deepening conception of them. Awareness of such a personality may become strong enough so that if he is known to be present in a given situation, the acquired sense of what would be his probable reaction may color the narrative's presentation of externalities and may license the artist's imaginative extensions beyond narrative and descriptive objectivity. Such enhancements do not drift beyond realism but deepen it, just as in actuality the presence of an intimately known person, who is watching and listening though doing or saying little or nothing, may condition one's sense of a situation and may even qualify one's understanding of it. A classic fictional example of such a reality subtly apprehended is in the concluding passage of Joyce's deceptively simple first-person story of a maturing lad, "The Sisters," in which the closure may be misread unless the old women's pious babble of funereal cliches is sensed as it must have sounded to the already disenchanted and withdrawn boy, whose canny self-emancipation is the story's whole theme.

Chapter XV in *Sanctuary* is omnisciently narrated, with some compressed factual details and scenes that are primarily dialogue, yet the errant and susceptible Horace Benbow's consciousness is felt in much of it as enhancing coefficient to the style itself. Midway in his flight from home, and after his Frenchman's Bend encounter with Popeye, Goodwin, Ruby Lamar, and Tommy, he stops near Jefferson at the house of his widowed sister Narcissa Sartoris and finds that his wife Belle had wired her that he "had left" and she "had gone back to Kentucky" and had sent for her daughter, Little Belle. Narcissa and Miss Jenny reprove Horace for his unconventional behavior, in passages of wry family dialogue, but Horace's mood in this situation is most felt in a description of Narcissa that is given a special tone merely from his presence:

He stayed at his sister's two days. She had never been given to talking, living a life of serene vegetation like perpetual corn or wheat in a sheltered garden instead of a field, and during those two days she came and went about the house with an air of tranquil and faintly ludicrous tragic disapproval.

A paragraph of economical omniscient third-person narration conveys subjectively attuned realities in summarizing what Benbow was telling his sister and Miss Jenny of the Frenchman's Bend menage:

the three of them, himself and Goodwin and Tommy sitting on the porch, drinking from the jug and talking, and Popeye lurking about the house, coming out from time to time to ask Tommy to light a lantern and go down to the barn with him and Tommy wouldn't do it and Popeye would curse him, and Tommy sitting on the floor, scouring his bare feet on the boards with a faint, hissing noise, chortling: "Aint he a sight, now?"

and then, though as direct quotation, Benbow's talk begins to vibrate with something of the fever his personal crises have induced in him, leading his discourse into increasingly fanciful projections. He had sensed "the woman just behind the door, listening"; he knew she and Goodwin were "not married," just as he knew Popeye "had that flat little pistol in his coat pocket." Besides which, there was

that blind man, that old man sitting there at the table, waiting for somebody to feed him, with that immobility of blind people, like it was the backs of their eyeballs you looked at while they were hearing music you couldn't hear; that Goodwin led out of the room and completely off the earth, as far as I know. I never saw him again. I never knew who he was, who he was kin to. Maybe not to anybody. Maybe that old Frenchman that built the house a hundred years ago didn't want him either and just left him there when he died or moved away.

It is a casual but characterizing remark by the man who will think to himself later at a more stressful time of "all the nightmare shapes it had taken him forty-three years to invent."

Sanctuary introduces many such objective-subjective, doubly telling passages with an oblique added effect such as Faulkner is to employ increasingly and variously in later works. The practice is not unique in art, but he develops it to a high degree yet subtly, and an awareness of it can be a factor in the close and just appreciation not only of theme but of enabling style. Its veiled potency springs from a further freeing of the artist's (and the reader's) empathic imagination, a licensing to extend the intonations of a character's already revealed temperament into descriptions not directly attributed to his stream of consciousness yet consistent with its bent. Thus with it established in Benbow's awareness that this is Saturday, when country folk come to town, they are pictured in a paragraph which has no connection with him except that he "moved among them, swept here and there by the deliberate current." Even so, it is something of the artist's conveyed intuition of Benbow's sensibilities which supports the more than prosaic image:

Slow as sheep they moved, tranquil, impassable, filling the passages, contemplating the fretful hurrying of those in urban shirts and collars with the large, mild inscutability of cattle or of gods, functioning outside of time, having left time lying upon the slow and imponderable land green with corn and cotton in the yellow afternoon.

Here the artist is doing his work, supplying words for what is there, and the presence of such a character as Benbow validates this imaginative perception, even if he is not seen as sensing it with that particularity, but narratively is merely their foil, his melancholy to their placidity. In fiction such subtle subjective emanations deriving from a character's known nature, not attributed to him yet felt more strongly through his presence, can have an elementary analogy in some types of painting. A landscape can undergo alteration through the addition of a figure, whose mere presence can make the scene more lonely, novel, ominous, or refreshing, and this by the viewer's attribution of a probable human response, even from an anonymous being. In a fiction such effect is increased because the character exists in a time frame, surrounded by and creating event, and often of a particular identity, whose ongoing reactions even when not narrated can be imagined and so lend intensity to the presentation. From these grounds it might be put that objections to Faulkner's style at certain points would melt away if the reader became more intuitively aware not of the novelist but of his characters' subjective existence there and then in that situation.

In the skilfully modulated presentation of *Sanctuary* Horace Benbow is a major force and factor, yet far less than a "central intelligence" in the technical sense of that term. There is too much else of the story that he has too little or no part in, especially as it involves Temple and Gowan at Frenchman's Bend several days after his stopover there, and then Temple and Popeye there and in Memphis, before Benbow finds her at Miss Reba's bordello in his attempt to gather evidence that will clear Goodwin of the charge of murdering Tommy. But Benbow is the character the novel looks most closely into, as the disconcerted, disenchanted, and obsessed man who is nevertheless the protagonist of justice in a very naughty world. It is through Benbow's troubled consciousness that Faulkner reaches to some of the subtlest and strongest effects of an objectively-subjectively modulated narrative. Arrangement, proportionate economy, and highlighting in *Sanctuary* make it an early example of the peculiar Faulknerian dynamism felt in terms of immediacy and momentum, in which action is given its meaning by what it progressively means to the actor in his own endeavors and his witnessings. Yet this element need not, and in *Sanctuary* does not separate the personal and the societal; rather, their intrication is constantly a thematic determinant, as well as narrative matter and means. Above all, subjectively individualized characterization with its measured involvement in the overt narrative action, does not eclipse what is representatively human in the actors, and indeed may deepen the realization of it, even in this novel with such regionally and situationally isolated and variously deviating personae.

Unusual as they are, each is all too recognizable in his appetencies and foolish pursuits grown ruthless. Being sparsely sketched, they disclose the more recognizably an obsessiveness of one kind or another. Faulkner deviated only once from this pointed epitomizing, in the Chapter XXX flashback-epilogue on Popeye, a rather clumsy naturalistic, sociobiological documentation. From its meanderings the deeper realism of Popeye's case is rescued through its actual closure, with the puny, impotent, deadly man now imprisoned for a murder he had not committed, and reduced to inert, supine fatalism by life's latest irony at his expense, beyond which he has nothing but one meager conformity, his well-combed hair, in what proves a doubly vain concern about putting up an appearance on the scaffold. Perhaps Faulkner could not let Popeye stand there as a simply melodramatic figure, the evildoer so deviously brought to retribution, yet the artist had already given the episode a massively reverberant overtone in that Popeye's conviction and execution for what he did not do has had, through Temple's perjury, its more deeply ironic counterpart in Goodwin's condemnation and savage execution, for Popeye's murder of Tommy. Possibly without the tardily injected factor of heredity Popeye would have been left with more dramatic stature, as one of life's inscrutible products, like the opaque Flem Snopes, also impotent, or, to a degree, Temple Drake, also grossly lecherous. Faulkner is surest when he reserves the enigma of personality, pointing to conditioned motivation, as in Sutpen, but then probing its manifestations to their depths, as he does with Horace Benbow in *Sanctuary* to give him a certain primacy. Pure melodrama abounds in revelations, and exists to spring surprises, but these are "elementary" and instantly obvious, as with the turn of a card. Conversely, humanistic narration, because of complexities and irresolutions in the matter itself, is gradual in its disclosures and soberly reflective upon what is an admitted relativism, to which modulations of the narrative itself are accommodated, to permit conveyance through subjective processes.

Thus the overt violence that traces a bloody course through *Sanctuary* is fictionally rendered in understatement and largely by indirection, whereas Benbow's mental turmoil is represented as clearly as such can be, from his felt aversion to the crude superficial sexually predatory collegians, sensed during his mere presence on the train, to his despairing mood after hearing Temple's account of her misadventure (for though he is bringing back her promise to testify against Popeye in Goodwin's defense, that will allow only the law's retribution and a stay against further injustice, no remedy for evils done and still in progress):

> Better for her if she were dead tonight, Horace thought, walking on. For me, too. He thought of her, Popeye, the woman, the child, Goodwin, all put into a single chamber, bare, lethal, immediate and profound; a single blotting instant between the indignation and the surprise. And I too; thinking how that were the only solution. Removed, cauterized out of the old and tragic flank of the world. And I, too, now that we're all isolated; thinking of a gentle dark wind blowing in the long corridors of sleep; of lying beneath a low cozy roof under the long sound of rain: the evil, the injustice, the tears.

For such *Weltschmerz* in a character so subtle and strained as Benbow's, only such imagining would suffice; this passage credibly penetrates to the dark center of his mind's volatile complexity and recurrent despair. Deeply too in like manner there is to be found this being's most private anguish, from suppression of his barely acknowledged incestuous feelings toward his stepdaughter. That is approached in several passages echoing with his recurrent unrest. Chapter XIX had begun with Lee Goodwin's woman, now in Jefferson, telling Benbow in her own despairing way of Goodwin's involvement with Gowan and Temple as well as Popeye — "with those men there, living off of Lee's risk . . . and I had gone through it and gone through it and I'd tell Lee to let's get away. . . . And then she had to come out there, after I had slaved for him, slaved for him." For the while Benbow listens, not only intent on gathering evidence to clear Goodwin, but with the intuitive understanding that has developed between him and this woman beset even beyond the limits, almost, of her remarkable courage and endurance. But later when Benbow goes out to Narcissa's house, there follows an enigmatic passage reflecting a more privately overwrought mind through what seems perhaps an intentional obscurity of antecedents in references to Temple, Goodwin's woman, and Benbow's stepdaughter Little Belle.

He disgustedly tells Miss Jenny how Gowan Stevens had "carried a little fool girl out there and got drunk and ran off and left her," adding (concerning Goodwin's companion) "If it hadn't been for that woman — " and breaks off from this to denounce Gowan's "impunity," his shallow pretensions as a baccalaureate Virginia gentleman. Benbow's scorn extends to all Gowan's likes, the crudely lustful young college men "On any train . . . on the street, mind you." At this phrase Miss Jenny seems to know what may be at the back of Horace's mind, beneath all this Frenchman's Bend series of catastrophes; and perhaps she guesses rightly. Early in Chapter II, at Frenchman's Bend, the middle-aged runaway Benbow was babbling in his obsessed mood to the indifferent men about having tried to protest lightly to Little Belle for her taking up with a young man she met on the train ("Honey, if you found him on the train he probably belongs to the railroad company") and her retort, "He's as good as you are. He goes to Tulane"; and Benbow may have told the same thing to Narcissa and Miss Jenny in reporting his vagrant adventures. In any case, now Miss Jenny says, "I didn't understand at first who you meant." That at least she well understands Horace himself and has some intimation of his ambivalent interest in Little Belle is plain in her further remark: "What is it that makes a man think that the female flesh that he marries or begets might misbehave, but all he didn't marry or beget is bound to?" Apparently he senses her drift, for he answers "Yes, and thank God she isn't my flesh and blood. I can reconcile myself to her having to be exposed to a scoundrel now and then, but to think that at any moment she may become involved with a fool"—which, as to his ongoing concern, clearly refers to Little Belle.

Following this conversation Benbow returns to the unoccupied family house in Jefferson, where he stays while preparing his case in defense of Goodwin, simply "using a bed, one chair, a bureau on which he had spread a towel upon which lay his brushes, his watch, his pipe and tobacco pouch, and, propped against a book, a photograph of his step-daughter, Little Belle." As he looks at it, this rational yet imaginative man is racked by his susceptibilities; in his tortured mind's rising fancyings there is seen a deeper and more devastating eroticism than in all the animality at Miss Reba's bordello. He thinks of "the grape arbor in Kinston," and Little Belle there in the "summer twilight" with one or another of her young men,

and the murmur of voices darkening into silence as he approached, who meant them, her, no harm; who meant her less than harm, good God; darkening into the pale whisper of her white dress, of the delicate and urgent mammalian whisper of that curious small flesh which he had not begot and in which appeared to be vatted delicately some seething sympathy with the blossoming grape.

In his present ardent unrest Benbow moved, the photograph "shifted . . . from its precarious balancing against the book" (an epitomizing image in itself), and became differently highlighted, as if "seen beneath disturbed though clear water," at which he looked "with a kind of quiet horror and despair, at a face suddenly older in sin than he would ever be, a face more blurred than sweet, at eyes more secret than soft." Then with it put flat, "once more the face mused tenderly behind the rigid travesty of the painted mouth, contemplating something beyond his shoulder." After this glimpse into Benbow's private melancholy the narrative turns for a while to his public role, and he is seen arranging for lodging for Goodwin's woman and her sickly child (while Goodwin awaits trial in the jail) and then tracing Temple to Miss Reba's in Memphis where Popeye had installed her. It is after hearing Temple's story that he falls under the spell of cosmic despair, thinking them all better dead, blotted out; in this mood, returning by night train to Jefferson and to the empty Benbow family home, he sees it "dark, still, as though it were marooned in space by the ebb of all time," while "The moon stood overhead, but without light; the earth lay beneath, without darkness." Finding his way to his room and turning on the light, again he compulsively picks up Little Belle's picture; "the small face seemed to swoon" with "a soft and fading aftermath of invitation and voluptuous promise and secret affirmation like a scent itself." He stands at that hour alone in the ancestral dwelling as the anxiously striving champion of human rights and security for Goodwin and the woman and child, but also as self-hypnotized victim of a veiled but tolerated lust; and in both roles his despair is real, in a dissociation privately poised just this side of the sort of overt disaster a less rational man might already have precipitated himself into.

Such liability, especially in certain volatile natures, is a typical concept among Faulkner's characterizations. He treats of it intensely, yet not sensationally, but with grave concern, as over any threat to humane values and order, and with compassion for individuals. In Benbow at this point, with issue joined yet in suspense, the conflict of will and instinct reverses existence itself as to assimilation and realistic perception. Arrested between recently enlarged knowledge of his world's rampant, violent evils and of his private confusion that darkly combines pseudoparental concern and quasi-incestuous lust for Little Belle, he is invaded by an acute sickness of body and mind. Along with the nausea which suddenly overwhelms him there runs a many-dimensioned delirium in which the referents of "she" or "her" might be both Temple and Little Belle. In the bathroom with no time to turn on the light

Benbow "struck the lavatory and leaned upon his braced arms while the shucks set up a terrific uproar beneath her thighs," as if during Popeye's crude assault. There is the dark flow of blood, but then (in a railway image perhaps linked to Benbow's anxieties about Little Belle) "she was bound naked on her back on a flat car" that shot "from a black tunnel in a long upward slant," through a darkness "now shredded with parallel attenuations of living fire, toward a crescendo like a held breath," in which "Far beneath her she could hear the faint, furious uproar of the shucks." Benbow's nausea, in its ambivalent sexual context comprising both Temple and Little Belle, epitomizes impasse; the reflexive upward thrust of vomit seems a self-punishment in a denial of what has been fed on, yet is also a release, with orgasmic fantasy as of a fire-streaked sky. While this may owe something to Bloom at the beach, Benbow is not altogether such a caricature of ineffectuality; there is that in him which must strive for good and would have prevailed had it not been for Temple's perjury. Earlier despairs have bred this waking nightmare of his which explodes into parody of sexual excitation rising to a soiled autistic consummation beyond present sense of any reality but its own. The passage is a phantasmagoric consolidating of thematic material and characteizations through the distraught but event-oriented consciousness and conscience of an idiosyncratic Faulknerian protagonist *manqué*.

Here in one of the novel's several specializations Faulkner is encompassing substantial subject matter and grasping a mode of maximum conveyance. Benjy Compson had been a technical problem masterfully solved; the representation of Benbow was at another extreme of complexity, and a challenge brilliantly met. From his role in *Sartoris* Horace must have reentered Faulkner's mind trailing clouds of morbidity. As the bootleggers and the woman at Frenchman's Ben variously regard him, there is a streak of absurdity in this "professor" with a book in his pocket, this incomprehensively voluble runaway husband, whose objectively narrated return to Kinston in the novel's closures is a descent into an arrest, suggesting the inevitable confinement of a too-ardent spirit, as punishment for a mind that cannot heal its own divisions. It required from Faulkner a full representation of subjective states to comprise this characterization of one committed to strenuous engagement as public champion of the falsely accused Goodwin and his pitifully beset woman, with the defender himself reduced to chronic despair by more widely pervasive evils he could neither forestall nor subsequently remedy, besides which there is the private man, hypersensitive and volatile, incurably though reluctantly the accuser and indulger of himself.

While one aspect of Faulkner's advancing consolidation of fictional techniques in *Sanctuary* is the almost iridescently modulated fusion of Benbow's subjectivity into the narrative's overt motion, this has its counterparts in equally functional but different and even opposite techniques. In Faulkner's growing valuation of the subjective element and with his already proven skill at highly experimental levels in representing it, he knew the more clearly that there are limits beyond which even the artist's most empathic intuitions cannot proceed, nor is a uniform depth of penetration into every character consistent with sequential dramatic action or with the maintenance of controlled vision in a holistic fictional composition. The Bundrens' successive monologues, at their varieties of pitch, circle around Addie's dying and her burial; representation of Benjy's flickering awareness and responses depends in part upon the presence of others who answer to him in ways that penetrate somewhat the darkness in which he moves; the mind of Popeye remains screened behind his manner and his laconic, personally uncommunicative speech, from which only the most elementary suppositions can be drawn. This, however, does not minimize him as a player in the drama; though characterization of him is only two-dimensional, his is the force behind the story's major catastrophes, and perhaps in his opacity he does not so much personify as epitomize evil. Abstractly it becomes the story's grimmest irony that this shadowy and evasive figure could radiate so much destructive influence, and in this light it was well for the novelist to further reduce Popeye from a probable source in a more impressive actual figure (the notoriously wily Memphis gangster Popeye Pumphrey, "a handsome man never seen with girls . . . the granson of an Arkansas attorney general"). Conversely it was ill-advised to attempt a sociological emendation through a loosely sketched case history as Popeye's part in *Sanctuary* approaches its closure. It seems superogatory, and a clumsy digression after the fact of his consistent role already but played out, and about to move effectively toward that abrupt end, the sheriff's answering Popeye's gallows request to "fix my hair" by springing the trap. But this most specific closure and the two immediately preceding chapters quite redeem the narrative from that discursion and set Popeye as character in true situational perspective.

CHARACTERIZATION AND CONSOLIDATION

Between those extremes of humankind, Benbow and Popeye, whose courses strangely crossed in their separate unease and frustrations, *Sanctuary* deploys a large variety of characters through regional scenes which by adjacency emphasize stratifications in Southern white society following World War I; there is as well the more widely presentational factor of individual uniqueness, focused upon with apportioned emphases and distancings. Popeye seen and heard is an almost robot-like representation of inscrutable evil; Horace Benbow, as one of Faulkner's most complex protagonists, pervades the novel with his highly charged subjectivity in those portions where he is either in half-hearted flight from his ambivalent private life or where he is strenuously endeavoring to save Goodwin and meanwhile to aid the jailed man's woman, but in both phases of his existence he moves under the shadow of profoundly pessimistic intimations, to which even his sardonic wit is made to testify. Temple, figuring centrally in the plot as victim of one outrageous offense and perpetrator of another, is to be subjectively known chiefly in her sensations and her frantic imaginings during crises; Goodwin's woman is directly though less extendedly presented as she supplies information to Benbow, but shining through her laconic yet always candid telling there is impressive revelation of a life and a credible personality, capable of fidelity, an integrated and enduring self. Faulkner's intiguing presentation of this woman, evoking empathic response, can show that Benbow's efforts in behalf of her and Goodwin are more than quixotic in attempting, against odds but rationally, to save Goodwin from a false charge, and to give them both some chance on a safer and smoother course. Nevertheless in their presence Benbow senses the shadow of evil more closely, for Goodwin though not a coward realistically fears reprisal if he were merely to reveal that Popeye was ever at Frenchman's Bend, and refuses to do so, leaving Benbow's case dependent upon Temple's promise to testify, which she does, but falsely, being perhaps herself intimidated, or drugged, or moved by one more incalculable impulse out of her naturally undisciplined and now disoriented existence — a "spoiled" person, barely pitiable and morally repulsive, who walks in the obscurity of those who have not learned to take and give account of themselves.

Though State Senator Clarence Snopes pops up in the story again and again (being about his nefarious business of peddling to both sides the word that Temple is hidden away in Miss Reba's Memphis bordello) he is given a totally objective fictional presentation, but a quite sufficient one, since out of his own inept palaver as well as the pettiness of his offenses he stands exposed. The detail of that portraiture suggests an accumulated bulk and weight of the matter of Snopes upon Faulkner's imagination, pressing toward its first full release in *The Hamlet*. Yet already the tribe's representative in *Sanctuary* has epitomized aspects of what is to come; the two-dimensional figure fixes the judgment that nothing is to be learned in sounding the depths of obviously shallow water, however muddy, and the tone of grotesquerie as to Clarence prefigures a general view among their fellow citizens that Snopeses are not explicable under normal societal assumptions, and are to be taken seriously as threats to the social order, human beings without normal awareness of that nexus. The wordly and sentimental Miss Reba is fully objectified too, but humanly more real, and much of what is in her mind spills out through her conversational fluency, while her labors in her calling, though professionally prudent, have nothing about them of Popeye's reflexive cruelty or Clarence Snopes's low craftiness. In fact, Miss Reba's assistance in Benbow's interview with Temple, as well as her benevolences to certain unfortunately circumstanced children, shows her as more humane than Jefferson's Christian ladies who hound Goodwin's woman out of the hotel where Benbow had placed her and her sickly child after their flight from Frenchman's Bend and Goodwin's imprisonment. Within the same geographical region but in a quite different world from Miss Reba's and that of Goodwin's woman is Miss Jenny, a striking matriarch emerita, resident at the Sartoris home with Narcissa. Miss Jenny rests her frequent interpositions upon sharply humorous irony, of which both Horace and Narcissa, as well as Gowan Stevens in a passing aspect as Narcissa's beau, are objects; but she understands Horace well enough to recognize the core of principle in his superficially erratic life, and gives it to him as her opinion that "you'll work harder for whatever reason you think you have, than for anything anybody could offer you or give you."

In *Sanctuary* Faulkner developed, to a degree almost comparable with his best later work, the skills of transition and apportionment involved in a fluent manipulation of an actual chronological order, as these imposed fictional patternings can be related to structure, tone, and characterization. Obviously one practical reason for the disconnecting and rearrangement of sequential units is the need to marshall most effectively events that are concurrent or overlapping but diverse. Modern fictionists, no longer openly presiding over the story as master of its ceremonies, have also refined communication beyond the use of annunciatory guideposts to what had been happening "meanwhile" elsewhere; and readers have learned to pick up *au vol* the discreetly unobtrusive coordinates of a new situation or, more often, to go on with a character returned to. As with the basic usage of beginning well along in the midst of things, curiosity and suspense can be excited to some degree by ingenious realigning of episodes, but this practice can serve more important effects, too. These have to do with expedited progressive penetration of the matter, not only logically (thus resembling history, where coincidence requires a great deal of chronological sorting out) but dramatically, for the reader's guided realization of the work's thematic and tonal organicism, and by entry into the psychological aspect of situations, for a maximizing of characterization. This last operates at every level from completely objective presentation to a recurrently predominating subjectivity, as with so central a person as Benbow. Moreover, the fictional segmenting and repatterning of chronology is complemented by modulations in narrative pace and proportioning of episodes, together with progressive reinforcements and extensions of insights into personalities. With Faulkner, all characterization at whatever level is cumulatively relative to situation. Even at the most acute extremes of his self-confrontations Benbow in *Sanctuary* exists as of that novel, as do all the other characters, in their various emergences and degrees of prominence. Fusion of plot and character at high levels of effect and significance is advanced remarkably in this ambitiously revised composition.

In more than one sense the authentic date for *Sanctuary* is 1931; what is marked is the release into publication of a work Faulkner had evolved by transforming the galleys of an earlier draft into a creation of a quite different and higher order. As such it constitutes a further chapter (beyond *The Sound and the Fury* and *As I Lay Dying*) in that impalpable but imaginable *biographié interieur,* the ongoing life of the artist as creative maker. Twenty years ago Mr. Linton Massey in his pioneering "Notes on the Unrevised Galleys of *Sanctuary,*" pointed out in that Ur-version a "dichotomy of purpose," as between a psychological study of Horace Benbow and the story of Temple Drake's misadventures and corruption. A comparable bifurcation may be seen imposing its strain upon that only recently published curiosity tokening a prolific realistic regionalism, *Flags in the Dust*. Its diffuseness came of an attempt to intermingle closely two family stories, along with teeming lesser materials, and this was expediently remedied by drastic editorial excision not only of subordinate and conspicuously superfluous matter but by reduction of the Benbow family factor in favor of the Sartorises, making publishable the 1929 novel bearing as almost heraldic title that family name. Conversely in *Sanctuary* the remedy Faulkner privately achieved was a new synthesis, a step forward into a more selective inclusiveness and strategic ordering of the matter of the galleys. The relative success of his attempt (even though on its much larger scale it could not achieve the remarkable integration of *As I Lay Dying*) may have given some assurance to the artist in his next essaying the massive construct of *Light in August,* and in his bringing it off uniquely as of itself in a concerted exercise of his multiple powers with relation to major regional themes.

What Faulkner did to rescue and project *Sanctuary* forecast what was to come, for instance as to design in the measured use of episode, which can give proportionate accent and predominance to characters situationally, and thus contain their interrelation in a unified dramatic action. Both the galleys and the reconstituted novel, for example, begin with Horace Benbow, but at different points within the story's total chronology. In the galleys it was far advanced, to the point just before Goodwin's trial on the false charge that he had shot Tommy, and Benbow as Goodwin's defense lawyer is depending upon Temple Drake to testify truly that the murderer was Popeye. The recreated novel is made to open before any of the tragic events set going when Gowan brought Temple to Frenchman's Bend, got drunk again, and abandoned her there. This not only means that the first impressions of Frenchman's Bend and the persons there can be conveyed through the wandering Benbow's hyperacute sensibilities, but it discloses him before he has got himself involved as Goodwin's lawyer and had sought out Temple as defense witness, tracing her to Miss Reba's Memphis brothel, where Popeye was detaining her both for his protection and to serve his perverted lust. Under this chronological rearrangement the inclusion of Horace Benbow's story and Temple's is no longer the dichotomy Mr. Linton Massey discerned in the galleys' version, but is an engaging fictional intrication. The crucial difference is that Horace is established at once as of his own chronically restless troubled self, before a point in the narrative where his distraction might seem incidental only to the anxieties of a defense lawyer with but one witness, possibly undependable. The revised novel's first two chapters show him briefly fugitive from his wife Belle at their home in Kinston and in a more enigmatic flight from Little Belle. There are real and significant ambivalences in Horace, and they are to be seen rising to the surface in his compulsive pseudoincestuous musings about this stepdaughter, as he drunkenly confesses them to an odd audience of strangers, the men at Frenchman's Bend. This then is Horace Benbow, under the dominance of contradictory traits. Only later do his repressions become his most intense private realizations, after his encounter in the unsavory atmosphere of the brothel with Temple, the raped virgin now besotted over Popeye's henchman Red (for whom she will likewise be a fatality) — all of which is later to bring upon Horace an acute attack of sexual nausea, further intensified by hallucinatory fantasies.

Not for its own introverted sake did Faulkner seek expression of his players' consciousness, such as in Horace Benbow; it was for characterization, and this in situational contexts. He evidently accepted as a first principle that fiction can make serious claim upon recognition and intuitive, empathic responses only by conveying what James had classically defined as a felt sense of life. Yet "life" is quite a bundle, a double handful and more, and so in the strategies of literary art a primary principle is selectivity, by delimitations to arrive at a certain concrete subject matter amenable to containment in a conceptual point of view and its presentational conveyance, while conversely the force of a "felt sense of life" will still depend upon a typicality of content according to the artist's more than incidental experience, evaluation, and concern. In this complex of factors is to be found the essential veracity and logic of a hmanistically realistic fiction. A comprehensive mastery in this can indicate honest commitment and be the measure of achievement in an approach to pure fictional art, and it differentiates at least as to zones between such animated imaginative endeavors and the expedient peddling of stereotyped fictional or dramatic entertainment.

In *Flags in the Dust* Faulkner had wrestled not entirely successfully to coordinate such factors, abstract and particular, within a unitary work of fictional art, to arrest incident as of great moment in its context, and to make unique gesture yield up representativeness. The intervenient attempt thereafter to amend the matter, delivering *Sartoris* largely by the amputation of parts, has left some critical doubts. Following these difficulties, Faulkner's two conspicuous experiments in techniques of conveying the subjective as a vital narrative thread may have had a reactive element of caution, too, in a closer restriction of narrative matter and action and of thematic scope. But with *Sanctuary,* as he was prompted to recast and revise it in the light of more comprehensive visions and an increasing facility and assurance in his craft, he began a consolidation of means and ends which was to be the bedrock under his major achievements.

The narrative (except for the meandering sociological postmortem on Popeye that begins the closing chapter) is economical and expeditious. The harshest events are subdued by indirection, as with the unvisualized, almost soundless shooting of Tommy; and the gruesome specifics of Popeye's attack upon Temple (Faulkner's *donnée* in this narrative) are made plain only later at the trial by an exhibit, and are mentioned thereafter by transient "drummers" in incidental conversations which are made to satirize the speakers' crudeness. Rearrangement of chronological blocks skilfully supports the story's diverse episodes as they impinge thematically from such incongruous points as Frenchman's Bend, the house of Narcissa Benbow Sartoris, Miss Reba's in Memphis, and Horace Benbow's domicile in Kinston; also the Jefferson jail and courtroom, a jail and a scaffold in Alabama, and the Luxembourg Gardens. Scenes are often brief, but of whatever length their dialogue is sharply pointed; they epitomize an element, large or small, in the conceptual structure yet with utmost immediacy and liveliness. Conducted thus, scenes become one aspect of Faulkner's pervasively felt capacity for interfusing the concrete and the abstract, and thus to unite a present motion with the momentum which maintains the work as a whole. This is simply yet centrally the desired mode in fiction, but Faulkner's genius in it, to be clearly sensed in *Sanctuary,* is to make his next two works, *Light in August* and *Absalom, Absalom!,* among the most highly charged in modern fiction. In reading this artist, page by page under its maintained light, there may be sensed the unceasing whisper as of a dynamo and the faint vibrations from its barely contained force.

Sanctuary is not as nearly a perfected work as were Faulkner's two immediately preceding works, *The Sound and the Fury* and *As I Lay Dying,* yet in the main it is a consolidation as of its time in his career, by its reach beyond the scope of those two family novels, and in its adjudication of the ascendancy of certain subjective elements within a broadly staged story and its multiplicity of variously attuned objective elements. Its chief lapses, whether in some brief stylistic excesses or in the thematically superfluous and narratively stumbling interjection of Popeye's naturalistic case history, perhaps stem from a not yet wholly acquired command over the grotesque, of which Faulkner is to make such dynamic but controlled use in most of his major works. As for Popeye, from the first and quite sufficiently there is to be felt the ulitmate irony that a creature so puny and insecure could exercise such fatal control in his compensatory ruthlessness, which epitomizes evil as a sickness—one that can also have less obvious but possibly as virulent forms, such as chronic irresponsibility in the puerile, pretentious Gowan Stevens and the self-indulgent Temple Drake. Yet beyond these all of *Sanctuary* has its paradoxically lurid brilliance, in that something of Horace Benbow's eccentric intensity and soiled integrity, established from its beginnings, permeates the novel as recalled echo of his insistent protests and strivings.

Except as to an overheard story of a peculiarly horrible rape, together with some acquired knowledge of Memphis gangsterism and prostitution, the artist's impetus in *Sanctuary* is not precisely identifiable; however, his inspiration was served further by what he had already evoked in *Flags in the Dust* of Horace and Narcissa Benbow Sartoris and of the genus Snopes. On this question of sequentially derived matter Faulkner's proportionately related emphasis and economy in *Sanctuary* are notable. One character, the state senator Clarence, suffices to detail Snopesism in its full flower of pernicious activity which (by circumstantial implication) is this time given its comeuppance. Narcissa Benbow Sartoris is shown in her aloof widowhood, caring for her young son, preserving the household's amenities and chiding her brother Horace for his socially untidy life; but while these two may rouse more extensive memories of them in *Sartoris* and as of earlier sources in *Flags in the Dust,* their roles in *Sanctuary* do not depend upon this antecedent material, and to that end the treatment of Narcissa is almost sparsely economical, yet of a measured sufficiency and pointed relevance within this novel's autonomy. There is also a more central and significant economy, in Faulkner's judicious adaptation of what he had learned from writing *The Sound and the Fury* and *As I Lay Dying* about representation of a character's subjectivity. For Temple this is closely contained in her sensation-bound mentality, and her awareness of surroundings and immediate event is more serviceable to narrative itself than revelatory of any deeper tides in her nature. Horace Benbow's more sophisticated, scrupulous, and variously tinged processes of consciousness are conveyed in modulations through his bizarre but anxiously concerned behavior and talk, his tensed private

responses to whatever falls within his quick awareness, and at
moments his absorption by intimations of predicament, his
own and that of others, and of mankind.

Considering the complexity of Benbow's nature, his grotesque and unamenable domestic situation with its undertone
of suppressed incestuous desire, his idealistic and sympathetic
compulsion to take issue on broader socioethical grounds, and
the multiform evils he confronts and consequent defeats he
suffers, the artist's combined penetrativeness and measured
economies in treating of him achieved a particular new
mastery. In *Sanctuary* Faulkner employs Benbow's insights
and sensibility as key and containment; lacking sufficient
recognition of this factor, the novel may be recalled flatly in its
most obtrusive overt events, and too largely in terms of
Temple and Popeye, Frenchman's Bend and Miss Reba's, in a
world where Clarence Snopes walks to and fro in merely grotesque guise, and violence is only a natural misunderstanding,
with fatalities scarcely more than mishaps. Conversely the
novel has so much not only of evil but of a general callous
indifference to it that a reagent was required to detect and
protest such human waywardness and indiscrimination and set
existence in a possibly humane perspective. This becomes
Horace Benbow's role, though acceptance of its obligations
cannot be the whole of his life; his sensibilities are not entirely
engaged by the emergence of dire socioethical issues, he being
(not altogether privately), so troubled in his personal life. Pure
genius led Faulkner to open *Sanctuary* at the point where the
distraught Benbow, after several days of questing "for a hill to
lie on for a while," stoops to drink at a spring in the woods and
finds himself being watched by the perceptibly ominous
Popeye, who takes him into precautionary charge and brings
him (whether only as prisoner or also as a curiosity, a man
with a book) to the Gothic and sordid *ménage* at Frenchman's
Bend.

Both plot and characterization, together with emerging
theme, are served here. While Benbow is to be sent off to Jefferson that same evening on Popeye's Memphis-bound boot-

legger's truck, within a few days he is to be involved again with these people — as lawyer for Goodwin jailed on a murder charge (prompting Benbow to seek out Temple at Miss Reba's in Memphis for a promise to testify it was Popeye who had killed Tommy), and Benbow is meanwhile the protector of Goodwin's woman as she waits in Jefferson with her sickly child. None of this is forecast, however, in the two chapters that open *Sanctuary,* nor has Benbow yet asserted to the disapproving Narcissa that he must involve himself and "cannot stand idly by and see injustice — ." Instead, in those few hours at Frenchman's Bend Horace appears and is lengthily heard at his most disconcerted, under his half-hidden personal stresses now poured out to these strangers. His desire for "a hill to lie on for a while" is not merely for relief from the flat Delta country around Kinston, where he lives with his wife Belle and his stepdaughter Little Belle; it is for respite from the flatness of that marriage. However, while an ardent symbolist might discover the implication of a particular *mons,* Horace's repressed semi-incestuous desire for his stepdaughter is to be most pointedly understood in his characteristic romanticizing of it, through the image of the blossoming grape arbor with Little Belle in the hammock there in the dusk. Nor is this extravagance the artist's, and Horace is made to pay for his equivocal fancies with a violent attack of sex nausea, after his interview with Temple more directly forced harsher realities upon him.

When Horace Benbow's sensibilities turn outward, however, what shows is his principled strength, even against odds, and though under the never entirely dissipated cloud of his melancholy. The interview with Temple had been in strenuous quest for evidence to clear Goodwin of the false murder charge; his compassion for Goodwin's woman was manifested not only after she and Goodwin fall into dire trouble, but from the first at Frenchman's Bend. She is a minor figure whose case after Goodwin is lynched calls for and receives no closure except the plain implication that what is to come will be much like what had gone before. At which, with his skilled

selectivity, the artist leaves it. Yet he has developed her character in some depth, particularly in her nuances of feeling
beneath her matter-of-fact stoicism, and this is done not
descriptively or analytically but in a narrative context of
encounters and exchanges which also reveal Benbow's positive
traits of compassion and beneficence. At Frenchman's Bend
the woman's surroundings are sordid, her life is unremittingly
hard. She keeps her sickly baby in a box to protect it from rats,
she must carry water from a mile away several times daily, and
serve as cook and caretaker for Goodwin and the others, who
include a totally blind and deaf old man and the full-grown
but mentally simple Tommy, as well as those engaged in illicit
distilling and transporting the liquor for Popeye's Memphis
enterprise. Popeye, with his automatic in his pocket, tyran-
nizes over the whole operation, and it is through his sadistic
verbal abuse of the woman (taunting her for being reduced to
wearing Goodwin's old army shoes) that the narrative identifies her as Ruby Lamar, formerly a Memphis prostitute. But
merely through Benbow's being brought to the house and then
in some tentative reactions between them, much more is
shown of her.

As she overhears this vagrant's rambling account of his
private griefs to the scarcely comprehending men sitting
drinking on that porch, first she states to herself a basic female
verdict: "That fool. . . . He better get on to where he's going,
where his women folks can take care of him." In his going on
about Little Belle, he declares "That's why nature is 'she' and
Progress is 'he'; nature made the grape arbor, but Progress
invented the mirror," and the listening woman says, "He's
crazy," but then, "The fool. The poor fool," and as she sees
him in silhouette coming toward the door—"a thin man in
shapeless clothes; a head of thinning and ill-kempt hair; and
quite drunk"—her feeling is that "They dont make him eat
right." As the two confront each other, he immediately enters
into her situation as she already has into his; he asks if she likes
"living like this" and suggests that being "young yet," she
could "better" herself in the city. She replies as to herself, yet

not of herself but him, somewhat aloof but almost maternally toward this older person: "'The poor, scared fool,' she said." He confesses he lacks courage — "The machinery is all here, but it won't run" — and having admitted his own demoralizing disenchantment, he fumblingly touches her cheek and repeats that she is "young yet" with "practically" her "whole life" before her. Still she doesn't answer for herself, but out of what she had overheard him tell the men she asks why he had left his wife. He tries to explain his reluctance to get the box of shrimp from the train and carry it home as he had done every Friday "for ten years, since we were married." In that uneasy marriage as a woman's second husband, he has obsessively fixed upon a detail, and he speaks not so much of the box of shrimp itself as its constant dripping and his almost schizophrenic fantasy of watching and following himself, and thinking, "Here lies Horace Benbow in a fading series of small stinking spots on a Mississippi sidewalk." Her reply is a monosyllable, but its mood and possible intonation may be apprehended from the spare context:

"Oh," the woman said. She breathed quietly, her arms folded. She moved; he gave back and followed her down the hall. They entered the kitchen where a lamp burned. "You'll have to excuse the way I look," the woman said.

She shows him her baby sleeping in the box; then Goodwin enters, to say Tommy will take Benbow to the bootleggers' truck, which will drop him off in Jefferson. Benbow thanks the woman "for the supper" and goes on hesitantly: "Some day, maybe. . . . Maybe I can do something for you in Jefferson. Send you something you need. . . ." She flicks her hands from a fold in her dress, hides them again, and says, "With all this dishwater and washing. . . . You might send me an orange stick." By his compassion, in suggesting more hope for another than he can hold for himself, the "poor, scared fool" has drawn this beset woman somewhat out of her enforced hardness, and if not into a seizing of the whole of a new life, at least as far as a womanly wish to give some care to her hands. He has given her a change of mood, in a respite from fatalism.

Then several days after this passing encounter, Benbow is fully involved, not just in Goodwin's defense against the false charge of having shot the harmless, pitifully innocent Tommy, but as the woman's protector against Jefferson's Christian ladies who have had her with her baby expelled from the hotel where Benbow had made arrangements for her. When all his efforts and the woman's faint hopes are brought to nothing by Temple's perjury, in violation of her promise to identify Popeye as Tommy's killer, there is a last glimpse of Goodwin's woman in the courtroom, where she with her child had been sitting beside her man at the table with his lawyer Benbow. The infant (perhaps disturbed by the murmur passing through the room at the trial's climax) "made a fretful sound, whimpering," the woman said "Hush. Shhhhhhh," and with that controlled motherly utterance in this moment of tragic defeat she disappears from the novel. It is one of Faulkner's nice economies in this closely controlled narrative, where elision often stirs echoes of latent implication; here hers is as of an already roughened hand raised above a stream that will drag her deeper. The story had brought her fully to life, in her fatalism that nevertheless had not broken her nor robbed her of sensitivity, but she is clearly fated, one of the lowly whose unfortunate life has had nothing to teach her except the folly of hope or belief. It had been epitomized before the trial when Benbow, after all he tried to do for Goodwin and for her, discovered she had been thinking she must pay the legal fees by offering her body; he is naturally appalled by what it shows of how uniformly harsh had been her knowledge of men, and her distance from any experience of another human being's disinterested compassion. Thereafter for Benbow himself, roused during the night following the trial by tumult in the Jefferson streets, comes the most brutal shock, Goodwin's immolation by the mob, which Horace does not witness except in the superfluous unabated flame, seeming to "live upon itself," imaging the fierce persistence of evil.

Hence the brevity and relatively flat objectivity of the following Chapter XXX, omnisciently framed and telling of

Horace Benbow's return, defeated and drained, to his house in Kinston, where he finds the nonmarriage resumed, his wife Belle having come back too. Now she repeatedly instructs him to lock the back door, since Little Belle, off at a house party, will not be coming in later from the hammock in the grape arbor. Perhaps in this chapter's terse and stark finality, fittingly objectifying Horace immured in an unamenable situation, Faulkner subconsciously relaxed his hold upon the novel, and so went on into the next and final chapter with a more permissive tentativeness that produced the loosely inclusive omniscient account of Popeye's antecedents and early life—from which lapse into an inconsistent determinism the artist rallied for the two effective closures, through Popeye's mistaken imprisonment and execution for murder in Alabama, to Temple seated in the Luxembourg Gardens with her father, both immobilized, and her face "sullen and discontended and sad." But these finalities, though contributive, run beyond Mississippi and out of Benbow's ken. So doing, however, they suggest that while the determining roles in the central action of *Sanctuary* are Temple's and Popeye's, Benbow has been the key figure, conveying the dominant theme.

From the novel's very beginning at Frenchman's Bend (with the vagrant equivocally taken in by Popeye, fed, listened to by the men, and overheard by Goodwin's woman so that those two can at once speak knowingly to each other before he is sent off to Jefferson on the liquor truck) Benbow is disclosed in all his pessimism, sensibility, and compassion, his private life a shambles, his stance toward the world both confessional and assertive, by nature an ironic aloof man yet capable of deep principled commitment. Though a shabby protagonist, he is quite other than a nonhero; in much of the story he is a humanistic central intelligence, and as a defining conscience he pervades the whole story, not only through his entering into Goodwin's precarious situation, and the consequent seeking out and interviewing of Temple at Miss Reba's, but by openly fending off his sister Narcissa's objections to what she deems not only quixotic in him but *déclassé,* and what the good Christian ladies of Jefferson consider disgraceful. In his endeavors he has touched upon circumstance at many points and levels, and in this event-crowded story it is his responses, both overt and subjective, which supply the measure. In the end he effects nothing except his own desperate flight from Kinston and his dejected return; beyond that, his attempts to reverse the course of material events in a freeing and saving of Goodwin are doomed to fail, under the succession of evils in which the last links are Temple's perjury and the mob's sadistic violence. Benbow had seen Popeye plain though briefly, and could estimate any trace of that ruthless creature he uncovered thereafter; what it came to with Temple and as to the mob he knew of more directly. The weighty knowledge of good and evil, humanly assayed, can be a doom, remaining poised in memory and conscience, and so it seems to have been with Faulkner as responsible realist and regionalist, profoundly committed to the art of fiction. In recasting *Sanctuary,* was the artist also steeling himself against any such impasse as Horace Benbow's, an arrestment in a chronic disconcertion stemming from irremediable instances of evil, which by casting gigantic monstrous shadows as abstracts of themselves may seem to eclipse the very light that discloses and defines them?

Certainly every sort of consideration, from fine details of narrative techniques and subtle matters of aesthetic effects to the broadest conceptual bases of his works, must have extended into the experimentation and further tempering the artist imposed upon his practice and himself in it before he would let *Sanctuary* go forth a second time. A most notable though simple aspect is an unusual economy of narration, accelerating an already eventful action. Sometimes this is little more than the common quality of good expedite storytelling, but Faulkner can make it even more compressed and of intense effect by eliding what soon enough becomes plain. Thus with narration obviously approaching a further point, passage into that is omitted, yet with no mark except sometimes a new paragraph. For instance, at Frenchman's Bend, when Goodwin's woman (who has served him his supper with the others) sees him in the dusk, "a thin man . . . quite drunk," approaching the door where she has been listening to his overwrought talk, she seems to continue her earlier thought that he needed the care of "his women folks," for now she tells herself "They dont make him eat right." Then the next words, in a new paragraph, take a minute leap ahead in time and space; he is now inside the house, and she is "motionless, leaning lightly against the wall, he facing her." A naturalistic regionalist, to reinforce the story's setting, might have mentioned Benbow's crossing that worn-down threshold into this decayed old house; symbolism (if, as reports allege, such can enter with pervasive dominance into the nature of fiction) might have seized the image for its more esoteric purpose; and a matter-of-fact storyteller would simply have seen to it that the reader got smoothly from there to here. Faulkner expected readers to take that little move forward with him, and merited that collaboration by making such minimizing of the merely transitional create the momentum for a striking passage in which it is as if these motionless strangers through their intently direct exchange of words both grapple and embrace and also make way for two further pages, fuller but still remarkably concentrated, in a culmination of episode. The passage merits particular review for its emergent virtuosity. Their immediate frankness (he asking, "Do you like living like this?" and she musing aloud over "The poor scared fool") would be harsh if a reciprocal compassion were not apparent. This continues in his urging her to "better yourself" and in her asking why he had left his wife. When he details his carrying home the dripping box of shrimp every Friday and confesses a distraction that finds its symbol in the trail of spots on the sidewalk, her "Oh" that is eloquent of pity is only a final step into awareness of a kindly rapport that leads her to ask to be excused for "the way I look." Here is seen one of Faulkner's acquired strengths that will increase, the blending of technical skill into conveyance of his humane vision, in a scene that plays itself absorbingly because its brevities resound with overtones of consciousness in situated beings.

Such weighted economy makes for a momentum which intensifies the aesthetic experience, and not just as to tempo but in a sostenuto, a maintained continuum, suggestive of the characters' incessant processes of consciousness. Yet like other technical factors in Faulkner, momentum is not uniform but fluctuant, also with correspondence to music, in narrative modulations which serve variety of tone and apportion a substantive emphasis through adapted modes of presentation. As in other matters, economy in fictional narration (if not made immoderately an end in itself) will allow preferential expenditure, in comparatively deliberate passages, often substantiating even minor points of reference which broaden the work's total scope and may extend the web of thematic design. One instance in *Sanctuary* is the place and treatment given the character Tommy, who figures in the novel's early chapters, in the Benbow and then the Temple episodes at Frenchman's Bend. A hanger-on, Tommy is full-grown but simple-minded, with a natural doglike amiability and a capacity for amused wonder and guffaws, especially over Popeye, yet with traces of a mind of his own even in his necessitous subservience to others. He considerately leads Benbow along the mile of rutted, leaf-choked road out to the bootlegger's truck for his ride to Jefferson. Tommy in expatiating on Popeye as "The skeeriest durn *white* man I ever see" shows an innocent's lack of apprehension of the sinister, or else may be nervously laughing it off, but he sensibly explains Goodwin's advantage in selling his illicit liquor by the truckload: "It's in making a run and getting shut of it quick, where the money is." At the truck Benbow extends his hand, saying, "Goodbye. And much obliged, Mister—," to which the other says, "My name's Tawmmy."

Tommy's involvement with events then becomes more complex after Gowan Stevens, continuing his carouse, brings Temple to Frenchman's Bend, gets drunk again, is bested in a fight, and abandons her there. When she turns away from the supper table frightened by the truck driver's attempt to pull her onto his lap, Tommy follows her with a plate of food and tells her to "set down hyer and eat a little bite wher wont nobody bother you," but she runs around to the kitchen for refuge with Goodwin's woman, while Tommy continues his muttering: "Durn them fellers. . . . They ought to quit pesterin her." Yet in the presence of this scantily clad girl and others' open lust for her, Tommy has felt stirrings he can't define, and in Chapter XIII, when he comes upon her hiding in the barn, terrified by the rats and more so by these rough men, there follows a laconic exchange, enigmatic beyond words, as such personal encounters can be. Tommy tells her that "Lee says hit wont hurt you none. All you got to do is lay down," and clumsily touches her thigh. That Goodwin would make Tommy, or anyone else, his envoy in such a matter is not credible; he too has an eye for this girl, especially after Gowan has left her there, and has slapped his woman in a quarrel about Temple, but thus far has made no move, except to dominate the other men and keep order within the house. Popeye lurks on the edges of the scenes, fearful of how a drunken brawl might expose his illicit liquor operation, but with his mind on the girl too, and Tommy's genuine sympathy inclines him to defend her most of all from this threat. But Tommy is a grown man, perhaps thirty, he thinks, and having been at Frenchman's Bend at least four years, not only has heard much lewd talk about women, as from the truck drivers, but has felt "surges go over him, like his blood was too hot all of a sudden, dying away into that warm, unhappy feeling that fiddle music gave him"; now he may be struggling to link this dim awareness with words he could have heard Lee Goodwin say. And when he repeats them to Temple while she feels "his diffident, hard hand on her hip," she answers, "Yes, all right. Dont you let him in here," and there follows this curiously antiphonal dialogue:

"You mean fer me not to let none of them in hyer?"
"All right. I'm not scared of rats. You stay there and dont let him in."
"All right. I'll fix hit so caint nobody git to you. I'll be right hyer."

"All right. Shut the door. Dont let him in here."

"All right." He shut the door. She leaned in it, looking toward the house. He pushed her back so he could close the door. "Hit aint goin to hurt you none, Lee says. All you got to do is lay down."

"All right. I will. Dont you let him in here." The door closed. She heard him drive the hasp to. Then he shook the door.

"Hit's fastened," he said. "Caint nobody git to you know. I'll be right hyer."

Their repetitions become something like a stutter induced by complex tensions at an uncertain verge of action. Intent as Lee Goodwin himself may be, those reported words of his, scarcely credible as an intended message, could have been an indifferent conversational minimizing of taken-for-granted facts of life, in a dismissal of any mere girlish squeamishness about them. Whatever Temple may have made of it, her saying "All right. I will" seems a choice, a consent not to Goodwin but to Tommy's hesitant advances. She knows from his manner and his attempted kindness that he is not ruthless but gentle, and perhaps from her experiences with collegians and town boys she may believe she can handle the ignorant, inept Tommy, to appease him while sparing herself and keeping him as her protector. But the story does not tell, for neither of them is to have time enough. Popeye has been in the barn loft; he comes down, shakes the fastened door to the corn crib, and demands that it be opened. He puts his hand on Tommy's face, shoves him back, looks up at the house, and then at Tommy, asking, "Didn't I tell you about following me?" Tommy says he wasn't following, he was "watching him," presumably Goodwin at the house.

"Watch him, then," Popeye said. Tommy turned his head and looked toward the house and Popeye drew his hand from his coat pocket.

To Temple, sitting in the cottonseed-hulls and the corncobs, the sound was no louder than the striking of a match, a short minor sound shutting down upon the scene. . . ."

At this crucial point Faulkner's narrative mode is modulated into economical implicativeness; only Temple and God are witnesses to Tommy's fall, and readers do not share even her sight of it. Then the rape which immediately follows is not described but indirectly conveyed as effect, by Temple's hysterical useless cries to the blind and deaf old man to be seen sitting on the porch of the house in the sunshine: "Something is going to happen to me . . . is happening to me . . . I told you it was . . . I told you! I told you all the time!" How the impotent Popeye has performed the act is not mentioned, nor is it clearly implied until much later in the novel, at the trial of Goodwin, falsely charged with both Tommy's murder and the rape.

Then in the two-page Chapter XIV (immediately following those outcries of the assaulted Temple) narrative economy becomes even more stringent; Goodwin's woman, with her child at the spring near the road, has seen Popeye leave in his car, and glimpsed the abducted Temple in it, her face "like a small, dead-colored mask drawn past . . . on a string and then away." Returning to the old house, the woman finds Goodwin shaved and putting on a tie and about to walk to a neighbor's and telephone the sheriff. She simply usurps that errand, and over Tull's phone she tells the sheriff "A dead man . . . the old Frenchman place. . . . This is Mrs. Goodwin talking." She has not named Tommy now, nor had he been mentioned in the scene's scant talk between her and Goodwin, in which her mood seems to stem not only from shock but from their earlier quarrel about Temple and his having slapped the woman repeatedly. Thus that terse, elliptical simplification emphasizes the murder not just in itself but in further strains on their situation and relationship. It can be assumed that Goodwin told the woman more than the story reports, and the reader can suppose what it could have been, as the fictional narrative now focuses upon the ongoing lives of these two not just involved in violent external events but in their own melancholy alliance. Such modulations between detailed or sparing but always strongly implicative narration will pervade Faulkner's art at its heights; in the carefully rewritten *Sanctuary* they appear as steps in perfecting an aesthetic economy of means and ends.

Under such dispensation Tommy, who dropped so suddenly out of life, is to have further place, in a deliberate passage at the close of Chapter XV, where his history is accorded an omnisciently narrated closure. That chapter had begun with Benbow returned to Jefferson and to his widowed sister Narcissa and Miss Jenny at the Sartoris place nearby, to endure a shrewd going-over for having left his wife and his home in Kinston. In return he wryly tells them of his pause at Frenchman's Bend, with "himself and Goodwin and Tommy sitting on the porch, drinking from the jug and talking, and Popeye lurking about the house," cursing Tommy for refusing to "go down to the barn with him," and Tommy chortling: "Aint he a sight, now?" Benbow left his sister's house next day and stopped in Jefferson, moving about among townspeople who remembered him "as a boy, a youth, a brother lawyer" who had practiced there with his father. He saw the country people too as they moved deliberately about the town square on Saturday; Faulkner's imagistic recounting of this seems to bear the tinge and warrant of Benbow's sensibilities. Then the chapter's last paragraph become simpler, more objective in its presentation, but with no less effect. On Monday the country folk are back in town—"All day long a knot of them stood about the door to the undertaker's parlor," where some "entered in twos and threes to look at the man called Tommy."

He lay on a wooden table, barefoot, in overalls, the sun-bleached curls on the back of his head matted with dried blood and singed with powder, while the coroner sat over him, trying to ascertain his last name. But none knew it, not even those who had known him for fifteen years about the countryside, nor the merchants who on infrequent Saturdays had seen him in town, barefoot, hatless, with his rapt, empty gaze and his cheek bulged innocently by a peppermint jawbreaker. For all general knowledge, he had none.

In that open societal area of the funeral parlor, where even if it is only from curiosity he is object of more attention than he had ever received, his is the double isolation of the anonymous dead. Lying barefoot in his overalls, he is an abstract effigy of all who have lived little known and less valued. In this he is like the figures of *The Nigger of the 'Narcissus'* as Conrad conceived of them, drawn "out of all the disregarded multitude of the bewildered, the simple and the voiceless." Murdered, he is classic as victim of iniquity in an ancient, absolute, and irreparable form; and such evil, juxtaposed to that poor creature's harmlessness and comparative innocence, becomes the more revolting and ominous. The note thus sounded will be heard as a recurrent lament throughout the Faulkner *oeuvre*. Even so, for one so ill-equipped and precariously situated, Tommy had an equanimity amounting to fortitude, he could be compassionate within the scope of his perceptions, and something other than a mere fool in his chortling sense of the grotesque, which in his situation and especially vis-à-vis Popeye seems a recognition of the profoundly absurd. Yet he is no philosopher; his is the unfortunate vulnerability of an innocent ignorance, encountering evil and comprehending it not in its chaotic darkness. More broadly, though Tommy is a minor and transient figure, he is essential to the plot and is made sufficient to that end, while in addition his presence as a being enhances scenes, multiplies implications, and reinforces theme. In this aspect his employment by Faulkner within larger manipulations of the fictional narrative is exemplary in itself and as of things to come. And despite the novel's celerity, there is time and place for him to be noticed though he goes unnamed.

In *Sanctuary* as a novel drastically recast before release for publication, the modulations of momentum and proportion, extending from a sometimes even elliptical economy to a delberate immediate fullness, and moving fluently within relative levels of objectivity and subjectivity, seem to disclose a strenuous forging ahead in the careful practice of an art. Given the novel's first draft as a variously peopled and too diversely eventful narrative matter unsatisfactorily conceived of and unrealized as genuine, serious fiction, Faulkner apparently made his revising it primarily a disciplinary and exploratory exercise in the techniques of his art. This was not with an assumption of instant full-blown virtuosity — which he had already approached in *The Sound and the Fury* and more precisely in *As I Lay Dying* on its limited scale, though these also were under the aspect of his vision as realist and regionalist. When Faulkner "tore the [*Sanctuary*] galleys down and rewrote the book," paying for having the type reset though he could ill afford it, this was a committed artist in earnest, with the confidence and competence given him by his two preceding novels and the roused imaginative grasp of what *Sanctuary* could be made to be. He did not bring all of it to levels of a controlled brilliance and approach to perfected autonomy he had achieved in those two earlier novels he hoped it "would not shame," but in making "a fair job" of it he extended events and projected their various enactors more fully within the regional milieu, developed more flexible modulations of narrative modes, effectively structured the overlapping of diverse concurrent scenes, and centered more directly upon evil in its most malignant forms, while making Benbow's desperate humane resistance to it a major theme.

Certainly in Horace Benbow at his moments of personal crisis Faulkner achieved the maximum realism possible in *monologue interieur,* but in the modulations of *Sanctuary* the subjective element is not restricted to such a purely introverted state. Indeed, Faulkner never leaned toward a strictly sustained, single protagonist's stream-of-consciousness novel. Nearest approaches to it are, most conspicuously, the series of separately personalized discourses in *As I Lay Dying,* (each individualized yet all coordinated to the family's situation), and, less specifically, the subjective quality naturally inherent in any sustained first-person narration, as in what "GRAND-FATHER SAID:", which constitutes the whole of *The Reivers,* where in the midst of multiple and diverse events the main thread is completely interior, young Lucius Priest's ongoing awareness of stages in his forced rapid maturation. However, such marked forms of centering on human consciousness in its singular involvement with events are not the only alternative to a sustained naturalistic objectivity — if such a mode can indeed be made recognizable as evocative fiction. Between the musing Bundrens and the boy Lucius tossed between exhilaration and anxiety lies the broad terrain of Faulkner's modulated objective-subjective presentations, with their more flexibly complex structurings and containments, and their informing pervasion by temperament. Though it was as to their unique inwardness that Faulkner probed toward his characters' reality and their interest as beings, in his commitment to the regional he treated them primarily through their socioethical involvements, to which even their most private introspections are to be seen as responsive, even if negatively. For Faulkner it is within terms of the human predicament, closely instanced yet as related to representatively significant issue, that individuality is to be most pointedly defined, and private fates disclosed, with greatest evocation of empathy.

In *Sanctuary* an authentic, palpable, and psychologically penetrated regionalism is contained by a powerfully conceptual realism which while certifying local instance tends to universalize some of its aspects. Reciprocally from within the story its subjective factors confirm this realism as humanistic. Thus even in the starkness of this novel's narrative economies and at an almost constantly hastened pace, it projects central Faulknerian concerns and characteristics. Where "the human heart" is detected in paradoxical "conflict with itself" what is seen to be at stake is some transcendent human value in its elusive but abiding verity. It was with a particularly acute realization and deeply intuitive sense of human consciousness as a constant yet flickering flame that Faulkner proceeded from work to work into a middle ground between theoretically and technically differentiated objective or subjective fictional narration, and inclined instead toward the more difficult practice in which they merge, while holding to what both predicated, the almost anonymous impersonality of the artist through self-restriction from direct entry into the work of art. This has not been unique in modern English and American fiction at its most serious levels and in its distinguished achievements. Rather, Faulkner has followed the main way of much of it. He is not an eccentric artist; he does not differ essentially from those in the fertile modern trend that derived its aesthetics of fiction, including control of point of view and narrative use of subjectivity, primarily from James and Conrad, and produced a remarkably various yet instrumentally conventionalized flowering in Faulkner's own time. Faulkner's distinction, which requires that he be named among the most distinguished of his contemporaries and immediate predecessors, is not in a difference from the most significant trends in fiction; rather it is in his superlative accomplishment, in its scope, grasp, vigor, and intuitive penetration, and the sheer virtuosity of his greatest compositions. If future times permit the further projection of English an American fiction in that freely creative and dynamic tradition which has evolved since the eighteenth century, Faulkner's centrality as an artist in his own place and right will be increasingly recognized.

Sanctuary can be turned to as a case in point, and one the more striking because at first it was unappreciated and grossly derogated by some who should have known better, and soon thereafter it was overshadowed by two of Faulkner's greatest novels. His going on to *Light in August* and *Absalom, Absalom!* may suggest that to a great extent the revised *Sanctuary* was a readying process, not as to matter but as to art, and at least it might be allowed such reflected credit. Even its most directly objective and apparently simplest passages are conveyed with subtle technical skill and judicious structural control, and there is also to be felt in them what only a humanely intuitive imagination and a commensurate fictional aptitude can offer: a pervasive emanation beyond words, actions, and the continuum of scenes and even the unfolding of theme in its rising constellation of elements; that implied subjectivity vivifying the represented passage of momentarily central figures, and validating this action as human experience. It is the virtue of fiction as a high art to beget such response in the consciousness of imaginative readers, something beyond passive superficial assent, an intuitive recognition. And the hopeful, faithful artist, though he knows that in a sublime sense he is playing with a kind of strange fire, trusts to it for conveyance in a degree of transferred awareness, believing with supreme optimism in empathy as a widespread human trait. While he may well consider this to be so common that a merely factual news story, professionally objective, can nevertheless rouse some readers to intimations of what those events might have meant to the ones experiencing them, he will know also that to many other readers of so bald an account the beings involved will move as mere puppets or stand as nothing but statistics, and that in all mankind and within various cultures there are these gradations between an unresponsive indifference and an acute awareness and sensibility to external human instances. For the fictionist, where readers' requisite responsiveness does not operate, the doors of empathic consciousness will not open wide enough to admit his story as he intends it, but he continues to believe in his art as a way of evoking a comparable imaginative projection from those of like mind, and as a sincere and concerned artist he will risk being potentially as evocative as it is given him to be.

Faulkner in his original version of *Sanctuary* may have toyed with this vocational relationship expediently, looking for much-needed commercial success by means of sensationalism, as he confessed (though perhaps exaggeratedly) in his preface to the reconsidered, recast novel. What was continuingly revealed thereafter of this artist's make-up might suggest shame over having written badly, under pressures extraneous to his real and already acknowledged calling. If so, then *Sanctuary* reborn is more than just the "fair job" he was willing to call it —more than an early consolidation of acquired aptitudes and an extension of further insights into fictional art—it is the point at which he could move beyond partial experimentation into a confident though wary release of his genius, knowing that for all its force and fieriness he could ride it and it would carry the artist toward his most ardently desired ends. His further creations were to surpass *Sanctuary* in regional representativeness and by realistic em-

bodiment of broader concepts; they would also extend evocative fictional techniques far more freely and variously, with
what seemed an inexhaustible originative power. Yet *Sanctuary* showed this too, in lively early stages. It makes what would
continue to be the typical Faulknerian demand for unremitting and wakefully imaginative attention to substantive detail,
narrative techniques, and the progressive structuring not just
of plot but of affective artistic composition, together with
empathic response to the resonances of subjective tonalities.
Perhaps such outright requisitions upon the reader, when only
dimly and thus disturbingly felt, gave more breath to the first
outcries against *Sanctuary* than did its shocking events and its
recurrent sordidness, though these could be singled out as
most open to certain basically impercipient attacks. But what
has given Faulkner his high place, beyond his gathering up
and intuitive penetration of significant matter in the light of
humane understanding, is a uniquely creative and spectacu-
larly originative fictional art, at the level of genius.

INCLUSIONS, CONVEYANCE, AND CENTRALITIES

In *Faulkner: A Biography,* Professor Joseph Blotner notes
that *Sanctuary* (1931) did not go without a measure of recognition from one distinguished Southern man of letters, Donald
Davidson, whose column in the Nashville *Tennessean* was also
carried by Knoxville and Memphis papers. Placing Faulkner
high among his contemporaries, Davidson praised him "as a
stylist and as an acute observer of human behavior" but felt
presciently from *Sanctuary* that the artist was still without a
theme or a character to draw forth his gifts at their fullest.
Possibly even now some readers of *Sanctuary* may underesti-
mate the strength and significance of its socioethical theme
because its supportive instancings, both in enactors themselves
and the *mise en scène,* are so much on the seamy side, narrow-
ing recognition and minimizing a sense of representative import. Moreover, some might consider it reductive that
Benbow, as the novel's indubitably principled protagonist, is

privately so flawed, shabby, and ineffectual a being. This, however, would be to look for something like a romantic hero, fearless and irreproachable, but that is not Faulkner's line; his realism pictures even the best persons as asymmetric and fallible, while it posits that the force of evil, as *Sanctuary* shows, is insidiously rife and sometimes rampant beyond control. In tempering his praise of Faulkner, Donald Davidson had made no prophecies that this young novelist would find his imaginative way, beyond *Sanctuary,* to broader themes and more impressive characters. However, this sagacious critic had discerned what many, then and since, failed to recognize, the important fact that Faulkner's intricate prose was neither loose nor confused but remarkably dynamic, the voice of a temperament perhaps capable of conveying larger projections of men and events and their profound meanings. Thus to recognize the artist's insight into behavior and his powerfully enabling style was to anticipate the major novelist.

Despite its lack of the heroic *Sanctuary* can be rightly described, though on its own immediate terms, as in the tragic mode. It is so in its spare and indirect presentation of the sensational, and in the amalgamation of that with the comprehensively evaluative, through the imaginative choruses of Benbow's subjectivity. Moreover, the novel in its totality is made classically tragic by the given view of life, of the waste and pity of it, conveyed even within such localized and limited terms. These though exceptional and random skirt a larger matter, the sad fact that while mankind possesses creation's highest gifts of mind and heart, men should be so darkly and fatally given to inordinateness. If in *Sanctuary,* as in later works, Faulkner admitted through his beset protagonist a melancholy *Weltanschauung,* this was at least an outgoing and confrontative opposite of that barren solipsism into which contemporary stream-of-consciousness fiction had too often tended to sink. Among Faulkner's characters, the recurrently acknowledged mutuality and further responsiveness to others even in a stratified and more specially fragmented society confirms the artist's primary assumption of a socioethical

view, in a kind of natural piety. *Sanctuary* can be seen not
only as one of Faulkner's most authentically regional novels,
lavishly yet pointedly furnished forth, but also exemplary of
his humanistic realism. Plainly the careful recasting of this
novel was under the imperatives of art, yet not for art's sake
but to make reality apparent in this clearest light, comprehensive of men's benightedness and abrasive oppositions but also
of heart's struggle to come to terms with itself by way of
human verities.

Donald Davidson's speculation that Faulkner's powers
might be stimulated more fully by other themes and characters was to be ratified, in two novels which soon followed
Sanctuary. What *Light in August* (1932) and *Absalom,
Absalom!* (1936) have in common is that they center on the
multiracial factor and its effects, without which Faulkner's
regionalism, whether treating of the deep South past or
present, would have been incomplete to a degree suggesting
either impercipience or avoidance. No one can prophesy a
future artistic creation, the artist himself can scarcely realize it
until it is done, textured as well as structured, but Davidson
saw from *Sanctuary* that at least here was genius enough for
fuller expression if it found its way to matter of greater
import, through characters able to enact it. Such matter,
turning upon the racial issue, was approached directly in these
two Faulkner novels not just as a possible subject but as
imperative upon him in his bent and commitment as
Mississippi regionalist. It might be opined that in some degree
Sanctuary, by its achieved ordering as if on a lesser scale for
more inclusive and intricate future constructs and with its
economies showing the feasibility of controlled abundance,
was a preparation for those two major novels; but rather than
to see *Light in August* and *Absalom, Absalom!* implicit in
Sanctuary, even for many modern minds it would be easier to
credit the Muses. Certainly Faulkner's gift is to be sensed as a
supreme bounteousness when the two novels are set side by
side and their utter differences are noted, though each turns
centrally upon the matter of race and the factor of miscegena-

tion. Each as a unitary work of fictional art is typically Faulk-nerian in that it is consummately realized in its own terms and way, and as beween these two novels in which the artist at last undertook regional-racial matter as centrally thematic, the techniques of presentation are uniquely at opposite extremes of his practice.

The fury latent in blood and sex in a biracial South is epitomized in its simple brutality and obscure psychology by the stark short story, "Dry September"; in these two novels such surfaces and depths are comprised in massive, multidi-mensioned, and brilliantly executed compositions. With the factor of race operating in each primarily as to miscegenation, society's antipathy to a mixing of bloods is probed, though from different sides of the issue, in its utmost complexities. In *Light in August* at the end of Chapter II is a passage which would almost seem to suggest that the question is a metaphysi-cal superimposition upon an incorrigible atavism. When Joe Christmas told Miss Joanna Burden concerning his parents that he only knew "one of them was part nigger," she asked how he knew that, and after a long pause he said, "I dont know it," and then added after another wait that "If I'm not, damned if I haven't wasted a lot of time." The evidence that the dark-skinned Mexican circus hand who seduced and carried off Milly Hines was "part nigger" rests on the crazed fanatical talk of Hines, who shot the man and brought his pregnant daughter home, then tried in vain to find an abortionist, and so let her die unattended in bearing the hated living child. When the circus owner had been called back to testify, his word that "the man really was a part nigger instead of Mexican" is apparently the easy way for an itinerant to escape being detained during a prolonged trial of Hines for murder—which will not happen if the "Mexican" is known to be a "nigger." The phrasing of that reported testimony is subtly suggestive; "a part nigger instead" eclipses and cancels out "Mexican," a supposed trace of black blood is the whole of the matter and the end of it, with now no need for the law's reprisal against the killer. The major implication of *Light in*

August becomes that of a life harshly beset and brought to nothing by a withholding of its right to full human identity, in a social order where mere rumor of mixed blood is fatal. The novel is the more powerful in that there remains this vacuum at its center, this absence of fact, and that Joe Christmas moves under the vast abstract shadow of a cruel lie, reinforced in this instance by the various punitive fanaticisms of Hines, McEachern, and Percy Grimm. (Such casting out and dismissal of the Negro from human consideration may raise the ghost of a bit of unconsciously cruel dialogue in *Huckleberry Finn,* when the disconcerted Huck is trying to play the role of Tom Sawyer which Aunt Sally has mistakenly thrust upon him, and fabricating about a steamboat accident, he says, "We blowed out a cylinder head." "Good gracious! anybody hurt?" Aunt Sally asks, and Huck tells her, "No'm. Killed a nigger," which leads her to say, "Well, it's lucky; because sometimes people do get hurt —". Which indeed they do, as Faulkner is instancing decades after a civil war.)

In *Absalom, Absalom!* it is again in terms of the dreaded recurrent threat of miscegenation that Faulkner treats the regional subject of a racially divided society. This still more ambitious novel, however, tells of miscegenation as both threatened and real; discovered, it breeds disasters among the Sutpens, whose rise and fall is the narrative's central thread, and Quentin Compson's anguished preoccupation. In *Light in August* the fate which isolates Christmas throughout his life is bred out of fanatically cultivated rumor; in *Absalom, Absalom!* the fact of miscegnation in a broader societal context is a family's doom, as obsession turns inward upon itself, a contagion to be transmitted by hearsay to Quentin, son of another family regressed and frustrated under societal change. What is similar in both novels is the fatalism which overtakes victims as different as Joe Christmas and Judith Sutpen, and then extends to Quentin. Faulkner did not exhaust the racial theme in these two novels; in *Go Down, Moses* its fictional treatment runs far, from the antebellum oddities of Uncles Buck and Buddy McCaslin in their grotesquely partial emancipation of the family's slaves and a reversal of its feudal life-style, to the poignant instance a century later of the octoroon woman and child repudiated by Roth McCaslin. Isaac as a boy had heard the story of how his father and uncle had handled the incubus of their inheritance by putting the slaves in the big house and locking only its front door at night; now in old age he grieves over this latest impasse stemming from the McCaslin patriarch's misuse of his female slaves, which leaves the intractable issue dramatized and furnished with actors, the separate lines of his legitimate descendents and their unlegitimatized relatives of mixed blood. For the resolutely idealistic but melancholy old Isaac, who had repudiated the material heritage reaped from his grandfather's slave-holding, fear centers on what the taboo on racial intermarriage can do to such defenseless victims of exploitative males as this woman and child, yet he feels that in the mid-twentieth century the time for remedy is not yet, and says so, while for himself he cannot dismiss the nightmarish intimation that the racial question is only one part of multiplying socioeconomic confusions and complexities that may prove irremediable and disastrous. However, the continuation of the racial theme in *Intruder in the Dust* presents a cheerful antithesis to the isolated, status-bereft Joe Christmas, through the remarkable Lucas Beauchamp, who had fought his white kinsman for recognition of equal manhood in "The Fire and the Hearth" and continues to boast of his McCaslin blood in assertion of an impregnable identity, and by so doing helps Gavin Stevens' young nephew, Charles Mallison, to outgrow the narrowly racial, potentially racist attitude Yoknapatawphan society has threatened to infect him with.

Though race in the particular aspect of miscegenation is the common theme of *Light in August* and *Absalom, Absalom!*, the segregated, fugitive existence of Joe Christmas and the turbulent Sutpen saga are each accorded the unique fictional presentation that such distinctly different histories merited and that it was well within the scope of Faulkner's genius to create. *Light in August* is essentially bounded with the thirty-three years Joe Christmas lived, extending into the third decade of the twentieth century, though two of the novel's three antiphonal subplots predate that whole life and not just the presence of Christmas in Jefferson during his last years. There ar Hightower's youth and young manhood during which his disastrous nostalgic fixation upon the Civil War proliferated to find its frenetic place in his semons; still earlier is the post-bellum history of Joanna Burden's now dead family, migrant into those parts, (and two of the men shot by Colonel Sartoris "over a question of negro voting") as this explains her social isolation and the philanthropic interest in Negroes which turns into sexual obsession with Christmas, assumed to be one. The third of these counterplots is Lena's contrasting story, assertive of earthy simplicity and natural survival, and she does not come upon the Jefferson scene until final stages in the main plot; as she first approaches the town she sees smoke rising from the burning house where Joe Christmas has just murdered Joanna Burden. The consequential interrelating and fluent nterweaving of these subplots with the story of Joe Christmas achieves a brilliantly ordered aesthetic and thematic composition. From a wider scope in time than his thirty-three years and through those other even more various circumstances than Christmas had known, all is drawn into a unity with the enigma he presented at first sight when he came to work at the sawmill and with the chronologically retrospective passages selectively sketching his earlier history. Even Hightower in the morbid grotesquerie of his ministry and the apparently related failure of his marriage is made adjunctive — for instance, the avidly involved Byron Bunch draws this superannuated and scarred man to give peculiarly fit ear to old Mrs. Hines, the long-suffering grandmother of Joe Christmas, and Hightower and Joanna Burden, though they do not touch in their separately self-destructive and essentially contradictory fanaticisms, become like different species of the genus whose more deadly forms include the ones who beset Joe Christmas first and last, those compulsive doctrinaire sadists, his grandfather Hines and Percy Grimm, the patriot hero *manqué*.

Conrad Aiken, writing in the *Atlantic Monthly* in 1939 in one of the rare early recognitions of Faulkner, and mentioning *Sanctuary* under perspectives provided by the novelist's subsequent works in the thirties, declared that "it betrays a genius for form, quite apart from its wonderful virtuosity in other respects." Certainly in *Light in August* that genius for form continued to make itself felt with a wider grasp upon a greater variety of realized characters, and in a skilful structuring of plot and enhancingly related subplots. One measure for estimating this novel's magnitude and intrinsic significations beyond those of *Sanctuary* (as well as the artist's more assured and extended techniques) would be from the further use of his favored device of multiple closures. The last three chapters of *Light in August,* dealing first with the bloody fate of Christmas, then with Hightower's immobilizing self-confrontation, and finally with Lena's further venturing into the wide world with her baby and with Byron Bunch as acquired protector, are all fully developed, each with its own peculiarly suitable mode of narration, and given its own tonal quality. Yet beneath these differences there is a common movement too, so that it is as if the novel's strands and stringencies are being loosened before the reader's eyes, while he is left with them all in mind, and not just with Lena's complacent remark at the Tennessee border, "My, my. A body does get around," marking it as the first relatively comfortable place for this predominantly melancholy story to cease. This quiet closure, however, still falls in with the novel's structural integration and fundamentally unitary quality, since it does not contradict the thematic characterization of Lena as herself a victim of betrayal, who had drawn humane aid from others and has kept her native resoluteness, though she really has as little defence and remedy as they have against a variously wicked though in some degree a kindly world.

Lena epitomizes endurance, a representative quality Faulkner admired, recognized in many guises, and gave high place as a verity; in many contexts he seems also to see it as complementary to the humane virtue of compassion, or conversely the tragic consequences of the lack of that. Lena's purposeful but adaptable expedition, with its *de facto* levies upon others, is richly illustrative of the regional but also more widely typical; specifically it is a counterpoise to the exceptional yet credibly revealing adversities of Joe Christmas. Having a chapter of her story told with humorous appreciation by the man who furnished her and her baby and the anbiguously attendant Byron Bunch a lift in his truck serves to lighten this somber novel at its close. It also precludes sentimentalizing Lena, who is scarcely archetype of the Earth Mother so much as of the natural woman of her time and place who will have her way quite as far as she can and then rest serenely in that. The truck driver, a dealer in refinished furniture, comes into the story out of the landscape, on a business journey, and later recounts to his wife in the privacy of their bed what recently he had had a passing glimpse of, yet he has a common folk quality of personal responsiveness to casual events and a tendency to correlate his impressions with his own store of wordly knowledge, and so (by the grace of the artist) he is made a rudimentary but telling documentarian. Thus one more Faulknerian episode is entrusted to a fictional person's conginzance and unique sensibilities for conveyance of a realistic-regional theme.

Lena, however, is but one of many; and within the wide reaches of Faulkner's *oeuvre* what she and a throng of others point to is this artist's power to assemble a variety of striking but humanly credible characters interconnectedly, and also to make that regional matter thematically complementary in an imaginatively unified and aesthetically attuned fictional work. This copious provision of players is not in an excess of artistic virtuosity; here as in other aspects of his art, prolific invention itself has its often insufficiently recognized counterpart in a conceptually controlled economy, and even supernumaries are made to contribute, through their glimpsed individual being, to the effects of scene within the action's larger context and progression. Typically this total motion is relatively arduous for its enactors, in their overt doings and more so in the suggested subjective stresses of confrontation, made conjunctive in terms of Faulkner's interrelated regionalism and realism. So steadily the experimenter but reaching toward specifically validated representativeness, Faulkner was no writer of sequestered neighborhood idyls—not even with the Bundrens—and his flashes of supportive imagery did not pause in locally colored vignettes. Conflict, acute, sometimes violent, and often of far-reaching effect is a common element in his stories, with a prismatic range of ethical refractions, both in societal situations and within the privacies of troubled minds. Differences extending to dilemmas imply the enigma of defining issues and also the vital need to deal with them civilly and in conscience. Faulkner's imaginative envisionings of human existence comprehend and judiciously treat the mutually conditioning factors of multiplicity and representativeness, of anomalies and verities.

More than most fictionists Faulkner could make a continuously present sense of milieu contain a company of diverse and responsive individuals in the privately intentioned course of their situationally interconnected lives, sometimes discordant, often significantly committed within their human limits. The achievement of momentum in the conveyance of such complex and subtilized matter is another aspect of Faulkner's economical narrative art which nevertheless maintains an immediacy of effect, yet not with such studied spareness as Hemingway's but through the controlled flow of a flexible intensity. Region, in shaping Faulkner, allowed him something in accord with innate teperament and outlook and amenable to his developing artistic intent, out of a stratified but mutually conscious society, committed in certain ways to custom and ceremony, proudly and painfully aware of its history, and uneasily preoccupied with biracial issues felt as a dilemma between close familiarity and uneasy incomprehension. All this Faulkner penetrated into as few of his townsmen did, with an absorbed observer's receptivity balanced by an artist's detachment which liberated his conceptualizing powers in their naturally humanistic vein.

That Faulkner's closely centralized regionalism was not an opportunistically chosen fixed stance is apparent not only in his fictional excursions from native ground but in the thematic range of his Yoknapatawphan novels themselves as unique artistic autonomies. He not only "watched and listened" but he pondered judiciously, with necessary strictness yet in an extension of empathy and civil commitment. He had realized early that his birthright of sociohistorical situation and accessible actors and instances was a bountiful heritage, from which beyond the factual he could derive assurance of verities, and within which he could advance for a lifetime, through an increasingly thorough appreciation and assessment, in works expressive of a region's infinite human variety and societal dynamism. In the place where he had grown up he came upon this early, still a young man and not yet risking creative flights beyond finely penciled sketches and rather derivative poems, to find that an area and its natives were arrested both in his attention and his envisionings, and had given his imagination points of reference for its transcendent conceptual trends. It was a fate that might have been envied by such different contemporary literary wanderers as Hemingway over three continents, or Willa Cather in her ranging with humanistic-regional concern from New Mexico to Quebec and several locales between—which, however, may bring to mind that Willa Cather in childhood experienced a striking change of environments, from Virginia to Nebraska, yet in a way that consolidated her views, whereas Hemingway at the verge of manhood had known war's drastic unsettlings, while Faulkner as fascinatedly attentive and recollecting artist continued to return to Oxford, Mississippi, and for most of his long working life to the same house, his chosen purchased habitation.

Yet absorbed as he was from his youth in the diversities of his native region, and its issues and evolution, and forever attached to it, Faulkner at the beginning of his career had already gone out into the world to live among other writers in New Orleans, to train with the R.A.F. in Canada, to sail from New Orleans and sojourn about Europe for several months. Just as anywhere in Yoknapatawphan County, everywhere else he would have watched and listened, though probably without quite the same habitual intensity. Whether he traveled to a distance or into his own back yard, he would have come away not with a clutch of data as commonplace as a tourist's postcards but intrigued by apperceptions bordering on the scarcely definable, yet to him apparent similitudes. So for the collegiate lyricist and maker of sketches, who had gone far enough in body and mind to see that the world, though round and all of a piece, was even more diverse than anything he had known, yet had its seasons and tides in its affairs, there ripened comprehensive intimations of the representatively human, which he was later to present in the aspect of verities. So there was nothing for it but fiction, and on his surest local grounds, that it might be as nearly veritable as he could make it. Here was the effective logic, represented not defined, of this artist's intuitive fusion of regionalism and realism. While the immediate pressed upon his perceptions in such multiplicity that mere enumeration might have seemed enough, he sensed the typical dramatic element, the unifying factor in men's existence not as picture but motion, both overt and conscious, in recognitions and conciliated arrangement, through men's projections of ethical principle, even in the midst of a constant roil of disconcerting passions, which Faulkner, like any man really in earnest, did not minimize or compromise with—an attitude he attributed to various protagonists of his.

Regionalism provided the rich substance and fluent modes of Faulkner's work, but the profound idiom of his communications is a humanistic realism. The fusion of such immediate knowledge with apperceptions of the humanly representative motivated the artist's imagination and enabled his creative consolidations. While naturalism in fiction is not without objective grasp in its constancy to profuse materials, in this aspect Faulkner's regionalism, though forcefully authentic, was more selective of detail, to further ends. For him emphasis by comparative limitation of substance and selective ordering of narration itself served to implement a dynamic realism stressing what in the local instance also suggests the more widely typical. Thereby as a regionalist whose developing concepts, though of always broader derivation, had feeding roots which ran close and deep in an immediate acquaintance, his fictions transcended entirely the dimensions of typical naturalism.

Faulkner entered into the mainstream of fiction and drama in aiming to convey the complicated realities of personal-interpersonal existence, as it moves in its intertwined societal and subjective ways, through his characters' words and overt acts and by intimation of their awareness and intention. A high Faulknerian achievement in fictional illusion is the suggestion of this private state without removing processes of consciousness too far or too long from the eventful narrative stream in which they swim. This implements a dynamic realism in sustained structural interplay between events and its participants' awareness, and it requires a subtler art than naturalism's steady data-laden march or than those fictional actions more confined within the orbit of a protagonist's private awareness less societally constrained or interpersonally constituted. (In this aspect Faulkner's touch can be of an utmost delicacy, seldom made note of and probably not yet fully appreciated.) From this preoccupied regionalist and committed realist working beyond naturalism under certain humanistic imperatives there was elicited a doubly selective procedure and creative synthesis, to serve the discovered opportunities of his vocation. The substantive and the conceptual, magnitudes o˜ two orders, required a functioning equation. Fiction as the pure art to which he aspired for the evoking of imaginative response needed, he knew, an opposite process from exposition's reliance on explicit definition and the impersonal momentum of logic. Intimately acquainted with what he found himself temperamentally committed to, he found a great superfluity of objective detail inherent in those regional subjects, and as his command grew he seemed to sense that the subjective element must have full complementary force, not as a fashion but for vital motion in his characters' locally conditioned singularity and more than regional representativeness.

It is in the arful fusion of regionalism and realism that Faulkner's calculated and proportionately sufficient injection of the enactors' consciousness into the narrative stream can most closely be identified. This typical Faulknerian practice appears as stringent economy with local detail, in a reliance on intensity rather than fullness — and imagery, aptly modulated as between precision and impression, along with Faulkner's succinct, often pointedly idiomatic and idiosyncratic dialogue, operates too by suggesting the personal reactions of characters. There is also a contributive effect through chronological rearrangement, not an unprecedented device, but made peculiarly effective by abruptly bringing the narrative again and again to a point of issue and tension where characters' personal response takes natural precedence. These may involve direct disclosures of consciousness, but not as a prolonged stream, rather so acutely that they project lingering mood into quickly resumed overt yet relevantly charged narration. Still, in the way of Faulkner's practiced art such recognizable fictional uses do not strike intrusively as something calculated, and are more than the mere devices they may seem when enumerated. Even paused upon, they still appear spontaneous within the driving narrative pace, and as instinctive as the reflexes maintaining equilibrium forward on a variable path. What is plain all along, however, is an artist's commitment to a central common principle as essence of any significant fictional action, the necessary nexus and reciprocity between events and participants' realizations thereof, with the latter factor as intrinsic key and the way of access for the reader's answering imagination.

Under Faulkner's synthesis of regionalism and realism what his technical accomplishment most differed from was not a simple objective naturalistic fiction but its opposite, stream-

of-consciousness narration, with its narrowed exclusive subjectivity along a more random and desultory way, with a
greater self-preoccupation and less involvement, in a diminution of dramatic tensions. The very life of each of Faulkner's
greatest fictional works is in its lives figured as interpersonally
situated, through which there fluctuantly interpenetrates a
variable fusion of forces, objective-subjective, communal and
individual, overt events and private responses tinged with relevant individual concern. Regionalism sharpens issue through
its situational immediacy in the pressures of milieu, and thus
frames the singular qualities of individual responses; correspondingly through that medium a humanistic realism makes
the local representative and further sanctions its specificity. In
this totality the private awareness of Faulkner's characters is
shown moving through attitude into action, and such purposeful consciousness implies subjective configurations, the gestalts
of organismic thought and feeling. Presumably out of comparable imaginative awareness and response there may have
loomed more largely the cloudy silhouettes of not impossible
fictional entities for this greatly gifted artist to arrest and
perfect into the totalities of inclusive concept and aesthetically
containing form. This apparently he had proved as the one
thing needful for himself, given the fruitful juncture of regionalism and humanistic realism in an achieved objective-
subjective juncture and functioning. That unity, ultimately
validated in the holistic work of art itself, could have increasingly stimulated him to the pure sorcery, through style and
structure, which liberated his genius and enabled consummate masterpieces.

8

Short Stories into Novels

FAULKNER'S career after 1940 saw the publication of six more novels and four other volumes of collected short stories, sketches, and novellas; it also included a book which was first put in this latter class but has been given consideration as a novel, and a great one, by reason of its substance and its subtle progression and interrelations. The original title on publication in 1942 was *Go Down, Moses and Other Stories,* and the First Printing carried the acknowledgment that "Some of these stories first appeared in *The Atlantic Monthly, Harper's Magazine, Collier's, The Saturday Evening Post* and *Story Magazine*." In subsequent American printings the phrase "and Other Stories" was deleted from the title, at Faulkner's request. This was obviously in accord with his view of the book as more than an assemblage of disparate tales, and stimulated a view already held by some, that *Go Down, Moses* may be considered a novel, a total composition with parts thematically related and reciprocally operative in fictional effects. That portions or earlier versions of five of its seven sections had been previously published in magazines was only in line with recognized procedures and not uncommon in Faulkner's career. Earlier, of the seven chapters in *The Unvanquished* the first five were published in *The Saturday Evening Post,* and the sixth in *Scribners Magazine,* and Faulkner had sought magazine publication for the seventh, the richly textured "An Odor of Verbena." By this time Faulkner had issued two volumes of short stories drawn from the much larger number he had published in a variety of magazines, but though many of these pieces had been reworked and woven in as elements of novels, neither in *These Thirteen* (1931) nor in *Doctor Martino and Other Stories* (1934) did the items aggregate into a novel, whereas *The Unvanquished* unquestionably is one. Its chapters are related episodes in the cumulative tale of Bayard Sartoris's maturation, through his boyhood during the Civil War and thereafter into the crucial episode of his young manhood. The victory the title indicates is compounded of a holding fast to the sense of honor which the Old South had engendered, though along with arrogance and violence; and with the war lost and the old order itself dissipated, the arduous transition is to an honor beyond bloodshed, in a courageous repudiation of an outworn code.

The Unvanquished has two simple unifying factors in that there is a single first-person narrator throughout and the progression is chronological. A subtler filament is that Bayard, growing from boy to man, is constantly learning from observation and hearsay in the course of direct contact and participation, and his expanding view evolves and contains the whole matter. The sections' varied tones nevertheless give the theme validity and reality, since personal maturation typically evolves out of disparate experiences. If *Go Down, Moses* is to be termed a novel (despite the original subtitle and the statement that "Some of these stories first appeared" in five different magazines) then at least it must be admitted that its unity is most subtly intricated, compared to that in any other of Faulkner's extended fictions. Correspondingly, this could be cited by advocates as a preeminent accomplishment. At least it may be seen that through the presence of McCaslins, dominant in all but one, even the minor stories have been given more entree than just as some pages in a collection. And as with others of his short stories adapted into his novels, most were somewhat revised, even reshaped, in their recruitment for a more extendedly related function. Even so, the operation is not in a change beyond tracing, as it was with those lesser castings which the passionate Cellini threw into the crucible and melted down for metal enough to complete his Perseus. No doubt comparably drastic transmutations overtake some wandering phantoms in a fictionist's imagination, but Cellini could well remember and record his sacrifices, while a fictionist works among impalpables, and could easily have forgotten an Ur-character in the more lively presence of his descendant. Indeed, with Faulkner the adaptation of earlier sketchings into a finished evocative literary work can be seen as creation in its stages, and to find a relation of parts in *Go Down, Moses* is almost to hear echo of the artist's footsteps, as careful as a hunter's, as intent as a pilgrim's. To sense in this intensely rendered work that kind of unity which constitutes a novel is to confirm the view that aesthetic autonomy (as also in Kantian ethical terms) is the result of an imperative. From what depths of intimation and into what breadth of coalescing vision Faulkner drew up the portions of this intriguing and cumulatively weighty book might be estimated from his other treatments of regional material, but how in working from one point and then another he gave it such total yet subtle resonance, like that of a bell whose precise stroke has not been heard, is a mystery not to be defined, and can merely be attributed to dedicated genius. Thus the stories published here and there and revised, refined to a larger purpose, sink fluently into place, like waves into a great tide.

The primacy of a configurative formal conception in Faulkner's working imagination is doubly obvious, from the unique total patterning given each novel and by the proving of it in readers' responses to its effects, such as in a paced momentum contained in a continuity, an engrossing cumulativeness, alternations and antitheses that become antiphonally composed, and an experiential immediacy borne up all the more strongly by the narrative's flow. The pervading and presiding creative intention, sustained throughout the long process of fictional composition, is at the center of a mysterious mentation, yet that it is there, felt and held to, is to be sensed. Some fictionists, notably James and Conrad, but others too since, have confided what was this or that story's *donnée*, but it would seem probable that in the evolving of a detailed complex work of fiction there must have been a stream of supplementary happenstances. It is also obvious, from the more general associative operation of consciousness, that the artist must combine extraordinary susceptibilities and spontaneity with a sustained purposefulness, to experience the vision and then give it embodiment in an evocative form. Conceivably the projection of some of the matter in short stories might be a stage in the clearer shadowing forth of the whole, and then a complementary reshaping of the short story would be required for its amalgamation.

Such procedure is to be discovered by collating some of Faulkner's short stories with what they become as parts of novels. Always there is a merging, a blending, an absorption into the larger purpose, and this repeatedly demonstrates that whatever his extravagances or involutions, Faulkner knew what he was up to. There is even an instance of his sure control in one negative choice which proves how far beyond the haphazard or merely expedient were his adaptations of shorter into longer works. This concerns the great story "Barn Burning," which, as Professor James B. Meriwether has indicated in his bibliography, "The Short Fiction of Faulkner," was originally meant to be the opening portion of *The Hamlet*. Given this novel as *fait accompli*, readers can see why Faulkner had decided not to open it with the already realized and structured short story. That the choice was made suggests the novel's larger dimensions and components were settling into the artist's mind with their own imperatives — to begin with, the deliberate tempo and indeterminate air under which the first incursion of Snopeses and the faintly ominous early glimpses of Flem himself were to be infiltrated into the not yet quite alerted speculations of the Frenchman's Bend folk. What then follows in *The Hamlet* is a series of panels: Flem Snopes' rise as clerk in Varner's store and recipient of Eula Varner when all her lovers have been scared off by her pregnancy; the long summer marked by the idiot's love affair with a cow and culminating in Mink's killing Houston; and the uproar over the auction of wild Texas ponies Flem had brought back along with Eula and her new-born child he could not have fathered. Moreover, in contrast to the short story in its compactness and finalities, *The Hamlet* is open-ended, pausing with Flem on his way to more lush pastures in Jefferson — there to wait in the wings of Faulkner's imagination and be brought on stage years later in *The Town* (1957) and *The Mansion* (1959), and be dealt with at last by cousin Mink.

"Barn Burning," a complete thing in itself as published in *Harper's* and included in the *Collected Short Stories,* is also of some magnitude, a miniature *bildungsroman,* for in a few brief episodes the boy Sarty has gone the whole agonized way of emancipation from his ruthless father, Ab Snopes, the compulsive arsonist and necessarily itinerant tenant farmer. To have begun *The Hamlet* with so explicit a confrontation and repudiation would have superseded a central theme of the novel and indeed the whole trilogy, the inexorable but gradual rise of Snopesism in all its pernicious mutations. Possibly Faulkner came to consider Sarty a distractingly improbable Snopes; certainly Faulkner took pains to emphasize the genetic factor when he explained the atypically conscientious Eck Snopes as presumably a product of "some extracurricular night work" by his mother. Not that Faulkner makes this a seriously propounded thesis; he individualizes each Snopes character, but in their variations they all illustrate thematically some degree of menace to the social order as they go carrying their own tribal culture alng with them. Thus when Sarty Snopes of "Barn Burning" set himself against all that, as it was typified in his father's malevolence, his flight, after having tried to alert their landlord against Snopesism rampant, carries him on out of *The Hamlet.* Only an uncertain mention of him remains in the novel, through Ratliff's wry report of Ab Snopes and his son Flem, and "another one too, a little one," who isn't "with them" now. In the story, with Sarty's warning too late and De Spain's barn already in flames, the boy as he ran away heard shots and supposed his father dead. In the novel, as Ratliff recounts it, Ab Snopes appears next morning to tell De Spain their rental contract is canceled, and De Spain says he would cancel a hundred like it "and throw in that barn too just to know for sho if it was you I was shooting at last night." The grotesque in Faulkner's fiction, as brought to quintessence through Ratliff's reports of the Snopes incursion, searches out an inverted humor in what is deplorable, yet not to exonerate but to take a stand at a distance and in that absolute separation which irony allows, with its rejections as quietly final as a raised eyebrow. The conclusion of "Barn Burning" is at the opposite extreme from this in Faulkner's tonal reach. Instead of native colloquial wryness there is a lyricizing of Sarty's absorbing a deep personal grief as concomitant of his more abstract realizations. Since the boy assumes his father's death, it becomes a fact in his story, but only as adjunct to the larger import that every drastic human severance is a kind of death. Short story and novel cannot be called inconsistent; they are embraced in Faulkner's outlook. And his instinctively sustained craftsmanship shows in his finding a more deliberate and tonally detailed entrance into the novel, while letting "Barn Burning" retain its separate existence, almost as if Sarty himself had demanded it by his resolute virtue and the price of grief he had paid for his own freedom.

Faulkner's criterion here as elsewhere was integrity of composition, in self-contained, consistently keyed fictional form. "Barn Burning" used complete as the novel's opening passage would have deflated a more variegated thematic development to follow; it would also have displaced the leisurely rustic yarning and folk humor with which the artist found it best to flavor *The Hamlet* at once in establishing an accordance with milieu. Yet that did not prevent his extracting from the *Harpers* story certain events for the novel's opening pages, especially Ab's deliberately staining the elegant rug in De Spain's front hall with a dung-covered boot and then ruining it in the cleaning he was ordered to do. This borrowed matter was much revised, though, as was usual when Faulkner wove a previously written short story into the texture of a novel. Here the transmutation is away from Sarty's unease, as a loyal son but a disturbed witness of his father's ruthlessness, and into Ratliff's ironic recounting what has become generally known when Ab brought the dispute before the Justice of the Peace. Then in the adaptation of "The Hound" (also from *Harpers*) into Book Three of *The Hamlet,* the change is in protagonists; Ernest Cotton's role as Houston's murderer is given to the reputedly "meanest" of the Snopeses, Mink. This extends, for the novel's purposes, the theme of Snopesism, and it also serves plot, showing the arch-Snopes Flem not only indifferent to his cousin's plight but successfully scheming to have Mink's prison sentence extended when he is caught in a bizarre attempt to escape, which in turn cocks a Eumenidean trigger for Flem's death years later, at the trilogy's end. In some such ways, it would seem, Faulkner furnished and shaped *The Hamlet* with steady regard for the modal aspects under which intimations of the work of art had come to him, and thus he achieved a unique accord with his ripened sense of the whole matter.

A scrutiny of modifications Faulkner made in his adapting some already published short stories into his novels can reach beyond simple collation to apprehend trends of his creative temperament in shaping and deepening unitary fictional works of art. One telling example is "Delta Autumn," as it first appeared in *Story Magazine* and then was reshaped, to give it under the same title a place with two other sections in a consummating realization of Isaac McCaslin's pivotal role in *Go Down, Moses.* As modified for its inclusion, the original short story was expanded and refined, and the betrayer's role was given to a younger McCaslin, to enhance the whole of Isaac's story as set forth in "The Old People" and "The Bear," as well as to provide a closure that became a basic resonance in those chiming reverberations which give *Go Down, Moses* in its seven parts its subtle unity, and a claim to be regarded as a novel, under the aspect of a sort of fictional symphony or suite. Yet the synthesis where existing narratives are recast for amalgamation into some larger work of art can show conversely the ratio in each of means to a particular end, and will repeatedly illustrate the usual rightness of Faulkner's touch in all degrees from overt simplicity to extreme elaboration and subtlety. Finally, the absorption of detail into the ultimate achievement, whatever its magnitude, emphasizes by what accretive steps the artist came into complete possession of his subject. To find him reworking toward larger and more complex structures what he had already given a unified and conclusive even if lesser form is to glimpse him in the very movements of imagination and to sense the daemonic impetus of genius, together with its imposed rational control in the light of envisioned conception.

As to Faulkner's whole way of apprehending and narratively substantiating his fictions, much is to be realized more clearly through relation to a regionalism usually confined for its illustration to one Mississippi county, where certain characters appear from work to work, with different degrees of prominence, showing additional facets of temperament, motivation, and response. Fundamentally they remain consistent, yet in their plasticity they are the antithesis of the stock character, through whom an expedient puppetry rests upon stereotyped attitudes and repetitious interjections, and is actually antidramatic, since it shows no new awareness in the character under the impact of emerging event. Even Faulkner's bit players, like Shakespeare's, enter into the action respondently in their own right and with thematic relevance, sometimes giving point and movement to merely transitional passages, as with the tenant farmers on the porch of Will Varner's store in the hamlet, a wry laconic chorus of judicious witnesses. And those of Faulkner's Yoknapatawpha folk who turn up conspicuously in successive but not always sequential works are made new not by striking changes (which might strain credibility or depreciate the character in one role or another) but are at once recognizable in extensions of themselves into further sectors of their experience, with consequent response. Such typical progression in a human life makes its total consistency the more credible. Like so much in Faulkner, this fictional practice is in essence nothing new, but his existential representation of human beings, through their struggles within themselves and under the pressures of all that impinges upon them, is extraordinarily dynamic. Few writers have had as acute a sense of unique human lives in process, between memory and expectation, and played upon by both while in the midst of the immediate, with which they deal according to the trends of their natures, which in turn are further conditioned thereby. The persistent sense of personal existence as motion within a ceaseless roil of multiple circumstance and intrigued consciousness was strong in Faulkner even from his youth (as his sage and sympathetic mother noted). Derived from the life about him, it was woven into the artist's evolved outlook as humanistic realist, making him most concerned with those characters in whom strivings were sufficiently consistent to be traceable through the intrications of purpose and predicament in the existential flux, without minimizing either values or hazards. Once again, this in Faulkner is nothing new in literature, but as always in any of its significant achievements the hand of the creator is perceptibly his own.

While his amalgamating of some short stories into the larger context of certain of his novels involved a reshaping, refinement, and further projection in both substance and art, undoubtedly the practice had its reciprocities. The matter and import already arrested in the short story may have disclosed larger possibilities, may even have made their realization imperative. It is through such returns upon itself, in its seemingly inexhaustible propagative power, that Faulkner's closely localized regionalism is most significantly creative, rather than in a methodical construction of a saga. He was conscious of world enough, yet after *Flags in the Dust* he did not try to see it whole, not out of timidity but because his immediate passion at any point was to penetrate the given and demanding subject to the full extent of the art he was rapidly mastering. As with the synthesizing of short stories into novels, so the reenlisting of already familiar Yoknapatawphan characters for further appearance in roles intrinsic to the new fictional composition is revelatory of Faulkner's particular creative tendencies during the course of his amazingly productive career. Its points of reference remained fairly stable. Though there were excursions from his regional base, he repeatedly returned to it, making it the grounds of most of his major achievements. Even so, his procedure was not a survey or census, nor did the successive works constitute a chronology. Though he had fixed his attention on the phenomena of Snopesism as early as 1925, *The Hamlet* did not appear until 1940, by which time he had done a large portion of his greatest work, with the brilliant experimental studies of the Compson and the Bundren families, in which he confirmed the centrality of the subjective in fictional representation; there was also the revised *Sanctuary*, which was his novitiate in conducting a multifaceted plot toward a closer confrontation of evil; and then triumphantly the superlative achievements of *Light in August* and *Absalom, Absalom!*, together with three other notable novels, one (*The Unvanquished*) going back to the Civil War and the other two (*Pylons* and *The Wild Palms*) in ventures beyond Yokanapatawpha County. Then after *The Hamlet* it was seventeen and nineteen years later before the volumes completing the Snopes trilogy appeared, and that long interval had included the remarkable variety and great conceptual and presentational achievements of *Go Down, Moses* (perhaps his greatest, next to *Absalom, Absalom!*), *Intruder in the Dust, Requiem for a Nun,* and *A Fable*—a monumental achievement perhaps underestimated by some readers simply because it was a projection so far beyond the like of anything Faulkner had done before, whereas it should be appreciated as one more instance of unfailing originality in the embodiment and particularizing of a new matter, to the demands of which the artist had totally given himself creatively.

In lengthening perspective it grows increasingly clear that Faulkner's practice epitomized fictional art ideally, by an alertness and spontaneous answering to envisionings, imaginative *Gestalten,* conceptual *données,* configurative inspirations, to which he responded with suitably particular inventiveness and compositional control, yet always in his chosen mode and accepted responsibilities as realist and regionalist. Whatever realism may be in other areas, in fiction it centers most truly upon human lives in their awareness of situation and their consequent concerned subjective-objective responses. Faulkner's acute observations of persons in their modes of behavior, joined to his empathic intuitions concerning certain ones in their essentially private ongoing consciousness, make his realism humanistic, postulating values, and broadly ethical in its main thrusts. These confront the evils that men do in various interpersonal contexts, whether immediate or more widely societal, as in *Sanctuary, The Hamlet, Go Down, Moses,* or *A Fable,* whether illustrated by Popeye as murderer and rapist or in the arrogant presumptions and moral evasiveness of Temple Drake and Gowan Stevens, or in meanly predatory Snopesism, or it is shown through Isaac McCaslin's grief and despair over slavery and its residual problems, or on an international scale by the agonies of millions entangled in the most monstrous of evils, war. Fortunately Faulkner's region and the felt influences of its well-remembered eventful history, with the fairly representative aspects of his immediate environment and his access to intimate acquaintance with all that, quickened his awareness of the human predicament yet reassured him in his gathered intimations that verities could endure.

Whatever the scope of a Faulkner fictional work, it depends upon deeply realized characters for enactment of the complexity and unrest of an intricated, shifting social order and the ongoing enigma of individual fates therein. The tension is constant, with something comparable to an alternating current as between event and what it may be meaning to one or another of those involved; and the dramatic flow is strong because of the always realized interaction by penetratively imagined individuals within a relevantly implied societal context. In this respect Faulkner is a most sound creator of well-balanced fiction, and that is the more apparent because of a pervading intensity which attentive reading will find to stem from purposeful over-all economy that nevertheless allows minute treatment of the enactors' personal realizations central to the story's import. Thus plot and character are merged in a unitary composition assimilative of both; situation exacts relevant response from its agents, and the story becomes what those so situated make of it. With the whole of the Faulkner *oeuvre* now possessed for over a decade by many serious readers, including a number of diligent scholars, the appreciation of his characters each as of his or her place and time, or places and times in separate works, becomes more crucial. When within the unique integration of any one of Faulkner's compositions a figure reappears out of another work, or when a short story is adapted with modifications into a more extended and intricate piece, this secondary use should be viewed totally and explicitly in its new context. There are perceptible consistencies between the Gavin Stevens of *Intruder in the Dust* and of *Requiem for a Nun,* but these roles are best perceived integrally, in their appropriate differences; and an attempt to coordinate them and make them precisely interexplanatory may diminish each, or at the least blur its firm outline, which has been achieved by a selectivity rigorously relevant to a certain work's total compositional unity and intent. Faulkner's ranging perceptivity and enabling inventiveness necessitate attention to each of his fictions in the details of its contextured autonomy. Sudious readers with the whole of his work in mind will repeatedly find themselves pondering instances as typical yet unique in their idiosyncrasy. Such returns to recognized similarities in their singularity are part of a maintained responsiveness to this constantly originative artist. What is representative in him may be described but cannot be contained in definitions; each of its manifestations is specifically constituted and asks to be noted as such as well as to its correspondences elsewhere. Interconnections themselves recur in modified terms and tones, too, so that the involved reader, both as judge and amateur of essences, is bound to get down to cases in this subtly but insistently specific as well as profoundly conceptualizing fictionist.

Even in some relatively simple Faulkner short stories his importantly functioning characters have a credible vitality which suggests they could be transplanted into another situation, to continue flourishing as themselves, through adaptation. It is by their intentness as dynamically integrated persons that Faulkner's characters make themselves so credibly felt, yet this effect must be sufficiently credited to Faulkner's art in limning them. It derives in part from the authenticity of Faulkner's regionalism, but that does not mean he picked up characters readymade off Jefferson's streets or in the outback of Beat Four as instances of local color. Under his purposeful realism they are made recognizable in terms of their ongoing human existence; they are not admitted to the story as picturesque supernumeraries but to serve with some relevance to the action's theme. To that end Faulkner treats all his characters with selective economy. It is amazing how many possible narrative developments he can pass over and omit and yet give the effect of a rounded major character, and under such dispensation even all those many who appear only briefly nevertheless leave the sense of their serviceable relation to the whole. The principle of a realistic and proportionately relevant characterization operates as well when Faulkner characters are allowed to reappear from work to work. Their dynamism is maintained not by repetitious trading upon what they have been elsewhere and at another time but as to this new situation, in which their immediate responses disclose as consistent realities new facets of the person. If his actions and reactions in another story are referred to, this will be made definitely as of that other time, when this same person was yet somehow other in a different portion of his life. In any story Faulkner's characters, whether appearing only there or recurrently from another narrative, are made to be seen within the containment of a present role in a present matter.

When Faulkner adapted some short stories into some of his novels there was in the practicalities of art a substantial amount of repetition, but what was most telling would be transforming modifications, for extended and deepened implications, such as between the *Story Magazine* version of

"Delta Autumn" and its use to conclude Isaac McCaslin's story in *Go Down, Moses*. In the magazine version, the hunter who asks Uncle Ike to give the packet of money and the word "No" to the woman who may come by looking for him is not an Edmonds nor anyone else of the old Lucius McCaslin line. Boyd is his name, and he is flatly presented as "ruthless" in his handling of animals, machines, or humans. Correspondingly, in the *Story* version the partly Negro woman who appears with the infant this Boyd has fathered is not James Beauchamp's granddaughter, and so does not contribute a further instance in that particular chronicle of tensions over mixed blood which the family patriarch Lucius Quintus Carothers McCaslin had set going six generations earlier. To give Boyd's place to Uncle Ike's kinsman, Roth Edmonds, lifts the story to a higher level of implication and irony, and makes Isaac's ordeal more severely personal. Boyd in his ruthlessness was two-dimensional; Roth (seen in "The Fire and the Hearth" as the exasperated but considerate moderator between old Molly Beauchamp and her all but intractable husband Lucas) here in another aspect but not contradictorily becomes the cynic and surly man of bad conscience, suffering for what he will not try to amend beyond indirect conveyance of some money. The disclosure that the infant son of Roth's mulatto woman is in the sixth generation of that illegitimate descent from Lucius Quintus Carothers McCaslin, through his miscegenous union with his slave Eunice and his incest with their daughter Tomansina, is the ultimate in a series of cumulative shocks for old Isaac, and his gradual absorption of this latest harrowing knowledge with all its implications provides a unifying closure to his life story as comprised in "Was," "The Old People," "The Bear," and "Delta Autumn." Here in process was a structuring which strongly combined a detailed regional theme and the accompanying subjective realities which were subtly the heart of the matter, as protagonist's crucial experiences and a sustained narrative's import.

The architectonic workings of Faulkner's creativity are almost mystical in their cumulative consolidating effects.

Specific concretions can project and merge into a larger unity, more hauntingly abstract yet immanent, the concept intrinsic in the event, the event absorbed into theme. This is illustrated by characters through their personal interactions with circumstance, in its extended elucidation yet not to their own eclipse. They gain greater individual stature by their human representativeness, for the sake of which synthesis Faulkner invents his demonstrations. It is therefore peculiarly hazardous to approach any work of his in a possibly fragmenting analysis. This can happen for instance in a too studious recalling of characters from work to work, with diversion of attention from the structural, tonal, and thematic unity of the particular narrative in hand. Such seems to have been the tendency of one esteemed critic in his weighing of "That Evening Sun." This famous short story, first published in 1931, is told by Quentin Compson, who had his prominent monologic part in *The Sound and the Fury* (1929) and who in a unique fashion is the central intelligence and sensibility throughout *Absalom, Absalom!* (1936). These two novels are correspondingly chronological in Quentin's life (overlapping through his year at Harvard), but they are vastly different in focus, inclusion, and mode. The earlier centers closely on stresses within the disintegrating, demoralized Compson family, and Quentin's is only one of three brothers' streams of consciousness traced in separate sections, the first being that of Benjy, whose clouded mentality apprehends only intermittently and fractionally what goes on around him. In *Absalom, Absalom!* the vast chronicle of the ill-fated Sutpen family is adumbrated as archetype through the youthful Quentin's observation, involvement, and appalled pondering, evolving into his ambivalent attitude toward the South. In "That Evening Sun" the adult Quentin is narrating detachedly but with implied insights a childhood experience shared with his younger sister Caddy and brother Jason, concerning the Compson's terrified washing woman Nancy, who senses that her husband will murder her for her prostitution to white men. To begin with, Quentin speaks reflectively of how it was in Jefferson "fifteen years ago," when the Negro washing women still carried the laundry bundles balanced on their heads; he mentions that he was then nine years old, Caddy seven, and Jason five, which would make the reminiscent teller of the tale twenty-four. This is, however, an age Quentin never reached in the two novels where he chiefly figures; a collating of them and the story indicates he was twenty at the time of his suicide, at the end of his freshman year at Harvard.

This discrepancy as to such a detail works no harm; Faulkner may have let it stand to assert the story's autonomy, and indeed that may have been his design. Yet a critic seemingly less concerned with each work's unitary consonance than with wider factual consistencies has found it "curious" that in "That Evening Sun" Benjy "is never mentioned." However, considering Faulkner's already demonstrated virtuosity, and the extremely careful fictional art of this story, what would really have been curious would have been any attempt to include Benjy. He was then only four, his mental age was not even that, and as always in such cases his abnormality would have conditioned the consciousness of the others, especially if improbably he had been included in the movements back and forth between the Compson kitchen and Nancy's cabin. It is true that the rest of the Compson ménage are included; it is while Dilsey is ill that Nancy comes to cook, but Dilsey returns, her strong self; Mrs. Compson, at the edge of events, is in character, exuding self-centered complaints; Mr. Compson, wrapped in resignation, coolly mandates among them all. He quietly reproves Nancy for her earlier involvements with white men but he now tries to allay her fears, and with the three children for company he conducts her through the dark lane to her cabin and tells her to bar the door. There would scarcely have been place even for bare mention of Benjy as he might be remembered from *The Sound and the Fury,* much less for any meaningful present allusion to or representation of him. The story's whole drift from the mature Quentin's deliberately descriptive recall of Jefferson as of his ninth year and the narrative's slow muta-

tion into pure memory with a quick cinematic flow of action
and dialogue is an extraordinary fictional unfolding, lucid
and indeed simple on its surface, yet full of hints. The simplicity inheres in the two younger children; five-year-old Jason
is toying with the question of who is or is not a nigger, and
Caddy in her seven-year-old superiority teases Jason about
being afraid; however, their tireless chatter is not entirely silly,
for each is projecting from what is impinging upon them,
Nancy's fatalistic "I aint nothing but a nigger" and her deep
terror. Quentin at nine, however, was already showing the
acuteness of intuition that finally was to make a hypersensitive
life insufferable. At that early point he had understood,
evidently, the import of general gossip about Nancy's prostitution, with her saying, "When you going to pay me, white man?
It's been three times now . . . ," for which public offense she
got her teeth kicked out. In quite another aspect, at home he
not only had estimated his mother as one who "believed that
all day father had been trying to think of doing the thing she
wouldn't like the most," but he and his father had some
mutual understanding about avoiding her unreasonable
demands, so that Quentin kept quiet when one was expected
involving them both and, already almost as between gentlemen, "So father didn't look at me."

The vastly different levels of understanding separating a
precocious Quentin from the two only slightly younger children (which would have made presence of the abnormal Benjy
still more complicatedly interruptive in this story) are implied
in its closure. Mr. Compson has come to Nancy's cabin to
bring his three children home. He cannot persuade Nancy to
let them take her to stay with her Aunt Rachel or even to put
out her lighted lamp and bar her door. Overtaken by the
inertia of fatalism, she has said, "I just done got tired. I just a
nigger. It aint no fault of mine." Now as the Compsons walk
away through the dark and cross the ditch where Nancy's
vengeful husband may be hiding, they can hear her wailing,
and Quentin says, "Who will do our washing now, Father?"
Here Faulkner may have risked an extreme subtlety, and

Quentin's question perhaps deserves to be read as the only way he could speak at the moment of all he is realizing. Possibly in a small boy's lack of words he has already come by the wise child's knowledge of how reticence as well as uncertainty can be served by understatement. After that, what remains of the story is a shrill interchange between the two self-preoccupied younger ones, with Jason now confidently asserting, "I'm not a nigger," and Candace saying, "You're worse, you are a tattle-tale. If something was to jump out, you'd be scairder than a nigger," and then the final words as Jason says, "I'm not," and Caddy says, "You'd cry," and calls him "Scairy cat" and Mr. Compson stops it with a heavier second reproof to her, "Candace!" It is interesting to note that the two elements in this closure might have been reversed, putting first the impercipient younger children's chatter in a customary spat and then using young Quentin's more ranging and reckoning question to his father as the last line. However, perhaps that might be read to make Quentin seem naively indifferent to anything beyond menial services for his family, but as it is placed it glimpses in passing that at nine he has quietly sensed realities in Nancy's situation and foreseen probabilities, while Caddy is still playing the more childish game of who's afraid, and Jason at five is just beginning to wonder about people of different color, and perhaps even feels the puzzling ambiguities of that in his environment, as in his saying earlier, "I aint a nigger. Am I, Dilsey?" Certainly the latent ironies here were opened up in Dilsey's answer: "I reckon not."

One of the enabling fictional effects in "That Evening Sun" is the measured but rapid drift of its first-person narration from the stylistic tone of adult perceptions in the first paragraph, colorfully descriptive of Mondays in Jefferson "now," and through the second paragraph's somewhat simpler diction but still elaborate sentence structure concerning the difference "fifteen years ago," and so on to the third paragraph, which begins with the word "Nancy" and tells (still without identification) how "we would" follow to watch her carrying away the bundle of laundry balanced on her head. So this is the story of Nancy, a Jefferson family's "washing woman" as of fifteen years ago, but it also becomes a matter of recollection which gradually transports its teller (and the reader) completely into that lost time, in the objective simplicity of the story's surface and details, and into the subtleties of the young witness's wakening intimations. Once "That Evening Sun" is under way, despite its fully detailed eventfulness it maintains that objectivity, as in its closure as well as at the earlier points where Quentin's acute intuitions are no more than implicit beneath the simple surface of a lad's naturally put account of events, with its large dependence upon purely colloquial dialogue.

It would be imperceptive to fault Faulkner for inconsistency of style as between the story's first paragraphs and its main body and closing passage. "That Evening Sun" is rather to be seen as one of the most adept and effective uses of first-person narration. The modulation from a sophisticatedly descriptive prose to a simple objectivity serves as induction into a chosen kind of fictional illusion, wherein the mature narrator's retrospection becomes like a vivid dream in that it returns him to levels of expression natural at that earlier age and by that veracity is capable of carrying as well the import of his inarticulated realizations. Perspective is augmented by the device, and this value is unobtrusively achieved and sustained, in full but rapid conveyance of the matter. Yet it is economical too; when late in the story Quentin takes twelve lines to identify a Mr. Lovelady as the collector of Negro burial insurance (the "coffin money" Nancy has mentioned) and then to summarize what he knows of that vaguely suspect man, it suggests a young witness's attempt to understand Nancy's life, and through her something of Negroes. In fact, the adult Quentin's rapid immersion into the remembered past, going to the distance of recapturing his nine-year-old self at that point of an articulated awareness, is a complex demonstration in brief of Faulkner's inclination toward character in the motion and tone of its consciousness and as at the vortex of that reality which fiction seeks to suggest and to evoke some sense of in its immediacy and flow.

In "That Evening Sun" such an intention is clearly shown in the rapid modulation of narrative style and the mode of progression toward the story's central events placed at a child's level of realization. The artist's choice here was to make apparent a return to past time to stress the pure and simple perceptions of a circumstantially limited but sensitive small boy. Some first-person short stories have plunged directly into an immature stream of consciousness, to show a process of maturation, as in Joyce's "The Sisters," but often to revolve perhaps ironically upon the juvenile narrator's impercipience. Conversely, if the matured protagonist looks back from a present vantage point, he may make himself felt throughout by style and retrospective comment, as Faulkner did with "Grandfather" really saying it all in *The Reivers*. But in "That Evening Sun" Quentin at nine is made to carry Nancy's whole story, so far as he then saw and heard it, and made a child's suppositions about its complexity of events. It was to serve this chosen approach that Faulkner called for some special attention to extended passages of unbroken dialogue where the younger children, Caddie and Jason, talk to each other and their elders, and are answered and then turned away from by concurrent talk that is other-directed and beyond them but overheard and productive of more questions; here who is speaking to whom must be gleaned from substance and context, and can be, with a striking sense of verisimilitude. (Again, though, where could Benjy have been placed in such scenes?) The reversion to these events of fifteen years ago, made in the story's second paragraph, had briefly allowed the adult Quentin who speaks in paragraph one a range of sophisticated imagery — the new street lights like "clusters of bloated and ghostly and bloodless grapes," the city laundry trucks on the recently paved streets, on which "the soiled wearing of a whole week now flees apparitionlike behind alert and irritable electric horns, with a long diminishing noise of rubber and asphalt like tearing silk." In the second paragraph, beginning "But fifteen years ago, on Monday morning," the imagery is more literal, and while that return to the past is still consciously reminiscent, there is a shift from impressionistic imagism to subtle effect of rhythmic and suspended sentence structure: "the quiet, dusty, shady streets would be full of Negro women with, balanced on their steady, turbaned heads, bundles of clothes tied up in sheets, almost as large as cotton bales, carried so without touch of hand between the kitchen door of the white house and the blackened washpot beside a cabin door in Negro Hollow."

That established image carries into the next paragraph and Nancy, with whom "we would go a part of the way . . . to watch the balanced bundle . . . that never bobbed nor wavered . . . her head rigid, uptilted, the bundle steady as a rock or a balloon." Here the chronology is turned back, with "we would go," but there remains that trace of the figurative as if to make the transition less abrupt. Young Quentin thereafter does not extend himself so far in his attempt to report the matter, though his perceptions are increasingly penetrating. For instance, "Dilsey was still sick in her cabin. Father told Jesus [Nancy's husband] to stay off our place. Dilsey was still sick. It was a long time," the family was "in the library after supper" and his mother querulously wondered whether Nancy was "through in the kitchen" and his father said, "Go and see if Nancy is through, Quentin. Tell her she can go on home." The boy obeys, and there follows this remarkably keyed passage:

> I went to the kitchen. Nancy was through. The dishes were put away and the fire was out. Nancy was sitting in a chair, close to the cold stove. She looked at me.
>
> "Mother wants to know if you are through," I said.
>
> "Yes," Nancy said. She looked at me. "I done finished." She looked at me.
>
> "What is it?" I said. "What is it?"
>
> "I aint nothing but a nigger," Nancy said. "It aint none of my fault."
>
> She looked at me, sitting in the chair before the cold stove, the sailor hat on her head. I went back to the library. It was the cold stove and all, when

you think of a kitchen being warm and busy and cheerful. And with a cold stove and the dishes all put away, and nobody wanting to eat at that hour.

Amid the clamor of insistent questions from the two attention-demanding younger children Quentin is restrained, but his repeated "What is it?" to Nancy is urgent with anxiety; and his sense of Nancy's desolation runs off into fragmentary expression, as of "blank misgivings" while "moving about in worlds not realized," but where unlike Wordsworth he is to find no "benediction" in the painful awareness he shows in his other, later question: "Who will do our washing now, Father?" This goes beyond simple practical concern into a child's way of fixing upon clear points of reference amid a cloud of indefinable apprehensions, and it shows not just in Quentin's two sober inquiries amid his siblings' babble of successive questionings as mere handholds on the moment, but in his scrupulous detailing of known facts throughout the story of Nancy. Beyond that psychological realism, Faulkner's structurally and stylistically modulated short story was designed to convey a mature protagonist's remembering from fifteen years earlier not as a tranquil recollection in perspective but as a dreamlike summoning up of that living experience itself, as of its own time and terms, and with its vast socioethical reverberations. It is credible that one like Quentin could be capable of such a literal recovery and sensitive playback because once it had so affected his extraordinary sensibilities (inherited from his only begetter). That this fictional artist, out of bits and pieces of his regionally based knowledge, could recover such a concept whole and alive is at the height of creativity, as of a phantast and a seer.

By its stylistic modulation into what is to be the pure tone of its persistent key, and with its open-ended structure which after all leaves its young narrator clearly intuitive of outcome, "That Evening Sun" is perfectly a contained and complete thing. No reader ignorant of The Sound and the Fury would feel any lack, nor could find it "curious" that "Benjy is never mentioned" in a short story which could not even answer to the question "Benjy who?" But readers who have lost such innocence will soon know this, as a certain constellation begins to appear. The third paragraph had told that "we would go a part of the way" to watch Nancy faultlessly balancing the bundle of washing on her head; the fourth paragraph, a single sentence, tells that "when Dilsey was sick . . . Nancy would come to cook for us." The fifth paragraph tells how "we" would go down to Nancy's cabin to call her," and on one of those times "Caddy" delivers the summons and "Jason" asks whether Nancy is drunk. The narrator does not report his saying anything to Nancy but does register the image of her coming to the door, "leaning her head around it without any clothes on." This may relate implicatively to the whole of the next page, which sets down the publicly spread talk of Nancy's prostitution to white men and her consequent pregnancy and that leads into this scene "before father told Jesus to stay away from the house."

Jesus was in the kitchen, sitting behind the stove, with his razor scar on his black face like a piece of dirty string. He said it was a watermelon that Nancy had under her dress.

"It never come off of your vine, though," Nancy said.

"Off of what vine?" Caddy said.

"I can cut down the vine it did come off of," Jesus said.

"What makes you want to talk like that before these chillen?" Nancy said. "Whyn't you go on to work? You done et. You want Mr Jason to catch you hanging around his kitchen, talking that way before these chillen?"

"Talking what way?" Caddy said. "What vine?"

"I cant hang around white man's kitchen," Jesus said. "But white man can hang around mine. . . ."

His complaint, prolonged in several more sentences, is correlative to Nancy's later fatalistic lament: "I aint nothing but a nigger. It aint none of my fault." That had been her reply, when his father having said "Let Quentin go and see," the now identified young narrator had found Nancy with her work finished and her hat on, sitting by the cold stove as if numbed, and he had intensely asked "What is it? What is it?" Seemingly there had fallen upon him then a vague intimation of the post-bellum Negroes' lingering plight, which does not form itself expressibly except in his figurative sense of desola-

tion, "a cold stove and the dishes put away," and the unfortunate woman immoblized, resigned to her doom, yet fearing to
face the dark outside and the husband in whom outrage
against the white man's continued demeaning incursions into
his house "woke up the devil in him."

Not only has the nine-year-old recollector of these entangled events been named on these pages, but his father too
has been allowed a first name, as Mr. Jason, in the customary
old combination of deference and intimacy. Students of
Faulkner's works have learned that this man is Jason III (in a
genealogy stretching back to Quentin MacLachan Compson,
born in 1799), and thus in "That Evening Sun" the
five-year-old so insistent in his inquiries about who is a nigger
is Jason IV. It can scarcely seem "curious," however, that
mention of Benjy was omitted from a story in which there is no
naming of any of them as Compsons, and, moreover, where
the pitifully benighted Benjy would have remained an
extraneous factor, diluting the thematic effect of counterpoise
between the two talkative but less perceptive younger children
and Quentin, who at nine has begun to understand—which is
why fifteen years later he remembers it all so explicitly and in
its true shadings. What might be remarked is that with *The
Sound and the Fury* published only two years earlier than this
short story, and with an impressive projection of Benjy as core
of the novel's opening section no doubt still vividly alive in
Faulkner's working imagination, he nevertheless refrained
from giving this character mention and identity in a story that
included all the other members of the family and Dilsey with
them. Yet this choice, to leave the then four-year-old Benjy in
fictional limbo in Quentin's veracious recall of events concerning Nancy, is only another clue to that judiciously artful selectivity by which Faulkner creates thematic focus and accomplishes the structuring of each holistic composition. Such a
basic fictional aesthetic (and not mere opportunistic and completely frugal recovery of earlier associated details) guides the
artist either way, whether in a heightened reconstituting of the
short story "Delta Autumn" for consummate closure of Isaac's

extended role in *Go Down, Moses,* or by the simple finality of a one-way journey back into Quentin's consciousness at nine, where the severe but barely expressible impact of milieu is as scrupulously noted by the artist as it was soberly apprehended by his young subject.

Were any assiduous reader of Faulkner to come away from "That Evening Sun" asking where was Benjy, it would only suggest a not-uncommon tendency to historicize the matter of Faulkner's fictional works in quest not only of a consistent but an interlocked chronology. This would run quite opposite to Faulkner's primary artistic bent toward unitary autonomous fictional entities. (It is true that in the Appendix focusing of the Compsons which Faulkner furnished for Malcolm Cowley's judicious and serviceable *Portable Faulkner* collection of excerpts from the works, as of 1946, the artist allowed himself some lively biofictive extrapolations on what had gone before, but this was more of sheer exuberance than a sober attempt to tidy things up.) Naturally enough in fiction as profoundly regional as Faulkner's and with his empathic attachment to his discovered characters, from work to work there are many consistencies among diverse matters. Quite as naturally, readers may find these amplifying—for instance, as with the trace in "That Evening Sun" of a rapport between the small boy Quentin and his father, which at other stages and levels, especially in *Absalom, Absalom!,* may contribute to tone as well as substance. There are Mr. Compson's installments of information about the Sutpens, that only Quentin's grandfather, General Compson, had known and had passed on within the family. Mr. Compson's memory-saturated, intuitively projected monologues and what he writes his son at Harvard are not only telling but communicate a sure sense of congeniality between them. However, none of this need be noticed, either fleetingly in the short story or extendedly in *Absalom, Absalom!,* to make the other understandable, for Faulkner has built these two structures, the slight and the monumental, each in its own unitary perfection.

The fourth and final section of *The Sound and the Fury,*

conveyed in third person from the chronological perspective of Easter 1928, eighteen years after Quentin's suicide, omnisciently included the idiot Benjy a grown man still bellowing for the vagrant Caddy, who has left her daughter named Quentin with the Compsons, and she in turn has run off, taking Jason's cash savings, and Jason has gone in savage pursuit; even so, within all this overt turmoil the most memorable aspect is the characterization of Dilsey. Scarcely able to climb and descend stairs, yet the household's sternly dutiful and responsibly commanding center, she found no respite except at the Negro church, where as she listened to the picturesque eloquence of the visiting preacher, her now-released "tears slid down her fallen cheeks in and out of the myriad coruscations of immolation and abnegation and time," and she becomes the epitome, as of Faulkner's own period, of the emancipated but not yet free and still direly circumstanced ones. Possibly Nancy's story may be considered as proceeding out of the roil of imagination which had produced *The Sound and the Fury,* where thematic and hence the supportive compositional emphasis was predetermined to fall upon the deterioration of the melancholy Compsons, allowing only lesser yet relevant weight, through Dilsey and her family, as to the Negroes' unhappy socioeconomic situation, in an inadequate and unstable postbellum commutation after collapse of the unnatural because inhuman attempt at symbiosis through slavery. Thus beyond Dilsey as of 1928 there had been no rounded role or even place for such as Nancy in *The Sound and the Fury,* but she can come among the Compsons in "That Evening Sun" at the racial extremes of her ordeal, and thereby can waken in the boy Quentin extended notions of agonies more acute than the tepid griefs of his own depleted yet still further fated family.

Here there is a converse process from that of extending, transmuting, and intensifying such short stories as "Spotted Horses" or "Delta Autumn" for inclusion in novels. Returning to the Compsons in a short story so soon after having displayed them in full, and several of them at subjective depth, Faulkner did not need to expand but to exclude everything irrelevant to young Quentin's tentative yet increasing awareness of Nancy. By his humane intimations of her predicament as "nothing but a nigger," Quentin at nine is the youngest of those Faulkner protagonists upon whom the strains and enigmas of an inequitable biracial society impinge, even if he can articulate it no further than his anxiously repeated question, "What is it?" A decade later, in *Absalom, Absalom!* his unrest as a Compson is to be quite overshadowed by his dismay as a Southerner. In different generations and situations, and with relatedly different responses, Chick Mallison and Isaac McCaslin confront the biracial problem during adolescence. Isaac, Quentin, and Chick are all precocious, as Faulkner was, in their ethical sensibilities, but this theme of cultural formation of temperament is treated with most extreme delicacy in the Quentin of "That Evening Sun," while his later absorption with the racial issue as played out at length and in all its permutations in the Sutpen story and Quentin's submission of mind and heart to its heavy burden make *Absalom, Absalom!* the most comprehensive and profound of Faulkner's regional works and properly allow its effectively lyrical narrative treatment.

In "That Evening Sun," with an all but complete assembling of the Compson family under their first names, and with the confirming presence of Dilsey, it is quite natural for a reader already acquainted with them in *The Sound and the Fury* to remember Benjy, but to recall him in his pitifulness is to recognize an inscrutible genetic accident in the midst of the world's other imperfections which also include matters of a quite different order, human conduct as personal and societal interrelations, where choice often might have operated to other and better ends than the brutal misuse of Nancy by white men, which thus roused her Negro husband to outrage he can vent only by even greater wrong, against life itself. "That Evening Sun" being largely a domestic story (played out not just in Nancy's cabin or through hearsay of the episodes on the street and in the jail, but chiefly at the Compsons' house), a merely factual linking of it to *The Sound and the Fury* could have put a four-year-old Benjy into the picture and even credibly underfoot in the kitchen where Nancy was substitute cook. It is unthinkable that Faulkner merely forgot to include him; he was left unmentioned because his extraneous being would have weakened the story's intense focus and unity. Conversely, Caddy and Jason are contributive. By their contending with each other and asking their naive questions that never get answered they become a unique chorus, in a paradox of irrelevance and a proportionate realism, and as foil to the not much older Quentin's attentiveness, anxious concern, and a beginning of wisdom that could darken further. This is not thematically inconsistent with Quentin's melancholy and his life's despairing early end as already set down in *The Sound and the Fury*. At its juvenile level the short story accords with the broader and more steadily anguishing sociohistorical view of the biracial South which he is to experience in *Absalom, Absalom!*, at the verge of relinquishing his despairing existence. However, neither of such views of what may befall a nine-year-old within a decade is written into "That Evening Sun" or is necessary for the fullest reading of it, and possibly Faulkner disregarded or even calculated its minor chronological inconsistency with an already published novel in order to give over the short story completely to the boy's sufficient merit, within the immediacy of Nancy's ongoing ordeal and her projected fate. (It might even be fancied of so protean an artist that Faulkner gave Quentin a life beyond his short span in *The Sound and the Fury* for the sake of conceptualizing a speculation on how early there had begun to accrue a certain portion of that knowledge of his particular world which was to bring him down.)

In fictional composition inclusion and exclusion are central to an art as nearly perfected as Faulkner's. Proportionately, innumerable economies and outright omissions of the feasible are correlative to his elaborations. These fuller passages could be seen as functional within the work's selectively aggregated unity if they were more responsively read by those who call them extravagances, yet who do not bring the same charge against less imaginative, more literal naturalistic novelists whose inclusions are on a more nearly uniform scale and cast in a style less modulated to the narrative's motion, and consequently are less proportioned to the emphasis of theme and the symmetries of an autonomous organic structure. Faulkner as storyteller will casually admit some forever unredeemed hints along the way but does not descend to mention and dismissal of this or that as "another story"; he silently turned away from many a road not taken. The "Appendix: The Compsons," which he furnished for Malcolm Cowley's *Portable Faulkner,* shows how his Pegasus, given its head, could have galloped off distantly in all directions, instead of remaining under the artist's rein in favor of compositional unity, his early-achieved masterful practice in story or novel.

In the *Portable* appendix the most notable spurt for its own sake is the extended entry on "Candace (Caddy)," which after sketching her psychology, especially in reference to her brother Quentin, elaborates an open-ended biography, taking off in 1910 from Caddy's socially respectable marriage "when two months pregnant with another man's child" and her divorce in a year, and a second marriage in Hollywood in 1920 and divorce five years later, and disappearance "in Paris with the German occupation in 1940, still beautiful" and not looking "within fifteen years of her actual forty-eight, and was not heard of again. Except . . ." Here begins the more than five-page cadenza, impelled by Faulkner's talent for discovering minor characters as a supposed situation might require, and then becoming infatuated with them in whatever human uniqueness he had endowed them with—after the manner that led him to say he had fallen in love with Ratliff, which fortunately for his readers he never recovered from. For the postscript on Caddy the odd supernumerary was "a woman in Jefferson, the county librarian," a "mouse-sized" spinster who "had passed through the city schools in the same class with Candace Compson." That this antithetical pair had been friends is scarcely to be presumed, but the whole town must have been conscious of the Compsons, so one day in 1943 the little librarian closed and locked the library in midafternoon and called on Jason Compson at his farmers' supply store to show him "a picture, a photograph in color clipped obviously from a slick magazine," of an elegantly dressed woman in an expensive sports car, her face "ageless and beautiful, cold serene and damned; beside her a handsome lean man of middleage in the ribbons and tabs of a German staff-general." The librarian tells Jason, "It's Caddy! We must save her!" Jason recognizes Candace and breaks into laughter, as might be warranted by the grotesqueness of her whole story, but then he denies it (probably wary of involvement), and says it must be Caddy's illegitimate daughter. Next day the librarian journeys to Memphis to show the picture to old Dilsey, retired there to the little house her daughter Frony keeps for her. To the visitor's excited assertion that "It's Caddy!" Dilsey's immediate intuitive response is "What did he say?" Understood, she is told Jason had said it was Candace, "But as soon as he realized that somebody, anybody, even just me, wanted to save her, would try to save her, he said it wasn't. But it is! Look at it!" Dilsey says, "Look at my eyes. How can I see that picture?" but as the librarian is asking her to call Frony "the old Negress was folding the clipping carefully back into its old creases, handing it back." The librarian returns to Jefferson in tears, thinking Dilsey didn't want to be told whether it was Caddy. Dilsey's first asking what "he" had said seems meant to remind Melissa Mink of realities, and painfully in some degree she senses what Dilsey well knew of Compsons, that Caddy was beyond wanting a retroactive redemption such as the sentimentally nostalgic librarian was conjuring up.

Concerning the Appendix about the Compsons, a series of further inventions he supplied for Malcolm Cowley's anthology of excerpts, *The Portable Faulkner,* Faulkner commented that to him the novel was "still alive and growing." Accordingly he took the chance to summarize a family's history, from pioneer days and to project its postbellum decline from General Compson on, with none left in midtwentieth century to mourn it, since its one survivor *in situ* lacks that natural piety. As of the Appendix, Jason Compson IV is the pragmatic one, industriously acquisitive and completely expedient. In middle age, with his parents and brother Quentin dead, and Benjy in an asylum, and his adventuresome sister Candace and her thieving daughter Quentin lost track of, he prospers as a merchant and cotton dealer, living in a room above his store, a bachelor visited weekly by "a big, plain, friendly, brazenhaired pleasantfaced woman no longer very young . . . his friend from Memphis." He "would say" that "Abe Lincoln freed the niggers from the Compsons" and he "freed the Compsons from the niggers," meaning in particular the formidably devoted Dilsey and her family. The deeper fact further illustrated by the Appendix is that Jason had freed himself from trying to be a Compson, in a line that had run out not just genealogically but (after his antebellum great-grandfather Governor Quentin MacLachan Compson) had declined from accomplishments or even the ability to hold on to its land, the Compson Hundred, most of which General Compson had gradually sold off to keep financially afloat, and almost all of the rest went for Quentin's year at Harvard and Caddy's necessitous wedding. The penultimate phase of the Compson family story was marked by the stoic detachment of the father, Jason Compson III, dipsomaniac reader of the classics, and the lassitude, complaints, and faded pretensions of Mrs. Compson; then came the divergent fates of that family's last generation. Jason's acquired freedom is by escape into mediocre mercantile anonymity, and through avoidance of conventional sexual alliance and ongoing familial responsibility. Hence when he is shown the photograph from the slick magazine he says, "It's Cad, all right," but when the librarian exclaims, "Jason! We must save her!" he answers, "Dont make me laugh," though he has already done so; now called upon, he evades by adding, "This bitch aint thirty yet. The other one's fifty now," implying that the German general's mistress is Caddy's runaway daughter Quentin. This notion is canceled out in the Appendix itself, where the subsequent entry on Quentin (largely parenthetical about Jason's own malfeasance) concludes with her at seventeen running away with the money, "And so vanished; whatever occupation overtook her would have arrived in no chromium Mercedes; whatever snapshot would have contained no general of staff." Complementary to this is the instinctive awareness the librarian shares with old Dilsey, that the greater part of the money Quentin had stolen from Jason had been withheld from what Candace had sent back to the Compsons for her daughter's support. In any event, the self-liberated, self-seeking Jason would have had no desire to confront Candace now.

Something fundamentally relative to Faulkner's dealing with character in relation to situation and theme is pointedly illustrated by that middle-aged little county librarian ("Melissa Meek, from Jefferson," she reminds Frony when after Jason's rebuff she leaves the library locked up for a second day and carries her quest to Dilsey in Memphis.) The story of this woman's bursting out of her vocational routines she had so primly and censorially pursued and undertaking the quite madly quixotic project of "saving" Candace is narratively sustained and detailed to greater length than is the treatment of any other person touched upon in the Compson Appendix, yet she is not a Compson, and out of the whole of the Faulkner *oeuvre* she is from nowhere else but these few pages. She was evoked by Faulkner's prolific imagination for a particular purpose, yet she grows into more than a device; evidently her creator became intrigued with what he could make her be and show, but this to his purpose as well as for the artist's most real reward, his own zest. Miss Melissa Meek's case thus seems the more comparable in miniature to that of Ratliff, whom Faulkner hit upon as a shrewdly contributive intelligence in *The Hamlet* and continued to develop and depend upon throughout the Snopes trilogy, along with a more involved Gavin Stevens and a grown-up Chick Mallison. Yet the artist's summoning the librarian to her incongruous and faintly grotesque as well as pathetic minor role went beyond an indulgence in improvisation, to illuminate Candace herself by antithesis and enforce the theme of the whole Compson history in their mutations and extended rise and decline. For these services Melissa Mink is allowed something like her own complete short story, with what seems probably her farthest excursion into worlds beyond library walls, and may constitute her one greater assertion than keeping *Forever Amber* out of the hands of highschool students. Most importantly, this little tale has its development and denouement, placing its protagonist implicatively in a context with Candace Compson, who may have paradoxically dazzled such a mousy little schoolmate of probably unthreatened virginity, yet who now aroused in the aridly seasoned middle-aged spinster the aptitude for fantastically embracing a lost cause.

It was a distinct achievement to make the little librarian so memorable within her allotted less than six pages, and a real feat to turn that narrative into an appropriately diminutive yet well-sustained and affecting fictional fragment. As such it stands out on its own among the Compsons, who are enumerated in chronological order in that Appendix. For the most part such entries are supplementary in two aspects, as condensed biographical summaries and as psychographic epitomes of characters in their major tendencies and relationships — for instance, an abstract of Candace, "Doomed and knew it," neither "seeking or fleeing it," and loving her brother Quentin "despite him," loving in him "that bitter prophet and inflexible and corruptless judge of what he considered the family's honor and its doom" — this preceding the mere data of her marriages and divorces, and then her disappearance in Paris. This is the chosen point at which such documentation is interrupted, with a marked shift and smooth entry into what becomes fairly sustained narration. The sentence concerning Candace's vanishing in Paris concludes with "was not heard of again"; the following sentence making the adroit turn into Yoknapatawphan locale and personae begins unobtrusively almost like an afterthought but quite discernibly a rising curtain on further disclosure: "Except there was a woman in Jefferson, the county librarian . . ." Melissa Meek moves beyond the data and epitomizing of the Appendix, and beyond anecdote, and takes on a fictional protagonist's initiative, in which momentum is generated by her mania, and the denouement is epiphanal, her realization of not just the impossibility of her desire but the emptiness of her beliefs.

Faulkner explicitly makes the little librarian quaint, but

there is more to her than static outline and fixed local coloration as an odd regional figure. She is genuinely a Faulknerian
character, which is to say a person in motion, and very much
so in this case, spatially as well as subjectively, and inter-
relatedly, with dramatic outcome and thematic overtone. The
few pages given Melissa Meek in the "Candace" section of the
Appendix are the more valuable because in their comparative
brevity and simplicity they most clearly disclose the artist at
work, shaping and placing a structured fictional episode in its
designed connections with a larger context. To note a typical
but not always credited economy in such an introduction of
character and occurrence is to give Faulkner's controlled procedures further recognition. It is simply because the little
librarian appears only in the "Candace" section of the rather
compressed Appendix on the Compsons that she is treated so
selectively; she is enlisted only to elucidate Compsons, and in
so doing to sound a related but larger Faulknerian theme.
Faulkner must have relished creating those brilliantly incisive
pages, but there is no extravagance and no detail except as
needed to substantiate Melissa Meek within the larger context,
the Compson story. That the dynamic Caddy had been
Melissa's schoolmate presumably enters as more than a factual
connection, perhaps hinting a silently attentive fascination;
decades beyond this, what still might have moved the quiet
little librarian out of her now long-sequestered life could have
been that Candace was a Compson.

So Melissa sets out to recruit others to a crusade, going first
to Jason in his store, and then after his rebuff journeying to
Memphis to appeal to Dilsey, living at last in retirement, with
her daughter Frony. The librarian's altogether impracticable
appeal to Jason and his rough reply is made into a more sustained dramatic scene and gives a more specific characterization of him than any comparable passage provided by the
"Jason" entry in the Appendix. Thereafter the librarian's brief
exchange with the now detached Dilsey leaves her without further resort in her fantasy of "saving" Candace, but the helpless
little woman's tearful grief as she returns on the bus to Jeffer-

son seems over more than that. In their extremes Dilsey's abrupt realistic dismissal of the whole matter and Jason's grossly expressed indifference to another Compson's fate seem to comprise for Melissa Meek the death of a long-sustained retrospective dream, however compounded of a family's history, the shy remembering of a dazzling schoolmate, and now Candace's latter-day glitter and audacity and peril. Melissa has been too long immured in the library, and too intent on repeatedly shelving out of reach *Forever Amber* and its likes; her foray into the world to "save" Candace is this side of madness in something nearer the sheer innocence of locally nourished sentimental illusions, which suddenly fade when brought out into the open air in 1943. Then she sees in the mediocre, unfeeling Jason the last of a once-notable line, and finds that the Dilsey whom so many had so often called upon had laid down her burden as of no impelling worth. From Dilsey in Memphis the librarian fled toward refuge, on a bus so crowded with war-time travel that a soldier "rose and picked her up bodily and set her into a seat next the window," and as she wept she knew that

presently now she would be home again, safe in Jefferson where life lived too with all its incomprehensible passion and turmoil and grief and fury and despair, but there at six o'clock you could close the covers on it . . . and turn the key upon it for the whole and dreamless night.

Within the narratively represented character of Melissa Meek on her brief crusade there inheres the implication of long-delayed disenchantment as irreversible defeat. This effect is enforced by the very structuring of language in a downward all but disintegrating spiral as she painfully formulates acknowledgment of Dilsey's wholly self-possessed abstention from involvement in what has become pointless:

because she knows Caddy doesn't want to be saved hasn't anything any more worth being saved for nothing worth being lost that she can lose.

The little spinster librarian is a furthest adumbration of the incongruity of making any last stand for the Old South as late as midway into the twentieth century. In a paradox of specific impracticality, an utter irrationality in disregard of circumstance is figured by her seeking what would require a high strategic foray during a great widespread war, for rescue of the less than hypothetical "honor" of a latter-day Compson. Thus like many other Faulkner characters she enacts a broad abstraction, but with idiosyncrasy approaching uniqueness. Melissa Meek is not certifiably insane, but merely fanatical— although, as Faulkner depicted in a shaded variety of manifestations, that can be very like madness. Yet among her own she is comprehensible, and there could have been many, including both Quentin Compson and Chick Mallison, who despite their own ironic detachment might have been the one to pick her up and get her settled, on the principle that a lady who has some necessary tears to shed in a crowded bus ought at least be given the minimum privacy and easement of a window seat.

The more than five pages of consecutive and substantially developed fictional narration about the librarian are anomalous, yet in a usefully illustrative way. Standing out from the rest of the Appendix by its consistently sustained mode, the passage seems a short story, perhaps extractable as such, yet it is not, though it could have been made one, complete and autonomous, by sufficient supportive additions. These would have involved the gist of what in its present position it derives not only from the Compson Appendix but also from *The Sound and the Fury*. Such sources are what make Jason's behavior clearly comprehensible and give credibility to the presence of middle-aged Candace where the picture shows her; they also underlie the logic of the librarian's venturing to Memphis to appeal to Dilsey, and give that old woman's reply its depth of calm relinquishment. The all-inclusive anomaly in considering the librarian's story an adequately realized short story of itself is that without its connections to all Faulkner had written and was writing about the Compsons, this passage would lack its abstract overtone, the regional-historical-familial theme of rise and fall, and of all lingering backward looks reluctant to let it be. Without this dimension the character of Miss Melissa Meek, county librarian, would lack the pathos that as it is outweighs the otherwise the faint grotesquerie of her eccentric superannuation.

Two most interesting aspects of her narrative as inserted into the "Candace" section are, first, its fundamental illustration of this artist's regulated interrelating of plot and character in strong thematic development, and second, more specifically, Faulkner's ranging and brilliant inventiveness, together with a skilled conducting of narration. As to the first, those pages on the librarian could have been dispensed with, though they do enrich the section and augment its reverberations. Still, this addition does not substantially round out Candace's story, nor is anything of her present inner self revealed by that photograph; rather, its very pose suggests a future of drastically changing circumstances, and the "fur piece" she has come carries no such promise as surrounds Lena at the end of *Light in August,* in her own maintained stability and under trustworthy Byron's protection. What has moved the librarian is some particularly conditioned sensitiveness to hazard for Candace, with remembrance of her in earlier local contexts, and perhaps as well a temperamental affinity and professional concern with a more extended regional history, including that of the Compson family. Credibly there is that in Melissa Meek which can spur her out of life-long reclusiveness into an attempt to set going a fantastical crusade. She thus illustrates how in fictional creation of the first order the summoning-up of characters to optional minor roles is for enhancement of the total action, yet they themselves must be made part of it by having a related coloration and thrust, giving them something beyond the neutrality of an anonymous messenger entering with tidings. Melissa Meek is perfectly serviceable to Faulkner's purposes in the "Candace" section, and to that end her discovery of the magazine photograph and reaction to it are neat inventions. For once she projects herself actively into her surroundings and thereby takes on dimensions as a genuine protagonist in a story of her own, yet this stands only on her coexistence at school with Candace in an apparently intense awareness of her and of her "old Jefferson family" as such.

There is a notable subtlety in the way Faulkner first introduces and then orders the revelations in the librarian's story. Candace "Vanished in Paris . . . was not heard of again. Except . . ." leads into identification of the "mouse-sized" county librarian, a spinster, of an age with Candace Compson in the Jefferson public schools, and now a timid woman who "One day in 1943, after a week of distraction bordering on disintegration" locked the library and hurried to Jason Compson's supply store for farmers, and passing through all its clutter came to Jason's desk and laid something upon it, the photograph from the magazine, Candace in the Nazi general's sports car. Only with that is the cause of her distraction known, and the impetus for her leaving her post. Meanwhile she has been imaged as the library's patrons had seen her and noted her strange state, and Jason, last of the long line of Compson men, is found ensconced in a rough and ready mercantile establishment which becomes backdrop to his raucous, indifferent, and evasive refusal to agree that "We must save her!" The narrative reserving of a detail, the discovered photograph, allows a reader's attention to move through such expectant wonderings as to what could be disturbing the little librarian so deeply, and why she finally breaks away before closing hours, and now what is she doing in this gloomy store so crammed with farmers' equipment, confronting its not entirely respectable proprietor. An eccentric minor character thus comes round into an extended intrication with the main immediate context, Candace, and its still larger perimeter, the Compsons.

As episode, the Melissa Meek tale is an atypical instance, thrust as it is into the documentary rather than fictionally narrative Compson Appendix, in a unique containment which determines to some degree the inclusion of detail (such as to Jason's store) and the proportioning of emphasis (as placed upon Dilsey in Melissa's brief interview). Though her two short excursions from the library provide some momentum and lead to a distinctly epiphanal closure, that total passage is scarcely extractable as a unitary composition. Placed within her subjective experience, it would fail without supportive knowledge from beyond that. Presumably during all her otherwise unnoted life the librarian's one real adventure has been fantastically into no wider world than that she imagined of the Compsons, as she conceived of it from being at school with Caddy, and from Jefferson's accumulated but superficial common knowledge of a notable family, while in the Appendix and *The Sound and the Fury* there trail surges of deeper, darker clouds than she could have conceived of. By this it illustrates all the more Faulkner's genius in amalgamating entities into a larger construct, for enrichment. There is no formula for it; it is never done twice alike. It can be as incidentally inserted as the largesse of the little librarian and the discovered photograph, or as centrally purposeful fictionally as the enriching revisions of "Delta Autumn" for rounding out Isaac McCaslin's life story in *Go Down, Moses*. It can become what amounts to an enhancing translation, that of "Spotted Horses" from its first-person version in *Scribner's*, June 1931 to its use of that auction of Texas ponies as opening section of "Book Four: The Peasants" in *The Hamlet* (1940). Here the extended narrative reach and stylistic range of omniscient, third-person narration, while including the farcically grotesque, modulates into other keys, suggesting more fully the ominousness of Flem's craftily indirect exploitations and the pathos of some of its victims, thus bringing the short story's substance more definitely within the novel's main thematic containment. This then made possible interconnectedly a brilliantly presented regional postlude, a two-part episode, the abortion, by a Snopes's perjury and through the law's obstructive intricacies, of both the Armstid and the Tull suits against Flem Snopes over injuries from the Texas ponies. At these further denials of remedy against Snopesism, the venerable old Justice of the Peace (who had advised silent prayer to begin with) adjourned the court crying, "I cant stand no more!"

Miss Melissa Meek, given no world of her own beyond the library except through her care for Candace Compson, is made to render a considerable return, through Faulkner's unceasing yet selectively controlled inventiveness. In coming upon the photograph, the librarian furthers, by one more chapter, the middle-aged Candace's still open-ended history. More largely, this serves to place both Candace and Jason as what these surviving Compsons have come to, in an echoing of Faulkner's theme of a family's decline, and by implication in the aspect of the Old South so fated. Finally, under the liberties of the Appendix and with perhaps as greatest reverberation, the librarian is made conductive of latest word on Dilsey, found still in her firm self-possession and unshakable dignity, "in faded clean calico and an immaculate turban wound round her head," sitting by the fire in deserved security and ease, in the neat little house in Memphis with Frony. Later in the Appendix that detail is extended by another entry, a simple sentence:

FRONY. Who married a pullman porter and went to Saint Louis to live and later moved back to Memphis to make a home for her mother since Dilsey refused to go further than that.

With what zest Faulkner must have seized the given notion of bringing Dilsey live into that brief episode, during the little librarian's frantic furthest thrust of illusioned effort, and showing Dilsey in contrast still herself, having endured much acquaintance with others' ingrown griefs and willfulness, and now in restful privacy, yet in her natural vitality still capable of intuition and decisive acceptance of realities. Her foreknowledge that Jason (even if it were of any use) would have had no concern for Caddy draws upon a dark store of matters under which Dilsey no longer suffered, as shown in her handing back the picture in a gesture of dismissal. Yet in so doing Dilsey has given the little librarian more than she knew she needed, a realization of actualities in a tearful dissolution of who knows what extravagant retrospective dream of Caddy, who was a Compson. And by recalling Dilsey, Faulkner could align the librarian's venture and ultimate realization with the most veritable referent to realities and indicator of theme, that knowing, decisive, forever incorruptible, and now fully emancipated old servant of Compsons.

Sarty Snopes, after the barn-burning, ran quite through his adventure and on out of Yoknapatawpha County and his creator's fief, except as a rumor. This left Faulkner free to begin again with *The Hamlet,* at a more deliberate rate of disclosure and eventuation, and on a conceptual scale inclusive enough to comprise, in time, a trilogy. Yet the short story was not canceled thereby, nor even eclipsed; it endures within its own frame as one of Faulkner's most brilliant compositions, through its immediate regionalism and by instancing a typical Faulknerian theme, a youthful maturation whereof the subjective thrust is toward socioethical verities. In an opposite instance, this time after the event of a novel, there is a chosen imaginative return in a closely contained short story, with an outcome only foreshadowed and a young protagonist's tenuous intuitions cryptically implied. Revisiting the Compson family with a fictionist's privilege soon after he had classically posed them as if beset by furies in that four-paneled and subjectively variegated novel, Faulkner found them in place in "The Evening Sun" but chiefly as of an earlier and more innocent time than either 1910 or 1928. Yet while the artist's more focused view now went back into the end of the nineteenth century, it also called up a Quentin older than he lived to be in the novel, to have him recall how fifteen years earlier, at nine years of age, he had lent his wakening sensibilities to a feeling perception of Nancy's fate and of its most weighty element, her basic racial reading of it as one who was "nothing but a nigger." This gives her story, so barely contained yet pointedly intuited by the boy, a socioethical scope complementary at least in its factors to that of the Compson family's disintegration. Again, the connections and contrasts

to be seen when corresponding subject matter is treated repeatedly but with a difference of mode and dimensions can
bring to fuller light not only the uniqueness of separate works
but the persistence of a fictional practice, under a temperament's commitment to the principles of an art. Melissa Meek,
the county librarian glanced at with sketchily fictional notice
in the documentary Appendix, depends for her motion and
very breath upon connective references to a family not her own
except in her continuing and finally obsessive awareness of
them. Her brief emergence is from the fringe of that host of
Faulkner's minor characters, their faces barely read in
passing, repeating uniquely the recurrent human suggestion
that "perhaps a tale" could be made of this. Their common
plea is that they be seen each as a self, solitary, yet a being
given shape and movement through circumstance and by
interpersonal relations and consequent private realizations.
Thereby Faulkner showed that no two fictional episodes can
be alike and each must be projected in its telling factors and
its essence by answering to the subjective heart of the narrative's matter, the positioned character's inmost experience of it.

The apparition and episodic passage of the little Yoknapatawpha County librarian intent on "saving" a middle-aged
Candace Compson successfully established as courtesan to the
enemy in the midst of World War II is peculiarly suggestive,
not only about particular qualities of mercy or its absence or
inapplicability if not irrelevance, but theoretically concerning
the fragment of narration so like a short story yet in and of
itself not quite that, lacking holistic autonomy. Yet in its approach so close to the condition of a total fictional entity that
it leaves a shimmer as persuasive as a mirage, this potentiality
can suggest what more should go into a fictional *fait accompli*.
In fiction seriously endeavored under conventions seen to
inhere in the most dynamic achievements in this art, accomplishment naturally requires more than a simply factual eventfulness. Under the grammar of fiction the sequentially
impinging cogs of plot are subordinate, however substantively
essential and as defining qualifiers. Though imagined events,

synopsized as to their overt inpingements, can validate the logic of their consequences, that is not fiction, in which the central matter implied by it and empathically realized from it is human experience, conveyed by suggestion of the characters' existential passage through cumulative realizations. Yet states or even streams of consciousness cannot exist alone as works of fictional art; indeed, even with the purest lyric in its arrest upon the moment there is some objectively related motion. The mind in its own place still must sojourn in a locale and hold itself up upon the flowing surface of occurrence. What makes the asymmetric instance of Melissa Meek illustrative of fiction's requirements is that it has the very essence but insufficiently sustained and contained, in that as the account stands, beyond herself the librarian is too largely beholden to the Compsons for her motivations, and it is peculiarly as thrall to Candace that she is impelled to venture out from the library. This insufficiency is no one's fault and indeed no real lack; Faulkner was not writing a short story but a documentary appendix to all he had already written of the Compsons. To note what elements of related matter would have to be built into a sustained narrative structure to make up what could be imaginatively comprised and intrinsically impelling as a short story about Melissa Meek is to realize appreciatively what has been accomplished in "Barn Burning" and "That Evening Sun," in each uniquely, in both completely, the first beyond any need for further connections, the other without undue dependence and submission to a larger context to which it is recognizably related, yet without essential dependence.

Quentin Compson of the story, remembering his world and himself in it at age nine, like Melissa Meek out of nowhere but Faulkner's appended improvisations about the Compsons, brings into clearer light the substance of human interrelations and private awareness, in the dynamic nexus required to animate fictional representation. They show in miniature the psychological complexity of such composition, in its essential imaginative synthesis of objective and subjective factors.

Specifically they silhouette Faulkner the artist in his grasp of potentialities and in the disciplined *élan* of his projection into particular endeavor, as realist and regionalist. The boy Quentin at nine images Faulkner's own lifelong awareness, reflectiveness, and ready empathy; Melissa Meek epitomizes an extravagance in the human heart's demands, which Faulkner understood and repeatedly risked showing under little control except the artist's own. Judgment of Faulkner requires what was only tardily and too reservedly granted him, a distinction between what he represents—which he properly centers in his characters' human experiences—and how he invigorates and yet controls that representation, by a penetrating imaginative power and a mastery of structuring, selective expansion and contraction, and stylistic effects. As regionalist he had at hand, and in hand through observation and participation, the immediate and intuited sense of concrete experience that is an indispensable factor of fiction; as realist he was equally committed to a complementary factor, the nature of individual and interpersonal experience as the fictionist's own possession of it qualifies and illuminates his temperamental intuition of it in his imaginatively conjured characters. It is memory in them, beyond controlled strengths of Faulkner's own, that the narratives must ride upon, yet not in reverie or deeper introversion, but with recall and expectation as the stabilizers of the thrust of present purposes in their existenial continuum.

In an age when experimentation has galloped off in several directions purposing to represent the "stream of consciousness," Faulkner is a standing point of reference, in his most finely developed short stories as well as novels, concerning what may or may not be feasible in representing the subjective element fictionally and how certain possible means may be made contributive within unitary and dynamic works of art. Centrally notable are his skilled rearrangements of chronology, with exploitation of various advantages under that flexibly transcendent point of view. Thus in the essential dramatic narrative he can hold events suspended, so that when they finally emerge they may have their fullest impact in the light of all they have led to, while with more purely subjective matter at issue he can drop into a character's consciousness at a crucial point—and in complement, at times this shift into something immediately arresting is his way of breaking off from a consummated climactic passage where further detail is dispensable and would retard momentum. Faulkner's ingenuity and economy in such orderings of the narrative and proportioning of emphasis within it are traits that went too little recognized by reviewers and are too seldom fully weighed even by carefully appreciative readers. The looseness of his earliest work, along with his continuing tendency to allow the extravagant its natural place in representations of reality, have combined into vague notions of an artist somewhat too intense and profuse.

Indisputably Faulkner may be that to some tastes, but others more eclectic may look closely over his shoulder to see in his workings an example of genius functioning creatively within the tradition. To relish a fictional work's effects it is not necessary to analyze its techniques and procedures, and indeed the purest experiences of any artistic creation are to be had in a direct, spontaneous, absorbed receptivity to those effects within the work's aesthetic totality; but if that is to be analyzed it may come down to a noticing of operative techniques, and such exposition sometimes can be of service in defense of the artist against impercipience compounded into derogation. Conversely, attention to techniques under the aspect of adapted tradition can instruct any admirer who naively credits an artist with complete originality in his ways and means. Faulkner did not invent the fictional tactics he so brilliantly employed in the unique strategies of each of his scrupulously unitary works. His reliance on admired predecessors (not just Balzac but more especially James and Conrad) is obvious; so too is his acceptance of an artist's responsibility to whatever already demonstrated literary mode he chooses to employ, to make it his own and thus paradoxically to prove and strengthen it through his singular personal specialization which illuminates its general validity and infinite possibilities. Such distinctions will bring to light how disciplined are Faulkner's originations, which despite an ardor that now and then verged on excess or an inventiveness that skirted self-defeat, were in the main one of the great consolidations within the tradition.

Detailed study of Faulkner will increasingly disclose the fact that this conspicuously idiosyncratic writer was at bottom a conventional artist, with quiet but abiding regard for certain enduring yet pliable modes of fictional art. His originality was not tangential but, as with other geniuses, an emanation out of the intensity of a temperament committed to its insights, and by good fortune focused upon matters that were amenable to his extraordinary powers of conception, structuring, and evocation which they enjoined. Specifically a sufficient acquaintance will show how organically functional was his grasp of the character-situation nexus, how steadfastly he served his belief that in fictional narration the very point of their juncture must be seen in the actors' awareness of themselves circumstanced, and how well that was made to implement his total thrust as humanistic realist and closely committed regionalist. The extent of Faulkner's accomplishment and its means are to be appreciated most closely, however, through a distinguishing between artful techniques themselves and the intentions of the sheer originative power behind them. Though Faulkner acknowledged the inheritance, in his Yoknapatawphan "postage stamp" of territory and population, of more matter than he could write about in a lifetime, he viewed all that as transposed into the realm of his imagination from the beginning, where it acquired fiction's freedoms of substance and treatment and its responsibilities as to tone and import. He was never historian nor documentarian and certainly no practitioner of "new journalism"; as his admirable piece on "Mississippi" in *Holiday* magazine showed, he was rather the imagistic lyricist of essences, with implication of issues and the human verities at stake.

Faulkner's idiosyncrasies as fictionist were indeed the virtue of so extraordinarily dynamic a creative temperament that to allege any immoderation is beside the point. The truth about him is that his intensity, though it may have admitted some excesses in his early work, was rapidly brought under a control which regulated it to his artistic aims without diminishing its power, and instead found further outlets for it. There is a distance as of a different order of nature between the opening pages of *Mosquitoes* (1927) and those of "Was" in *Go Down, Moses* (1942); meanwhile in *Absalom, Absalom!* (1936) the artist had shown he could release his powers to their fullest while keeping them under a control conducive to maximum compositional and tonal effect. He had soon taught himself to avoid outright interpolation, and while he continued to exercise a fictionist's privilege of omniscient third-person narration and description (with sound results, such as in *Light in August* and *A Fable*) he predominantly tended to a more purely fictionized mode, to which he imparted a recognizably Faulknerian vitality. In this what the artist empathically intuits of his characters' experiences is transmuted in some degree from fictionally represented ongoing consciousness in them; typically these entrusted conveyors of aspects of the narrative are key figures, whose responses operate centrally from within the fictional web of circumstances and with some import concerning theme, and they may be protagonists in the advertency or even the adversary role Faulkner often assigns them for his fables of good and evil. It is in representing the processes and effects of interpersonal engagement, the very substance of drama, that Faulkner becomes most dynamically subjective, imaginatively projecting a continuum of responses in the consciousness of characters evoked primarily to so serve him.

For fiction to build upon states of mind in the private flow of enactors' consciousness might seem a blanching out of dramatic force, and that can be so in a projection bent on sustaining a constant subjective tone by restricting itself to a character's free association in a languor of narcissism. Such subject matter would not have suited Faulkner, either as regionalist or as humanistic realist. His characters are out of a complex and stratified yet traditionally intimate society and are represented through their stressful, value-oriented engagement with each other within it. In such human relations, whether cooperative or in conflict, there can be shown something of psychological reality, in the quickening of consciousness rising to issues according to temperamental bent yet with alertness to whatever may be unique in its present emergence. In the midst of contention and strenuous overt action there is a vibrancy of response in those chosen minds through whose awareness and intent Faulkner is letting the reader see the story unfold in its human implications for its participants. They cannot merely mime his works, wherein narrative "action" goes far beyond what is completely visible as such. One basic factor is the lively implicativeness Faulkner can infuse into scenes through the individualized overtones in his closely keyed, aptly colloquial dialogue. Beyond that, yet still connected to situation, is the further suggestion of what is inward and of the essence as operative consciousness in certain characters functioning crucially in the action; this is still more subtly implied by the modulated tones of the narrative account, made resonant with the sense of the characters'experiences. These are matters which still await thorough critical appraisal pointing to an incomparable achievement in the aesthetics of fiction, where again it is not so much what Faulkner experimentally devised as what he brought to fuller uses under the perceived potentialities of the art.

It can be pointedly indicative of what the artist has advanced into if note is taken of how Faulkner balances substantive details, obligatory developments, evocative enhancement, and rigorous limitations or exclusions in a whole economy of plenitude, ellipses, and modulated momentum. All this implies of course no more than the basic complex strategy of any effective fiction (and in fact the simpler the work may appear to be the more imperatively these principles may have operated), but as always with Faulkner the remarkable achievements are not so much by sheer innovation

as by the conceptual reach and imaginative vigor in his extensions of what was latent within the conventions of fiction.
Central to this is his way of bringing the subjectivity of certain
key characters pervasively into the story's fabric, yet allowing
consciousness its own chronology, transcending that of overt
events in the fictional work. This too is realism, and of the
most telling kind, since it closely suggests human experience in
its very process and context, with the enactors' minds
remembering and anticipating and with whatever appeal the
reader may find in all this to his ranging intuitions and
empathy. Faulkner's bold use of this factor can contribute to a
peculiarly intense effect of complex narrative motion. Within
an instant in the time sequence of overt happenings a character's awareness may move backward in associative recollection
and forward in further realization. Yet this transcendence is
not by "free association"; its stimulus is out of the immediate
new event, under which memory may set some past matters in
a new order or may reconstruct expectation, yet with instantaneous response to what is externally current. How far and how
dramatically this runs beyond "stream of consciousness"
fiction as conventionally thought of must be fully understood
to appreciate Faulkner's accomplishment, or at least not to
misapprend or misjudge it.

The interrelations which abound in Faulkner's works,
especially through his highly localized and conceptually
focused regionalism, produce resonances of all kinds, echoes,
reflective pauses upon old matters, and further apprehensions
stemming from formative memories. Recurrences to bygone
event as that reappears in the guise of consequences is of
course a substantial factor in any plot; so likewise is the reappearance of characters in projections beyond their already
known bent and potential. At a higher conceptual level,
theme may be repeatedly sounded by related imagery; this
Faulkner most effectively does by locating the realization not
in authorial narration but as passing recollection by a concerned character. Still more pointedly, at a crucial moment,
the story may be volatilized totally into the ongoing motion of

a protagonist's consciousness, in a compendious further realization, epiphanal and something more too, in the extent of its socioethical reference. Not that the conning mind in such interrelation is ever quite disinterested, but its rearrangements of things past will serve not only to characterize but to support the large Faulknerian theme of the human heart's struggle with itself. Sometimes in consequence there is a rise to the heightened tone which the self may allow itself in secret, while behind all of such fictional representation is the empathic and just mind of Faulkner the artist, maintaining realities in their various shadowings-forth of import. Sustained timbre in Faulkner's varied narratives is a natural outcome of his humanistic concern with the individual's "buried life," and of this artist's brilliant strategies in representing the continuities of subjectivity within its circumstantial context. With Faulkner a constant wakeful awareness in characters (and echoed in readers) becomes the sustained incidental music of the fluctuantly represented fictional actions. His intensification within his narratives of the sensed presence of ongoing human lives at deep levels of their awareness of self and surroundings is a determining aspect of his art, and exemplary of the subjective factor rightfully poised in fiction, while also clearest index of Faulkner's genius. It is to be found in his best short stories, it surges and pulses like an aurora borealis in the skies of the worlds that are his novels; and though in this mode he speaks with the syntax of fictional art, the special resonances so strongly prolonged are in his own inimitable voice.

To recognize recurrence as memoried reference proceeding beyond mere repetition into an advance of awareness, to see a Faulknerian story's permutations as having the higher consistency of a fictional motion conditioned overtly by circumstance and subjectively through the enactors' conscious responses, and to sense this altogether as more than plot, as aesthetically an action distilled out of a conceived human situation—this is essential to a full realization of Faulkner. The effects in his fiction, though of drastic import, are not abrupt, much less peremptory. Modulations between matter and mind proceed almost like the unobserved change of light upon the same object within some minutes that have just passed; yet this aesthetic gradualism, however richly referential, sustains the synthesized continuity of event and realization, and prolongs that motion which gives Faulkner's compositions their extraordinary vigor and credible vitality. In this, however, no fictionist could stand further than Faulkner does beyond a primary dependence upon mere curiosity as to the final outcome of plot in an overt disposition of the several major characters. Even in *Absalom, Absalom!,* that fable of hubris set in a maze of secrets, while the characters surprise themselves with speculation and each other with facts (as when Quentin gets round to telling Shreve that Sutpen's child by Milly Jones was not the sought son but a mere female), the reader is kept more contemplatively and empathically absorbed in tracings of inpingements of events upon consciousness, both in the enactors and the reconstructors of the tale. For Faulkner ultimately suspense is endless this side of God's judgment and disposal. What is chiefly and progressively disclosed in his fictions is further revelation concerning character as of its inmost being in its existential progression amid vicissitudes. In consequence his stories are essentially open-ended; the only finality is metaphysical, in that the enactors still live within ongoing time and their own progressing awareness, which will carry them by chance and by choice into further confrontations with issues unpredictable but certain to impose upon them other shaping influences that will evoke further realizations. Even *Absalom, Absalom!,* despite its seeming finalities of devastating violence, is inconclusive; Shreve points out that in Jim Bond "You've got one nigger left. One nigger Sutpen left," while Quentin still has the South as his heritage to deal with in an ambivalence of hatred and love. Throughout Faulkner's work it is demonstrated that in open-ended narratives an organic unity is to be found beyond summary denouement, in the represented aspect of characters' subjective responses to the transitory, both in events and as of

themselves, modified by passing event, but of a fabric somewhat more enduring and self-renewing.

When Faulkner had second thoughts granting him a more
expansive way to open *The Hamlet* than through young
Sarty Snobes as his agent, perhaps he more readily surrendered "Barn Burning" completely and conclusively to that
young protagonist, knowing that as artist he might never
again be granted so prime, substantial, and lucid an epitome
of man in motion as his working premise. Perhaps likewise two
years after creating *The Sound and the Fury* and with
Absalom, Absalom! in the offing, when he turned back in
"That Evening Sun" to Quentin Compson at twenty-four
remembering himself at nine, the artist similarly could have
been conscious of illustrating a principle, through a protagonist's stirring awareness of entry into what was to be the self's
anxious ongoing inner dialogue with circumstance, in empathic suppositions about others under the aspects of human
verities and the solitariness of personal dooms. Faulkner too,
and also out of local situation intimately experienced, repeatedly turns to his Yoknapatawphan characters — as young
Quentin anxiously did to the frightened Nancy, asking "What
is it?" — but with the artist's deeper and more intuitive sense of
the whole matter of fact and fatality and the pity of it. And
somewhat like Sarty, though less acutely and more abstractly,
Faulkner was agonized by the imperative that he distance
himself somewhat from his flawed heritage in its regional
aspect and repudiate what remained socially unamended in it,
though this was done without surrender of affection and all
possible pride. Here analogy, as sometimes may be, is most
illustrative by its lack of complete correspondence; Sarty's
father, Ab is no personification of the South at any stage, but
one of its worst aberrations, and while there was no salvation
for Sarty except by denunciation and flight, Faulkner could
best assert his integrity by the natural piety of an unbroken
attachment to his region, with his humanely appreciative
judgments upon a variety of individuals in it.

Consequently Faulkner's close devotion to a Jefferson incorporated by artistic fiat in a mythologized Yoknapatawpha County did not hamper but stimulated a profuse inventiveness, and through the strength of his temperament he found there an ample stage for humanistic realism. His lifelong, intimate acquaintance was with a limited but variously peopled area possessed of a lively and tragic history, yet one where life was pervaded by the paradoxical tendency to live dynamically as individuals within the stresses of its multiple conventions. So since for Faulkner the central realism is in the subjectivity of primary characters, he did not write ordinary biographical, cradle-to-grave novels, with their miscellany of events and diverse crises and their comparatively loose linkage of periods and major episodes. (In this he is specifically the opposite of Dickens, whom in other ways he has been found to resemble.) Instead, the unitary effect desired for thematic emphasis, fluent modulation and intensities of tone, and narrative celerity is sought by Faulkner through close focus not only on select events but on specific determinants, basically subjective. Thomas Sutpen and Isaac McCaslin appear in what are life-stories, but each account takes its holistic aesthetic form from a protagonist's conditioning in adolescence, and each man is dealt with in actions given place because they dramatize that determinant operating as intensely conscious motivation. The same subjective mode holds with Faulkner characters who move from story to story, and through quite different events. In Quentin Compson the recognizable consistency as he appears at various ages and in contrasted circumstances in the two novels and "That Evening Sun" is in the extremity of his extended sensibilities. Ratliff, through the volumes of the *Snopes* trilogy and over the more than a generation that they cover, becomes more sophisticatedly articulate, but his native sagacity, humor, and poised good will remain to be drawn out in different but always veracious responses according to circumstances ranging from the farcical to the ethically outrageous and deeply pathetic. Though

Ratliff's is a more restricted habitat, and he a simpler man, in his versatile adaptability he is comparable to Conrad's Marlow, another example of the power of a vital character's subjectivity to illuminate a tale as well as to extract its essence out of its ongoing motion, while remaining within its unitary autonomy, even in so focused and subjectively framed a short story as "Youth."

Since there is about Faulkner's characters this uniquely strong aura of passage that suggests any appearance is only a glimpse of what is evolving uniquely yet with complex response to situation, and could play its idiosyncratic part accordingly in other encounters, for this artist no fictional persona is a whole man, arrived at a steady pose for portraiture. Character is not to be summed up in its lively reactivity until after some last glimpse, since from the first it has been materialized as of a being moving through discoveries and compounded responses which aggregate into a mutant silhouette in transit. Basically this conforms to a refined narrative mode that has supported some of the most specialized developments in excellent modern fiction. However, no other artist than Faulkner has more soundly and effectually intensified within fluent yet thematically weighty narratives the sensed presence of ongoing human lives at deep levels of their awareness and response in the personal-societal crux, of which they convey a deep sense, on their own terms and to the reader himself alone, in the unique reciprocities of representative art.

A special aesthetic result of the subjective element in Faulkner's fictions (beyond conveying an ultimate realism through an immediate sense of individual lives in experiential process) is the pervasive force of this mode in support of the narrative's unitary effect. In fiction of such high calibre as Faulkner's, plot can be no more than mere contrivance except as it is enacted by characters from whose being and becoming its real motion is derived. Indeed, with Faulkner—as with James or Conrad—the *donnée* becomes imperative and operates essentially as an illustrative imagining of certain beings' progressive idiosyncratic responses to situation and a personal strategic engagement therewith. This is true throughout Faulkner's most significant work, whatever its narrative scope, whether in Quentin's rapid but careful retrospective return into his ninth year and a surrender of the story of Nancy to the tones of his intuitive experiences then and there; or Sarty's sober claiming of moral self-possession by a quick detachment, however painful, from his savage father; or Chick Mallison's four-year progression, more gradually but also through points of crisis, until he was ready to repudiate not a father but that something in his society which he had been forced to see not as the faces of men but as the visage of a mob. Yet it is not only or peculiarly as to the maturation of Southern youths but also in the still cumulative insights of old age that the enhancing factor of subjectivity enters into Faulkner's fictions, vitalizing plot and enhancing the sense of composition as it advances into an organic totality—representative, thematic, and tonal.

If it be postulated that in the most potent fiction its evocative force has its primacy in the consciousness of major personae moving responsively as individual beings through the narrative's overt events, this may seem most revealingly exemplified at close range when Faulkner, through revisions, transferred "Delta Autumn" from *Story* magazine into its greater place in *Go Down, Moses*. What is especially illuminating is that the changes were not in the basic skeletal plot; in the enhanced version this still tells of a white man's fathering a mulatto woman's male infant, and then refusing to see her when she comes to the hunting camp looking for him, but imposing upon Isaac McCaslin the awkward task of telling her "No" and giving her an envelope stuffed with money, as if in settlement. This is painful enough for the austerely ethical old man, and the magazine version shows his deep compassion for the abandoned woman and child, and also his agonized reading into this secret offense and its private grief an omen of general doom, extending beyond a disordered society to the misused land itself. As it stood in *Story* magazine "Delta Autumn" is a powerful and brilliantly realized short story, and much of this merit was brought over directly into the revised version, but what makes the greatest difference (and not just in its strengthened connections with the rest of *Go Down, Moses*, but within its own containment) is that the roles of mulatto woman and white man are now assigned to characters different from those in the original version, with more intense involvements for themselves and more acute and portentous realizations for Isaac. Boyd, in the *Story* version, is a rough, totally cynical man, briefly treated in just those terms; in the revision the faithless lover and evasive betrayer is Carothers ("Roth") Edmonds, a somewhat complex and ambivalent person, whose harshness is often a cloak for his shame. Moreover, he is Isaac's younger cousin, to whom Isaac had taught the hunter's craft and code; and as for the rejected mulatto woman, she is a fifth-generation descendant of Isaac's grandfather, slave-holding founder of the Mississippi branch of the McCaslin family and also begetter by miscegenation and subsequent incest of the so-called Beauchamp line. Isaac as a young man had known this woman's grandfather, James ("Tennie's Jim"), and also Jim's sister Fonsiba and the younger brother Lucas Beauchamp, all of that third generation of mingled McCaslin and Negro blood. Consequently when Roth's rejected mistress reveals her identity Isaac is the more severely shocked; bitter knowledge of this irregularly pro- liferant family history has restrictively shaped his whole life, and he must now take something of the woman's grief and Roth's shame upon himself, in a sharpening of his more general despair. In this course of events (which connect with the book's preceding section, "The Bear," and derive much from it) the surprises certainly are major and the turn in the plot is powerfully dramatic, yet it is most of all in what this means to Isaac and how it weighs upon him in his old age that the story as revised takes on its greatest intensity. It is a com- plete illustration of Faulkner's power to extend and deepen import by absorbing the already formulated into a larger con- tainment, and plainly his intention here is typically focused, beyond events themselves, upon what they mean to his protagonist.

Ratliff once remarked that for lawyers nothing was right until it had been "complicated up" enough. A Faulkner plot as such may be quite complicated too (as in *Light in August* with its interlocking patterns of life-stories, or more specifically in *Intruder in the Dust*), but in no case has it been made so for plot's sake. Events may be drawn into a more intricate and tighter knot, yet the central and most powerful effect is not found there but in terms of subjective impact upon certain of the characters; and by such typifyings of crucial human experience it runs beneath the narrative of overt events like a series of shudders as of the ground itself, through a parable of socioeconomic doom in which personal factors merge into the ultimate incalculabilities of the human predicament. His consequent apocalyptic vision is shown to strike old Isaac quite as severely in both versions of the story; and indeed the two texts, after the woman's departure and on to the end, are essentially the same, the minute revisions being stylistic rather than any modification of substance. However, most readers as they come to the closure of "Delta Autumn" in the context of *Go Down, Moses* will feel Isaac's experience more strongly, in its implied greater depth for him through the change in the players from Boyd to Roth Edmonds and the identification of the mulatto woman as of that particular Beauchamp lineage. With this fact revealed, there looms out of the past but still beyond propitiation the specter of Isaac's grandfather, Lucius Quintus Carothers McCaslin, whose miscegeny and resultant mixture of bloods were to be deduced decades later by the youthful Isaac out of the antebellum McCaslin plantation commissary records, influencing him to repudiate his McCaslin heritage and refuse the inheritance, with the consequent failure of his marriage to an embittered ambitious woman, who had stipulated his conformity as the price of her bearing him a son. All of which the reader of *Go Down, Moses* will have known by the time he reaches "Delta Autumn," but it is returned to explicitly enough in this revised version to make clear such profound unforgettable conditionings of Isaac's ongoing conscious responses, and to suggest in some measure the depths of that despair which his last words in the story suggest has quieted into stoic resignation.

Though in Faulkner's continuing struggle to remain financially afloat he did hack out some uninspired short stories, most of his work in this form was with genuine and complete commitment, and when he adapted some of these stories into his novels it was never a mere mercenary compounding of assets in hand but a further conceptual and imaginative thrust, from a sound base, and into deeper import. Of such ongoing vital creativity, and at the level of genius, "Delta Autumn" in its adaptation into *Go Down, Moses* is a superb example. Yet it cannot illustrate a "method," for the practice was never that. Any instance of fusion of a Faulkner story into one of his novel's more extended and complex total structure gives a glimpse through only the barest of his synthesizing imagination at work. This was more than the fabrication of a plot or the assembling of a puzzle into complete visibility; it was the arresting of reality in the processes that circumstanced human existence. Because this was the passionate concern of the artist in his very habitude, he looked with compassionate vision into the fancied representative lives of others, and with more than ordinary insight, and what he thus saw he made his stories of. They came out of everything he knew and felt, and out of nowhere but himself. The associative echoes in the minds of Faulkner's characters derive from the artist's own resonant and keyed consciousness, his regard for the humane injunction to "connect," his empathic polity that could set even the lowly and inarticulate within other men's hearing, his unyielding partisanship as between the evils men do and the enduring human verities. He could make the ironies of a situation resoundingly typical, yet transpose it into the unique minor air of a private fate. He built massive novels in which he sometimes approached the spectacular, yet often what is made most memorable is the pause, the quiet solitude at the heart of the human matter, all out of artist's concerned remembrance and speculation.

And the virtue that was in him, so lively and yet judicious, could find right containment in many forms. Such achieved compositions as "Barn Burning" and "That Evening Sun" not only could stand alone but were not amenable to fusion within their more voluminous familial contexts. However, the imaginative story "Delta Autumn" led to the enhanced revision which not only could take a significant place in a larger company but could supply through its closure a gathering up of Isaac McCaslin's life story, and thus weave into *Go Down, Moses* further associative and thematic strands to bind its sections into the most subtly integrated and hauntingly attuned of all Faulkner's novels.

9

Go Down, Moses

IN 1940 (as he reminded his publishers the following year) Faulkner had "mentioned a volume, collected short stories, general theme being relationship between white & negro races here." The book's title was to be *Go Down, Moses;* the first story was to be "The Fire and the Hearth"—which evolved into a three-part novella concerning Lucas Beauchamp, young and old. A portion of this material, "A Point of Law," had appeared in *Colliers* in June 1940, and a further section, "Gold is Not Always," in the *Atlantic Monthly* in November of that year. The other stories, in their proposed order, were to be "Pantaloon in Black" (from *Harpers,* October 1940), "The Old People" (from *Harpers,* September 1940, "Delta Autumn" (which was to appear in *Story,* May-June 1942), and lastly "Go Down, Moses" (from *Colliers,* 25 January 1941). "I will rewrite them, to an extent," Faulkner promised, and then added that "some additional material might invent itself in process." It did, and these additions made *Go Down, Moses* one of the most powerful, intriguing, and characteristically opalescent of all his works, supportive of opinion that this is not an adventitious roundup of discrete narratives but an aggregation into a basically unitary composition, through structural and tonal variations abstracting a complex theme. As such it is one of the most subtly imaginative of creations within the modern novel's ongoing originative trends. And Faulkner's knowledgeable craftsman's phrase, when first suggesting the project, that

334

more "might invent itself in process," was piously tentative yet full of a faith which was amazingly rewarded, out of what at the time was forming and emerging from his imagination's depths, in a climax of vitality. The mentioned stories were not only extended but deepened, especially as to the proposed general theme of "relationship between white and negro," through development of a racial and also universally representative crisis in "The Fire and the Hearth" between Lucas Beauchamp and Zack Edmonds, by a larger regional abstraction through an episode between these two men's sons, and in the more acute focusing of Isaac McCaslin's story through the recasting of "Delta Autumn." There were also significant additions of units beyond the table of contents Faulkner first suggested to his publishers. The new opening was reconstituted out of an unsold story called "Almost," that had a nine-year-old narrator named Bayard; "Was," the revision, moved to third person with McCaslin Edmonds, nine, as central intelligence witness and conveyor, but significantly was prefaced by that unique page-and-a-half abstract of Isaac as Uncle Ike, which not only shows him as inheritor from his elder cousin McCaslin of this grotesquely tinged tale out of the decade before he was born, but may seem an intended fair notice that *Go Down, Moses* will unfold itself in its own way yet with sufficient resonance to hearing ears. Of most import, there is also the insertion, between "The Old People" and "Delta Autumn," of the lengthy five-part narrative "The Bear," which extended itself far beyond that portion of its matter contained in the earlier short story "Lion" in *Harper's Magazine* of December 1935, and in so doing became the dynamic epicenter of *Go Down, Moses.*

"The Bear," together with "The Old People" and "Delta Autumn" and as framed by them, makes Isaac McCaslin's life story one of the most impressive novellas in modern fiction, fit to rank with the work of such masters as James, Conrad, and Mann in this felicitously refined-substantial mode. Nor does this three-part novella eclipse the book's other four sections or minimize their essential intrication within the novel as an orchestrated whole, as it can be sensed in the reading of *Go Down, Moses* from first to last. Yet concerning this point, beyond the text itself a great deal of interest and relevance is to be gathered from Professor Joseph Blotner's account in his meticulously detailed biography of the stages by which *Go Down, Moses* grew to be more than "Go Down, Moses" and "other stories," as the first-edition title page had indicated. Professor Blotner shows that when Faulkner was assembling the units which were to constitute the book and was revising — sometimes extensively and pointedly — those which had been published earlier as short stories, he had typed fourteen pages of the newly constituted "Delta Autumn" and then stopped. If he had got to this story, then according to the original plan suggested to his publishers and within the chronology of Isaac McCaslin's life, this would mean he had already dealt with "The Old People," that story now given over specifically to the boy Isaac's initiation into the hunter's craft and code by old Sam Fathers, the man of mixed blood and all its collective wisdom. This for Isaac was supplemented through kindly fostering by his cousin McCaslin Edmonds, seventeen years his senior, and the medium (out of his own boyhood antebellum memories) as the central intelligence in the opening story, "Was," and McCaslin is concerned debater with Isaac in the crucial section 4 of "The Bear." If Faulkner had typed fourteen pages of the revised "Delta Autumn," in the fourth paragraph he probably had already changed the offender Boyd to Roth (McCaslin Edmonds' grandson, Zack's son Carothers), then in the fifth had identified Roth as Isaac's kinsman, and on that page had gone on with Legate's not too cryptic jesting about Roth's pursuit of a certain doe, "the one that walks on two legs — when she's standing up, that is. Pretty light-colored, too. . . . The one I figured maybe he was still running when he was gone all that month last January."

At this early point in the process of revision (and though Legate's talk is left essentially the same as in the *Story* magazine version) even if Faulkner had not yet fully determined his course, it might seem that with the transfer of the faithless

white man's role from Boyd to Roth the artist might also have
been feeling his way toward making the rejected woman of a
latter generation in that Beauchamp line of mixed blood,
descended by way of what Faulkner was yet to set forth in
section 4 of "The Bear," Isaac's grandfather's cohabitation
and incest with two of his slaves, mother and daughter. Certainly with the youthful protagonist's role in "The Old People"
now reassigned, this time to young Isaac McCaslin, and with
old Isaac's younger cousin Roth Edmonds being given that
shameful place in the intensifyingly revised "Delta Autumn,"
Faulkner was finding more impressively structured and potently circumstanced means of treating the theme originally
stated to his publishers, "relationship between white and
negro races here," and in terms of a family history and of a
protagonist whose oppressive heritage it became as he
matured. And the artist in him may have been realizing
imaginatively that here was the whole flow and range of a significantly lived existence to be traced, by inserting a major
section between a twelve-year-old boy's shooting his first buck
under Sam Fathers' tutelage in a hunter's proper ways, in
"The Old People," and the final disenchantments of a bereft
but principled and stoic old man, in "Delta Autumn." Only
through a reading of that magnificently composed creation,
"The Bear," in itself and with its enhancement of a protagonist envisioned previously as a younger boy and later as old
man, can it be imagined with what strenuous surmises of
immensities moving into his ken Faulkner had stopped in the
midst of revising "Delta Autumn" and began to write a first
section of what was to be the heart and crucial substance of a
life-story, Isaac McCaslin's.

"The Bear" opens with Isaac a youth of sixteen, the well-
tempered disciple of Sam Fathers, accepted into the companionship of a select party of experienced hunters including
his elder cousin McCaslin Edmonds. However, the narrative of
this story's part 1 (which Faulkner dispatched to his publishers
in July, 1941) soon reverts to its main substance, the boy's
earlier solitary proving of himself by trailing the legendary old

bear, without a gun and finally leaving his compass behind, until at a remoteness in the leafy summer woods he and the wily old creature come near enough to exchange glimpses of each other. That encounter, as if by the old bear's consent, implies a further initiation in a more mystical connection between man and nature than that in a hunter's however atavistically rooted taking of an animal; and in the factual context of Faulkner's compositional procedures at this point those exchanged glances may seem comparatively to suggest the artist in his questing approach to realities and the good fortune of a granted closer vision.

The techniques and strategies generally empowering Faulkner's creativity can be looked at with some profit by tracing what he chose to include from some of his published short stories, how he merged such material into the larger fabrics of novels, and with what modifications and additions. In such processes it would seem a frugal scissors-and-paste practicality was not what moved him; with him apparently the completed achievement is to become more than the result of a sudden and sufficient inspiration, but rather at any such beginning he sets foot into a new land which he pioneers, maps, develops, and thus increasingly takes possession of. With "The Bear" as ultimately and greatly realized in *Go Down, Moses* the artist's growth into his subject in the course of creating the work is an edifying history in itself. In his bibliography, "The Short Fiction of William Faulkner," Professor James B. Meriwether has a useful section, "The Collections," which lists not only the contents of volumes of short stories but, beginning with *Absalom, Absalom!,* names the published short stories assimilated into the novels. Concerning "The Bear" as in *Go Down, Moses* Professor Meriwether notes that it "incorporates, extensively revised, 'Lion', *Harper's,* December 1935, and 'The Bear', *Saturday Evening Post,* 9 May 1942." The *Harper's* story is related briefly to section 1 of "The Bear" in the novel, but more fully to sections 3 and 5, furnishing an index to the kind of further intrications Faulkner would venture upon whenever he compounded earlier material by more amplified and deepened treatment in extension of work in progress.

Written about five years before Faulkner began to put together the units that were to constitute *Go Down, Moses,* "Lion" in *Harper's* was a detailed and firmly ordered story, characteristically Faulknerian in its vigor and picturesqueness, though more episodic than climactic, and (with fictional propriety) set at the comparatively simple level of its young first-person narrator, one Quentin, sixteen, there with his father, but himself observant and responsive to events and persons. Returned to for larger uses, "Lion" provided a store of substantial material, amenable to enhancement for fusion into the novel's more profoundly conceived and brilliantly set forth central piece, "The Bear," which was to make Isaac McCaslin its youthful protagonist but to trace him more fully in experiential motion and maturation and to convey these deeper matters in their more subjective colorations through the further reach of third-person narration. The *Harper's* story began with details similar to what would constitute scene and atmosphere in the first pages of "The Bear" in the novel, with Isaac too at sixteen, an already seasoned hunter and woodsman, admitted as an equal into the company of experienced men at Major DeSpain's camp for the annual December bear hunt, that will focus on the patriarch of those ancient woods, Old Ben. The short story "Lion" touched only briefly on these introductory details, mentioning the men's customary good talk, reminiscent of other seasons, over whisky, the hunter's drink, and then moved into events that will be part of section 3, in this novel to come. Section 1 of "The Bear" will suggest the acutely conscious youth always listening, but then will drop quickly drop back into a new and richer substance, the boy's privileged apprenticeship in the big woods from his tenth year on, under the incomparable Sam Fathers' guidance, and those milestones in the boy's increase in skills and wisdom — his trailing the old bear with Sam to show him the marks and even the print of the maimed foot, and the next summer his compulsively going alone unarmed into the woods to catch sight of Old Ben, and, as it chanced, to be looked back at, as if in an acknowledgment. Sam Fathers' formative presence in the boy's life is not shown in "Lion," and theoretically speaking, the characterization in *Go Down, Moses* of such a man and his influence is of a dimension and recurrent thematic reach that could not be encompassed in a short story. The poignant matter of Sam Fathers' death and presumably requested Indian burial and the glimpse of his devoted disciple Isaac's passionate defensiveness that closes section 3 of "The Bear" may not yet have been conceived when "Lion" was written; at any rate the short story does not include it. Yet since chronology in the ten pages of "Lion" extends between details specifically corresponding to those at the opening and the closing of "The Bear" in *Go Down, Moses,* a juxtaposition of the story as comparatively incomplete skeleton and the 140 pages of the novella as Faulkner's fullest realization of the matter suggests a reciprocally constructive interaction in an artist's creative processes. This is more complex than that of a painter (such as Cezanne) from preliminary sketch to final version, since for the fictionist an elementary plot may give rise to further envisionings of the chief enactors, which might stimulate invention of circumstances to draw those potentials into play, and so on in further converse and commerce between plot and character, as artistic imagination realizes and consolidates its creations. The short story "Lion" sketches matter which will enter into part 3 of "The Bear" in the novel; Boon is sent to Memphis to get more whisky and sixteen-year-old "Quentin" (here the first-person narrator) is sent along to see that the strong, impetuous, childlike man gets back to camp with the supply. On the train and in Memphis Boon's boasting tells of the great dog Lion, but the detailed account of Sam Fathers' trapping and training this animal for the bear hunt was not yet made part of the matter. In "The Bear" in the novel Quentin will become "the boy . . . Ike . . . Isaac McCaslin," sixteen years old and the central intelligence in a third-person narrative, besides being in the midst of the action when the old bear they have hunted for several seasons is finally brought down, though not by a bullet but with Lion's jaws fixed in his throat and Boon astride Old Ben, stabbing him to save Lion. In the *Harper's* short story Quentin does not have any part in that hunt or sight of it; he can tell only of its passing clamor from his assigned "stand" in the woods. He does see Lion brought back to camp, mortally mangled, and hears the manner of it, but there is nothing in the short story about Sam Fathers' death soon after from exhaustion, he having collapsed at the climax of the hunt; neither is anything told of the youth's poignant watching by his childhood mentor after Boon and he have placed the body on a platform in accordance with Indian tradition. In the novel Faulkner rounded out the portrait of Sam Fathers and related Isaac's part in the great hunt to the theme of his earlier apprenticeship as hunter in the book's preceding section, "The Old People." Finally, though, the *Harper's* story "Lion" has something of what will be developed in the novel version's section 5 of "The Bear" — the youth's nostalgic return to the big woods in summer, seeing where Lion had been buried, and finding Boon crazed by his ineptitude with a gun and hostile in his embarrassment. However, the story puts little emphasis upon the progressing destruction of the great woods by the timbering operation, which in the novel will sound the note of devastation, an analogue in nature to what is to be Isaac's private fate, as compounded of disenchantment and personal deprivation. Faulkner found his way to all this within the great central section 4 of "The Bear," through two climactic events, Isaac's shocking discoveries in the commissary ledgers about his grandfather McCaslin's miscegenation and then incest with two of his slaves, which impelled the grandson to renounce his inheritance when he came of age, and brought on his wife's conjugal rejection of him for his refusing to reclaim it, thereby leaving him "father to no one." His resolute acts of conscience and patient endurance of their results situate him as the book's central figure, by whom others may be justly measured, yet he is of such probity and magnanimity as makes him "uncle to half a county." While Faulkner admits into their major roles in the book such various characters as Lucas Beauchamp, Sam Fathers, the Edmonds generations — McCaslin, Zack, and Roth — and Boon, Rider, Gavin Stevens, the conception of Isaac in a chief protagonist's dominance — basically as Sam's disciple in woodsmanship and thus as inheritor and contemporary adapter of Sam's ethic growing out of primitive man's pious relation to nature — could have been what led this dynamic artist imaginatively during the expansion and integration of *Go Down, Moses* to construct "The Bear" as heart of the larger work, with its section 4 as peak and thematic center in the story of Isaac McCaslin, and with significant realtion to the major theme of the whole book.

Quite another matter than "Lion" in *Harper's*, "The Bear" in *The Saturday Evening Post* scarcely can be considered Faulkner's source material for refinement into the novel. Instead, here the process of incorporating anew was reversed; the magazine story is an offshoot, a quickly drafted expedient recasting. Less inclusive chronologically and in detail than "Lion," it does not tell of the final organized hunt, but only of episodes resembling pages in parts 2 and 4, the first the boy's ambushing the old bear but not shooting and instead running in close to rescue his fearless little fyce, the second his elder cousin McCaslin's trying to help him understand the idealism that may have prompted his actions. Faulkner explained to his agent and so to the *Post* editor that the story was a rewrite from "a book under way," a "first draft and in haste because I need some money badly," and he fell in with the editor's suggestion that he add to the story's conclusion to make it more accessible to readers. It was real financial need — more of the same that had caused Faulkner to write some acknowledged potboilers and periodically had driven him to what for him were the "salt mines" of Hollywood — which led him to make extracts at two points from work in progress and structure a story he titled "The Bear," with hopes of getting a thousand dollars from the *Post* for what would pass as another hunting story. Yet in the midst of these expediencies he chose valued matter, revealing the boy Isaac in a complex but spontaneous act of forbearance and courage, and his cousin McCaslin's attempt to explain these traits to him as veritable and honorable aspects of the heart's truth. While this second episode in the *Post* story was extracted out of that masterful complexity which was to constitute part 4 of "The Bear" in the novel, it does not relate to the main plot factors there (Isaac's discoveries in the ledgers, his consequent refusal to inherit the McCaslin holdings, despite his cousin McCaslin Edmonds' protest, and with the further consequence of impasse with his wife). In the *Post* story the exchange with McCaslin is from a flashback at a pause in the strenuous argument in the commissary on Isaac's twenty-first birthday, as he recalls one of his elder cousin's earlier sympathetic attempts to help the youth understand himself in his strivings toward maturity. Faulkner was after a needed thousand dollars, but he turned away from cheaper material at hand and instead extracted something of pertinence, out of what at the time his imagination was suffused with. Aside from that, whether in extracting this material from the novel in progress he strengthened his grasp on those episodes would lie beyond conjecture even were there a day-to-day log of work done, yet it is evident that *Go Down, Moses* is a product of organic creative growth, a feat of the imagination at its height, with the novel's tonal-thematic unity its ultimate fruit. Certainly in section 4 (pages 254 to 315) of "The Bear" in the novel, Faulkner was working at the top of his bent. "Some additional material," as he had put it in his prospectus for the book, continued to "invent itself in process." Explaining a delay at this point, he wrote his publishers, "There is more meat in it than I thought . . . which requires careful writing and rewriting to get it exactly right." There spoke the artist who (though he was not being credited for it) did not stint or begrudge his craft. The result here was exactly right and more; it is one of the greatest compositional movements in all of fictional art.

IMPLICIT STRUCTURE

That *Go Down, Moses and Other Stories* was the book's title in its first edition, in 1942 but when it was reprinted the phrase "and other stories" was dropped may have roused second thoughts in other minds. Although in first offering such a volume to his publishers Faulkner had called it "collected short stories," he had indicated later his belief that "Moses is indeed a novel," and this in him is realization of what his devisings had grown into. The view is supportable, not only because Faulkner's prospectus of a "general theme" of "relationship between white & negro races here" is sustained by tides moving back and forth from first to last, but because the seven main sections retain their separate titles not as chapters but as unique integers, yet to greater or less degree expanded and deepened, in recastings and thematic coordinations which carried the matter far beyond original formulations. Indeed, as Faulkner discovered, these exceeded his original conceptions, especially in those two main consolidations, "The Fire and the Hearth" and the triptych depicting Isaac McCaslin's life. Nevertheless some will still raise the question whether *Go Down, Moses* should be termed a novel. Certainly it shows no such sustained intrication and close subjective containment in a single character and his interpreter as does *Absalom, Absalom!,* and in its spread over a larger time span than *The Hamlet* occupies it also lacks one prevailing theme as specific as that of Flem Snopes' incursion. Yet interconnections among the seven parts of *Go Down, Moses* are close, and motifs recur, with their modulations refining a delicate intimation of structure, as in a musical suite. Nevertheless, naming this remarkable work in its entirety a novel must rest upon a judging (and more strictly with fiction than music) just how far and with what variation can composition extend and yet aggregate into an aesthetic, an imaginatively evocative unity.

Such a sensing of it can be supported by noting its aspects as another Southern family saga, of further extent and variety than the Sartoris, Sutpen, and Compson histories, and one more interfused than even *Absalom, Absalom!* with the biracial theme. This has two aspects: the ancestral McCaslin factor operates most crucially and persistently in *Go Down, Moses,* three of the seven parts are conveyed through Isaac, last of the direct male McCaslin line, and the episodes in their onward course come up into the contemporaneous, as far as the verge of World War II in "Delta Autumn."

All but one of the book's sections ("Pantaloon in Black") are peopled by descendants, legitimate and illegitimate, of old Lucius Quintus Carothers McCaslin. Isaac McCaslin is his grandson, and direct male heir by one of his twin sons, Theophilus ("Uncle Buck"), and Sophonsiba Beauchamp. The Edmonds line are also of legitimate McCaslin descent, by way of Lucius McCaslin's daughter. But the Negro Beauchamps, who have taken that name from slaves held by Isaac's mother's family, also stem from Lucius McCaslin's mating with his slaves, first with Eunice and then with their daughter Tomasina. Thus two chief figures in *Go Down, Moses,* occupying the most substantial roles are both grandsons of old Lucius, but their reactions to this ancestry are quite different. It is a discovery, in the old plantation ledgers, of his grandfather's cohabitation with slaves treated as mere chattel which spurs Isaac to repudiate his inheritance and turn over all the McCaslin landholdings and other property to his elder cousin, McCaslin Edmonds, who protests the move but accepts it as a continuing family responsibility. Lucas Beauchamp, one-quarter white from his McCaslin grandfather (and born a decade after slavery and living on the plantation in a cabin with a ten-acre lot deeded him by Zack Edmonds) is proud of his ancestry, though it comes to him through the subjected Eunice and her incestuously used daughter Tomasina. In "The Fire and the Hearth," after Lucas's most crucial self-assertion, that violent reclaiming of his young wife Molly from service in the Edmonds' house as nurse to Zack's motherless son, he thinks, *"So I reckon I aint got old Carothers'* [McCaslin] *blood for nothing, after all."* And later, in *Intruder in the Dust,* Lucas calmly tells an abusive poor white at the country store, "I aint a Edmonds. . . . I belongs to the old lot. I'm a McCaslin." He even speaks of his cousins the Edmonds men as woman-made, as if his descent in a male line through Tomy's Turl (Tomasina's Terril) outweighed the preceding illegitimacy and incest.

From the beginning of *Go Down, Moses,* in the grotesque rustic comedy of "Was," there is foreshadowed a curious circumstantial link between Isaac McCaslin and Lucas Beauchamp, though it becomes evident only later. A card game between Uncle Buddy and Hubert Beauchamp only temporarily reprieved Uncle Buck from marriage to Sophonsiba Beauchamp (from which strange match after the war came Isaac, their only child). But Uncle Buddy's gamble also provided that the slave Tennie Beauchamp was to be given to the McCaslins' Tomy's Turl (from whom came Lucas, youngest of their six children). And in the final and title story, "Go Down, Moses," it is the grandson of Lucas and Molly, Samuel Worsham Beauchamp, an executed murderer, whose body must be brought from Illinois for burial back home, "back where he was born," as Miss Worsham insists, to satisfy Molly's notion of propriety—which Gavin Stevens then willingly serves. Thus the last section of *Go Down, Moses* introduces into full view the character who is to play a major role as advocate extraordinary in five of the seven books Faulkner was yet to write. And thus first and last the stories "Was" and "Go Down, Moses" frame the book's more substantial matters chronologically, as between old Lucius Carothers McCaslin's reactively non-conformist antebellum sons, Uncles Buddy and Buck, and that twentieth-century eccentric Gavin Stevens, an "amateur Cincinnatus" of a more sophisticated type, with wider range and propensity for benign interference in matters seen as less than rightly ordered. Yet the immensely comforting benefit Gavin Stevens conveys to old Molly and to her white friend and lifelong confidante Miss Worsham is a small matter for a county attorney who has more than provincial know-how and address, and the measure of Gavin Stevens will be more fully shown in various aspects in *Intruder in the Dust, Requiem for a Nun,* and the two volumes completing the Snopes trilogy. It is the McCaslins who dominate *Go Down, Moses.* Lucas is shown there at more points in his life and in more telling aspects than will appear in *Intruder,* and his white McCaslin cousins, Zack Edmonds and his son Roth, are also given full dimensions. However, the preeminent figure in more than half the book is Isaac McCaslin, traced through stages of his exemplary though beset life, and his experiences suggest themes that resound implicatively throughout the other sections, and in sometimes contrasting tones.

"Was"

This priority is asserted in a unique Faulkner passage, the isolated untitled first three paragraphs of "Was" — and therefore of *Go Down, Moses.* Throughout the book, because of its chronological scope and numerous characters and the intricacies of their experiences and relationships in separate situations and episodes, there recur some similar but not unique passages. These are generally quite lucid but syntactically abbreviated and of great density, in an economical compacting of substance, to give supportive immediacy to multiple events over a wide time span. (It is a very sophisticated fictional device, soliciting involvement, and its psychological validity is indubitable; it offers the reader all at once a large part of what would have suffused memory and the active consciousness of one participating in and attempting to understand ongoing developments.) Usually such passages, as they also occur elsewhere in Faulkner, are absorbed into an already established narrative flow, but in "Was" it uniquely opens the story. Yet it is not introductory as in an old-fashioned novel, with the presiding author deliberately setting a scene and introducing its characters. It merely names and gives a kind of poetized *curriculum vitae* of an old man who could not have appeared in the pell-mell happenings of "Was," not having yet been born. Isaac McCaslin knows the story only "from the hearing, the listening" to "his cousin McCaslin ["Cass" Edmonds] born in 1850 and sixteen years his senior" and, for the early-orphaned Isaac, "rather his brother than cousin and rather his father than either." What McCaslin Edmonds has told is now transmuted into the further distancing and depersonalizing of third-person narration (beginning "When he [Cass] and Uncle Buck ran back to the house from discovering . . ."). It is an antebellum yarn from McCaslin Edmonds' early boyhood, when he took part in one more sporting chase after the McCaslin slave Tomey's Turl, who had again run off to the Beauchamp plantation "to hang around" their slave girl Tennie, but the genealogical relevance to *Go Down, Moses* through the resultant marriages of Isaac's parents and of Lucas Beauchamps' is not mentioned, only prepared for, for those who care to attend. "Was" does tell in passing how the twin sons of the McCaslin patriarch, Uncles Buck and Buddy, had moved out of the big house their father "had not had time to finish," and had "moved all the niggers into" it. Not until the pivotal fourth section of "The Bear," however, and in a further thematic linking, is this elaborated to tell of Uncle Buck's and Uncle Buddy's quixotic semiabolitionism in building their cabin without slave labor, and shutting in the Negroes every night by nailing up the front door of the big house, on the "unspoken gentlemen's agreement between the two white men and the two dozen black ones that . . . neither of the white men would go around behind the house," which had no back door at all, "provided that all the negroes were behind the front one . . . again at daybreak." Yet this is more than a comedy of humours. Old McCaslin's twin sons' dealing thus with the unfinished pretentious big house and the drove of slaves was a way, within their limits, of staving off rather than adapting to their confused and confounded heritage. Likewise, their intended avoidance of marriage is not just inborn male recalcitrance; it sees the hazard as what a woman may expect in the way of security, amenities, and position, entailing conformity to the current societal norms. This issue can be especially severe in a stratified socioeconomic culture, and "The Bear" will tell of its cost to Isaac; it also relates to structure that his father and his uncle were the ones whose entries in the old commissary ledgers were deciphered by the lad Isaac, uncovering the miscegenation and incest his Grandfather Lucius Carothers McCaslin had committed. The decisive turn which this effected in Isaac's attitudes and conduct is but one, though greatest, of the major events coded within the book's cryptic opening.

What makes that segment of three paragraphs in "Was" unique is not only that Isaac, as yet unborn, can play no percipient part except as listener to that bizarre pastorale as his cousin tells it later, but that then he appears only briefly and incidentally, a young married man, in the section, "The Fire and the Hearth" and not at all in the third, "Pantaloon in Black." Yet beginning at almost the middle of the book, the next three sections are his—"The Old People," "The Bear," and "Delta Autumn"—and in themselves they constitute a short novel, a chronological life-story with a classic turning point and substantial elucidation of major themes echoed from first to last in the whole of *Go Down, Moses*. Thus in that prologue to "Was" it is as if Faulkner lays a claim in advance, with something like prophecy or even annunciation, and almost as epigraph or text, or the "argument" of what beyond the separate seven facets of *Go Down, Moses* is to be shadowed forth as an insubstantial yet unified and haunting morality. Though Isaac could know of the trivial-consequential happenings in "Was" only by hearsay, his imagination was to be involved from his youth on in much earlier antebellum events, and having pondered them gravely under the aspect of Western man's traditions, his country's and region's evolution, and his own basic tutelage, he was to carry consequent attitudes and commitments throughout life and into his diminished but still resolute old age. Therefore Faulkner uniquely opens the book Isaac is to dominate: "Isaac McCaslin . . . past seventy . . . a widower now and uncle to half a county and father to no one," the "why so" of which will be told in

"The Bear," as well as why Isaac is not possessed of an inheritance which, as the prefatory page tells, "some still thought should have been" his, he "who owned no property and never desired to since the earth was no man's but all men's, as light and air and weather were." In those few phrases, scarcely fictional narrative, Isaac is abstractly, transcendently "placed" and revelation is implicitly promised.

The preeminence Isaac is to have, suggested by this somewhat enigmatic opening, is fully established later in his highly charged story sustained through three stages, from early boyhood with its particular conditionings, into young manhood's crucial determinations and a detached and melancholy but no less principled old age. This major fictional conception, one of Faulkner's most intense searchings-out, required a strategic positioning of the book's four other parts. The three units of Isaac's story gain strength by standing together, and in turn contribute a structural core to which the other units can be related, with an enhancement of theme. Yet Isaac's history entered upon too early would have made anticlimactic even that many-dimensioned, widely inclusive account and portrayal of Lucas Beauchamp in "The Fire and the Hearth," which Faulkner chose to follow "Was." Then comes "Pantaloon in Black," intrinsically one of Faulkner's greatest stories, of a profound pathos and craftily structured. The compressed but vivid tale of Rider is a buffer between the more broadly dimensioned dramas of old Lucius Carothers McCaslin's differently descended, differently constituted and fated grandsons Isaac and Lucas. This third story has no closer connection with the legitimate McCaslin folk and their land than that the Negro protagonist, when he married Mannie, had rented one of Carothers McCaslin's cabins and proudly put it into repair; the link with Lucas is that Rider "built a fire on the hearth on their wedding night as the tale told how Uncle Lucas Beauchamp . . . had done on his forty-five years ago and which had burned ever since." It is by such immemorial themes, and especially as to the discovery of love and its loss and confrontations of fate, that "Pantaloon in Black," though autonomous as composition, becomes a movement in *Go Down, Moses,* and supplements it by a more than familial highlighting of the regional-racial subject.

"The Fire and the Hearth"

Professor James Meriwether's bibliography of Faulkner's short fiction not only notes the incorporation in revised form into this section of *Go Down, Moses* of "Gold is Not Always" from the *Atlantic Monthly* and "A Point of Law" from *Colliers Magazine;* it also cites "several versions, none complete" yet extending to a number of typescript pages, which are to be connected with a portion of "The Fire and the Hearth." It will grow into a novella, to constitute the next-longest and next most important unit in the book which Isaac McCaslin's life-story dominates.

Those various preliminary draftings suggest an artist's successive thrusts as he evolved his concepts and devised their expanding embodiments, which were to contain much besides the wilful humours of Lucas, and to turn in an antiphonal pattern upon Lucas's wife Molly, young and old. In their old age Lucas, while still farming his plot of ground, had also continued his more private enterprise, producing moonshine; then having found a gold coin in a caving bank of earth, he spends his nights with a gold-divining machine he has "bought"with one of Edmonds' mules and in turn has swindled the machine salesman, in a series of deals that have more of hearty mischief than iniquity about them, and seem largely his means of asserting individuality in the role of a free man. The effect is comic, but Lucas is formidably ingenious, and his passages with those about him are lively folk humor, neatly turned. Then the matter becomes serious when old Molly, worn out, decides to divorce him for hunting gold every night and leaving the chores to her. Roth Edmonds (McCaslin Edmonds' grandson and present holder of the McCaslin inheritance) tries to intervene, for the sake of the old Negro woman who had nursed and reared him when he was left motherless, but Lucas insists, "I'm the one to say in my house, like you and your paw and his paw were the ones to say in his." When Molly is missing and is found exhausted, Edmonds resolves to help her get the divorce. He takes the odd pair to Jefferson, to a hearing before the Chancellor. Only at the last minute does the stubbornly assertive Lucas yield and tell the Chancellor, "We dont want no voce. Roth Edmonds knows what I mean." Then before they start back to the farm Lucas brings Molly a nickel's worth of candy as peace offering, putting it into her hand and saying, "You aint got no teeth left but you can still gum it." But Lucas is to make a larger gesture. He cleans the gold-divining machine, brings it to Edmonds, and tells him to get rid of it, and when Roth suggests he'll keep it and perhaps Lucas will want to use it occasionally, Lucas insists that it be got rid of. His reason is not that he doubts there is gold to be found, but he reckons finding it "aint for me," he being too close to the end of the "three score and ten years on this earth" which "the Book says" that "man has got." (Molly, in her appeal to Roth and with her old woman's wisdom, had put it more simply: "He dont look it, but he's sixty-seven years old. And when a man that old takes up money-hunting, it's like when he takes up gambling or whiskey or women. He aint going to have time to quit.") Yet for Lucas it is a realistic renunciation, and in its way as resolute as young Isaac's far different and greater ones, yet as much a matter of honor, in the knowledge that it scarcely becomes an old man to pursue a lust for gold to the edge of the grave. It also resembles Isaac's principled act in that Lucas too takes some authority from the Book, and in that it suggests a crisis of inexpressible emotion, in avoidance of what would be shameful, yet the basic return has been to Molly herself, in all that the fire on his hearth has stood for through the years.

Lucas's stubborn declaration earlier of his rights, equaling those of any McCaslin or Edmonds, to be ruler of his own house and life had been prefaced by an unconditional claim: "I'm a man." In thematic complement to the shadowed comedy of old Lucas's obsessive gold-hunting to the verge of domestic disaster, there had been in his early years a more drastic assertion of manhood, in a life-and-death struggle with Zack Edmonds. This was at a time when Zack's motherless infant son Carothers (Roth) was dependent on being nursed by Lucas's young wife Molly, two years married, who also had their own infant at her breast. During this six-months' episode (which takes up most of section 2 in Chapter One of "The Fire and the Hearth") Lucas and Molly helped Zack all they could, following his wife's death in childbed, and thereafter. Indeed Lucas had swum the flooded river to summon the doctor in vain. But then Molly was kept on in the widower Edmonds' house, and Lucas moved from impatience to affront and finally a rage in which "he caught himself" standing over "the fire which was to burn on the hearth until neither he nor Molly were left to feed it," now with "the cedar water bucket already poised" and then set it "back on the shelf, still shaking, unable to remember taking the bucket up." Instead he goes to Zack, says, "I wants my wife back. I needs her at home," and he will not discuss the matter, will not let Zack swear there has been no guilt in it; he simply demands that Molly "be in my house tonight." Though she returns, she brings both infants, and though she patiently explains she couldn't leave a nursing child behind, Lucas is confirmed in what had smouldered in him all day: "I got to kill him or I got to leave here." So he takes out his store of cash from under the brick in the fireplace, wraps the money in a rag and fatalistically puts it in Molly's shoe near the bed where she is sleeping with the two children, gets his razor and starts out for Edmonds' house. Yet he will not set upon Zack in the dark; he waits till dawn and then enters the unlocked front door, then the bedroom, determined to kill the man who had used him presumptuously, and made him jealously doubt his marriage.

There ensues a scene in which the character of Lucas is given largest dimension, in the overflow of a suppressed rage moving with the potential of tragedy, which is avoided not by decision but by accident. Zack Edmonds is admirably cool; lying quietly in bed, he repeatedly tells Lucas to put down his razor so they can talk. Finally Lucas hurls it out the window, but that is only in his raging wish for an equal contest, and he says he will come at Zack with his bare hands. In his outpour of words he exposes the heart of his complaint: "You thought that because I am a nigger I wouldn't even mind." (It is almost as if he speaks for the ghost of his Negro great-grandmother Eunice, who had drowned herself after old Lucas Carothers McCaslin had impregnated her daughter and his, Tomasina.) When Lucas tells Zack to "get the pistol under your pillow," Zack calmly says it's not there but in a drawer, and he rises and gets it but tosses it onto the bed, for them to struggle over. He too will not take an advantage. At this offer of man-to-man encounter Lucas begins to tremble, says "No," and would have Zack Edmonds take the pistol. The storm in Lucas's mind might be seen as having a clear center; perhaps he wants the white man to retain the advantage he has always had and is felt to have abused, so that Lucas can put him down from that height; perhaps more explicitly Lucas thinks that to struggle on equal terms would be to exonerate Edmonds from a suspicion of guilt. In "a strangling voice" Lucas says, "For the last time. Take your pistol. I'm coming." Zack answers sharply, "Come on then. Do you think I'm any less a McCaslin just because I was what you call woman-made to it? Or maybe you aint even a woman-made McCaslin but just a nigger that's got out of hand?"

At that questioning quip "Lucas was beside the bed," not remembering "moving at all . . . kneeling, their hands gripped, facing across the bed and the pistol the man whom he had known from infancy, with whom he had lived until they were both grown almost as brothers lived . . . had fished and hunted together . . . learned to swim in the same water . . . had eaten at the same table in the white boy's kitchen and in the cabin of the negro's mother . . . had slept under the same blanket before a fire in the woods." Now Lucas repeats, "For the last time," and cries out, "I tell you! Dont ask too much of me!" and Zack thinks, *I was wrong. I have gone too far,* realizing the tortures of mind that have put Lucas into an irreversible position. Then Lucas has the pistol and they spring up, with the bed between them. Lucas glances at the cylinder's load and says, "Because I'll need two of them," and Zack realizes that Lucas in his trance of emotion "cant even see me right now." When Lucas goes on to say he may just use the last one and "leave you something to think about now and then," at this more open threat of suicide Zack grapples with him, "grasping at the pistol and the hand which held it," but Lucas "jammed the pistol against the white man's side and pulled the trigger and flung the white man from him all in one motion, hearing as he did so the light, dry, incredibly loud click of the miss-fire." It is one of the great scenes in Faulkner, expressing the black man's proneness to a fatal rage under a sense of irreparable wrongs, at the heart of which is the white man's assumption of superiority and dominance, (though Zack's bearing throughout suggests he is guiltless of sexual offense), but beyond race it typifies the despair of any murder-suicide in which thwarted desire for human status and acceptance brings down everything with it in a vengeance.

With that misfire which spared both men Faulkner breaks off the scene, and the narrative moves to Lucas plowing, with Molly bringing his noon meal, and his musing over the live cartridge dented by the firing pin. At suppertime Molly is preparing to return to Edmonds' house with the two small children, but now with rage purged and feeling himself vindicated, Lucas is conciliatory. He asks if she can "tote them both all right" and she answers with perhaps some overtone that she's "been taking care of both of them a good while now without no man-help." She adds, "I'll come back when I gets them to sleep," and "gruffly" but with an implication of patience he answers, "I reckon you better put your time on them. Since that's what you started out to do." Yet she leaves him thinking, *"Women. I wont never know. I dont want to,"* and as he "turned toward the room where the fire was, where his supper waited" he speaks aloud: "How to God can a black man ask a white man to please not lay down with his black wife? And even if he could ask it, how to God can the white man promise he wont?" This is not a surrender. Lucas has as-

serted himself over Zack Edmonds, and Molly will be returning to their warm hearth as soon as she cares for the little children—white and black, Zack's by his lost wife, Lucas's by his
living one. In the pause after so much tumult of mind he is
pondering the enigma of the natural situation, and its intensification by racial difference and his own temperament—no
man (and he least of all) can say "please not" to another man,
he can only fight for a presumed sole possession or let the
woman go; and no man (not even Zack Edmonds, the companion of his youth, and a decent person) can promise absolutely that he will never yield to promiscuous impulse.

In the midst of all the plot elements, the divers persons and
drastic events of such a representatively Faulknerian piece as
"The Fire and the Hearth," there is to be seen the artist's
stringent selectivity, an economy in the interest of emphasis
and pace. Action is not extendedly shown for its own sake,
neither when a conniving older Lucas is using Roth's authority
to put a prospective son-in-law safely out of business as a
moonshiner, nor specifically probing for gold in the double
dark of night and his obsession, nor a younger Lucas exhaust-
edly swimming the dangerous river to get the doctor for Zack's
dying wife. Nor does the narrative go into Zack's ordeal at that
time and what must have been his enduring grief thereafter,
for this would diffuse a concerned attention beyond Lucas.
Yet in the confrontation between the two men thereafter,
while the affective force of it is largely through Lucas's consciousness, Zack is solidly emergent, enough is told of the bereaved man to suggest a calm detachment and ironic resignation, and Lucas is revealed further through Zack's estimate of
the man's disturbed state of mind. Yet Faulkner can break off
an accelerated narrative momentum to prevent its diminution
into a less than obligatory and perhaps an awkward or sluggish
scene. Here when the break comes with the click of the pistol's
misfire, Faulkner emphasizes transition not just by showing
Lucas back at his plough, but by changing to a deliberate
tempo—"That had been a good year . . . He would make
more . . . some of his corn had not had its last ploughing. He

was doing that now . . ."—allowing an incidental enhancement through the reader's amazed sense that this is still the same day, and lives are going on beyond recent hazards. At the same time the agile fictionist has avoided, for himself and for the reader's credence, the problem of what to show between the two men in the moment and minutes after that releasing click. By the story's earlier accounting, there were four other cartridges in the revolver; the abrupt breaking-off of the scene tells that pulling the trigger once had accomplished a catharsis for Lucas, through an awesome intervention of fate that later leaves him "musing" alone in the field, over the nicked cartridge itself, "large enough to contain two lives."

It is not only in episodes of great dramatic force that Faulkner exercises his skill as fictionist; the selectivity which makes way for development and containment of such scenes continues to operate more closely within them; and this practice, in its ratios of economy and intensity, is seen in briefer passages, as for instance that laconic but telling exchange between Lucas and his young wife which reasserts their fidelities amid situational stress. Years later, in the grotesquerie of old Lucas searching for gold but brought back to more proportionate behavior by Molly's resolute either/or, these humors contrastingly frame the retrospectively disclosed heart of the story, while in this novella's last passage Lucas, by absolute renunciation of what for an old man is doubly a folly, asserts his fundamental self, in its quaintly engaging blend of serene craftiness and invincible dignity. The fine hand of Faulkner is also to be felt throughout his works in the treatment of characters who move into and out of the story playing subordinately contributive parts. These folk pass the ultimate fictional test for their kind, being so acutely realized that they can be imagined taking the scene into the purview of their own consciousness and transforming it into quite another fictional enaction, yet they are never allowed a vaudevillian turn of their own, and in being supportive they accelerate the central action. Faulkner as literary artist also excels in brilliantly strategic placings of segments of action out of their chronological order. Basically this is, of course, a classic usage, entrance upon the narrative *in medias res* to provide immediate dramatic momentum while arousing a secondary curiosity about causative factors and giving these a more affective impact when they are disclosed. However, Faulkner specialized the usage in many variations of it. The extreme of this, working through his modernistic tendency to locate narrative "point of view" in the ongoing consciousness of one major character or another, sometimes makes for a flickering subjective play between past and future within brief passages of a present awareness, and in this Faulkner is comparable to Joyce, especially as in *Ulysses* (though never with such artifices) or in a more fluently iridescent use as in Virginia Woolf, in *Mrs. Dalloway* for example (though not with such minute suspension). Basically Faulkner is a more intent storyteller, seeing inner states in their contexts of interaction, and his characters' associative processes are made contributive to an ongoing action in which they become fully themselves as participants.

In that most sustained and centrally dramatic return upon their past, the fourteen pages in "The Fire and the Hearth" which compress the encounter between Lucas and Zack as young men, is introduced on the thirteenth page of that nearly 100-page novella, and Lucas once more has remembered it when Zack's son Roth, "a young man still, a bachelor, forty-three years old last March," comes out of his house to be told about the glib George Wilkins, in Lucas's self-confounding attempt to eliminate this putative son-in-law as a reckless competitor with a poorly concealed illicit still of his own, and the whisky kept under his back porch. (No wonder that later when both stills are discovered, the commissioner at the federal courthouse in Jefferson asks Roth, "What the hell kind of Senegambian Montague and Capulet is this anyhow?") But all that is still to come; during the moment's pause Lucas is remembering that this man was left motherless at his birth, the infant whom his young wife Molly had looked after in Zack Edmond's house and had nursed along with her own firstborn, with results Lucas "would never forget," and with this phrase the narrative drops back to its substance. Placing that memorable history so early in the novella gives a key to Roth Edmonds' considerate, almost dutiful, sometimes irritable relationship with Molly and Lucas; it also gives Lucas a further human dimension and a kind of attestation as a human being proven in his passionate young manhood and more than a merely foolish and stubborn old man, and it enhances his renunciation at the last for Molly's sake, and in one more reassertion of a hard-won, stoutly held poise.

An earlier assertion of it, carried off with a style of its own, brings Isaac McCaslin briefly but revealingly into "The Fire and the Hearth." It connects this story with "Was" by mention of "old Carothers McCaslin's twin sons, Theophilus [Isaac's father] and Amodeus," the Uncle Buck and Uncle Buddy who in antebellum days had "made an especial provision . . . for their father's negro son," who was Tomey's Turl, Lucas's father. When Isaac at twenty-one "relinquished, repudiated even" the title to the McCaslin estate, he conscientiously retained trusteeship of that fund set up by his father and uncle. The money was never claimed by Tomey's Turl (Terril) though he had remained on the land after emancipation. Then Terril's eldest son, James, at twenty-one, had "fled, quitted the cabin he had been born in, the plantation, Mississippi itself," and though the youth Isaac had spent a week looking for him to give him a third of the legacy, he couldn't be found. When Terril's daughter Fonsiba "married and moved to Arkansas" Isaac traveled there to put her share of the legacy into the bank for her. Then years later, reading the paper, he stares at the date and realizes Lucas Beauchamp is twenty-one that day and is not surprised when his wife tells him Lucas is in the kitchen. There follows a ceremony of taking possession of an inheritance (the obverse of Isaac's renunciation when he had come of age) and Lucas formalizes it in his own assertive way. Isaac has taken him to the bank and explained he can leave his money on deposit there and draw checks on it just as other men do; Lucas draws a check for the entire amount, and sees it counted out, then counts it himself, and finally says, "Now you can put it back. And gimme my paper." Thus Isaac has carried out his father's intention, and Lucas has been set up with money in the bank and has written his first check "in the cramped though quite legible hand" Isaac's mother (Sophonsiba Beauchamp McCaslin) "had taught him and his brother and sister too." Thus are threads of McCaslin history woven in from one section to another in *Go Down, Moses,* yet in this scene as in others, character is in the foreground — Lucas laying his claim to his standing as grandson of old Lucius Carothers McCaslin and also a man in his own right; Isaac as trustee carrying out a just family duty as scrupulously as he has refused to possess what to him is a tainted family heritage. (This crucial matter in *Go Down, Moses* is not told of until in part 4 of "The Bear," but Faulkner implied just enough of it to allow a revealing glimpse of Lucas Beauchamp at twenty-one.)

Within the bounds of "The Fire and the Hearth" there is a repetition, in successive generations, of a thematic pattern which also appears in other Faulkner novels — prolonged companionable relationship between a white and a Negro boy. In *The Unvanquished,* between Bayard Sartoris and Ringo, it lasts throughout the story, from the days of their boyhood games mapping the progress of the Civil War through the precocious starkness of their revenge on Grumby for his murder of Grandmother Millard, and on to Ringo's coming, a young man of twenty-four, riding forty miles to bring word that Redmond has shot Colonel Sartoris, Bayard's father, and to ride into Jefferson with Bayard, his "boy" still but his second too in an affair of honor, even though he doesn't understand Bayard's confronting Redmond unarmed. In *Intruder in the Dust* the main narrative is confined to the period from Charles Mallison's twelfth to his sixteenth year, but the resourceful and wily Aleck Sander, son of the Mallison's cook Paralee, is Chick's good companion throughout. As told in "The Fire and the Hearth," Zack Edmonds

(McCaslin Edmonds' son) and Lucas have grown up together, and when Lucas risks death swimming the flooded river to get the doctor for Zack's dying wife, it presumably is in a devotion beyond conventional duty. Yet this connection is only briefly touched on, as Lucas is struggling with Zack for the pistol; what is traced out more closely is the course of a later boyhood relationship between these two men's sons. It is given that greater emphasis because it involves painful stages in Roth's (Carother Edmonds') relationship both with his father and with his playmate, Lucas's and Molly's son Henry.

Presumably this companionship was made more close because of Roth's absolute dependence from the first on Molly as foster-mother, making her care of him parallel to and often simultaneous with what she gave her own child — as is figured in her nursing both infants and "toting" the two of them back and forth between Edmonds' house and Lucas's cabin. Roth's lasting sense of this care is in his troubled mind when Lucas's gold-hunting mania and consequent irresponsibility in old age impel Molly to want a divorce. In his solitary life Roth is sometimes surly and often irritably ironic, but he is always gentle with Molly, and when she has turned to him in this crisis he thinks tenderly of her as having "surrounded him always with care for his physical body and for his spirit too, teaching him his manners, behavior . . . who had given him, the motherless, without stint or expectation of reward that constant and abiding devotion and love which existed nowhere else in this world for him." (There are interesting resemblances to this in Faulkner's dedication of *Go Down, Moses* "To Mammy — Caroline Barr," a servant who had died in 1940 at the age of one hundred, and who, Faulkner put it, "gave to my family a fidelity without stint or calculation of recompense and to my childhood an immeasurable devotion and love.") For orphaned Roth Edmonds, Molly, "who had been the only mother he ever knew," retained some such fixed and increasingly appreciated aspect — and all this comfortably within the unexamined mores of the only community he had acquaintance with. In this same context, however, Roth's boyhood companionship with Molly's son Henry, his contemporary and a natural playmate in their isolated plantation world, was vulnerable to stresses having to do with a Southern boy's growing consciousness of the complex and uneasy relations between the white and black races in the postbellum South.

In early childhood Roth had accepted Lucas as "adjunct to the only mother he would ever remember, as simply as he accepted his black foster-brother, as simply as he accepted his father as an adjunct to his existence." He and Henry slept "on the same pallet in the white man's house or in the same bed in the negro's" and ate "the same food at the same table in either," with Roth "actually preferring the negro house, the hearth on which even in summer a little fire always burned, centering the life in it," more life and more of home than there was in his bereaved, solitary father's house. Then "one day he knew," without "remembering when or how he had learned" it, "that the black woman was not his mother, and did not regret it; he knew that his own mother was dead and did not grieve," and still he preferred Lucas's house, and Molly's and Henry's, to his own. Still he and Henry pursued their intent young lives, riding "plantation horses and mules," having "a pack of small hounds to hunt with and promise of a gun in another year or so" (though they were only seven). Here Faulkner epitomizes youthful minds, their receptiveness and evolving independence—"they were sufficient, complete, wanting, as all children do, not to be understood . . . but only to love, to question and examine unchallenged, and to be let alone." Yet nowhere for long does the world allow such pure privacy and untaxed freedom; readiness of intuition and self-defensive instinctual response as of the moment carry on into crises beyond innocence.

Conscerning this stage of Roth's early childhood Faulkner conducts the account with remarkable finesse and evocativeness, in balancing an omniscient narrator's explicit abstractions and the small boy's crucial assertions which he cannot examine until he has made them, and then only to discover himself under a larger dominance than he can give a name to or had hitherto apprehended. Nothing in the Faulkner *oeuvre*, despite his recurrent concern with the matter, comes more acutely upon an individual's susceptibility to a society's pervading atmosphere, with cultural influence as an early unconscious assimilation, antecedent to adequate personal experience and learning, and largely though not altogether impervious to rational modification. This force, broadly acknowledged in Faulkner's fiction, is often particularized in terms of a youthful development, a consolidation into manhood, but it is always made relative to the South, in the artist's unflinching fidelity to his known material and its milieu. It is at the heart of Thomas Sutpen's story, in the pathos of his early seduction by an overweening element of a society which refuses the frontier directness he knows and induces him to compete on its more advantaged grounds, through which not only he is destroyed but also those melancholy half-brothers, his two sons. Opposites in the South's cultural situation as Faulkner treated it existed in an impasse not to be compromised, and despite his natural intelligence and endurance Joe Christmas, unable to know himself as either black or white or of what mixture, finds no world to live in with self-possession. Sometimes however the theme is treated as an emancipative growth, as in young Bayard Sartoris in his progress beyond a code of "honor" linked to arrogant violence, or less drastically and more constructive societally in young Charles Mallison through relationship with old Lucas Beauchamp, or finally with less of racial stress and more awareness of the whole miscellaneous community, as with the hero of *The Reivers*.

The issue had beset Roth Edmonds very early — even sooner, more abruptly, and with less informative referents than in the precocious case of Sarty Snopes in "Barn Burning," where, as with Bayard in *The Unvanquished*, the conflict turns on criteria of family honor and personal rectitude rather than on the more obscured question of racial relations. Since Roth and his black foster-brother Henry are only seven years old, emphasis falls on the instinctual element in Roth's crisis, yet there is an awareness that is somehow the fruit of his limited but intensely focused experience, and like his one day knowing "that the black woman was not his mother" and "that his own mother was dead," this further knowledge is without his "remembering when or how he had learned it." In Faulkner's telling, having mentioned the desire of children "to question and examine unchallenged, and to be let alone," he now speaks of something destined which, no matter how sequestered and permissive the child's rearing, will invade and will not forbear: "Then one day the old curse of his fathers, the old haughty ancestral pride based not on any value but on an accident of geography, stemmed not from courage and honor but from wrong and shame, descended to him." Pointing up the possible insidiousness of a cultural influence, under which men are fated to conflicts which ancestral voices continue to prophesy, the story adds that "He did not recognize it then." But the form which his almost reflexive action takes is explicit. He and his playmate "had finished supper at Henry's house" and Molly is sending them to the bed these two use there when "suddenly he said, 'I'm going home.'" Henry innocently says, "Les stay here. I thought we was going to get up when pappy did and go hunting." But former arrangements no longer hold; Roth, "already moving toward the door," says, "You can. I'm going home." Still unaware of tension, Henry agreeably says, "All right," and follows him, with Roth walking just fast enough so that "the negro boy never quite came up besides him," and so they enter the McCaslin house and "the room with the bed and the pallet on the floor which they slept on when they passed the night here." Roth purposely undresses slowly enough to let Henry "beat him to the pallet and lie down," and then he takes the bed for himself. Henry, with a child's custom in companionship, says, "Well, all right" and approaches the bed, and waits for Roth to move over, but Roth says "No!" speaking "harsh and violent though not loud." Henry, slowly beginning to understand, asks, "You mean you dont want me to sleep in the bed?" and Roth neither moves nor answers, "rigid on his back, staring upward." Again

Henry says "All right," his naiveté now tempered with instinctive realization, and returns to the pallet, but when in "slow equable voice" he says "I reckon on a hot night like tonight we will sleep cooler if we —" Roth answers, "Shut up! How'm I or you neither going to sleep if you keep on talking?" Henry hushes, attempting no further amelioration, and falls asleep, but the white boy does not, "lying in a rigid fury of the grief he could not explain, the shame he would not admit" — a stage of not-yet-defined experience which Faulkner's phrases profoundly epitomize.

Afterward "he slept and it seemed to him he was still awake, waked and did not know he had slept until he saw in the grey of dawn the empty pallet on the floor." Now the artist Faulkner briefly tells of finalities, not only that "they did not hunt that morning," but "never slept in the same room again and never again ate at the same table." Then the narrative passes into the episode in which the white boy tries, too late, to recapture something lost. In his impasse of emotions he has stayed away from Henry's house and for a month has seen him only at a distance, "holding the reins of the team while Lucas plowed." Then "one day" knowing his grief and wanting to admit his shame, Roth "went to Molly's house" and "trembling a little" in embarrassment, he speaks, "lordly, peremptory: 'I'm going to eat supper with you all tonight.'" Her face expressionless, Molly says, "Course you is. I'll cook you a chicken." Briefly "it was as if it had never happened at all," when Henry comes, and the two of them kill and dress the chicken and Roth goes to the barn "with Henry and Lucas while Henry milked." Molly calls Henry "and then a little later himself, the voice as it had always been, peaceful and steadfast. . . . But it was too late." The table was set in the kitchen as usual, but Lucas was not there, Henry was just leaving, "and there was just one chair, one plate, his glass of milk beside it, the platter heaped with untouched chicken." Roth cries out to Henry: "Are you ashamed to eat when I eat?" and the other small boy, similarly caught by circumstance, answers from his own required vantage point: "I aint shamed of nobody. Not even me." In two small boys Faulkner showed psychologically the inherent postbellum strain between the races—endemic, inscrutable. So too the adolescent Chick Mallison found he had breathed in the feel of it and required several years to adjust himself to the self-possessed Lucas Beauchamp. So Huck Finn had to live on a raft with Jim to realize him as a fellow human.

At which point the narrative breaks off. It is not told what the white boy found to do next. With the sentences that follow, his story passes on further—"So he entered his heritage. He ate its bitter fruit." Like the historian, the fictionist cannot supply a complete chronology, giving each hour its sixty minutes; and even more than the historian, the fictionist is to be estimated by the judiciousness of his lacunae, for a closer weaving of an affective continuity. Faulkner, so often sternly charged with profuseness, has yet to be sufficiently credited for his rigorous economies in structuring his narratives toward successive climaxes and that sustained claim upon attention which can create the spell of art. The next step shown in the boy Roth's painful and constricted maturation is his pondering of the relation between his father and Lucas. He notes that Lucas says, "Mr Edmonds," never "Mister Zack," and Roth understands that the first is men's custom as equals, whereas the second is an equally established usage that makes it the familiarity of a trusted servant; furthermore, Lucas avoids "having to address the white man directly by any name at all," with such "calculation" and "finesse" that the boy "could not tell if even his father knew that the negro was refusing to call him mister." At last he speaks about it to his father, not reproachfully but in a stumbling search for protocol that will declare the Edmonds' rights. Zack explains to his son that he and Lucas "grew up together . . . ate and slept together and hunted and fished together, like you and Henry" and adds significantly, "We did it until we were grown men."

He does not tell the boy the rest, their almost fatal clash over Molly, but Zack's consciousness of it is so strong that he utters it cryptically: "Except that I always beat him shooting

except one time. And as it turned out, I even beat him then."
It gives the boy an intimation in passing, though it also precipitates a generic childhood experience as the offspring
"realizes with both grief and outrage that the parent antedates
it, has experienced things, shames and triumphs both, in
which it can have no part." Thus he can only accept the
"trade" his father offers—"You let me and Lucas settle how he
is to treat me, and I'll let you and him settle how he is to treat
you." It is a paternal gesture of equality and an allowance of
self-determination, but the sense of a concealment lingers,
and in his adolescence Roth begins to have notions of
"something which had happened between Lucas and his
father . . . because they were themselves, men," and neither
from difference of race nor the same McCaslin blood in them
both. Then his intuitions carry him on to thinking "*My father
and a nigger man over a nigger woman,* because he simply
declined even to realize that he had even refused to think *a
white woman.*" He concludes that "*Lucas beat him else Lucas
wouldn't be here,*" and attributes it to that in Lucas which is
"*impervious to anybody.*" This has been felt by the growing
boy himself, and his speculations stop short there; since his
father will never tell him about it, he cannot realize how he
had taken the first step correctly in assuming it happened because "they were themselves, men," nor can he know with
what formalized equality they had striven, and most of all that
neither had beaten the other but fate had spared them both.
In his own struggle Roth Edmonds comes to see a Negro of
mixed blood emergent in quite different aspect from that of
Jim Bond as the Canadian Shreve sees the homeless degenerate
creature at the end of the Sutpen line. Roth images Lucas as
"*both heir and prototype simultaneously of all the geography
and climate and biology which sired old Carothers and all the
rest of us and our kind,*" Lucas "*intact and complete, con-
temptuous, as old Carothers must have been, of all blood
black white yellow or red, including his own.*"
Roth had wavered from the first, in that awkward vain
attempt to recapture the unexamined natural mutualities of

innocent companionship, lost through societally inherited pride and arrogance. Instability is to be traced into his mature life, and finally a demoralization, in what some have blamed as a fictional inconsistency, whereas it accretes into a more telling characterization, giving him representative stature in his state of dilemma racially induced and festering into cynicism. From the small boy in a simple and miniaturized situation, upon whom barely intuited cultural pressures had fallen stealthily but all the more specifically, he becomes the mature man still kindly toward his black foster-mother but sometimes irritable and often aloofly ironic with Lucas; finally in "Delta Autumn" he show the cynical bitterness that skepticism about a whole social order compounded with personal frustration and bad conscience have brought him to. In this episode as finale to Isaac McCaslin's three-part story the fruits Roth Edmonds has gathered from submission to his heritage and not always honorable use of it give a clear perspective on Isaac, poised in his romantic faith that nature, with its bounties and beauties and unequivocal requirements, is a better teacher than society as either he or Roth has known it. And it is Roth's unprincipled behavior, raising again the old specter, an irresponsible intermingling of the legitimate and miscegenated McCaslin lines, which renews and accentuates in Isaac that melancholy the absolute idealist is fated to encounter and must learn to bear to the last.

But to follow Roth Edmonds into the Delta on what probably was Uncle Ike's last trip to the hunting camp is to go not only beyond the pattern of "The Fire and the Hearth" but the larger order of Isaac McCaslin's story in its three sections and the place of all these in the still more intricated totality of *Go Down, Moses*. In "The Fire and the Hearth" the postponement until its final chapter of Roth Edmonds' recalling his early boyhood alienation from Lucas's son Henry there is an echo, with variations, of Zack's remembering earlier the outright combat between him and Lucas in their young manhood, with the common factor, in both generations, of racial tension. Thematically in this final chapter of "The Fire and the Hearth" another recurrence to the assertive young Lucas Beauchamp is at his twenty-first birthday, when Isaac as trustee helped him execute his claim on money that came down from old Carothers McCaslin's estate, along the line of miscegenation, by old McCaslin's incestuous union with Tomasina that produced Lucas's father, Tomey's Turl. Finality in "The Fire and the Hearth," however, is of middle-aged Roth Edmonds' dealings with Molly and Lucas in their old age; first Roth assists Molly toward getting the divorce, because he feels she can bear no more of Lucas's gold-hunting mania, and then Roth is the receiver of the gold-divining machine and witness to Lucas's recovery of his self-possession and dignity through the unequivocal forswearing of that folly.

"The Fire and the Hearth" can be called a novella because of its scope, its thematic focusings and dramatic finalities, and its developmental characterizations. Among novellas it is one of the most remarkable achievements in modern fiction; its less than one hundred pages firmly contain a plenitude of happenings and a number of sharply realized scenes, with tonal variations from bucolic comedy to representative pathos, and the over-all chronology of interlocking events is subtly manipulated, stressing by strategic interjection the antecedent influences upon the racially bifurcated McCaslin lineage, and therein developing Lucas Beauchamp as a protagonist, first and last and at various points, while bringing both Zack and Roth Edmonds into full view, along with Molly Beauchamp. There are external as well as internal connections; the McCaslin and Edmonds strains appear more nearly harmonized in Zack Edmonds than in his son Carothers (Roth), in whom they seem to struggle; Lucas's supple enterprise seems as if derived from his father's aspects in "Was," just as something like Lucas's own aplomb is evident even in the brief appearance of his young son Henry, glimpsed in the scenes of the boy Roth's rejection of his companionship; while for those who read through the book's parts in their order, old Molly at the end, in "Go Down, Moses," is to be found still as definite in her intentions and as effective in accomplishing them.

"Pantaloon in Black"

All in all, "The Fire and the Hearth" is so richly inclusive and engrossing, and so steadily keyed to the inter-racial theme — even when Lucas's compensatory assertions are comic — that an encompassing structural intention might be presumed from the placing of "Pantaloon in Black," as third among the sections of the book, preceding its most substantial portion, the three sections focused on Isaac McCaslin. Indeed, since "Pantaloon in Black" is the only portion of *Go Down, Moses* not concerned with McCaslins (whether so named or whether called Edmonds or Beauchamp) perhaps the brief, idyllic, and tragic story of the Negroes Rider and Mannie, their devotion in marriage and their harsh untimely fates was meant as a tonal-thematic interpolation between the two stressful life-stories of Lucas and Isaac. Providing a point of reference detached from either, "Pantaloon in Black" also widens *Go Down, Moses* by extending a view of postbellum Southern Negroes in a pure state, economically subject to the white race, but unvexed by miscegenation and able, while fate spares them, to create a completely private felicity. Such a compositional functioning within the totality of *Go Down, Moses,* however, in no way impairs the perfected sufficiency of "Pantaloon in Black," in itself one of the most brilliantly realized and structured of Faulkner's short stories. Yet it is tied to the locale of *Go Down, Moses,* and specifically the McCaslin plantation, for when Rider marries Mannie, he rents a cabin from Roth Edmonds, and it connects with the latter years of the preceding narrative's period, for Rider had "built a fire on the hearth on their wedding night as the tale told how Uncle Lucas Beauchamp . . . had done on his forty-five years ago and which had burned ever since."

Rider, a big powerful young Negro, almost an idealization of man as splendid animal, and head of the timber gang at the sawmill, where he would show "the vanity of his own strength," had been orphaned and was then reared by a timorous, pious old aunt and her husband, but has lived riotously, having "the women bright and dark and for all purposes nameless he didn't need to buy" and drinking and gambling each weekend. Then "he saw Mannie, whom he had known all his life, for the first time and said to himself: 'Ah'm thu wid all dat,' and they married." (The compacting phrases are Faulkner's style at its most intent.) There is only a glimpse of Rider's transformation and their completed contentment. On Saturdays, shortly after noon, he would be home with his week's wage, "and ring the bright cascade of silver dollars onto the scrubbed table in the kitchen where his dinner simmered on the stove and the galvanized tub of hot water and the baking powder can of soft soap and the towel made of scalded flour sacks sewn together and his clean overalls and shirt waited, and Mannie would gather up the money and walk the half-mile to the commissary and buy their next week's supplies and bank the rest of the money in Edmonds' safe and return. . . ." That is how it was for him with her, "de onliest least thing whut ever kep up wid me one day, leff alone fo weeks"; then in a few months this with its niceties and frugalities, its consummations poised in the first peace he had known, was over. Nor has the story begun there, but at Mannie's graveside, where he energetically helps shovel the dirt into the grave, not insensitively as it appears to some but desiring to have it over with and carry his grief away alone, refusing both his aunt's solace and the jug his loyal companions have provided.

It is in this context that his having found Mannie has been looked back to, with the sweet details of his having her completely and beautifully, but then only to lose her so soon. How that came about is not told; the story is of his desolation. So it shows him at her grave, and at the house haunted by her, in memory and literally to his eyes; then next day he is strenuously back at work as if still in duty to her. But he breaks from that trance before the day is out, and refuses his old aunt's consolations and her husband's counsel of prayer, to which he says, "Whut faith and trust? Whut Mannie ever done ter

Him?" So he drinks from a jug of raw illicit whiskey till he can hold no more and staggers into the midnight dice game at the mill, the players three of his timber gang and others of the mill crew and the white night watchman. Yet Rider is not so drunk that he cannot detect what he has suspected, that the white man is cheating; Rider grabs his wrist, but speaks quietly, and something of Mannie's humanizing influence seems to linger in is expressed concern: "Ah kin pass even wid missouts. But dese hyer yuther boys—" Rider twists the watchman's wrist, "the second pair of dice [the missouts] clattered onto the floor beside the first," the watchman draws his pistol, but as he fires Rider kills him with a razor-slash across the throat. Here the story moves into a second part; again Faulkner has used structure and a narrating witness to distance what otherwise might seem merely sensational and melodramatic. The conveyor of the remaining narrative is the deputy sheriff, whose grotesque account is saturated with his insensitiveness as he tells his wife what happened after he found Rider asleep at his cabin, readily confessing the murder but asking not to be locked up. He is taken into custody, again refuses his old aunt's comforting words, tears the cell door out of the brick wall in his raging despair over Mannie's death, is "delivered" from the jail and lynched by a mob. The deputy's review of the whole affair is prefaced by his more general view: "Them damn niggers . . . it's a wonder we have as little trouble with them as we do. . . . Because they ain't human . . . when it comes to the normal human feelings . . . they might just as well be a damn herd of wild buffaloes." The deputy has seen a lack of feeling in Rider's helping to close Mannie's grave, not having heard and unable to imagine the rest, the black man's haste to get away from others with their useless consolations, either his aunt's religion or his friends' whisky jug. Lack of "normal human feeling" is seen too in Rider's returning to work next day, thinks the deputy, without sensing the automatic momentum of a committed life, and, in Rider's realizing the loss of its object, what must have been the mood in which he had single-handedly lifted a larger log than ever and flung it down the sawmill incline and then walked away. As final evidence of the Negro's subhuman nature the deputy cites Rider's hysterical laughter and his tears "big as glass marbles" as he says, "Hit look lack Ah just cant quit thinking. Look lack Ah just cant quit." The deputy having asked his wife what she thinks of that, the story closes with her indifferent response from the next room: "I think if you eat any supper in this house you'll do it in the next five minutes. I'm going to clear this table then and I'm going to the picture show." Thus in this dearth of the humane, antithesis may bring into ghostly remembrance the brief idyl of Rider and Mannie, whose hearth was so brightly warmed but briefly.

In its full effect "Pantaloon in Black" is not only a feelingly sketched, brilliantly composed short story of love and disaster; it speaks directly to Faulkner's proposed "general theme" for the book, "relationship between white & negro races here." This it does with close regional acquaintance and racial representativeness, yet without stereotyping Negro or white. Its most sensational events are subordinated in favor of individual particularity, humanizing many of the characters, including Rider's sympathetic fellow-workmen, his old aunt and her husband, and even the moonshiner who, sensing Rider's desperation in his grief, tries in vain to refuse his four dollars for a gallon of liquor by offering to give him a pint. No less real, however, are the deputy and his wife, whose presence and talk fills the story's closing section, permeating it with their human insensitivity. The deputy tries to make a comic tall tale of Rider's tearing his cell door out of the brick wall but not trying to get out of the jail, and lying on the floor laughing and crying large tears and saying, "Hit look lack Ah just cant quit thinking." A mob of his victim's relatives having taken him, next day he is found lynched, hanging from the bell rope of a Negro country schoolhouse. The deputy's wife, with her mind between a disappointing afternoon card game and the prospective evening "picture show," is impatient with her husband's talk and indifferent to its human import, in a dearth of empathy. The closure, casual and grim, completes with strong regional implications a story brilliantly conducted in its chronological arrangements, economically modulated emphasis, and tonal richness. A test of Faulkner's focusing control can be made if it is remembered that Rider and Mannie had rented a cabin on the McCaslin place from its present proprietor, Carothers (Roth) Edmonds, and Mannie bought their food at his commissary, while Roth kept their weekly savings in his safe for them. Why then was he not brought into the story, to provide the added dimension of his awareness of them, and thus to tie "Pantaloon in Black" more closely to the other narratives in *Go Down, Moses?* To see the correctness of Faulkner's restraint in not doing so is to appreciate further the sheer skill of this focused, succinct fiction of love, a death, and subsequent personal devastation and catastrophe.

Nowhere in any of its nuances does "Pantaloon in Black" raise or even imply, it only shadows forth, the rhetorical question whether a Negro too does not have "organs, dimensions, senses, affections, passions." Moreover, as in the very title itself, the story answers to that only ironically, with its closure in that vignette of the impervious deputy and his impercipient wife. Resonant within its own selective brevities and artfully faceted narration, "Pantaloon in Black" is also consonant with the artist's announced major theme for *Go Down, Moses*— "relationship between white and negro races here"—and by its intentionally slightest of connections with McCaslins and Beauchamps it becomes the more widely representative, while yet its brilliant realism is lightly held to a familiar regional base.

THE STORY OF ISAAC MCCASLIN

With rhetorical formality and apparent thematic emphasis "Isaac McCaslin, 'Uncle Ike,' past seventy," had been given brief mention in the first lines of "Was," opening *Go Down, Moses.* There he was named as having been auditor, in boyhood, to his elder cousin McCaslin Edmonds' account from before his time of social manoeuvres that eventually had brought Isaac's father and mother together. Beyond that, Isaac had learned from McCaslin's tale how his father, "Uncle Buck," and the twin brother, "Uncle Buddy," dealt indifferently with their father's unfinished great house and even in antebellum days presided loosely over their semiliberated slaves. In "The Fire and the Hearth," the book's second section, Isaac is again mentioned in a passage of McCaslin family résumé as "'Uncle Ike,' childless, a widower now . . . past seventy," but he appears too as a young married man in the briefly told earlier episode of his turning over to Lucas Beauchamp on his twenty-first birthday the three-thousand-dollar McCaslin inheritance Isaac had held in trust for him. The third section of *Go Down, Moses,* "Pantaloon in Black" showed nothing about Isaac, though the present McCaslin (Roth Edmonds) is their landlord, and though Rider's and Mannie's love story may be felt later as counterpoint to Isaac's connubial impasse. Then came the three sections recounting in sustained chronological order the crucial events of Isaac's life, from formative boyhood to resolute old age, and constituting not only the greater portion of *Go Down, Moses* but the book's heart. The main narrative thread connecting "The Old People," "The Bear," and "Delta Autumn" carries Isaac's strangely patterned story of precocious development from early boyhood through adolescent maturation to decisive assertion upon arrival at his majority, beyond which he maintains a stance he will not surrender, even in the weariness and melancholy of old age. A common element throughout the three sections is a vivid and tonally varied rendering of the sensory, especially of the big woods, images echoed and interpreted by Isaac's responsive, meditative consciousness. The factor which gives magnitude to his whole history is his movement under acquired and revered principles into crises of conscience, to which he gives absolute and irrevocable answers.

Isaac McCaslin is sometimes condescendingly viewed, and even superciliously judged, without regard for his situation, upbringing, and emergent nature as a youth who then made his binding choice at the age of twenty-one. An orphaned child who "could not remember . . . his father's face," he had the protection of his cousin McCaslin Edmonds, but he was more open to the predominating influence of Sam Fathers, a remarkably skilled and honorable woodsman, and himself an outsider, with his mixture of three racial strains and in his chosen austerities and aloofness. His gifts to Isaac included not only a hunter's skills but their inclusive code, based on a primitive piety (of American Indian derivation) toward the whole creation, giving the boy an immediate personal example of abiding integrity. Beyond this upbringing Isaac is quite the regional character, growing up on the McCaslin plantation he is heir to, and inheriting also as the child of his times, born in 1867 into the defeated South's melancholy and exacerbation, its vulnerabilities and confusions and the chronic anxieties of a failed culture. This is the book of life out of which he learns to read, and it is no wonder he prefers the lucidity and satisfying consistency of Sam Father's surer word. A complementary factor is the Bible, the only book Isaac seems to know much of, though he has a smattering of history; reverence for nature in its enduring manifestations carries his mind to first causes, and he evolves (chiefly from a Southern Protestant's fundamentalist view of Genesis) criteria which he applies to the contemporaneous world of men with all the strictness he had learned in the big woods. "Sam Fathers set me free," said Isaac at twenty-one to his cousin McCaslin Edmonds, but that freedom like any other came at a price, on which Isaac made payments all his life. To the youth of sixteen situated and conditioned as Isaac was, his discovering evidence of his grandfather's miscegenation and incest, offenses entered into as a landholding slaveowner's *droit* and with the most arrogant assumption of the Negro's natural subservience, was so massive a shock that it could be countered with no less outright an answer from Sam Father's disciple than repudiation of the inheritance upon reaching his majority. Yet from a man's refusal of undue advantage, however strongly principled, it is not always possible to infer his sincerity, whether in the sportsman or the citizen. At no point in the narrative of Isaac's life, however, does he appear timorous; even in old age, in "Delta Autumn," he is as strongly assertive of humane values as ever. But such absolutists make their morally less strenuous fellows uncomfortable, and incline them to evade the fact that some traitors to their class have proved themselves friends to mankind, and not all apostates become professing cynics, some have turned up as saints.

"The Old People"

It is at formative stages in his early boyhood that Isaac is seen in this story. These "People" are known to him only by hearsay, in what Sam Fathers, son of a Chickasaw chief and a quadroon slave woman, tells of his ancestors' ways. As young Isaac's cousin McCaslin comments about Sam, "When he was born, all his blood on both sides [Indian and Negro], except the little white part, knew things that had been tamed out of our blood." Sam's privileged place on the McCaslin plantation is as blacksmith and carpenter, but he works or not as he pleases, hunts whenever he wishes, and though not responsive to questions, he will discourse to Isaac of the older times and their ways, and he becomes the boy's mentor in the hunter's skills and his code. Sam Fathers is not only learned in every aspect of woodsmen's lore but is devotee in a primitive piety of close relationship to the natural world and to its wild animals, especially those he kills for food. So he "taught the boy the woods, to hunt, when to shoot and when not to shoot, when to kill and when not to kill, and better, what to do with it afterward." What Sam Fathers stands for in Isaac's life story is a primary formative influence that is extrafamilial, extrasocietal and antedates by far all he knows or is to learn of his own heritage as a McCaslin. Credibly enough, so early and positive an influence abides, and at Isaac's decisive entrance into manhood, formally declared by rejection of his heritage, he reveals a kind of pantheistic mysticism underlying his Biblically based ethos. The primitive pagan element had entered as a powerful intimation while the boy would listen to Sam's retrospective talk, until "gradually" those "would cease to be old times and would become a part of the boy's present" and "as if they were still happening. . . . And more: as if some of them had not happened yet" and "he himself had not come into existence yet" nor had his ancestors come here yet, with "the other subject race" they had brought, and so their hold on the land was "trivial and without reality," and so hunting on what "someday would be his own land . . . it was he, the boy, who was the guest here and Sam Fathers' voice the mouthpiece of the host." For the entranced child it is as if Eden were still to be and his innocence in it yet to be known; it is a type of the Arcadian dream some men in every age have come upon, in deep consciousness of existing within nature, and with a related humanistic faith in natural law.

"The Old People" contains two chief dramatic incidents, thematically related. One is Isaac's shooting his first deer, at the age of twelve, and Sam Fathers' marking his face with the deer's blood, as an initiatory rite, which the boy felt "had marked him indeed, not as a mere hunter, but with something Sam had had in his turn of his vanished and forgotten people." This confirmation in his discipleship has been preceded by much instruction; by the time Isaac was nine, on the plantation, Sam had told him "I done taught you all there is of this settled country. You can hunt it as good as I can now," and so the boy waits for next year when at ten he will be allowed to go with the men in November to hunt bear and deer in the big woods, at Major DeSpain's camp. Here he has his own allotted "stand," not one of the best, but with Sam Fathers still there, "a little behind him and without a gun himself, as he had been standing when the boy shot the running rabbit when he was eight years old." Now on these annual hunts not until his twelfth year, in this third November with the hunting party, does he see a buck, running but within range, and Sam says "Now, shoot quick, and slow," and as he tells McCaslin later, "He done all right," the boy has got his first deer properly. Faulkner opens "The Old People" with this occurrence, and then drops the narrative back into the

preceding apprenticeship and growing awareness and seasons
of waiting that illuminate it as a climactic event. In suggesting how fully and particularly formed was Isaac's outlook even
at twelve, it establishes the factor of a precocious and specifically conditioned maturation which makes the more credible
Isaac's responses, in his latter teens, to discoveries in the Mc-
Caslin plantation records that appall him.

The second major event for Isaac in "The Old People" hap-
pens on the afternoon of that same rainy November day of his
initiation. It is their last that season; they have broken camp
and are moving out of the big woods, by horseback and with
Isaac and Sam in the wagon with the boy's trophy, the deer's
hide and antlers. As they journey a big buck breaks cover near
the narrow wagon track, and Ewell, with Boon and Sam and
Isaac, stay behind on the horses and take positions in the
woods to watch for the deer to circle back. As Isaac and Sam
wait at their spot they hear "the flat single clap of Walter
Ewell's rifle which never missed" and "the mellow sound of the
horn." The boy, regretful that he has not had a chance at this
deer too, is impatient, but Sam says "Wait," and then Isaac
sees the big buck "coming down the ridge, as if it were walking
out of the very sound of the horn which related its death." As
it passed them Sam Fathers raised his arm palm outward and
said, "Oleh, Chief. Grandfather." Not until after midnight
does the hunting party reach Jefferson, where Isaac and his
cousin McCaslin are to stop overnight at Major de Spain's
house before going the seventeen further miles to the plantation. As they lie in bed the still excited boy tries to tell McCaslin about that living apparition of the buck in the moment
after its death. McCaslin quietly says, "Why not?" and suggests to the twelve-year-old that since "you always wear out life
long before you have exhausted the possibilities of living . . .
all that must be somewhere," yet not beyond the stars, "knock-
ing around out there, when it never had enough time about
the earth as it was, when there is plenty of room about the
earth." The boy says, "We want them too. There is plenty of
room for us and them too," but when McCaslin in agreeing

says, "That's right. Suppose they dont have substance, cant cast a shadow—" Isaac breaks in to claim "But I saw it! I saw him!" McCaslin (concluding this last episode in "The Old People") says, "Steady. I know you did. So did I. Sam took me in there once after I killed my first deer."

What has preceded this denouement, however, raises the episode beyond a demand for simple assent to a supernatural occurrence, and suggests a larger transcendent reality. When Isaac and Sam had reached Ewell, he was "standing above a little spike buck which had still been a fawn last spring" but the tracks are, as he says, "pretty near big as a cow's," and adds, "If there were any more tracks here besides the ones he is laying in, I would swear there was another buck here that I never even saw." Sam Fathers does not comment, nor does Isaac until later to his cousin McCaslin. A cautious reader may believe that there were two bucks, the little one Ewell shot and a larger one that had left the print, and so the big buck Isaac had seen and Sam had saluted was a real deer, as also the one must have been that Sam had showed McCaslin earlier—as real as the renowned big bear the boy has already seen in its remote domain. An intermediate and broader reading could be that Faulkner is trying to pass beyond both a supernatural phenomenon (such as what the boy vehemently declares he had seen) and a factual explanation as well, to suggest a more diffused but insistent quality known in art and discerned in nature by man's imagination. In "The Old People" as primarily a story of a boy's growth in wisdom, such a realization passes beyond things like Rider's seeing Mannie's ghost, which can be supposed a real one or an illusion bred in Rider's grieving mind by the commonly accepted superstition that so soon after burial "She be wawkin yit." A more definite though inscrutable phenomenon is old Mollie Beauchamp's extrasensory perception, in "Go Down, Moses," that her grandson is in trouble—"I dont know whar he is. I just knows Pharaoh got him"—and Gavin Stevens, who however imaginative is anything but a mystic, "would not have been surprised" had she "also been able to divine where the boy was and what his trouble was."

What then if anything might Faulkner be suggesting that would lie between supernatural phenomenon and factual explanation, and yet fall within the realm and viable modes of realistic art, with correspondence to the trend of Faulkner's imagination? Perhaps an intimation can be drawn from Sam Fathers' primitive and profound gesture, the raised hand, and his acknowledgment: "Chief. Grandfather." This is not Sam's regular practice in the big woods; evidently he is recognizing what for him is a manifestation. A deer has been shot, the annunciatory horn has sounded, a great deer passes and Sam salutes it. Instance of death and of generic life coexist in nature under its own laws. Not that Sam thus abstracts it; he has his own unspoken wisdom, nor can vision be denied so intent and pious a follower of it. Here may be one more symbol of the artist's idealizing identification of essences that transcendently persist within the flow of time and under the aspect of mortality. Such is the bedrock of Faulkner's belief, as indicated in his Nobel Prize speech by a naming of enduring "verities," and it is the *sine qua non* of his creativity, under his dramas' requirements of abiding human referents. Moreover, since concepts make their particular demands upon expression, and with especial subtlety and refinements in literary modes, this central concern of Faulkner's often is a determinant in his style. This may occur at points where style has come under question, and where in turn such judgments may be questioned. Critical dubiety might be dispelled by closer looks at what Faulkner is trying to make imaginatively accessible and indeed demanding, an awareness through intimations of the enduringly representative within the momentary. This is of course the crux of the literary artist's function, to bring abstraction within the bounds of existential time, giving the revealing flow of consciousness a native human voice, and furnishing it a dimensioned, colorful, and peopled habitation. In giving substance to the essence of the matter Faulkner works with prodigalities of image and rhythm, unremittingly soliciting attentive and responsive engagement, but these are an artist's means to signification.

Faulkner's art is not more complex than his subject as he conceives it in his duty to it. What that fidelity is can be seen in simplest fusions of mode and meaning, as in an envisaging of motion implicit in the inert, or action memorialized in its arrest. Here consciousness is at its most vital, totally of the instant and yet transcendent too through memory, lively intention, and ranging supposition. When Isaac runs up to stand over his first buck, he sees it "where it lay on the wet earth still in the attitude of speed." It is not just Faulkner's phrase; all that has gone into the conditioning of this boy as woodsman and hunter is implicit in his gazing thus at his first trophy only a moment after its severance from life, and a moment before the boy's bleeding of the carcass under Sam's careful instruction about cutting its throat and then being ceremoniously marked with its blood. The physical immediacies and resonant mood of this passage form an explicit preface to Isaac's more abstractly conceived response, that afternoon, in sighting a great buck moving past just after Ewell's horn had announced a kill. Time and its transcendence by representativeness, abstraction endowed with vitality as a heritage from its instances, this reality is emergent in the boy Isaac's intimations.

"The Bear"

"The Bear," with its five sections and 140 pages, is by far the most substantial of the book's seven parts, it shows Isaac McCaslin as boy and young man in fullest detail and contains the most crucial events of his life, but Faulkner did not put his whole story into this one narrative unit. Beginning with Isaac at sixteen, "The Bear" recurrently gathers up some earlier events from "The Old People," yet that preceding unit has its own rightful place, to establish Sam Fathers as a racially and ethically significant character, making credible his formative influence on young Isaac, and above all to frame in a kind of separate purity the boy's first coming into the big woods and his formal initiation as a hunter and nature's devotee, to whom it vouchsafes revelation. Following "The Bear" and also a story of hunters, "Delta Autumn" is not just epilogue or tonal postlude, but a necessary view of Isaac as an old man, his bodily strength depleted but his stance still held, with its deepest cost the lost hope of progeny, and now its immediate sorrow the seeing of an old pattern of evil come round again, in an Edmonds, one who bears with blood-right the McCaslins' progenitor's name, Carothers. "The Bear" is prodigally furnished, crucially dramatic, and massively structured and orchestrated, but it takes on a multiplied richness when viewed in this containment between "The Old People" and "Delta Autumn." For its full realization Isaac McCaslin's life story must be read in its continuity and complete context, with the separate but coalescing focusings and complementary enrichment its three parts furnish each other. That totality gains further from its flexibly wider inclusion between the antebellum data on Isaac's parentage as foreshadowed in "Was," with its grotesquery of the old socioeconomic order's local collapse, and at the end, almost a century later, in "Go Down, Moses," the death of Molly's grandson, electrocuted for murder but brought home from the North with all the conventional dignities insisted on now and at various other times by the Negro Beauchamps, especially Lucas, as in "The Fire and the Hearth."

"The Bear" nevertheless is pivotal and preeminent in *Go Down, Moses*. Ranging back and forth over Isaac McCaslin's conditioned realizations, early and late, under the requirements of his temperament and within the context of an environment that includes heritage and exacts commitments, this lengthy narrative with its five differently keyed movements draws all things into it through the intense subjectivity of its protagonist. A maintained sense of Isaac's consciousness as the stage of action (together with the alert attention required by any closely and subtly wrought literary work) will show memories returned to because those events are taking on further relevance or evoking a fuller emotion as they enlarg-ingly relate to some present event or reflection. Faulkner is not confused nor is he inadept in this not unprecedented way of narration; he is simply but very skillfully claiming for his char-acter the transcendent play of what is the mode of operant intelligence and feeling. In such a complexity the recurrences are not only of former matters made new; sometimes what is enduringly remembered is called up as witness and support in a present response, which may deepen drama in marking out motive. Yet however frequent and sometimes abrupt are memory's shifts of chronology in "The Bear," the steady, strong thrust beneath such variations is supportive, through that ongoing receptivity of mind which brings about Isaac's maturation, especially in those realizations which fixed his judgments and intentions and supported him in his severe consistencies.

As "The Bear" begins, Isaac "was sixteen" and "For six years now he had been a man's hunter . . . had heard the best of all talking . . . of the wilderness, the big woods, bigger and older than any document." Already, under Sam Fathers' tutelage and out of his own deeply sensed experiences, he had formulated his regard for the natural world as a living crea-tion existent in its own right, and older than the oldest legal paper by which men had "pretended" to "convey" ownership of it. Thus early in "The Bear" Faulkner again sounds a major theme with relation to Isaac, as he had done similarly at the beginning of Go Down, Moses, with brief mention of "Isaac McCaslin . . . past seventy," who "loved the woods" and "owned no property and never desired to since the earth was no man's but all men's"—this stipulated in preface to "Was," which narrates hearsay of antebellum events his father Theo-philus ("Uncle Buck") played a part in before Isaac was born. Thus when it comes to Isaac's discussion with his cousin McCaslin in section 4 of "The Bear" the reader knows Isaac's assertions are propounded out of conviction that had long been growing in him. Its taproot reaches to an intimation of universal mystery, with a pious regard for undespoiled nature itself as the lively yet stable and provident creation, seen with a primitive awareness that antedates by far the Biblical metaphors which Isaac uses to represent it and its consequent imperatives. Beyond argument between middle-aged ameliorist McCaslin Edmonds and Isaac McCaslin at just twenty-one, already shocked by a recently discovered heritage of shame into an absolutism he makes manifest by relinquishing title to the McCaslin holdings, beyond Isaac's extrapolating his cousin's tentative hypotheses about "this Arbiter, this Architect, this Umpire" into a historically furnished notion of worldwide predestination that dwarfs Miss Rosa Coldfield's finding the South's doom and damnation illustrated in the Sutpen debacle, deeper than all this is Isaac's immediate stay and assurance, an indefinable natural mysticism, confirmed by his senses and instincts, and bred in him from boyhood on in the big woods, with its mysterious realities as Sam Fathers leads him into them.

Isaac's primary awareness has been conveyed in the narrative through suggestions of his sensory responses, as on that morning when, waiting to shoot his first deer, he stands with Sam Fathers behind him in "the faint, cold, steady rain, the gray and constant light of the late November dawn, with the voices of the hounds converging somewhere in it and toward them." The feel of the rain is intensified by all three adjectives; under clouds the "late November dawn" comes as daylight that is "constant," growing no brighter; in the hounds' voices "converging somewhere in it" but "toward them" there is indefiniteness pregnant with the impending explicit moment when Sam will say "Now, shoot quick, and slow," and Faulkner has got the mounting urgency of the preceding moments into the very rhythm of the phrase "converging *somewhere* in it *and* toward them." Static but equally strong in "The Bear" is the boy's feeling on his solitary and most venturesome penetration of the big woods in the summer of his eleventh year, when for a moment he stood "alien and lost in the green and soaring gloom of the markless wilderness." That gloom, "green and soaring," is under ancient trees grown tall and thick; and "markless" makes it stranger than "unmarked" would be, in this place where not only no trace has been left by man but where there is nothing to indicate it as anything the boy in all his explorings has ever come upon before.

Yet this passage, like any other, must be returned to its context, which moves through sensory impressions in tracing a boy's continuous quest for self-discovery and membership in an admired order of men, under a remarkable mentor. So well has Sam Fathers already trained him by rabbit-hunting on the more open plantation land and so much has young Isaac learned from the men's talk of hunting in the big woods and of the legendary bear, that instead of merely watching the wagon leave with men, dogs, and supplies for the November trip to the Big Bottom, he was allowed to come along, at the age of ten, with the assumption, of course, that Sam would still be with him. The boy's rare ardor is of the kind that can be known by the young in early realizations of a chosen all-absorbing course that promises immeasurably more, "a next time, after and after," in return for one's constancy. Now as the wagon carries him into "his novitiate to the true wilderness with Sam beside him as he had begun his apprenticeship in miniature to manhood after the rabbits," it seems to him he is "witnessing his own birth." Nor is it strange to him; with true imagination that consolidates what he has heard about the camp, "he knew already how it was going to look." Many happenings lie ahead, and much exaction and some hazards, but the heart of Isaac's story from tenth to sixteenth year as seasonal hunter in the woods of the Big Bottom is not what game he bags with what rigorous efforts but in his witnessings and the sweep of his realizations. In this "novitiate" the big woods and the life in them stimulate Isaac's instinctual self, drawing upon atavistic depths in the masculine nature. This force is exemplified in Sam Fathers' formalism, out of his preserved Indian heritage, and an older and purer propriety than the white men's codes as hunters or in their general contacts with the natural world.

Sam Fathers trains the boy Isaac in more than techniques;

he is a guide into natural mysteries and a mentor in conduct. Practical instruction begins at once. As they wait at their stand for what the baying dogs may be driving their way, Sam says, "Now, slant your gun up a little and draw back the hammers and then stand still," and after the chase has passed beyond them he says, "Now let your hammers down. . . . I want you to learn how to do when you didn't shoot. It's after the chance . . . has done already come and gone that men and dogs get killed." Beyond such matters of prudent practice, for Sam the big woods is one world, in which he senses that the wild animals return men's curiosity about them. In the second week of Isaac's first season in camp Sam suddenly tells him to listen, and the boy hears the dogs differently, "no ringing chorus strong and fast on a free scent but a moiling yapping an octave too high . . . taking a long time to pass out of hearing, leaving even then in the air that echo of thin and almost human hysteria," and the boy knows it's the bear, Old Ben. "He do it every year," Sam tells the boy. "He come to see who's here, who's new in camp this year," and Sam explains as to the chase that "He'll let them follow him to the river. Then he'll send them home." Sam and Isaac return to camp to find the dogs "huddled back" in the dark space under the kitchen; then in mid-afternoon the eleventh dog returns, and the boy and Tennie's Jim "held the passive and still trembling bitch while Sam daubed her tattered ear and raked shoulder with turpentine and axle grease," and Sam remarks "Just like a man. Just like folks. Put off as long as she could having to be brave, knowing all the time that sooner or later she would have to be brave once so she could keep on calling herself a dog, and knowing beforehand what was going to happen when she done it." This may seem a too fanciful anthropomorphizing for the laconic Sam Fathers in his practical role, but he is a primitive mystic too, and what he is grasping at with those words is a common factor in the animate world, including dogs and folks and bears, the force of native instincts and the ascendency some of these can take over others less vital.

In the sweeping montages of "The Bear," one of modern fic-

tion's most opulently furnished and subtly commanding creations, a notable passage is that which comprises Isaac's first
experiences of the big woods, in November with the hunting
party, and then during the second visit the following June, a
season the men have arbitrarily chosen not for hunting but to
celebrate Major de Spain's and General Compson's birthdays.
For Isaac there in his tenth and eleventh years these two
sojourns are crowded with experience, learning and realizations, and this complex objective-subjective process in maturation is brilliantly recounted. What it holds to thematically is
the boy's preoccupation with the famed Old Ben, "the bear
which had run in his listening and loomed in his dreams since
before he could remember." In his second week that first November he has heard the terrified dogs' strange barking and
seen the little bitch come back wounded, "as if the wilderness
. . . had patted lightly once her temerity," and Sam has told
him the bear comes close once each year "to see who's here."
Then for three mornings Sam is gone; when he comes back it
is with knowledge of what territory the bear is in, and that day
he takes the boy to a distance where "in the thick great gloom
of ancient woods and the winter's dying afternoon, he looked
quietly down at the rotted log scored and gutted with claw-
marks and, in the wet earth beside it, the print of the enormous two-toed [trap-maimed] foot." The next day he stands
where Sam placed and left him and waits, holding the gun
"too big for him," and hearing where, invisible nearby, a big
woodpecker "clattered at a dead trunk." Then that drumming
stopped short, as if the bird had sensed a special presence, and
somehow the boy "knew that the bear was looking at him. He
never saw it. . . . He did not move, holding the useless gun
which he knew now he would never fire at it." Then "the
woodpecker's dry hammering set up again" and the moment
had passed. When Isaac tells Sam, "I didn't see him," Sam
answers, "He done the looking," and the boy, recognizing his
fear, knows too that he *will have to see him . . . will have to
look at him . . ."*

Not until the next summer can he answer to that challenge. In this off-season he assumed the others (celebrating those birthdays in camp) supposed he was squirrel-hunting when he set out each morning, but what he does is to range the area around the place where he thought the bear had come and looked at him. He finds the spot where last November, standing with Sam, he had been shown the unmistakable footprint, but he does not see the bear. And returning "in the twilight of the third evening," he learns that, not surprisingly, one person knows what he is up to, when Sam says, "You ain't looked right yet" and adds, "Likely he's been watching you. . . . It's the gun. You will have to choose." So next morning he left before dawn, without breakfast (fanciers of ecclesiastical symbols may see that as fasting before partaking of a sacrament, but his solitary enterprise is something even more austere and private) and with nothing but "the compass and a stick for the snakes" and his dead father's "old, heavy, biscuit-thick silver watch." In going disarmed he is accepting what he feels as a condition imposed by nature, and thus he passes even beyond the distinction Sam had made—"Be scared. You cant help that. But dont be afraid." Now the boy knows he would not be afraid, "not even in the moment when the fear would take him completely: blood, skin, bowels, bones, memory from the long time before it even became his memory." The instinctive visceral reaction, rooted in the primitive racial psyche, is completely natural, and is even a bond with the animate world through his oldest progenitor's experience in it. Yet in that recognition the boy also knows his human identity more clearly, in "that thin clear quenchless lucidity which alone differed him from this bear and from all the other bears and bucks he would follow." In the flame of the hunter's consciousness, besides response to preconditioned involuntary reactions, there is place for current choices, and not merely practical ones but rising to the acceptance of a code of conduct.

At noon, nine hours after his leaving camp on what is not a hunt but a quest, he is "farther into the new and alien country than he had ever been," traveling by compass and knowing it will be dark before he can get back, but pushing on. Then he senses that leaving the gun behind "was not enough. . . . It was the watch and the compass." So he hangs these on a bush, and leaving even his stick behind, he circles further into the wilderness, in a complete relinquishment to it. Beyond a supposition that the bear might take this into account (besides its actually detecting the gun by smell if not by sight) there could be the psychological implication that the boy's voluntary act liberates and extends his instinctive responses. At any rate, his realizations are not defined, they are merely represented as he loses himself and circles and then comes upon the crooked print so recently made in the damp earth that, while he looked, "it continued to fill with water." He follows the trail; it brings him back into a little glade, and there is the bush with his compass and watch glinting in a ray of sunlight; and "then he saw the bear. . . . it was just there, immobile . . . looking at him." Then "it moved . . . crossed the glade without haste, walking for an instant into the sun's full glare and out of it, and stopped again and looked back at him across one shoulder." After such deliberateness it is suddenly gone, "back into the wilderness." And that accomplished rendezvous, instinctively pursued with courage and humility and consummated in an exchange of looks, completes the first of five sections in "The Bear."

The second section opens in typical Faulknerian manner, with an enigmatic statement, that promises revelation which, after that has been fully given, recurs with fuller thematic significance. "So he should have hated and feared Lion," it begins. He was "thirteen then . . . had killed his buck and Sam Fathers had marked his face with the hot blood, and in the next November he killed a bear." He was competent in the woods, knew all the territory within twenty-five miles of the camp, had often found the big bear's trail and once "saw it cross a long corridor of down-timber where a tornado had passed." And he has confronted the bear "at bay . . . on its hind feet" when he drops his gun, rushes in, and snatches back

his impetuously brave little dog from certain death. This time
Sam Fathers presses the boy: "You've done seed him twice
now, with a gun in your hands. This time you couldn't have
missed him," and Isaac answers, "Neither could you. . . . Why
did't you shoot him?" but Sam "didn't seem to have heard."
The two haven't really questioned each other; they have
obliquely confirmed that they would not want the old bear to
die yet, nor in such a mere ambush, but in a proper hunt.
Which the lad implies when he says, "It must be one of us. So
it wont be until the last day." Whereupon the narrative repeats the sentence section 2 began with three pages earlier —
"So he should have hated and feared Lion" — and it is then
developed what Lion is, a great Airedale capable of holding
Old Ben at bay. The animal had been running wild in the
hunting-camp area, killing a doe and its fawn and a colt, but
Sam Fathers, having trapped it, slowly tamed it, with the
youth Isaac watching in fascination, and had named it Lion,
and Boon Hogganbeck becomes the dog's devoted caretaker.
In November of that year Lion runs and corners the old bear,
but it escapes; the next November, with Lion's help, the hunt
comes closer, and Boon in his notorious way shoots five times
and misses, but in an earlier encounter General Compson
"drew blood." His shots have not seriously wounded the tough
old bear, but the boy had seen drops of its blood on the
ground, and no doubt read their omen. The concluding paragraph in section 2 of "The Bear" then again repeats the phrase
with which that section opened — "So he should have hated
and feared Lion" — but it continues with "Yet he did not."
What is suggested is the maturing youth's intimation of a fate
that will come out of "something . . . beginning . . . already
begun . . . like the last act on a set stage." The similitude from
drama suggests awareness of the foreordained, with chosen
action moving inevitably toward larger and irrevocable ends;
and the youth's readiness echoes an august conception of the
witnessing of tragedy in a frame of communal participation
and understanding: "It was the beginning of the end of
something, he didn't know what except that he would not

grieve. He would be humble and proud that he had been found worthy to be a part of it too or even just to see it too."

Here the story passes into its section 3, as of a cold December in the following year, which is to include for Isaac at sixteen not only Old Ben's and Lion's conjoined fate, but the maturing youth's decisive confrontation of a full knowledge of evil in his heritage. (This latter, with its ensuing consequences in his later years, is to be a detailed part of the crowded, variegated, and brilliantly rendered section 4 of "The Bear," after which section 5 is no more than a postlude in a minor key, an aesthetic diminution following upon the series of crises that make up Isaac's passage into manhood and a fixed stance.) In section 3 Boon Hogganbeck, one of Faulkner's most colorful primitives, plays a conspicuous part, and some association with him enters into Isaac's experiences at this season, laying responsibilities upon him and in the end evoking a passionate partisanship. Boon is one-quarter Indian, grandson of a Chickasaw squaw; he is six feet, four with "the mind of a child, the heart of a horse"; he has his virtues, in his loyalty to Major de Spain and his almost equally submissive devotion to the great dog Lion; he is, besides a notoriously bad shot, a gregarious and cheerfully contentious man, and tireless in the field. He is to be given new entity as conniver in those adventures into low life which mark the initiation of the boy Lucius Priest in *The Reivers,* Faulkner's last novel, but Isaac, at sixteen in the 1880s is no such innocent. When that year the hunting party stayed on waiting "for the weather to soften so that Lion and Old Ben could run their yearly race," Major de Spain and McCaslin Edmonds send Boon to Memphis with a suitcase to get further supplies of whisky from the distiller, and Isaac is sent along "to see that Boon got back with it or most of it or at least some of it." Which Isaac accomplishes, though not until they have missed one returning train and he has been irritated not so much at Boon, who had begged a dollar for drinking in a saloon, as at himself for impatience with the childlike, goodhearted man.

The larger part of section 3, the next seventeen pages, constitutes a powerfully narrated account of next day's fateful hunt, in which Isaac is assigned not just a man's part but a foremost one at the insistence of General Compson, who praises the youth's woodsmanship and surrenders to him the advantage of riding the one-eyed mule that won't bolt at the scent of bear or of blood. In the hunt's furore Isaac finds himself riding alone with Sam Fathers; then joined by Boon, they swim the river with their mules in close pursuit. The bear is brought at bay, standing among the hounds too close to permit shooting; Lion leaps, takes the bear by the throat, and clings in spite of the great beast's raking forepaws; to save Lion Boon leaps onto the bear's back and knifes it, finally reaching its heart, and it "fell all of a piece, as a tree falls." Boon, though clawed on head, arm, and leg, pays no attention to that but works, with Isaac's help, to pry Lion's jaws from the dead bear's throat. And then he cares for Lion, whose entrails have been torn out of him. Hurrying, they find the hunt has had a further cost; Sam Fathers is down, "lying motionless on his face in the trampled mud." With the skiff they bring Sam and the wounded dog and the dead bear back across the river. There Major de Spain takes charge, giving Tennie's Jim his mare to ride to summon the sawmill doctor, and seeing to getting Sam back to his hut and Boon and Lion back to the camp. The doctor comes, Boon will not be touched until Lion has been sewed up, and then, with Boon's wounds disinfected and bandaged, they go to look after Sam, still lying in his bunk where Boon had placed him. The doctor says Sam is exhausted but will be all right after a day or two in bed, but "the boy knew that Sam too was going to die."

Next day at sundown Lion died, and "with lanterns and lighted pine-knots" they go with Boon to bury the great dog on a knoll in the woods, and General Compson, standing at the grave's head, "spoke as he would have spoken over a man." Then the party is to break camp that night, leaving Boon and Tennie's Jim to stay with Sam "until he feels like getting up." Isaac refuses to leave, his cousin McCaslin insists he has already missed too much school, General Compson intervenes

and arranges for the boy to be allowed to stay until the following Sunday night. What follows is dramatically narrated:
"That was Thursday. On Saturday morning Tennie's Jim left
on McCaslin's woods-horse . . . and late that afternoon rode
through the gate on the spent horse and on to the commissary
where McCaslin was rationing the tenants and the wage hands
for the coming week." What Tennie's Jim then tells McCaslin
is not given, only that McCaslin takes his surrey and goes in to
Jefferson to get Major de Spain, "and they drove thirty miles in
the dark of that night" and "as the sun rose" that Sunday
morning they reach the spot where Lion had been buried.
Now it is apparent what news Tennie's Jim had carried which
brought McCaslin Edmonds and Major de Spain back to the
Big Bottom in such haste. What they find beside "the low
mound of unannealed earth where Boon's spade-marks still
showed" was "the platform of freshly cut saplings bound
between four posts and the blanket-wrapped bundle upon the
platform and Boon and the boy squatting between the platform and the grave." Boon springs up with his gun, McCaslin
grasps and calmly takes it away from him by patient insistence, and the anguished Boon explains: "He told us exactly
how to do it. And by God you aint going to move him. So we
did it like he said, and I been sitting here ever since to keep the
damn wildcats and varmints away from him . . ."

The traditional Indian burial makes obvious Boon's and the
boy's vigil, and Isaac does not rise into action until his cousin
McCaslin presses Boon to know what other old custom may
have been carried out at Sam Fathers' bidding. "Did you kill
him, Boon?" he asks, and Boon cannot answer, moving as if
drunk and blind, his chest heaving, while McCaslin repeats
the question; then to Boon's agonizingly repeated "No! No!"
McCaslin says, "Tell the truth. I would have done it if he had
asked me to." At this the youth moves in "between them,"
facing his cousin McCaslin, and in tears as if "not from his eyes
alone but from his whole face, like sweat," he cries "Leave him
alone! Goddamn it! Leave him alone!" It is in this paroxysm of
Isaac's grief, anger, compassion, and assertion that the story's

section 3 ends. Faulkner doesn't tell that Sam Fathers' body was taken down from the raised platform and buried there next to Lion's grave. That is only incidentally made apparent in section 5 of "The Bear," when while still in his teens, in June, Isaac visited the camp one more time before the lumber company moved in to cut the hitherto untouched big woods. Major de Spain had reserved out of the sale the plot with the two graves and had its corners marked with concrete posts, and Isaac goes there and finds them. But nowhere in "The Bear" has it been detailed how McCaslin Edmonds and Major de Spain calmed down Boon and Isaac as his indignant defender and reconciled them to proceeding with a more conventional burial for Sam Fathers. The intrinsic possiblities of such a scene, with Sam's young disciple Isaac as participant, would have tempted many a fictionist, but it would have followed lamely after the powerful overflow of Isaac's emotions, and as usual Faulkner knew what to select in what proportion, and when to break off an episode for thematic climax. For it is all contained in Isaac's gushing tears and earnest youthful profanity and angry command; it is not only Boon whom he defends, it is Sam Fathers' body disposed as he had desired, still according to his own tradition and nature. Isaac's outburst also breaks the silence of a sustained melancholy in his realization of the simultaneous ending of eras: the many-faceted, formative years of his instructive companionship with Sam Fathers, their special acquaintance with Old Ben, the three seasons of hunting him with Lion, and encompassing all that and much else, a decade of tutelage in more than woodsmanship under Sam Fathers, who (as he puts it five years later to his cousin McCaslin Edmonds) had set him free.

The sixty pages of section 4 in "The Bear" draw all the other four parts of this 140-page novella to it as center of a field of force, in representing how Isaac McCaslin at twenty-one and thereafter consolidated his ethical position and bore himself accordingly. While this section has received a great deal of admiring attention, it has also been criticized for alleged extravagances and diffuseness. Actually it is solidly compacted and masterfully controlled, and not too difficult if read with deliberate attention and upon the bases of the three sections preceding it in "The Bear" and the four stories preceding it in *Go Down, Moses*. Nor is it monotonous, as might be suggested by some criticisms which arouse suspicion that the reader is remembering only a portion (for instance sections of the dialogue between Isaac and McCaslin) and has come to think that the whole sixty pages are in that mode. Actually section 4 opens with three classic Faulknerian paragraphs as prodigal prologue to that debate between Isaac and his older cousin McCaslin, until now his guardian; actually their dialogue is broken into several times by Isaac's privately intruding consciousness, meditative but also extending to vivid objectification of other episodes recalled. Considering the weighty import of section 4, it is remarkably pointed and its manipulation of detail is fluent and expedite; in the variegated pattern a compositional totality of related personal, familial, societal, and historical factors is achieved, with intriguing effect; and the whole is resonant with the vital force of Isaac's deeply engaged consciousness as he stands fast in his convictions at his young manhood's most crucial points.

The powerful first three paragraphs launch section 4 with sustained momentum and abundant substance, and with an almost incantatory tone as if to forecast epical disclosures. It begins with a complete clause but not capitalized: "then he was twenty-one." Identity in this *bildungsroman* has endured and progressed; Isaac having arrived at his majority, now "He could say it." Basic to his declaration is an ethical judgment of the plantation system's economic and human aspects, as he now finds himself "juxtaposed not against the wilderness but against the tamed land which was to have been his heritage." Knowing the wilderness from his early boyhood (as "The Old People" and the first three sections of "The Bear" have shown), he has found his way in it and among its creatures bravely and with humility, seeing its immemorial and vital equilibrium as of the Creation itself and under that providence, with required deference to an ordered reality. The land he stands to inherit as direct legitimate heir of his grandfather Lucius Quintus Carothers McCaslin has been "tamed" only because "the human beings he [the grandfather] held in bondage . . . had removed the forest from it and in their sweat scratched the surface of it . . . to grow something out of it which had not been there before and which could be translated back into the money he who believed he had bought it had had to pay to get it and hold it and a reasonable profit too." In Isaac's particularly developed view this transaction and similarly all the earlier ones reaching back to the Chickasaw chief Ikkemotubbe had had no validity, because "not even a fragment" of the land had been any man's "to relinquish or sell." (Here centrally in this section 4 as it carries "The Bear" to its largest dimensions as Isaac's life-story, a motif is sounded, but not for the first time. It had been introduced in those cryptic two pages, a separate first section of the story "Was," which opens *Go Down, Moses.* Naming "Isaac McCaslin, 'Uncle Ike,' past seventy . . . a widower now and uncle to half a county and father to no one," the passage characterized him as a man who "loved the woods; who owned no property and never desired to since the earth was no man's but all men's, as light and air and weather were" — all this in a kind of chronological and compositional paradox through a thematic preemption, in advance of the narrative substance of "Was," its setting being 1859, eight years before Isaac's birth, and its source a recollection by Isaac's elder cousin McCaslin Edmonds, nine years old at the time he witnessed those frantic events not unrelated to two unions, Isaac's parents and those of Lucas Beauchamp, those two grandsons of Carothers McCaslin, the dynasty's patriarch, who figure most significantly in *Go Down, Moses.*)

The second and third paragraphs in section 4 of "The Bear" move the camera eye into the McCaslin plantation commissary, with Isaac "himself and his cousin" McCaslin Edmonds positioned in what is "not the heart perhaps but certainly the solar plexus" of those holdings and that ongoing enterprise which their direct heir Isaac, come of age in 1888, is now declaring himself unable to accept in good conscience. The commissary shelves and walls contain everything from cheese to harness, and also the ledgers "in which McCaslin recorded the slow outward trickle of food and supplies and equipment which returned each fall as cotton made and ginned and sold (two threads frail as truth and impalpable as equators yet cable-strong to bind for life them who made the cotton to the land their sweat fell on)." There are older ledgers too, "clumsy and archaic in size and shape, on the yellowed pages of which were recorded in the faded hand of his father Theophilus and his uncle Amodeus during the two decades before the Civil War, the manumission in title at least of Carothers McCaslin's slaves." And in these same old ledgers Isaac during his crucial sixteenth year had read secretly at night of many other and earlier matters, contributive to his disillusionment about his grandfather and the methods and mores of the social order within which that man had operated, so that now Isaac is resolved to refuse even what remained after the war of a presumed right to own and exploit. But this is not yet told, it is gradually unfolded later, along with its grounds in successive decipherings and deductions from the antebellum ledger entries. What Isaac's story moves into in the fourth paragraph of that section is a colloquy between himself at twenty-one and his cousin McCaslin, seventeen years his senior, until now his informal, concerned, and benevolent guardian, and manager of the plantation pending Isaac's fully taking over his heritage. Which he is refusing to do.

The next six pages are occupied by some of this debate, with McCaslin Edmonds arguing for "what that man [Isaac's grandfather, "Old Carothers" McCaslin] accomplished," something "worthy of bequeathment for his descendants' ease and security and pride." To Isaac, though, this is not a matter for family pride but shame, after his discoverings from the ledgers of his grandfather's miscegenetic use of the slave Eunice and then his incest with their daughter Tomasina, causing Eunice's suicide. Beyond all that, and as an absolute determinant, is

Isaac's broader view of legitimacy, on which he bases his refusal of the inheritance, in his belief that the land itself "was never Ikkemotubbe's fathers' fathers' to bequeath Ikkemotubbe to sell to Grandfather." In pursuit of this natural theology Isaac turns to the Genesis account of the Creation, affirming that God had made man "to be His overseer on the earth . . . not to hold for himself and his descendants inviolable title forever, generation after generation," but "in the communal anonymity of brotherhood." Faulkner does not develop Isaac's view of what happened to brotherhood between the first men born of woman, nor does Isaac's argument take into account the more crucial matter of what his Book soon states of the Lord's early promise to Abram that through a son of his own begetting his descendants are to inherit the land from the river of Egypt to the Euphrates, a territory already occupied by ten named tribes. In this portion of their speculative talk McCaslin is skeptical about God's entering into or even noticing men's affairs, and he not only says his younger cousin has "taken to proving your points and disproving mine by the same text," but he laconically cites "The sons of Ham. You who quote the Book: the sons of Ham," suggesting thereby that if Isaac is right in supposing "maybe" God's purpose was working through a substitution of his grandfather for Ikkemotubbe in control of the land then perhaps the Negro's fate (as sons of Biblical Ham) is as fixedly ordained as the favoring of Abram's people, who themselves were dispossessed, as Rome then was by the barbarians. McCaslin's wider historical view forces Isaac to admit some possible fallacies in his source, but to that he appends two assertions. One is that "He didn't have His Book written to be read . . . by the wise of the earth . . . but by the doomed and lowly . . . who have nothing else to read with but the heart"—which brings him close to the emotional fundamentalist Christianity that in his postbellum South is the one congruity (though separately maintained) between most of the Negroes and many whites. Isaac also puts it that those "who wrote His Book for Him . . . human men . . . were trying to write down the heart's truth out of the heart's driving complexity," and that "What they were trying to tell, what He wanted said, was too simple."

He is naturally resorting to the highest authority for human conduct he knows, but like most amateur theologians he has compounded his exegesis beyond the biblically based Creation myth into speculations about the Creator's ongoing will. In returning to rest on the explanation that "what He wanted said was too simple," he asserts his own more than physiocratic simplicity, as a devout absolutist. His strongest link with biblical religion is in a mysticism resembling a Franciscan piety toward the whole creation; yet for Isaac the fundamental source of that has been not biblical but his novitiate under Sam Fathers, who salutes the wild creatures of the big woods filially and in fealty and has insisted on unequivocal conduct as a hunter, respectful of aspects of reality outside himself. Specifically, as to the boy's desire to see the old bear, Sam had said, "You will have to choose," which meant putting aside the gun, and, as Isaac then chooses further, dispensing with all advantage of man-made accouterment and facing without watch or compass the realities of the natural world as one of its beings, not only trusting but obeying the instincts which lead him on to what he values and seeks. This is beyond any ancient book's authority or the expedient customs of his own times; and it is in that same absolute light and with that same fidelity to what he feels that Isaac, later in this dialogue, is to tell his cousin McCaslin, "I'm trying to explain . . . something which I dont quite understand myself. . . . I could say I dont know why I must do it but that I do know I have got to because I have got myself to have to live with for the rest of my life and all I want is peace to do it in." If Isaac is to be condemned, it comes down to calling him a fool for seeking a supposed peace such as the world cannot give; and indeed what he is to find is emotional deprivation in his childless manhood, and in his latter years a renewal of an old anguish, to be met with nothing more comforting than honest stoicism.

In this first, five-page portion of exchanges between Isaac at twenty-one and his older cousin McCaslin, concerning Isaac's rejection of inheritance and heritage, Faulkner establishes a structural formality which will be adhered to in resumptions of this dialogue throughout this section of "The Bear." Their speeches, usually half a page or more, are argumentative and crowded with detail but coherent, direct discourse made up of complete sentences. Since there is no internal attribution such as "said Isaac" or "said McCaslin," there is no cause for a scramble to avoid repetition by having the two men successively state, declare, reply, object, point out, and so forth. Indeed, Faulkner does not let even that much incidental characterization enter here. Instead, at the paragraph's end of a speech by either man, two words are attached — "and McCaslin" or "and Isaac" or simply "and he" — and these, without terminal punctuation, lead inobtrusively into the next paragraph, the quoted response by the other. This not only keeps the reader sufficiently reminded which one now speaks, it sustains the sense of urgently continued exchange (even when it is only McCaslin's occasional "Ah" as if signaling both his attentiveness and his suspended judgment, or a concessive "Habet" or a "Go on.") The device also suggests a conventional mode, as if in the miming of a morality play, with the cousins the masked dialecticians of a universal quandary. It is not a mannerism but only one of Faulkner's many ingenuities, and in its uniformity and slightness is just sufficiently perceptible to create its supportive effect.

The formality which such succinct indication of its speakers gives this vigorous debate prolonged at intervals during section 4 of "The Bear" also calls close attention to McCaslin Edmonds, an especially interesting character as seen in his significant relations with his younger cousin Isaac. Those annunciatory pages which open *Go Down, Moses* as a novel, with their effect of foreshadowing Isaac as a named but yet-unborn character who will emerge from the wings into a leading role, also describe "his cousin McCaslin born in 1850 and sixteen years his senior" as having become "rather his brother than cousin and rather his father than either." In that first story,

"Was," McCaslin Edmonds is only a small boy hurriedly accompanying his uncle Buck McCaslin [Isaac's father-to-be] on a chase to the Beauchamp plantation to recover a runaway slave, their part-Negro half brother, Tomey's Turl, gone once more to woo the Beauchamp's slave Tennie.

However, "Was" is not told by the boy McCaslin in naive first-person (after the manner of *Huckleberry Finn* or Hemingway's "My Old Man"); instead, the third-person narrative inclusively gathers into its remembering and enhances what Isaac could have been made conscious of by his cousin's later recountings, and could transmute into an extended relevance. There is much of such assimilated hearsay and of Isaac's own penetrating reactions to it in "The Bear," especially section 4, where — still in third-person, as in all of *Go Down, Moses* — the story looms the more powerfully as of Isaac's evolving awareness in central crises of his discoveries and his self-determination. For instance, the boy born after the Civil War knows from his elder cousin how scarce food was then, when McCaslin, an orphan in his teens, was being cared for by Uncle Buddy on the plantation while Uncle Buck (Isaac's father, Theophilus) was fighting in Bedford Forrest's Confederate cavalry. It must be by way of young McCaslin's boyhood memory that Isaac can know how at sixty Uncle Buck, "lean and active as a cat," would mount "the horse . . . already moving, already running" by the time he "came into the seat." Certainly his cousin has conveyed not only what the whole county knew, how in 1837 "as soon as their father was buried" the twin brothers moved out of his unfinished big house, built a cabin with their own hands, and put the two dozen slaves into the big house, but also how its front door was formally nailed shut every night with no check on the open doors and windows at the rear, in reliance on "an unspoken gentlemen's agreement" that all the slaves would be "behind the front one" when it was opened "at daybreak." And McCaslin has even told Isaac that his father's last entry in the ledgers, in 1869 and "almost indecipherable . . . from the rheumatism which now crippled him," had been written "with the left hand." Certainly it was through McCaslin that Isaac could visualize an event that had occurred two weeks after his birth. When his father, back from the war, finally had married Sophonsiba Beauchamp, she insisted that with her dowry they complete the big house begun by Old Carothers McCaslin and move into it; and it was there, "the first time he [Isaac] and his mother came downstairs," his nurse Tennie carrying him, that Isaac's uncle Hubert Beauchamp presented and sealed up in burlap a silver cup with fifty gold coins in it, to be opened by Isaac on his twenty-first birthday. This later event, over a decade after Hubert's death, was to have an ironic overtone as to inheritances, with the silver cup found transmuted into a tin coffeepot and the gold coins replaced by I.O.U.'s from Uncle Hubert, grandiosely signing himself Beauchamp and promising "twenty (20) percentum compounded per annum."

McCaslin Edmonds was present at that mannered bestowing, as he had been there all along during Isaac's twenty-one years. Orphaned and growing up with his uncles on the plantation, McCaslin was living and working there when Isaac's father and mother moved into the restored big house, and when Theophilus McCaslin died soon after Isaac's birth, McCaslin Edmonds in his early twenties apparently took over management, to rejuvenate and hold the postbellum operation until Isaac would be of age in 1888, and to be Isaac's most immediate source as to what those years had been like. When Sophonsiba Beauchamp McCaslin died, before her son was ten, McCaslin became Isaac's beneficent guardian, closer than mere kin, and later he disinterestedly contested against Isaac's repudiation of his inheritance, though without success even in persuading his cousin to receive money from the plantation except as a loan until Isaac could establish himself as a carpenter.

It has been the at least suggested if not always indicated supplementary accounts by McCaslin Edmonds to his cousin, and not just the facts and implications which the maturing youth exhumed from the plantation ledgers, which substantiate the reach into the past by Isaac's ranging consciousness in and beyond the two cousins' passages of dialogue in section 4 of "The Bear." Besides former events recalled by Isaac himself there are actions directly realized with McCaslin a participant, as well as more condensed and relatively subordinated enlargements of the complex narrative in terms of Isaac's consciousness but still with reliance in part on what his cousin has communicated to him. McCaslin Edmonds thus has been the steadiest contributive factor in Isaac's growing up within his environment and heritage (though the more particular influence of Sam Fathers has been the greatest single determinant) and there is pathos in both Isaac's and McCaslin's situations when separative strain mounts as their contesting becomes that between men each in his own right and conviction. It appears sharply, though with emotion suppressed into matter-of-fact succinctness, in a great Faulkner passage, the brief scene in "the little cramped icelike room in Jefferson" to which Isaac moved immediately after the renunciation on his twenty-first birthday. On the night before, he and McCaslin had opened Hubert Beauchamp's burlap-wrapped gift and found the tin coffeepot substituted for the silver cup and I.O.U.'s for all the gold pieces, with the "handful of copper coins" that had still furnished a promising jangle; and McCaslin, wryly pointing out that these are "not old enough yet to be either rarities or heirlooms," adds, "So you will have to take the money"—presumably meaning at least a substantial rent from the plantation which Isaac refuses to inherit, live on, and operate. This next night, in Jefferson, when McCaslin Edmonds tosses some "folded banknotes onto the bed," Isaac stipulates, "As a loan. From you. This one." But McCaslin, still pressing his insistence that the property and its yield are Isaac's as the direct male heir, says, "I have no money that I can lend to you," and tries to cover with gruffness his intention to continue such allotments, telling Isaac he "will have to go to the bank and get it next month because I wont bring it to you." Then Isaac, "looking peacefully at McCaslin, his kinsman, his father almost yet no kin now as, at the last, even fathers and sons are no kin," suggests McCaslin spare himself the immediate return, "horseback and in the cold," on the seventeen-mile journey he has made (plainly in much concern for his younger cousin), and McCaslin, leaving, answers, "Why should I sleep here in my house when you wont sleep yonder in yours?"

So Isaac is left, amidst all the self-willed tensions of his just-achieved majority, looking at the tin coffeepot "and thinking and not for the first time how much it takes to compound a man (Isaac McCaslin for instance) and of the devious intricate choosing yet unerring path that man's (Isaac McCaslin's for instance) spirit takes among all that mass to make him at last what he is to be, not only to the astonishment of them . . . who believed they had shaped him but to Isaac McCaslin too." The passage could serve as *locus classicus* for all of Faulkner's work, in his meditative regard for his many characters as human natures uniquely compounded out of heredity and circumstance and ongoing choices scarcely scrutable to the choosers. Isaac admits to himself at the time he makes his renunciation, moves to Jefferson, and sets about earning his living there that his "ends" sought, "although simple enough in their apparent motivation, were and would be always incomprehensible to him," and as for his life, "invincible enough in its needs, if he could have helped himself . . . he would not have chosen it." Yet from those who know him best he does not meet with absolute incredulity, and certainly not repudiation, nor do they condescend to him with the suggestion that at twenty-one he doesn't know what he's doing. His elder cousin McCaslin presses on in their dispute, but flexibly and with unmistakable affection and concern, and other experienced, just, and well-intentioned men show bafflement over Isaac's drastic move along with undiminished regard. Major de Spain offered Isaac a room in his house; and the patron of Isaac as a youth in the woods, old General Compson, who had put the sixteen-year-old in the forefront of the final hunt and then defended the boy's right to miss school and stay on with Sam Fathers after his collapse, now offers to share his room and bed for the winter, saying, "I have watched you in the woods too much and I dont believe you just quit even if it does look damn like it."

At this early but considered and unrevoked turn in Isaac's life Faulkner is not lightly sketching singularly eccentric behavior which readers may feel about as they like, one way or another. Ambivalence, inherent in this particular human situation, suggests too a broadly representative element, possibly existing in various terms in those excellent men—Major de Spain, General Compson, and most of all McCaslin Edmonds. The major characteristically treats Isaac's case like any emergency, with prompt and steady practicality. The old general, with a more intuitive personal interest, admits the appearance that Isaac had "just quit" but refuses to believe it, and his wanting to know reasons seems not a casual curiosity but a desire to see Isaac vindicated, while Isaac's quiet suggests his awareness that young men cannot always explain to their elders. However, circumstances as well as familial and personal loyalty dictated that he must answer to McCaslin Edmonds; he does so painfully and at times lamely, and McCaslin obviously thinks him extravagant and perhaps fanatically unrealistic, yet the strained tie holds, for between tempered men a good man's private reasons under ordeal are of less weight than his resoluteness. Moreover, Isaac's three benevolent intimates—the reliable major, the imperious old general, and the practical but empathetic cousin who had been as a father and brother too—all had lived through the severe exactions of their times, variously participant at their different ages in the wrenching transitions from antebellum South through war and into its troubled aftermath. Their responsive concerns for Isaac certainly would have been tinctured by some not too closely analyzed private experiences of involuted necessitous choice productive of further necessities, becoming imperative as to further conduct, and definitive of one's fate. Perhaps too their concern for Isaac is sharpened by regret that he should have been brought so early to this full accounting with himself, and had to take his first grasp upon his rightful manhood under such a deep and lasting shadow, whatever it was, since any experienced man can sense somewhat the weight of another's necessity without knowing its substance and shape. To suggest how men thread such rapids in their lifestream where there is no turning back is a classic commitment of fiction and drama, and Faulkner's complete acceptance and brilliant accomplishment of the task is a primary distinction in this work.

While Major de Spain and more particularly General Compson withhold judgment as to Isaac's drastic act of repudiation, McCaslin Edmonds' attitude is more complex, not unclear but apparently ambivalent. He is conditioned to a responsibility for the family plantation, which from early manhood he has been carrying on throughout the orphaned Isaac's boyhood and youth, and during the peculiarly rigorous economic and political postwar period; he remains, as always heretofore, Isaac's loyal kinsman, and respectful of him in his year of decision, while still allowing himself the gruff ironies which presume a mutually dependable regard and trust. In Isaac's upbringing, McCaslin and Sam Fathers have had complementary roles, and while Sam's influence is lasting, he is no longer there after Isaac's sixteenth year, or could he (nor indeed anyone else) have supplied the knowing and critical examination of Isaac's decision furnished by McCaslin. In the long run and on the broadest terms McCaslin remains Isaac's closest associate, in a complex of family ties, shared experience and awareness, and similar destinies oppositely dealt with. McCaslin Edmonds, so substantially and compellingly realized especially in section 4 of "The Bear," is more than a "minor" character, and though subordinate in the design of *Go Down, Moses* he is not just first but preeminent among the other Edmonds, his son Zack and grandson Roth, who also loom as three-dimensional and thematically contributive figures, through "The Fire and the Hearth" and "Delta Autumn."

It is essential to the complementary structuring of *Go Down, Moses* that Old Carothers McCaslin's legitimate white descendants by his daughter (married to an Edmonds) should be stressed as a continuity with some variations, for these men as well as his grandson Isaac are also closely interactive with Old Carothers' illegitimate line of mixed blood by way of the slaves Eunice, Tomasina, and "Tomey's Turl," who will father "Tennie's Jim," Sophonsiba, and Lucas Beauchamp. Yet apart from these interactions, though they sometimes become the dramatic heart of the matter, there is more sustainedly the more direct familial and circumstantial relation between Isaac as boy and young man with his elder cousin. This culminates in the debate wherein McCaslin, pressing the argument but far from quarreling, shows a reluctant concessiveness which suggests an unease possibly precipitated by the large dilemmas that surround them both and loom as they peer into the past or speculate about the future. Considering how strikingly and with what virtues and sensitivities of his own McCaslin Edmonds is set forth in "The Bear," is it a possible supposition that the uneasy ambivalence he shows toward Isaac was shared by Faulkner in creating this character, or at least in looking back on him? The question itself would be not only extraneous but of questionable propriety, directed at a work of art so great per se as *Go Down, Moses,* but it has obtruded by way of repeated reference to comments wrung from Faulkner in questionings put with the journalistic assumption that the artist, having created his work, is now obliged to define and explicate it.

In one of Faulkner's encounters with an interviewer he was led to say, "I think a man ought to do more than just repudiate. He [Isaac McCaslin] should have been more affirmative instead of shunning people." And in the course of discussions at the University of Virginia, Faulkner put it that "Isaac McCaslin says 'This is bad and I will withdraw from it.' What we need are people who will say, 'This is bad and I'm going to do something about it, I'm going to change it.'" It is painful to see such adventitious remarks set beside the work of art, like a yardstick at the base of the Washington Monument, which, beyond a suggestion of linear measurement, would really be most illustrative of a vast and utter difference as to

substance, mode, and implication. Yet a critic can choose to
take such exacted statements as basis for declaring Isaac's life
"a failure," in that he "rejects all opportunities for affirmation"—which in fact does not accord with the fictional character, and in essence overlooks the supremely positive fortitude that can be required in saying "No" and sticking to it,
even at great personal sacrifice. At Charlottesville Faulkner
said other things too about Isaac which seem to counter-
balance a negative view, as that Isaac fulfilled his destiny on
the basis of what he learned as an adolescent in the woods and
had thus achieved "serenity," and also that no matter what
argument his wife could have used for returning to the plantation, Isaac "would have stuck to his position," defined by
Faulkner as a refusal to "profit from this which is wrong and
sinful." But for readers it is a better practice, more respectful
of the essential artist, and more rewarding, to find the strange
truth about Isaac McCaslin in the fiction itself. Therein it is
perhaps allowable to estimate Faulkner's personal outlook, not
definitively emergent but as overtone from the display of his
characters, juxtaposed individuals, as envisaged in the reciprocal dynamics of their encounters.

Having been moved to comprise in *Go Down, Moses* the
McCaslin family saga through both its lines, and to set all this
against a background of Mississippi history from settlements
by white slave-holders near the end of the eighteenth century
to the eve of World War II, Faulkner not only illustrates the
complexities of this milieu in the rapidity of its modifications,
but brings the book to its thematic climax in the comprehensive fourth section of "The Bear." Here it would seem that the
artist placed the full weight of the matter, under the convergence of the several basic issues, on Isaac McCaslin, a character carefully prepared for such an exacting role. Yet he is
not to play it alone, nor to have it all his own way. The elder
cousin McCaslin Edmonds, also well established fictionally,
enters in section 4 as Isaac's concerned inquisitor but sometimes too his collaborator, as their discussions (supplemented
by Isaac's remembering of McCaslin's earlier communica-

tions) range far in time and in undimensioned speculation. Where so much is being figuratively reconstructed and analytically reviewed, is the voice of Faulkner to be detected in either speaker? Consideration of characters as mouthpiece, in a use of fiction as ventriloquized advocacy or even propaganda, were sometimes advanced about Faulkner novels preceding *Go Down, Moses,* concerning traits as various as Horace Benbow's inclusive melancholy or Ratliff's wry assessings. Later to some readers it seemed beyond doubt that Gavin Stevens in *Intruder in the Dust* is Faulkner behind nothing more than a token mask. To pursue such a question in terms of Isaac McCaslin or McCaslin Edmonds, however, may serve only to caution against all such identifications, and will certainly reinforce the need to find significance in the autonomous fictional work rather than in speeches by any one character or, still less, in whatever fragmentary explanation may be got from the author beset by the niggling questions of not very percipient interviewers.

To conceive of Isaac McCaslin as mirroring his creator's temperament and intention is impossible, since Isaac has taken the stance of an absolutist and Faulkner the fictionist, in a life's commitment no less resolute than Isaac's, conceived realities of the human condition as under impingements of mutability, and also relatively. In whatever Faulkner conjures up, the verities he formally espoused are given unquestioned preeminence, but whatever conduct ensues in his fictions under these imperatives as only dimly apprehended by most of his characters is tentative and fluctuant, often a settling for less than the whole loaf, and at times for only a crust. To suppose, however, that this is what Isaac is left with would be a distorted view. (Such has been contributed to by readers' belittling reference to Isaac's "pension" of fifty dollars a month from the plantation exchequer. To paint Isaac as a kind of meek remittance man is without regard not only for Faulkner's total treatment of him but also for particular contexts in *Go Down, Moses* and for chronology of circumstances in Isaac's life. In "The Bear," section 4, Isaac at twenty-one insists on treating "As a loan" the thirty dollars his cousin McCaslin leaves with him after Isaac's move to Jefferson, and he treats likewise the thirty-dollar monthly installments McCaslin continues to deposit in the bank for him. Out of his earnings as carpenter Isaac is able to repay all this within less than two years, and when the banker tells him McCaslin Edmonds has forbidden having it repaid by transfer to his account, Isaac keeps it in bills and cash, wrapped in a handkerchief in the now doubly symbolic tin coffeepot, become an icon of Isaac McCaslin's fidelity to principle, as it had been token of Hubert Beauchamp's flabbiness. The monthly "pension" of fifty dollars from the plantation is mentioned earlier in the book, in "The Fire and the Hearth," when Lucas Beauchamp comes on his twenty-first birthday to claim the Carothers McCaslin legacy to his illegitimate son, Tomey's Turl, Lucas's father. This bequest Isaac is holding as trustee, after having attempted even before his majority to deliver their portions of it to Lucas's elder brother Tennie's Jim (whom Isaac never found) and Lucas's elder sister Fonsiba (for whom after her inauspicious marriage Isaac deposited the money in an Arkansas bank). But by the time Lucas at twenty-one appears as claimant, Isaac is twenty-eight, and not only has married but has reached an impasse in that. While it is not told how Isaac has been persuaded to accept the monthly allowance, it could be assumed that combined pressures from his wife and his cousin McCaslin may have prevailed. Anyhow, Isaac's motivation is sound, but it is of the intangible kind others may not appreciate, and in dealing with the aggressive young Lucas, Isaac imagines him thinking Isaac had made a surrender, and only for "obliteration and a little food" and not for "peace" — which, as he had tried earlier in his life to explain to McCaslin, was the only condition under which he could live with himself for the rest of his life.

It is not then so much for lack of interactive dramatic force in itself but because its influence is inhibited by his very absoluteness that Isaac McCaslin cannot be considered an approximate silhouette of Faulkner the protean-minded, liberally inclusive, and tentatively empathetic artist, whose imagination constantly recreates that which bears it up in its full force, a sense of human life's continual and changing flow and men's sometimes basic uniqueness. Isaac's decisive act is less than representative, it is indeed exceptional, and a finality well this side of death. Having done exactly what he felt he must do, Isaac maintains his position consistently, and his story is not of defeat or merely partial success but of an absolute victory which he himself, in spite of its severe personal cost, never called Pyrrhic. As a fictional character, however, he becomes immobilized in his abnegation, self-arrested except as passive exemplar of principle, or its melancholy spokesman, as in "Delta Autumn," near his life's end. Except for his honest trusteeship that set up Lucas at twenty-one with a bank account, what further could there have been to tell of Isaac between that ultimate display years later of a life-long consistency and the earlier disclosure of its greatest price, which he had incurred well before his twenty-eighth year and for life, as tersely recounted in the episodes closing section 4 of "The Bear"?

No such abeyance and consequent arrest as a dramatic figure occurs in McCaslin Edmonds, who moves with energy and thematic significance through many events in *Go Down, Moses*. His appearance as an antebellum nine-year old breathlessly trailing Uncle Buck as he pursues Tomey's Turl in "Was" is prelude to his assumption in his postbellum early manhood of overseeing the plantation after the McCaslin twins' deaths; it also establishes him as conveyor to Isaac, sixteen years younger, of some sense of those rapidly changing times. His considerate guardianship of Isaac after his mother's death left the small boy totally orphaned is paralleled by McCaslin's understanding of Sam Fathers, so perceptive that it amounts to a protectorship and enables him, for instance, to explain to Isaac that a certain look in Sam's eye, being in recollection of his descent from a Chickasaw chief, goes back further than his lightly worn subservience to the McCaslin establishment, of which he is perhaps the freest member. McCaslin puts young Isaac under Sam's tutelage, but supplements it, as by suggesting larger verities than sportsmanship involved in the boy's refraining from shooting Old Ben. McCaslin plays a man's part not only among the hunters at de Spain's camp but as his cousin's concerned questioner, until the absolute finality of Isaac's enacted decision makes discussion pointless, though still evidently he did not leave off pressing Isaac to accept an allowance from the plantation. Yet for all his blended virtues of fidelity, committed energy, and compassion, McCaslin Edmonds wears no mask behind which can be found the full aspect of his creator's genius. No average man, he is of a valuable minority (like such other Faulkner characters as Gavin Stevens and Ratliff and Sheriff Hampton) in his principled application of a wordly wisdom. In controversy with Isaac at twenty-one he is strenuous and shows some sweep of imagination and wit, yet he seems constantly to sense a rare worth in his adversary cousin even while questioning the viability of his assumtions. Their inconclusive colloquy grows increasingly speculative on both sides, as the cousins become primarily opposed yet complementary forces in the kaleidoscopic flow of this section of "The Bear," wherein is equilibrated as if on vacillating scales Isaac's absoluteness and McCaslin's relativism.

In this intense representation a felt consciousness of the artist himself may suggest his particular closeness to the subject, and perhaps the distillation of a special and recurrent concern, expressed elsehere in Faulkner's works, but here more specifically dramatizing an ambivalence inherent in any comprehensive view of certain realities, particularly the flux of societal trends and the dilemmas of involved individuals. The seriously realistic fictionist, feeling impelled to conceive of his subject as comprehensively as is permitted by his own temperament as well as his immediate narrative design, may go beyond one character's side of the matter and find in a division between intimately associated figures the dynamics of an episode, if not of a whole tale. What can empower such creativity may be a larger conception than anything personified by any one character. And in Faulkner there was a regional-historical pre-occupation he seemingly came to regard as more than oppor-tune, as his daemon, which let him believe "that something worth saying knew better than I did how it needed to be said." This dictation came to him thematically in terms of heritage, not material and not only familial but societal, and ambiva-lently, as to its defense and conflict with it. Involving not just conviction but affiliation, such situation is painful, and (with weightier truth than in Auden's description of Yeats as "hurt . . . into poetry" by Ireland) it could be said Faulkner was lashed into fiction, in a whole series of fables envisioned at various reaches of perspective, within a well-known, penetratingly viewed milieu.

For such a character as Quentin Compson the legacy of ambivalence is insoluble, inescapable, and at last fatally dis-concerting, as foreshadowed in *Absalom, Absalom!* and en-acted in *The Sound and the Fury.* (Such an instance provides one criterion for a more positive evaluating of Isaac McCaslin, in that Quentin's fate came out of what he could neither bear nor abjure, whereas Isaac travels that road all the way.) *Light in August* is permeated by destructive ambivalence, societally and circumstantially imposed upon Joe Christmas for his pre-sumed mixture of blood, and more deeply working disintegra-tively in Hightower and in Joanna Burden. (This novel also illustrates, in the separate examples of Hines, McEachern, and Percy Grimm, the threats of outright evil in an absolute adher-ance to fanatical belief.) That a willed resolution of conflict which has arisen from ambivalent tendencies can be the road to maturation is shown in *Intruder in the Dust,* where indeed it is the real story, transcending all the overt circumstances. The adolescent Chick Mallison passes from a stalemate in maneu-vers between himself and Lucas Beauchamp over a private matter of ascendancy and personal pride into a broad sector of societal conduct where he is repeatedly tempted to avoid responsibility but stays to see out the maintenance of operative law and the protection of an innocent Lucas from the threat of mob violence. He does not accomplish that result alone, overtly

Miss Habersham and Aleck Sander play full parts, yet the choice not to run away but to stand against a racially tinged public disorder and social evil is made in the privacy of Chick's conscience, and against recurrent temptation to yield — which, along with much further about his ongoing consciousness, makes him protagonist, under Faulkner's perfected mode of interpreting and intensifying events through an accompanying subjectivity, in organismic fictional action.

It is in "The Unvanquished" that ethical dilemma in a familial-societal context comes closest to Faulkner's own family heritage, drawing chiefly upon the life story of his great-grandfather, Colonel William Clark Falkner, who raised a regiment and led them with distinction in important engagements in the Civil War, built a railroad afterward, quarreled with the partner whom he had bought out and who became his opponent in politics and finally shot him on the street at close range, though the Colonel had forsworn going armed after all the killings in the War. In *The Unvanquished* this ancestor is prototype of the character of Colonel John Sartoris; the novel's more fictionalized protagonist, however, is his son Bayard, seen growing from boyhood during the War in close company with a Negro playmate, Ringo. Childishly they map the Colonel's battles in the dust, but soon thereafter they take a most violent vengeance upon the horse thief who had murdered Grandmother Millard. Yet after the War has passed, when the unarmed Colonel's death at his former partner Redmond's hand seems to Yoknapatawphans to lay a duty upon his grown son Bayard to make the conventional gesture of retaliation as a matter of honor, he too goes unarmed to face Redmond in his office, so disconcerting him that he fires intending to miss and immediately leaves Jefferson and Mississippi.

There are interesting analogies between Isaac McCaslin and the matured Bayard Sartoris: Bayard too says, "I must live with myself," in a context meaning not only that he is not afraid to break with tradition but that he must act to prove it; and his Aunt Jenny realizes that the proof is not directed toward family or community, but inwardly to his conscience, when she says,

"Then it's not just Drusilla. Not just him [his father]? Not just George Wyatt and Jefferson?" And the young man Bayard's panting private agony over all such external confrontations is a parallel to what Isaac experiences even before twenty-one, solitarily at night in the commissary, reading the old ledgers, and asking himself, *"But why? But why?"* and when he comes to the answer, his grandfather's miscegenous incest, thinking, "No No Not even him," and painfully realizing the suicide of the doubly dishonored slave Eunice on "Christmas Day 1832" as "ceremonial, in formal and succinct repudiation of grief and despair who had already had to repudiate belief and hope."

The connections Bayard Sartoris and Isaac McCaslin have with their fathers are suggestive in themselves; and the contrast, showing Faulkner's versatility in working on such different scales, defines in particular the larger dimensions of Isaac's ordeal. Bayard, born two decades earlier than Isaac, experienced in his adolescence some typical instances of upheaval in the South's slaveholding plantation system. While his reactions began as child's play in collaboration with his Negro "boy," the ingenious Ringo, the two were increasingly drawn into grim realities. After the bushwacker Grumby murdered Grandmother Millard, they track him down and Bayard shoots him; then they nail his body like an animal's hide to the door of a cotton compress, except his severed right hand, which they lay on Grandmother Millard's grave. This is not comparable to the sadistic pleasure juvenile gangs take in stomping old men to death on city streets; it is a true vendetta, yet it shows the pitch Bayard and Ringo have been brought to, and only in its greater bloodiness does it exceed the wartime acting-out of a regional law in the absence of any other, as does Colonel Sartoris after the war when he shoots Northern carpet baggers who would stuff the ballot box and exploit both whites and blacks, and then sees it stuffed by his own men, who will do the best they can according to their lights. Bayard is not brutalized, and in early manhood he chooses to repudiate violence by facing his father's murderer unarmed. Isaac, born shortly after the war, is shown in boyhood and until sixteen chiefly occupied in shaping a

woodsman's outlook derived from Sam Fathers' already displaced Indian culture and its lore and mystique. Yet Bayard at
fifteen, however savage his revenge on Grumby, was acting out
family loyalty and pride; Isaac at sixteen, reading the ledgers,
was taking on a burden of shame as the real heritage from his
grandfather. While Bayard saw his father closely as a strenuous
and impetuous man of affairs and cavalry commander, Isaac,
orphaned too early to remember, knew his father only as what
his imagination could reconstruct from others' telling, chiefly
his cousin McCaslin's, beginning with that nine-year-old's
portrait of a dashing horsemen still at sixty, who had ridden
four years with Forrest's cavalry, and returned a lagging
Benedick to marry Sophonsiba Beauchamp at last. Isaac had
heard too (as it is told in "The Fire and the Hearth") that his
father and the twin brother Amodeus (Uncle Buddy) "in the
early fifties . . . put into operation their scheme for the manumission of their father's slaves," having already moved out of
the big house in 1837 ("as soon as their father was buried") and
put the loosely supervised slaves into it. He would have learned
too that upon their marriage his father and mother had
restored and reoccupied that house (an obverse to what in a
later time he refused to do), and he had been born there, and it
was there his uncle Hubert Beauchamp made the grandiose
gesture with the gold coins in a silver cup, his gradual sur-
reptitious repossessing of which symbolized final decay of a
tradition, its pretensions dissolved into shabbiness. For Bayard
the issues were simpler; his father, for all his impetuosity and
wilfulness, has exemplified his courage as well as flexibility by
finally repudiating violence. Bayard's following that same pattern must be by his own volition in the face of some dubiety
from others (including his father's young wife Drusilla, his boyhood Negro companion Ringo, and members of his father's old
command), but the issue is explicit, and though the situation is
permeated by cumulative griefs, as "An Odor of Verbena"
intensely shows, his dealing with it can be conclusive, though he
and Drusilla lose each other, she leaves on his pillow as accolade
a spray of verbena. Isaac, in contrast, is left to endure an

ongoing paradox, as "husband but no father, unwidowered but without a wife," as fate redefined it in his own generation and his marriage, but still through the old lusts for possession and dominance, which he must resist with unaltered conviction. While he had the example of his father's leniency toward the family's slaves and the twin brothers' scheme for their eventual liberation, these merely ameliorative measures in a separately necessitous bygone time give no precedent for him in his own day, the South of the 1880s. Yet with his personal life become paradoxical he at least refuses to let it deteriorate into dilemma, of the kind perhaps attributable to this nation itself as an unsettled state between conscience and comfort.

Though Faulkner was not there as of that postbellum era to decide how to confront the man who had killed Colonel William C. Falkner, his great-grandfather, not in a duel but a kind of assassination, the novelist could translate the problem into fictional terms and delegate its solution to those who, being his approved creations, are presumably surrogates though not alter egos. Faulkner too had read in his people's ledgers, his region's history, and had come upon grievous facts; he too had been shaped by the impacts of an environment saturated with legend and firmly sustained conventions, yet shaken by chronic uneasiness. There in his own time a primary separation and stress remained in the relation between whites and blacks, and a concern with it enters crucially even into his fictions set in the twentieth century, such as *Light in August* or *Intruder in the Dust,* or the latter narrative stages of *Absalom, Absalom!* and *Go Down, Moses.* These are of the very world where he lived on, a native son whose sentiments remained attached to his heritage, while as an artist he moved at some distance from it into his necessary perspectives. How he arrived at that proper detachment and bore its disciplines is a mystery, as always with the emergence of genius into its singular combination of intense engagement and retained antonomy. However, certain factors operative in *Go Down, Moses,* and particularly as to Isaac McCaslin but also vitally involving McCaslin Edmonds, are sufficiently characteristic to define some persistent traits born

of issues in Faulkner's work and art, as it reaches into antebellum history and extends into the comtemporary, in such
instances of young men's moral crises as Bayard's and Chick's,
but neither as centrally and drastically as with Isaac.

Prominent is a permeating awareness of history, regionally
operative but often most specialized in the sense of family. This
becomes a determinant of actions, as well as being a presence
variously recurrent in the characters' associative reflections. It
has to do with tradition and enterprise, with fortune and
disaster, with radical change and persistent memories. In it the
Civil War exists as a great divide, major referent and salient
feature in a landscape two centuries broad in the Faulkner
oeuvre. The coexistence in this milieu of two races is, in this
view, not the total reality but a fortuitous and uneasy condition,
like a trying climate under which life ranges from inertia to
violence, its average stability achieved by the artifices of custom
where no more assured way is seen, rather than by intended
procedure. Less conspicuous, but a distinct regional element in
Faulkner's fictions of whatever period, is his characters' readiness of expression, succinct or voluble — which in the realities he
represents may be related to its stresses. Within that, and indicated by it, are emergences of minor and unpresumptuous idiosyncrasy, given the passing tolerance which a historically conventionalized society can accord, perhaps finding quaintness
vaguely compensatory. But whether humorous or in earnest,
this Southern fluency and pithy vigor, this lively talkativeness as
an accepted mode, enters naturally and rightly into Faulkner's
style, and (though often misevaluated) is an important function
of his realistic regionalism. (All such characteristics, beginning
with a regionalized sense of the historical, distance Faulkner
somewhat beyond perceptions in other parts of the nation, especially under the new and thus far unexpressed regionalism of
the megalopolis, where so much of life is without roots in place
or past, denatured by expedient homogenization, and maintained by unexamined and transient clichés rather than conventions with at least an aura of rational tradition.)

The sense of an extended continuity with some persistence of

elected tendencies despite catastrophic upheavals connects
with another characteristic recurrent in Faulkner's fiction—
portrayal of an individual's private consciousness of his own ongoing and socially related personal history, as shaped by choice
amid the exactions of circumstance, including heritage and
present intractabilities, and productive of defiant refusal, or
surrender into conformity, or suspension in ambivalence.
Sometimes the issue, embodied as typical instance, occurs repetitively to the individual, no matter how decisively put down,
as with Isaac McCaslin in a further confrontation in "Delta
Autumn," still resolute but worn by the melancholy of old age.
With some who have not resolved ambivalence on whatever
personal terms it takes, the issue waits to fall full force, as it does
early with Quentin Compson in *The Sound and the Fury,* or
late, as in Hightower's overwhelming epiphany after the last of
his intermittent and inadequate efforts. More often the process
of existential response is in a significant growth as shown in boyhood, youth, or young manhood, as with Sarty of "Barn
Burning," Bayard Sartoris throughout *The Unvanquished,*
Chick Mallison from twelve to sixteen in *Intruder in the Dust,*
or Isaac up to a marital impasse, part 4, "The Bear," and it was
to a brief period in a boy's maturation that Faulkner returned
in his last book. However, the recurrent theme of development
in such separate accounts is given no fixed pyschological pattern nor close parallelings of circumstance, though there is
usually encounter with heritage, either familial or societal or
both, and an ambivalence to be transcended, yet in the unique
way of each personality in its particular situation.

These confrontations, complete and absolute, are not to be
met by mere gesture, but require total response, unequivocal
action in the light of fullest possible understanding, no matter
how hardly come by. Arising as such issues do at crucial points
in the full tide of maturation, they prompt review and inquiry,
in self-examination which poses questions comparable to those
of any history—what happened and with what past effects and
to what degree do these persist. Beyond the historian's concerns
the fictionalist projects another dimension, "What now?" This

relates to Faulkner's frequent use of young protagonists, whose pasts are so to speak still in process, their memories fresh and their curiosities lively, not yet perceptibly fated, their major commitments still to be made, but the stakes perhaps higher than ever again, and the exemplified values most explicit. Dramaturgically such material provides not only climax but prolonged rising action, and this Faulkner intensifies by two extraordinarily combined means, a close subjective tracing of the protagonist's experience and overtly a sustained collective inquiry by others more or less involved, including not only their discussions but attempts at detection. This last has to do not just immediately with actual crime, as in *Intruder in the Dust;* the latter half of *Absalom, Absalom!* is Quentin's and Shreve's prolonged and more or less cooperative investigation, based on evidence, clues, and supposition, into the lives of men and women dead and gone, to patch together intuitively something of the picture puzzle of incidents and motives; in *Requiem for a Nun,* conversely, the crime is self-confessed by Nancy and the real inquisition by Gavin Stevens tries to lead Temple back and then forward again through stages of her history to what she had arrived at to become Nancy's unconscious instigator.

Not that all questions get answered, even in the most investigative of Faulkner's stories. Always the thing ultimately proved is that any human mystery becomes too deep to walk into or even to sound. No perennial enigmas are unmasked, and even among the enactors' opinions a subjective diversity relatively persists. To serve his concern in his stories of personal-societal evolvement out of deep and intricate roots Faulkner employs ingenious narrative skills which sometimes have been criticized for the prolonged suspension of explanatory details and a circuitous approach which subordinates them to the story's greater subjective inclusions and deeper tones. Such a superbly skillful method can be relished for its requiring curiosity to wait not on mere precipitous and deflating surprise but on the classic service of plot, wherein happenings are gathered up into inclusive meanings. This practice also serves a larger realism, affirming that in most complexities much is learned late and more may yet lie beyond comprehension, yet not so far as to revoke the necessity of choice. It is an intensification of pathos in *Light in August* that no one, not even himself, knows certainly whether Joe Christmas is part Negro. The two legal actions toward the conclusion of *The Hamlet* end in partial or complete frustration for the plaintiffs and leave the conscientious old justice of the peace in despair over the law's limits, while in a hazy middle distance moves the shadow of Flem Snopes covering his tracks on his way to further enterprises, as the novel's conclusion will underline in a brilliant vignette.

Nowhere in Faulkner is this artful suspension of fictional data and its subordination to total meaning more brilliantly employed than in *Go Down, Moses,* and here it reaches some of its greatest effects in section 4 of "The Bear," though its largest dimensions are in Isaac's whole story. Debate between the cousins goes far beyond the immediate matter of Isaac's decision, but the excursions are natural, since principles of conduct are in question, and these turn upon large realities—present, antecedent, and permanent—which are their context. There in October, 1888, with Isaac arrived at twenty-one and McCaslin Edmonds thirty-eight, they speak on the same grounds but out of different lives and each with his own acquired perspectives. Their references to the immediate past and their specific heritage run on further into centuries of the Western world's history, in search of causation and process, the better to estimate present effects, and Isaac carries inquiry into the teleological, though somewhat uncertainly as to a Prime Mover's intentions past and present. The formal narration of dialogue ("and McCaslin . . . and he") suggests tension between concepts transcending the men who propound them, but it also implies an intentness and liberal speculativeness which characterizes the cousins beyond stereotypes and as more than debaters, each at the top of his bent, and considerable in his own right, but also a deeply congenial pair. Moreover, this striking device in section 4 is only intermittently used, as one part of a narrative fantasia in which instance and generalization, past scenes and synopses carry the matter forward. This momentum, going beyond the commissary and Isaac at twenty-one, brings him into Jefferson, and carpentry, and marriage, and the stasis of his middle years, untold but implied.

McCaslin in section 4 plays a significant role, though it ends after Isaac's immediate move to Jefferson (almost as abrupt as the recorded departure of the untraceable James — Tennie's Jim — Beauchamp at his own majority). Indeed, McCaslin Edmonds and Isaac McCaslin taken together could be seen, especially in their personifying an abstract of more formal debate, as an ambivalent state of mind, representative of a typical (though far from universal) condition among reflective Southerners in the early post-bellum decades. While the cousins' unfailing intimacy in the midst of contradictions celebrates a vitality of human relationship, more generally it suggests the inescapable force of previous conditioning in present choices and the relativity of all knowledge, with the ongoing strain of private uncertainties under societal divisions. There is intense pathos in that brief scene in "the little cramped icelike room in Jefferson" Isaac has moved into, with the formal "and he . . . and McCaslin" resumed for the two brief exchanges of speech, when McCaslin tosses the folded banknotes on the bed and the two men differ over whether it is a loan or Isaac's, while Isaac sees McCaslin as "his kinsman, his father almost yet no kin now as, at the last, even fathers and sons are no kin," and McCaslin will not stay the night, because Isaac will not sleep in his own house "yonder." With McCaslin gone horseback in the cold the seventeen miles to the plantation, no wonder that Isaac muses on "how much it takes to compound a man" and set him on his "devious intricate choosing yet unerring path," such as had brought him to this room, and conversely and with a more common logic, sent McCaslin back to the plantation, leaving them fundamentally divided after all those years of companionship, family loyalty, and affection.

Despite McCaslin's considerable presence and the inclusion of narrated episodes and synopses, the whole of section 4 in

"The Bear" moves around the felt center of Isaac's consciousness. Thus in the midst of the cousins' great debate not just Isaac's unvoiced reflections are represented but other concepts associatively recalled can emerge in a sudden shift. The cousins' ongoing discussion at one point was turning on characteristics of the Mississippi Negro, as slave and then as in some degree emancipated; Isaac has called their vices "aped from white men" or what "white men and bondage have taught them," whereas their inherent virtues, he says, such as "endurance . . . forbearance . . . fidelty," were "got not only not from white people but not even despite white people because they had it already from the old free fathers a longer time free than us because we have never been free." Whatever Isaac's suppositions about the Negro in Africa, it would seem they are without awareness that often Negroes were sold to the slave trader by their own chiefs, though Isaac must have remembered that Sam Fathers and his quadroon slave mother had been sold to Old Carothers McCaslin by Sam's father, the Chickasaw chief Ikkemotubbe. Even so, Isaac's racial heritage of "freedom" and their consequently integral virtues touches the cornerstone of his theologized rationale, premising a primitive innocence, comprising absolute virtues. For Isaac this is not altogether an illusion, he having seen it exemplified and been taught something of its spirit by that intact and tempered survivor out of older times, Sam Fathers. McCaslin Edmonds in his own boyhood has known that influence too, as is shown in one of his previous intimacies with Isaac, recounted in "The Old People," after the boy has killed his first buck and has seen another which may be an apparition, for Sam has saluted it and said "Oleh, Chief. Grandfather." This same night McCaslin, telling Isaac that Sam had conducted him too through parallel experiences, imaginatively expresses for the boy the mysterious possibility that something endures out of all life, even if it "cant cast a shadow," since lives wear out before they exhaust "the possibilities of living" and "all that must be somewhere." Such have been the intricacies in Isaac's upbringing, and such the part played in it not only by Sam Fathers but by that many-faceted man, his elder cousin McCaslin. Thus later, as the stream of Isaac's conciousness carries forward the whole matter of section 4 in "The Bear," a passage of this crucial dialogue in the commissary can be broken into by his remembering another instance of a different kind of communication with his cousin.

While Isaac is mentioning, in relation to freedom, a primordial influence on Negroes from "the old free fathers," his talk breaks off as "he had only to look at McCaslin's eyes and it was there, that summer twilight seven years ago." The events which his cousin's recognizable expression recalls are two: first, Isaac's behavior in not shooting the old bear when he and Sam stumbled upon it at close range, but instead Isaac's rescuing his little dog, and second, McCaslin's talking with him about it on an evening several days later, after he'd heard of it from Sam Fathers. McCaslin asks the boy how close he'd got to the bear and Isaac's description of seeing a tick on it shows he went very close, but he adds *"I didn't have the gun then."* McCaslin, pressing him further, says *"But you didn't shoot when you had the gun. Why?"* and not waiting but trying to help his inarticulate and perhaps self-evasive young cousin, he crosses to the bookcase above which hangs the mounted head of Isaac's first buck and reads him Keats' "Ode on a Grecian Urn," repeating one stanza (perhaps the last?) and after he has closed the book, quoting from the second: *"She cannot fade, though thou hast still thy bliss; Forever wilt thou love and she be fair."* Very creditably for a fourteen-year-old, Isaac comments that *"He's talking about a girl."* McCaslin says the poet *"was talking about truth"* and adds that *"Truth is one. It covers all things which touch the heart—honor and pride and pity and justice and courage and love."* At the moment, still thinking about his not shooting at the bear, the boy feels *"it had seemed simpler than that."* Then he finds himself reconstructing his memories of that encounter a bit closer to indefinable reality, thinking step by step that *"he didn't shoot. Because a little dog—But he could have shot long before,"* and realizing this, the boy hears McCaslin's voice continuing, *"the words as quiet as the twilight itself was,"* and telling him *"what the heart holds to becomes truth,*

as far as we know truth. " With the next line the narrative is back
in the commissary, yet with Isaac still hearing the words, "intact
in this twilight as in that one seven years ago," but now
McCaslin, still apropos of the Negroes and freedom, is saying
"Habet then. — So this land is, indubitably, of and by itself
cursed."

At this point in this last and brief resumption of their
formally indicated dialogue Isaac ("and he") agrees, "Cursed,"
yet he specifies "not the land, but us." Meanwhile McCaslin had
"merely lifted one hand" but here as so often in this section a
gesture, a single word is to evoke larger entities for Isaac and the
reader, "not only the ledgers but the whole plantation," that
"edifice intricate and complex and founded upon injustice and
erected by ruthless rapacity and carried on even yet with at
times downright savagery not only to the human beings but the
valuable animals too, yet solvent and efficient . . . brought still
intact by McCaslin, himself little more than a child then,
through and out of the debacle and chaos of twenty years ago."
(Again and again in young Isaac's mind the local instance
enlarges into the regionally representative, as with the plantation ledgers become "that chronicle which was a whole land in
miniature, which multiplied and compounded was the entire
South.") There was also what was "chronicled in a harsher
book," the destructive war and defeat's aftermath of carpetbagger exploitation, "and McCaslin, fourteen and fifteen and
sixteen, had seen it and the boy himself had inherited it as
Noah's grandchildren had inherited the Flood although they
had not been there to see the deluge." Faulkner did not add to
his several stories of youthful maturation that of McCaslin
Edmonds, but not only is its formative mark left on the man,
much of this is to be apparent in the course of section 4 in "The
Bear," and so acute and unforgettable had been the young
McCaslin's observations and his later accounts that Isaac "at
almost eighty" was to feel he "would never be able to distinguish
between what he had seen and what had been told him,"
another showing of close interplay between the objective and
subjective worlds. Thus in essence Isaac brings it all at twenty-

one into his sense of place and his already patterned convictions. In Isaac's thought there resounds for a third time the motif imaged as "the frail and iron thread" (the output of cotton, the intake of provisions for operation, subsistence, and profits) "strong as truth and impervious as evil and longer than life itself," as the ledgers have attested, so that Isaac now voices his resolution more specifically: "I am free. . . . And of that too." McCaslin adopts Isaac's biblically based mythologizing of further divine purpose to point out how slowly changes are wrought, and what may be impervious to change. If Isaac has been chosen "out of all your time as you say Buck and Buddy were from theirs," then "it took Him a bear and an old man and four years just for you." (Presumably that would run from Isaac's shooting his first buck and his refraining from shooting the old bear to his part in the last hunt, with its fatalities for the bear, the dog Lion, and Sam Fathers.) "And it took you fourteen years to reach that point and about that many, maybe more, for Old Ben, and more than seventy for Sam Fathers. And you are just one. How long then? How long?" Isaac concedes that it will be long but avers "it will be all right because they [the Negroes] will endure."

Ironically McCaslin remarks, "And anyway, you will be free," but then continues with direct abrupt statements that invite probing not just for the sense of this exchange but for significations in Faulkner's whole treatment of his subject in *Go Down, Moses.* As to any freedom from the sociohistorically induced impasse between the two races, McCaslin says, "No, not now nor ever, we from them nor they from us. So I repudiate too." What follows indicates he is repudiating not just Isaac's faith and personal assertion but its implied hope of an ultimate solution, in a perfection of the social order, for McCaslin is saying, "I would deny even if I knew it were true. I would have to." He calls on Isaac to see that he, McCaslin "could do no else," being "always what I was born and have always been." To this he adds, "And more than me" — implicating all other men similarly placed in traditionally and practically conditioned situations, existentially committed to minding the store and maintaining business as usual. Yet McCaslin Edmonds is no such caricature of impervious materialism as General Compson had suggested: "You've got one foot straddled into a farm and one foot straddled into a bank." In this dispute the old general's intention is right, having understood that indeed the youth Isaac has "got to stay" in camp with the dying Sam Fathers and not return to school until the following week. Not that McCaslin is unfeeling, ever; in this instance he is merely making the well-intentioned mistake by which dutiful people overlook what at the moment transcends the normal values generally pursued; and as for McCaslin and Sam, nothing could be more revealing of his fine nature than the matter-of-fact respectfulness with which he had assented and cooperated when the old hunter had announced he wanted to go to the Big Bottom to live. And also in "The Old People," explaining Sam to the boy Isaac, McCaslin had revealed a detached ironic view of the white race which showed he realized something merely necessitous in his own situation — putting it that all Sam's "blood on both sides [Indian and Negro] except the little white part, knew things that had been tamed out of our blood so long ago that we have not only forgotten them, we have to live together in herds to protect ourselves from our own sources." This McCaslin Edmonds, though bound and buffeted by circumstance from his youth on, is a man of parts, fit to carry his side in a contention with Isaac, to whom he himself has bequeathed shrewd and sensitive awareness of antecedents in the social order Isaac found himself repudiating.

Thus when McCaslin claims community or at least a common fate with other men ("More than me") as those called upon to strive for maintenance and amelioration of the imperfectible and this is echoed by Isaac's "And more than me," McCaslin denies an analogy. Borrowing Isaac's own arguments in support of his rejecting the inheritance from Lucius Quintus Carothers McCaslin, Edmonds traces a more mystical and exclusive genealogy for his young cousin: "You said . . . when Ikkemotubbe realized that he could sell the land to Grandfather, it ceased forever to have been his. All right; go on: Then it belonged to Sam Fathers, old Ikkemotubbe's son. And who inherited from Sam Fathers, if not you?" To this Isaac assents but in his own terms: "Yes. Sam Fathers set me free." He does not define the freedom into which he had been liberated, nor does McCaslin insist upon the implication that what Sam Fathers had to bequeath was woodsmanship, a hunter's ethic, and the oblivion of an outmoded way of life. At this point in section 4 of "The Bear" the intermittent dialogue between the cousins, which has been the central thread woven into the preceding 45 pages, ceases with an abrupt narrative shift forward which in a dozen lines locates Isaac in the Jefferson boarding house "with his kit of brand-new carpenter's tools and the shotgun McCaslin had given him with his name engraved in silver," (when Isaac was ten, for his first hunting in the big woods) "and the iron cot and mattress and the blankets which he would take each fall into the woods for more than sixty years and the bright tin coffee pot." That last article might seem part of a woodsman's camping equipment, but it has quite other significance, to which Faulkner gives nearly eight pages of narration, beginning "there had been a legacy, from his Uncle Hubert Beauchamp, his godfather." The "silver cup filled with gold pieces and wrapped in burlap and sealed with his godfather's ring" was often exhibited and shaken to hear the sound of the legacy within which awaited Isaac's twenty-first birthday, but the sealed-up object had changed shape, and opened it revealed not the silver cup but a coffeepot, repository of a few coppers and Uncle Hubert's promissory notes for the gold coins and finally for the cup itself.

The satirically narrated record of a heritage metamorphized is a thematic irony, and Hubert Beauchamp's successively dated notes of hand parody the ledgers while they also caricature the man; the passage also moderates tempo following the variegated intensities that have been played out in this section of "The Bear" between Isaac and his cousin McCaslin, including not just their talking but Isaac's recurrent concentrated consciousness of much that McCaslin had told and taught him and done for him. And the coffeepot is to figure as narrative link in another abrupt transition. McCaslin had witnessed its unveiling at the plantation, on the evening of Isaac's twenty-first birthday (presumably following that day's long discussion in the commissary office) and had said in his wry way that the copper coins weren't old enough to be valuable, "So you will have to take the money," (his inheritance or at least a stipend from it). The next few lines show a Faulknerian acceleration with its dynamics and its unpunctuated demand in return on the reader's close attention. At the plantation Isaac, not listening to McCaslin, is "looking peacefully at the coffee-pot and the pot sitting one night later on the mantel . . . in the little cramped icelike room in Jefferson as McCaslin tossed the folded banknotes onto the bed," doubtless because he knows Isaac would not take them from his hand. Then in less than a dozen lines the cousins ("and he . . . and McCaslin") are seen in two formal exchanges and a final impasse over a loan or no loan, sleep here or not, and in whose house "yonder." It is the same matter of opposed principles that has underlain their long debate in the commissary the day before over Isaac's decision to repudiate heritage and inheritance, yet beneath the present laconic exchange is a stratum of human kindness more than cousinly: McCaslin wants Isaac to be provided for and to accept money as his due from his plantation; Isaac, no doubt moved by this continuing evidence of McCaslin's magnanimous concern, wants him to stay the night rather than ride horseback in the cold the seventeen miles from Jefferson to the plantation.

Yet this marks the cousins' separation in the world of *Go Down, Moses*—Isaac at twenty-one plus a day, McCaslin Edmonds seventeen years his senior. They part unyieldingly opposed on principle, but in personal amity, not animosity. Those who are inclined to extrapolate the lives of a fiction's or drama's characters beyond their embodiment in the artistic work might imagine that Isaac and McCaslin could meet again, and were that to happen they would not be anything but cordial, in the deepest sense. Probably they would also be regretfully embarrassed over the rift between them, and like all who take their convictions seriously, could never talk with each other so freely and searchingly as they had. However, that need not be thought the reason Faulkner tells nothing of further meetings. For the artist, McCaslin Edmonds had served his purpose, in a role complementary to Isaac McCaslin as protagonist in "The Old People" and "The Bear," but especially in the great fourth section of the latter. What little besides is known of McCaslin Edmonds comes in obliquely. Presumably he had approved and implemented Isaac's search at nineteen for James Beauchamp, to give him his share of the legacy from Old Carothers McCaslin which James' father Terrel Beauchamp had never claimed, for in the ledgers Isaac himself records not finding James and returning the money to McCaslin as trustee. Similarly McCaslin must have provided Fonsiba's share for Isaac to carry to her in Arkansas at the end of that same year. (From "The Fire and the Hearth" it is known that at his majority Isaac "had retained of the patrimony, and by his own request, only the trusteeship," and there it is told in detail how Lucas, youngest offspring of Terrel and Tennie, came at twenty-one to claim his share, and Isaac showed him how to set up a bank account with it.) "The Fire and the Hearth" also tells that when Lucas within the year married a Negro woman not from the fields but from town, "McCaslin Edmonds built a house for them and allotted Lucas a specific acreage to be farmed as he saw fit" — showing McCaslin now in his mid-forties, still administering the plantation which Isaac, seven years before, had refused to inherit or live on. There is earlier (in "The Bear") just a glimpse of the elder cousin at seventeen like a figure in a bleached family-group photograph (merely in the naming of Isaac's "mother and his father and McCaslin" — and presumably there to Isaac's knowledge through McCaslin's later telling), the youthful McCaslin one of the plantation ménage when Isaac was born, and when Tennie as his nurse carried him downstairs for the first time, two weeks old, and his Uncle Hubert presented and sealed up the gift of the silver cup and gold coins. There is echo of an older McCaslin Edmonds' voice when the banker tells Isaac his cousin has ordered that the thirty dollars he has deposited monthly for Isaac is not to be transferred back into McCaslin's account. The name of McCaslin Edmonds' wife is discoverable, but there are no scenes presenting the two together, and this one fact comes out only in that "McCaslin's wife Alice had taught Fonsiba to read and write too a little" — yet certainly a fit trait in the spouse of one who himself was a patient ameliorist.

McCaslin Edmonds is a remarkable persona, engaging and impressive, and technically an instance of Faulkner's developed art of selective narration and characterization. Despite McCaslin's centrality in *Go Down, Moses* there is scarcely material to be pieced together as a life-story. And this is proper fictional practice, for the energetic, sensitive, and ironic elder cousin is after all, like Sam Fathers, only a dramatic adjunct to the subjectively dimensioned story of Isaac. If McCaslin were protagonist it would be obligatory to show by more than one *scene à faire* his experiences and reactions during the crucial years of a war he was just too young to fight in, and then himself in his early manhood, when the nearly simultaneous deaths of the elderly McCaslin twins thrust upon him a responsibility for the plantation and for the boy Isaac's upbringing. It may be assumed that the artist Faulkner, in omitting anything except indirect suggestion of all this (and only as Isaac remembers being told of it) was nevertheless not imperceptive of its intrinsic possibilities, but was exercising his acute artistic instinct for selective focus and proportioned depth of treatment, aiming at thematic and aesthetically organic composition. His primary engagement was with the ongoing realizations and consequent actions of Isaac McCaslin. Faulkner treated this perennial fictional subject of maturation more than once, but always under the form's necessity of focus on the objective-subjective nexus and crises in a central character's life, as with Bayard Sartoris, Sarty Snopes, Chick Mallison, or, more somberly and tragically, Quentin Compson. In the three parts of *Go Down, Moses* which center thematically on Isaac McCaslin he is given that fourth dimension which most fully empowers artistically implicative projection of a protagonist, by some admittance to passages of his consciousness. The maintenance of Isaac in this preeminent function by containment of McCaslin Edmonds in an objectively represented relative role is a superb but essentially typical example of Faulkner's judiciously employed technical skills. This modulated touch, this inflection of emphasis may even be felt in the story "Was." Its substance is known only later to Isaac "through and from" his elder cousin (the phrase conjoining objective-subjective factors), yet McCaslin is not obtruded into a conspicuous place as robust first-person narrator. The story remembered by Isaac "from the hearing, the listening" (again a complex function, aural and psychological) is translated into third-person narration, as redistilled in its having been laid down in Isaac's vicarious realizations. Through it there moves what may have been the closest and most sustained apparition Isaac ever met with of his unremembered father, and of the innocent bluster and comic helter-skelter that camouflaged the principled revolt of Lucius Quintus Carothers McCaslin's twin sons against his ways and those of his society. Then Isaac's cousin McCaslin Edmonds in adolescence had witnessed and could attest to a postbellum sequel, conveying word of Isaac's beginnings to him. There was his father back from the four years in the Confederate cavalry (disclosing a typical Southern complexity of attitude in this man who with his own brother had provided for the manumission of his leniently supervised slaves but leaped into the saddle to fight Yankee invaders). There was his marriage at last to Sophonsiba Beauchamp, and the two of them established (by her initiative, no doubt) in the restored "big house" where Isaac was born and would refuse to reside once he reached his majority, Yet of his childhood under her upbringing till her death some time before he was ten almost nothing is told, but one instance out of their visits to Uncle Hubert still living at "Warwick" is stamped on the boy's memory, as a first sensing of male-female relationship when his mother turns out her brother's mulatto cook and there is a glimpse of "silk gown" and "glint of an ear-ring" which "somehow even to the child" is "evocative." It is by such realized episodes rather than a plodding chronology that Faulkner structures this narrative that rapidly turns its facets while constantly resounding with mingled themes—in this case another aspect of the self-indulgent Hubert, the socially conscious Sophonsiba Beauchamp McCaslin, and the boy Isaac's continuing absorption of formative impressions, either at first hand or by what he learns from Sam Fathers, from his cousin McCaslin, or the commissary ledgers. And it is this maturation which is the story in "The Bear," through which all other characters move across his consciousness, not in orderly procession, but as summoned up under his associative drift and quest.

McCaslin Edmonds' seniority over his cousin Isaac by sixteen or seventeen years—and these the South's most stressfully eventful period, with drastic changes in which McCaslin had become more and more involved—gives him that certain authority to be drawn from direct observation and engagement. It is apparently from this, already communicated, that Isaac extends his socioethical summarizings and speculations which make some pages of section 4 in "The Bear" reverberate with the murmur of a subjectivized history, ethnology, philosophy, and even an elementary theology. By the time he is twenty-one, however, Isaac has not only absorbed woodsmanship and its related mystique from Sam Fathers and has acquired regional-historical worldly knowledge from McCaslin Edmonds (supplemented by schooling McCaslin had insisted that Isaac diligently pursue); by 1888 he is able with some detachment to see that in this multiracial society wracked by its recent ordeals some problems not only remain beyond reconstruction but still await adequate definition and thus continue to solicit his free conjectures rather than partisan action. In the revulsion from his own heritage which has deepened in Isaac during the five years since his reading in the commissary ledgers, he can understand to some extent the melancholy mood of his fellows, haunted by a regional record of institutionalized wrongs yet exacerbated by defeat in war, and thus made prey to ambivalence, as in that love-hate relationship with the South which Quentin Compson carries into the twentieth century, but in which Isaac has refused to entangle himself.

Though McCaslin's wide views (acquired in earlier, ex-

tended, and varied encounterings and under prematurely imposed practical responsibilities) seem to come into section 4 of
"The Bear" through Isaac's condensed realizations derived
largely from his cousin's telling, the earner of all this experience
is felt throughout such summary passages, as well as the inheritor who supplements them with conjecture, colors them with his
own melancholy, and answers to their inherent issues out of his
own explicit convictions. Confrontation between the cousins
became inevitable as Isaac's resolve to repudiate silently formed
itself during the years until his majority would let him speak,
but in this period the two were collaborators in attempting to
convey the McCaslin legacy to Terrel's offspring, and even in
debate their cordial good will is itself real beyond familial
habit. The separation and detachment Isaac arrives at has
nevertheless something of a counterpart (though of a quite different coloration) in McCaslin Edmonds, who has seen things
through practically and, while still trying to do so, eases the
cousin's man-to-man encounter in the commissary. In spite of
the matter's gravity, at points their talk becomes complementary, and even antiphonal, when for instance they pronounce in their different voices on the war that was lost twenty-
three years before. Isaac, citing picturesque examples, is com-
menting reflectively on the audacity of the Southerners who
attempted a war between the States believing that success depended not on "acumen . . . nor diplomacy nor money" but
"just love of land and courage — ," to which McCaslin ironically
adds, "And an unblemished and gallant ancestry and the
ability to ride a horse. Don't leave that out." Here Faulkner
briefly realizes the setting: "It was evening now, the tranquil
sunset of October mazy with windless woodsmoke" and the flow
of plantation life is epitomized in that "all day now the wagons
loaded with gathered corn moved between field and crib, processional across the enduring land." (The simple imagery becomes thematic through one word, "processional," making
ritualistic the routines immemorially sustained by nature.)
McCaslin elegaically continues their discussion by borrowing,
with mild ironic skepticism, from Isaac's mode of warranty by

his own reference to the Book: "Well, maybe that's what He wanted. At least, that's what He got." This genial communicating despite the cousins' different temperaments as well as outlooks now lets Isaac sympathetically remember the "harsher book" McCaslin had read from in his teens, during the war which Isaac thus has heard of most closely, though he was not born until two years after its last inclusive pages were set down. He has grown up into its sequel, however, with its residue of intractable problems and unrest, and after this wearily fanciful exchange with McCaslin the narrative moves into a compendium, yet vivid in its details, of the postwar years, the region's civic dislocations and vulnerability to exploitation and fanatical impositions, from without and within, with inert at its center the still inscrutable enigma of racial tensions.

Conceivably it was this last factor, in its historical, regional, and especially its disheartening familial aspects for him, which finally tempered Isaac to abjure participation in what he sees as continuing obliquities in the South's whole system, and the futility of expedient improvisations. What at sixteen he stumbled upon and deciphered from the McCaslin commissary ledgers was that the founder of the family in Mississippi, his grandfather, made sexual use of the slave Eunice, bought in New Orleans for that purpose, and then incestuously used their daughter Tomasina, whence Terrel (Tomy's Turl), from whom and Tennie Beauchamp came James (Tennie's Jim), Sophonsiba (Fonsiba), and Lucas Beauchamp. Beyond this data not without some parallels in the slaveholding South, and in broader sociohistorical terms, it might be asked whether Faulkner had not endowed Isaac at twenty-one, in 1888, with a prescience which more than half a century later, when the artist was conceiving this character's prototype and the substance of his story, was still scarcely credible. Some may say that Isaac's views were warped and darkened by a morbid melancholy, while others would make him a paragon of ethical sensitivity and a natural seer. Both expedient materialists and frustrated humanitarians could feel Isaac was right about one thing, that the racial issue would be with this nation for "maybe a long while yet," and some ecologists would agree that abuse of the land is a basic symptom of a societally rampant obtuseness as well as ruthlessness. Yet Isaac is a fictional character, not to be defined but realized; and it seems obvious from text and tone that his creator, as humanistic realist, considered him not only credible but positively significant. Some such fictional reality emerges under a regarding of him as one peculiarly preconditioned by Sam Fathers and determining, while still a rather isolated youth, not to be overset by findings in the family's history but moved to disavow his heritage as product of the larger pattern it illustrated. When Isaac during their debate tells his cousin, "Sam Fathers set me free" he means an avoidance of bad conscience, for the priceless reward of peace. His fear (shown when as helpful trustee he is dealing with Lucas about Terrel's untouched McCaslin legacy) is that others, not crediting Isaac's motive in his own remembering because they cannot imagine its grounds, will think he sold out for a pittance and a release into irresponsibility—though had that been his aim he could honorably have accepted at least half the value of the plantation. But Old General Compson, having watched Isaac as a youth in the woods, refuses to believe he "just quit," however much it looked like it, and Major de Spain, asking no questions, offered the young man a room in his house. Buying carpenter tools on what he takes only as a loan from McCaslin, and punctiliously refusing not only his friends' endorsing offers of shelter but the use of what McCaslin deposited monthly in the bank for him, Isaac shows both diligence and resoluteness. (It is to be noted that while Ike McCaslin had been incidentally mentioned in *The Hamlet* as owner of a "farm" on which he raises cotton, and where he had hired the Ab Snopes family to work by the day "and let them winter in an old cottonhouse he wasn't using," Faulkner makes different reference to him in novels following *Go Down, Moses.* In *Intruder in the Dust* he was still alive at ninety, and has passed on the story of the one-eyed mule he rode that wouldn't spook in the big bear hunt; in *The Town, The Mansion,* and *The Reivers* he is identified as junior partner operating a hardware store, where Mink Snopes, planning to shoot Houston (this in *The Mansion*) tries to buy two buckshot big-game shells. Here Faulkner reidentifies the man of probity he created in *Go Down, Moses;* Mink knows as soon as he sees Ike's eyes that *"Hit wont do no good. He has done spent too much time in the woods with deer and bears and panthers that either are or they aint, right quick and now and not no shades between. He wont know how to believe a lie even if I could tell him one,"* and Isaac, asking twice what Mink wants the shells for, says "No," both to the story of a bear and to a promise to pay when Mink's cotton is ginned, and explains, "I aint going to let you have them. There aint anything out there at Frenchman's Bend you need to shoot buckshot at." This image of him through Mink's reaction corresponds to the glimpsed essence of "Uncle Ike" in "The Fire and the Hearth," as one "born into his father's old age and himself born old" but who "past seventy . . . had acquired something of a young boy's high and selfless innocence."

Whatever degree of such serenity Isaac McCaslin achieved was at a high cost, and (as with some other worthy Faulkner characters) under a series of demands. At the opening of section 4 of "The Bear" the first two clauses ("then he was twenty-one. He could say it") imply a deliberated intention that has awaited his right to declare it with a man's authority, in so grave a matter as rejection of heritage, and to so valued and concerned a person as his elder cousin, the patron of his orphaned youth and strenuous, faithful preserver of the plantation for Isaac to have as the heir first in line. In their very closeness they find themselves at greatest difference, as it can become between friends when the issue is abstract, beyond personalities. The antithesis between Isaac's inflexibly absolute idealism and McCaslin's relativistic practicality reveals in each man an integrity transcending Isaac's melancholy disenchantment and McCaslin's restiveness released in ironies. Each in his way is an integrated man; as each declares, he is doing and being what he must. Each has met circumstance resolutely and with commitment, in an acceptance of responsibility to conceived values, which, however they have been conditioned in him, are real to him. As of his time and place neither can be a representative figure; it is when viewed together — "juxtaposed not against the wilderness but against the tamed land" — that they embody the conflicting forces which internally affect some of Faulkner's major characters. In these an ambivalence, whether enervating or exacerbating, is a fate circumstantially imposed upon personal susceptibilities, but does not necessarily disclose a weakness, rather a strong humane awareness.

The recurrence of their kind in Faulkner's fiction may point toward one of the inestimables concerning literary art — the degree to which any persistent inquietude as part of the creator's disinterested viewing of the human condition requires some representation of its fluctuantly conflicting factors if the artist is to maintain his pyschological impetus and morale as a realist. (Not that the apprentice need first resolve his ambivalences; such recently fashionable therapy may serve most when it mollifies and perhaps cures an adventitiously contracted case of *cacoethes scribendi.*) The proved artist, creator of valid autonomous work, may instead have drawn upon his ambivalences not to display a possible resolution but to exercise under their tensions a breadth of ventured insights that raise him above propagandist, sentimentalist, or solipsist. Inscrutibly even to himself his opposed uncertainties may function in creative imaginings; elements distinct and even at variance in his own nature may people his drama with contenders who suggest mysteries large enough to constitute a field of action for them all. In the artist's tentative intuitions of these embracing themes he finds proper scope and scale for any elected character and weaves the idiosyncrasies of each unobtrusively into the larger pliancies of the narrative continuum. At such levels of sustained invention, variety and even opposition of personified tendencies can merge into a dynamic totality directly expressive of the artist's intent and power, conceptual and evocative — as with Isaac McCaslin and McCaslin Edmonds. They come to readers straight from the imagination of one who, choosing to remain on native ground, and observing closely and receptively its people and their doings, related these immediacies to what he could learn of their larger contexts and representative implications. Thereby the artist assumed a unique complexity of attachments and obligations in personal attitudes developed through such a purposeful and intensive exercise of temperament, and through remembrance of his fictional characters as evoked out of known realities for use in his practice of a metamorphic art.

Hence there seemed some presumptuousness and even imposition in certain questions directed at Faulkner, especially by private interviewers or by inquisitors at his public appearances, asking for a quick estimate or specific judgment of this or that event or character. If these have been given fictional vitality, then for their creator even more than for the reader they exist as in their conceived world, through the interactions and tensions in that fancied web, where as with any actual human existence events fade at their edges into the penumbra of ambiguity and the nullity of the untold. In some of Faulkner's reported answers to interviewers, beneath his scrupulous gentility and patience there would seem to have been a trace of diffident improvisation, as if in an awareness of attempting the impossible, the resuscitation in a sentence or two of an imagined but dimensioned being whose only habitat was the story's action, in which the character too was progressively in motion, a continuum in which every act, thought, and feeling took shape out of memory and intention. With major characters the question of the whole fictional truth, besides growing more complex, may suggest in larger dimensions a silhouette of the artist's concerns and strategies. The strivings between Isaac McCaslin and McCaslin Edmonds, enacted against the epical background of their times, disclose with a special clarity and intensity the artist's widely ranging awareness and concern, even perhaps to the extent of some ambivalence. This appears to allow certain validities to each man in their extended debating which, whatever its immediate matter, seeks to "turn upon the poles of truth," even while granting that these may be opposed at furthest extremes. What McCaslin and Isaac have in common, deeper than blood relationship and the habits of a shared life, is consistent responsibility to ethical imperatives. That they read these differently in part 4 of "The Bear" is not a merely devised fictional conflict, nor is the spectator furnished a melodramatic key to simplistic right versus wrong in it. Faulkner's profound dramatized use of subjectivity reveals that the situation is not single, it is separately integral for each man, while each besides is acutely aware of the other's difference, of a degree of his right in it, and his absolute right to it. It is thereby to be seen that the roots of temperament cannot be completely traced, and also that of necessity conscience is autonomous. Hence the ethical dignity of sound fiction and drama.

In such representations, behind these instances of the human verities which paradoxically make for individual uniqueness, there is to be felt the force of the artist's informed and dynamic imagination, judicious and empathetic, struggling mightily with immeasurable intimations, and offering their essences in the containment of an evocative art. It approaches a full bespeaking of "weakness which impairs" and "griefs which bow," but likewise of resoluteness sufficiently supported by conviction and supplementary faith. Presumably it was such lofty sightings, not mere caprice, which wakened Faulkner's visions, and drew out his amazing artistic ingenuities as means of evocative representation. An example is his intricate rearrangements of chronology, as in section 4 of "The Bear." In general such practice can enhance effect by reducing the claims a straightforward narrative would make for obligatory scenes (in this case, for instance, the marriage of Isaac's parents and their settling in the big house, by way of McCaslin Edmonds' telling). The economies of such omissions or minimizings heighten momentum and allow comparatively more prolonged emphasis on crucial scenes—a classic and increasingly practiced technique in imaginative narration; it is also easier (or Faulkner makes it seem so) in a "floating" chronology to pass into synopses and emerge directly from them into further scenes in process that come on fully, as with a curtain suddenly opened. And rearranged chronology withholds revelations not for suspense in the fashion of ordinary plotting but for entrance into narrative substance at key points of psychological penetration and measured recurrence of motif. For some example of all this, at the beginning of section 4, with Isaac and his elder cousin in the commissary discussing the young man's first declared intention of his majority and the most crucial decision in his life, he is basing his arguments primarily on a mystical regard for the created natural world and men's proper and ultimately most wholesome use of it, taught him basically by Sam Fathers, and extended through a belief in the Creator's providential will, as conceived of from "His Book." But these influences had come to their full tide in Isaac's sixteenth year, with the last big hunt and the death of Old Ben and of Sam Fathers. More deeply while he was sixteen Isaac's outlook had been supplemented by what "The Bear" does not tell of until section 4, his disillusionment about his grandfather, as the youth had deduced it, a detective story the drama of which is in the discover's shock. After this, but before reaching his majority and his right to tell McCaslin that he repudiates what he now inherits, Isaac had twice made what might be considered expiatory pilgrimages; he tried unsuccessfully to find James Beauchamp and give him the Carothers McCaslin legacy unclaimed by James' father Terrel, and he did find Fonsiba in Arkansas and deposit money for her guaranteed subsistence. Along with these attempts in those same years of maturation between sixteen and twenty-one, there was all the learning from McCaslin's accounts of a past he hadn't known (as in "Was" or more substantially in an accumulated awareness of what the first years of Reconstruction must have been like), and there were also his own experiences, most crucially from the ledgers themselves, and his rearranging of attitudes following a loss of innocence through deprivation of belief in what he stemmed from, which he must have been judging most directly by the admirable McCaslin Edmonds. This is the major content of section 4 up to Isaac's twenty-first birthday, but given a strategic reordering by Faulkner for the concentration of all such complexities into a surge of constantly rising action, soon to be augmented by a second critical factor, impasse in his marriage.

Certainly the cousins, being not wholly at odds, do influence each other. Isaac's asserted principles give McCaslin sufficient pause to evoke serious response, and McCaslin's combined practicality and probity affect Isaac. Even as a youth he has no superficial notion that wrongs can be erased by good will, the wronged be set on their feet by proclamation, or freedom be translated from abstraction to reality by anything less than sustained and responsible action. His full realization of this has been illustrated by the moving instance of Fonsiba. Her origin was recorded in his father's rheumatically cramped last entry in the ledgers: *"Miss sophonsiba b[orn] dtr t t @ t* [Terrel and Tennie] *1869"*—the "Miss" a postbellum politesse and perhaps ceded the more readily because her continuingly faithful parents had given her his wife's name. Then when Fonsiba was seventeen, two years younger than Isaac, suddenly a Northern Negro appears and, with a studied propriety that declares his assumption of equality, notifies McCaslin "as chief of her family" that he intends to marry Fonsiba and take her to live on an Arkansas farm he has, through his father, as a grant from the United States army. Isaac, in his familial concern that extends to the McCaslin descendants of mixed blood, cries out "Call aunt Tennie!" McCaslin, realizing after a few severe questions that the matter has been settled with Fonsiba, merely tells the pretentiously formal man they are to "be off this place by full dark." Afterward when Isaac asks incredulously, "How did she ever know him?" his elder cousin replies in a typical tone: "Ha. Even their parents dont know until too late how seventeen-year-old girls ever met the men who marry them too, if they are lucky." But young Isaac is to be most fully instructed in this instance when five months later he journeys to Arkansas, carrying gold in a moneybelt, Fonsiba's share of the McCaslin bequest her father Terrel had never claimed. Like "a disguised one of the Magi travelling incognito and not even hope to draw him but only determination and desperation, he would tell himself: *I will have to find her.*" And he does, in a two-room log cabin, with "no barn, no stable, not so much as a hen-coop . . . a farm only in embryo, perhaps a good farm . . . but not now, not for years yet and only then with labor, hard and enduring and unflagging work and sacrifice." He finds the husband in a rocking chair "before that miserable fire for which there was not wood sufficient to last twenty-four hours," reading a book, wearing gold-framed spectacles which had no lenses in them. Isaac senses the man's "baseless and imbecile delusion" and as he orates of the now-lifted curse upon the South the youth can sense that a part of it remains upon the Negro, in the form of a passivity and continuing dependence induced through generations of enslavement. When the man says the curse "has been lifted . . . voided . . . discharged" and "We are seeing a new era . . . dedicated, as our founders intended it, to freedom, liberty and equality for all . . . the new Canaan," Isaac asks "Freedom from what? From work? Canaan? What corner of Canaan is this?" The man blandly explains, "I have a pension. I have my father's pension too" and he also has a hog running loose that "probably" he can track down. Isaac turns away in anger and dismay from the pretensions as empty as the spectacles are of lenses, and as he goes out through the other room he sees Fonsiba "watching him without alarm, without recognition, without hope." He repeats her name and asks, "Are you all right?" and she says, "I'm free." He goes to the bank in the town, deposits her thousand dollars there, and arranges to have it paid her at three dollars a month, so that for some years "at least she would not starve." (The positioning of this episode of further maturation in Isaac's nineteenth year usefully shows he entertains no naive illusion that on anyone's way to Canaan there will be manna aplenty; and it emphasizes that when, after declaring Sam Fathers set him free, he then uses his freedom at twenty-one to repudiate inheritance, he is also accepting obligation to work for a living throughout his life.) The melancholy situation of Fonsiba scarcely veils what is at its deep core, dilemmas inherent in freedom, that two-faced coin, cryptically stamped, of variable currency. Something of this Faulkner had comprised at the close of "Retreat" in *The Unvanquished*, when Granny Millard protests that two Sartoris slaves who are leaving to follow the marauding Union soldiers will be led "into misery and starvation" and the husband Loosh says, "I going. I done been freed. . . . I belongs to me and God," while the more prudent wife Philadelphy, protesting she has tried to dissuade him, follows him in tears. And in greater complexity, Isaac's renunciation of inheritance, spurred by discoveries in the antebellum ledgers, and believed to promise him freedom, peace, and self-possession, is not only to divide him from his cherished cousin McCaslin, but in his ongoing personal life to make a second and most severe charge upon him during his first decade of manhood, in the climax which terminates the massive and momentous section 4 of "The Bear."

After the painful and essentially conclusive separation between Isaac and his cousin McCaslin the narrative goes ahead quite rapidly, condensing a great deal of significant material with sometimes a kind of shorthand, almost a précis in style, as it moves toward the denouement in Isaac's personal life, his young wife's turning against him. He had taken money from the plantation only as a loan from McCaslin and returned it, he had refused the free lodging offered both by Major de Spain and General Compson, he had set up as carpenter and acquired a partner whose skill he repaid by caring for him after his drinking bouts. In all this, "to earn his bread" because he "had to" and "for more than bread," to make his own way honorably as a free man, he is doing what, as he had put it to McCaslin, "I dont quite understand myself," yet knows he must do. Now embarked on his endeavor, he detachedly and resignedly thinks, "Isaac McCaslin's ends, although simple enough in their apparent motivation, were and would be always incomprehensible to him, and his life, invincible enough in its needs, if he could have helped himself . . . he would not have chosen." What is seen here is no dogmatic relishing of rebellion or even the exuberance of one set free, but one gravely steadying himself in an instinctive revulsion from the way of life that has engendered him. To that passage's phrases is added "and paid it back," a quick Faulknerian transition recurring to the loan, but more broadly shadowing forth all that this man must do.

On a farm where he and his partner had built a barn "from

the ground up" he meets the girl he married. All Faulkner tells of their getting together is that she watches him working most of the day and asks about what her father had told her, that "That farm is really yours, isn't it?" When he says "And McCaslin's" she presses about the will, and he says none was needed, "His grandmother was my father's sister. We were the same as brothers." Her answer, as assertion and a shrugging off, is equivocal: "You are the same as second cousins and that's all you ever will be. But I dont suppose it matters." It seems Isaac innocently took for granted that curiously professed supposition. Yet it is to matter, crucially, as it would for any honest man; and the particular cost that Isaac must pay for his consistent adherance to his principles is to be most harshly exacted.

For Isaac at first his marriage is an utter fulfillment — "it was the new country, his heritage too . . . beyond the earth yet of the earth . . . and that room wall-less and topless and floorless in glory for him to leave each morning and return to at night," and "because each must share with another in order to come into it" there was for him the sense of community and peace which he had thirsted for in the abstract, and now found even more immediately and instinctively than from anything Sam Fathers had led him to in the woods or anything his distracted world could bequeath. His felicity was not to be for long, his separation from it to be more traumatic than his discoveries in the ledgers. One night, they "not even touching yet, her face strained and terrible, her voice a passionate and expiring whisper of immeasurable promise," she says, "You know I love you. When are we going to move?" At first Isaac thinks she means the bungalow he and his partner are building on a Jefferson lot her father had provided, all of it intended to be a surprise for her, but she says, "The farm. Our farm. Your farm." His "No! No!" she stifles with her hand upon his mouth, and whispering "of love and of incredible promise," she again asks "When?" He begins to answer her as before, but she rises from the bed and, in what "seemed no voice of hers he ever remembered," gives him a series of commands: "Stand up and turn your back and shut your eyes. . . . Lock the door. . . .

Take off your clothes." Now she reveals herself as she had refused to do before, completely naked, and draws him to her with a conditional hand upon his chest as she seeks to lure him into a promise that would negate the principled act with which he had entered into manhood. He repeatedly refuses her: "No. . . . No . . . No, I tell you. I wont. I cant. . . . I cant. Not ever. Remember."

There follows what might be considered an enigmatic passage. As Isaac, while speaking his repeated refusals of her demand for a promise, is enticed into this sexual union, "he said Yes and he thought, *She is lost. She was born lost. We were all born lost* and "then he stopped thinking and even saying Yes, it was like nothing he had ever dreamed . . . until after a no-time he returned and lay spent." Specifically her being born lost was into one of the common human cravings, in this case for possession and place (as had been hinted in her first known conversation with Isaac). Is his "Yes" the mindless, wholly instinctive assent to passion itself in an eclipse of all other regard (as with Molly Bloom's quick repetitions of the word, remembering her young lover on Gibralter), and does Isaac mean humans are "all born lost" to such susceptibility? This seems more probably the implication, rather than that Isaac in his sexual eagerness has quite consciously consented to the demand he had just refused, repeatedly and emphatically. Furthermore, with the act completed, his wife seems to be bearing away from the encounter no assurance but rather a realization that this man cannot be induced to yield up his previously defined convictions in return for sexual access; she has turned from him and, while laughing loudly in a way he first thought was crying, is exclaiming, "And that's all. That's all from me. If this dont get you that son you talk about, it wont be mine" — all this with "her back to the empty rented room" that he had thought the boundless heaven of his delight and hope.

This moment, which so climactically concludes the stupendous section 4 of "The Bear," is catastrophic for Isaac, the ultimate exaction from him for his principled refusal of the inheritance, leaving him in early manhood fated for life to stoic endurance of a deep human deprivation. That seems to have been insufficiently taken account of by some readers, especially those who charge Isaac with inertia, but Faulkner had implied it as fate and lifelong factor in the book's first three lines: "Isaac McCaslin, 'Uncle Ike,' past seventy . . . a widower now and uncle to half a county and father to no one"—and what man could carry such desolation of selfhood, however privately, without some shadow of inexplicable aloofness? It is not told when his wife died, but she had lived to a time when her niece had children and being widowed could come, with them, to keep house for Isaac, as mentioned in "Delta Autumn." All this was in the little bungalow he and his partner had built, on land and with materials supplied by his wife's father, to be a surprise for her, but before it was finished and they had moved in, Isaac already "had lost her in the rented cubicle." In "The Fire and the Hearth," when Lucas Beauchamp at twenty-one presented himself to claim his McCaslin legacy from Isaac as trustee, Isaac and his wife were living in that bungalow, they still in their twenties, he subject to her sarcasms in her "tense bitter indomitable voice," but this he suffers "with pity for her and regret too, for her, for both of them." And on the second page of *Go Down, Moses,* in "Was," in that preliminary placing of old Isaac McCaslin, it had been recorded that his wife had willed the bungalow to him, and (as that brief prologue also says) though he "owned no property and never desired to," this legacy "he had pretended to accept, acquiesce to, to humor her, ease her going." Isaac has lived with this woman without resentment or bitterness, despite her denying him a man's greatest human fulfillments, and he has brought away from the debacle of their union and its long unease the lenient faith that having at one time come into touch through love, "they voluntarily and in advance forgave one another for all that each knew the other could never be." However, section 4 of "The Bear" can end on no such elegaic note but dramatically, in that first hour of a searing crisis, with the painful sound of a woman's bitter "laughing and laughing."

The fifth and final section of "The Bear" is a postlude, in a minor key, and retrospective, but thematically reverberant. With the closure of section 4 in such a thunderclap of individual doom, either a further unfolding was obligatory, or else some marked shift and subsidence. The repudiation of Isaac, signaled by his wife's scornfully hysterical laughter, has been succinctly prepared for in the only passage given of their talking before marriage, which reveals her alert interest in the inheritance he had already transferred to McCaslin Edmonds, and also—"But I dont suppose it matters"—her calculated waiting until after marriage to press him to reclaim it. The glimpse of Isaac's disappointed wife given in "The Fire and the Hearth" suggests that her proneness to sarcasm meets an equal inflexibility in his maintained refusal despite her counter-measure; the passage also shows him enduring her mood with "pity and grief." In "Delta Autumn" old Uncle Isaac, widowed, will think of his wife compassionately, in that he had "lived with her and lost her," long before her death, "because she loved him." The next sentence bring this enigmatic phrase into somewhat clearer light by a cryptic generalization: "But women hope for so much. They never live too long to still believe that anything within the scope of their passionate wanting is likewise within the range of their passionate hope." (In him this seems a kind softening of her special trait into a generic determinant.) However, recollection of his wife is incidental to the story, which more resonantly echoes the stipulatory phrase at the opening of *Go Down, Moses:* "Isaac McCaslin . . . a widower now and uncle to half a county and father to no one." In that Delta November hunt (the last readers are to know sustainedly of Isaac) he is seen in the company of "the sons and even grandsons" of men he had been with in the big woods during his boyhood and youth. Two grandsons are Roth Edmonds and Will Legate; two other men, "sons of his old companions," are ones "he had taught not only how to distinguish between the prints left by a buck or a doe but between the sound they made in moving." Distinguishing between bucks and does, figuratively speaking, is thematic in "Delta Autumn," but this mention also underlines what *Go Down, Moses* repeatedly touches on, that Isaac had had no son of his own to initiate into the hunter's craft and its properly related attitudes.

It must be presumed that if Isaac remainded "father to no one" it was because his wife had held to her terms, "That's all from me." Yet he had lived on with his wife in the little house her father had given and Isaac and his carpenter partner had built for her. The detachment from things of this world he had asserted in relinquishing heritage is compounded in the patience, compassion, and melancholy with which he thought of his wife. Thus the deadening immobilizing pressure on Isaac through his wife's spurning of the man he had already declared himself to be looms as a factor essential to comprehension and judgment of him. Absolute idealism such as his would be peculiarly vulnerable to frustrations, yet had his wife accepted the honorably purposeful carpenter she had married and given him children, he might have borne himself differently in his milieu. But such a development was not what Faulkner looked to beyond the evocation of a uniquely conditioned young man's resolute personal response to impingements peculiar to his heredity, region, and generation. Hence Isaac has no further connubial history except his regrets for them both, in his arrest in the stoicism he is seen already fated to. He is not to be found further on in life, after that dreadful moment of his wife's estranging laughter, until as an old man in "Delta Autumn," where he shows himself still calmly resolute in his ethical convictions, but with reason still beset by "pity and grief." This is the whole man, as of his life, which a just reading should answer to, and one test of understanding would be the weight given that long hiatus in his history and its implied arrest and barrenness, from early in his marriage to his reappearance, a widower nearing eighty and father to no one, in presumably his last hunt. However, "Delta Autumn" is an ultimate matter, projected far beyond the great hunt in section 3 of "The Bear" and the momentous substance of section 4, comprising Isaac's refusal of heritage, his turning carpenter and marrying, and his wife's rejection of him. All this is made to await for the full closure of Isaac's story by that movement into his old age, with a subsidence leaving multitudinous events and realizations in a suspension as fixed, dimensioned, and yet shimmering as if in depths of limpid water.

For its conclusion, "The Bear" required of its creator a further section, an area of pause, a plateau this side of those major determinative events in section 4 which would require a man's lifetime to endure and translate into finalities. Hence in section 5 the drop backward in chronology, to a point between the year of the great hunt and the day of Isaac's majority. The return is to June in his eighteenth year, and his mood is not only intently retrospective but valedictory. From his tenth to his sixteenth years, with McCaslin's consent and under Sam Fathers' tutelage, he had been in the big woods for the annual November deer hunts, and at sixteen he was assigned a man's part in the forefront of the course of epical events (the substance of section 3) which saw the death of Sam Fathers and of the big bear, Old Ben, and the great dog Lion. These constituted a climactic turning point for Isaac, especially in the loss of his mentor in woodsmanship. It had constituted what he had intuitively foreseen, "the end of something," indefinable, and fully realized only in the event, but a major formative influence. That following November there had been another hunt, old General Compson's last, in company with McCaslin Edmonds, rifleman Walter Ewell, Isaac himself, and Boon, Tennie's Jim, and old Ash the camp cook. But not Major de Spain, and not at his camp in the big woods, or on the large holdings of ancient forest he had sold to a lumbering company. Instead the hunters went in two wagons, "and drove two days and almost forty miles beyond any country the boy had ever seen before and lived in tents for two weeks."

Nothing is told of the hunt; presumably it would have been anticlimatic for them all. Then the next June Isaac revisited Major de Spain's camp "one more time," to walk those big woods again before they "began to cut the timber." Punctiliously he has asked the Major's permission, and graciously the Major arranged to have Boon and Ash the Negro cook there to meet him. Isaac rides his "three-year-old filly he had bred and raised and broken himself" and starting at midnight, he is at Hoke's, the log-line junction, six hours later. He rides the logging train into the woods, and old Ash is there with the wagon to meet him and give him word from Boon that he'd be at the Gum Tree, which stood in a clearing and often was full of squirrels. But Isaac first takes a different direction on foot, intent on a more compelling engagement. As he makes his way accurately and with confidence in the woodsman's skills Sam Fathers had taught him, he muses on more than just the practical aspects of that influence from one "who had been his spirit's father if any had, whom he had revered and harkened to and loved and lost and grieved: and he would marry someday and they too would own for their brief while that brief unsubstanced glory . . . but still the woods would be his mistress and his wife." In this complex mood he journeys on through solitude to the plot Major de Spain reserved from the sale, where Sam Fathers and the great dog Lion were buried; there he feels their transcendent presence, defined as "not in earth but of earth," and Old Ben's too. After this nostalgic pause he turns and walks on toward the Gum Tree where he expects to find Boon, but first he has another encounter. "And watch your feet," Ash had warned him. "They're crawling," and now he freezes in midstep, sensing and then seeing and smelling the rattlesnake, "more than six feet of it," not yet coiled, its head elevated "higher than his knee and less than his knee's length away . . . the old one, the ancient and accursed . . . evocative of all knowledge and an old weariness and of pariah-hood and of death." He holds; it does not strike, and as it glides away Isaac stands "with one hand raised as

Sam had stood" and "without premeditation" speaks as Sam had: "'Chief,' he said: 'Grandfather.'"

A little more than a page completes this section and concludes "The Bear." Isaac, hearing the sound of hammering, found the Gum Tree full of "frantic squirrels," with the inept Boon, sitting at its base, pounding at the breech of "his dismembered gun" with the barrel of it. Not looking up, he shouted, "Get out of here! . . . Dont touch a one of them! They're mine!" It is a curious finale for so great a novella as "The Bear." Yet the hunting of Old Ben itself had ended unconventionally, when Boon, attempting to save the dog Lion, fearlessly used his knife to bring down the great creature. He thus enacted from an earlier season a revised and bloody version of the boy Isaac's forbearing rescue of his little fyce without shooting at Old Ben; Boon also had superseded his fellow hunters, Isaac and Sam, and in so doing had changed the hunt from its ritual into something more primitive. And Boon's churlish behavior concluding section 5 and "The Bear" as a whole has its peculiar fitness in its tracing of a decline, in essence and on a scale from a particular greatness in men and animals, under the exactions of nature's realities, to incompetence, triviality, and what would be meanness were it not simply childish. And while this is the doing of a subsidiary figure, its passive spectator is his familiar, the youth who pervades "The Bear" dramatically as protagonist, and as its central sensibility gives it wide ranges of tone and vision all along the way from his early initiation and continuing development as hunter and virtually a man among men through to his uncompromising break at his majority with what he has come to consider an ethically ambiguous socioeconomic order, provoking consequent rejection later by his ambitious young wife, fating him to be "father to no one." The tale has been of personal aspirations, immense realizations, and searing disenchantments, with the trend become retrograde, into despoliation and irrevocable losses. Yet it scarecely can have the large dimensions of tragedy, since the youthful protagonist has already disengaged himself in spirit from the overt struggle, and so is to become the nostalgic devotee of an increasingly disregarded code and of verities which are its referents. Thus he can be stoic witness to Boon's grotesqueness and the story can halt there.

Furthermore, structure in the five sections of "The Bear" is not primarily shaped to chronological sequence, but rather to a series of climaxes in Isaac's progressing experience. In section 1 it is his hard-earned first glimpse of Old Ben, got by precocious woodsmanship and commensurate courage; in the second it is his intimation of "a fatality . . . like the last act on a set stage," the inevitable culmination of these yearly hunts. The third section comprises that finality, with not only Old Ben's death but Sam Fathers', and Isaac's passion of grief. The lengthy and crowded section 4 turns upon his renunciation as direct heir of the McCaslin inheritance, and later, in consequence, his wife's rejection of him and of his hopes for a son. These events have been at a high and higher pitch, continuing a rising action thus far throughout the four sections; a subsidence in a return to an event before he was twenty-one is not without effect as closure, especially in a tale so flavored by his subjectivity and when he has already lost his mentor and read the commissary ledgers' dark story. It finds him chiefly solitary, and shows him in June rather than the season of the great hunts, but visiting those old haunts where he had been able to range for miles without map or compass and now witnessing the progress of lumbering which means the death of the great woods itself, which stirs his apprehensions of further losses. At that time he cannot suppose what shapes some of those will take, such as the reader already knows of them from section 4 as they reach to the life-determining events of his early manhood, but his present melancholy suggests how acutely they will impinge upon his spirit in the privacy of his maintained resolution. However, "The Bear" is not the whole and the end of Isaac McCaslin's story; it had an earlier part, "The Old People," giving Sam Fathers

his substantial place and permanent footing and showing
Isaac's formal blooding, and it will be followed by "Delta
Autumn," reaching into Uncle Isaac's old age, and bringing to
full circle not only his maintained ethical stance but his sense
of emotional deprivation throughout his long life and a
further disenchantment through the recrudescence of old evils
striking close through the offense of a kinsman.

The abrupt overt closure of section 5 in "The Bear," with
Boon's violent assault on his own gun and his hostile outburst
against his friend Isaac as a mere intruder, is to be conceived
of most truly through a sustained sense of the youthful
protagonist as witness, and by relevant intuition of how it may
have appeared to him, making that the real culmination of
this section for the imaginative reader. Isaac's immediate
awareness, deliberate recollections, and reflectiveness have
constituted the quiet continuity in this account of a farewell
visit to the big woods. His consciousness has swung between an
ongoing knowing observation of an everchanging yet enduringly familiar natural life of its own, and the thus evoked
recall of overheard lore and personal experiences. The section
is introduced through the youth's punctilious call upon Major
de Spain in his office to request permission for a visit to the
hunting camp where there have been no more summer
birthday parties or November hunts after the great one when
Isaac was sixteen, when Old Ben was killed by Boon's knife,
and the dog Lion who had held him died of injuries, Sam
Fathers of exhaustion. Major de Spain consents, and in
another demonstration of how he values Isaac, will send a wire
to Boon, now marshall at Hoke's, to meet him, and will dispatch his attendant, old Ash, by train, to cook for them in
camp, but says he "will be too busy" to go himself. Here to
begin with a retrospective image is evoked, the youth seeing
Major de Spain

sitting at the desk, with a paper in his hand . . . the short plumpish grey-
haired man in sober fine broadcloth and an immaculate glazed shirt whom
he was used to seeing in boots and muddy corduroy, sitting the shaggy

powerful long-hocked mare with the worn Winchester carbine across the saddlebow and the great blue dog standing motionless as bronze at the stirrup.

With entry into the main episodes there is a particular sounding of a theme recurrent throughout this section and in its closure, that of desolating change. On Isaac's arrival after six hours horseback at the log-line junction he had "looked about in shocked and grieved amazement" at the new planing mill, the stacks of rails for more log-train tracks into the woods, "feeding-troughs for two hundred mules at least and the tents for the men who drove them." Boarding the log-train caboose, Isaac "did not look any more, . . . looked no more save toward the wall of wilderness ahead within which he would be able to hide himself from it once more anyway." The closely spaced phrases, "any more . . . no more . . . once more," are not monotonously prolix; they become a lament, in the way Faulkner's repetitions and rhythms can lyricize a character's realizations, and even the ordering of "any . . . no . . . once" is narratively effective in an account of influences that are making this visit a farewell. Beyond this, the section's chief effects, up to the conclusive focus on Boon, are through Isaac's recall. Even incidental and commonplace bygones become resonant in his reveries. Their narrative movement is reflectively associative, yet momentum is sustained as theme is unfolded.

Two illustrative instances are of the treed half-grown bear and of the Negro camp-cook Ash's one venture as hunter. The first begins for Isaac as the log-train leaves the junction, with "a rapid churning of exhaust, a lethargic deliberate clashing of slack couplings traveling backward along the train, the exhaust changing to the deep slow clapping bites of power as the caboose too began to move. . . ." Watching from the caboose cupola, Isaac sees the little locomotive "vanish into the wilderness, dragging its length of train behind it so that it resembled a small dingy harmless snake vanishing into the weeds, drawing him with it too until soon it ran once more at its maximum clattering speed between the twin walls of unaxed wilderness as of old. It had been harmless once." But with this new spur line snaking deeper into the wilderness, it becomes a threat. Isaac remembers his cousin McCaslin Edmonds' recollection of the half-grown bear on the track, frightened by the warning locomotive whistle and scrambling into a small tree from which it would not come down, and so Boon and Ash had "sat under the tree all that night to keep anybody from shooting it," and when at sundown next day thirst drove it to the ground, Major de Spain (who had orderd the train held at the junction) and "not only Boon and Ash" but "General Compson and Walter and McCaslin, twelve then" (and now Isaac's doubly resonant source for the story), were there to watch it run off into the big woods. Following its pictured escape, which significantly becomes not McCaslin Edmonds' story but the youthful yet experienced Isaac's remembrance of how bears run (and instances how old tales get reconstituted by other tellers), the next paragraph begins with dependence on one of Faulkner's thematically filamentary rather than syntactically determined antecedents, "It had been harmless then" (echoing "it had been harmless once" from amidst the preceding paragraph), as Isaac remembers how the hunters at night would hear the train's whistle out at Hoke's from Major de Spain's camp deep in the still untouched, uninvaded forest.

The little train slows down as it nears that area, and while it is still in motion Isaac with gun in hand swings off; it picks up speed again and is soon out of hearing, leaving him there where "The Wilderness soared, musing, inattentive, myriad, eternal, green; older than any mill-shed, longer than any spur-line." Since Ash, waiting for him, has word where he can meet Boon, Isaac doesn't get into the wagon and return to the camp but strikes off through the big woods, "not alone but solitary," as "the solitude closed about him, green with summer," as changeless as in those other seasonal recurrences, "the fire and rain of fall and the iron cold and sometimes even snow." The thought of snow, together with old Ash's recent truculence about when he and Boon are to be back for dinner, leads the youth to muse on something out of his own earlier days, Ash's disgruntlement after Isaac had killed his first buck (as told in "The Old People"), and so when another hunt started with the men riding after hounds, the boy had taken the impatient Negro, on foot and with Boon's gun, into the snowy woods which Ash, even after all his years as camp cook, knew nothing of; they come across a half-grown bear that escapes Ash's inept efforts with an unreliable gun, but he was appeased, he had been on a hunt. The wryly conveyed ancedote brings back a homely touch of intimate camp life, with something besides intrepid endeavor and perfect markmanship, an undefined mutual companionability; then the incident of the treed bear supplies other realistic ingredients, by the men's serious concern for the young wild animals, and their relishing good true stories retold.

Recollections of one young bear up a tree and another one that Ash couldn't hit with all his trying take their place in section 5 mainly as modal antistrophes in the melancholy consciousness of a youth bidding farewell to the great stage of his life's most stirring events between the ages of ten and sixteen. It is only because the ancient irreplaceable big woods is to be cut over for timber that Isaac has come there once more, and after seeing the large-scale preparations at Hoke's junction for this inroad and devastation he knows "why Major de Spain had not come back, and that after this time he himself, who had had to see it one time other, would return no more." Like any genuine nostalgia, Isaac's has a whole history behind it, and an unusually rich and formative one. His present pilgrimage to the site of Sam Fathers' grave and that of the dog Lion renews a sense not just of the great hunt but of Isaac's extended training under Sam. There is a fine deliberate passage which epitomizes the slow growth of the boy, in the telling of Isaac's approach to those graves through the as yet unmarked deep woods. Now at eighteen he muses that not many years earlier he wouldn't have been allowed there "without someone with him," and then after he had learned a little even if allowed he wouldn't have dared to go this far, and later still he would have needed a compass — "McCaslin and Major de Spain and Walter and General Compson" having "taught him at last to believe the compass regardless of what it seemed to state." As for the sun, which doubtless Sam Fathers had shown him the use of, now he is not even noting its position except subconsciously, "yet he could have taken a scaled map and plotted at any time to within a hundred feet of where he actually was; and sure enough, at almost the exact moment when he expected it, the earth began to rise faintly, he passed one of the four concrete markers . . . of the plot Major de Spain had reserved out of the sale." Because of the reversion in chronology in section 5 of "The Bear," with Isaac at eighteen remembering Sam Fathers and showing the competence derived from that past schooling, a complementary thematic echo sounds paradoxically from the known further side of time to come, where as told in the preceding section 4 Isaac, a man at twenty-one finally free to speak, and out of weighty knowledge of his heritage, absolutely knows where he stands, remembers exactly how he had come there, and thus can do no other, though renunciation of inheritance costs him a disingenuous wife's supposed genuine alliance, and wrecks hope of having "that son" he had talked of to her.

Faulkner's manipulations of a narrative's chronology call for appreciative recognition of their functions in broadening and intensifying fictional effect, through evokings of sustained attention as of the moment and a more intuitive response to a character's enhanced subjectivity. Moreover, the closing section of "The Bear," (with the telling of Isaac at eighteen made to follow what has been reported of him at twenty-one and after) can set the reader at a vantage point for sightings in both temporal directions. Thus the fictionist who rearranges chronology so that the story returns upon itself is not necessarily capricious nor confused, but properly has in mind the effects of a subtly intricated yet powerfully integrated aesthetic construct, through the transcendent presence of memory and expectation in a human consciousness. Of course the reader will be presumed to have noted indications of chronological movement back and forth along the way. Given duly attentive reading, these indications are plain enough in Faulkner, though skimming reviewers sometimes have missed them, and having lost their sense of direction, will charge the artist with a confusion that is their own. Admittedly some of Faulkner's transitions in manipulating chronology, while explicit, are sudden and brief and must be caught on the wing; it is almost as if he is muting them in a subordination of plot elements to the tonalities of situation, for a more subjectively interfused and transcendently total imaginative effect. Perhaps the unique richness and intensity in Faulkner's novels cannot be come at by any other way than in this response of his temperament to the inclusive truth that nowhere in any life's continuity are all its conditionings and perceivings simultaneously present, while the weightiness of any circumstance is nothing fixed in its own right but only as it is determined and may subsequently be modified situationally, and so to sort out events into a straight chronological line may minimize their dynamic subjective recurrence in all their protean appearances. This deep exploring of modulations in the awareness, attitudes, and intentions of his personae is the very opposite of the random; neither is it indifference to the overt event that must structure any fiction. Faulkner is a superb fabricator of plots, but in each the scale and shaping of components keeps it adjunctive to the artist's larger concern, an evoking of intuitive response to the conscious motion of his characters in their existent reality. Thus in the closing section of "The Bear" Isaac's June pilgrimage into the doomed big woods in his eighteenth year is quite other than an ordinary fictional "flashback" to matters previously left untold for the sake of "suspense." Isaac at Sam Fathers' grave in that season stands midway between those seven November hunts, ending in his sixteenth year, and the choices he will assert on the first day that can give them a man's and an heir's independent authority. Meanwhile, the narrative pause is also a point around which there orbit Isaac's slight but significant gestures that dimension his whole story. There is his back turned on

Hoke's junction with its raw preparations for large-scale lumbering and his steady gaze instead at the wall of forest as the
no longer "harmless" snakelike train approaches and enters it;
there is his leaving at Sam's grave the little gifts of tobacco,
bandanna handkerchief, and sack of peppermint candy,
which, with his deep sense of a wilderness full of creatures,
he knows will be "gone . . . almost before he had turned his
back, not vanished but merely translated into the myraid life
which printed the dark mold of these secret and sunless places
with delicate fairy tracks, which, breathing and biding and
immobile, watched him from beyond every twig and leaf until
he moved;" there is finally (in the manner of Sam Fathers), the
gestured and spoken salute to the snake, not only dangerous
but sinister in its real embodiment of myth, yet with its ancient
place in the self-maintained order of nature.

From this point on, with one long paragraph and one burst
of short hysterical exclamations from Boon, "The Bear" is
concluded. The incident is grotesque, and trivial in itself but
not in all that its connections imply. Approaching the Gum
Tree, Isaac hears a hammering sound; he comes into the
clearing and sees first the tree "alive with frantic squirrels" and
then Boon seated with his back against it, beating on one part
of his disassembled gun with another. What Boon cries out is
"Get out of here! Dont touch them! Dont touch a one of them!
They're mine!" It has been quizzically noted by one reader of
this passage that Boon doesn't look up to see who is approaching; actually he doesn't need to, he knows without looking, for
Major de Spain (who had got Boon installed as town marshall
at Hoke's junction) has sent him word of Isaac's coming, and
Boon has told Ash that Isaac can find him at the Gum Tree.
Boon the childlike man who "had been ten all his life" (and
whom Isaac at sixteen had been sent along with to Memphis to
make sure Boon got back with "at least some" of the suitcase
full of whisky he had been sent for) now does not look up
because he is angry with himself over his ineptitude with guns,
and is abashed before Isaac, just as he had confessed himself
disgraced when with the great dog Lion "looking right at me"

he had shot five times at the old bear in close range and missed. And as can happen in anger and shame, he declares his own alienation in telling Isaac to get out. Yet this is the Boon whom the youth Isaac has known as "brave, faithful, imprudent, and unreliable," who "had neither profession, job nor trade and owned one vice and one virtue: whisky, and that absolute and unquestioning fidelity to Major de Spain and the boy's cousin McCaslin." And this is the Boon who at the height of the hunt, when Lion has Old Ben by the throat and the bear is ripping at the dog's belly with its claws, leaps on Old Ben's back and, striking with his knife, probes until the bear falls dead; then afterward Boon will not let the doctor treat his own wounds until Lion's exposed guts have been sewed back into the quietly dying dog's belly.

Since encompassment of "The Bear" in the closure of its section 5 is neither a dramatic crux nor a consummative denouement but a diminution coming to rest upon a minor figure, any objective force can derive only from that character's relation to main aspects of the story. Yet because Boon is a subordinate he can serve the better as catalyst through his multiple connections with more important characters and events. The sight of him at the story's last moment hammering the parts of his gun against each other does more than remind of his general incompetence, and his defiance of his accustomed companion Isaac is not malicious but an old discontent with himself expressed often before in bluster. Boon's claiming the squirrels is a fierce hold on what little is left him. With the end of the hunts at Major de Spain's camp and surrender of those woods to the impending lumbering operation, Boon's scope is sadly reduced. He had been doubly secure in his status as liege man and retainer under two masters, Major de Spain and McCaslin Edmonds, and their patronage continues, but it is no longer in the hunting-camp's embracing hierarchy that gave everyone a reassuring sense of participation. Isaac had realized a phase of such a feudal structure when Boon became keeper of Lion and even had him sleeping on his bed, and the boy had wondered if this slighted Sam Fathers, who had trapped and wisely tamed the great dog to the precise degree of tempering which made him obedient without lessening his virtue, but later Isaac concluded "it had been all right," because "Sam was the chief, the prince" and Boon "the plebeian," who should have looked after the dogs. Generally this camp is a humane order; its leaders are firm but courteous, as in McCaslin Edmonds' quick consent when Sam Fathers wants to go to live in the big woods, and in Major de Spain's deferring to Boon in his distress over the injured dog.

Boon, along with the insistent Isaac, has loyally stayed on in the woods with the failing Sam Fathers to the end. Having carried out the old man's wishes for his body's exequy as by Indian custom on a raised platform, Boon temporarily resisted McCaslin Edmonds and defied Major de Spain when they approached, and in this closure of section 3 of "The Bear" was defended by the weeping Isaac ("Goddamn it! Leave him alone!") in an overflow of the youth's cumulative emotions over the multiple fatalities of that year's hunt, and no doubt a sense of the collapse of what for him had become a ritual, expressive of the mystique he had derived from Sam Fathers and had seen played out in their ways by the men who also were contributing to his maturation. Boon's momentarily turning his gun on his respected patron McCaslin Edmonds to protect the body on its Indian bier, and Isaac's weeping, cursing demand upon his guardian and always beneficent cousin McCaslin, that he let Boon alone, are plainly excesses out of their prolonged anguish over this succession of deaths at the heart of their present world—Old Ben, Lion, Sam Fathers. But McCaslin Edmonds deserves to be seen rightly too. His fearless advance upon Boon, his taking the soon released gun, and his painfully direct questioning are all well intended; plainly he is trying to help Boon assimilate whatever he had done at Sam Fathers' request. "Did you kill him, Boon?" Edmonds asks, and when Boon collapses, chest heaving, with his back against a tree, he goes closer and asks again. Boon's answer is "No!, No!" Then McCaslin, the man of unswerving rectitude and intuitive compassion, becomes explicitly the therapist, urging Boon to "Tell the truth," and adds the ultimate in sympathetic identification with the distressed childlike man: "I would have done it if he had asked me to." It is then that Isaac, perhaps too overwrought to realize what his elder cousin is attempting, possibly at sixteen still too young, or conceivably with a closer understanding that this is not the time, makes his tearful and compensatorily profane demand that Boon be let alone. It has been a brief scene but one in which all the characters are deeply etched. After so strong a consummation of Isaac's story to this point, in major ways conclusive, it may well have seemed imperative to leap ahead into section 4, beginning "then he was twenty-one. He could say it," he in the meantime having made his determinative discoveries in the McCaslin commissary ledgers.

Substantially as well as chronologically, the real finale of "The Bear" is not in section 5, its last, with the demoralized Boon's raging tantrum; thematically that is only reflective to the recent disruption of the purposeful, zestful little fraternity at Major de Spain's hunting camp. This had been Isaac's graduate school in real woodsmanship under Sam Fathers for annual sessions, winters and summers, from his tenth to sixteenth years; it also had been Boon's assured base, as a retainer yet a full participant. In "The Bear" the multiple determining crises for its protagonist Isaac McCaslin (following upon the last of the great hunts and the death of old Sam Fathers from exhaustion in section 3,) are all in section 4. They may be said to stem from his shocking discoveries in the antebellum commissary ledgers as these intensified a growing private dissatisfaction with his milieu in its variances from the simpler and unequivocal ethic inculcated by Sam Fathers. There was a kind of family shame too with his finding while still an idealistic youth that his grandfather, patriarch of the McCaslins in Mississippi, had made miscegenous use of two of his slaves, Eunice and her daughter Tomasina, which through Tomey's Terrel set going the related Beauchamp line of mixed blood. This sharper knowledge of the real world he occupied, and to which he was committed by tradition and blood at least, no doubt sustained Isaac in his more broadly based and principled rejection of the family inheritance on the day he became twenty-one. Section 4 begins with that, in the wide-ranging, severe, yet mutually respectful debate with his foster-ing cousin McCaslin Edmonds, who has kept the plantation going and held it for him. What Isaac holds to for life, how-ever, are his deepest convictions, and with a certain piety, and this a short while later surprisingly brings about a major impasse in his still-new and supposedly compatible as well as delightful marriage. In all conscience he cannot accede when his wife makes their reclaiming what Isaac considers a tainted property put to still exploitative uses the price of his holding any further hope of having a son — her emotional declaration after their making love once again being the closure of section 4.

Throughout "The Bear" the subjective factor, operating fictionally to advance the action, is shaped to realize Isaac as this story's protagonist, in such culminations as round out its five sections. There is a striking pattern here, structured with the first two as the youth's private epiphanies, the third as his most strongly assertive recorded speech, the fourth and fifth in words he hears addressed to him. In section I the boy's coura-geous solitary quest is completed by a first sighting of the legendary old bear; in section 2 he progresses to a resolutely accepted apprehension of inevitable finalities in those pat-terned November hunts. Then in 3 he is to find that catas-trophe can run beyond the implicit pathos of tragical dramas, as it carries with it his first major grief, over Sam Fathers' death, which underlies his violent outcry ending this section in defense of Boon's having carried out Sam's last wishes. Then in a greater span than the six successive years of Isaac's seasons with the hunters, section 4 extends chronologically from his disenchantment soon after by secret discoveries about the McCaslin patriarch, his grandfather, and so his renunciation of heritage at his majority, and the painful separation of minds between him and his deeply valued elder cousin

McCaslin, and ending during his early manhood in a private doom, with his wife's conditional pronouncement of what, under his deepest earlier commitments, he knows will mean a lifelong personal deprivation. At the story's end, in section 5, what has subjectively formulated itself during the youth's farewell summertime return to the big woods (a year and a half after the last great hunt there) continues only implicatively, wordlessly through the latent suggestion of Isaac's presence as a comprehending spectator and presumably sympathetic auditor despite the harshness of Boon's words. The youth's primary reaction in this final episode must have been in further realization of change and loss, through their having so pitifully disoriented the faithful Boon. Presumably Isaac would calm him down, for his own sake (just as he had understandingly and firmly looked after him earlier on their trip to Memphis to buy whisky from Major de Spain's favored distiller and get it all safely back to the hunters) and now would take him back to camp, before arbitrary old Ash lets their dinner cool. And here closure of "The Bear" can be with this minor character's uncharacteristically hostile words, for the reader already knows Isaac fully enough, and indeed through section 4 has already learned all he will know about him until in the third and final installment of the Isaac McCaslin story, "Delta Autumn," when he is encountered as an old man, still a hunter and Uncle Ike to younger generations of men, still competent and resolute among them, and now fated to be almost but not quite overset by yet another shock, on which he will utter the last word.

In "The Bear" the chronological rearrangement of the last two of its five narrative units is striking, and the artist has purposely made it plain (by resumé on page 316) that Isaac's pilgrimage, the main matter of section 5, takes place in the summer a year and a half after the great final hunt in Major de Spain's holdings in the big woods, timber rights to which he has sold this last spring, so that if those seasonal haunts are to be revisited in their primeval actuality it is now or never. Certainly Faulkner might have injected the substance of section 5 into 4, with less outright rearrangement of chronology, for though 4 begins with Isaac on his twenty-first birthday discussing his self-declaration with his cousin McCaslin, it includes flashbacks into his latter teens in the matter of his researching the commissary ledgers and then in the whole shabby-comic history of the Hubert Beauchamp cup, and even includes an arrest of chronology and a long return upon it in a remembrance mutually recognized by Isaac and McCaslin: this elder cousin's quoting Keats to perhaps help an idealistic boy of fourteen understand why he had rescued his little fyce rather than shoot at the old bear. But Faulkner has made no ordinary disposal of chronological units as between the fourth and the final sections of "The Bear," and judged for its effects rather than its conformities, it may be seen as the artist at his most prodigal, ingenious, and subtle as a deviser. Section 5 does not show itself as aimed at a typical dramatic irony, where generally the action would at least approximate the chronological as to the central character's ongoing life, but with him excluded from some part of the narrative, which the spectator remembers and can see as impending threat to a naive protagonist — whether with comic, satiric, or pathetic effect. Essentially what Faulkner accomplished in "The Bear" by chronological relocation of the matter of section 5 was a preferable apportioning of emphasis, a maintenance in its sufficient unity of the amazing plenitude and gathering momentum of section 4, and an almost lyrically sustained as well as defining and implicative subjectivity within this novella's conclusion. Had section 5 been wedged into section 4 as of its mere chronological right there, it would have been a crowding into what is magnificently symphonic as it stands, and 5 itself would necessarily have been diminished in both substance and essence and hurried beyond its widely thematic resonance and tonally effective deliberate tempo. More importantly, had section 5 been incorporated into section 4, through enough compression to admit it as a chronologically placed recollection like several others in that richly detailed narrative, then the present resounding conclusion of 4 would have offered a

perhaps enigmatic closure for the whole of "The Bear."
Thereafter the story of Isaac McCaslin, completed by "Delta
Autumn" as it stands following "The Bear" in *Go Down,
Moses,* would have summed up with somewhat augmented
emphasis how within his flawed marriage and lost hope of a
son Isaac had stoically absorbed his wife's early affront to his
declared identity and the shock to his natural expectations.
After her calculating ultimatum, her hysterical "laughing and
laughing" recognizably shows she realizes Isaac had meant it
when he said, "No, I tell you. I wont. I cant. Never"; and
added, "I cant. Not ever. Remember." Admittedly then to
have had that eerie laughter end the whole of "The Bear"
(rather than the present closure in section 5) would have made
more conspicuous Isaac's resoluteness, but as within the private context of his frustrated connubial life, and would have
stressed further his endurance of such an impasse as a continuing influence tempering the personality of the highly-regarded
Uncle Ike, while to that degree minimizing a positive stance
and force in Isaac's earlier and later years. Such added emphasis through a closure's special effect perhaps might have
led some readers to give more weight to an inhibited domestic
life as causative in at least a certain aloof passivity they variously charge Isaac with. But Faulkner's ordering of sections 4
and 5 is a precautionary balanced weighting of themes. As for
the reputable Southern man of letters who defended Isaac's
wife, whether a further emphasis by chronological finality on
what has led into the closure of section 4 in "The Bear" would
have affected his view that this young farm girl's plea was
really for stable socioeconomic values would depend on something further—how he had read the few earlier but adjacent
lines which tell of her pressing the young carpenter early in
their acquaintance about legal ownership of the McCaslin
place, retorting to Isaac's "same as brothers" of McCaslin Edmonds with "same as second cousins," but falling back to "I
dont suppose it matters," waiting, it seems, for the more opportune time after their marriage. With that in mind, her defensive critic would have to judge whether her attempt to use

connubial sexuality and Isaac's desire for a son to overset her young husband's basic and already professed and enacted convictions was acceptable—perhaps on the grounds that those who know better have a right to try to manipulate by any means (for their own good, of course) the supposedly more naive?

Even in his teens, Isaac was far from naive. Sam Fathers' conversations about the "Old People" had evoked for him in miniature an anthropological view of cultures, and confirmed him in piety all the more certain in its primitive simplicity, yet with functional extensions into the ecological long before its vogue, and in old age Isaac shudderingly predicted a decline into fatalism about that concern. McCaslin Edmonds, born in 1850 and postbellum restorer of the plantation to economic viability, had bridged that war-haunted era for the early-orphaned boy not so much with battle tales (which Isaac would have heard everywhere anyhow) but with particulars on local and familial grounds, and for young Isaac this subjectively tinged historical view was vastly deepened by those private perspicatious and disenchanting readings in the commissary ledgers. And the pragmatic McCaslin was also young Isaac's preceptor in philosophical ethics when he read Keats to the boy still bemused by his own spontaneous rescuing of the little fyce and refraining from shooting the old bear—this by McCaslin to illustrate the "truth" which is "one" and "doesn't change," because "It covers all things which touch the heart—honor and pride and pity and justice and courage and love." Isaac's instruction runs wider than this too, especially in his association with the hunters, and he knew the emancipated Negroes remaining on the place and had shown concern for their welfare—as with Fonsiba. Isaac's decisions, though formulated before "he was twenty-one" and then "could speak," were well-founded, and though provincially acquired, had a general rational applicability, for whatever that meant in a "practical" world.

A measure of Isaac is in his endurance of what men may find can be one of the costs of moral resoluteness in a perverse

context — a multidimensioned melancholy. To this Isaac coun-
terposes a stoic's temperate cheerfulness and equanimity. This
was to be briefly glimpsed in the course of "The Fire and the
Hearth," in his toleration of his young but already withdrawn
wife's sarcasm and his benevolent assistance to Lucas Beauchamp, come at twenty-one to collect his token McCaslin
legacy from its hereditary trustee. That Isaac, then twenty-
eight, is not seen at a later date (except in incidental mention
elsewhere) until he appears as an old man in the conclusion of
his life story has not only a biographical propriety but a
thematic one, in showing him in "Delta Autumn" still enduring resolutely, even in a deepened melancholy under added
disenchantment that comes cruelly near, and once more in the
guise of that interracial ethical issue he had encountered all
too closely in the commissary ledgers' disclosures about his
paternal grandfather. When in "The Bear" its section 4 carried him chronologically beyond twenty-one to the married
state ("and it was the new country, his heritage too as it was
the heritage of all" who in "sharing" become "one"), but soon
there came his ambitious wife's extortionate attempt which
evolved into rejection of the man himself together with his
hope for a son, such a personal defeat might have furnished a
sufficient denouement to an episode, yet it would have been
only a fractional one for the novella as a whole, or even within
the totality of that massive, intricate, and widely revealing
fourth section. The structured transcending of chronology in
"The Bear" distributes emphasis and modulates tone, and
makes both pace and proportion factors in the total compositional effect. That debating with his elder cousin McCaslin
over Isaac's resolve to renounce his inheritance which opens
the section is recurrent on a widening scale as a major element, after the drop back to Isaac's earlier exploration of the
ledgers. There was also his concern over Fonsiba, daughter of
the former slaves Terrel and Tennie Beauchamp, and therefore in the line of miscegenous descent from Isaac's grandfather, with this too submerging into the pure subjectivity of
Isaac's reflections; besides, there are recollections of his

mother and her brother Hubert Beauchamp and the disreputable business of Hubert's gradually retrieving the gold
coins he had pretentiously sealed in a silver cup for the child
Isaac to have at his majority—with its clutter of I.O.U. notes
almost a parody of the ledger's sober successive entries, and
also an abstract of the Faulknerian theme of latter-day pampered male weakness. Then out of the nearly 150 pages of
section 4, there is only a page for the poignant scene of McCaslin's visit offering money to Isaac in the room he had rented in
Jefferson, and two pages on his settling himself independently
as a carpenter, with a dipsomaniac old shipbuilder as partner
to teach him the trade and to be cared for and sobered up in
return. After that, a little more than four pages rapidly
comprise his meeting the girl on a farm where they were
building a barn, his entrancement in their marriage, and her
unprincipled attempt to reverse him from the pattern of life
he had chosen on principle.

Here the narrative acceleration stresses the suddenness of an
unforseen stroke of fate, showing (as Faulkner not infrequently does in his characters) that disaster is not always the
chastening of a ruthless inordinateness. Nothing was further
than that from Isaac's course of action. It had been out of
youthful shame over his grandfather's offenses, and apparently in doubt that he could contribute to real advances
toward interracial equity and peace through what might persist as a veiled feudalism in sizeable agricultural operations and
in the postbellum South's persisting and not very pliable socioeconomic structure. He acts at twenty-one, in 1888, on
grounds of ethical conviction and an idealist's intuition that
an exploitative society's squanderings of human as well as material resources would ultimately destroy it—which in his last
days he is to believe more strongly than ever. In saying all he
wanted was peace he implied that his identification with society could not be through a role as inheritor of all that his
grandfather had set going. He does not propose to drop out of
his world; to earn a useful, constructive, and honorable way in
it he will learn and practice the carpenter's trade. Then in

what apparently was complete intersexual naivete Isaac married a farm girl more shy than he in marriage's early days, yet one who bared herself to him in what emerges as a passion for conventional status, with a demand that her young husband renounce his basic convictions and reclaim the hereditary property he had resolutely repudiated. That his maintained stand costs him further connubial relations and any hope of having a son should be held in mind when judging the tinge of aloof melancholy in his further behavior, as the sobering effect of his consistency at such a price.

Though his wife's words and scornful laughter, bringing Isaac to an unforseen and personally severe and permanent impasse with what is a break in presumed marital trust, constitutes a highly dramatic closure to the last five pages of section 4 in "The Bear," this scarcely sums up that entire section, and still less the whole of his story, which has embraced, besides this searing private grief, the shaping from boyhood on of the man who cannot now yield up the sum of his convictions and purposes made clear to everyone in his actions from the day he came into his majority. Moreover, that was before he encountered this woman who loves him, but loves her own ambitions more, and as the story evidences, lets them move her to a sort of treachery. When from her hysterical dismissal, more scornful than the slamming of a door in his face, "The Bear" is projected into a fifth section reverting chronologically to Isaac in his teens, he already felt himself under the hand of a general change invading his life through mortality itself and men's abetting it in their accelerated ravaging of nature. With his mind so suffused, a sufficient closure to this section and the story as a whole is that he is known to stand near enough to hear Boon's bitter childish outcry, and will understand this is not trivial, and not really meant for his young companion of the old days, but confesses Boon's own inadequacy, now so coldly exposed in his diminished and denatured world.

Certainly Faulkner did not extend his craft into its remarkable intricacies and subtleties just to intrigue by novelty or enigma, but rather for evocative fictional effects comprised in consummate narratives. It is presumable, then, that his reversal of chronology in the last two sections of "The Bear" was carefully intended, with multiple purposes. Not only did it avoid overcrowding section 4, it preserved adequate range and allowed a more deliberate, elegiac section 5 for a younger and not yet formally and fatally committed Isaac to make his farewell pilgrimage to the doomed great woods and the grave of Sam Fathers, whose death from exhaustion following the final hunt had so darkly rounded out the youth's basically formative years. It is thus, and not in lesser guise as comedy or satire, that a veiled dramatic irony enters into the closing section of "The Bear," through its manipulation of chronology in Isaac's life story. In this summer of his eighteenth year he has behind him the sense of a curtain fallen on all those years of elated growth in a primary wisdom under Sam Fathers and by wider insights got from his elder cousin and guardian McCaslin Edmonds; and from that same sixteenth year he has held as well his private intuitions of shocking family history drawn from cryptic entries in the McCaslin plantation's antebellum commissary ledgers. But at this point in Faulkner's ordering of periods in Isaac's life, the youth may still be groping toward what the reader can be ironically certain of from section 4, the scope and depth of conviction behind the drastic self-assertion he will make on the day he is twenty-one. Yet in further irony, not even for that day could Isaac in his human trust have any intimation of a doom that will befall him maritally not long thereafter, though this too the reader has already learned from the closure of the ample fourth section, with its rapid reach into Isaac's first years after renouncing his inheritance.

Faulkner must have been certain of the rightness of ending section 4 with the wife's rejection of Isaac *lui-même*. Chronologically it is the furthest point (well into his twenties) in a story as revealed thus far, and not to be resumed until near its end in his old age. Thematically it is the most drastic emotional test that his rooted convictions will be put to. But it cannot be such a closure to section 4 as his impasse with

McCaslin Edmonds might have been, after their lengthy, strenuous, but mutually respectful argument, broadly concerned with principle. The whole import of the section thus far would have been comprehensively summed up had it proceeded only to the brief scene in Isaac's boardinghouse room when his cousin brings money, tosses it onto the bed, and goes, after succinct words between them that are full of their unyielding opposition, mutual love, and present sadness, and then Isaac is left "thinking and not for the first time how much it takes to comprise a man," himself for instance, and not only to the "astonishment" of those "who believed they had shaped him, but to Isaac McCaslin too." Closing section 4 at this point would have provided the consummative effect of an epiphanal realization which Faulkner often relied on, as in sections 1 and 2 of "The Bear," but again his instinct as narrative artist would seem, in his doing otherwise, to have been correct, for closure with Isaac's musings on the makings of a man would have been a pause in which an only recently assertive protagonist could not be left untested without perhaps stirring too much question from the reader and possibly raising a misleading doubt about his constancy in such a drastic course. Therefore ensuing events are quickly disclosed — Isaac's setting up as carpenter to certify his economic independence and for its further justification by contributing a constructive share in the economic order; then his finding a wife, his glorying in the "new country" of marriage, and finally in a most dramatic catastrophe, a real overturning, her setting the price he must refuse to pay, now or ever. In these last few pages of section 4 this movement beyond the moment of Isaac's parting from his cousin McCaslin into the variously decisive events of the several years thereafter, Faulkner's sure purpose is shown by a stylistic quickening of pace, almost into a précis, even to the extent of beginning certain paragraphs in lower case, sometimes in the midst of a syntax only remotely referential ("as a loan"), or with a narrative leap forward ("and had the wife now"). This momentum of an idealistic and purposefully oriented young life passes into his intense erotic realizations in the episode the woman arranges with quite opposite purposes. Then at its outcome her wild laughter so like weeping shows that her ruse has failed, and marks their arrival, by the separate paths of her craft and his trust, at denial and a certain isolation for them both, to which she responds thereafter with irritable spite, he with a patient endurance he is to sustain by attributing her inordinateness to her sex but also by remembrance of known love, to which his feelings remain faithful.

To have closed "The Bear" on this bedroom catastrophe, however, would have maximized a private injury and grief and muted the larger socioethical theme of Isaac's maturation and resoluteness. From the preceding chronologically projected plenty of section 4 it is known in 5 that, out of a rich though specialized experience thoughtfully responded to, Isaac will consolidate a view of his present world and its challenges to himself in it, and will resolutely claim an unequivocal socioethical status and course of action, beginning on the day of his majority. His rejection of his wife's seductive demand that they move to "our farm" shows as the obverse of what his announced and enacted rejection of that inheritance had been. His resistance to her is confirmation by severe test of the man himself as he had chosen to be and live; the major significance of his marital impasse is not so much the severe entailed losses as it is his consistency in bearing them rather than reverse himself by abandoning positive, identity-asserting principles he had accepted as the imperative from all he had derived out of the rich experiences of maturation. Purposefully though cryptically at the very opening *Go Down, Moses,* in the story "Was," its first phrases connote these factors concerning "Isaac McCaslin, 'Uncle Ike,' past seventy . . . uncle to half a county and father to no one"—this obviously prologue to the book rather than part of the short story, since the events of "Was" took place before Isaac was born and are told him by his cousin McCaslin Edmonds, seventeen years his senior. Another precursory reinforcement of major theme preceding the Isaac McCaslin story's consolidation (in "The Old People,"

"The Bear," and "Delta Autumn") occurs on two pages of "The Fire and the Hearth" which review his repudiation of inheritance, retaining only as family duty in reparation the trusteeship of his grandfather's now augmented bequest to the line he had begotten upon his slave Tomansina. These pages also mention what "The Bear" tells of in detail, how when the grandson James ran off toward the North, the youth Isaac took a third of what McCaslin Edmonds was still holding as trustee and tried unsuccessfully to trace "Tennie's Jim"; later Isaac did get her share of inheritance to Fonsiba, "free" on a farm in Arkansas, and in need, married to a pretentious impractical Northern-bred Negro. The third of Tennie's and Terrel's children Isaac did not need to look for; Lucas Beauchamp had remained in Yoknapatawpha County, and with a reverse in miniature of Isaac's decisive action, he came to claim and take his share on the day he was twenty-one. This occasioned sarcasm from Isaac's wife, which he bore "with pity for her and regret too, for her, for both of them"—he then only twenty-eight and she still younger—in a brief scene which chronologically goes beyond anything in "The Bear" about Isaac's marriage. So this too, as well as the novel's first words, stresses that factor in Isaac's experience contributive to an ironic pathos in those later confrontations in "Delta Autumn," with his cousin Roth, and with the involved woman.

At that point of latest acquaintance with Isaac, however, though experience has infused his melancholy detachment with stocism, yet it has reinforced his positive socioethical outlook, under more general aspects than the private failure of his marriage. Correspondingly in "The Bear" the addition of one more section, with that return into Isaac's eighteenth summer, may have seemed thematically obligatory to Faulkner to restore the balance of determining factors in Isaac's behavior—by suggesting those late adolescent ripenings of attitude which were shaping toward such major determinations. In the detailed narration of actual return to the big woods, with all its associations felt under the present encroachment of its certain doom, things to come are not directly forecast, and

since this last portion of "The Bear" is sustained largely in the
youth's retrospective subjectivity as it is intensified during his
pilgrimage to Sam Fathers' grave, they exist only in the
reader's ironic knowledge of them. Yet this could support supposition that Isaac's resolve to reject inheritance is forming,
and prompt further reflection that he cannot know how the
materialistic conventions he is to go against will take their
private revenge upon him through a dissembling and then
demanding wife. Strikingly then section 5 emphasizes that as
he confronts the impending, permanently decisive events of
young manhood Isaac though vulnerable will not go completely unarmed nor be totally put down.

Dramatic irony in fiction, as occasioned by readers' knowing in advance what lies waiting for a protagonist, invites their
expectations and also some intuitive speculation about what
his responses will be. It will seem obvious to most that in "The
Bear" the nostalgic melancholy accumulating in Isaac's consciousness during section 5 will be sharply added to by his encounter with the demoralized and even disoriented Boon at
the place of rendezvous Boon himself had set. But is "The
Bear" in its totality to come to its compositional fulfillment
with an arrest upon this merely ancillary character — and one
so plastic that Faulkner could reshape him to a quite different
role in *The Reivers?* It is true that sometimes Faulkner was inclined to close on a subsiding note, more impressionistic than
dramatic, but Boon's outburst is scarcely that. For Isaac,
however, it must be deeply symbolic of disintegration under
loss of an old order, and hence may be so for readers. In mere
chronology the termination of "The Bear" occurs in its section
4, with its latest as well as last event the young wife's mordant
laughter implying her realization that not even by seduction
can she turn Isaac from his chosen and declared course. Hence
it might be thought that Faulkner, in a liberal use of the dramatic irony created by the drop back into the youth's eighteenth summer, was now depending upon the reader's remembering that early in his maturity Isaac's basic resolution will be
challenged and will hold at that most crucial point in Isaac's

marriage. Certainly then the already resolute and humane youth can now deal with a distraught Boon, despite his own sharpened melancholy, and will do so patiently and compassionately. What Faulkner may have intended was that beyond the clatter and clamor Boon was raising as of the text's last lines, then, in that silence wherein any story is surrendered wholly to a reader's sensibilites and judgment, there would stand the existential reality of Isaac McCaslin, come these further steps and to this pause in his quest for self-realization under an acceptance of such verities as he has progressively been laying hold on. Access to such a conception by the reader can be aided by the light cast through Faulkner's chronological rearrangement of the last two sections of "The Bear." Seen as technique in a needed balancing of factors following that closure in section 4, the final section can also assist wider awareness of the concentrated explicitness of parts, yet in their controlled relation to total thematic-compositional effects. What the shift backward in chronology, with its largely reflective pause in Isaac's eighteenth year can do in its heard reverberations and its ironies is to evoke a consolidated sense of its protagonist that will be found consistent still in the Uncle Ike of "Delta Autumn," where half a century later new events reiterate old issues and, despite his deepened melancholy, evoke this man's reassertions of undiminished virtues.

"Delta Autumn"

Sixth of the seven units in Go Down, Moses, "Delta Autumn" is one of Faulkner's most effective fictional accomplishments. First published in Story Magazine, it is made far more than a short story through enlargement and pointed adaptation into the novel, absorbing extended connections with Isaac McCaslin's life, early and late, and echoing major themes from throughout Go Down, Moses. Structurally "Delta Autumn" is a distanced and time-attenuated, time-enhanced epilogue to "The Bear," as "The Old People" had been a closer prologue. This opening had pointed to what would fully evolve, in that the early tutelage under Sam Fathers would not just fix Isaac's skills and code as hunter but enter into his total outlook and his resultant principles of conduct. "The Bear" had unfolded Isaac's youthful proof of himself in the woods and, more weightily, his completed maturation as the precociously disenchanted McCaslin heir and as an engrossed and then thwarted husband, in the grave personal renunciations which he found a deceptive marriage required him to enforce upon himself. In "Delta Autumn" he is an old man but a hunter still, and, as the annunciatory first sentence of *Go Down, Moses* had put it, "a widower now and uncle to half a county and father to no one." Often prodigal of detail, Faulkner can also communicate through a clearly framed ellipsis. In "The Bear" section 4 had brought Isaac up into his early manhood and through his two major crises; now "Delta Autumn" finds him nearly an octogenarian, and here in his longest backward look the scanty glances at his life's middle decades touch only the few points needed to trace stages of a lonely journey through aridity and barrenness, under his wife's stubborn denial of her body and of his hope for a son. So even more than most old men, Isaac is preoccupied with memories. And as may be with those whose earlier acts have included formative discoveries and hard choices, his musings are not just a mirrored recapitulation; they become extended reshapings and shadings that gather up past events under the aspect of their overt effects and in an increased perspective.

More broadly, such a way of remembering is not unique with Isaac, even though circumstances have peculiarly constrained him to it. Its likeness is recurrent in the subjective life of a number of Faulkner's most positive protagonists. Ordinarily they do not lose themselves in passive reverie, nostalgically calling up immutable ghosts; neither do they isolate experiences and so becloud what was once an immediate reality, yet they are alert to later disclosures of further import. This awareness can be a subtle but active force in the trend of any human consciousness, and Faulkner's fictional realizations of it support the sense of a continuum of existence in which nothing is fixed nor ever wholly lost, and sometimes when strangely transformed is yet the more fully recognizable. This flows out of individual characterizations into the narrative movement, as it abounds in surprising recurrences of the familiar. It is one of those masteries in his art which make Faulkner infinitely rereadable, and is at its height of effect in Isaac McCaslin, in whom a resolute high-mindedness came to find itself not just skeptically questioned but cynically rejected by a younger Edmonds cousin, while in that changed world an old woe recurred in a new guise to test his stoic endurance. Just as in musical composition a phrase does not become motif until it is repeated, and the more strikingly so because of a modifying new context, so it is in Faulkner's fiction. The narrative's returns upon its own substance contribute to its aesthetic organicism, through intrications of character, plot, theme, and as to tone and tension, dramatic or stylistic. Details recurred to, especially over a long time span, can greatly extend the sense of sequence, connection, and effect, and within shorter ranges can make continuity fluent and enliven its motion into a degree of opalescence. As with motif in music, recalled matter in fiction can take on a dynamism which permeates its new context, while making the reiterated factor perhaps the most novel element in the passage, through the force of its further relevance. In such narrative effects as Faulkner creates them there is a mingling of imaginative appeals, as recognition is intensified by surprise and the challenge of new linkings, with their significance extended beyond origins in a primary time frame, while the conceptual is made manifest in an immediate presence, and the moment would be almost arresting were it not for its resonances and further lure.

Well along in "Delta Autumn" there comes a passage which richly illustrates this artist's skill in a purposeful employment of reiteration. The hunting party, with Isaac its customary and veteran member, have arrived under the November rain at their chosen spot in the Delta's big woods; they have set up their tents and eaten an evening meal to the jangle of some assertive talk, and then have all settled down and the younger men have fallen asleep. Isaac, still awake, lies on his back "peaceful and quiet as a child," looking up at the rain-soaked canvas "upon which the glow of the heater was dying slowly away," and perhaps it is that image, here in the big woods, which turns his mind back to his initiation as a hunter. Sam Fathers, that skilled and primitively intuitive woodsman, "son of a Negro slave and a Chickasaw chief," had ceremonially marked the boy's face with the blood of his first buck, shot when Isaac was twelve, and under Sam's guidance. Faulkner has already told this at the beginning of "The Old People," and readers remembering that can see in Isaac's recalling it nearly a lifetime later its confirmation as a lastingly formative experience. Isaac now projects that realization through several stages, joining it to other incidents and realizations in a multiplying of dimensions—a characteristic of Faulkner's extensions and deepenings by repetition. Isaac remembers how, when Sam "marked his face forever," in his consciousness of that initiation he had "stood trying not to tremble, humbly and with pride too," genuinely feeling what he could not phrase till later, *"my bearing must not shame your quitting life,"* and beyond that *"my conduct forever onward must become your death."*

In what immediately follows in the text—"marking him for that and for more than that"—the "more" is given a condensed summary in the old man's musings on his life's major confrontations and how he had conducted himself in them. First there is "that day," his twenty-first birthday, "and himself and McCaslin" in prolonged debate over his refusal of his inheritance, "in repudiation and denial at least of the land and the wrong and shame even if he couldn't cure the wrong and eradicate the shame, who at fourteen when he learned of it had believed he could do both when he became competent and when at twenty-one he became competent he knew he could do neither but at least he could repudiate the wrong and shame, at least in principle, and at least the land itself in fact, for his son at least: and did, thought he had." At least, at least, at least—the phrases are like steps in a pilgrimage carried on only by the relinquishment of one desired possibility

after another. And his musings this night finish the account of
his arrival at impasse and resignation—his marriage, and his
ambitious wife's attempt to sway him, "the first and last time
he ever saw her naked body, himself and his wife juxtaposed in
their turn [as he and McCaslin had been] against that same
land, that same wrong and shame from whose regret and grief
he would at least save and free his son and, saving and freeing
. . . lost him," the son he never had. The next sentence, "They
had the house then," is one of Faulkner's elliptical transitions,
where antecedent is to be found in what follows, for "They"
are the elder hunters, Isaac's patrons in his youth, and "the
house" is Major de Spain's lodge in the Big Bottom, where
they went each November during the years of hunting "Old
Ben"; and then, the year Isaac was eighteen, he visited those
woods in midsummer alone and for the last time, before
they were cut over for lumber. But if Isaac's preceding reverie
has set his life story into the perspectives only time can give,
and has emphasized that since he couldn't "cure the wrong
and eradicate the shame" of a whole socioeconomic system, he
must repudiate it, it has also confirmed that his wife's denying
him a son had been unrelenting. Most of all, it has sounded
the theme of "wrong" and "shame" which soon is to be re-
capitulated in ways that come agonizingly close to Isaac. On
that note of a recurrent and apparently irremediable evil,
against which there seems no recourse except a stoic endurance, "Delta Autumn" continues and concludes, and with it
the three-part chronicle of Isaac McCaslin, which has preempted nearly half of *Go Down, Moses*.

Before his story's end, however, and even before old Isaac's
wakeful review of his life's decisive turns, issues have been approached and Isaac has met them still with his inbred quiet
resolution. Though the matter of "Delta Autumn," as with
earlier episodes in Isaac's life, is rooted in an account of a
hunting trip, it contains only the party's journey to the Delta
woods, their setting up a tent camp, and Isaac's first hours
there, during which his concerns with bucks, does, and fawns
are only figurative, and in an altered context from his earlier

years of hunting. Now it is a long journey (by rapidly driven cars along straight concrete highways through land cleared for its timber and then planted to cotton) to reach the shrinking area where some game was still to be found. Now two in the group are grandsons of men whom Isaac as a youth had been allowed to hunt with. And one is Isaac's forty-year-old cousin, Roth Edmonds, grandson of the McCaslin Edmonds, that "cousin (his older brother, his father too)" of Isaac's boyhood and majority. As they drive along through the November rain there is still, as in earlier days, the free and easy interruptive man-talk of hunters, but without the old tacit solidarity. In this later generation's uncertainties and restiveness some private ironies, skepticism, and even acrimony creep in. These turn on Legate's jesting allusions to a doe, one Roth "was after them nights last fall . . . that walks on two legs . . . light-colored, too." Isaac thinks to himself how last year a box of food was lost and "his kinsman had gone back to the nearest town for supplies and had been gone overnight." Isaac recalls too his impression on Roth's return that "something had happened to him." This season Roth hadn't intended to come on the trip and then changed his mind and now, suddenly stopping the car, seems about to change it again, but then says, "I'm going in. . . . Because this will be the last of it."

It develops that Roth is speaking not just about his personal affairs but about the country, as it was moving out of a decade of the great depression and Hitler's rise, and toward involvement in a World War. By his present indecision and bitterness, Roth seems like some other Faulkner characters—such as Jason Compson of *The Sound and the Fury* or Temple at times in *Requiem for a Nun*—persons in whom an element of self-loathing is diverted into broadsides of cynicism. When Legate says any dictator would be stopped "in this country," Roth, not without point, asks, "How? By singing God bless America in bars at midnight and wearing dime-store flags in our lapels?" Isaac, still of a firm mind, tells his kinsman that the country "is a little mite stronger than any one man or group of men, outside of it or even inside of it either" and that even those, including his father, who "tried once to tear it in two with a war" had failed. Roth summarizes his view of what is "left"—unemployment, the dole, with people "that wont work" and others "that couldn't work even if they would," with "too much cotton and corn and hogs, and not enough for people to eat and wear." In a way Roth's view resembles a larger pessimism which is to appear in Isaac's later apocalyptic vision of society evolving into a denatured swarm. Legate breaks in to remind Roth, "We got a deer camp—if we ever get to it. Not to mention does," and Isaac takes that cue, to assert figuratively the only moral basis for war, "to protect does and fawns." Roth reduces this almost inhumanly: "Haven't you discovered . . . that women and children are one thing there's never any scarcity of?" Isaac has not protested to his younger cousin, Roth, but it becomes more and more evident that the very presence of this childless landless patriarch of the McCaslin-Edmonds clan is felt as a reproach by the restive surly Roth Edmonds. The sensed tension between the kinsmen is set off by contrast through Legate's considerateness: he had asked if Roth's suddenly stopping the car had hurt Uncle Ike. That the old man has the younger hunters' genuine respect is evident throughout; and they still listen seriously to him on more matters than that.

As the revised version of "Delta Autumn" in *Go Down, Moses* is deepened by implicit relation to "The Old People" and "The Bear" through Isaac's wakeful rememberings after the hunters have retired, so Roth too, being already known from "The Fire and the Hearth," is to be seen in fullest dimensions under such complementary lighting, as not altogether an obdurate and cynical man. He is only so in "Delta Autumn" through rage and shame over his present impasse with "the woman." Similarly unifying connections run referentially through all Faulkner novels, but perhaps most subtly in *Go Down, Moses,* with its harmonic echoes and climactic returns upon its multiple elements, its earlier substance transposed into the modes of present situations, its essential dramatic tensings in the course of the individual life reconstitut-

ing and extending itself through confrontations with circumstance and consequence, in which change may be slow or
rapid. Something of what had been talked about during the
trip to camp is recurred to as the men eat their evening meal
in the cook tent, and there emerges not just a set piece of topical discussion but a dramatizing of individuals separately yet
contibutively weighing realities of their social order and the
beings it attempts to comprise. Between the cousins the issue is
inescapably drawn, by their opposed natures within the bonds
of blood, and out of casual remarks Roth Edmonds seems to
force a conflict. When one man says, "Times are different
now" and Isaac "quietly" agrees that "there was game here
then," Roth answers him: "And better men hunted it. Go on.
Say it." Isaac will not have those words put into his mouth, but
he takes up the subject broadly: "There are good men everywhere, at all times. Most men . . . are a little better than their
circumstances give them a chance to be." Roth is not only
scornful but abusive; if that's what Isaac "finally learned
about the other animals you lived among" so long, then his
question is, "where have you been all the time you were dead?"
This is too much for one of the men, who protests, "Well, by
God, Roth — " but Isaac remains one who can answer for himself, "his voice still peaceful and untroubled and merely
grave," to tell his kinsman that "if being what you call alive
would have learned me any different, I reckon I'm satisfied,
wherever it was I've been." From "The Bear" readers can
know that Isaac would never forget where he has been, disillusioned in youth, then stranded upon his wife's sustained
attempt to break his resolution, denied love, denied a son, yet
steadfast in his convictions. But Isaac does not explain that to
this audience; instead he listens as one of the men presses Roth
and gets his answer that a man behaves only because someone
with a badge is watching him. Isaac says, "I deny that," while
Roth's questioner carries on the debate himself, telling Roth,
"I'm glad I dont have your opinion of folks," and proceeds to
an interestingly phrased reassertion of Uncle Ike's view: "now
and then, maybe most of the time, man is a little better than

the net result of his and his neighbors' doings, when he gets the chance to be." Here again is the Faulknerian theme that sometimes virtuous individual assertions can rise above the inadequate approximations of a social order, and even if such persons cannot make a verity generally operative they can at least exemplify it — which has been Isaac's sustained achievement.

This invincible integrity in Uncle Ike which Mink Snopes as well as others could recognize at a glance was, though mildly maintained, a felt rebuke to any misdoing, and it impinges sharply upon the already disconcerted Roth Edmonds. Yet Roth cannot be judged solely by the lapse which "Delta Autumn" exposes, and his bitterness may be seen as an attempted cover for the sense of dishonor he admits at one point and scarcely conceals by his generally unabated harshness. The elements are strangely mixed in this man too, as has been seen in "The Fire and the Hearth," in the irritable patience and matter-of-fact considerateness with which Roth helps settle matters between old Mollie and Lucas during that stubborn man's gold-hunting obsession. And as in the course of "Delta Autumn" it seems Isaac is carefully probing toward a vein of integrity in this kinsman so obviously troubled by his own guilt, it appears too that for a moment Roth may be on the point of responding. As the hunters' talk had drifted on beyond whether conduct is with regard for anything more than a law officer's badge, Uncle Ike discursively refers to Roth's having said earlier that there is never a lack of women and children; then as the others listen, held by "his quiet and peaceful voice," he goes on to speak of God and his creation and man in this world, not yet "quite God himself," and when Wyatt asks when he will be, Isaac affirms in quaint phrasing that whenever there has been complete love between man and woman, "at that instant the two of them together were God." (It seems Isaac has kept intact the memory of his marriage in its ecstatic early days, before his wife's opposing herself against the man he felt himself obliged to be, and this night in his reveries he is to excuse her under the softening generalization that "women hope for so much.") But for Roth Edmonds the suggestion of a divinity in the conjoining of man and woman brings on a rejection that is also a confession: "Then there are some Gods in this world I wouldn't want to touch, and with a damn long stick," to which he adds, with a look at Wyatt, "And that includes myself, if that's what you want to know. I'm going to bed."

With Roth gone but with the others still listening, Uncle Ike elaborates his faith, and his apprehensions about its violators, in an analogy with the woodsman's status and obligation: "He put them both here: man, and the game he would follow and kill, foreknowing it. . . . But He said, 'I will give him his chance. I will give him warning and foreknowledge too, along with the desire to follow and the power to slay. The woods and fields he ravages and the game he devastates will be the consequence and signature of his crime and guilt, and his punishment.'" Then with no change of "voice and inflection" he announces bedtime and orders old Isham to have breakfast ready at four oclock. Going to the big tent, he finds it warmed by the sheet-iron heater and his old cot set up, and Roth Edmonds "already rolled into his blankets, motionless, his face to the wall." Isaac retires, knowing he would not sleep, but thinking, *"Maybe I came for this. Not to hunt, but for this."* For the old man associative surroundings and reflective remembering are enough. He lies on his back with eyes closed, isolating himself just to that degree, "while the others undressed and went to bed and the last of the sporadic talking died into snoring. Then he opened his eyes and lay peaceful and quiet as a child," looking up at the glow of the heater on the tent canvas, and falling into recollection of great days in his youth, when the peerless men who went each November to Major de Spain's hunting camp in the Big Bottom just thirty miles from Jefferson allowed him to come along with his elder kinsman, McCaslin Edmonds, and when Sam Fathers stood beside him through the stages of his basic education. In old Uncle Ike's wakeful receptiveness, and under the stimulations of life-long familiarities, his reverie runs on to his refusal of his heritage at twenty-one and then to his young wife's sexual rejection of him because he would not reclaim the plantation and install her in the big house. However, at many points the drifting associative résumé would be cryptic and even enigmatic except for remembered connections with more fully developed episodes in "The Bear," and in like manner at other points with reference to "The Old People." Thus "Delta Autumn" compositionally requires a regard for Faulkner's whole chronicle of Isaac McCaslin as a "life," a narrative continuum despite its flickering transcendings of chronology and its large ellipses, and with impelling flow and enriching resonances.

As Isaac pursues his rapid crowded recall of things long past, a shadow looms against the heater's dying glow upon the canvas ceiling, and Isaac takes it for that of the young Negro who is to tend the fire; then he sees "sharp against the red firelight the sullen and ruthless profile" of Roth Edmonds, and speaks, but his kinsman answers, "Nothing. Go on back to sleep." Isaac must have sensed an uncertainty, and as if to make way for communication he alludes to Legate's teasing suggestion that Roth had "had some trouble sleeping in here last fall too." Whatever Roth might have been inclined to say or do, he turns away from it and goes back to his bed without answering. Perhaps he had been about to make his statement and a request, but decided to wait until he was ready to leave the tent after breakfast; possibly in his troubled mood Roth stood for a moment on the verge of a confession to his kinsman, and even a plea for counsel; or he might have been about to leave the camp again this year, in some further excess of impulse. Isaac does not ponder such possibilities; he drifts into sleep, thinking of the men he had first hunted with, "moving again among the shades of the tall unaxed trees and sightless brakes where the wild strong immortal game ran forever before the tireless belling immortal hounds, falling and rising phoenix-like to the soundless guns." The phrase "phoenix-like" may recall from "The Old People" that moving apparition of a great buck a moment after an ordinary deer has been shot, and "soundless guns" has the dream-like reality of imagings on the verge of sleep.

Soon Isaac is wakened by the men's rising for the hunt; then it is Roth carrying a shotgun. He hurries irritably past Uncle Ike's question—"Since when did you start having trouble getting meat with your rifle?"—to say, "There will be a message here . . . give the messenger this and tell h— — say I said No." "This" is an envelope containing "a thick sheaf of banknotes;" again a kinsman is tossing money onto Isaac's cot, but this time the grandson of McCaslin Edmonds, and not out of concern for a cousin's welfare but as the price of his own escape from a responsibility. Isaac says "Wait. Wait," and is listened to as more than Roth's blood relative and his senior; it is the voice of one without property or an heir, yet speaking as the McCaslin, and with the manly authenticity that has made him Uncle Ike "to half a county." Now he asks Roth, "What did you promise her that you haven't the courage to face her and retract?" Roth answers, "Nothing! Nothing! This is all of it. Tell her I said No," and "was gone." His haste is shown to have perhaps more reason than just an escape from his kinsman's stern interrogation, for soon thereafter the one Roth had called a "messenger" is brought to Isaac still abed. He senses something peculiar in that Old Isham had delegated the conducting to the youngest of the three Negro servants, instead of officiating himself, but at the moment there is more to think about than that—"the woman entering, in a man's hat and a man's slicker and rubber boots, carrying the blanket-swaddled bundle on one arm and holding the edge of the unbuttoned raincoat over it with the other hand."

The scene that ensues is central and the most powerful in "Delta Autumn," and along with its immediate intensities there is a reaching back and gathering up of substance from all the preceding chapters of *Go Down, Moses*. Isaac asks the woman "Is that his?" and having been told so, offers her the envelope, saying "He left you this. . . . He said to tell you No." All the while she has been regarding him "with that immersed contemplation, that bottomless and intent candor, of a child," and now she says, "You're Uncle Isaac." Then opening the envelope and having looked in vain for anything besides the bank notes, she says, "That's just money." Isaac asks what else she had expected and she admits Roth hadn't promised marriage, he "didn't have to." But she goes on in a spill of words illustrative of what had been in Isaac's compassionate night thoughts about his dead wife, that "women hope for so much." Now this woman with Roth's baby is refining the matter to the real truth of her ambivalence—"And we agreed . . . agreed again before he left . . . that would be all of it. I believed him. . . . I mean I believed myself. . . . I must have believed it. I dont see how I could have helped but believe it, because he was gone then as we had agreed and he didn't write as we had agreed, just the money came . . . but coming from nobody as we had agreed. So I must have believed it. I even wrote him last month to make sure again and the letter came back unopened and I was sure. So I . . . rented myself a room to live in until the deer season opened so I could make sure myself and I was waiting beside the road yesterday when your car passed and he saw me and so I was sure." And "so" nevertheless here she is at the camp, as Roth had thought she probably would be.

The passage acutely realizes a conciousness in conflict with itself, in its refusal to acknowledge what it has repeatedly made "sure" of. Isaac tries to prompt her toward a clarifying distinction, asking "What do you want? What do you expect?" but she is not listening to that; she answers "Yes," while again in her eyes is "that grave, intent, speculative and detached fixity like a child watching him," with her musings now turning back far beyond her involvement with Roth, and even into the reaches of hearsay. She is tracing Roth's ancestry to his "great great *great* grandfather" who "was your grandfather McCaslin. Only it got to be Edmonds. Only it got to be more than that." This more, as she knows of it, contains salient genealogical facts young Isaac had heard from McCaslin Edmonds (as in "Was") and deciphered them further from the plantation ledgers. "Your cousin McCaslin was there that day when your father and Uncle Buddy won Tennie from Mr Beauchamp for the one that had no name but Terrel so you called him Tomey's Terrel, to marry." Isaac knows Terrel was given no other name because what was rightly his could not be allowed, he being the son of old Lucius Quintus Carothers McCaslin, by miscegenation and incest, through the slaves Eunice and her daughter Tomasina. This history had had its part in stimulating the abnegations which had so severely shaped Isaac's life, but now there is still more for him to learn, in a further compounding of the same bitter-flavored knowledge. The young woman has lived in the North, she has come back to Mississippi from Indianapolis after her father's death, she teaches school, and is living with an aunt, a widow with a big family, who takes in washings.

With that last bit of stigmatic information, a full awareness of what had been indicated by Isham's not conducting the visitor himself but sending her with the Negro boy now flows over Isaac, and "not loud, in a voice of amazement, pity, and outrage" he cries, "You're a nigger!" The complexity of his emotion — *amazement* at one more dubious situation, *pity* for the woman and child, *outrage* at another such offense by a McCaslin — sums up the ongoing ordeal that had been and is Isaac's inescapable fate. And there is to be more: the woman consents to his word for her and states a more particular identity: "Yes. James Beauchamp — you called him Tennie's Jim though he had a name — was my grandfather." "And he knows?" Isaac asks, meaning Roth (and in further amazement at this complication), to which she says, "No. What good would that have done?" She thus implies a more particular acknowledgment — how could Roth's knowing that she is of the spurious miscegenatic McCaslin branch have inclined him to accept her and the child? Seeing that she understands this, Isaac asks, "Then what do you expect here?" and she says, "Nothing," and adds that she is "going back North. Back home." While in saying she expects nothing she no doubt "believes it," yet this trip to the camp (after being passed by on the highway after having her letter returned unopened) has the aura of all those earlier attempts to make herself be "sure." The pathos of her mere silent presence in this aspect brings on the grieving tone in Isaac's response as he tells her to go, get out, he can do nothing for her, no one can.

As she turns to go, Isaac says, "Wait," and lays on the blanket at the foot of the cot "the sheaf of banknotes" she had dropped indifferently as she looked into the empty envelope and then tore it open, making indubitably sure that there was no message from her lover in it. As to the money, she says she doesn't need it, but adds what shows she feels the degrading indifference in this further gesture of rejection: "He gave me money last winter. Besides the money he sent to Vicksburg. Provided. Honor and code too. That was all arranged." The "outrage" Isaac had felt before against Roth flares again, and he must control his voice from rising as he says, "Take it. Take it out of my tent." She picks it up, and what recurs out of old Uncle Ike's complex life-long grief is "pity"; again he says, "Wait," and puts out his hand to her. "But, sitting, he could not complete the reach until she moved her hand, the single hand which held the money, until he touched it — the gnarled, bloodless, bone-light bone-dry old man's fingers touching for a second the smooth young flesh where the strong old blood ran after its long lost journey back to home. 'Tennie's Jim,' he said. 'Tennie's Jim!'"

The name is a pivot about which Isaac's most meaningful and durable memories turn. Jim's mother Tennie was the Beauchamp slave of whom it has been retold this morning in this tent [by her great-granddaughter] that she was won by Uncle Buddy McCaslin and married to the slave Terrel, who was Tomey's son by Lucius Quintus Carothers McCaslin, the family's patriarch and begetter of its genealogical confusion and shame, all of which Isaac had taken upon himself and sought to mitigate by renunciation. In "The Bear," as Old Ben had fallen with the great dog Lion fastened upon him and Boon's knife in the bear's heart, it had been Tennie's Jim who "ran forward" with Isaac, and together the two youths "prized

Lion's jaws from the bear's throat." It was Tennie's Jim who was entrusted to ride Major de Spain's mare to get the doctor for the injured Boon and for Sam Fathers, who had collapsed. When the party broke camp, Tennie's Jim stayed behind with Isaac and Boon to look after the exhausted Sam Fathers in his cabin and to tend its fire day and night; but then when he saw how things were going it was Tennie's Jim who on his own initiative took the woodshorse and rode in to report to McCaslin Edmonds and to come back with him and Major de Spain to settle properly the vexatious matter of Sam Fathers' Indian burial.

And Isaac's memory can hold some of this history from its beginnings more formally imaged out of the McCaslin plantation ledger's pages he had read surreptitiously. There he found set down the record of *"Amodeus McCaslin Beauchamp Son of tomy's Turl ⍺ Tennie Beauchamp 1859 dide 1859"* and of *"Dauter Tomes Turl and tenny 1862," and "Child of tomes Turl and Tenny 1863"*; and then some explanation of those brevities, along with significant fact and flavor, emerged in another entry:

James Thucydus Beauchamp Son of Tomes Turl and Tennie Beauchamp Born 29th december 1864 and both Well Wanted to call him Theophilus but Tride Amodeus McCaslin and Callina McCaslin and both dide so Disswaded Them Born at Two clock A, M, both Well

Those ledger items after 1861 were in the hand of Amodeus McCaslin (the Uncle Buddy of "Was" who had won the slave Tennie from Hubert Beauchamp at cards, after which she was *"Marrid to Tomys Turl"*); in 1864 the twin brother Theophilus McCaslin was gone to the war as a cavalryman, and only thereafter did he marry Sophonsiba Beauchamp and father Isaac, in 1867. Evidently then James Beauchamp, born at the end of 1864, was the fourth offspring of Terril (Tomy's Turl) and Tennie, but the first to survive. The first son, named Amodeus, had "dide" in 1859, the year of his birth; the second, in 1862, a *"dauter"* and evidently named Callina [Carolina] presumably died in infancy; the *"Child"* in 1863 seems not to have lived long enough to be named, and in those starved times may have been stillborn. It is this succession of losses which Uncle Buddy could have used to *"disswade"* them from naming the fourth child Theophilus [and presumably McCaslin], they having *"Tride Amodeus McCaslin and Callina McCaslin and both dide,"* and hence the avoidance of whatever might bear the trace of a family curse; instead the emergence of James Beauchamp, with reinforcement by a middle name, Thucydus, nominally this child's great-grandfather, a slave, husband to the unhappy Eunice, and according to the ledgers, father of her daughter Tomasina, whom actually old Lucius Quintus Carothers McCaslin had begotten, and on whom, his own daughter, he was to beget Tomey's Turl, whose parentage the falsified ledgers had also attributed to Thucydus, saddling him with the McCaslin's incest too. Yet in the same old entry there was the added phrase, *"Fathers will,"* and Isaac in his youth had known it included a thousand-dollar legacy to the son [Tomey's Turl] of "an unmarried slave-girl," and by adding that piece to the puzzle had put together the whole somber story of his family's secret dishonor, leaving himself stunned, thinking bitterly that not only had this earlier cash settlement been *"cheaper than saying My son to a nigger"* but that this son was by Tomasina, *"His own daughter. His own daughter"* by miscegenation with Eunice, purchased carefully under slavery for sexual use.

Terrel (Tomy's Turl) had never collected that legacy; it had been added to for his children by Isaac's father and Uncle Buddy, and certainly the appearance at the hunting camp of Terrel's great-granddaughter must have turned the old man's anguished mind back to an entry he himself had made in the McCaslin plantation ledgers in 1886, when he was not yet twenty-one. The birthday referred to there shows the subject to be Tennie's Jim, whose disappearance from the realm of the McCaslins and of *Go Down, Moses* it records, while incidentally revealing something of young Isaac's deep familial concern and scrupulosity:

Vanished sometime on night of his twenty-first birthday Dec 29 1885.
Traced by Isaac McCaslin to Jackson Tenn. and there lost. His third of
legacy $1000.00 returned to McCaslin Edmonds Trustee this day Jan 12
1886

All that history and much more could have flowed through old Uncle Ike's mind as he briefly touched "the smooth young flesh where the strong old blood ran," in this granddaughter of the Tennie's Jim he had "lost" in Jackson, Tennessee in 1886. Now James Beauchamp is found here in this his great-grandchild of mixed descent, repudiated by a father who is great-great-great grandson of old Lucius Quintus Carothers McCaslin, whose unruly blood has come down directly for six generations to this infant, through two separate lines, white and black, and lately with compounded dishonor to the McCaslin name, even though it had "got to be Edmonds," through the married sister of Uncles Buck and Buddy.

"It's a boy, I reckon," says Isaac. "They usually are . . . ," and the nameless young woman says it is, and "just for an instant" seems about to uncover the child's face, "But she did not." The contact with old Uncle Isaac has been not only too tenuous but too strained for them both; her extensive knowledge of the family, like her connection with one of its members, is not legitimatized, and with her obvious sensitivity as well as intelligence she certainly was aware of Isaac's deep distress beneath his exacerbation. So she turns to go, having picked up Roth Edmond's money as Uncle Isaac told her to, but "once more he said Wait," and directs her to take down the hunting horn (covered with buckskin and bound with silver) that hangs on a nail on the tent pole. (It is "the one which General Compson" — who in his life had accorded the youth his patronage, and in Isaac's troubled young manhood his trust — "had left him in his will.") Had Isaac had a son, no doubt this heirloom would have come to him; now Roth's son, the great-grandson of Tennie's Jim, is to have it, and Isaac's proffering it is a gesture of affiliation. In what woods this child in his youth may sound this old hunting horn and to what end is not to be conjectured; yet as with many objects made symbolic by association, its very inutility enhances its significance, while in this instance certainly it serves the giver more than the receiver. The woman thanks him, and now Isaac knows "his voice was running away with him and he had neither intended it nor could stop it." He tells her to go back North and marry, a black man, and adds his general view: "That's the only salvation for you—for a while yet, maybe a long while yet. We will have to wait." By that "we" he identifies himself with mankind and with this woman's plight and her child's future. Yet she does not welcome it, especially as he goes on to say she could thus "forget all this, forget it ever happened, that he ever existed." As he sat there in his huddle of blankets "she blazed silently down at him," and then subduing that flash of outright anger and standing "in the gleaming and still dripping slicker, looking quietly down at him from under the sodden hat," she said, "Old man, have you lived so long and forgotten so much that you dont remember anything you ever knew or felt or even heard about love?"

The passage can be made too much of; it should not be disconnected from the total situation and the characterization of the woman herself, nor should it be extracted and disjunctively applied to Isaac. She is in the midst of an acute crisis, and for the present it has not let her off from repeated attempts to "make sure" that what she may "expect" will or will not come up to what she "wants." There is both prudence and probability in Isaac's suggestion that she can move beyond this impasse between a recurrent hope and its fixed denial. But Isaac (like many when they try to console and to reorient the disconcerted) extends a substitute hope even more tenuous, that all will be forgotten, the episode itself, the lover's very existence. Her answer, while an outright reproof, also suggests a real incredulity that even age and its forgetfulness could remove anyone from remembrance of love. The implied idealism in her question has its antithesis not in Isaac's "outrage" but in what was its object, Roth's careless wronging of this woman and his cynicism about personal relationships and human conduct in general, as when at supper the evening before he declared men's behavior is restrained only by knowledge of a man with a badge watching. (That there is some validity in all these three persons' separate views sets this narrative beyond didacticism, presenting each character through ideas that are not abstractly detached from a unique temperament but reveal it situationally in motion. This is exemplary of that intentness upon existential individuality which enables Faulkner to make conceptual material dramatic, and give weighty issues a fictional hold and unfolding.)

In this story's great central scene the last word was the woman's. Having so spoken of love and forgetfulness, "she was gone . . . and once again the tent held only silence and the sound of rain. And cold too: he lay shaking faintly and steadily in it, rigid save for the shaking." Not that it need be thought the woman's parting question had shamed him; out of his transient early experience of sexual love and the strained but not unconcerned relationship that endured beyond it till his wife's death, Isaac has held to a diminished but positive concept. During the wakeful night thoughts that had turned back to his youthful seasons in the big woods, and their finest hours in sterling company, there was also that part which summed up out of his ill-starred marriage a preserved knowledge of love and a woman, with that special form of constancy which consists of understanding and remembering. Throughout the condensed subjective passage, vibrant like the silences of the deep woods, those perceptions had been made explicit and his experiencing them is cryptically epitomized. Two losses of love are acknowledged; the first was early in their marriage, when his wife had made her fullest physical appeal to him but tied a further granting and hope of a son to demands he could not accede to without betraying his convictions; the second loss was at her death, after the years he had "lived with her," and this in the knowledge, despite their divergence, that "she loved him."

A glimpse of what that frustrated conjugality had been like may be found in "The Fire and the Hearth," when Lucas

Beauchamp at twenty-one comes to claim his McCaslin legacy from its trustee, Isaac. (This money—which Tomey's Terrel had never claimed and which Tennie's Jim had left without claiming—Lucas is now as prompt in demanding as Isaac had been seven years earlier in repudiating the whole inheritance and all the works and ways of the McCaslin patriarch.) Isaac's wife, "a young woman then," has announced Lucas with ironic reference to the larger McCaslin inheritance Isaac had refused, and her "tense bitter indomitable voice" and facial expression Isaac well knows and accepts "with pity for her and regret too, for her, for both of them." At twenty-eight, though resigned to their differently prompted, mutually endured incompatibility, Isaac compassionately holds to what remains in their hampered relationship. On that same day when Lucas at twenty-one came with his demand and Isaac as trustee patiently showed him how to put his newly received legacy into a bank account, Isaac as husband was privately consolidating his view as to the "pity and grief" of his marital situation: that "it was all right" if "husband and wife did not need to speak words to one another" over their differences because "they had touched and become as God when they voluntarily and in advance forgave one another for all that each knew the other could never be."

Half a century later old Uncle Ike, "a widower now . . . and father to no one," is trying to convey to younger men a mystique of passage by way of loving sexual relationship into a transcendent state of being, one wherein he had known mutual forgiveness to be an attribute. (When Isaac told his hunter-companions that "every man and woman," in the fulfillment of their coming together, are "God," that is perhaps less hyperbolic in essence than as to its commonalty. He himself having known unforgettably this fullness of experience, like the benevolent idealist he is—and perhaps like Faulkner—he attributes such capacity for realization and openness to revelation to all fellow-beings.) As Isaac's quaint but apt definings suggest, their interchange of absolution was in a bond paradoxically affirmed by their recognizing each other as of different natures. Reciprocation as the mode of physical love thus had entered also into something more constant; they had maintained a marriage by personal conciliation in the face of the conceptually irreconcilable. Each having been sharply hindered had endured deprivation—property and status for her, fatherhood for him, and presumably conjugal passion for them both—yet compassion had remained. It is thus that the aged and now solitary Isaac in his nocturnal reverie can feel he had lost his wife more than once, since after her refusal of herself to him she had remained with him, and even in her irritability under the strain of their separately necessitated, mutually contrived frustrations, she had "loved him." Indeed, had Roth's mistress stayed for an answer to her scornful question, Isaac could have told her more about remembered love and its proliferations of unforgettable human insights than could be understood by anyone so young and still so suspended in an immediate ambiguity and the most private of sorrows.

As "Delta Autumn" approaches its concluding episode, after the departure of the woman and child whom Roth Edmonds had rejected, it might be sensed that so too Isaac's wife had lingered, waiting through the years to "make sure." Though it takes more than two instances to constitute a law of nature, in his encounter with Roth's deserted mistress Isaac might at least have recognized further illustration of his recent night thought that women never relinquish the belief "that anything within the scope of their passionate wanting is likewise within the range of their passionate hope." This view, extracted in essence from a melancholy life of acute human deprivations to be endured by resignation but without loss of compassion, must have echoed in his consciousness as he had tried to lead the granddaughter of Tennie's Jim to distinguish between what she wanted and what she could expect; and her self-deception exposed in those successive maneuvers to "make sure" was enough to disconcert Isaac through associated recurrence of an old anguish at the heart of his own life.

With her gone, Isaac lies back on his cot "the blanket huddled to his chin and his hands crossed on his breast," trembling not just in the chill of the rainy November morning but in a crisis of comprehensive realization. This finds its presentment in a characteristic Faulknerian vein, the evolving history of his region and its accelerating absorption into the nation's ominous trends, raising in bitter caricature the specter of a drifting materialistic heterogeneousness:

This Delta, he thought: This Delta. *This land which man has deswamped and denuded and derivered in two generations so that white men can own plantations and commute every night to Memphis and black men own plantations and ride in jim crow cars to Chicago to live in millionaires' mansions on Lakeshore Drive, where white men rent farms and live like niggers and niggers crop on shares and live like animals, where cotton is planted and grows man-tall in the very cracks of the sidewalks, and usury and mortgage and bankruptcy and measureless wealth, Chinese and African and Aryan and Jew, all breed and spawn together until no man has time to say which one is which nor cares. . . .*

From this Uncle Isaac's mind drops back to the mystical foreboding he had uttered similarly to the other hunters the night before: "No wonder the ruined woods I used to know dont cry for retribution! . . . The people who have destroyed it will accomplish its revenge." In his devout belief that God is not mocked, that whatever the seed sown it will spring up anew in its kind, he apprehends beyond simple ecology that ruthlessness, in all forms from a hardened indifference to the entrepreneur's calculated exploitations, will eventually bring down a society's shaky expedient improvisations upon its own head.

A reader who has followed out Faulkner's whole design knows from "The Bear" that Isaac's use of the word nigger is still (in 1940) merely colloquial and suggests no derogation or even a mild condescension; neither can Isaac's reaction to miscegenation be taken to mean a notion of racial superiority. Indeed, a part of what had shocked him in the plantation ledgers was discovery of his grandfather's arrogant assumption of chattel status for the carefully selected, expensive young female slave Eunice. Yet as for his grandfather's begetting

"Tomey's" Terrel on Tomasina, at first the idealistic youth had tried to imagine some human mitigation, in that for the lonely widowed old man *"there must have been love . . . Some sort of love"*—thus approaching the concept of reciprocal acceptance of differences such as Isaac is to discover in quite another guise through his own marriage. But then for the inquiring youth the old ledgers' puzzle pieces had suddenly locked together, and he realized Tomasina was his grandfather's daughter by Eunice, and hence came Eunice's suicide, hence his grandfather's bequest to Tomey's Turl, the son-grandson, by double miscegenation and by incest, whom the McCaslin would not acknowledge, and so made the ledgers attribute the fathering of both Tomasina and her child Terrel to the slave Thucydus. Then when as an old man Isaac tells Roth Edmonds' mistress it will be "maybe a long while yet" before there can be a mingling of bloods in marriage, he adds what allies himself with both races in that future coming together: "We will have to wait." Nevertheless, as for "now" in 1940 in the United States, and on a more general, impersonal basis, old Isaac is revolted by a nightmarish apprehension of what is to come within the nation's materialistic scramble and cultural diffusion and leveling-off, as "Chinese and African and Aryan and Jew, all breed and spawn together until no man has time to say which one is which nor cares."

This cannot be called mere racism, to which there is no inclination in Isaac. Indeed, he had been shaped and guided from boyhood on by the revered Sam Fathers, a man of three racial lines, son of a Chickasaw chief and a quadroon slave woman. Conceivably what so phantasmagorically moves Isaac in the aftermath of his agonizing encounter with Roth Edmonds' mistress may be a kind of instinctive folk prudence which would caution any tentatively stable societal group to rest in its present approximations of order without risking the strain of added factors, especially those most apparently even if superficially discrete from a current pattern of familiarities and mores. Such instinctive reaction can and does exist in modern societies, and in forms too deeply and positively

derived for a simple labeling as racism or religious or class
prejudice — though often it is superficially left at that, even by
some who profess to be dealing with it correctively. At that
point in old Uncle Ike's traumatic experience and resultantly
fantastic vision, what he flinched at was not the future intermingling of races in itself but the lack of care about wasted resources, not just ecological but human, as in the special and
even uncommon cultural values, inherent and potentially
operative in many still distinct groups, classes, and kinds of
people, with certain particular concepts set forth and validated by the lives of those adhering to them. Isaac's saying the
generations would "have to wait" for full racial integration,
including unquestioned intermarriage, is only relatively opti-
mistic; he seems to see that it or any other such advances
would require a precondition paradoxical in itself — the evolving of societal aims which are rational and dynamic yet not
preclusive of mutual allowance for all those differences which
can cease to be separative when they are recognized as distinct
manifestations of infinitely various human vitality and creativity. Faulkner's conceivings here may seem to be a long way
ahead of not only some sentimental liberals but many sociolo-
gists.

What is explicit throughout Isaac's life as his humane
regard for his fellow-beings and his troubled concern for a
maintained equity, honor, and accommodation among them
is also implicit in Faulkner's treatment of many of his most
highly individualized characters. Their singularities are not
made into oddity but suggest a convincing animation as social
beings in the various stresses and realizations of ongoing
human involvements. In fiction generally idiosyncratic characterization when closely geared to role is a potent factor in a
narrative's movement and evolution, and Faulkner excels in
putting this potential to dymanic use. In this aspect, what is
perhaps most remarkable throughout his work is the intricate
yet fluent blending of the dramatic and the psychological,
societally and subjectively. Typically the action is briskly and
vividly conveyed, but the actors' interpersonal experiences are
often intensified by transmission through the accompanying

movement of some key figure's intuitive observations and secret consciousness, supplementing overt matters by unique responses which give a large containment and provide theme with its core. Ultimately of course all effects stem from Faulkner's organic art, but here, for a representative instance, the realization of James Beauchamp's granddaughter as a character is not only in her speech and manner but through Isaac, both by his direct exchanges with her and in his constrained reactions. The somber issue's acuteness and the painfulness of the instance both find a universalizing antiphony in Isaac's private and apocalyptic lament. Substance such as formerly the classic chorus and conventional soliloquy added to imaginative works as complement is drawn here into a sustained mingling, synthesized into a more potent unity, in this advanced fictional mode of which Faulkner's art is a particularly brilliant instance. "Delta Autumn" is only one exemplification of it, but strikingly so, as through the racked and shaken but still steadfast mind of old Isaac McCaslin narrative continues the thrust and increasing momentum of "The Old People" and "The Bear" and gathers up a life in its fidelities, recurrent ordeals, and stoic resignation.

In "Delta Autumn" the proportioning of episodes (or more subordinately of "scenes," in the dramaturgical sense) and the variation of intensity in their successive climactic waves are clear illustrations of Faulkner's judicious flexible craftsmanship. The long trip by car through the November rain to the Delta woods for what deer hunting is left gives a somber tinge, and Roth's sudden indecision about continuing with the others leads into oblique remarks about his pursuit of two-legged does the previous season. The hunters' talk at supper is a contest moving across two sectors; further slyness at Roth's expense arouses his bitterness, which he extends in both sociopolitical cynicism and self-derogation, while that and the others' excursions into ethics by way of the woodsman's code and the game laws evoke Isaac's consistent assertion of principles, which holds attention and draws a degree of assent. Echoes of that ranging and sometimes contentious discussion

prompt Isaac's wakeful reverie in its return to his chief points
of reference: his entry into woodsmanship as craft and piety
and arena for life-long testings and realizations, his conscientious dissociation from his McCaslin heritage, and his connubial love frustrated but not effaced by clash of wills, over
irreconcilably different values. All this prepares for the narrative's central and most fully developed episode, his encounter
next morning with Roth's mistress. As on the night before in
the hunters' talk, here too this experience of Isaac's is dimensioned to encompass the interlocking issues of his life. Roth
McCaslin's clandestine use of the woman and his harsh
abandonment of her and the child replays in modern dress
and five generations later old Lucius Quintus Carothers Mc-
Caslin's more outright and fatal offenses which, as traced in
the ledgers, had turned young Isaac against a corrupted system that purgation by war and the palliative of emancipation
could not wholly set into a just order, especially while in larger
ways the deterioration of an unsound society was being extended and accelerated. This portentous appearance, compounded of histories private and societal, illustrated anew
from within the McCaslin clan and also by what seemed to
Isaac the disordered twentieth-century drift of the whole
nation, becomes in the end the most persuasive apologia for
young Isaac's sensitively prescient refusal of his McCaslin inheritance. Given rejection as the only sure weapon for one
man's resistance to corruption, a life-long constancy to principle under continuing stresses becomes the badge of his
honor.

With the woman gone and Isaac lying chilled by more than
the dank November weather and an old man's bodily debility,
the newly suffered knowledge of his kinsman Roth's wrong-
doing had sunk into Isaac's wider grief for the ravaged Delta
and all that such continuing trends forebode. Here the story
could have closed as if on a drum roll and cymbal clash in that
signaling of fatal convergence between human excesses and
natural law, according to which the offenders become their
own executioners, under a revenge accomplished by inevitable
consequence. However, in Faulkner's narrative art closures

usually tend instead toward either a reduced intensity and a tonal diminuendo, and even a distancing by delegation to minor characters, or, as in this case, by closer focus and a more direct conveyance. Evidently quite well aware of the momentum and sonority his climaxes often reach, this judicious artist inclines to avoid the shock effect of abrupt finalities, and even though the terminating matter is sharply conclusive, its narrating may be modulated toward muted resolution with an almost severe simplicity. This is definitely so in the twenty lines which make up the last episode of "Delta Autumn."

Some one enters the tent, and the darkly musing Isaac opens his eyes. It is Legate—the hunter who had been considerate of the old man, asking if he had been hurt by Roth's sudden stopping of the car on the way in, later (in vain) urging Isaac to stay dry and let the younger men put up the camp tents in the mud and rain, and telling the others at four next morning to "let Uncle Ike sleep" because "he aint got any business in the woods this morning"—this probably not just to keep the old man from overexertion, but to avoid his exposure to worse than weather, the sight of Roth hunting deer with a shotgun. Now Legate is looking for Roth's knife; they have "a deer on the ground." Isaac, having seen the shotgun and reproved his kinsman when he stopped to leave the money and the message for the woman, now asks, "Who killed it? Was it Roth?" Legate, raising the tent flap to go, says, "Yes," and Isaac says, "Wait," and rising on his elbow, asks, "What was it?" Legate, pausing beneath the lifted tent flap, "did not look back" as he said, "Just a deer, Uncle Ike. Nothing extra." This brief answer, made "impatiently," is obviously evasive, but the further attempt to spare Isaac is futile. Then Legate

was gone; again the flap fell behind him, wafting out of the tent again the faint light and the constant and grieving rain. McCaslin lay back down, the blanket once more drawn to his chin, his crossed hands once more weightless on his breast in the empty tent.

"It was a doe," he said.

If there were to be an effigy of Isaac McCaslin—represented as postulant confirmed by Sam Fathers, as abdicator from patriarchy, doubly bereaved of one wife, an anchorite, "and uncle to half a county and father to no one"—it should be shaped to this closure, in this death-in-life but also as of a stony lifelong integrity.

Isaac's last recorded words are merely a recognition, not a consent, and they imply a further judgment consistent with his principles. In its simplicity this pictures a stoic calm, following the storm of his outrage over Roth's ruthlessness toward the woman and his child by her, together with the vision it projects of a collapse of societal values. Even more than for most solitary men deprived of love, there has been for Isaac as he approaches his end a loneliness of utmost severity. An abiding human relationship is the needed complement to the "freedom" Sam Fathers had given him; that freedom at least has endured as worth having, a resolute self-possession under the auspices of trusted principles, and while these in Isaac's case were circumscribed as of time, place, and a particular practice, their force is extended in that, as with any virtue even the most simple, they served to validate and enjoin idealism. Yet as Isaac learns (like many other Faulkner characters, and like aspirants in real life) no one can completely transcend circumstance, one man's repudiation of evil cannot prevent another's falling into it, nor is any man's ideal necessarily another's salvation. "Delta Autumn" elucidates what Isaac's consistently sustained resolution has cost, in a knowledge of evil that alienates him from his McCaslin heritage, and by the impasse of his marriage, and through his growing disenchantment and apprehension over the present tide of human affairs. This (though he still trusts to widespread individual virtue) has set him at a cautious distance from his fellows, but has not alienated him or them. As an old man approaching decrepitude he is no mere hanger-on in the company of hunters, but takes his part in setting up camp, and in his own right he is the unpretentiously firm spokesman of the old values, one in whose presence fallible younger men must at least pause to listen, and some to give assent.

In the finality of his austere composure there is one frequent element of melancholy he need not suffer; he shows no regret for any road not taken. Hence his quiet and even cheerful assurance; he for one is not disconcerted as Roth was by an ambivalence that runs to harshness against himself as well as the world.

The evocation of Isaac McCaslin as a fictional persona, emerging and rounding itself out in the triptych of "The Old People," "The Bear," and "Delta Autumn," is one of Faulkner's most remarkable achievements in its consistency and cumulative force. Beyond largely local containment and referent groundings in five generations of family and regional history, Isaac's story reaches further backward and forward, into lore and augury. It channels a torrent of events and convokes striking individuals in unique situations, yet all this is conveyed in essence through Isaac's alerted discoveries and principled determinations over a span of more than seventy years. Boy, youth and young man, and old man, Isaac in his being and becoming is the same and not the same, faithful to himself in the midst of changes wrought externally upon him. It is the subjective reality of this modest but sturdy protagonist which sustains the regionally and racially conditioned socio-ethical themes that run throughout this life story in a multiplicity of strenuous events and their impassioned enactors, with a plenitude of effects, in climactic surges, and with all the momentum of urgent human concern.

Much can be discerned more plainly about Faulkner's full intentions for "Delta Autumn," in itself and as terminal chapter in the saga of Isaac McCaslin, by comparing it as it stands in *Go Down, Moses* with a shorter and simpler version which appeared, under the same title, in the May-June 1942 issue of *Story*. In its definitive form, "Delta Autumn" is made to merge more explicitly into the total pattern of Isaac's life, drawing particularly upon major revelations and crises in "The Bear"—woodsmanship as paradigm of the ethical, the land as providence and inheritance, anomalies in a biracial society, stresses in marital love. In the *Story* version the man who leaves money and the word "No" for the woman whose child he had fathered is not Roth Edmonds but one Boyd, flatly characterized as ruthless in his use of "animal, machine or human," and the woman, though she does have some Negro blood, is not the granddaughter of James Beauchamp. Thus this "Delta Autumn" evokes no ghosts out of the plantation ledgers through recurrence of infamy within the McCaslin clan; the woman has no hereditary right nor evidently any knowledge out of which to call the old man Uncle Isaac, nor has he any reason to touch her hand and murmur "Tennie's Jim" or in the end to give her General Compson's hunting horn as heirloom and perhaps amulet for this child. Nevertheless in the simpler magazine version Isaac is moved to compassion and anguish, thinking as to racial separation and tension that *"Maybe in a thousand or two thousand years it will have blended in America and we will have forgotten it. But God pity these."* In the narrative's version in *Go Down, Moses*, with the intensifying fact that the offender is Roth Edmonds, the passage becomes *"Maybe in a thousand or two thousand years in America. But not now! Not now!"* In both versions of "Delta Autumn" it is evident, from the "voice of amazement, pity, and outrage" in Isaac's recognizing the woman is of Negro blood, that his distress is not primarily over miscegenous cohabitation in itself but the man's outrageous ruthlessness and irresponsibility, and the pity of the resultant social dilemma under existing mores. The story as revised to merge with "The Old People" and the much more extended matter of "The Bear" takes on greater thematic force and not only shows another facet of the latest McCaslin heir, Roth Edmonds, already well dimensioned in "The Fire and the Hearth"; above all it sums up and conclusively embodies the stringencies of Isaac's life and his hardihood. This last revealed episode, by its connection with other parts of *Go Down, Moses* and echoes of its themes, also clearly shows why Faulkner wanted the book to be called a novel and considered as such.

Specifically the most significant distance between the full realization given "Delta Autumn" in *Go Down, Moses* and the earlier *Story* magazine version is that there the widowed old

Isaac had been allowed "a wife and children once though no more." In the book, "Delta Autumn" treats his marriage by the light of that early but decisive clash between their wills which is the climax of section 4 in "The Bear," and which gives fullest meaning to the characterization of Isaac as "father to no one." This if recalled should weigh in estimating Isaac as he stands resolutely cheerful but at a certain distance from more fortunate men who have not "lost" a wife twice, the first time early in an ongoing marriage. It is something the old man had mused on in his reverie the first night in camp and defined with charity toward his wife, under the depersonalizing assumption that women "hope for so much." Another difference in the story's two versions is that the supper-table conversation (almost five pages in the book) does not occur in the magazine text. While its insertion adds realistic substance, it also widens thematic scope, by references to right conduct and to love, in terms of game laws and conscience, and with Isaac's word on the nature of the whole creation and the Creator's entrance into it (though not in terms of Christian theology) through love between man and woman. In the scene at table the strain of next morning's somber events is presaged through Roth's uneasiness, with its compensatory harshness and cynicism, and Isaac's equally forceful, utterly opposite, but calmly expressed principles and sentiments, which soon are to be put to their severest trial since his youth and young manhood.

It might perhaps be suggested that in the *Story* version the matter of interracial sexual union with its responsibility for offspring is given wider representativeness by keeping the two parties to it simpler characters than they become in *Go Down, Moses*. In this latter, through their bringing together the legitimate McCaslin-Edmonds line and the illegitimate, originally miscegenous and incestuous McCaslin line passing through the slaves Eunice and Tomasina to become Beauchamp, the plot must turn upon Roth's presumably chance encounter with this particular woman. Yet that is not incredible, and Faulkner, with his fine sense for selection, avoids presenting the incident or anything of its sequel directly, letting significance arise from accident and covertness and the slow disclosure of resultant complexities and their peculiar stresses. These then take added force from their supposedly fortuitous beginning, giving coincidence an uncanny aspect as a familial fate that overshadows socioethical abstractions. In the scales of effects there is another ponderance, and as to the situation in its most acute aspect, it does not return upon Roth, whom the woman has not told she was James Beauchamp's daughter. ("What good would that have done?" she had said, seeming to echo generations of dire experience and implying her reluctant acknowledgment that if what she wants is not assured through love then it will not be.) Having left as he did, the evasive Roth presumably will never return to her, and in this tale he returns to Isaac only through the intimation that he has killed a doe with a shotgun. Thus Roth, though of restive conscience, for lack not only of knowledge but of heart has not fully sensed the impact of the situation, while he remains centrally a devastating influence in several ways. So it is Isaac who is at the historic crossroads of this hunting-camp crisis of human consequences, and not just as conveyer of money and message but the one knowing most fully the irony and pathos of this return of heritage upon itself. Thereby the Isaac McCaslin of *Go Down, Moses* is made not only a more detailed figure than the Uncle Ike of the *Story* magazine version, he is incalculably more impressive. Which may allow some specific pondering of Faulkner's creative imagination in its ongoing dimensioning and deepening of a story. In particular a comparison of the two versions may suggest Faulkner's paradoxical genius for making a narrative action more illustrative by individualization—the Shakespearian quality of lively representativeness through some conjured interfusion of idiosyncrasy and verisimilitude, the kind of characterization more tellingly achieved by Conrad and Faulkner than by Dickens, with a deploying of any character into larger and more sustained relation to evolving theme. In the great central scene of "Delta Autumn" as given in *Go*

Down, Moses, not just the events of Isaac's whole life but his qualitative experiencing of them are the roots of his present reactions, and the key of their fullest tones; and a reader who did not know and remember this context might prefer the simpler magazine version.

In the *Story* magazine "Delta Autumn," while it is established at once that Isaac has been coming on these hunting trips for fifty years, and with him now are sons of former companions who refer to him as "Uncle Ike," the narrative text from the first and throughout refers to him as "McCaslin." In the expanded *Go Down, Moses* version, though he is given his identity for readers of the book by being called "Uncle Ike," in the narrative text up to the point of their settling down to sleep he is termed "the old man," and "Old man" is what the woman coldly, impersonally calls him next morning in her parting speech reproaching him for having forgotten what love is; however, to begin with she had knowingly said, "You're Uncle Isaac." The change from "McCaslin" to "the old man" in the story's first part assumes that what has gone before (in "The Bear," "The Old People," the prelude to "Was," and a significant passage in "The Fire and the Hearth") will plainly establish that an "old man" called "Uncle Ike" is Isaac McCaslin; it also gives some stress to these scenes in "Delta Autumn" by their following so long after the sequences of a crucially eventful youth and young manhood, yet with connections that substantiate themes. Then as the definitive version of "Delta Autumn" proceeds there occurs an implicative change in references to the protagonist. Once the men have gone to bed and dialogue is ended and Isaac lies musing, "he" is a sufficient naming, but when Roth Edmonds is up and restless and Isaac rises on one elbow and Roth says, "Nothing. Go on back to sleep," then the reply is from "McCaslin," not just the old Uncle Ike whose word is respected by hunters for ripeness of experience, but the McCaslin, the voice of moral authority among his kinsmen. He does not directly reproach Roth, he simply lets him know he has connected Legate's jibes about hunting two-legged does with Roth's behavior the year before. Next morning, though, when Roth, carrying a shotgun, leaves the envelope with money and the message "No," it is "McCaslin" who asks, "Since when did you start having trouble getting meat with your rifle?" and "What did you promise her that you haven't the courage to face her and retract?" When Roth has gone and "the woman" comes—that undifferentiating reference an aspect of her desolation—it is the protagonist as "he" who extends the envelope and answers her "You're Uncle Isaac" with a "Yes. But never mind that. Here. Take it. He said to tell you No." Throughout their conversation, so racking for them both and without any recourse for either, it is "he" and "she," and after she is gone it is "he" who lies shivering in a solitary confrontation, thinking his dark thoughts about racial tensions and wrongings and the deeper darkness he had acknowledged earlier, that the "ruined woods" will have their "revenge" in a "retribution" their "destroyers" will bring upon themselves, by debasing and denaturing a whole society. Then when Legate enters the tent and rummages in "Edmonds' bed," it is as "he" that the old man asks, "What is it?" but thereafter when he is told Legate had come for Roth's knife because they have "a deer on the ground," it is "McCaslin" who asks, "Who killed it? Was it Roth?" and "McCaslin" who moves "onto his elbow" again and says, "Wait. What was it?" Finally, undeceived by Legate's "Just a deer, Uncle Ike. Nothing extra," it is "McCaslin" who "lay back down," with "crossed hands once more weightless on his breast" as he tells himself "It was a doe," out of a weighty knowledge fallen upon him through events and in stages long before he was "Uncle Ike."

In the ultimate "Delta Autumn" evolved for its place in *Go Down, Moses* the various extensions, alterings of proportion and emphasis, and heightenings of stress, and even so minute a matter as the movement from "the old man" to "McCaslin," point to Faulkner's readily associative, inventive, and broadly constructive force. And it is an illuminating paradox that the simpler version of "Delta Autumn," less potent, also seems less rapid. Given attention, the refinement by which detailed effects are made incisive, the illustration of theme by reciprocities of structure, the intensification of scene by a synthesis of issue and individual response, together with a robust realism and an adaptive style both vivid and expedite, all enter into the sustained dynamics and remarkable momentum of Faulkner's fiction. In the telling of Isaac McCaslin's whole story, man and boy, these powers are as fully evinced as anywhere (except perhaps in *Absalom, Absalom!*) and they make a corresponding levy upon readers' amply rewarded imaginations. Since the McCaslin story is constituted as a triptych, with its massive central panel "The Bear" itself divided into five sections, "Delta Autumn" can furnish a peculiarly illustrative example of how Faulkner's effects and their significations accumulate, accelerate, and compound. Those last hours concretely known of in Isaac's life draw upon the whole of it, yet keeps those antecedents subordinate to this time, this finality — as should be of any mortal still possessed of memory and actively responsive.

When Isaac at twenty-one told McCaslin Edmonds, "Sam Fathers set me free," presumably he was implying liberation from socioethical ambiguities under which even upright and humane men like this elder cousin must make some accommodations. Earlier Isaac had wholeheartedly embraced the more explicit imperatives of the woodsman's code, with the hunter's skills sanctified under a primitive natural piety. Early and late, however, he was fated to be beset by issues that ran beyond the reach of this rule, basic though it was. Still he never surrendered it. Something of his virtuosity and merit in it is suggested by a passage occurring in both the *Story* version and the final form of "Delta Autumn," at the point when Legate has considerately told him to rest and keep dry while the younger men made camp, but he "did neither." Instead, having directed the Negroes to raise the cooktent, cut firewood, and prepare supper, he went to bring the "backing and snorting" horses across the river:

He took the leadropes and with no more weight than that and his voice, he drew them down into the water and held them beside the boat with only their heads above the surface, as though they actually were suspended from his frail and strengthless old man's hands, while the boat recrossed and each horse in turn lay prone in the shallows, panting and trembling, its eyes rolling in the dusk, until the same weightless hand and unraised voice gathered it surging upward, splashing and thrashing up the bank.

Transferring this haunting image, readers might envisage something of Faulkner himself, the artist as *magister* and *magus,* explicit and mysterious in his powers, through the radiations of a gifted and intent temperament. Certainly the passage, showing a quiet strength that seems literally a virtue, related to both skill and integrity, also complements the effigy-image of Isaac at the story's end; it is Isaac's unsurrendered fidelity that requires confrontation and a stoic endurance under continuing trial.

Considering its relative brevity and simple narrative structure, "Delta Autumn" as placed and furnished forth in *Go Down, Moses* has depth and potency that must be credited to its consolidation of effects drawing their reverberance from antecedent disclosures, chiefly in "The Bear," but also from certain details elsewhere in the book. A central example is Isaac's long apprenticeship and careful initiation under Sam Fathers and then the rapid collapse of that whole structure of associations in the season when General Compson mounted Isaac in the forefront of the hunt and he and Tennie's Jim closed in to pry the wounded indomitable dog's jaws from the great bear Boon had finally knifed, for in that very action Sam Fathers had collapsed and would soon die, as did the dog Lion, and there would never be another bear like Old Ben nor those woods to shelter him, with the Big Bottom sold for lumbering. In this same period of ongoing loss the youth Isaac was to cross back over the great divide in his region's history and decipher from family ledgers an even more shocking offense than exploitation of the land — his grandfather's humanly degrading use of the slave Eunice, bought in New Orleans at a relatively high price and evidently for that carnal purpose, and then his incest with their daughter Tomasina. A despoiling of the natural world itself and an extension of that arrogance to the ruthless treatment of human beings — these are the factors, complementary in the socioeconomic order as he sees it, which had precipitated Isaac's rejection at twenty-one of the McCaslin inheritance. Thereafter it was his fate, under a recurrence of similar factors, to take an ambitious wife who having accepted him less than candidly then used her body to bargain with, leading him to turn back from a momentary surrender to sensuality and reassert his principled stand, at the price of relinquishing both conjugal love and hope of a son. And now in old age, as hunter still and faithful still to larger convictions drawing upon the hunter's unequivocal code, he encounters not just neglect of that but a kinsman's reenactment of old Lucius Carothers Quintus McCaslin's kind of ruthlessness, in a relationship with a woman whose mixed blood ironically is also of that McCaslin strain. In either version of the story the theme of an accumulated weight of sobering experience is strongly set forth, but in this concluding chapter of the Isaac McCaslin saga as incorporated into *Go Down, Moses* and linked with it, the effect is immensely intensified. This old man is he who in his youth had been Sam Fathers' disciple, had hunted Old Ben with Major de Spain, General Compson, the admirable McCaslin Edmonds, and Tennie's Jim, and having made appalling discoveries in the plantation ledgers, had renounced his inheritance and had been renounced by his wife and denied a son. Now he must see in another McCaslin kinsman not only a repetition of irresponsible fatherhood but, in the rejoining of lines generations later, a more than lifesize symbol of miscegenation and incest, and an abstract of evil grown the more monstrous by its turning in upon itself. In the series of denouements each crisis is acute, but successively they do not eclipse what has preceded; cumulatively they gather it up into the heavy darkness of one man's fate, and when Isaac told himself, "It was a doe," all the rest of it was there too.

In drawing together many strands out of other portions of *Go Down, Moses*, "Delta Autumn" not only gains significance from them but reciprocally illuminates them, and recognition of these roundings-out can be rewarding, but as the interconnections become more complex, readings need to be close and careful, with regard for Faulkner's conception of the book as a novel. There is an exemplary instance when Roth's woman, who had just showed an acquaintance with the McCaslin-Edmonds genealogy but (in the skilful narrative ordering) has not yet fully disclosed either her mixed blood or her Beauchamp connection, says of Roth, "I would have made a man of him. He's not a man yet. You spoiled him. You, and Uncle Lucas and Aunt Mollie. But mostly you." Naturally Isaac is astonished—"Me?' he said 'Me?'" Her illogic recognizably springs from a wish to exonerate the one she loves, and his wronging her she minimizes by the familiar gambit of blaming those who brought him up, and most of all the one who a decade before Roth was born had given over the plantation to the McCaslin-Edmonds line, by which through McCaslin's son Zack it had come to Roth. Apparently she knows that when Zack Edmonds' wife died giving birth to Roth, young Molly Beauchamp became Roth's nurse and brought up the motherless boy. But of that postbellum turn of the century matter so wrought with interracial tensions and so scrupulously and affectingly treated in "The Fire and the Hearth," what else is it likely she knows—even given the assumption that such a relationship as Roth's with her had included intimate confidences about his early boyhood.

If those bygone events are remembered by readers, however, and together with those the still earlier situations of Isaac McCaslin and McCaslin Edmonds as boys and in their different entrances into manhood, there might be less critical inclination to find in this distressed young woman's reproach any support for condemning Isaac's renunciation of inheritance. Both Isaac and his elder cousin McCaslin had grown up on the plantation; Isaac, child of a late marriage, was born in the big house, in 1867. His cousin McCaslin Edmonds, born in 1850, had been raised by his grandmother Edmonds, the sister of the twin McCaslins, Theophilus and Amodeus. McCaslin saw the odd life those bachelor coheirs had lived with their semi-emancipated slaves before the Civil War, and is the conveyor, from his observation at age nine, of the rampant and comic events of "Was." But in his adolescence McCaslin Edmonds had seen too the struggle to maintain hold on the plantation and secure bare subsistence for its people during the war, and then in his early manhood it had fallen to him to carry on, through the miseries of "reconstruction," holding and managing the inheritance until its direct heir came of age. Fatherless before he could store a meaningful memory of his father, Isaac has known the plantation only as once more a going enterprise, with many of its former slaves remaining and working on the land by choice and securing their supplies through the commissary administered by his cousin McCaslin Edmonds—"rather his brother than cousin and rather his father than either." And there too, as if foreordained, was young Isaac's chosen mentor, absolute in his skills and principles, the woodsman and hunter Sam Fathers, who had "belonged" to the McCaslins since his own boyhood, when he and his quadroon mother were traded to Isaac's grandfather by the Chickasaw Indian chief Ikkemotubbe, Sam's father. "The Old People" shows Sam Fathers' tutelage as the primary formative influence upon the orphaned Isaac, and this is supplemented by his cousin McCaslin, himself a hunter and a man of honor and imagination too, as when he explains to the boy the primitive wisdom and untameable conflict of bloods in Sam Fathers, or reads Keats to the youth to help him understand his instinctive reactions in confronting the great bear. Yet besides such positive influences there came upon Isaac familial shame over what the ledgers evidenced of his grandfather's compounded inhumane offenses against those slave women, mother and daughter. It was a complex heritage indeed, with its accumulated ethical enigmas more weighty than any mere administrative tasks. Extending the sense of old wrongs, there was the present sight of blacks emancipated but still subordinated, and (as with Fonsiba Beauchamp and the deluded Negro who carried her off to Arkansas) a people without a center to hold them, in a society itself increasingly disoriented under economic exploitation of both land and men.

Though from the first, Isaac was closely and congenially associated with his elder kinsman McCaslin Edmonds and though scarcely a generation lay between them, they were separated not merely by natural differences in temperament. Children of the same plantation, they nevertheless were not similarly shaped, since the years of their maturation lay on opposite sides of that great circumstantial and cultural divide, the Civil War. In the South of the 1880s young Isaac felt himself within yet not of a society presumably settled but obscurely adrift, and found himself at the threshold of decision and commitment required by a series of crucial experiences that weighed against each other. What must be seen as determinative in his choice is that to him the apparent alternatives were not equally explicit, and so he chose not to play a major operative role in a materialistic system riddled with ambiguities and infected by inequalities and acquisitiveness he could not assent to without equivocation. He did not propose a revolution; he simply elected to pay his way in the world as he found it, and constructively, with a set of carpenter's tools. Certainly his decision must have been easier since his cousin McCaslin had already "inherited," by an early impressment, the responsibility of rescuing the enterprise, and had proved himself a humane as well as judicious administrator. Thus without offense or disservice to anyone else—he had not yet married—and with what most would call potential benefit to the Edmonds line, he simply stepped aside, but now at the end of his life of renunciations for the sake of principle there appears the great-granddaughter of Tennie's Jim and mother of Roth Edmonds' illegitimate child, to charge Isaac with having "spoiled" Roth—"You, and Uncle Lucas and Aunt Mollie. But mostly you."

It is impossible to trace the descent of any such malign influence along such a route. As for Molly's alleged part in it, as seen in "The Fire and the Hearth," what had she done but nurse and nurture the orphaned child from the hour of his birth—and years later when Lucas's obsession with divining buried gold drove old Molly to think of divorcing him, the middle-aged Roth as mediator remembers her as "the only mother" he "ever knew" and one "who had surrounded him always with care for his physical body and for his spirit too, teaching him manners, behavior," giving him "without stint or expectation of reward that constant and abiding devotion and love which existed nowhere else in this world for him." Nor had there been any inherently adverse influence from Molly's son Henry, Roth's foster-brother and inseparable playmate, the two even eating and sleeping together in either his father's house or Lucas's cabin until they were seven. What marked the child Roth at that point could not have been Molly's devotion or Henry's cheerful fidelity but something larger than such comfortable domestic intimacy, and utterly impersonal, harshly emergent as an abstract interdiction:

Then one day the old curse of his fathers, the old haughty ancestral pride based not on any value but on an accident of geography, stemmed not from courage and honor but from wrong and shame, descended to him.

Though "he did not recognize it then," he acted decisively. They had finished supper at Henry's house and were to sleep there but the white boy suddenly said, "I'm going home." Henry wants to "stay here" so they can get up early and go hunting, and Roth takes the chance to say, "You can. I'm going home." But Henry says, "All right" and follows, and Roth must roughly make it plain to him that he is to remain on the pallet where they sometimes used to sleep together, and is not to get into the bed with his companion. So Henry goes to sleep on the pallet and Roth lies awake, "in a rigid fury of the

grief he could not explain, the shame he would not admit."
(That the child cannot articulate his remorse over his impulsive actions realistically suggests an ambivalence in a more
than childish knowledge of good and evil.) The pallet was
empty when Roth awoke in the morning, and for a month he
did not go to Henry's house, but then went to reestablish the
old relationship—"only it was too late then, forever and
forever too late," as the boy dubiously senses and is soon to
learn. He announces he's come "to eat supper with you all,"
and Molly says, "Course you is. I'll cook you a chicken." Roth
has seen "nothing in her face" and so felt he "could say it
almost any time now, when the time came," presumably to
admit grief and shame over his behavior. But when Molly calls
him in, the table is set for him alone, and Henry is leaving the
room; and when Roth cries out, "Are you ashamed to eat
when I eat?"—that "when I eat" subtly suggesting an uneasy
avoidance of the more direct "with me"—Henry pauses to
answer "slow and without heat: 'I aint shamed of nobody. Not
even me.'"

Those less than three pages comprise one of Faulkner's most
brilliantly accomplished episodes, epitomizing several aspects
of his genius. It moves quickly from a grave generalization into
several brief scenes that mark off a drastic transition in human
relationships; there is deep psychological penetration implicit
in its terse colloquial dialogue with overtones of complex unspoken attitudes; out of its entirety is distilled a fable of loss of
innocence with Roth's instinctive discovery of racial aloofness
and his own supposedly rightful place in the social order.
There is also, as would be in any decently inclined being—
most naturally in a child, and more constrainedly in the
embittered middle-aged Roth of "Delta Autumn"—the other
voice of grief and shame, disconcertingly bespeaking a recognized unremedied wrong. In "The Fire and the Hearth" the
man Roth is to remedy his childhood's offense and to make
ample amends to Molly, especially by his humanely sustaining
her through the ordeal with Lucas in her old age, but in the
episode between the small boys it had been Molly who must

carry on past this major turning point, Molly and not Lucas, who was not given a role in that almost ceremonial supper scene. That Lucas is not present and that the episode's closure in words and gesture is given to his young son Henry is clear example of Faulkner's sense for dramatic-thematic inclusion and exclusion, as between the obligatory or at least the enrichingly contributive and conversely the superfluous or even the incongruous. There is plenitude in Faulkner but a genuine economy too, and while a constant relevance gives pace even to copiousness, what is most typical is a pointed selectivity.

This pervades Faulkner's characterization, with theme in mind. He shows various types of Negroes in their reactings to the constant sense of racial separation, and Lucas Beauchamp's style is a confident assertiveness, carried off shrewdly but not often with finesse. Molly, in dealing with the boy Roth (and evidently in having shown her son Henry how to transcend the change in the playmates' relationship) goes beyond finesse. She not only recognizes the irreversible realities they have arrived at as of that time and situation, but with the *noblesse oblige* of a wise young matron she conducts them all through it and into a conciliated way of going forward as best they can. That neither this nor other acts in bringing up Roth have utterly spoiled him is shown in his dealings with the Beauchamps when the plantation has come into his hands; he is gruffly reasonable with Lucas, tender with Molly. Roth is no villain, he is a man of average sensuality, guilty of a not uncommon offense he is not capable of setting right, and on bad terms with himself because of it. The woman he has turned his back on has now seen him at his worst, but her verdict that he's "spoiled" and "not a man yet" is a limited judgment, scarcely borne out in the larger scope of *Go Down, Moses,* especially in that portion of "The Fire and the Hearth" where in his troubled but finally helpful dealings with Lucas and Molly he is of about the same age as in "Delta Autumn."

If as the wronged woman preposterously charges it had been

chiefly Isaac who at twenty-one had "spoiled" the not yet born Roth Edmonds by giving Roth's grandfather McCaslin Edmonds the plantation, then McCaslin and in turn his son Zack, Roth's father, would seem to have transmitted that supposed injury. However, other parts of *Go Down, Moses* show the immediate problem is not the land itself but a prudent and even piously beholden use of it, and equitable and humane relations between the races in operating it effectively as a cotton plantation, and in this three generations of Edmonds men, including Roth, have performed honorably and well. McCaslin had brought the enterprise through the dire times of Reconstruction and into a productivity that has some benefits for all, but the complexity of that and its personal stress are shown in part 4 of "The Bear," first in the detailed description of the commissary, "not the heart perhaps but the solarplexus" of the organized inflow of supplies and outflow of cotton, and more profoundly McCaslin's moving declaration that as between the races, at a full generation after emancipation, freedom is not to be found, "not now nor ever; we from them nor they from us," and he must be what he "was born" and had "always been," just as other men, including Uncles Buck and Buddy, had had to deal with what was left them, as inheritance and encumbrance. But while McCaslin Edmonds was helpfully influential on Isaac in his youth, Roth never knew this grandfather. "Then McCaslin Edmonds died and his son [Zack] married and on that spring night of flood and isolation the boy Carothers was born." Yet this birth brought him under influences more immediate and pervasive than consciousness of being heir to the plantation. His mother's death in bearing him made him *de facto* the foster-child of Molly, and Henry's foster-brother, as the two were nursed together at her breasts and were taken back and forth with her in her work in Zack's house and Lucas's cabin.

When in early boyhood Roth instinctively separated himself from Henry as playmate on equal terms, and thus "entered his heritage" and "ate its bitter fruit" as conscious member of a biracial society with a fixed assumption of white superiority, he found that this acquisition though less substantial than a legacy was of wider extent than a plantation. It might be speculated that the issue came upon the small boy too early in his isolated but intimate and privileged existence. Therein he had not been given such direction and prolonged cultural conditioning as Isaac had under Sam Fathers and more broadly in the senior but brotherly companionship of McCaslin Edmonds, and no such stimulating association with remarkable men as told of in "The Bear." However, a contrasting of the two men as they exist within Faulkner's fictional design should take account of their different times, and especially as of the South. Isaac was born two years after the war's end, Roth two years before the beginning of the twentieth century. Isaac's somewhat earlier beginnings and greater span of experience make him heir of several epochs and thus support him in a biographical role. The mature Roth in "Delta Autumn," under Faulkner's allocation of fictional emphasis, is not brought forward under so sustained a regard. Even the central matter of his secret involvement with "the woman" is not fully played out from its beginnings by the defecting offender himself; minimum fact is obliquely conveyed by Legate's jests about "doe-hunting" the year before, and by Roth's gruff hurried entrusting of message and money to Isaac. Roth does not stay to answer Isaac's question about what he had promised "her," and when "the woman" begins to speak openly to Isaac she reveals how compliant she must have been under little or no commitment from Roth. Whatever the earlier influences on Roth, certainly in this episode between them she had "spoiled" him by indulgence and self-subordinating accordance. Faulkner is not indifferent either to her or to Roth as characters, and he develops traits in each which enhance their largely implied story; yet it is, as always in fiction, a question of whose priority in which scene, and in this technique Faulkner is a superb dramatist. Elsewhere, in "The Fire and the Hearth," Roth had been represented in some detail and with nuances of behavior and mood, and not only in the boyhood issue with Henry but as a mature man,

third-generation Edmonds proprietor of the McCaslin plantation and overseer of Lucas and Molly in several creditable
guises, especially in a real devotion to his old foster-mother
and in the man-to-man tolerance he extends at the story's
close to its wilful protagonist Lucas, only to find him sobered
into moderation at last. Roth emerges as a rounded character,
sardonic in temperament, fundamentally humane, forcefully
assertive at times, occasionally as irritable at himself as at
others, but a man seen glancingly, never set forth in a sustained
narrative development, simply because "The Fire and the
Hearth" is more the Beauchamps' story than his. He furnishes
an example of Faulkner's power to project a character in less
than a sustained primary role yet as a factor and living being
in his time upon the stage. But in "Delta Autumn" any
supposed "spoiling" of him, whether by "the woman" herself
or those whom she charges with it, is not a perceptibly developed theme. His dereliction exposed there takes on appreciable weight not so much in itself and as to himself as by impact
upon the woman — in only the single scene, but illustrative and
revealed in some psychological and emotional depth — and by
effect upon Isaac, for whom Roth's indulgence and failure of
nerve are a further affliction of an old kind, and reiterate the
enigma of interracial connections, in their circumstantial
closeness and their deep stresses.

The placing of episodes and apportioning of thematic emphasis also makes evident that Roth's nature had not been
dominantly influenced by his father, who had let the small boy
live on equal terms with Henry as playmate, as Zack himself
and Lucas had done in childhood and youth. This allowed
Roth and Henry to move back and forth between Zack's house
and the Beauchamp place to eat and sleep, and they rode the
plantation horses and mules and hunted with a pack of small
hounds, and Zack had promised a gun when they were a bit
older, meanwhile according them their natural desire, "to be
let alone." Not that Zack lacked concern or directness, and he
had showed admirable coolness in the physical encounter
forced upon him by the jealously suspicious Lucas in their

young manhood (after Zack's wife's death in bearing Roth, when so much had been required of Molly with menfolks and infants in two houses to care for). The stamina they mutually proved then allowed them a degree of steady understanding and a kind of equality beyond race. The two men have made an uneasy peace, which suffices for them, but not for Roth in the course of his growing up. So he protested to his father about what Roth saw as a tolerated presumptuousness in Lucas, and Zack explained not the whole story but that he and Lucas had grown up as companions "like you and Henry," adding in what could be a veiled reproach that the close association had continued "until we were grown men." Roth is still disturbed, says, "That's not enough," and sees the barrier between them, as at "that instant when the child realizes with both grief and outrage that the parent antedates it, has experienced things, shames and triumphs both, in which it can have no part." Seeing his son at this impasse, Zack tries to resolve it by saying, "I'll make a trade with you. You let me and Lucas settle how he is to treat me, and I'll let you and him settle how he is to treat you." This is Roth's real heritage, not the title and husbandry of the land itself that McCaslin Edmonds had had to accept from Isaac and then bequeathed to Zack, from whom Roth inherited it. At forty-three Roth for a generation "had run it, tried to" as his forebears had done and still has Lucas to cope with in this season of old Molly's threat to divorce that wilful man. This immediate and demanding involvement is with Lucas as of McCaslin blood, the acknowledged legatee at twenty-one of a thousand dollars come down to him from the clan's promiscuous founder, and now owner of a house and a portion of plantation land provided for him by McCaslin Edmonds and further assured by Zack. These considerations, however, were not the essence of that heritage whose "bitter fruit" Roth had eaten early. They could not have entered into his mind when at the age of seven in an unhappy confusion of impulses he harshly broke off what had been a close and constant companionship with Lucas Beauchamp's and Molly's son Henry. The instinctive move is not shown to have a local cause; it seems prompted by what penetrated into his sequestered and satisfied young life from the larger postbellum society that enclosed him by containing the plantation itself and conditioning a whole region's economic modes and social mores. Certainly in renouncing Henry's cheerful, agreeable companionship the boy was impelled by something other than an atavistic reaction against physical dissimilarity; his inner rage of ambivalent feelings suggests an obscure yet insistent apprehension of racial strain in a whole regional order, something insidiously encroaching upon his present immediate satisfactions and robbing him of his innocence. This disenchantment was real and cruel, though he could not then or later have defined what was in the very air itself, nor could he have identified the "fathers" from whom he was inheriting what the narrative calls "the old haughty ancestral pride" nor have documented it as "based not on any value but on an accident of geography." In this wide sense "geography" was to bind Roth Edmonds for life, in what seems a melancholy and irritable isolation; and clandestine excursions beyond the pale have only added to his disconcertion. Yet here again, in "Delta Autumn," the artist Faulkner shrewdly avoided a diffusive complicating of issue, by holding Roth apparently unaware that "the woman," though "light-colored," is also of that Negro line with a strain of McCaslin blood, her grandfather the elder brother of Lucas. (At least Roth need show no morbid sense of incest diluted to a distance of five generations, a far piece for even a postbellum Southern notion of cousinliness.) Faulkner's economy of emphasis reserves this most affecting element in the woman's situation for its private realization by the protagonist, Isaac, upon whom it will fall with fullest weight not only because of all his earlier knowledge and experiences, but because this so acutely symbolizes the "bitter fruit" of the "heritage" Isaac had resolutely abjured, yet was to suffer from, through his wife's fixed ambition to identify with it. Narratively Roth is circumstanced enough by what in this "geography" must be his uneasy awareness that (as Legate's phrase suggested and as Isaac could perceive) the "light-colored" woman is not white. This fact is assumed with wider reference by one critic who considers it improbable that Roth would have married her "even if she had had no trace of Negro blood." However, to realize "Delta Autumn" a reading need not extrapolate beyond the text the element of Roth's irresponsibility, and to do so may neglect the effectively focused economy in Faulkner's treatment of men and issues, together with the pertinence of this Roth Edmonds episode to the announced "general theme" of the book—"relation between the white and negro races here." Certainly the factor of racial strain which Roth had become aware of so early enters sharply into his whole life, and is to be understood in proportionate relation to his boyhood and his later experiences told of in "The Fire and the Hearth" as well as this latest glimpse in "Delta Autumn." Such connections to him as boy and man, though latent, can be recalled as explicative and enriching, in supplement to the realistically supplementary constrained treatment of Roth in "Delta Autumn." All such ranging references contribute to the book's subtle unity as a symphonic novel. Another such instance, and one more stressed, is in the echoings out of "The Old People" and "The Bear" that give Isaac major stature among Faulkner's protagonists, making the revised "Delta Autumn" larger than itself for remembering readers, in transcendent crescendo toward the story's great climax.

Neither in his boyhood or middle-aged at the Delta hunting camp could Roth Edmonds resolve the restive ambivalence which follows upon the severing of a human attachment and cessation of familiarity, whether with his rejected youthful companion or with "the woman" he would no longer see. Here is what Isaac has refused to endure, an equivocal state of mind, however painful its resolution; and it would be a curious logic if readers were to accept the woman's argument that Uncle Isaac is responsible for "spoiling" Roth Edmonds by turning over the plantation to Roth's grandfather McCaslin. Refusing to inherit, Isaac has declared against an evil inherent not in the land itself but in the uses it had been put to and the inequities and wrongs such privilege tolerated. Moreover, this is not just as to the McCaslin property (despite dark chapters in its early history) but as to the conventions of an inequitable socioeconomic order of which this plantation is inescapably a part. By implication young Isaac had denounced all this, including what in the 1880s and thereafter still surfaces from it as racial tension, chronic symptom of misalliance and pervading maladustments. The fateful weight of this, acutely sensed but imperfectly answered to, had "spoiled" Roth's boyhood companionship with Henry—and perhaps Roth is to be most accurately perceived as a human being in the "grief" and "shame" soon following upon this offense that marked a change beyond remedy, and then its more fierce likeness in the ambivalent guise of his cynicism and self-loathing in "Delta Autumn," along with his other quite different behavior at about the same time of his life, as at the conclusion of "The Fire and the Hearth," in his offering Lucas a degree of indulgence, once Roth has tenderly saved old Molly from the disruption of her accustomed life.

Allowing that except for the most severe traumatic experience persons are not "spoiled" by one act, it still can be seen that the woman has come close to apprehending a major influence on Roth, but she has seen him in only one atypical episode, and most ironically her reproach falls upon the one man who is free of blame if anyone can be, having renounced completely and in its entirety the system which aggravates a corrupting influence and complicates the problem of coping with it. An appreciatively humane view of his fellowmen and an adherance to the austere pieties of an ethic formed in his youth define Isaac's concept of responsibility. Consistent support of his code has required relinquishment of far more than the plantation itself; especially a wife doubly lost, destining him to be "father to no one." In "Delta Autumn" he is seen still keeping and professing his faith, and required to suffer further for it, by reminders of past evils through present recurrences, and under a baseless reproach that he had "forgotten anything" he "ever knew or felt . . . about love"—he who had bespoken it ideally and mused on it humanely the night before. According to "The Fire and the Hearth" Isaac had carried into old age "something of a young boy's high and selfless innocence." Here though is not the conclusive nor the definitive image of the man, but rather in that speaking effigy at the end of "Delta Autumn," acknowledging with four words. "It was a doe," the somber symbolism of a deplorable fact, but suggesting in his fixity the retention of an opposing principle. It is best to take Isaac where Faulkner left him, to refrain from seeing him either as saint or apostate, but rather as member of a rare and always endangered species, the enduringly principled and purely disinterested man.

In some readings of Faulkner there occurs, at the least, an implied dissatisfaction with the man Isaac McCaslin, if not outright disapproval. This can turn on his nonconformity in refusing to accept inheritance and its responsibilities, economic and societal. Thus one study even approves his wife's attempt to lure him back to a conventional and privileged local position as the McCaslin, hereditarily in residence. Any such argument, however, cannot offset what Faulkner so subtly built into her brief conversation with Isaac before they were married, showing her intention and also a certain deviousness, when she presses the question of title to "the farm" and then draws back—"But I dont suppose it matters" —having discovered Isaac's simple disregard of the presumptions of primogeniture, in his brotherly view that his cousin McCaslin Edmonds has an equal claim. Others disapproving of Isaac have been most explicit about his receiving a small stipend from the plantation's profits, taking the attitude which Isaac suspected in some of his contemporaries, notably Lucas Beauchamp on the day he came at twenty-one to claim his McCaslin legacy. This was from the money which Isaac, still a youth, had tried ten years earlier to deliver a fair portion of to Lucas's elder brother James ("Tennie's Jim"), searching for him all the way to Jackson, Tennessee without finding a trace of the northward-bound young man. Isaac then returned this "third of legacy $1000.00 . . . to McCaslin Edmonds Trustee" and so recorded it in the ledgers. Then almost a year later Isaac, still in his teens, set off on another such errand, again carrying a thousand dollars in gold, as share of the legacy for Fonsiba, James' younger sister, who at seventeen had married a pretentious impractical Negro from the North (a wearer of gold-rimmed spectacles without lenses). Finally Isaac found them, on a rundown farm in Arkansas, with Fonsiba "thin, too thin" and withdrawn as if into a trance, and so he deposited the money in the town bank as a trust from which a small allotment was to be delivered to Fonsiba each month, assuring that "at least she would not starve." It further mirrors the man Isaac that when he came of age and relinquished title to the land to his elder Edmonds cousin, he conscientiously retained this trusteeship for the Beauchamp heirs, considering it his real responsibility as present head of the McCaslin line, even while repudiating his own larger inheritance.

With Lucas presenting himself promptly on his birthday, Isaac's wife has made the sarcastic suggestion that perhaps Isaac's cousin McCaslin has sent Lucas to announce stoppage of "even that fifty dollars a month he swapped you for your father's farm." It had been no "swap," and when Isaac renounced the inheritance despite McCaslin's attempts to dissuade him, his distressed cousin had followed him to town and left some money, which Isaac had insisted on repaying from his carpenter's income. If later Isaac accepted a monthly allowance from the land's earnings, it was for "peace," through that much appeasement of his acquisitive wife and perhaps even some conciliation, and no doubt to relieve the generous-minded McCaslin's quite different concern about his younger cousin. But Lucas, Isaac thinks, will not understand, will consider that Isaac had "reneged . . . sold my birthright, betrayed my blood for what he too calls not peace but obliteration, and a little food." It is with this probably correct assumption in his mind and with his wife's scorn echoing in his ears that Isaac still can wish Lucas "Many happy returns" and patiently show him how to deposit his money safely in the bank. So much for the surface of the episode; the truth about Isaac is to be discerned at some depth, implicatively. The phrase "what he too [Lucas] calls not peace but obliteration" shows Isaac's sense of that isolation a conscientious man can feel when what positively motivates him is not merely misunderstood, it is not even perceived, being mistaken for some lesser thing. But Isaac's concept of manly virtue makes absolute demands upon him, and, as he had repeated to McCaslin in their long debate in "The Bear," he craved the peace that could come only with the sense of being honorably answerable to his conscience.

It is an aspect of McCaslin Edmonds' largeness of spirit that he understands this in Isaac, and accords him the ultimate recognition, by debating the matter objectively in broad terms, with reference to past and present circumstance, running beyond local problems of husbandry, but also coming back to such immediate obligations in a present context. For McCaslin these would include an heir's duty to maintain a socioeconomic enterprise, and since Isaac declines to assume it, McCaslin then does so. This is in a continuation of what he had taken over at nineteen, upon the deaths of Isaac's father and his Uncle Buddy shortly after the war; and McCaslin has carried on through difficult times for the next nineteen years until his younger cousin arrived at his majority. Now despite his own honorable convictions, which make Isaac's correct legitimate inheritance of the land more important to McCaslin than his possessing it himself, he allows Isaac his different convictions, and never descends to derogation, no matter how ironic he becomes in the established vein of their deep intimacies and loyalties. That long, wide-ranging, searching debate in the commissary is a severe struggle, but one in which the contenders' earnestness, sincerity, and mutual concern become more continuously moving for the reader than any of the opposing points they raise. That is proper to a humanistic fiction, as also is a concurrent representation of environmental issues in their immense complexity; and Faulkner's proportioned balancing of these compositional factors here is exemplary.

This extended discoursing between the cousins on the day of Isaac's majority and his most decisive act defines him conclusively, yet not just in that instance but as a being with a life story. For such a disclosure's full perspectives, however, McCaslin Edmonds too is indispensable; he is not a mere interlocutor but conceptually the adversary, given emphatic and credible voice by an artist who is no mere ideological dogmatist in representing human beings in the existential crunch. Any who are made uneasy by Isaac's absolute austerity, with its implied reproach of ambiguousness, will be more tolerant of him if they recognize that with all his virtues Isaac is not superlatively Faulkner's exemplary man. Neither, however, is McCaslin Edmonds, though he has been made thoroughly admirable, and steadier and more sturdy than the earnestly principled but volatile Gavin Stevens, who often may seem his author's *alter ego* because he is so strenuously active in a twentieth-century context. More broadly, these and a number of other favored figures are all Faulkner's men, surrogates of his multiple sensibilities, representing his selective interests within wide range of other observed individuals in their behavior, and conveying his acute intuitions of sentient humans as they live and move in their acquired quiddities, the visible sign of their persistent elusive dreams.

Faulkner will most readily abide questions if he is allowed his distanced objectivity and relativism in imaginatively evoking unique lives, conscious beings, each creating out of his or her own bent both tangible and impalpable effects, and doomed to endure them. In such fluent private intensities among a throng of players there are no saints and no complete heroes, and not even any villain without the twisted pathos of his self-imprisonment even in his devastations. Frequently too characters are paired and set opposite each other not just as ideological pawns but for the fuller dramatic tension that discloses temperament through stress over issues. Besides the cousins McCaslin and Isaac there is Quentin Compson with his Harvard roommate. Shreve, established humanly in *The Sound and the Fury,* is then retroactively the collaborative inquisitor in *Absalom, Absalom!,* bringing to Quentin's agonized meditations on the South the cool incredulity of a Canadian and the natural responsiveness of a friend. There are Gavin Stevens the lawyer and Ratliff the sewing machine salesman and county intelligencer, differently circumstanced and temperamentally opposites, yet drawn to each other as perspicacious men of principle; though not infallible, they provide Faulkner's most cheering illustration of a possible commonalty through moral sentiment put into effect, in an affiliation sustained by mutual approval and flexible companionability. And in more drastic debate yet paradoxically closer by blood tie than even Isaac and McCaslin, there are the General and the Corporal in *A Fable,* less individualized than Faulkner's Yoknapatawphans because they must represent more formally some of the most profound abstractions that beset mankind. Yet Isaac on his own limited field plays out with his cousin a dialectic of comparable magnitude and not entirely dissimilar in its elements.

Familiar as Isaac has become in the course of his maturation, his renouncing inheritance with a degree of resort to the mystical may create uneasiness in professedly pragmatic minds. Yet in the fullest sense McCaslin and Isaac were both pragmatists; their difference is in their estimates of the situation to be dealt with, what ends they have in view, and their choices of approach. Certainly Isaac deserves the respect implied by McCaslin's meeting him on equal ground, and in Major de Spain's asking no questions about the rejection of inheritance but offering him a room in his house — which Isaac declined. More specifically Isaac's virtue is curiously certified in similar ways by two quite different characters — General Compson, who says it looks like Isaac "just quit," but his old patron won't believe it because "I have watched you in the woods too much"; and later, when Isaac is a storekeeper, Mink

Snopes knows it will be useless to try to lie to a man with such an alerted sense of realities, and the habit of unequivocal response, one who *"has done spent too much time in the woods with deer and bears and panthers that either are or they aint, right quick and now and not no shades between."* Perhaps the ignorant but natively shrewd Mink has defined in his quaint way the distinguishing quality which makes Isaac a problem, for his cousin and for some readers less sympathetic than McCaslin. Conditioned in the woods as the boy Isaac had been by Sam Fathers, he has grown into an either/or man regarding ethical problems as well, especially concerning the society he was born into but finally refuses to affiliate with unquestioningly. Yet though that refusal was absolute, the decision had not been made easily, nor by a simple-minded ascetic or a merely indolent young man seeking "obliteration." Indeed, a rightful assessing of Isaac McCaslin becomes peculiarly relevant to the more general understanding of Faulkner.

A great merit of "Delta Autumn" is that within its chronological scope of an afternoon, night, and morning it comprises not only the weighty matter of all those summary denouements in the Isaac McCaslin life story but his recollections which keep touch with his crucial past experiences, not only a hunter's development of an ethos and then an heir's disenchantment and a husband's frustration, but most tellingly a recapitulation of stages in arrival at his major decision and its still more painful reconfirmation. At sixteen, having realized "wrong and shame" from discoveries in the ledgers, Isaac believed that when he reached maturity he could eradicate the shame by curing the wrong; the idealistic youth definitely holds in prospect his assuming a corrective control of the plantation. At twenty-one, tempered by those five years of varied experiences which are touched upon in "The Bear," Isaac knows he cannot effect a sufficient transformation within this unit of the postbellum socioeconomic order, and therefore he must in conscience repudiate title to the land, not only to hold to his freedom and keep his peace, but to "save and free" from such ambiguous involvement the son he hoped to have. That in so doing he "lost him" is not Isaac's fault, but an accident, an unpredictable repercussion, through his wife's betrayal of the trust implied by her acceptance of the young carpenter in marriage. At that point, unless he were to renege, he must reaffirm his earlier decision and action, even if at a further price that ironically robbed him of related values he had had in view, and this must have clouded the peace he sought. Thus, though he kept consistent faith with himself, the rest of his long life was transposed into a minor mode; and though "Delta Autumn" shows the old man still of firm mind, the story resounds with unease and is saturated with gloom. It culminates in the further shocks under which Isaac must continue to bear out to the edge of existence a doom that pursues him into the woods which had been his first sanctuary and were his last resort.

But the woods have their relative darkness too, even by day, as Isaac had known from his youth, whether under summer's full foliage when he stood alone "in the green and soaring gloom of the markless wilderness" before relinquishing compass and watch lest the old bear sense them, or whether when, "standing beside Sam in the thick great gloom of ancient woods and the winter's dying afternoon," he looked at "the print of the enormous warped two-toed foot." In "Delta Autumn" it is "in the beginning of dusk" that the old man brings the horses across the river, and by supper time the only light left in the woods was "the thin stain of it snared somewhere between the river's surface and the rain." Then next morning, with Isaac still abed in the tent, there are further images of fluctuant illumination. As Roth goes out after leaving the one-syllable negative message and the envelope with the "sheaf of bank-notes" for the woman, the tent flap "lifted on an in-waft of faint light and the constant murmur of rain, and fell again"; to Isaac, deeply perturbed, even stunned by what Roth had partially revealed, with the envelope clutched in a "shaking hand," there seemed no interval between "the tent flap falling on the same out-waft of faint and rain-filled light like the suspiration and expiration of the same breath and then in the next second lifted again," by the youngest Negro, and "then the woman entering," bringing with her a further burden of knowledge. Once more, when she leaves after their painful conversation "The waft of light and the murmur of the constant rain flowed into the tent and then out again as the flap fell." Soon Legate comes in, hurriedly, for Roth's knife to dress the deer they have got, and having answered that Roth had killed it, evasively calls it "Just a deer. . . . Nothing extra" and "was gone; again the flap fell behind him, wafting out of the tent again the faint light and the constant and grieving rain," and leaving Isaac to provide his own answer, "It was a doe."

This closing line is enhanced in the revision Faulkner imposed upon the *Story* magazine version. There the last two sentences following the repeated image of "the faint light . . . the constant and grieving rain" were these:

McCaslin lay back on the cot.
  "It was a doe," he said to the empty tent.

In the expanded and deepened version for *Go Down, Moses* the last two sentences read thus:

McCaslin lay back down, the blanket once more drawn to his chin, his crossed hands once more weightless on his breast in the empty tent.
  "It was a doe," he said.

That utmost brevity stresses another shameful finality with its bleak claim upon Isaac's stoical endurance, and his not just thinking but speaking the words denotes his unequivocal acceptance of ethical issue on which he will not yield. It is a germane and potent image, this empty tent where there has been so much coming and going while old Uncle Isaac still lies abed — Roth's hurried exit leaving behind money and message and taking with him the shotgun rather than rifle; the woman's relatively brief visit, the story's central scene and done at the intense height of Faulkner's artistry; and then Legate's sudden entry to get Roth's knife and his evasion of Isaac's searching question and Isaac's answering it himself, unequivocally in a stoic acceptance of disreputable family history repeating itself in essence. But the final revision of those closing lines, transferring the empty tent image with all its recent external connections, leaves Isaac's four words where they have an ultimate isolated force, in his pained consciousness still bent on facing the facts in any matter of conduct.

The intermittent wafts of faint light into the rain-darkened tent seem the artist's signature of his represented glances into darkness deeper than the gloom of an unmarked wilderness, and as hardly penetrable as the still more ancient night. Yet whatever of such light can be projected into the obscurities of men's doings, it it wafted, it has its transient motion, and though darkness cannot be banished, it may be probed, again and again, by its momently declared antithesis. In those latter pages of "Delta Autumn" that closely recurrent imagery is not monotonous, its wafts derive from nature and from the very pulse of the artist's committed imagination, it takes on the vitality of breath. While the rain becomes a "grieving," there has been light enough to see Isaac by, and above the rain's constant murmur can be heard in his final words not just an infinite melancholy but resoluteness in a further confrontation. By that measure, at least, Isaac is his creator's veritable surrogate.

Epilogue to the Story of Isaac McCaslin

Faulkner's comprehensively delineative and penetrating account of Isaac McCaslin — as boy and youth, at his assertive majority and in his marriage, and in widowed old age, under a life's formative experiences and various stresses — presents a person of consistent virtue in the word's basic sense, yet that cannot be taken to mean he is Faulkner's man, in the guise of perfect exemplar. Anything so nearly monolithic and stereotyped, or even vaguely approaching the extreme fabrications of popular fiction's and television serials' characters held in permanent detention apart from the existential realities of being and becoming, was the opposite of Faulkner's intention, working imaginatively as realist, and for the most part close in on his regional subjects. Though he lets Miss Rosa label Thomas Sutpen a demon—which Sutpen may have seemed to his Yoknapatawphan neighbors in his incursion—the artist characteristically found a way around any such simplistic view, by the man's puzzled but illuminating confidences to General Compson that became Quentin's only inheritance from his grandfather. For Faulkner characterization of a persona is to be projected in the classic way, by the particulars of his concerned responsiveness, overt and subjective, to situational realities. Therefore in the popular sense Faulkner has no heroes, which may at least partially account for the opinion of unsophisticated or merely careless readers that he is obscure. Of more grave though temporary effects during Faulkner's emergence had been the muttered distaste of anxious academic humanists, who protested against what they saw as Faulkner's nihilistic sensationalism, in his morbid preoccupation with evil as it erupted into violence. Conversely there are significant realities and profundities of insight in Faulkner's work, together with a potently enabling art, and these are quite accessible to intent and intuitive readers. For them the great distance and difference of Faulkner's work from sensational melodrama defines the truth of the matter. Instead of melodrama's simplistic view arriving at finalities, with its stock figures essentially static in black and white under absolutes of good and evil, there are Faulkner's characters as beings realized in a living fusion of overt and subjective motion. Herein this artist's vision and his commitment to the human condition is inescapably fluid and necessarily tentative except for the fixed lights of those primary and imperative verities distilled from the experience of generations.

Thus Faulkner, in transcending the reductive antitheses of simple melodrama, offers some admirable characters, some sadly flawed, but all quite naturally fallible, each in his way and degree. As creations by a genuinely humanistic regional realist they are not expediently fabricated out of unexamined platitudes, nor mere facsimiles of provincial types; they are given identity and tendency in some singular complex of humanly recognizable traits, which this sharply observant and highly intuitive artist has laid hold on. Projected situationally, Faulkner's predominating characters move in their many-sidedness through a range of aspects, in tensions between emergent circumstance and their own variable but basically purposeful courses. The stage is sometimes crowded, but the action is usually expeditious; Faulkner is a superb director, especially in maintaining fluidity by proportioned emphasis and by adept transitional nuances. To serve his genius as fictionist Faulkner claimed a resource for characterization in the midst of action such as the modern stage does not provide (nor has the cinema developed it to any extent)—a use of a protagonist's centrally poised consciousness, which frames events in its own concurrent awareness and responses, thereby absorbing the overt action into the persona's own ventured existence. Here Faulkner's art earns comparison with that of James or Joyce, though there are also the natural contrasts in accord with each artist's temperamental inclinations and unique creativeness. While James remains unequalled in penetrations and definitive refinements without blunting fictionally implicative subtleties, and Joyce is a very Prospero in projecting dramatically a cloaked and smoothly masked self-preoccupation, Faulkner is notable for measured flexibility in using his characters' consciousness to support conveyance of his realistically conceptualized fictions. He seeks always to give narration its maximum containment, pace, and import within an organismic subjective-objective nexus—notably as with Isaac McCaslin in the continuum of each of the successive stories he preempts, under transcendental rights Faulkner bowed to and piously tried to serve.

In fictional structurings to all such ends, Faulkner employs dialogue as complementary element with brilliant effects, giving it a primarily synthesizing function at the crucial point of subjectively colored response to personal involvement with situation, projecting identity as seen in motivation, and deploying characters functionally in proportion to the thematic course of the total action. In such an economy, dialogue however idiosyncratic is never merely picturesque, for static local color. Faulkner's characters, given some scope, are as befits their time and region notable talkers, and may even become broadly speculative, but it is always to a point, with its inquiry, assertion, or controversy geared to the narrative thrust in its immediate issue. Exchange keeps major characters related to the narrative's thematic as well as its overt movement. Not separated from the struggle, neither are its central actors wholly subordinated to its intent, though they are not exempt from its subjective exactions. In Faulkner's dialogue inherent thematic stress individually answered to produces uniquely intense dramatization which unites the commonalty of human concerns and animated personal response. Both of these as factors in consolidating a fictional effect operate in the *Absalom, Absalom!* discussion between the Harvard roommates, predominant in the book's latter part. Though their engrossed suppositions in pondering the Sutpen saga sometimes take on an almost impressionistic tone that places their exchanges beyond ordinary conversation, this is made real enough through their opposed but humanly credible and representative traits of detached curiosity and anguished involvement, in the so differently conditioned Canadian Shreve and Mississippian Quentin Compson. Curiosity and involvement, detachment and anguish might be thought to represent elements in the artist's complex awareness of the matter so masterfully synthesized in this most remarkable, and for some the greatest, of American novels. Certainly Faulkner's conducting of the narrative so largely through Quentin's sensibilities, at first alone and then with Shreve's cool but interested collaboration, allows a distancing of the artist's oversight and a widening of his range and control; and the prolonged dialogue in itself, beyond its different degrees of subjectivity in Shreve and in Quentin, objectifies the story's substance and thus imaginatively illuminates its august and somber themes.

A most profound use of dialogue as the sustained drama of earnest inquiry, surpassing even that in *Absalom, Absalom!*

through its immediacies of issue for both participants, is that in section 4 of "The Bear," in the McCaslin commissary and briefly thereafter, between Isaac McCaslin at twenty-one and his cousin McCaslin Edmonds, seventeen years his senior. The conjunction of Quentin and Shreve had been of that quite fortuitous yet steadily acquaintive kind, as college roommates. The connection between Isaac and McCaslin, though they are adversaries in their dialogue over matters of principle, is not just familial but close, affectionate, and mutually respectful. Orphaned, McCaslin Edmonds had grown up on the plantation under the guardianship of his grandmother Edmonds' brothers, Isaac's father, Theophilus, and Amodeus; then after their deaths McCaslin as a young man, "himself little more than a child," and in the midst of the difficult reconstruction period, had kept the estate "intact" and solvently operative "out of the debacle and chaos . . . where hardly one in ten survived." In turn McCaslin Edmonds had taken the orphaned Isaac under his guardianship and guidance until he would be of age to assume title as the direct McCaslin heir. No wonder that in the cryptic preface to "Was" and thus to his whole story, old "Uncle Ike" is pictured remembering McCaslin as "rather his brother than cousin and rather his father than either." However, in section 4 of "The Bear," which begins with the commissary scene and the searching discussion there betwen Isaac and McCaslin Edmonds, the familial aspect of Isaac's contention with his elder cousin is specifically in terms of Isaac's rejection of the inheritance, on this first day of his majority. Legally he is the indubitable heir, and McCaslin in his concern for a rightful continuity and the order symbolized by primogeniture wants him to assume that role. It is not that McCaslin seeks to escape responsibility for the ongoing enterprise he has so strenuously labored to maintain and pass on; nor can it be doubted that this remarkable man would willingly remain as collaborator, to induct Isaac further into material complexities and continue to assist—just as he had tried to help the boy Isaac understand more abstract values in citing Keats to illustrate the concept of "truth" as "all things which touch the heart," or as even earlier, in section 3 of "The Old People," where McCaslin's lengthy mystical reflection becomes a paean to life itself, with a genial apologia for such persistent ghosts as that of the great buck Sam Fathers has led Isaac to see, as before in McCaslin's own youth. Yet McCaslin Edmonds is the long-recognized *de facto* head of the McCaslin family, preserver of the estate through difficult postbellum years, and Isaac's protector since he was early orphaned; and thus Isaac himself at twenty-one, declaring independence by rejecting the legacy, puts it that "I'm trying to explain to the head of my family something which I have got to do." There is no such basic confrontation between Quentin and Shreve. Theirs is a collaboration in an assessment of the Sutpen family story, though in different moods, with Quentin's so painfully close a societal and personal involvement that he becomes the subjective protagonist of the novel as a fictional whole, while Shreve's view is detachedly inquiring and some of his responses are ironic. But he too does get caught up in that grotesquely somber drama of hubris and its spreading destructive effects, and finally he ventures to try to bring Quentin's ambivalence to the surface, asking him the question the youth must too protestingly deny, "Why do you hate the South?"

There is no indication that Isaac hates the South; apparently he loves what he sees as what is left of it to him, though not the McCaslin inheritance with its title not only stained by its patriarch's misuse of female slaves but spurious in itself. Isaac seeks a responsible place in the South's postbellum order, as a workingman, a carpenter, and he aspires to marry and rear a son on these his native grounds, actually and mystically too, in the larger boundaries of belief. Isaac's progress toward this societally and individually honorable goal (and his achieving it except for its ultimate part, a son, forestalled by his wife's duplicity) is swiftly traced in the condensed, energetic narrative which follows his parting from McCaslin Edmonds on the night of the first day after he is twenty-one, in the rented room in Jefferson, where he will accept only as a loan the money the anxious McCaslin has ridden in to town to bring him. Here for those few tense moments both men are outwardly obdurate, McCaslin arguing sophistically that he has no money to lend Isaac and saying Isaac hereafter will have to go to the bank for what will be left for him monthly, presumably as a still undisputed heir's share of profits from the plantation—all of which Isaac refuses and in due course resists. But at the deeper level of personal concern Isaac, "looking peacefully at McCaslin, his kinsman, his father almost yet no kin now as, at the last, even fathers and sons are no kin," says "It's seventeen miles, horseback and in the cold. We could both sleep here"; and McCaslin answers doggedly, "Why should I sleep here in my house when you wont sleep yonder in yours?" and is gone. The words "my house," implying that this Jefferson property, rented out, is one of McCaslin's investments, suggests the further irony, in that part of Isaac's payments for room and board would be returning to McCaslin. Yet deeper than the grotesqueness of situation is the conveyed sense of this resolute man's sorrow at the severance that has fallen between him and the young cousin he had fostered from childhood and for whose sake, really, he had maintained "intact" and further strengthened the McCaslin inheritance. Here then is the shatteringly separative outcome of that debate early in section 4 of "The Bear" between affectionate and mutually respectful cousins, yet each an unyieldingly principled man.

McCaslin Edmond's code was one he had accepted out of the best he had known of men and their affairs as a small boy in the South's last decade before the Civil War and as one too young for it, yet not spared the rigors of those times and their aftermath, during which at still an early age he was virtually conscripted by the necessities of situation itself, to which his dutiful, strenuous answering was a wholly responsible and in one way a disinterested act. All this set and held him in a course he did not waver from, and in which he displayed admirable traits, not only resoluteness and industriousness but a fostering compassion for his younger cousin Isaac and just dealing and human kindness for all who depended upon the enterprise he had saved out of a general debacle. He is a sound, sympathetic, and wittily ironic character about whom one could wish to know more, not only out of curiosity but in admiration. At various points Faulkner as artist must have had to control impulses to go further with McCaslin Edmonds, and the artist's having restrained himself from so promising an opportunity implies a superb sense of proportionate emphasis, primarily to maintain the subjective-objective priority of Isaac McCaslin in "The Old People" and "The Bear." In "Delta Autumn" McCaslin Edmonds is to be felt if at all only as a shade in absolute contrast to his grandson Roth, privately but plainly eaten by shame over his deplorable conduct. Old Isaac, who has to deal with all this, might well have been reminded of that irreproachable elder cousin, yet Faulkner did not take this up; he was too intent not only upon a telling resolution of Isaac McCaslin's whole history but on the purest possible resonances from this final story in his commemorative triptych.

An inclusive survey for perspective on what comprises that story may point out the massively substantial and tensely dramatic section 4 of "The Bear" as the peaking promontory in that whole range, yet the widest view will show how relevantly supportive, especially through thematically contributive climaxes, is the matter in all three of the *Go Down, Moses* stories which convey that widely spanning, diversely eventful, and intensely lived existence. The setting of the cousins' crucial dialogue in the plantation commissary concretely suggests that socioeconomic operation for which it is the controlling center, and where ledgers contain the long history of that ongoing process which war and federal emancipation have not yet essentially modified in its physical factors. In the third paragraph of section 4, just preceding the first extended passage of the cousins' dialogue, there is that image (which will recur more elaborately later) of the two strong threads which bind through the necessary exchange of labor and its product for operating supplies and subsistence. This reciprocation has its rigors; it requires both sweaty labor and constant forethought, frugal oversight, and regulation. It has also its internal order and ethic, as to a right relation of laborer and overseer, and of all men toward their domestic animals and in the care of the land itself. Central to Faulkner's veracity is his duly noting that certain realities persist of necessity despite the fluctuations in men's sporadic rearrangements of affairs. The South's agricultural processes had continued in much their usual ways after the war, with seedtime and harvesting its means and with only a degree of adjustment in methods. Conversely, while this pertained too in the story of Isaac McCaslin, there some interracial changes at the local level had preceded the war and emancipation by several decades. When old Lucius Quintus Carothers McCaslin died in 1837, his direct male heirs then in their late thirties, the bachelor twin sons Uncle Buck (Isaac's father Theophilus) and Uncle Buddy (Amodeus), had mollified the system for all concerned by trading dwellings with the slaves, building themselves a cabin and installing the slaves in the big house, into which they were checked and locked up every night with ceremonial formality while the back doors and windows were left open for them to run free, with the "gentlemen's agreement" that they would be present to file out the front door when it was reopened next morning. (When Tomey's Terrel, L. Q. C. McCaslin's son by the slave Tomasina, stretched these provisions by running off to court the Beauchamp's slave Tennie, his recapture was made a kind of sporting event in which he played a foxy evasiveness, while there was also the secondary hazarding for Uncle Buck of Miss Sophonsiba Beauchamp's all-out coquetry, as known at nine by the uncles' ward McCaslin Edmonds and so reconstructed in "Was.") The twin heirs also had given the McCaslin slaves "manumission in title at least," a token but also a liberality then so scandalously nonconformist that only their general eccentricity could have sustained it.

It was only when Uncle Buck was well along into his sixties, and after he had ridden off to sample the Civil War, that he resigned himself to the role of Mr. Theophilus and married the long-awaiting Miss Sophonsiba Beauchamp and moved with her into the restored main house, where Isaac was born. The possibly formative influences of all this familial example and ambience on both McCaslin Edmonds and Isaac McCaslin could be widely speculated upon, but that would enter a range of extrapolation more to be frequented by some practitioners of social science and psychiatry than by careful students of so scrupulous a humanistic realist as Faulkner. As meticulous artist in fiction, he limited himself to showing the matured McCaslin Edmonds balancing considerate treatment of the postbellum Negroes with an efficient ordering of what provides sustenance and stability for all those involved; Isaac was shown to have found more abstrusely the equilibrium of a consistent attitude in a synthesis of what Sam Fathers had taught him (and his elder cousin McCaslin had helped him understand) and what he had understood all too well of his family from commissary ledgers. Conveying Isaac McCaslin's story as it sketches his growth into maturity and in particular comprises his deepening yet finally divergent relationship to his cousin McCaslin Edmonds, Faulkner is exemplary in an avoidance of undue extension beyond represented sympathies and opposition. Yet these are made credible in that they are seen supported by adduced formative experiences as influences leading to different attitudes and their enactments, by two congenial but uniquely assertive men, though of the same blood and less than a generation apart. If the War between the States was indeed a great divide, they found themselves at last on its opposite slopes, yet within sight and hailing distance. Their mutually suffered ordeal at Isaac's majority can be reminder that beyond war's bloodshed, and decades after the material devastation now largely remedied, later scarrings were to be taken by Southerners sharing something of these two men's reflective and ethically concerned natures, and so similarly were to find themselves alienated to some degree and in one way or another from those whom and that which they loved.

McCaslin is the first of three generations of Edmonds

cousins, older and younger, whom Isaac is to know during his long life; they stem directly from old L. Q. C. McCaslin through his daughter Mary, Isaac's aunt and McCaslin Edmonds' grandmother. The first and third of these Edmonds cousins, McCaslin and Carothers (Roth) enter directly into Isaac's life story—McCaslin most steadily and profoundly, in "The Old People" and "The Bear," Roth most startlingly in Isaac's old age, through an episode during the hunt described in "Delta Autumn." Zack Edmonds, McCaslin's son born in 1873, and father of Roth, is not developed as of a relationship with Isaac, though they hunted together; as seen in the matter of "The Fire and the Hearth" Zack is a man of stamina but dramatically subordinate to the story's protagonist, Lucas Beauchamp, and his young wife Mollie. Whether Zack offends by miscegenation with her is left in doubt, through focus instead on Lucas's natural suspicions and his fortuitously aborted murderous rage under the postbellum black man's continuing vulnerability to the white man's possible ruthlessness, especially in this most sensitively personal area. In elucidation of the multiracial theme that runs throughout *Go Down, Moses* perhaps the most telling and certainly the most broadly implicative and subtly set forth episode in "The Fire and the Hearth," however, is that of the seven-year-old Roth's instinctive separation of himself from his hitherto constant companion, his foster brother Henry Beauchamp, son of Mollie and Lucas. Yet when Roth as third-generation Edmonds inheritor is seen as operator of the enterprise, he is fondly attentive to his old foster-mother Mollie and impatiently lenient with the assertive Lucas, who has the house and portion of land within the family acres which McCaslin Edmonds had given him to farm as he pleased and to which Zack had certified his perpetual title. However, Roth's continuation of the Edmonds' tradition of humane dealings with the postbellum Negroes is the period too of his miscegenous relation with the woman of "Delta Autumn," whom he will not see, though he leaves money with Uncle Isaac for her and their infant son. With her identifying herself as Tennie's

Jim's granddaughter, she impinges upon old Isaac as a veritable apparition out of the commissary ledgers, and a shocking reminder that the inherent human ruthlessness he had repudiated and separated himself from remains incorrigible and seems endemic — as it had in another guise to Quentin Compson.

In Roth's grandfather, the admirable McCaslin Edmonds, there had been no corruptibility whether by lust or by greed and either during Isaac's impressionable boyhood or youth. And at Isaac's majority, in the crisis of his life as a McCaslin, his elder cousin is candid and judicious in his principled opposition, but with no diminution of respect and constancy. Having been confronted by the postbellum modification of the old system, and having labored strenuously to bring the family holdings through that adjustment, McCaslin Edmonds naturally is conscious of what its operation still requires, and sees it justified by its productivity, and commensurately by the living and a degree of stability it has given the emancipated Negroes who have chosen to remain upon it, as Terrel (Tomey's Turl) and his wife Tennie Beauchamp did, as their son James and daughter Sophonsiba did not, but as their youngest, Lucas, was to do under McCaslin's patronage. Not inconceivably McCaslin Edmonds at thirty-eight, with the plantation soundly reestablished and largely by his efforts, may wonder why Isaac, the more direct heir, does not see in his inheritance something he might honorably put his shoulder to; and at the beginning of their discussion (before it becomes historical-theological) he is reproaching Isaac for indifference to that. But Isaac is looking at his situation from another aspect, and when the image of a binding recurs it is not of two threads, the plantation's output and the commensurate perpetuating material returns; instead it becomes singular, "the frail and iron thread strong as truth and impervious as evil and longer than life itself and reaching beyond record and patrimony both to join him with the lusts and passions, the hopes and dreams and griefs, of bones whose names . . . even old Carothers' grandfather had never heard." Isaac having just said "I am free," now immediately adds "and of that too," meaning an ancestry beyond tracing but with hints of its iniquities centered in what the ledgers have let him discover about his grandfather's unfeeling use of human beings he had held as slaves.

Isaac's concept of freedom is not escapist; it is a responsible attempt to avoid being drawn into a way of life which would equivocate the primitive piety engendered by Sam Fathers, and also would shadow his related hope (in accord with the Book's myth of an unfolding purpose) that in time the wrongs his people have done the Negro may find some amendment. McCaslin, though he cannot wholly agree with Isaac and would dissuade him from relinquishing the inheritance, is no less a principled man, but merely more pragmatic, as product of a different formative experience, which has taught him the vulnerability of even best-laid plans and a consequent imperative for setting a firm hand to the plow. In his present, accepted situation McCaslin soberly judges that any notion of freedom is invalid, "we from them nor they from us," possibly meaning weighty involvements with a specific heritage as it includes the disturbingly related Beauchamp line, but certainly suggesting the larger, perhaps unamenable complexities of the given unwieldy multiracial society. Yet McCaslin too claims his identity and defends his course of action, saying of his carrying on the plantation's work that he "could do no else," having been born into it, along with other men, "more than me" — those many who have found themselves heir to some task immediately at hand, among whom he cites Isaac's father and uncle, Buck and Buddy. However, McCaslin is no mere simple conformist. His strenuous dutifulness has not muted or diminished this forthright, judicious, humanely tempered, quietly ironic man. As its maintainer, he is primarily conscious of the plantation, with its socioeconomic complex of interactions that must be kept smoothly and equitably operative. Conceiving of the tamed land as man's basic resource and means of subsistence, he considers its careful productive use an honorable occupation and derives from that an almost physiocratic sense of values, not merely of property and enterprise, but of free human interchange in mutual respect for persons and opinions. Concretely he is to be glimpsed at many moments that reveal a steady, humorous, intuitive, benevolent man. In "The Old People" there is his dealing with Sam Fathers when he wants to go live in the big woods near Major de Spain's camp, and McCaslin (after jesting about whether Sam can get away from the boy Isaac or will he take him along) quietly says, "Yes. Of course. I'll fix it with Major de Spain." There is McCaslin's calmly resolute disarming of the distraught Boon and his conciliatory suggestion of assent to whatever Boon may have done at the dying request of Sam Fathers. There is, retrospectively in "The Fire and the Hearth," the fact that McCaslin Edmonds had "built a house" for young Lucas Beauchamp and his wife and "allotted Lucas a specified acreage [of McCaslin land] to be farmed as he saw fit." In "The Bear," section 4, there is an equal concern expressed for Terrel's and Tennie's daughter Sophonsiba Beauchamp, through McCaslin's sharp interview with the presumptuous impractical man, son of a one-time slave, who wants to marry the seventeen-year-old girl and take her to a farm in Arkansas; and later McCaslin as trustee had let Isaac, still a minor, carry her portion of inheritance to her and bank it there as a supportive trust fund.

Of greatest importance to McCaslin Edmonds has been the guardianship of his early-orphaned young cousin Isaac. His concern runs far beyond duty to family. The boy had been admitted to unstrained companionable talk, of which much conveyed the essence of earlier times, such as stands transmuted into "Was." There is more direct and reciprocal intimacy too; in "The Old People" McCaslin imaginatively explains Sam Fathers' perceptible unrest as from consciousness of previous slavery and an earlier intrinsic freedom, and when the boy cries, "Let him go!" McCaslin liberally alludes to a deeper and now unanswerable imperative in Sam's awareness, of things "tamed out of our blood," suggesting comparatively a kind of reduction for white men, who having forgotten such

experienced insights, "have to live together to protect ourselves from our own sources." Himself having known Sam
Fathers in the big woods, McCaslin Edmonds does not dero-
gate such racial wisdom, nor the mystique the man Isaac has
laid hold on and held to from it. Still, even as adversary in
their most crucial discussion on the day Isaac was twenty-one
and "could say it," McCaslin is his younger cousin's real friend,
trying to bring him around to what is presumed a more prudent
and socially positive course, yet respectful of Isaac's achieved
identity as well as his just-acquired status. That last meeting
the story records, twenty-four hours later in Isaac's newly
occupied room in Jefferson, with McCaslin proffering money
under a pose of gruffness and Isaac resistant yet tentatively
friendly, reveals both men wracked by the pain of their
severance.

Their suspension in this impasse is not static; it projects
enigmas compounded of variant individual circumstances,
values, and fates. Under aspects of reality, each man is impinged upon in unique terms. Yet they are joined too, and not
just by blood or to a locale and common associations, but in a
regional and societal situation that is broadly typical and
widens beyond boundaries into even more representative
human problems of right conduct. For the greater part of
section 4 of "The Bear" (there in the commissary, the base of
McCaslin's years of responsible efforts and the locale of Isaac's
probably determinative discoveries) the interrogation and
defense of Isaac's renunciation, running on in the dialogue
and enlarged by Isaac's rememberings and speculations,
extend beyond family matters into meanings of the South's
history, and the country's future, and into both men's more
speculative considerations of the human lot. Isaac's drama,
emerging by stages in "The Old People," mounts in "The
Bear" through his personal advances and the dramatic climaxes of that story's parts, and at its high point is rendered
throughout section 4, the most impressive realistic mélange
and sustained compositional medley in American fiction.
Beyond mélange, its elements are tactically ordered and pro-

portioned; beyond medley, its effects become contrapuntal; as composition it approaches the architectonic with its massive intrications. Cumulative references, rememberings, and affirmations, often expressive of opposed outlooks and personalities, repeatedly tend beyond regional instance to broader issue, but the essence of their evolving concepts is volatilized through the experiential, concretely represented. And this is not mere virtuosity; it has an end in view.

Such an acute personal factor is no more than is required for any dynamic fictional movement and effect, but it is not easily sustained when weighty thematic elements draw the imagination into wider associations, beyond the immediate scene and even into generalizations. Yet in that great section 4 Isaac's and McCaslin's active counter-presences, and the merged conveyance of past instances and reflective syntheses through Isaac's intense consciousness, keep the matter continuously in motion, with its protagonists always as its felt reactors. Such a reach of Faulkner's genius shows strongly throughout his work. With the broad deep panoramic backdrop of region and history which his stories must have, the characters nevertheless are not dwarfed or even distanced; they loom, and even the barely whispered *secretae* of their inmost awareness are clearly audible. Man's fate presses its claims upon empathy most closely as it is particularized in such animate men and women, while their separative uniqueness obversely insists upon implications of the representative. These reciprocations not only increase persuasiveness but add a peculiar validity in literary art, and such scope can hold accomplished fiction above the simplistic reductiveness which lurks in abstractions that descend into clichés.

For his concerned and searching presentation of Isaac McCaslin as a major protagonist, seen in his particular shaping and the early nonconforming thrust of his life, Faulkner required a character as adequate foil, a man of proven virtues, flexible intelligence, and human sensibilities. McCaslin Edmonds is so well shaped to these ends that he becomes a memorable figure in his own right, shown in detail to certify his stature and worth. That he is a McCaslin, on the distaff side, who has energetically sustained and consolidated the McCaslin estate through most difficult times and has held it with familial loyalty for its direct male heir at his majority, not only abets the narrative but makes it possible for Isaac to act with single purpose, knowing that he does not leave the enterprise and those dependent on it without someone competent to maintain it. However, this does not lessen the painful stress between the ideologically separated but attached and mutually respectful cousins, and this personal element enhances the drama of their adversary positions and thus fictionally vitalizes the large questions at issue. McCaslin himself having had the incomparable Sam Fathers, of mixed but predominantly Indian blood, as his tutor in the hunter's skill and ethic, he has allowed the boy Isaac to become Sam's devoted listener and pupil. However, this had evolved into discipleship, and McCaslin was to find from Isaac's first statements in the commissary debate that his young cousin is indeed a convert, and that the very base of Isaac's refusal to accept the inheritance is his conviction that the legal title to it is invalid, because the land never belonged to the Chickasaw chief Ikkemotubbe to sell, because (as that annunciatory preface to "Was" had put it concerning old Uncle Ike's beliefs) "the earth was no man's but all men's, as light and air and weather were." Now Isaac supplements Sam Fathers' Indian faith by reference to "the Book," which he interprets as telling how "He made the earth first and peopled it with dumb creatures, and created man to be his overseer on the earth . . . not to hold for himself and his descendants inviolable title forever" but "mutual and intact in the communal anonymity of brotherhood, and all the fee He asked was pity and humility and sufferance and endurance and the sweat of his face for bread." McCaslin informedly and eloquently argues otherwise, from the empirical grounds of man's history ever since he "was dispossessed of Eden," with its realistic implication of the inherence of evil. Yet McCaslin cannot prevail, for he confronts a pure form of intractability, conscientious objection to a generally accepted assumption—though in this matter as in others neither had the good McCaslin's conscience gone unexamined, and it would be hard to find a more admirable traveler upon the middle road of active and broadly referent responsibility. But Isaac has emerged from his shapings as one of those rarer men who, like Hamlet and with the same regard for the whole truth in the drama of mankind's existence, would not have its enactments "overdone, or come tardy off," and to whom its "reform" if "indifferently" accomplished is not enough, it must be outright, "altogether!" So in the absence of such a possibility Isaac will separate himself from what he deplores.

The belief Isaac embraces instead is that of "the old people," Indians of an earlier time, Sam Fathers' "vanished and forgotten people," with their reverence for the land itself and for its wild creatures, whom they honorably may take for food but do not heedlessly slaughter. So on the day when Isaac at twelve had shot his first deer, Sam Fathers had marked his face with the animal's blood and "he ceased to be a child and became a hunter and a man." The equation of the two in this context and under what Sam Fathers has inculcated suggests value-concepts (as with the physical-ideal components latent in the word virtue), and even intimates "verities," and this the full passage continues to illustrate. That same day, when a large buck passes Sam and Isaac fearlessly at close range and very like a phantom, Sam raises his right arm with open palm outward and salutes it: "Oleh, Chief. Grandfather," and years later Isaac on his solitary farewell journey at eighteen into the doomed great woods ritually makes the same gesture and repeats the same words to a large old rattlesnake that crawls past. Then as an old man, in "Delta Autumn," it is a sobered but still faithful Isaac who speaks simply to the younger hunters of the Creator's providence and "most men's" inclination to live correspondingly by principle, "not just because there is a man with a badge to watch us"—as with shooting only bucks, not does. When Wyatt points to the obvious pragmatic reason, "because if we did kill does in a few years there wouldn't even be any bucks left to kill," and Isaac calls that "just the mind's reason a man has to give himself because the heart dont always have time to bother with thinking up words that fit together," he seems to be asserting a deeper natural desire to preserve the providentially given. Among those men on that last Delta hunt for him, Isaac was still accepted as traditionally one of the group; he was also genuinely respected for his woodsmanship, out of which fullness he had taught several of them as boys. Yet as the story proceeds, there is to be felt a natural division in various degrees between him and them, more a matter of his atypicality than the gap between generations, and such as probably had always existed between him and others during the untold middle decades of his life, while nevertheless he became nominally "uncle to half a county." A consistent pietist, even one like Isaac who will state his beliefs but does not intrusively evangelize, is not easily suffered by the general run of men. Indeed, even some genial readers may not react congenially toward Isaac; they may well think he should have come to recognize that a primitive world view, out of isolated situation and a simpler societal context in which there was more elbow-room and less necessity for complex material organization, should give way to emerging realities. (In larger, looser terms this nation generally has been indifferent or even hostile toward American Indians who, on theocratic grounds similar to what Sam Fathers had taught Isaac, have protested against a federal abrogation of its treaties, in a utilitarian encroachment.) But Isaac had grown in a rural environment, with vestiges still of the frontier in its portions of primeval forest; moreover, he had been indoctrinated early in a fundamental attitude toward the natural world, even before he entered at ten into a hunter's life in the big woods with Sam Fathers still at his shoulder.

Since Faulkner is so dependably sure in his disposings of proportion and emphasis, it would seem that the detailed stress on Isaac's discoveries from the commissary ledgers of his grandfather's miscegenation and incest with a slave woman and their daughter may have precipitated and at least

must have spurred his gathering intention to sever himself from what to him was a tainted inheritance. It is not
surprising that McCaslin Edmonds showed no surprise over
Isaac's possession of this family history and its ongoing consequences. Doubtless the elder cousin has known it since his boyhood; cryptic entries by the patriarch's sons Uncles Buck and
Buddy showed them puzzling it out from the earlier pages of
that same record, and they had probably talked freely (as they
do in "Was") in the presence of their young Edmonds ward,
while later he constantly used the ledgers himself. McCaslin
may even have given the gist of it to Isaac, but not in detail,
for the incest is a horrifying surprise to the sixteen year old,
whose thought is almost a cry: *"His own daughter His own
daughter. No No Not even him."* Certainly the Beauchamp
Negroes of McCaslin blood possessed the knowledge and
handed it on; there is evidence from "Delta Autumn" that
Tennie's Jim (forbear of the woman in this story), who left the
plantation the night he was twenty-one, carried it northward
and had told his family of it. And though it does not enter
specifically into the dialectical opposition between the cousins
in the commissary, it may have tempered the just-minded
McCaslin Edmonds' tone, for this man who believes that
personal shame is intolerable can see Isaac's distress over what
he conscientiously feels he must say and do. However, from
the first Isaac bases his argument with McCaslin on Genesis
fortified by what Sam Fathers had told him of "the old
people," the Indian view that men's use of the land is not by
title to it but under the Creator's providential allowance,
which requires care of it too, and of all its living creatures. It is
in confronting this argument that the elder cousin carries the
matter beyond Isaac's correlation of Genesis with primitive
Indian religion, into the larger historical perspective since
"man was dispossessed of Eden," and on beyond "the tedious
and shabby chronicle of His chosen sprung from Abraham" to
the "five hundred years during which half the known world
. . . was chattel to one city" and "the next thousand" after
Rome's fall "while men fought over the fragments of that col-

lapse," and then "a new hemisphere" was discovered. Here McCaslin does not state but is implying the continuousness of courses of action men have followed from the first, for he asserts that their McCaslin ancestor "did own" the land, he "Bought it, got it, no matter; kept it, held it, no matter; bequeathed it: else why do you stand here relinquishing and repudiating?" Having thus extrapolated from history the on-going realities of men's aggressive acquisitiveness, McCaslin returns to Isaac's theological premise, asking where "this Arbiter, this Architect, this Umpire" had stood, for if He saw, He "at least did nothing," so was He "perverse, impotent, or blind: which?" (Such passages as these given McCaslin Edmonds exemplify Faulkner's stylistically representing a natural and fairly common human tendency, especially in men, to become declamatory over a crucial issue, thereby disclosing character dynamically in its real concerns and tendencies.) Thematically what emerges here is McCaslin as skeptical ameliorist, whose assertion of identity and integrity has comprised seeing something needful to be done and doing it; he has brought the property through the debacle of defeat, made the land productive of useful commodities and supportive of all those who have tilled it, and maintained humanely a degree of order and amity among them, according to his lights.

Isaac holds to his position, taking up McCaslin's terms to posit that men, from the dream of Eden on, have repeatedly "dispossessed" God of his realm, and that through Columbus He opened to them "a new world where a nation of people could be founded in humility and pity and sufferance and pride of one to another." Now against that plan's failure Isaac can do nothing but repudiate men's frustration of it, and piously attempt an honorable life on simpler, less vulnerable, and more nearly innocent terms. He tries to explain this to the cousin he prizes and the man he recognizes as the real head of the family, not just *de facto* but in his competence, fidelity, and integrity, but Isaac does not set up as evangelist of a contrary and heretical doctrine. He comes to Jefferson, but he does no explaining to the community or even his close friends. Old General Compson, who had given his place in the forefront of the hunt to a well-deserving Isaac at sixteen, admits that "It looks like you just quit," but this he will not believe, because, he says, "I have watched you in the woods too much." Evidently Major de Spain had the same view, for he asked no questions but offered Isaac "a room in his house as long as he wanted it," and no doubt he sensed a propriety in it when Isaac refused, settled in the boarding house, and went to work as a carpenter. It is not to be overlooked that in his youth Isaac had precociously proved himself to such men, in a milieu with its own exacting criteria, where he was judged at first hand in explicit situations. And it has not been a passive following of Sam Fathers, even from the first; in the summer of his eleventh year he had ranged alone far into the woods on a kind of search for a vision, had got lost and found himself, and finally putting gun and compass aside had come close enough to see the legendary old bear crossing a sunny glade and even pausing to look back at him.

As Isaac, between his tenth and sixteenth years, came upon nature's realities in the big woods on those November hunts and summer outings at Major de Spain's camp, he was also establishing his sure footing in its select company of hunters, all idiosyncratic men, and was independently shaping his wider convictions. Growing up on the comparatively isolated McCaslin postbellum cotton plantation seventeen miles from Jefferson, he nevertheless had experienced from day to day the milieu of a biracial little society fairly complex in its operations and necessities, in which interpersonal awareness was constant and could be insistent. Beyond this there were inevitable wider influences upon a youth whose formative years coincided with a period of postbellum regional reconstruction, and among a people still circumstantially constrained to look before and after, in a concurrence of difficult adaptations and melancholy retrospection. Born after the war, Isaac had escaped the immediate impact of such consuming stress and the haunting presence of afterthoughts. As a boy, perhaps he envisaged it chiefly through two immediate aspects, his elder cousin's accounts and the presence on the plantation of emancipated Negroes, some of whom, notably of the Beauchamp line, had been there before and during the war, as had his mentor Sam Fathers. An orphan yet safely ensconced while also given entrance at ten into the hunters' mature company, Isaac was thus allowed an unusual perspective, in a degree of separation from those who had been there long before him and had known drastic changes beyond which traces of earlier ways and views had endured. Presumably his secondary knowledge of the world had been extended by his formal schooling, about which his guardian McCaslin Edmonds is seen to have been insistent. Under Sam Fathers' matchless tutelage and through his own commitment he rapidly made a place for himself among the hunters and secured the trust of Major de Spain and General Compson, and he had his cousin McCaslin's companionable help in assimilating his experiences into concepts broader than the specifics of a hunter's life. Well this side of his majority Isaac McCaslin is a deeply even if not broadly experienced young man. The multiple factors in his cultural heritage run from both Hebraic and American Indian theology about a Creator's expectations concerning men's use of His earth to a sure knowledge of how to "shoot quick, and slow," but at a rocklike median his convictions rest upon a self-engendered imperative to take a self-defined but mutually responsible and humane place in his society, other than what has evolved for him in a sequential but fortuitous, miscellaneous accumulation and dead weight called a heritage. Hence the prolonged and deeply probing discussion on Isaac's twenty-first birthday with his elder cousin McCaslin Edmonds in the not only steadily frequented but on this occasion symbolic setting, the commissary.

At the opening of that massive section 4 of "The Bear" Isaac steps fully into his expanding and decisive role as the clearly motivated protagonist of his own story in its dramaturgical unfoldings by his realizations and assertions throughout "The Old People" and "The Bear," to find its epilogue in "Delta Autumn," with Isaac's consistency maintained under further stress. McCaslin Edmonds in that commissary scene is a character already sufficiently set forth by Isaac's story to that point, and also man enough (not just through seniority and greater experience but in the finest sense of the word) to take an impressive adversary position against Isaac without demeaning his younger cousin or himself, and without obscuring the divergent claims of opposite positions. In fact, what makes the encounter so acute and gives it a degree of pathos is that these devoted cousins are both men of conscience, and very much alike in their declaration of that — McCaslin at one point saying of his own strenuous endeavors with the plantation, "I could do no else. I am what I am." and Isaac at another point putting it that his renunciation of inheritance is "something I have got to do." Isaac is not meaning to affront McCaslin, but only to try to explain what he scarcely understands yet senses to be supremely valid for himself as he formally takes a place in the world of men. He must know too that his elder cousin (and until today his concerned guardian) cannot easily consent to, though he would not presume to forbid, the rejection of a family heritage duly and frugally held for a rightful heir to accept. Faulkner is not thus deploying the elder cousin primarily to create the drama intrinsic in a close personal confrontation, much less a sheer spectacle of altercation, which this scene rises above throughout and is often its opposite. As human encounter this is of the subtlest order, outspoken yet not blunt and certainly with no element of personal antipathy, but touched instead with melancholy under sudden inescapable strain upon a long and devoted relationship between men who find themselves of necessity at a parting of ways, on matters of principle. However, neither is this antithesis coldly for its technical sake, in an undergirding of narrative action by dialectic. The fictionist's significant end in view at this point is a thematic stressing of relativism as a constant. This particular narrative deployment of these familiar characters, each with his established credentials as a man yet in basic ideological opposition, is for a precautionary glance at perplexities in the best-intentioned human conduct, which not only separate otherwise congenial persons from each other but may evolve into apparent ethical dilemma and evoke readers' contemplative recognition of enigma. All of which places Faulkner, by his own careful and candid intent, beyond the barren terrain and white/black hats of melodrama, and points toward a deeper reality, in that his two adversaries are both troubled by imperfections, liabilities, and riddles with no easy answer, and that their predicament is mankind's.

Toward the closure of section 3 in "The Bear," after the finale of the great hunt in which Old Ben has been killed by Boon's knife, the implacable dog Lion has been mortally clawed, and Sam Fathers has collapsed, there is a telling episode when General Compson intervenes in a contention between Isaac, then sixteen, and his conscientious guardian McCaslin Edmonds. The men are leaving camp, with Boon and Tennie's Jim assigned to stay behind and take care of Sam Fathers, whom Boon has carried into the old man's hut and put to bed. The summoned doctor had pronounced it a case of exhaustion and perhaps shock, yet added, "He'll be all right," but "only the boy knew that Sam too was going to die." Though Isaac will not explain to the others why he wants to stay (not choosing to set his deeper intuitions against McCaslin's reasonable decision that it is time for him to get back to his schoolwork), he does plead his case, with promises to return on Sunday and make it all up, but McCaslin bluntly says, "No, I tell you." At that point General Compson takes over, in Isaac's behalf, while admitting only as of lesser worth McCaslin's prudence and practicality. Having said, "Hold up, Cass," and asked, "What is it, bud?" and being told only, "I've got to stay. I've got to," he declares, "All right. You can stay," depending on Isaac's promise to be back by Sunday. Then the old general (whom Faulkner summarizes elsewhere as being himself no very practical conserver of the Compson estate) puts it thus to McCaslin Edmonds:

You've got one foot straddled into a farm and the other foot straddled into a bank; you aint even got a good hand-hold where this boy was already an old man long before you damned Sartorises and Edmondses invented farms and banks to keep yourselves from having to find out what this boy was born knowing and fearing too maybe but without being afraid, that could go ten miles on a compass because he wanted to look at a bear none of us had ever got near enough to put a bullet in and looked at the bear and came the ten miles back on the compass in the dark; maybe by God that's the why and the wherefore of farms and banks.

As always with this artist, no such explicit speaking by a character is to be taken for the voice of Faulkner; that can only be sensed as cadences and in the resonance of context within larger contexts composing the total fictional entity. In this scene there are subtler aims, and implications beyond the old general's blunt intrusion. However, that has touched veraciously on Isaac's virtue and prowess already shown in his eleventh summer, and they are indeed of a higher order than the merely utilitarian. Beyond this, General Compson projects though unknowingly the irreversible separation to come between the cousins at Isaac's majority. And even now in this situation, as again then and again thereafter to his wife, Isaac has spoken *in character:* "I've got to stay. I've got to." As between him and his wife there can be no question who is the virtuous one, for she has been disingenuous and devious in the closest of personal relationships. So in any just estimation of Isaac his resoluteness as well as his consistency at that point cannot be overlooked, for he has surrendered a great hope and a lifelong expectation and resisted the most tantalizing of bribes to maintain his principles. Thereafter Isaac stoically has made the best of it, as of his time, place, and local culture; he has endured. Though her invalidating his expectations and her derogating his very way of being shadows his life with a certain futility while he is still in his twenties, he refused to deny his own idealism, and even in old age he will recall the act of love as a sharing in which for its while at least the two became one. Yet when in "Delta Autumn" he mused generically that "women hope for so much" he was being charitable to her (perhaps because he could not bear to be anything else), for had he judged his wife by his standards he would have said she hoped for so little, in putting mere property and status above what they might have had in a modest, mutually devoted life. Yet while Faulkner succinctly made all this quite plain in "The Bear" and "Delta Autumn," he has not implied any such contrasting of right and wrong as between Isaac McCaslin and McCaslin Edmonds, and the text would have to be blinked at to come to such a conclusion.

Old General Compson was intuitively right in insisting that if Isaac feels he must stay he should be allowed to, even though the lad is unwilling to explain more than by naming it a necessity. However, the general does not comprehend and cannot do justice to the McCaslin Edmonds Isaac has known as his kind, careful guardian, who has helped form the boy's spirit, and who even in the future hour of their separation will be "no kin to him at all yet more than kin," in the painful paradox of divergence between those who continue to honor and care for each other. As McCaslin Edmonds stands in Isaac McCaslin's story he could remind superficial advocates of the feasibly opportune that a man more resolute and capable than the best of them did not denounce his younger cousin for renouncing his inheritance, and even during the boy's upbringing had tried to help him lay hold upon his formative idealistic realizations. And Faulkner has enforced this aspect of the matter by making McCaslin Edmonds a person of impeccable honor and enduring fidelity and a fine, strong, subtly sensitive man in his own way and right. It is possible that compositionally McCaslin Edmonds in the commissary debate may seem at first to be dramatically projected as a corrective foil against Isaac McCaslin in his radical self-declared freedom at twenty-one. Yet while Edmonds' strenuous adversary stance is plainly an attempt to dissuade Isaac from an announced purpose, that is scarcely to be taken as a fictional soliciting of the reader's preference between the cousins in this opposition, even though their searching arguments are over major issues that naturally stimulate opinions. At this point in the well-detailed course of their long, close, and more than cousinly connection, with its habit of intimate personal communication, even to consider needful an explicit judgment favoring one or the other may obscure wider implications, and these in their inclusiveness seem to show the artist's main intent. As adversary McCaslin Edmonds is in no way antagonistic, but instead consistently and quite humanly the opposite. Had he been a materialistic pragmatist or a mere unimaginative conformist, McCaslin probably would have washed his hands of Isaac on the spot, though such a man scarcely would have denounced a direct heir for letting his inheritance pass to this elder cousin next in line, nor conversely could that final scene in Isaac's boardinghouse room even have occurred, with McCaslin Edmonds' need to mask by gruffness the melancholy of his deep personal concern.

Isaac, too, had been not just nominally respectful toward the admired and valued cousin he calls the head of his family, to whom he feels he owes an explanation; and to a degree he is even apologetic in his comparative inability to define his side of the matter. Not only was there never any acrimony or disdain in their exchanges; sometimes as if out of well-established habit they spontaneously supplement each other's statements. Most tellingly at one point there is that wordless recurrence of characteristic rapport between them when during a ranging discussion of Negroes' traits something (perhaps the word "dogs") makes them simultaneously remember (and Isaac can see that "it was in McCaslin's eyes too") an incident seven years earlier, when McCaslin had tried to help the youth realize the idealistic nature of his not shooting at the old bear but impulsively and hazardously rescuing the little fyce instead. Most significantly concerning basic Faulknerian outlook as conceptually recurred to in this scene on Isaac's twenty-first birthday, McCaslin Edmonds is quite other than a foil to him; he is rather a counterpoise, a makeweight, dramatizing a complexity beyond exclusive antithesis, at one of those points where a man of principle and of profound civility will know what he must or must not do yet will not presume to prescribe that choice for others, and privately taking such a positive ethical stand is sure index of character. If due yielding to the text's continuities in itself discovers that it is not devised primarily to extract a preference between these two cousins, conversely it may be found to elicit recognition of an impasse more than personal, and indeed typical of ubiquitous occurrence and inescapable stringency. Nowhere more pointedly and brilliantly than in Isaac McCaslin's story has Faulkner illustrated this large matter. Isaac and his elder cousin McCaslin, so much alike through their holding certain conceptual bases for their drives toward honorable conduct, are opposite in their applied courses of action; beyond that debate over the latter which severs them, McCaslin Edmonds through some substantial concurrence between them becomes an adequately complementary figure to his younger cousin, Faulkner's drastic protagonist.

This involving of the complementary within the antithetical is not only the most inclusive and complex representation of characters confronting issue, it is the most humanly realistic. Moreover, through such a comprehensive view the artist has projected the inescapable factor of relativism, not as a stark philosophical abstraction, much less as chance for an opportunistic kind of situational ethics, but as an intensifying element recurrent as issue in considered human conduct. Here and consistently elsewhere in Faulkner's works, relativism does not indicate any retreat from his fundamental humanism. This he maintains credibly in persuasive fictional contexts whose enactors are conceived of as called upon by given situation to establish some truce this side of total reconcilement between hardly amendable circumstance and their basic faith in abiding principles. It is not in the compromise that verges on surrender; it does stipulate that the half-loaf which the world rations for ethical subsistence must be entirely wholesome and worthily partaken of. And it is through an undeceived acknowledgment of such relativism that Faulkner's humanistic realism attains its consistency and strength.

Certain "verities" Faulkner attempted to delineate operatively in fiction and formally pronounced at Stockholm are not exclusively his articles; they are made referents in the represented lives of many of his major characters, and it is only the plot element of a debate (as again it will in *A Fable*) that gives them such definition between McCaslin Edmonds and Isaac McCaslin. In the commissary, in their simultaneously recalled incident from seven years before when McCaslin had read the Keats ode to the scarcely comprehending fourteen-year-old, he had explained that the poet "was talking about truth," as it "covers all things which touch the heart — honor and pride and pity and justice and courage and love." This had been to counsel the boy to trust his deepest urgings according to their widest relevance, as in his saving the little dog and not shooting the old bear. Now at Isaac's majority he defends Genesis as trustworthy authority because "the men who wrote his Book for Him were writing about truth and there is only one truth and it covers all things that touch the heart." Though there is irony in Isaac's returning McCaslin's earlier words upon him in argument, more broadly it instances McCaslin's strong influence upon his younger cousin, especially as that continues to show in the two men's fundamental likeness despite differences, through their reliance upon what they conceive of as humane principles. Nor is Isaac merely echoing McCaslin' imperatives as they constitute the one truth; he too has enumerated certain verities inferred from "what He told in the Book" in that "all the fee He asked" for men's holding the earth "mutual and intact in the communal anonymity of brotherhood" was "pity and humility and sufferance and endurance and the sweat of his face for bread." Furthermore, it is revelatory of theme that McCaslin Edmonds doubtless would grant the validity of Isaac's abstractions. McCaslin himself has demonstrated a commitment to labor, to resuscitate the plantation with both productive and humanly beneficial results, as Isaac will strive to do as a carpenter, and it is striking how alike the cousins are in their distaste for the impractical pretentious Northern freedman who carries off Fonsiba to a rundown Arkansas farm which Isaac finds he has left unimproved while this proclaimer of a "new Canaan" sits reading through lensless spectacles beside an insufficient fire. Moreover, McCaslin too not only has named pity as an element of the truth he finds ideally conceived of in the Keats ode, he has shown himself a compassionate as well as just man again and again. And in the same explanation of the heart's truth to the lad Isaac, McCaslin had named "honor and pride," which also he shows in his life and which virtues seem animated by his conviction that the one intolerable thing is "shame," such as he would feel if he violated his sense of what he must do and be. So doing and being, in middle age he could say to Isaac, "Even you can see that I could do no else. I am what I am."

This is a key to the intended dramatic realism in Faulkner's accounts of these cousins' circumstantially intertwined lives. For all the range and venture into abstractions of their crucial commissary discussion, these men are not just theorists but activists, and they differ less about honorable and proper ends than about viable means. Hence there exists between them an enlarging empathy as Isaac matures, in the recognitions each accords the other. Their dialogue is saturated with existential motion, under the impulses in both of that "human heart" by which, says Wordsworth, "we live." Isaac had made up his mind early and apparently was never in any doubt as he waited until "he could say it" and settle it. He is not to be dissuaded by McCaslin's arguments, and later neither would he buy his way back into his wife's favors by installing her as spouse of a gentleman farmer, in abandonment of his manhood's primary declaration of principle. McCaslin's continued regard and concern for Isaac at his majority took into account the man of conscience, as no light matter. Correspondingly, at the close of "The Old People" when McCaslin was affirming "living, pleasuring . . . grieving and suffering too, of course . . . but still getting a lot out of it," he had added his basic declaration, "There is only one thing worse than not being alive, and that's shame." Certainly in these contexts this means more than that loss of general esteem called disgrace. As McCaslin must imagine it, because he has never let himself know it, shame is inward, a self-confrontation over one's self-violated convictions and in the light of whatever principles one has valued.

These in their operative force, however, are not explicitly engraved on any stone tablet or ancient stele; their enduring validity is as of something more arcane, that can be approximated only as a sort of folk wisdom felt as consensus of human experience, by which responsibly endeavoring beings have come into realizations in sociopersonal good conscience. Moreover, each must arrive at his own intimation of what is incumbent upon him in his situation and as truly himself, which will allow him an honorable pride, in an experienced self-possession and humane involvement. Verities thus dynamically conceived of in Faulkner's fiction are synthesized into drama and become its energizer; this can produce an utmost thrust of realism, psychologically and in its interpersonal contexts. Such narrative stressings will pass into an entirely different order of perception and evocation beyond that of melodrama, with its narcotic illusion that good and evil are obvious and absolute opposites, and good is always to be fully realized, with evil completely put down by infallible heroes. Instead, Faulkner's protagonists suffer the common human lot of bafflement and uncertainty, under changes to which the changes in themselves are not always commensurate or even acquiescent. Hence there is liability to disenchantment and inhibitive dilemma, under the kaleidoscopic light of relativism. This difficulty Faulkner does not resolve or even seem to mitigate except through its pathos that may quicken a liberal empathy; what this artist does as responsible realist is to show the factor of relativism as it bounds and limits the endeavors of representative human beings, and to imply that this is what may evoke in fallible men of good will a contrary corrective alertness to verities and a commitment to whatever possible application of them. If Faulkner achieves any conciliation and precarious equilibrium between verities and the relativism of self-verified human insights, it is as these latter shape into understanding and consequent acceptance of imperatives, but the names for them will remain cloudy symbols beyond full realization by individuals in their approximating enactments.

With Isaac the constantly present protagonist of "The Old People," "The Bear," and "Delta Autumn" (whether actively or in consciousness as ranging recollection and imaginings), McCaslin is also very much there during the first two, in a wide spectrum as a youth's guardian and a young man's foil, to become in sum his cousin's counterpart. At many points, in positive manly traits, the two are essentially in accord, and most of all in that neither would descend to what in his own eyes he deemed shameful. Yet McCaslin has committed himself to a specific course which Isaac absolutely refuses to follow, and for each cousin his action has been according to his lights. Faulkner, maintaining that distance and measure which are of his own integrity as a fictionist, has not led on to a relative evaluation of the two, much less enforced it. His real emphasis between them is a matter of fictional technique, in making Isaac protagonist, presumably with an instinct that here lay the existential center of a matter which was to include vitally such other actors as McCaslin Edmonds, Sam Fathers, and Boon Hogganbeck, as well as an old bear, a little fyce, and a big dog. Correspondingly Faulkner chose to "place" McCaslin firmly enough and give him sufficient dimension for a reciprocal role in a story where any genuine promptings of conscience are such as it would be shameful for an honorable man not to answer to. Undertaking the subject of these two men's involvements with environment and inheritance in comparable but separate and separately assessed situations where each could "do no else," Faulkner's telling discloses that circumstantial factors no matter how similar do not operate identically with different persons, and may evoke responses utterly at variance, wherein each may seem to have some grounds in the broad areas of possible conduct. On such a base the story becomes profoundly representative, yet it is held at the proper fictional distance, this side of advocacy, leaving to readers whatever implications they may apprehend in so rich and subtle a bodying forth.

That Isaac has not wholly failed is implied in that the melancholy circumstantially forced upon him is held in a way which can contain and preserve his essential convictions. This is developed in "Delta Autumn," but it has been made implicit in "The Bear" together with earlier allusions and instances, and Faulkner has scrupulously left it at that. Isaac's suggested stance is not a cultivated apathy or even an inert fatalism such as some Faulkner characters are shown falling into. His resignation is not a benumbed and impervious negativity. Rather, in Isaac a uniquely conditioned stoicism has certain positive and historically classical elements, running beyond a disciplined composure. He has discovered and pursued that large accord with nature which supplies a sense for order and a paradigm of right reason. He has committed himself to a dynamic good conscience, as it points to what he considers sound societal relationship and its duties, and for the sake of peace and blamelessness. This separates him to a degree from more pragmatic men—and completely from any merely expedient behavior or opportunely accommodated opinion. If to some readers this seems to isolate and even immobilize Isaac McCaslin, he cannot be charged with falling short without still fully crediting what is exacted of any (and of this man as of his time and place) in taking a contrary stand and holding his ground. Especially if the sustained action is of the order to which the poet of "Carcassonne" aspired: *Something bold and tragical and austere,* as it proves to be for Isaac McCaslin.

Isaac has made and paid his way in the world, yet his real work has been his life itself, in following a vocation by waiting upon and obeying his intimations of what is needful toward a right relationship to his fellowmen and for an inner peace. This "uncle to half a county," a childless patriarch, becomes one whose example and word will linger in various minds, even as it has been with Mink Snopes in "The Mansion," when he realizes he cannot carry off a lie to someone as committed as Isaac is to the fact of the matter and the truth itself. To many others, and especially the hunters, who know him more closely, he is of an incorruptibility rarely seen and possibly somewhat disturbing—as it has been for certain readers. Plainly Isaac is one whose accepted inheritance from Sam Fathers, as the world transmuted it for him, included a vast loneliness. Yet he is not isolate, for he typifies a universal, the solitude of consciousness itself, and its unrest in a hunger for perfection, under the relative restraints of actuality. As of his times and Southern milieu, in a life that ran from postbellum days to the verge of World War II, Isaac personates the prophet, with an unflinching view that finally apprehends society's further doom. More enduringly, Isaac resembles the poet Faulkner envisaged in "Carcassonne," surrealistically situated between a romantic past and modernity's harshness, but mounted "on a buckskin pony with eyes like blue electricity and a mane like tangled fire, galloping up the hill and right off into the high heaven of the world." Written during the New Orleans period of Faulkner's early endeavors, but then placed as the concluding piece in both *These Thirteen* and the *Collected Stories*, "Carcassonne" thereby seems a sort of signature to an affirmation that was to be repeatedly made good, as what was latent in Faulkner evolved into controlled torrents of creativity. Yet among his world of characters, many of them overheard in the secret dialogues of subjective consciousness between itself and its external points of reference, perhaps no one would more deserve to have that poet's aspiring words for epitaph than Isaac McCaslin.

"Go Down, Moses"

Given his concept of a work of several distinct narrative sections throughout which certain thematic elements recurred in one embodiment or another, it would have been uncharacteristic for Faulkner to have concluded his novel *Go Down, Moses* with "Delta Autumn." Even though this section, taken with its immediate precursors, "The Old People" and "The Bear," completes a masterful triptych of Isaac McCaslin's life as it emerged, asserted, and sustained itself through more than seventy years, and even though this connected narrative in its entirety is the most massive, intricate, and weighty portion, it is but half the book. Constituting a brilliantly rendered novella, it is directly though cryptically presaged from the first by "Was" and "The Fire and the Hearth"; then "Pantaloon in Black" and "Go Down, Moses" frame it on either side at some distances in circumstance and differences in tone, yet with the marked relevance of racial themes. And though Isaac's concluding speech in "Delta Autumn," by merging resolute confrontation under relentless odds, has the force of a maintained premise and an earned epitaph, neither it nor any other phrase could sum up a life so strenuously ethical, in a tangential striving beyond moderate accommodation to a world of economically pragmatic men. Nor was Faulkner as fictionist given to heavily orchestrated finales or emphatic curtain lines, but rather favored a modulation into a coda going perhaps somewhat beyond the climactic point into a tempered closure, granting the reader the possible effect of a subsidence from being possessed by the work to possessing it reflectively. Furnished with its own distancing and iridescent closure, the brief story "Go Down, Moses" as an entity does something comparable to this for the Isaac McCaslin tripartite novella and for *Go Down, Moses* as a subtly synthesized novel.

The fifteen-page final story is structured out of brief scenes, concrete yet economical in themselves, and running preponderantly in simple chronology, with an especially significant connection between a short first section and all the rest. To begin with, a young Negro, modishly dressed, is lying on his cot in the penitentiary at Joliet, Illinois answering a census taker's questions, and instead of using the name under which he had been convicted of murdering a policeman, he identifies himself as "Samuel Worsham Beauchamp. Twenty-six. Born in the country near Jefferson, Mississippi." Then, with the census taker gone, the Negro "lay on the steel cot smoking until after a while they came and slit the expensive trousers . . . and led him out of the cell." What follows sectionally, marked 2, constitutes the rest of the story, and it begins connectedly with a transitional and localizing device: "On that same hot, bright July morning the same hot bright wind which shook the mulberry trees just outside Gavin Stevens' window blew into the office too . . . fluttered among the county-attorney business on the desk . . ." On this same morning as in the preceding scene in Illinois there comes into this room in Mississippi the same wind which moves in the mulberry trees outside — the not entirely parallel constructions emphasize a shift not only in locale but in focus and tone, yet also a coincidence in more than time and in local windy weather. Stevens is speaking to "a little old negro woman," and his first word, "Beauchamp?" repeats not only what a census taker in Illinois has written down today but what apparently the old woman has just told him. He then adds his further recognition, that she lives on "Mr. Carothers [Roth] Edmonds' place," and he finds she is presently staying in town with her brother Hamp Worsham, and what she wants is "to find my boy." Stevens, beginning to assemble some memories, realizes this means her grandson, and asks how she knows he's in trouble if she doesn't know where he is. Her answer is firm. "I dont know whar he is. I just knows Pharaoh got him. And you the Law." (Pharaoh figures symbolically in the Negro spiritual which calls upon Moses to "go down" and set free the enslaved, from whatever the form of their restriction.)

And Gavin Stevens does indeed embody the law, to the full extent of a county attorney's functions and more, and Faulkner has introduced him with data to prepare readers for this atypical officer of the court. He is not just a Harvard graduate, Phi Beta Kappa, but a Heidelberg Ph.D., his office "was his hobby, although it made his living for him," and his "serious vocation" is extravagantly represented as "an unfinished translation of the Old Testament back into classic Greek." However, if such a work by such a hand were in progress there, at least its being "unfinished" would be credible, since Gavin's efforts (not just in "Go Down, Moses" but in his many appearances elsewhere) extend beyond legal formalities into the fullest possible service, personal as well as professional, to his fellow-beings. Which is why old Mollie comes to him. She leaves him remembering more about that lost grandson, Mollie Beauchamp's daughter's child, orphaned at birth by his mother's death and his worthless father's desertion, and raised by his grandmother, but having gone wrong and then broken out of jail and disappeared, an untraced fugitive from Jefferson. *"And that's who I'm to find, save,"* Stevens muses, but never doubting "the old Negress' instinct," nor would he have doubted "if she had also been able to divine where the boy was and what his trouble was." Wondering how to proceed, Stevens thinks *"not the sheriff, the police"* but something *"broader, quicker in scope,"* and so he goes to the editor of the county newspaper, to find that old Mollie Beauchamp's intuitions, though they had not extended to extrasensory perceptions, were acute. The newspaper editor has a press association dispatch just received; the matter had caught notice when a "Mississippi negro, on eve of execution for murder . . . exposes alias by completing census questionnaire." Gavin is assailed by a particular ambivalence, but one which could take many equally representative forms. In telling the editor that he is out to find the locally disreputable Butch Beauchamp because of his grandmother Mollie's apprehensions about him, Gavin had just said he hoped for her sake and the public's that "his present trouble is very bad and maybe final too," but then the editor showed him the dispatch, and as Gavin, returning to his office, is compassionately wondering how old Mollie had made the seventeen-mile journey into town, he says aloud to himself, "So it seems I didn't mean what I said I hoped." For the moment societal considerations are outweighed by his pity for one old Negro woman in her familial grief from which he will not be able to spare her.

Stevens reenters his office to find anothe visitor waiting (and here style itself conveys rather than describes the surprise: He "entered his office. He stopped. Then he said, 'Good morning, Miss Worsham'"). She is old, the impoverished only survivor of the family from whose slaves Mollie was descended; Belle

Worsham and Mollie were of the same age and had grown up like sisters, and Mollie's brother Hamp had remained with the Worshams after emancipation, as had Mollie until she, "a town woman," married Lucas Beauchamp, and "McCaslin Edmonds built a house for them and allotted Lucas a specific acreage to be farmed as he saw fit." Now Gavin must tell Miss Worsham what he has learned from the news bureau dispatch. She says Mollie "mustn't know" the details but that she "will want to take him back home with her" (for burial on the land where she had reared him), and when Gavin shows surprise, Miss Worsham explains, "He is the only child of her oldest daughter, her own dead first child. He must come home." When Miss Worsham states that she will "defray the expenses" he assures her they will not be much, since "a box" will be furnished and "there will be only the transportation." Miss Worsham's reply is an epitome of situation and character:

"A box?" Again she was looking at him with that expression curious and detached, as though he were a child. "He is her grandson, Mr Stevens. When she took him to raise, she gave him my father's name—Samuel Worsham. Not just a box, Mr. Stevens. I understand that can be done by paying so much a month."

Recognizing the necessity as Miss Worsham knows Mollie will feel it when she is told, again Gavin assents by repeating the words, "Not just a box," and begins to speak of securing contributions besides his own, "if you will permit me," but Miss Worsham says, "That will not be necessary," and he merely "watched her count onto the desk twenty-five dollars in frayed bills and coins ranging down to nickels and dimes and pennies," which she says "will take care of the immediate expenses." Gavin does not deny her this illusion; instead he asks if he should give the news to Mollie, and when Miss Worsham repeats that she will tell her, Gavin suggests that he come out to the old Worsham house to see Mollie that evening. "It would be kind of you," Miss Worsham says, and (with one of Faulkner's rhythmic stylistic effects) "then she was gone, erect, her feet crisp and light, almost brisk, on the stairs, ceasing."

By this point in the story the artist's skill in conducting a fictional composition has been typically demonstrated. It is truly an economy, in its discriminating allotment of emphasis, its ellipses accelerating the narrative flow, with a piquant and regionally enriched colloquial dialogue, and its pauses upon details incidental in themselves—either as imagery or in a character's momentary consciousness of situation—yet evoking imaginative response. (There is, particularly, the well-born spinster's assumption of a genteel understanding when Miss Worsham passes from "Not just a box, Mr Stevens" to the cryptic "I understand that can be done by paying so much a month.") One of Faulkner's simplest and most directly conveyed short stories, "Go Down, Moses" is the more clearly illustrative of his art in its prudence and providence. The less than two introductory pages, showing the Negro murderer in his Chicago cell, provides all that is needed to let the Jefferson, Mississippi scenes of the story follow without an obscuring mystery and suspense that would be aside from the work's main intent. The very spareness of this opening enters into structural effect by antithesis to what will follow in Jefferson. A laconic objectivity of Faulkner's narrative style in that first passage is carried over into Samuel Worsham Beauchamp's speech, as a brittle mask, its rigid fatalism his last mode of defiance. (It is not unlike the fixed hardness with which Popeye, awaiting execution, had played out to closure his affected role of sinister indifference in the latter pages of *Sanctuary*.) Beauchamp's coldness seems a posed acceptance in advance of the stark quality in his doomed life and its impending end. This is more than miles away from the tides of emotion as well as action that his fate will set flowing through Jefferson, in the nine successive dramaturgical scenes which the thirteen pages of section 2 contain.

One simple, inconspicuous example of a complication of economies occurs when Gavin tells Miss Worsham what he has learned from the newspaper dispatch and she says Mollie "mustn't know." Gavin then assures her that the editor "has agreed not to print anything." This is the first mention of that decision, but there is recorded a gap of time during which it could have been arrived at. As the reader may remember, the scene in the editor's office was broken off after Gavin's having scanned only the first lines of the news bureau dispatch, with the story's next paragraph showing him "five minutes later" recrossing the square and returning to his office to find Miss Worsham waiting. However, it is not necessary that a fiction reader hold a stopwatch on narrative episodes or in this instance even that the mention of a five-minute interval be remembered, though it probably would be, especially since the gist of what presumably happened then (the editor's agreeing not to print the story) is disclosed in the next event and on the next page by Gavin's reporting it to Miss Worsham as *fait accompli*. Thereby it enhances this more central scene, and also spares the previous scene a no doubt interesting but slightly tangential dialogue between Gavin and the editor. This is the more dispensable in that the two of them will return to the Beauchamp matter twice. The first occasion immediately follows that decisive and comparatively extended scene with Miss Worsham in Gavin's office, after which Gavin again crosses the square to tell the editor he expects him to contribute to the Beauchamp funeral expenses and asks, "All right?" The editor wryly says, "No it aint all right. But it dont look like I can help myself." Still, he thinks, "the novelty will be almost worth it," in his having "paid money for copy" he'd promised not to print. (His ironic understatement characterizes him; the wire service was already paid for and he will be paying out of sympathy for impoverished Miss Worsham and grieving old Mollie.) The second recurrence to the matter is between the two of them alone at the story's end, yet in a way to bring Mollie back into a central position and in a further aspect. Thus narrative economy can be a means not only of acceleration and thematic development but of distributing relative emphasis, and still can make place for such enhancements as the detailed vignettes of Mollie and then Miss Worsham, as Gavin has seen them in his office.

Only a dozen lines are given to describe how Gavin spent the rest of that hot July afternoon, not attending to the county's routine legal business but going about the town square, soliciting in the stores and offices "with his set and rapid speech: 'It's to bring a dead nigger home. It's for Miss Worsham.'" A certain tact is to be seen here; apparently Stevens doesn't identify the dead man (briefly notorious in Jefferson) nor tell how he died, nor does he add that it's primarily for Mollie Beauchamp; Miss Worsham's name is still enough to draw contributions from many, nor is it untrue that the endeavor is for her also. That evening Gavin is not catching up on office work; instead he walks out to the timeworn lamplit Worsham place at the edge of town to call on Mollie and give her what assurances he can. But the situation has its difficulties. Mollie and her brother Hamp are lamenting in their own way, responsively, with typical resort to Biblical analogy—"He dead. . . . Pharaoh got him. . . . Oh yes, Lord. . . . Done sold my Benjamin. . . . Sold him in Egypt. . . . Sold him to Pharaoh and now he dead"—and neither mourner pays attention to Miss Worsham's "Hush, Hamp. . . . Hush, Mollie. Hush, now." Gavin had begun by saying, "He'll be home by day after tomorrow, Aunt Mollie," but she "didn't even look at him." Gavin tries again, saying he had "telephoned Mr Edmonds" and he would "have everything ready when you get there"—presumably for a burial on the plantation—but the nearest response Stevens gets is, "Roth Edmonds sold my Benjamin," (another Biblical reference, to Jacob's youngest son—as also with Benjy Compson). Edmonds had expelled the Beauchamp youth from the place for breaking into and stealing from the commissary, but when Gavin tried to remind Mollie, "It wasn't Mr Edmonds," in what had followed (the crimes and jailbreak in Jefferson and the flight to the far-off North and further offenses there), she only repeats her lament, "Roth Edmonds sold my Benjamin." Realizing she isn't hearing him, Gavin says he'd "better go." He hurries out, disturbed by this racially typical mourning, so private and separate yet so rooted in a complex of local circumstances and lifelong familiarities. Miss Worsham has followed him to the door, and he says, "I'm sorry. I ask you to forgive me. I should have known. I shouldn't have come," but she tells him "It's all right. It's our grief." For her the lifelong alliance with Mollie and Hamp remains complete and natural.

The story moves at once into the penultimate episode: "And on the next bright hot day but one the hearse and the two cars were waiting when the southbound train came in." There was also a larger crowd than usual of curious bystanders. The two cars waiting were Stevens' with a hired driver, to convey Miss Worsham and old Aunt Mollie in the wake of the hearse out to the burial place, and the editor's car, in which he and Gavin will follow part way for the sake of appearances, for old Aunt Mollie's sake. As the little procession circled the Confederate monument in the town square it was watched by "the merchants and clerks and barbers and professional men who had given Stevens the dollars and half-dollars and quarters and the ones who had not" — the various contributors and the non-participants in this communal support of a strangely constituted ceremonial observance. To comprise its incongruities Faulkner's simple narrative style rises to the baroque concerning the four people in the two cars following the body in the hearse " — the high-headed erect white woman, the old Negress, the designated paladin of justice and truth and right, the Heidelberg Ph.D. — in formal component complement to the Negro murderer's catafalque: the slain wolf."

As the procession passed Jefferson's city limits and picked up speed, Stevens "reached over and cut the switch, so that the editor's car coasted" and he could brake it to a stop. Stevens' gesture not only suggests that they need not follow for the seventeen miles out to the old McCaslin place; it wordlessly says that the editor, whom he had so imperiously conscripted into this kindly project, has done quite enough. But the editor has further news for him, and the telling, with Gavin's reflective understanding of it, constitutes the story's closing scene, as the two men sit in the car that has been turned around but not started back toward town. The editor now reports that "this morning, back there at the station," Mollie has told him, "I wants hit all in de paper. All of hit." The editor was inclined to ask her if she wanted "how he really died" included, but he had only said, "Why, you couldn't read it, Aunty," and she answered, "Miss Belle will show me whar to look and I can look at hit." Stevens' only answer to the editor is "Oh." But his mind, that has been so busy with practical details in appeasing Mollie's grief, now muses on the essence of this outcome:

Yes, he thought. It doesn't matter to her now. Since it had to be and she couldn't stop it, and now that it's all over and done and finished, she doesn't care how he died. She just wanted him home, but she wanted him to come home right. She wanted that casket and those flowers and the hearse and she wanted to ride through town behind it in a car.

Once her "boy" has been "found," all Mollie's subsequent wants have been obviously conventional ones, and Gavin might have been no more than wryly amused that part of his labors supposedly in her behalf (persuading the editor not to print the story lest word of it leak back to Mollie out on the plantation) have been wasted. As the hearse and two cars with their four passengers traversed the town square doubtless some of the noncontributing spectators would have thought it was all too uppity and wondered why the county attorney and the paper's editor were taking this trouble over a no-good dead nigger — and they may think so still more when they read the paper's next issue; but no doubt the editor, having gone along with Gavin in the whole project with Miss Worsham's and Mollie's comfort in mind, will now do what the old Negro woman wants.

And now Gavin is seeing into the flow of Mollie's life, through her simple insistence on having her grandson "come home" but "come home right." Her desire that all of it be put into the paper, besides showing the importance which the lowly of this world attach to at least that much distinction for their lost loved ones, also symbolizes her acceptance of what *"had to be and she couldn't stop."* After such formal bewailing as Gavin had heard on his visit to the old Worsham place two nights before, Mollie's turn to this intentness on satisfying the funereal proprieties is, he sees, her acknowledgment of on-going realities. Whatever anyone's confrontation may be it is out of such engagement with "all of it" that the admirable trait of endurance is bred and accretes into human integrity. This old Aunt Mollie Beauchamp is she whose people had belonged to the Worsham family, she who had grown up with them like a sister to the daughter Belle; she is the "town woman" whom Lucas Beauchamp married and brought to live on the McCaslin/Edmonds plantation, she who in "The Fire and the Hearth" carried the others through crises follow-ing the death of Zack Edmonds' wife, and smoothed over the alienation in boyhood between young Roth and her son Henry, and in old age shook Lucas out of his obsession with divining gold by threatening to divorce him, she whom Roth Edmonds remembered from her unstinting role as the only mother he ever knew, and so now in her old age once a month would bring her "a tin of tobacco and a small sack of the soft cheap candy which she loved and visit with her for half an hour."

No doubt much of Mollie's story is known to Gavin, but even without that in any detail what he has witnessed and chosen to take an implemental part in during the last two days would be enough for this man's intuitive vision of a resolutely enduring life, open to hardship and grief, calm in acceptance of what had to be, yet assertively determined not just to make do but really to make whatever best of it was possible. It is through Gavin Stevens' ranging, acute, and generous aware-ness of such representative matters that he becomes this story's subjectively communicating protagonist. More broadly, his humane engagement in this comparatively minor episode serves to validate in their essence the thematically comple-mentary thrusts of the six other narratives which make *Go Down, Moses* a novel in the mode of a suite. But Gavin is yet to play his most revealing roles, in *Intruder in the Dust, Requiem for a Nun,* and the latter volumes of the Snopes trilogy; and as *Go Down, Moses* itself shows, Gavin has been preceded in earlier generations by just and compassionate Yoknapatawphan individuals whose involvements have been more tryingly personal than his in answering to socioethical issues, often with racial complications. Moreover, in "Go Down, Moses" Gavin has not acted alone; the editor has been an ironic but sincere ally, and was still to play a part according to Mollie's insistence, of which (under Faulkner's superb craft of narrative arrangement) he has just told Gavin. Yet as the two men sit there outside Jefferson in the motionless car, both bemused by what they have just had a part in, Gavin does not try to express his felt response to this latest aspect of the episode. Instead, he speaks what furnishes the story's sufficient closure: "'Come on' he said. 'Let's get back to town. I haven't seen my desk in two days.'"

And it is also the right closure for the novel. Anything weighty would have unduly overshadowed the much more broadly dimensioned and significant denouements that have gone before in matters of greater moment. Yet for those readers who come to "Go Down, Moses" by the straight right route of the six preceding narratives, and especially "The Bear," there is suspended in this closing story a somber factor sufficient to give pause. The "slain wolf" within that passing hearse, within that ceremonial flower-covered casket, is the cold corpse of Samuel Worsham Beauchamp, the great-great grandson (by way of the slave Tomasina) of the patriarch Lucius Quintus Carothers McCaslin, whose reappearing ghost has effectually, even fatally haunted the whole of *Go Down, Moses*.

10

Requiem for a Nun

REQUIEM FOR A NUN is centrally a succinct drama, but in substantial parts it is liberally impressionistic prose; it conjoins those two in alternation and contrapuntally, despite their antithesis as literary modes. The prose as background poises views of locally based events deriving from prehistory, history, or legend, all given a mythic tinge, while the drama is a specific contemporary tale of kinds of culpability and responses to them, constrained into dialogue but with some extension into Shavian effects through stage directions and descriptions. Both the force of the law and its operational limits are acutely illustrated, as Lawyer Stevens' philosophical interventions rise above adversary procedure toward intuitable areas of the ethical, while for Nancy Mannigoe, the assertive house servant, and Temple Drake Stevens, her errant mistress, the question of guilt moves beyond conventions of conduct or the law's provisions into a theological context. Gavin's humanistic existential dictum that the past is "never dead" and "not even past" is illustrated in both women, and while this comprises a private hell for each, Nancy is levitated out of hers by unquestioned religious faith, with presumed assurance of her eternal salvation, whereas Temple, desperately attempting that route without achieving its condition of unquestioning self-surrender, arrives at a restless impasse from which no exit seems forecast in any probable drift of subsequent events.

As a drama *Requiem* is written with versatile skill, ingeni-

583

ously ordered for fluent inclusion of earlier happenings needed to give present action its full significance, conveying abstract concepts through credible, forceful, and idiosyncratic dialogue, and shaping various scenes into a total literary structure. Nevertheless, Temple and Nancy are such distinctive characters that the august factor of consequence (with which Temple is entangled through inordinate self-will, and which Nancy for all her previous miseries has transcended by an invulnerable mysticism) needs the broader illustrations of history and its edifying abstractions, provided in the three introductory and supportive prose structures, as they variously illustrate the inexorable progression of causes into their effects. That these prose overtures are to be felt integral to the organic literary creation is suggested by their primary place within each of the drama's acts — and not as a summary prologue but a substantial cycloramic background and clearly sounded motif. The typography itself emphasizes this, beginning with "ACT ONE/ THE COURTHOUSE (A Name for a City)," and recounting the erection of such a structure in pioneer times, with a series of bizarre events that include the opportunistically calculated naming of Faulkner's Yoknapatawpha County seat, Jefferson.

The pioneers' improvisations, mingling instinct and calculated motives, left its creators "a little amazed, with something like humility too, as if they were realizing, or were for a moment at least capable of believing, that men, all men, including themselves, were a little better, purer maybe even, than they had thought, expected, or even needed to be." Their constructive actions, expressing the sense of community, had thereby strengthened confidence in it. The detailed and turbulent story of that quaint early endeavor is thus broadly illustrative, through those men's sensing of the basic mystique of a social order within which judge and jury are to render disinterested, equitable decisions under enacted law. And while "The Courthouse," set at a distance in time, is told with a degree of Faulknerian grotesquerie, this is to find its more starkly gripping opposite in those tensions which Temple and

Nancy are to play out with such immediacy, toward crises and cruxes beyond adjudication.

Only after that 42-page prose account of a settlement's consolidation into a town called Jefferson and the erection of its central civic structure—"symbolic and ponderable . . . protector of the weak, judiciate and curb of the passions and lusts, repository and guardian of the aspirations and the hopes"—does the narrative merge into staged drama with its brief but descriptively programmed Scene I, the sentencing of Nancy for having murdered Temple's infant daughter. Fluctuantly aspiring men, with scanty resources and limited capabilities, had built Jefferson's first courthouse as symbol of their societal intent, looking to the law for its regulating force and guarantees, but the drama of *Requiem* is to give thematic perspective to the gap between even the fullest reading and reach of the law and the human spirit's utmost travails. In the first scene of Act One this is epitomized dramatically but almost as abruptly as if in an announced text or definitive title. The described stage is the courtroom; evidently the jury has already given its verdict, and in what remains there are only four speeches, by four different voices. An unidentified one says, "Let the prisoner stand." The judge in regular order asks Nancy if she has anything to say before sentence is pronounced, and when she remains silent he details what her crime has been, sentences her to "be hanged by the neck until you are dead," and concludes with the usual formula, "And may God have mercy on your soul." Now Nancy speaks, "(quite loud in the silence, to no one, quite calm, not moving) Yes, Lord." She is not mistaking the judge's proper title, she is speaking over his head. From the spectators there is "a gasp, a sound . . . of shock at this unheard-of violation of procedure." The judge "bangs his gavel," and as the curtain descends the bailiff is shouting, "Order! Order in the court! Order!" In the liberal stage directions Faulkner describes that "gasp" as "the beginning of something which might be consternation and even uproar," and it could well be so, in this impingement between two worlds. Not replying to the judge, saying nothing in her defense or as confession, and then having been sentenced, Nancy addresses the higher court she envisions, and her answer to it as always is consent. The play in its entirey will not establish any viable channel of appeal between those two courts; it will dramatize the dichotomy of their conceptual relationships, and their actual separation.

The next two scenes of Act One are still prelude to the play's central action. In Scene II, later that same day of Nancy's sentencing, Temple, her husband Gowan Stevens, and Gowan's uncle Gavin Stevens are at the Gowan Stevens' house, and while Gowan is out of the room Temple wants to know how much Nancy has told Gavin as her legal representative, and learns he knows that "there was a man there" the night of the murder, but knows too it was not Gowan, who was out of town. Temple and Gowan are almost hysterically bitter, and in their different styles are sardonic about themselves as well as Nancy. They are going to California, to remain out of town until Nancy's execution, and they bluntly invite Gavin to leave them now. He lingers, Temple goes upstairs, and Gowan, showing how seared he is by thoughts of events eight years earlier, reviews his casual, irresponsible connections as well as Temple's more serious ones with the evil events of *Sanctuary,* which their propitiatory marriage and parenthood thereafter could not amend. Scene III of Act One is in the same room, four months later, and just before Nancy's scheduled execution; the Gowan Stevens have returned from California in response to Gavin's pricking telegram to Temple: "You have a week yet till the thirteenth. But where will you go then?" Now Gavin is pressing Temple to go with him to the Governor of Mississippi, "Tonight," and to speak out not just as Mrs. Gowan Stevens but as Temple Drake—this obviously because her disastrous involvement with Pete, Red's blackmailing brother, had its roots in the bordello episode in *Sanctuary.* Temple refuses, but after Gavin has gone she telephones to say she will be ready in half an hour, presumably to offer a personal confession as an appeal for pardoning Nancy. This makes way for placing Scenes I and III of Act Two in the office of the Governor.

The fact that even before Nancy's murder of their baby both Gowan and Temple had been beset, in different ways, by the unforgettable *Sanctuary* episodes eight years earlier has been underlined by parallel details at the conclusions of Scenes II and III in Act One. In the first of these Gowan had berated himself sarcastically, remembering not only that his drunkenness had exposed Temple to the rape at Frenchman's Bend and her captivity in Miss Reba's establishment, but that she had "loved it," meaning the visits by Popeye and his performing henchman Red. Now Gowan, still tortured despite or because of his gentleman's gesture in marrying Temple, almost takes to drink again, after his abstinence for the eight years since that precipitating accident with the car, but finally he upends the whiskey bottle over himself, (as if in a baptism confirming renewed resolution), repeatedly muttering, "So help me, Christ," and then tries to wipe himself off and restore some order to the room. In the next scene, in that same room four months later, when at first Temple refused to go to the Governor's office and let him hear of all her unsavory involvements preceding Nancy's act of desperation, but then telephones Gavin to say she will go, she is asking him how much she will have to tell, and as she listens, "quiet, frozen-faced," it can be surmised Gavin's answer is "Everything." Which, as it is gradually unfolded to the Governor in Scene I of the next act, must revert not only to the Frenchman's Bend episodes but to their sequel in Miss Reba's bordello, since her passionate letters written then to Red are now his brother Pete's ground for blackmail, in the course of which approach Temple had become infatuated and prepared to run away with Pete, which Nancy strove to prevent, for the children's sake, with ironically disastrous success. Thematically this constitutes Faulkner's demonstration that the past isn't even past. Facing Gavin's call upon her to make this complete admission, from which no link in the chain of cause and effect can be omitted, as Temple puts down the telephone she "speaks quietly, without inflection: but reiteratively, 'Oh, God. Oh, God.'" Comparably Gowan, in his repeated "So help me, Christ" at the conclusion of the preceding scene, is "tense, barely articulate." This minute litany of subdued anguished voices typifies Faulkner's strategic patterns to comprise unique instance and some common denominator of human experience. Gowan and Temple, sadly yoked to each other's errors and offenses, must each cope privately and alone with their separate situations, yet with no exemption from an answering to the inexorable fact of consequence.

Opening "ACT TWO/ THE GOLDEN DOME (Beginning Was the Word)," the prose passage locates at Jackson, Mississippi, "Capital of a Commonwealth," this "already decreed . . . rounded knob, this gilded pustule, already before and beyond the steamy chiaroscuro, untimed unseasoned winterless miasma not any one of water or earth or life yet all of each." Here, in this style so closely conforming to the primordial welter it would suggest, there seems a linguistic connection between the Capitol's golden dome as "gilded pustule" and the earth's geological and climatic evolution in "steamy chiaroscuro" and "winterless miasma," with fog and mist rising on its surface in some such rounded shapes, out of the "boiling moil of litter from the celestial experimental Work Bench," the clouds portending man-made domes. In the next paragraph of this prose passage opening Act Two the reach into the prehistoric is less far but more figurative of an ongoing creation, in the ice age with "still this knob, this pimple-dome" in prospect as "this gilded crumb of man's eternal aspiration, this golden dome preordained and impregnable." Then with the retreat of ice "baring to light and air the broad blank mid-continental page for the first scratch of orderly recording," the account rushes on, of Indian tribes and French and Spanish explorers and the Anglo-Saxon pioneer, "innocent and gullible, without bowels for avarice or compassion or forethought either, changing the face of the earth: felling a tree which took two hundred years to grow, in

order to extract from it a bear or a capful of wild honey."
Then too "those days were gone, the old brave innocent
tumultuous eupeptic tomorrowless days." Then men "built the
statehouse, thirty by forty feet of brick and clay and native
limestone yet large enough to contain the dream; the first
legislature convened in it in the new year 1822." And "in 1903
the new Capitol was completed—the golden dome, the knob,
the gleamy crumb, the gilded pustule longer than the miasma
. . . more durable than the ice and the pre-night cold, soaring,
hanging as one blinding spheroid above the center of the Commonwealth, incapable of being either looked full or evaded,
peremptory, irrefragable, and reassuring;"—and there, left in
suspension with only a semicolon, ends this cadenza, one of
the richest flowerings from Faulkner's sense of men's hazards
and dreams, individual and collective, seen against the backdrop of environment and under winds out of the past's far
ranges.

Yet there is more to this whole prose passage announcing
the three substantial dramatic scenes of Act Two. It concludes
succinctly with a complete reversal of tone, just as there had
been, but in an opposite direction, in the prose passage preceding the scenes in Act One. There the movement was from a
pioneer strenuousness with its idiosyncrasies into the poetized
stasis of the enduring old courthouse, restored after the
war, and further embellished by "a cupola with a four-
faced clock and a bell to strike the hours." Yet not even civic
monuments last forever in a young country on the move, and
"every few years the county fathers, dreaming of bakshish,
would instigate a movement to tear it down and erect a new
modern one, but someone would at the last moment defeat
them" and "for a little while yet the sparrows and the pigeons"
would inhabit the cupola "until the clock strikes again which
even after a hundred years, they still seem unable to get used
to, bursting in one swirling explosion out of the belfry as
though the hour, instead of merely adding one puny infinitesi-
mal more to the long weary increment since Genesis, had
shattered the virgin pristine air with the first loud dingdong of

time and doom"—a thematic imaging of continuity, disruption, and dissolution. Conversely, in the prose of Act Two the change of key is from imagistic evocation to a laconic irony. There is first the vast progression by stages toward the golden dome's emergence—"the conflux of a hundred rivers into one vast father of rivers carrying the rich dirt, the rich garnering, south and south . . . flooding the Mississippi lowlands . . . raising inch by foot by year by century the surface of the earth which in time (not distant now, measured against that long signatureless chronicle) would tremble to the passing of trains," and so from the august imaging of the achieved Capitol dome, "peremptory, irrefragable, and reassuring," a sudden shift to a wry staccato parody of guidebook statistics about Jackson, Mississippi—its altitude and population as of 1950, its connections with a larger world by four railroads, seven bus lines, and two air lines, its two radio stations, and besides, its "Diversions: chronic," such as Red Cross Water Pageant, Basketball Tournament, and Girl Scouts Horse Show, and its "Diversions: acute: Religion, Politics."

Such changes in Faulkner's style are not in a careless drift nor an affectation of randomness; their opalescence reflectively carries his concepts into narrative and dramatic progressions. Faulkner allows himself an elaborateness that asks to be read with deliberate appreciation of every nuance and all enriching accretions; he can be succinctly colloquial, too, with a crystalline firmness and containment. Within the antiphonal structuring of *Requiem* he could range to wide extremes, but he composed these into mutually enhancing effects. There is a gusto and celerity in *Requiem* which may suggest the artist's balancing out this practice in relation to the massive epical consistency of *A Fable,* with which he was occupied in the same period. Such reciprocal creative practice would have been all the more possible in that these two novels so differently proportioned and materialized were both artistic transmutations of significant apperceptions discovered in historical vistas and made to contain twentieth-century instances in which cultural heritage is both boon and fate. As such, each is a unique thrust of Faulkner's imagination, while reiterating his acute sense of the insistent sociopersonal riddle, as variously illustrated in his other works, especially *Absalom, Absalom!, Light in August, Go Down, Moses* and the Snopes trilogy. In any of these a unique structuring and adapted modulations of style, whatever any reader's judgment of their effects, are beyond reproach as to their supportive intention, under the aspect of enduring abstractions, against which is silhouetted the individual life in its ultimate privacies as well as its immediate involvements. Uniquely in *Requiem* the liberally ranging style of its prose prefaces to the three acts sets off the dialogue's predominant succinctness despite excursions into theological and humanistic abstractions. This book is a novel, in which prose narrative, as vast backdrop to a compressed action, prevails over drama, yet does not outweigh it, and gives it the last word.

The three dramatic scenes following the golden dome prose passage which opens Act Two are structured for rapid inclusiveness and climax, but they also run deep psychologically. Scene I is of Temple's hesitant confessions, to which the Governor gives audience as they proceed under Gavin's probings and his supplementings when Temple falters. Sometimes though she rushes ahead volubly, conceding what Gavin had previously demanded, that she is to speak not just as Mrs. Gowan Stevens but as Temple Drake, elaborating with further perspectives the misadventures and degradations of the *Sanctuary* story, and of its recent sequel in which her lust and wilfulness had spread catastrophe, explicitly in provoking Nancy's fanatical smothering of an innocent, her infant daughter, and consequently the impending execution of the pitiable murderess. Temple herself is pitiable as she writhes under torturing memories, but she is almost repellent, too, in her sardonic talk that may seem to disclose more complaint about what has impinged upon herself than regret for what her conduct had brought upon others. Yet apparently it is only with harshness, like the snarls of a cornered creature, that she can force herself through this self-inculpating recital. It comprises the whole story, in its essential factors. The incident of the rape she suffered at Frenchman's Bend and the murder of the good-hearted Tommy when he had tried to intervene was a matter of court record and town talk, but now Temple lets the Governor know she had perjured herself in that trial causing the innocent Goodwin to be condemned, after which he was lynched and burned. Temple goes on—sometimes with Gavin's man-to-man supplements to the Governor in the more indelicate parts—to tell of her confinement in the brothel, her infatuation with Popeye's henchman Red, encountered under his master's voyeurism, and Popeye's quick revenge when Red tried to be with her alone. (This attempt had been made because of her direct enticement, and in *Sanctuary* her language at that point showed her utterly besotted.) Therein is the seed from which an old aberration rises up in new form. As Temple tells, it was to fill the hours between Red's conducted visits to her that she had written him those letters which have outlived the two men and that sordid situation, to reappear in the attempted blackmail by Red's younger brother, Pete. In Temple's perverse response to the blackmailer, she was soon ready not only to give him money and her jewels but to run away with him, taking her baby daughter with her. (This seems to symbolize the finality of her intention to desert her husband; Gavin cannily sees Pete's willingness to take the small child along as a calculation that it would help in "extracting . . . money later at . . . leisure," and Nancy, in her attempt to dissuade Temple, is to give this contingency an ironically harsh elaboration.)

At any rate, Temple has furnished the Governor a comprehensive and objectively phrased explanation for her desperate purposes: "Because Temple Drake liked evil." And later her sardonic self-analysis implies a fascination with violence, as in Popeye's ruthless shooting of Tommy—"her bad luck too: to plump for a thing which didn't even have sex for his weakness, but just murder."

The far way Temple has gone toward an unstable ambivalence (in which she can glimpse values but cannot summon up commitment that will move her to enact them, and instead evades them by cynicism) is seen in her glance at what she and Gowan might have achieved together had they risen to confession of errors—"just to kneel down, the two of us, and say 'We have sinned, forgive us.'"—and thus to pass beyond suffering into the bond of mutual forgiveness. Yet that hadn't been possible for them, and she blames the gratitude that they have had to give and accept for each other's tolerance. This is psychologically penetrating, but Temple does not broadly acknowledge that forgiveness must be earned by real penitence, and penitence requires humility. So Gavin takes it up and going beyond "Temple's good name" and "her husband's conscience," he blames Gowan's "vanity: the Virginia-trained aristocrat caught with his gentility around his knees," in his primary responsibility for what happened to Temple at Frenchman's Bend and, consequently, thereafter.

Temple turns sarcastically to their later facing it down, "the Gowan Stevenses, young, popular," with "a country-club younger set of rallying friends" and "a pew in the right church" in which to recover from "the Saturday-night country-club hangover." This is a cynical impasse, acknowledging a fate which defies correction, with its tangled strands of innate temperament and cultural conditioning, and its privileges celebrated by social rituals that engender scornful dissatisfaction. "My father's a judge" had been Temple's insufficient talisman and claim for privilege, but what that stood for in part at least was imaged at Goodwin's trial when her father approached the Bench and asked whether the Court was "done with this witness," and as she rose, her platinum handbag slipped from her lap, whereupon "with the toe of his small gleaming shoe the old man flipped the bag into the corner where the jury-box joined the Bench, where a spittoon sat." This is more than abandonment of an object in a moment of personal stress, it is an overriding gesture that almost seems to despise its own incidental power; it is tinged with the kind of arrogances that marked the Sartoris clan till Bayard repudiated it, even at the cost of losing Drusilla. It signals the claims of a conventional structure that had seduced Sutpen with its pretensions, and that had moved Isaac McCaslin to reject it entirely and (like Bayard) refuse to reenter its confines even to appease a woman's ambitions, and so reclaim both her and the hope of having a son.

Temple, going on at length to the Governor, had passed from satire of the country-club younger set's Saturday night and Sunday morning and arrived at something more central: "Then the son and heir came; and now we have Nancy: guide, mentor, catalyst, glue, whatever you want to call it, holding the whole lot of them together . . . in a semblance at least of order and respectability and peace." Gavin interrupts her, saying, "Now, the letters," and then takes up the story himself, leading toward its denouement by telling of Temple's getting together the money and jewels to give the blackmailer, and Nancy's taking and hiding them. At this point in the drama Faulkner makes theatric adaptation of the device he so often used narratively, a rearrangement of chronology with also a shift into direct objective representation. As the stage lights dim and go out, Gavin is heard saying to Temple, "Now tell him," yet when the lights go up for Scene II this is not the Governor's office but Temple's dressing-room several months earlier, and the events are not to be narrated in retrospect but will be played out by Temple, Nancy, and Red's brother Pete, in a dramatic scene, more incisive in its dialogue than some of Temple's outbursts before the governor, and rapidly paced toward its dreadful climax. Temple's bags are packed, and the room is in disorder; Temple and Pete have been looking for the money and jewels Nancy has taken and hidden. The two of them talk, each offering the other an "out," as if both are aware of hazarding too much in an involvement they cannot resist; Pete offers the letters for Temple to burn, she starts to do so, but refrains. Nancy appears, Pete implies he may put a cigarette to her foot to find where the money and jewels are hid, but Temple sends him out to his car. Now Temple and Nancy sharply argue Temple's intention, Nancy always pressing, Temple evasive and at one point striking Nancy but finally admitting defiantly that yes, she's going to run off, "Money or no money. Children or no children." Fatalistically Nancy had remarked, "It ain't even the letters any more. Maybe it never was. It was already there in whoever could write the kind of letters that even eight years afterward could still make grief and ruin." She insists, though, that her concern in not for husband or wife: "I'm talking about two little children." And she forces the point: "You cant no more leave a six-months-old baby with nobody while you run away from your husband with another man, than you can take a six-months-old baby with you on that trip." Yet Nancy realizes that the latter is what Temple means to do, and it must have weighed in her final action, considering with what sombre emphasis she put the prospect: "Or maybe taking her with you will be just as easy, at least until the first time you write Mr Gowan or your pa for money and they dont send it as quick as your new man thinks they ought to, and he throws you and the baby both out. Then you can just drop it into a garbage can and no more trouble to you or anybody, because you will be rid of both of them." Temple moves as if to strike her but holds back; Nancy tells her to go ahead, or to carry out Pete's threat of a lighted cigarette to her foot, and saying she's "tried everything else," reckons she "can try that too."

Here Faulkner employs a descriptive and explanatory stage direction for the reader, and what it suggests about Nancy is something an actress might convey: "She doesn't move. She is not looking at Temple. There is a slight change in her voice or manner, though we only realize later that she is not addressing Temple." Yet at this point, when Nancy is saying, "I've tried everything I know. You can see that," the reader like the play-watcher should be able to sense that the "You" who "can see" is the one to whom alone she had spoken at the time of her sentencing, remaining silent until that was pronounced by the Judge, and then answering, "(quite loud in the silence, to no one, quite calm, not moving) Yes, Lord." Now in this the drama's central and most purely direct, immediate scene, Nancy repeats her plaint to Temple herself: "I tried everything I knowed. You can see that." Then as she turns, purportedly to warm the baby's nursing bottle, she adds "I've hushed." From here on she speaks no more, though as Temple finishes packing for her adventure Nancy returns, puts back on the table the wages Temple has given her, and goes out by the other door. She had not answered the lame succession of conciliatory words from Temple: "Don't think too hard of me . . . You tried. But you were right. It wasn't even the letters. It was me. . . . I'll leave your money here on the table . . . Nancy!" But with Nancy gone the scene ends in silent acts and a scream. Having put Nancy's money under a paper weight, Temple takes up a blanket and goes out, presumably to get the baby. Then the scream, the stage in darkness, and next Scene III of Act Two, again in the Governor's office, and continuing Temple's confession beyond what has just been played out. Temple, kneeling before the Governor's desk, does not know that he "has gone" and her husband has taken his place behind the desk. "And that's all," she says. "The police came, and the murderess still sitting in a chair in the kitchen in the dark, saying 'Yes, Lord, I done it,' and then in the cell at the jail still saying it —"

The thought revives Temple's memory of the jail itself, and how when passing it one could see not the imprisoned Negroes themselves but their hands lying quiet in the spaces between the bars of windows where they looked out — hands "that can see the shape of the plow or hoe or ax before daylight comes; and even in the dark . . . can not only find the child, the baby — not her child but yours, the white one — but the trouble and discomfort too — the hunger, the wet didy, the unfastened safety-pin, and see to remedy it." Continuing, evidently with no pause, she says, "You see. If I could just cry." She cannot, yet beyond that self-engendered impasse she has moved into imagining the many Negroes held in the jail over the years, standing at the barred windows to watch the street, their faces unseen, only their work-habituated hands lying inert on the window sills; then out of that generalization she recalls not Rider by name but only in his known story, and from "before my time in Jefferson," the tragic protagonist of "Pantaloon in Black," driven wild by his cherished wife's death, and when restrained saying, "I just cant quit thinking. Look like I just cant quit." Rider's story had sounded in Faulknerian manner one of the antiphonal modulations of *Go Down, Moses;* Temple's reference to it not only discloses a degree of awakened empathy in this still dry-eyed woman, it suggests generally the play of reactive influence in a closeness of community among its members, despite racial and socioeconomic stratifications. To a degree they are known to each other as persons, and may know something of each other's lives, enough for intuitive recognitions, with some measure of paradoxically operative integration in Faulkner's South as of his time and his insights. Thus even in the finally stressful relationship with Nancy, and despite Temple's perverse resistance to acknowledgments, she had become momentarily penitent and had said, "I'm sorry," regretting having struck Nancy and screamed at her "when you have always been so good to my children and me—my husband too—all of us—trying to hold us together," and Temple credits Nancy in this even though it's "a household, a family, that anybody should have known all the time couldn't possibly hold together, even in decency, let alone happiness."

Now in Scene III (four months later, back again to the drama in the Governor's office, and on the eve of Nancy's execution) Temple's reflections gradually pass the jail where Rider of "Pantaloon in Black" and so many others had been confined and where Nancy is being held; now Temple is aware that at the trial Nancy, in saying only those two words at her sentencing—"Yes, Lord"—had transcended "the whole edifice of corpus juris . . . we have been working to make stand up by itself ever since Caesar." It is typical of Faulkner's genius, working through his characters' sensibilities, to merge a conspicuously regional story with wider socioethical import and to make these elements reciprocal in the imaginative work they enlarge.

The enigma this implies is explored after Temple has realized it is Gowan not the Governor who is listening to her, and after Gowan has cofirmed her despair about themselves by saying that eight years earlier they should have hidden "in two abandoned mine shafts, one in Siberia and the other at the South Pole maybe," but to her "I'm sorry" he answers, "Dont be. Just draw on your eight years' interest for that." He leaves to pick up their son Bucky and take him home; Temple lingers to question her questioner, sensing that there never had been a chance of reprieve for Nancy, and the whole of Gavin's devising had been to bring Temple to a complete self-confrontation, so that, as he puts it, she may sleep at night. Beyond that, the scene elucidates thematic antitheses inherent in *Requiem*. When Temple realizes in Scene III that the governor must have said No and insists on hearing "exactly what he did say," Gavin quotes but with what sounds like an emotionally tinged paraphrase: "Who am I . . . to set the puny appanage of my office in the balance against that simple undeviable aim? . . . to render null and abrogate the purchase she made with that poor crazed lost and worthless life?" The bare fact, stripped of its humane aura, is that the governor had no formal grounds for official action. The law, as symbolized by the Capitol's golden dome, is indeed "peremptory" and "irrefragable," but it can be "reassuring" only within the intent and letter of its writ, which does not run to assurances for "the human heart in conflict with itself," or even to such communally conceived intangible values as decency and civility, which must be grossly and openly violated before the law can seize upon them with its cumbersomely gauntleted hand. Indeed, there is no steady gradation; beyond the verge of the law's pale the landscape quickly alters into a wilderness of incalculable and hence unamenable human contentions, with their wrongs and consequent griefs. This stern reality explains the more than professionally concerned presence of Lawyer Stevens; while in its shadow Temple's consciousness runs beyond mere sleep at night to her speech with a "sleepwalker air" closing this act: "To save my soul—if I have a soul. If there is a God to save it—a God who wants it"—phrases that will reecho, still unanswered, at the drama's end.

Act Three of *Requiem,* like the work's preceding acts, begins with another extended prose passage; and once more an architectural structure is its central image. This time it is the old town jail, in Jefferson, and again, as with Yoknapatawpha county's courthouse and the domed State Capitol, there is sounded the motif of societal functions operant under the law. The jail itself is to be locale of the act's single scene as Temple, still under Gavin's severely benevolent direction and escort, visits Nancy on the night before her execution. And in this third prose prelude, amid a profusion of data molded into highly colored epitomes of times past and presently in passage, a window (not of a cell but in the jailor's living quarters) is frame to a portrait and a town legend that projects, out of a melee of circumstance, a faint enduring assertion of singular human identity. This also becomes a thematic element in the concluding action of *Requiem,* wherein the three primary dramatic movers, confronting august abstractions, approach each other on lines that intersect only to pass beyond that, on the distancing tangents of their separate natures. However, the atypical circumstances and trends of Temple's and Nancy's lives and the fatal acuteness of their involvement with each other have a complementary preface in the prose section. By its broader scope, with individuals standing out separately and less persistently against the panoramic, it serves to make way for that drastically constrained terminal enactment between Temple and Nancy with Gavin as moderator.

"The Jail" is of twice as many pages as that single scene which concludes Act Three and the book. As in the passages opening the two preceding acts, the discourse drops back, this time not all the way to prehistory, but far enough to show the enduring antebellum jail as the oldest building in Jefferson, yet of a concealed antiquity (like so much in Faulkner's South) with its original walls of "notched and mortised logs" now encased by a "veneer" of brick outside and plaster within. "The Jail" may be cited as *locus classicus* for one major aspect of Faulkner's idiosyncratic art in its service to his inclusive yet particularized conceptions. No doubt more than a few readers have considered this passage inflated and verbose; actually it is succinct in what it states, and urgently expeditious. Masses of detail are cast in staccato phrasings and gathered up into the accelerant flow of prolonged sentence structures; this not only is syntactically economical but imparts a suggestion of lengthy time span and the passing appearance of individuals within pulsations of large events. It traces Jefferson's mutations as halting place, settlement, village, town; there are detailed allusions to notable Yoknapatawpha names—Habersham, Ratcliffe, Compson, Sartoris, Sutpen, Redmond—and the parts they played as the forest land was razed and adapted to cotton planting, and war was fought and lost and their system overthrown, yet reconstruction was survived, and continuity was reasserted with the symbolic rebuilding of the burned-out courthouse around those "two columned porticoes" that still stood. Throughout there is a pondering of the past, that "vast weight of man's incredible and enduring *Was*," and the present sense of a rapid motion called progress, "faster and faster," into "One nation . . . one towering frantic edifice poised like a card-house over the abyss of the mortgaged generations." The cyclorama of events, imaginatively colored, is scanned at hypnotic speed but with vision from a held point, merging multifarious events and the uniqueness of individual lives—"the shapes and motions, the gestures of passion and hope and travail and endurance, of the men and women and children in their successive overlapping generations."

The opulent style in "The Jail" evolves out of the imaginative rehearsal and recoloration of matters drawn from throughout the body of Yoknapatawphan lore. There is the swearing-in of the regiment raised by John Sartoris with Jefferson its headquarters—"a voluntary association of untried men who knew they were ignorant and hoped they were brave, the four sides of the Square lined with their fathers or grandfathers and their mothers and wives and sisters and sweethearts, the only uniform present yet that one in which Sartoris stood with his virgin sabre and his pristine colonel's braid." (Here the effect is not merely from modifiers but more subtly in the creation of an image of crowd and the sense of mood by the enumeration of six kinds of onlooking relatives, two-thirds or more of them women.) Or stylistic recurrence may be to the more broadly abstract, as in Faulkner's lyricizing a vast socioeconomic movement in terms of footwear, "the prints of men — the fitted shoes . . . brought from the Atlantic seaboard, the cavalry boots . . . the moccasins . . . worn not by Indians but by white men, the pioneers, the long hunters, as though they had not only vanquished the wilderness but had even stepped into the very footgear of them they dispossessed," till they themselves were dispossessed first by "the husbandman printing deep the hard heels of his brogans," and then by "land speculators and traders in slaves and whiskey," and "now indeed the last moccasin print vanished . . . the last toed-in heelless light soft quick long-striding print pointing west for an instant, then trodden from the sight and memory of man by a heavy leather heel engaged not in the traffic of endurance and hardihood and survival, but in money—." Here there is both elaboration and economy; the sparseness of "a heavy leather heel engaged . . . in money" is a classic trope, and as to that "last toed-in heelless light soft quick long-striding print pointing west," every mobile word carries its justification. With such style, reading can witness the shaping of an effect as if out of clay, each modifier a further finger stroke, disclosing as aspects the planes which give dimensions and containment to the whole. It is art itself in progress. In Faulkner everything is motion, and in this moccasin-print passage the sustained stride carries imagination all the way out of Mississippi.

Not that the thrust of Faulkner's most impressionistic prose is always so expeditious; it may eddy, even repetitiously, since its criterion is conformity to the effect of whatever present instance. This Faulkner shows with Gavin Stevens, "the town lawyer and the county Cincinnatus," who "was wont to say, if you would peruse in unbroken—ay, overlapping—continuity the history of a community, look not in the church registers and the courthouse records but . . . on the walls of the jail." Here a humorous sense of Gavin's wryly affected quaintness (which his creator's indulgence abets) enters through archaic idiom—"was wont . . . nay . . . look not"—yet with some correspondence to the theme of retrospection itself. And the rest of this passage indirectly attributed to Gavin rises to more than mannerism in conveying how "only in that forcible carceration does man find the idleness in which to compose, in the gross and simple terms of his gross and simple lusts and yearnings, the gross and simple recapitulations of his gross and simple heart." These repetitions, suggesting the tomorrow and tomorrow of any imprisoned life, turn most significantly at their center on the compounding of "lusts and yearnings" and thus link with its gross animality the natural humanity of man's "simple heart"—which Faulkner had described generically at Stockholm as "in conflict with itself." Following that paraphrastic reference to Gavin Stevens, the prose is then more completely claimed by the artist himself—but still in terms of prisoners' graffiti, "the scrawled illiterate repetitive unimaginative doggerel and the perspectiveless almost prehistoric sexual picture-writing." The passage moves on through larger time perspectives than even a prisoner's life term; it scans three centuries of the region's history during which those who still can be discerned, however darkly, are "saying no to death across twelve generations, asking still the same old unanswerable questions," and it is all as "in the shadowy fathomless dreamlike depths of an old mirror which has looked at too much too long." Such "depths" show that the mirror, its silver back having changed with age, has acquired surrealistic perspectives and dimensions, which suggests what Faulkner's fiction often concedes, that envisagings of the past can become illusory; but the fuller weight of the passage is in the "too much" of circumstance, looked back at "too long," and of this Faulkner's Yoknapatawphan tales had touched on many instances centrally.

"The Jail" is pervaded by a melancholy, approaching the dimensions of *Weltschmerz,* that allows one of the closest sensings of this artist as Southerner of a certain generation and as meditative human being. There are traces of what was so fully expressed through young Isaac McCaslin, the regret for lost integrities of an unequivocal existence in a still unspoiled land; there is the more acute regional recollection, not without nostalgia, of an antebellum "little minute yet while time, the land, the nation, the American earth whirled faster and faster toward the plunging precipice of its destiny," but beyond the war itself (and beyond the carpetbagger, "symbol of a blind rapacity almost like a biological instinct, destined to cover the South like a migration of locusts") there is the dominating power of "Cotton: a king . . . a destiny of which (obvious now) the plow and the axe had been merely the tools; not plow and axe which had effaced the wilderness, but Cotton . . . altering not just the face of the land, but the complexion of the town too, creating its own parasitic aristocracy not only behind the columned porticoes of the plantation houses, but in the counting-rooms of merchants and bankers and the sanctums of lawyers" and reaching "the county offices too: of sheriff and tax-collector and bailiff and turnkey and clerk," making the old jail itself "a moveable pawn on the county's political board . . . converted indeed now, elevated (an apotheosis) ten feet above the level of the town, so that the old buried log walls now contained the living-quarters for the turnkey's family." A rise of ramifying power from an economic base is not unique with cotton or as of the South; here Faulkner created in regional terms a realistic profile of modernity. Yet in the freely chronological rangings and rearrangings of the broadly implicative and discursively descriptive prose that constitutes the nearly fifty pages of "The Jail," this site, these living quarters, will be returned to in successive mentionings, until through such accretions an obscure interpersonal enactment there during Civil War days and grown into local legend becomes humanistically contrapuntal to the sweep of cultural history, as sensed in mirrorings of deterioration, viewed with melancholy misgivings about the twentieth-century United States which occasionally tend toward the apocalyptic, a recurrent Faulknerian insight that may increasingly be credited to him.

Throughout "The Jail," where the persistent theme is of *gone, gone too, fast* and *faster now,* however intently it may turn to "legend and record and history, indisputable in authenticity yet a little oblique, elliptic . . . washed thinly over with a faint quiet cast of apocraphy," the melancholy is nevertheless more than a sentimental antiquarianism or a residual separatism. The socioeconomic and more general cultural shifts in the life of the South, in the wake of the Civil War and two World Wars all within less than a century, are made to demonstrate that "victory or defeat both are bought at the same exorbitant price of change and alteration." Reaction to such inordinate costs underlies the mingled tones of regret and apprehension in "The Jail." Given Faulkner's heritage and the supposition of humanistic "verities" he had arrived at, nowhere better than from such a base as his in twentieth-century America could it be discerned that in crucial eras most "reconstructions" are little better than improvisations, spawned chiefly by opportunistic materialism, its private thrusts aggregating into the confusions of a seduced and stultified people. Thus the changes in Faulkner's Jefferson are named in a way that evaluates relatively what has been replaced and what is its replacement — "and now the last forest tree was gone from the courthouse yard too, replaced by formal synthetic shrubs contrived and schooled in Wisconsin greenhouses, and in the courthouse (the city hall too) a courthouse and city hall gang, in miniature of course . . . but based on the pattern of Chicago and Kansas City and Boston and Philadelphia . . . which every three or four years would try again to raze the old courthouse, not that they did not like the old one nor wanted the new, but because the new one would bring into the town and county that much more increment of unearned federal money." There are the glass-fronted stores, too, with "interiors bathed now in one shadowless corpse-glare of fluorescent light; and, now and at last, the last of silence too: the county's hollow inverted air one resonant boom and ululance of radio: and thus no more Yoknapatawpha's air nor even Mason and Dixon's air, but America's: the patter of comedians, the baritone screams of female vocalists, the babbling pressure to buy and buy . . . one air, one nation: the shadowless fluorescent corpse-glare bathing the sons and daughters of men and women, Negro and white both, who were born to and who passed all their lives in denim overalls and calico, haggling by cash or the installment-plan for garments copied last week out of *Harper's Bazaar* or *Esquire* in East Side sweat-shops: because an entire generation of farmers has vanished, not just from Yoknapa-tawpha's but from Mason and Dixon's earth." This is attrib-uted to "the machine which displaced the man because the exodus of the man left no one to drive the mule, now that the machine was threatening to extinguish the mule," — a nicely involved representation of the crosscurrents in any economic complexity, and dimensioned beyond any table of statistics.

Out of all such detail as it laid its dire hold upon Faulkner's intuitions come the melancholy mirrorings and echoes of "one cosmos: contained in one America: one towering frantic edifice poised like a card-house over the abyss of the mort-gaged generations . . . one swirling rocket-roar filling the glit-tering zenith as with golden feathers," until for man "the vast hollow spere of his air, the vast and terrible burden beneath which he tries to stand erect and lift his battered and indomitable head . . . is murmurous with his fears and terrors and disclaimers and repudiations and his aspirations and dreams and his baseless hopes, bouncing back at him in radar waves from the constellations." Then, in Faulkner's next line, "And still — the old jail," in "its almost seasonless backwater in the middle of that rush and roar . . . not isolated by location so much as insulated by obsolescence." From the first, because of its closeness to events, the jail had been personified as "this mirror, these logs: squatting in the full glare of the stump-pocked clearing," and as such, when the last remnant of the indigenous Chickasaws departed westward "the jail watched that," and when the Sartoris Confederate regiment was sworn in, there was "the jail watching that too." Log jail, old mirror; watcher as mirror, mirror giving back from "shadowy fathomless dreamlike depths" — these images abruptly juxtaposed at a transitional point may suggest the artist, as he continues to perceive through whatever veneers may have been imposed by vicissitudes, and mirrorlike projects his imaginings from dimensioned depths produced through life's chemical influences upon the metal of his sensibilities.

The severe melancholy which colors many portions of "The Jail," however lurid some of its imagings, is not a private Byronic grievance against the world, nor is Faulkner's mid-century estimate of his region as within the nation an elegy for the old South. Though spoken in Faulkner's voice if not in person, his apprehensions are social not private, his negative judgments are not unique as of his time and place, and his regrets are over the obscuration of human values and verities. Faulkner's projected misgivings are not strictly pesimistic, he does not charge the cosmos with absurdity, and while Jason Compson may shake his defiant fist at the heavens and Horace Benbow may sadly come to doubt that existence has any perceivable meaning, these are fictional projections of recognizable types out of a milieu that contains their opposites in a spectrum of all sorts and conditions of men. In some Faulkner characters a disruptive evil seems innate and incorrigible, but others are equally intent in their commitment to certain "verities," which they find adhered to by other men and women, and thus to a degree made operative in a social order. Yet despite this emphasis in his work, Faulkner is not primarily a sociological novelist; his chief concern is not with abstracted patterns of behavior but with identities, uniquely represented yet humanly recognizable and evocative of personal response. It is chiefly in this respect that Faulkner can be compared, as he has been, to Shakespeare or Dickens; and a uniquely illustrative twentieth-century parallel would be with Conrad, whose intense narratives functionally comprise strikingly disparate beings convergent over typical human issues, so that characters are enhanced not simply by the action but through encounter as individuals.

And the artist Faulkner has vitally embodied too many en-

gaging and admirable fictional characters to be seen lamenting, as in Hightower's generic terms, over poor man, poor
mankind. He does consider all men fallible, and not a few as
culpable, but in part because modern men's unexamined
ingenuities have outrun control, in the lack of a comprehensive ethos, under a Janus-faced aspect of progression and disintegration. Therein, however, Faulkner sees the deepest root
of a saving unrest, prompting man's sporadic but inexhaustible drive toward community and consensus. And in "The
Jail" Faulkner had a further end in view, a presented exemplar
of an identity, simple, obscure in her own day and untraced
beyond that, but of a legendary fame in her recognizing and
accepting involvement with another instinctive and purposeful
being. At several points, beginning with factual correspondence as at the eve of the Civil War, and recurred to intermittently in the loose chronology of "The Jail" until it becomes
at last the whole story, there is this counterpart, an antiphony
to history's alarums, in a heartening legend levying upon the
human imagination's power to sustain transcendently an
instance that embodies a common ideal.

The old jail had "survived, endured; it had its inevictable
place in the town and county," yet it is now recurred to
climactically not just as to its outlasting the generations of
men it had seen, but for a minute something it contains. This
could be shown to the tourist as a curiosity, and the Chick
Mallison of *Intruder* would go look at it not for its antiquity
"but to realize the eternality . . . of youth." Faulkner touches
upon it similarly in *Requiem,* making thematic the dimensions of time and timelessness, of passing instance and its
lasting significations. On a windowpane in the old jail,
scratched there with a diamond, from the days when one
Farmer was jailor, is his daughter's "fragile and indelible
signature of her meditation . . . and the date: *Cecelia Farmer
April 16th 1861.*" The date sets her in her innocence and
frailty against a great backdrop of history; the war was getting
under way by stages, through secession, the raising of troops
on both sides, the firing on Fort Sumter. Yet Cecelia Farmer's

connection with all that and its sequelae is incidental, as Faulkner gives this watcher at a window her simple part in a little tale that became a local legend. In "the spring of '64" there was a sudden brief rearguard action by cavalry against Federal troops then entering Jefferson; as a Confederate lieutenant galloped through "firing a pistol backward at a Yankee army," the girl "musing in the blonde mist of her hair beside the window-pane" and "the soldier, gaunt and tattered, battle-grimed and fleeing and undefeated," had looked at one another "for that moment across the fury and pell mell of battle." Yet it sufficed, for when his part in the war was over he returned, in May of 1865, riding the mule he had "swapped" his blooded mare for, and having "traded his lieutenant's saber for the stocking full of seed corn," and married the girl at once, to take her off behind him on his mule to his father's farm in Alabama. Exemplary of love at first sight, it is an extreme instance yet offered not sentimentally but for the truth that personal recognitions can transcend circumstances and in so doing may modify them.

It becomes a fantasia (in which during the town's retelling the girl's hair had changed "from blonde to dark and back to blonde again"), and it sets those almost secretly fleeting but intent lives against this prose section's larger evocation, the impersonal and massive depersonalizing confluences of history, through which the town's jail has stood in its "thin durable continuity" for over a century. To draw together these narrative elements — illustrative fragments out of decades of turbulent regional history, which Faulkner continues to delineate evocatively, and a local legend of the romantic intersection of two private lives — there is the experience of a tourist taken ("now, in 1951") to see the name and date scratched "in a sheet of old barely transparent glass" and supposedly to conceive of another's existence, by using that "so vast, so limitless in capacity . . . man's imagination to disperse and burn away the rubbledross of fact and probability, leaving only truth and dream." Thus "The Jail" concludes with the suggestion that for those who have seen and remember the inscription on glass in the old jail window "there is the clear undistanced voice . . . from the long long time ago," saying, *"Listen, stranger; this was myself; this was I."*

Such a voice which can speak "undistanced" from the distant past is that of human identity intent on its self-realizations, and thereby generically representative, to be conceived of through such a reciprocally personal response as to "know again now that there is no time: no space: no distance." It is this in life which literary art cannot exactly imitate but can evoke as intimations. So doing, Faulkner's fiction discloses as inherent in reality those self-evident human values the law seeks to protect, but also, beyond society's formal effectuations, the unbounded reaches where intuitive good will extends its attempted ameliorations, or shares griefs for which no amend is found. A fictionist could spin out Cecelia Farmer's simple story through the further chapters of her fortunes and fate in postbellum Alabama as wife of a cavalry officer turned farmer, but this done at such long range could be based only on presumed human typicality. Yet the artist who (like Faulkner) had observed in detail and concernedly enough to sense what is individually representative in real situations could borrow instances and arrange them consequentially to make such a fiction persuasive. It could even be arresting in an extended assertion that this was I, Cecelia, and these were our years of love, and these our children and all our joys and griefs; this was what came of my standing at a certain moment looking out the jail's window where in an earlier time I had scratched my name on the glass with my grandmother's diamond ring.

Though Faulkner does wryly hazard her having borne the impetuous cavalryman twelve sons, heirs to their jailor grandfather's ineptitude, he not only did not write out any such further story, he limited the one he told to its local details, colorful but almost hastily brief, yet infinitely suggestive. Fictionally it serves the purpose of isolating a symbol, of selfhood, which appeals to imagination the more strongly through the given opportunity to carry on. The verity of Cecelia Farmer at the window where she left her name inscribed, illuminated in its immediacy and isolation amidst multitudinous historical data, becomes a bridge into Act III, with its single scene at the jail which concludes *Requiem*. It also allows a characteristic Faulknerian use of antiphonal structure, for the dramatic episode, with Gavin Stevens as interlocutor, centers on two women in their identities, as they connect and contrast, at extremes of temperament, character, and fate. This matter having been so fully and subjectively explored throughout *Requiem,* and with references in depth to the pasts of both women (including the extent of Temple's role in *Sanctuary* and during the subsequent eight years), it conversely marks out Cecelia Farmer's brief transit as a glimpse in silhouette. However, that does not diminish her common human claim to selfhood, and still her singular fate is aligned, through its mystery, with aspects of Temple and Nancy as characters, neither of whom close scrutiny can comprise or entirely penetrate.

One of the most enigmatic of Faulkner's novels, *Requiem for a Nun* is inconclusive not just as are others by their cessation within unfinished lives, but in its enigmatic treatment of good and evil in human conduct. Quentin Compson, for instance, in *Absalom, Absalom!* is left at a climax of ambivalent devotion and aversion, yet his further action (that suicide already known to readers of *The Sound and the Fury*) is conceivable, as also is Hightower's continued nostalgic arrest and Lena's further progress. Temple at the end of her drama is adrift in speculative gropings, and it seems less credible that any advance may come of this than that she may shake herself loose from the line on which Gavin has drawn her up into the light of self-scrutiny, and may more naturally sink back into the dark instinctual existence, so productive of havoc, that seems her creature habitat. Temple at the end links doom and damnation, and in her lack of a firm purpose it seems a proximate self-judgment, but they are to be separated in some other Faulkner characters, especially those innocents whose

doom far exceeds anything they can be damned for. Not so for
Temple. It is not just the sensual letters to Red that can implement her fate; she has been blackmailed by her unregenerate
self. This she has admitted to Nancy: "It wasn't even the
letters. It was me." Yet even such specific confession does not
always mean repentance, much less a genuine purpose to
rectify. And by whatever system of values Nancy's final and
fatal counterattempt may be examined, its economy, along
with that of Gavin's entry into Temple's deplorable present
affairs, might be questioned. Nancy has blocked the only road
to realization that Temple knows, a surrender to self-gratify-
ing impulse, without which she wavers, almost as inert as when
Faulkner had left her on that gray day at the end of
Sanctuary, seated with her father in the Luxembourg
Gardens. Had Nancy allowed her to run away with Red's
brother, Temple would have been forced to confront no doubt
rigorous consequences, and while the interrogations put to her
would have been neither as central nor as subtle as Gavin's,
they could have been as severe as the inalterable and paralyzing knowledge of those ends to which the intrications between her and Nancy had brought them separately, but under
an inclusive knowledge of doom.

Gavin Stevens can do nothing for Nancy but be there beside
her in court, and what professional part he may have played as
her defense attorney is not told of, but at least he had
symbolized her right to full legal procedure and judicial consideration, and had made *pro forma* and in earnest the plea
for clemency which the Governor is bound to refuse as beyond
legal provision. Gavin can do little more for Temple than to
prompt conscience and provoke full self-acknowledgment, as
basis for a perhaps possible reintegration this side of her admitted inclination toward evil, since Temple Drake had even
"liked evil." With such intent, having taken Temple all the
way to the governor at his seat of power, Gavin has now drawn
her on the further experiential journey to the condemned
Nancy in her cell. Yet Gavin cannot arbitrate between Nancy's
mystical belief and Temple's uncertainties. "Is there a heaven,

Nancy?" she asks, and is told, "I dont know. But I believes."
Then Temple, in the melancholy to which her self-confrontation has reduced her, says, "Even if there is one and somebody
waiting in it to forgive me, there's still tomorrow and tomorrow. And suppose tomorrow and tomorrow, and then nobody
there, nobody waiting to forgive me—" and pauses. Nancy,
about to be taken away by the Jailor, simply says, "Believe,"
and to Temple's outright question, "Believe what, Nancy?
Tell me," she repeats "Believe" as she passes out of the room.
It is in this context of unexamined orthodoxy that Temple, on
her way to join her husband Gowan and leave the jail, repeats
a motif from the end of Act Two and says, again almost as if in
a dream: "Anyone to save it. Anyone who wants it. If there is
none, I'm sunk. We all are. Doomed. Damned." Consequently
Gavin's reply is in the same context: "Of course we are. Hasn't
He been telling us that for going on two thousand years?"

By continuing in what had been the simplistic terms of
Temple's dialogue with Nancy he seems merely to be trying to
steady Temple at that elementary stage of her struggle with
uncertainties and misgivings. It would be a sentimentalizing of
Gavin's role in *Requiem* to see his advocacy as theological
rather than ethical; likewise it would be erroneous to interpret
this last page of the novel as a conceptual resolution. Temple
has come only as far as "If," and Gavin is only pointing her to
what Nancy offered, for something to go by. It is not Gavin's
customary line and limit of thought, nor Faulkner's, nor that
of any of his ethically concerned protagonists. Isaac McCaslin,
in the extended argument with his cousin McCaslin Edmonds
about ownership of the land, bases his refusal biblically, but
that is with reference to God as creator, immanent providence, and hence ultimate eternal possessor of the land,
a more nearly universal conception of deity than that of a God
as Savior by incarnation and propitiatory sacrifice, and
requiring only belief for forgiveness and eternal salvation. It is
at this Christian level that Faulkner most often admits
mention of his characters' religion, the most memorable of
these instances being Dilsey at church in *The Sound and the*

Fury. As for Faulkner's Christian clergymen, those who are treated in any psychological depth are an odd lot. Tull in *As I Lay Dying* sees Whitfield as one whose "voice is bigger than he is," and the reader is given access to the terminological hocus-pocus in which Whitfield's adultery with Addie Bundren is tossed about in a mind that hears God commanding open confession, and then thanks God because "He in His infinite wisdom . . . restrained the tale from her dying lips" and now as for a confession to the husband Anse, a merciful God "will accept the will for the deed." What infinite mercy amounts to for such as Whitfield is almost *carte blanche* as long as appearances are kept up and the clichés of faith are repetitively uttered. Hightower in *Light in August* is of a different sort, no hypocrite, but curiously bound as a sort of hostage to the South's past and his progenitors' part in it, and thereby unnerved both in his vocation and his marriage. Though he proves capable of compassion and is at last drawn though hesitantly into degrees of kindly human involvement, his had been a curious ministry, in that the preacher's license for rhetorical excess was made to release his private, life-destroying nostalgia. As for the French priest who, in an oppressive confusion of institutional and personal demands, paradoxically makes suicide a penitential act, all that is a far piece from Yoknapatawpha folk culture, and can be estimated only in a viewing of *A Fable* beyond its mythic parallels, which (like those in *Ulysses*) are simply a compositional structure eclectically used to contain socioethical rather then explicitly theological themes.

The simplistic Christian faith as pronounced by Nancy's "Yes, Lord" in the play's first scene and her final word in the last scene, "Believe," has its more somber and even sadistic counterpart in other works where religious fanaticism is made the mask for cruelty. *Light in August* shows the clearest example in McEachern's bringing up the adopted Joe Christmas so rigidly "to fear God and abhor idleness and vanity despite his origin," and also in the outright mania of Hines, believing himself "God's chosen instrument" to preach against the Negro race as an "abomination" and to practice early and late his hatred against his own supposedly half-Negro grandson. Whitfield in his pseudopious verbal sway over his conscience, McEachern with his reduction of Calvinist righteousness to a severity that becomes an unconfessed vice, and Hines as the monstrous evangelist of hate and desolation, all at their various distances may seem irreconcilably antithetical to Nancy in her constant belief and calm acceptance. Yet she stands legally condemned to be executed for murdering an infant, which considered as a sin is worse than Whitfield's adultery and a greater violence than McEachern ever was guilty of. When all argument failed, Nancy drastically obstructed Temple's deserting her older child by smothering the younger one; this must seem an act beyond human consent, and quite beyond any approbation. Its severity exceeds that of the law's retaliations, and it raises wonder about what Nancy's religion is except that pitiful last recourse of the downtrodden, a tempering of despair by endurance, through a dream of all set right by belief in a future existence, with past realities obliterated in a felicitous eternity. In that stark first scene of *Requiem* Nancy's startling reply after the judge's sentencing, but not to him—"Yes, Lord"—has a pathos like that of the repeated response, "Yes, Jesus," from listeners to the sermon (Dilsey among them) in *The Sound and the Fury,* with their moans "like bubbles rising in water." Yet what purity Nancy's act possesses is that of simple ignorance; and with her absolutes which she is incapable of examining, she seems as far beyond estimation as is Temple, adrift in her wilfully instinctual life. Nancy as remedial agent, as rigidly severe as the law, seems more cruel, for the law's lacks are merely of scope or application, while the execution Nancy performs is willed in isolation—unless, fantastically, as a pre-Christian nun she is seen to be enacting the grim redemptive ritual of human sacrifice. It would seem more charitable to consider (as did the Governor) the harshness of her former life and the anguish of her human concerns in her servitude to Temple, and to pronounce her "crazed." No model in the correction of evil, she may suggest instead (and with utmost emphasis) how evil is multiplied by reactions it provokes. Besides her fatalistic activism the law's discreet limits that often leave it powerless may seem a blessing, since her religion without rationality had carried her beyond realities into the slaughter of an innocent.

The undeniable pity of it seems involved in Faulkner's having commented, at the University of Virginia, that the Compsons' laundress Nancy who figures in "That Evening Sun" and Nancy Mannigoe of *Requiem* are "the same person, actually." That last word is a conscious qualification; the characters are not literally identical, they do not exist in the same time period, and one is doomed to death by her vengeful husband's razor, the other by hangman's noose, for quite different offenses. Still "actually" they could merge in their creator's memory, as servants and prostitutes and women badly used in other ways by men, and both approaching their terrible ends fatalistically. This qualified identification of them gives a glimpse of Faulkner's busy imagination, conscious of having individualized the two while "actually" they are fused in his memory by an inclusive representativeness. His comment in retrospect may remind acquainted readers of the balanced tension he maintains with uniquely rendered characters in roles contributive to theme. It is a common fictional and dramatic necessity that actions should progress by disclosures and with surprises, conceptual as well as overt, and yet these should aggregate into thematic structure while validating individual portraiture. In Faulkner's work here is one of the areas of particular mastery, especially considering the animated idiosyncrasy of most of his actors and the strenuousness of events that might descend to melodrama without the smoothly maintained tension of fictional elements. For all her resignation, though, the Nancy of "That Evening Sun" cannot control her terror of the bloody vengeance that lurks in the dark. Conversely, despite a grim inevitability under the law Nancy Mannigoe is unflinching, and what steadies her can be nothing else out of her unfortunate existence but her religious belief, held with boundless assurance. Thereby she becomes the enigmatic figure obliquely pointed to by a title replete with the terminology of Catholic orders and observances—though none to which she is immediately related or which she properly serves, and of which doubtless she has no specific awareness.

This Christian coloration in a work of regional fiction raised in simpler forms questions that were to abound concerning *A Fable* (often to the bewilderment and annoyance of the literal-minded). Though *Requiem* (1951) was written during the period in which Faulkner was more extendedly occupied with *A Fable* (1954), specific connection between the two does not go beyond the common element of conceptions deriving from the Gospels; on the whole the novels stand in great contrast to each other, in scope, focus, structure, presentational devices, and adaptations of style. In *A Fable* the far-reaching analogies, only loosely drawn from biblical history, are narratively transmuted into modern times; there they are less freely poetized while being given more massive and abstracted treatment than was the regional lore and geological record, as retained in their own chronological context and elaborately fantasied, in the prose passages of *Requiem*. Whereas in the confrontations between Temple and Nancy the issue moves from the conventionally ethical to the specifically theological, in *A Fable* the enacted stresses set forth as of stupendous twentieth-century world events are distanced into the perspectives of ethical allegory, more mystery play than miracle. Most strikingly, while the prose passage, "The Jail," opening Act Three of *Requiem,* uncovers scars left by the Civil War and suggests the secondarily disintegrating effects of any war, the matter of evil is atypically set forth in Temple, Pete, and Nancy, whereas in *A Fable* evil looms over all the characters as an abstract constant, in the arresting dimensions and terrifying overtness of war, the most titanic and tragic of socioethical failures, outcome of inscrutable compulsions and unremedied by its harvest of martyrdoms.

Despite its massiveness and multiplicities *A Fable* may be more readily perceived as a unified composition than can *Requiem for a Nun.* Here the freely ranging prose passages preceding each of the drama's three acts of tightly written dialogue are in even wider structural and stylistic contrast than there is, for instance, between the two plots of *The Wild Palms,* where sections of them narrated in alternation provide what Faulkner termed "antithesis . . . counterpoint." Yet in *Requiem* too there is counterpoint; the prose passages not only enhance the play but, as "Old Man" does for "The Wild Palms," they give it primary claim. "The Courthouse," "The Golden Dome," and "The Jail" are not prologues to the three acts of *Requiem,* much less stage directions (these being conventionally placed within the scenes themselves). Rather, the prose generalizes such themes as the law's efficacy and limits, society's looser systems, expediencies, and drifts, and within those larger contexts the volatile yearnings, constraining habituations, and impulsive thrusts of the individual life, to be assessed by its fellows or go unregarded, and to judge itself or evade that severest trial. This becomes antiphonal to the singular mischances and offenses and the private intensities which fatally shape Temple's and Nancy's lives, bringing them into a moral confrontation and finally a theologically based interchange.

Nothing in Faulkner's *oeuvre* points more intriguingly than does *Requiem for a Nun* to the mysterious ways of his dynamic imagination. What was it that led the artist to project Temple Drake's life as of eight years later and to find her still shadowed by the disasters of *Sanctuary,* in a morbid marriage with Gowan Stevens that is exacerbated by shame and pride and made still more unstable by Temple's wilfulness in another surrender to sensuality? And how did this projection, as given background, causative factors, and credibility by the earlier novel, now draw into itself for key figure the Negro Nancy Mannigoe, admittedly a semblable of the laundress and prostitute in "That Evening Sun," with besides a simple religious faith like Dilsey's of *The Sound and the Fury?* And how, above all, did Nancy's and Temple's fatally intersecting courses make imperative their presentation in dramatic form and yet evoke for total structure a framing and complementary augmentation by the interpenetrating sense of the historical, conveyed in those three panels of impressionistic prose? The process can be conceived of only as a song some siren sang to the favored and faithful artist. Yet while its inception remains inscrutable, the achieved work abundantly proves itself. Social history complements the Temple-Nancy interaction, with their intense, oppositely oriented drives and their overt offenses imprecisely adjudicated. The wide scale of reference established by the prose passages contributes conversely to the suggested separateness of each woman — Temple in her contumacious restlessness and Nancy poised in her simplistic religious trance. At the moment of judgment Nancy did not even answer society's legally empowered judge; Temple's wavering confessions scarcely reveal a sufficient purpose, leaving her not just adrift in her shabby history but only dimly related to anything larger.

These subtly implied themes in the stark drama are brought into wider relevance through the historically based passages, especially "The Golden Dome," shadowing forth generations in which the longer human struggle has gone on, with individuals making do under whatever approximations of community they may have arrived at, but with the more extended, larger life of society less susceptible to examination and adequate correction, and less controllable in its sometimes disastrous drives, so that history with its recent catastrophes and ominous accelerations is set against legend with its reassuring core of human identity and purposeful realizations. Such scales of reference are useful too in an estimation of Gavin Stevens' strange role in the *Requiem* drama, where though he is so insistent an agent he is also forbearing, waiting upon Nancy as well as Temple, and pausing with them when they have come as far as they can. Gavin as defense attorney has no debatable case to press; as catalyst he cannot be credited with any final effect; as investigator he comes away only obscurely answered. His merit is less by achievement than in a realistically measured compassionate attempt, beyond his merely professional competence, to comfort Nancy in ways she can understand and to prompt Temple toward a requisite next step, without which she will remain not just what she describes as "doomed" and "damned" but existentially lost for lack of present self-possession and any inner direction beyond impulse. Yet while Nancy seems to stand calmly beyond time and mortality, believing herself eternally "saved," Temple has experienced not a conversion to such a belief but only a catharsis by her abased admissions that leave her repeating a litany of questions, if, whether, and how.

The divergent enigmas of these two women's lives are set forth and held in dramatic suspension in the open-ended last scene of *Requiem,* when Gavin brings Temple to the jail to visit Nancy the night before her execution. They are admitted by the Jailor (the Mr Tubbs of *Intruder in the Dust*); he still talks too much, this time out of not knowing what to say in Temple's distressed presence; thus it comes out that Gavin has been visiting Nancy to sing hymns with her, in which other Negro prisoners have joined. The Jailor fumblingly expresses what "all of us home folks" in town and county feel, that Lawyer Stevens is "all right" even if "he got a little out of line defending a nigger murderer" and then coming to sing with the condemned woman. The Jailor's explanation for the community's approval of Gavin is that they "know him." What the Jailor cannot express is the fact that with all Gavin's unconventionalities he walks in a kind of immunity, as one recognizably reaching out across gulfs, not in an identification and not always in approval, but open-heartedly, and with a convincing assumption that men's ethical contract extends to individual human responsibilities the law cannot define. The deepest dramatic factor in this jail scene is that Temple has come to face Nancy as the last and hardest of the confrontations Gavin has led her to force upon herself, and also to try to glimpse the deepest source of that principled assurance Nancy had shown in her earlier struggles to persuade Temple not to desert her family and run off with Red's blackmailing brother. Those past events are not discussed now; the talk moves between Temple's still evasively and almost petulantly expressed despair and Nancy's matter-of-fact replies which always end in absolute assertions of belief in salvation, for herself and for the world.

In a telling passage Temple has turned to the grave matter of consequences and asked why her baby and Nancy too "have to suffer just because I decided to go to a baseball game five years ago." In this apparent attempt to turn obvious cause and effect, as they arise out of ill-considered conduct, into a cosmic mystery she seems still to be avoiding the why and wherefore of all that followed upon her intrusion with Gowan at Frenchman's Bend, including Tommy's and Goodwin's deaths, the second because of her perjury, and thereafter the disruptive entry of Red's brother into her life and her yielding herself to him. There seems too a typical sort of evasion in her removing the question of responsibility to an inaccessible theological level as she continues — "Do you have to suffer everybody else's anguish just to believe in God?" Nancy answers with more of her quaint earthy speculation to prop up her simple creed. God, she says, "cant help Himself. He's like a man that's got too many mules" and so must handle them cautiously and turn them loose from Saturday noon till Monday morning "to run free in mule sin and mule pleasure." This perhaps oddest formulation ever given the doctrine of free will prompts Gavin to ask, "You have got to sin too?" and Nancy says, "You aint *got* to. You cant help it. And He knows that. But you can suffer. . . . And He will save you." Gavin asks, "You too? A murderess? In heaven?" — not to contradict her faith but to concede to her what the question will evoke. Nancy says, "I can work." (When Mollie Beauchamp in old age proposes to divorce Lucas because of his gold-hunting mania and Roth Edmonds sympathetically asks how she will get along alone, Mollie too has said, "I can work.") Now Gavin enters into a series of what are not so much questions as another of his speculative discursions, as if on the biblically based theme of the required sweat of man's brow, especially as men had doubly enforced it on the Negro in the South: he says "The harp, the raiment, the singing, may not be for Nancy

Mannigoe, — not now." Still there's "the washing and sweeping
. . . the children to be tended and fed and kept from hurt and
harm and out from under the grown folks' feet? . . . A heaven
where that little child will remember nothing of your hands
but gentleness because now this earth will have been nothing
but a dream that didn't matter?" Nor is that all Gavin asks,
and the whole of his speech is to be understood in the light of
its last three words — "Is that it?" This is explicitly interroga-
tive, beyond what Gavin knows as mundane reality, wherein,
as he had told Temple and Gowan, there's no such thing as
immunity or as past either. As it had been with them in the
first two acts, Gavin's part is still to question, and now chiefly
to draw out Nancy for Temple's benefit, though beyond doubt
he is also thoughtfully attentive to this extreme instance of
pure belief, and the believer's insulation in it. Gavin's sympathy is genuine, too, as is seen when something Temple says
brings out that Nancy had lost a baby by miscarriage when a
man, perhaps the one who fathered it, had kicked her in the
stomach. Gavin's shock at this shows in his incredulous questionings, from which Nancy turns aside almost indifferently to
talk instead about whether that baby of hers will be in heaven
too.

And, "Is there a heaven, Nancy?" Temple finally asks.
Nancy doesn't know, she just believes. "Believe what?" Temple
asks, and Nancy repeats, "I dont know. But I believes." That
is how it stands as the Jailor comes to take Nancy back to her
cell for her last night. Temple repeats her appeal — "Believe
what, Nancy? Tell me." Nancy, as she goes out, is down to her
simple imperative, "Believe." And Temple, turning to leave
the jail, is left in dark uncertainties and speaks despairingly:
"Anyone to save it. Anyone who wants it. If there is none, I'm
sunk. We all are. Doomed. Damned." Although her "we all
are" is to that degree an identification with humanity, in the
context of Temple's behavior it does not rise perceptibly above
a fatalistic acknowledgment of impasse for herself, in a world
where she had discovered no verities transcending her own
wilfulness. The measure of her mood had been given when she

asked, "What kind of God is it that has to blackmail His customers with the whole world's grief and ruin?" As in many a recalcitrant, such bitterly desperate statement accuses the cosmos, however personified, in an avoidance of more acute issues nearer home. She who had contributed so much to others' sufferings (as looked back on in her reluctant admissions to the Governor) still resisted enduring her full share in it in the painful form of self-confrontation. Conversely, Nancy had accepted all suffering not just of necessity but by seeing it a means of grace, as when she says, "He dont tell you to suffer. But He gives you the chance." Nancy's mystical concept unites her in abasement with fallible mankind yet raises in her the hope of salvation; set beside that, what Temple wants seems a poor thing, little more than a further present indulgence, by promised exoneration from the results of her past offenses. Lacking faith, she calculates all this in terms of "nobody waiting to forgive me." Temple's despair is of that form which overtakes frustrated ego; Nancy's endurance is in that acceptance of suffering which converts the stoic secular *C'est la vie* into the anodyne and elixir of otherworldliness.

In *Requiem* it is consistently with a fictionist's interest that Faulkner touches upon theological abstractions; he shows their entering into the consciousness of individuals and drawing them into transcendent speculations on life and death, time and timelessness, and thus evoking the reality of the subjective, the spirit, the buried life in its immediate unique contextual motions. It is by this light that Gavin had required Temple to stand forth not just as the present Mrs. Gowan Stevens who had been about to desert her husband and home but as the Temple Drake of *Sanctuary,* and his aim is not a religious conversion through which she may find divine forgiveness but a present reintegration, by confronting what she had evaded earlier, that she, like everyone else, must "pay for your past." Resentfully she had asked, "Why dont you go on and tell me it's for the good of my soul — if I have one?" and he answers, "I did. I said, so you can sleep at night." He had said more than just that, though; he had mentioned pity, courage, honor, honesty, or, he concluded, "a simple desire for the right to sleep at night" — a right presumably secured through good conscience. Here and elsewhere in *Requiem* Gavin is not arguing theologically but ethically, yet not to denounce Temple but if possible to help her find herself, and not just because she is a Stevens by marriage but quite as much for the same reason he sings hymns with Nancy — because she too is a human being in dire straits. Such a scale of reference is necessary for understanding of Gavin in this drama, and for the measure of Faulkner's conception.

In his final speech, answering Temple's feeble speculation about forgiveness and salvation and her melancholy certainty of the alternative, doom and damnation, his assent — "Hasn't He been telling us that for going on two thousand years?" — is put in Christian terms because that has been the idiom of their dialogue with Nancy; and if this is the point Temple has been able to reach, then the best Gavin can do is to steady her there. This is not to deny that Gavin may have professed himself a Christian (and indeed he does know the hymns) but neither does that make him a Southern Protestant fundamentalist, nor does he ever sound like one. He is to be seen in his trend, and in *Requiem* as elsewhere it is toward immediate endeavors in terms of humanistic verities, which he promulgates through the law's remedies and beyond, if need be and if he can. In dealing with Temple he is increasingly pointed but still tentative, seeking to lead her not for confession's sake but as along the only way out of confusion. He has brought Temple to Nancy not for theological indoctrination or "conversion" but for his same reason in taking her to the Governor, to prompt a responsible self-confrontation. Thus at Temple's challenging him to admit that his efforts were "for the good of" her "soul," he immediately equated it not with salvation hereafter but with a human being's earned "right to sleep at night." The largest implications of *Requiem for a Nun* would not be recognized but reductively sentimentalized, and its essential Faulknerian qualities would not be realized, if Gavin were seen as Christian evangelist and Temple as saved by religious conversion. Indubitably Temple has been benighted, entangled in her wilfulness, and at the close of *Requiem* she

seems not notably advanced toward either the ethical assertions Gavin had attempted to prompt or the consolations of
Nancy's theology. Her last speech, the single word "Coming,"
might be given some implicative weight, but it seems only a
natural answer to her husband Gowan's calling her name from
offstage; and against the context of their whole history (not
just the matter of *Sanctuary* but its sequel in an inadequately
expiatory marriage, Temple's foiled but the more disastrous
intention to defect from it, and their expressed dejection over
themselves and each other) it would be more credible to
imagine an uneasy future for the Gowan Stevens than any
saving reversal and regeneration. Properly there can be no
projection of Temple's future, considering what has been
made thematic, her suspension, restless but resourceless, in an
ambivalence in which she unconsciously echoes Rider of
"Pantaloon in Black" when she says, on her return from
California, "If I would just stop struggling . . . but I still cant
seem to quit." Nor will circumstance permit it, but even turns
the sharp edge of coincidence against her, as when Gavin's
nagging telegram ("You have a week yet until the thirteenth.
But where will you go then?") had been prepared for by her
small son's asking whether they would stay in California "until
they hang Nancy" and adding, "Where will we go then,
mamma?" More generally, Faulkner does not picture soul-
saving conversions or denouements that suddenly make all the
difference. With his artistic intentness upon that primary
matter of fiction, the ongoing flow of conscious individual
existences, Faulkner does show accretions of awareness, or a
precipitation of insight, sometimes fulfilling, sometimes forbidding and even productive of despair, as with Temple,
beyond tears in her chronic intractability, while painfully
beset by the associative thrusts of a restless and sardonically
fanciful but not unsubtle nor wholly impenitent mind.

The darkness of *Sanctuary,* overflowing into *Requiem for a
Nun* in the morbidities of Temple's and Gowan's marriage
itself, and recurring through the sinister and corruptive incursion of Red's brother, illustrates the hazard of relationship as

it extends adventitiously to Nancy and augments the special
pathos of her life and fate. But for all her devotion and endurance in the course of a harshly beset, pitiful existence, its culminating act cannot be sanctioned. Nancy's offense, on both
legal and conventional scales, is worse than Temple's intent
had been, yet as Temple penitently admitted after striking
Nancy, she had "always been so good to my children and
me — my husband too — all of us — trying to hold us together"
(like Dilsey with the deteriorating Compsons) and this had
climaxed in Nancy's ruses and persistent arguments, for the
sake of "two little children," to dissuade Temple from running
off with Red's brother. Yet that scene concludes with the child-
murder — an act in defense of nothing knowable as of greater
value than the potentials of the untried, unrealized life she
snuffed out — and more drastic than anything Temple had
done or intended. Here the two women, despite their extremes
of difference, become strangely similar through the factor of
excess. In such a psychological drama this intensifies the large
question of their natures, extending to their separate cultural
conditionings, the one through presumed privileges and indul-
gences as a judge's daughter, the other through deprivation
and abuse made stoically bearable by primitive, strongly
mystical religious belief. Nancy's final act, if it be not madness, stems from a lapse into despair, but this she transcends
remarkably, through her inclusive and integrated view of sin,
suffering, and salvation. Answering Gavin's question, "You
have got to sin, too?" she continues, in summing up all its
factors simply but in essence, to set free will above predestination, and to credit that will with the providentially given
power of amendment.

You aint *got* to. You cant help it. And He knows that. But you can suffer.
And He knows that too. He dont tell you to suffer. But He gives you the
chance. He gives you the best He can think of, that you are capable of
doing. And He will save you.

It is an ignorant, alert, beset, resolute, earnest human being's
consistent workaday concept of the grace of God. Firmly as-

sumed, it makes plain the way to eternal life, not by works but by faith, and though Nancy cannot have known it, there is a preponderance of formal fundamentalist theology on her side. Nancy herself has cut clean through the intrication of knowing and believing, which more often is evaded by merely nominal affiliates of theological, political, or other fixed persuasions. As to religion, the issue is not often confronted as candidly and unequivocally as here when after Temple had asked, "Is there a heaven?" Nancy answered, "I dont know. I believes"; and then, when Temple put it more closely—"Believe what?"—Nancy compounded her absoluteness: "I dont know. But I believes." If this is the price of eternal salvation, Temple cannot pay it; conditioned in the seized freedoms of sensuality and defiant irresponsibility, but finally brought to some self-confrontation by Gavin's amateur yet penetrating therapy, she does not responsively intone that paradoxical confession of faith. Nor is she too different here from the ordinary skeptic who is not averse to revelation but honestly incapable of mysticism. Conversely, this scene illuminates Nancy's all but canonical exaltation under the elegaic ironies of the book's title. She who "can get low for Jesus," in an abasement which is an affiliation with the highest, thus is figuratively garbed as of a spiritual community, to be accorded at the last one of the Western world's most solemn rites.

Weighted though it is with abstractions, the drama in *Requiem* is succinct and celerate, because its flow is primarily from the temperaments of the pointedly engaged speakers rather than through an overriding expository progression. This is plainly to be felt in the differences of range, tempo, and tone between Temple and Nancy. In the final scene, where the talk for the most part becomes conceptually based, the dramatic action is still expeditious, along the tacking course of intent personal exchanges. Here at the end, as in the catastrophic central scene in Act Two, the dynamic factor is of confrontation between Temple and Nancy. At that turning point, when Temple's intention to desert her family would be halted by Nancy's smothering the baby, the conflict had been severe, with Nancy pressing relentlessly and Temple violently defiant; now in this finale at the jail Temple has become the shamed yet unsatisfied inquirer, with Nancy quietly firm at the verge of her death and transcendently confident in her beliefs. These two great scenes and the always impelling drama which frames them are only a moiety of a literary work made whole through the narrative passages — "The Courthouse," "The Golden Dome," and "The Jail." and throughout those discursive prose passages and this explicit drama in their three alternations a more immediate issue is implicated, and one more pressing for most than that of the soul's salvation hereafter; it is that of the perplexing ethical entanglement to which in some degree every mortal is fated beyond prescience, avoidance, or final estimation. Made thematic throughout, and exemplified by historical panorama, legend, and a specific contemporary dramatic instance, this is the unifying factor in *Requiem for a Nun*. It concerns the awesome, multiple-dimensioned matter of involvement and consequence, and it indicates the wide extent of that field upon which are played out the multitudinous contests between good and evil. It is on whether "good can come out of evil" that Gavin Stevens becomes dogmatic: "It not only can, it must." That too declares a faith, but based on possible assurances from mankind's history as it shows that evil may imperatively prompt the counterassertion of human verities. Yet such a hope presumes no guarantees, and Faulkner, who symbolizes men's aspiring drive toward order and justice in "The Courthouse," also apprehends "America" in socioeconomic perspective as "one towering frantic edifice poised like a card-house over the abyss of the mortgaged generations" and now "whirled faster and faster toward the plunging precipice of its destiny."

This novel in all its parts and structuring strongly suggests that if being involved in mankind means one may hear another's passing bell tolling for himself too, this is not entirely a matter of empathy but also of hazard apprehended — a particular pity and an immense terror, yet not so much of death as of life's threats as an inescapable venture into diverse and not always voluntary participations. Gavin Stevens' stipulation that the past is not dead, it isn't even past, is pressed upon both Temple and Gowan in their own continuing frustrations and calamities, as these stem from their ill-starred entanglements with each other and society, in effects still being precipitated out of the *Sanctuary* events eight years ago. Faulkner found many of his earlier characters recrossing his vision and would invite such as these into new situations; and also there were published stories still vibrant in his memory, some perhaps quarried out in his first tentative approaches under intimations of a larger subject, as with "A Name for the City," which settled into the larger frame of the opening portion of *Requiem,* "The Courthouse," while similarly Temple is made to know the local tale of Rider as evolved in "Pantaloon in Black," and in thinking of Nancy in jail for murder, enlarges it into typicality and an analogy with her own unabatedly troubled mind. Temple was a giddy coed and almost stupefied victim in *Sanctuary,* and Faulkner raised her into a keen young woman, more wilful in her own young matron's right and the more rebellious against that imperfect situation, being newly besotted with another embodiment of nihilism; perhaps Faulkner's *donnee* in *Requiem* was not so much an impulse simply to go on with her for her own sake as a sensing that the protagonist of *Sanctuary,* left passively suspended, could bring all that history of offenses, that not yet dead past, into a more extended illustration of involvement and ongoing consequence. He had frequently explored that theme; the most towering exemplar is Thomas Sutpen of *Absalom, Absalom!* who would not estimate the cost to those he involved in his compulsions and could not understand the moral arithmetic of the consequences he himself suffered, fatally at last. But Temple still lived, trailing along with her a dark past that would neither completely destroy her nor go away. By contrast Nancy's fatal involvement has no such antecedents, having come about only through her entry into the Gowan Stevens family as their servant, but it is the more representative, since in every life the chain of consequence is shaped and linked by fortuities, yet often irrevocably and sometimes fatally. Temple's desperate affair having precipitated Nancy's offense, that in turn will be a reactive force beyond Nancy's life. Short of being raised up into the consolations of religion, Temple is to feel herself doomed by her own actions in what they had laid her open to, and damned for what they had brought upon others.

Involvement and consequence are, obviously, the skeletal logic of plot in most fiction and drama. Used merely for surprise and shock or other sensational effects, they lower imaginative works to the level of melodrama, but properly they give narrative its continuity and momentum; and that simple claim upon attention is relatively compounded by whatever the conceptual substance of the work. What is remarkable in Faulkner is that unusual intensity of overt event is more than sufficiently complemented by sharp individuation and psychological penetration, and made commanding by some representative magnitude. In the great closing scene of the *Requiem* drama characterization is *in situ*, but not as with the stock pawns of simplistic conflict; the two women are revealed each as in the light of her earnestly turning consciousness, and poignant in a reaching toward the other. Temple here as well as earlier is allowed an urgent fluency, in verisimilitude of one under the pressure of a searing crisis; Nancy has willed her own calmness drawn from her inner assurances and yet keeps her ready native aptness. Meanwhile now that Temple has become genuinely engaged in this crucial confrontation, Gavin is the moderator sympathetic to both, concerned for both. Here where error and offense have such singular circumstantial shadings, evil is a miasma, stifling but invisible, and scarcely definable, its incidents having passed into ongoing consequences that establish tragic realities. However, the plain agent of specific evils, Red's brother Pete as Temple's blackmailer and lover, has lapsed from the scene and from consideration, having been only briefly glimpsed (through the dramatist's descriptive commentary) with his "definite 'untamed' air . . . a hard, ruthless quality, not immoral but unmoral," and it is as if it was not Nancy's desperate gesture which had eliminated him, but that willed simplicity of an unprincipled man, in which he lacks sufficient human dimensions and stature to sustain a more than causative role in this morality play, wherein the discussed abstractions of good and evil are a chorus he would be deaf to. Specifically, though Pete may dominate Temple, he can reach her in but one way in that highly sentient ambivalence without which hers can be only a gothic tale. She had been brutally and degradingly acquainted with sex, and conditioned to ruthlessness until in her own wilfulness she was made responsive to it, as an escape from a too stratified society's patterns and in an addiction that could not easily be appeased and could never furnish a life center that would hold. Thus in her impulsiveness Temple can suffer only momentary arrestment, an ominous syncope, under Gavin's queries and Nancy's forthright chidings, for she can no more commit herself to the constant rule of his humanistic verities than she can take Nancy's firm stand in this world by projecting her concern infinitely beyond it. It may well seem at the end that the dire consequences of Temple's involvement with mankind have all but overset her self-indulgent wilfulness and left her disoriented beyond any rescue. What Faulkner touched on here runs too deep to be resolved by a dramatic conversion; Temple's past remains an albatross still hung about her neck.

Nevertheless, since both Temple and Nancy are atypical characters, each with an uncommon history, and in their conjunction in *Requiem* are seen proceeding into further aberrance, in themselves they do not present a wide view of involvement and consequence, though they do show that effect follows inexorably upon even the most bizarre causes. The prose panels have their place in *Requiem* as a composition because they broaden instance and make more representative this unifying theme. It is given massive substantiation by extensions at various distances into the past, as it illustrates the widest human complications, through mankind's societal improvisations and procedures, which like those of individual life show aspiring endeavor, partial achievements, and sometimes calamitous, often insidiously corruptive effects. These matters, while given opulently detailed and rhetorically forceful expression, are still only glancingly sketched so that they may sound motif without rivaling the central *Requiem* story, with its tight structure and sustained intensity. But though only adjunctive, in their preceding the drama's acts and giving place to the third of these as climax and closure of *Requiem* as a whole composition, the prose passages have created an immense backdrop suggestive of the very world of all mankind, playing out the innumerable and never wholly known complexities of involvement and circumstance. This effect includes aspects ranging from something as central as a pioneer construction of a seat out of which law could make its pronouncements or to such extremes as the sense of an *élan vital* moving through prehistoric darkness and old night into the raising up of the Capitol's golden dome, or, minutely yet of primary significance, the soundless voice of Cecelia Farmer etching her words upon the imagination: *"Listen, stranger; this was myself: this was I."*

Like any clearly illustrative as well as distinctly individuated figures in drama and in fiction, Temple and Nancy continually bespeak intuitive attention, and given it, each takes on lifelikeness by becoming less simply appreciable and less inclusively definable the more they are seen and heard; thus they grow into recognizably human mysteries. As the drama's last scene swells into a strangely poignant kind of fundamentalist theological colloquy there in the jail, sight may be lost of the privacies as well as distances from which the characters speak. Gavin, having insistently brought Temple into meetings with others for the sake of inducing her self-confrontation, now leaves the talk largely to her and Nancy, entering into it interestedly and sympathetically himself yet mainly to expedite it for both their sakes. Yet these women are not on the same plane, and the obviousness of this may make it seem that

Temple's asking Nancy to tell her not *how* to believe but *what* is almost as if to test not only a credibility but its worth — which Nancy assumes and takes for granted as the grace of God, though that is not her phrase. Concerning her belief in the supernatural and her certainty of a saving relationship to it, her most implicative comment is also a most intimate disclosure of herself as of this life. She tells that when "Mr. Gavin" hadn't come the night before to sing hymns with her she "guessed" he and Temple had gone to see the Mayor in her behalf, and when she is told it was the Governor, she is still sure it was to no avail. She had not allowed herself to hope, and now she calls hoping "the hardest thing of all to break, get rid of, the last thing of all poor sinning man will turn aloose." She even connects man's hoping with sin, in that "sometimes before he even knows it, he has throwed salvation away just grabbling back at hoping." Gavin, pressing for clarity, asks, "You mean when you have salvation, you dont have hope?" and Nancy, with all her successively disappointed hopes of this life already surrendered, answers, "You dont even need it. All you need, all you have to do, is just believe."

This is almost like a voice from the other side of tomorrow's appointment for Nancy. Yet earlier when Temple had asked whether to "Trust in Him" was only "because there isn't anything else," Nancy had called the trusted promise of salvation "maybe your pay for the suffering." Then Gavin, probing, had asked Nancy whether what she meant was that the world's salvation is in man's suffering, and she said, "Yes, sir." It is no sophisticated orthodoxy she is affirming, not sacramental Trinitarian Christianity with its belief that the crucifixion of Jesus Christ was sufficient sacrifice for the sins of the whole world; yet stripped of theological subtleties and ritualistic observance, this comes into simplistic fundamentalist evangelism in the symbolic phrase, the blood of the Lamb of God. The sermon Dilsey listens to near the ending of *The Sound and the Fury* is on the announced and repeated theme, "I got the recollection and the blood of the Lamb," and hearing it, she "sat bolt upright . . . crying rigidly and quietly

in the annealment and the blood of the remembered Lamb."
Whatever hymns Gavin sang with Nancy, this must have been
their drift. Even so, Nancy's saying the world's salvation is in
man's suffering had a religious insight beyond her defining;
and it is an import Gavin must have sensed responsively. Since
human suffering often springs out of societal disorders, or
from interpersonal offenses through falsehood, greed, and
cruelty, or by self-inflicted harm through ignorance, illusion,
and recklessness, a mundane view if not of sin at least of
human misdoings and consequent sorrows may be suggested,
and present ameliorations might be envisioned. This is Gavin
Stevens' tangent; he has not only been compassionate toward
the condemned Nancy, he is trying to orient Temple in her
present state by urging a self-confrontation and acknowledgment of responsibilities under the light of values such as he
named — pity, courage, honesty — as means of sound sleep at
night now and in this life through fidelity to such principles.
These hold out no such infinite and absolute promises as
Nancy has found in her religion, yet they aggregate into an
ethic and a resultant degree of present assurance. For Gavin the
pursuit of verities is not to be relinquished exclusively to philosophers; it is the work of ordinary men in all their adaptative
and progressive existences, and this assumed fact is at the
heart of Faulkner's realism, as he proclaimed at Stockholm. In
his various works his protagonists' reactions suggest that disorder and confusion, with their flavor of the random and
chaotic and their enormous levies of human suffering, are
conversely challenging, even imperatively, by shadowing forth
an approachable order with its cumulative realizations, for
mankind and for men.

It is thus that what Nancy says of suffering and salvation has
also a worldly truth, and though this is far short of the transcendental absolute, it is the factor of ongoing human achievement, though only relative even at its highest level. Temple
therefore has two examples set before her, different yet not
totally antithetical, since both are idealistic projections; and if
she is seen without a resolute grasp on either it is not from a

dilemma of choice but from paralyzing incapacity. She has answered to Gavin's promptings and undergone the ordeal of confession to the Governor and to Gowan, but beyond that she seems either reluctant to surrender her habitual wilfulness and assumption of privilege to the priority of the larger conceptions Gavin invokes, or unable in her exhaustion and despair to rally to them. As to the recourse Nancy exemplifies so strongly, Temple cannot trust its assurance, and even near the end of the drama she fears the risk that, after believing, she will find no one to receive and forgive her. Not even her own past and Gavin's interpretations have taught her the sufficient prudence of recognizing that even now she is creating her future; and Nancy's example cannot carry her into the mystery of knowing by believing. Temple has come as far as a stifling sense of doom, and anything beyond that would be not only another story but one dependent upon assertions she cannot presently rise to.

Nancy, moving serenely under her own doom, has spoken one word, "Believe," as she goes to pray with the preacher and sing hymns in her cell on the last night of her existence. Temple, leaving the scene of her last meeting with Nancy, has answered her husband's voice with the single word "Coming," yet with no sign that she knows in what fixed direction, to what lasting purpose. The harshly detailed illustration by these two women's lives of complex human involvement and drastic consequence is distilled into starkness by these laconic last utterances, but immediately before that Faulkner has begun a closure in a modulation that is one more unique instance of his art as it contributes to organic composition. Having taken Nancy back to her cell after the interview, the Jailor returns to escort Temple and Gavin out through the locked doors whose metallic clanging have been the incidental music to this scene. They have heard the Jailor tell Nancy that he has found a "preacher" to come see her "about sundown, he said," and now with her gone the Jailor remarks, "If I was ever fool enough to commit a killing that would get my neck into a noose, the last thing I would want to see would be a preacher. I'd a heap rather believe there wasn't nothing after death than to risk the station where I was probably going to get off." This single different note struck after all the colloquy extends the range of the scene, and like any other variation, by that slight difference it shifts the whole episode's center of balance. It is with such multiplication of diversities that the narrative artist distances himself and the reader from the work, allowing a perspective in which its conceptions are not given over to conveyance by any one voice but are left to an augmenting intuitive comprehension still only relatively defined. Such designed furnishings forth subtly enlarge imaginative appeal, and as comprised within the total composition of *Requiem for a Nun,* they give range on a new tangent to Faulkner's characteristic traits, with their unique effects. And for all its literary experimentation, the novel is centrally expressive of Faulkner as humanistic realist and Southern regionalist. However, the unusual and undeniable darkness in this drama admits most openly a relativism in Faulkner's humanistic faith, and in his confidence in his fellowbeings, while the prose overtures in their larger dimensions disclose a narrator's bleakly apocalyptic lyricized visions not unlike what old Isaac McCaslin finally experienced, but here much more fluently, fully, and ominously set forth. While Faulkner does not step onto the stage in *Requiem for a Nun,* in this aspect his voice resounds throughout the theatre—nostalgic, apprehensive, ironic, and uncompromising.

Achievement and Celebration: Faulkner's Last Two Novels

11

Faulkner in *The Mansion*

UPSTART Flem Snopes, insidious villain of *The Hamlet*
and *The Town,* has met his end in *The Mansion,* in retribution for his lack of fellow-feeling; the avenger Mink Snopes has
escaped, to move on through darkness toward his own place in
the ground; Linda, Flem's daughter he never fathered, has
left Jefferson again and perhaps finally, after abetting Mink;
and Gavin Stevens would seem to be temporarily out of avoca-
tional employment as witness and intervener in a world the
Snopeses almost made. Thus is the trilogy completed—the
fine house is emptied of its usurper who could never fully
occupy it, and the tale ends upon a pause, its implications suspended as in the complementary reflections of Stevens and
Ratliff:

"You see?" his uncle said. "It's hopeless. Even when you get rid of one
Snopes, there's already another one behind you even before you can turn
around."

"That's right," Ratliff said serenely. "As soon as you look, you see right
away it aint nothing but jest another Snopes."

Once more a Faulknerian theme has been evolved, in an opulently detailed yet scrupulous fable of the human condition,
with conflict between ruthless aggression and a principled
resistance only partially successful, barely forestalling despair.
    There is, however, no oversimplified reduction to absolute

This essay first appeared in *The Virginia Quarterly Review,* Spring 1960, pp. 273-92.

extremes. *The Mansion* continues to set forth a complex involvement of relative good and evil in their qualifying interactions. Faulkner's note prefacing this terminal volume admits "contradictions and discrepancies due to the fact that the author has learned, he believes, more about the human heart and its dilemma than he knew thirty-four years ago [when Faulkner began this work] and is sure that, having lived with them that long time, he knows the characters of this chronicle better than he did then." Actually, the discrepancies are minor and insignificant, and extensions of characterization do not disrupt earlier concepts but supplement them. Yet not only do familiar Yoknapatawpha folk reveal themselves further, sometimes surprisingly; the present brings past event into drastic reassessment, discovering beyond the overt action more of motive and mood.

The extended view is bent primarily upon Mink Snopes, twice a murderer, in young manhood and old age, briefly a tenant farmer and an almost lifelong convict, a formerly flat character emergent in the round, a primitive done with arresting detail. The opening chapter of *The Mansion* probes further Mink's ambushing of Houston after a quarrel over an impounded cow. In *The Hamlet* where this killing was first narrated, Mink's elemental fury was singled out; and the brutality which drove his wife from him led Ratliff, in *The Town,* to pronounce Mink "out and out mean." In *The Hamlet* psychological emphasis is on Houston's bitter aloofness after a stormy youth and the accidental death of his young wife; Ratliff re-estimated Houston in *The Town* as "proud to begin with and then unhappy on top of that" and so "a little overbearing." In his conceit, sorrow, rage, and compensatory arrogance Houston was both unamiable and pitiable, a typical victim of self under the stress of event, whose unease rebounds upon others. Now in *The Mansion* Mink's side of it is looked into, and in his more meagre pride and sorry efforts he is found pitiable too, yet not without a certain dignity.

Those "discrepancies" Faulkner acknowledges are "actively"

(as Ratliff would say) an aspect of reality, being of the kind which may exist between a man's outward showing — the brute starkness of his wrong-doing or his folly — and the intricate conditioning of personality through which the explicit act was triggered. Such a variance is to be charged, if at all, to another creator than any fictionist, who has done his part when he brings to the commonplace event the revealing light of its private motive and cloaking mood, by which it becomes united in its very incoherencies with the whole history of "the human heart and its dilemma." Faulkner, moreover, deals forthrightly with incoherencies as such, for comprehensiveness and that truth in depth which touches upon permutations and dramatizes discrepancy as reality, with all its appeal to curiosity and its challenge to judgment and compassion. Thus Houston, the tortured man of *The Hamlet,* turns under changing lights in *The Mansion* to become the simpler, more removed figure, while Mink's "meanness," seen into more closely and literally reviewed in fuller relations, is seen beyond.

Mink lives by that endurance Faulkner finds in mankind, with a quietly courageous persistence making survival something more than a brute matter. He plays the game, too, according to dim but steady lights of his own. At first it is only one of the minute economic expedients of his marginal existence — he thinks to let his strayed cow stay and be wintered with Houston's herd and then claim it, fattened and perhaps bred, in the spring. When Houston charges for the cow's keep, Mink doggedly works it out digging post-holes, but when Houston demands a dollar impounding fee, Mink does the added work and then shoots Houston from ambush, in an assertion of pride carried out almost ritualistically. On trial, Mink asserted the human claim in elemental terms, as to blood, clan. His naïveté in supposing Flem would come to anyone's aid gratuitously lays him open to a traumatic disillusionment, and he goes to prison in the added bonds of an obsessive conviction that he must kill Flem. After Flem schemes to prompt Mink's futile attempt at escape, so that his sentence is extended, Mink's determination to be revenged is increased.

He holds it through long years and achieves it at last against all that baffles an ignorant, almost penniless, and aged man, sustained by his code and by his underdog philosophy that "Old Moster jest punishes; he dont play jokes."

But *The Mansion* is not just a tale of the Flem-Mink opposition. A related element, more obliquely set forth, is the rôle of Linda Snopes Kohl and Gavin's concern with her, which becomes the business of Ratliff and Charles Mallison, and all of which develops connections with Flem's whole story, his end, and Mink's agency in it. Linda's position in her home and her home town being anomalous, and her experiences having been excruciating and injurious, she reappears in *The Mansion* as one so impaired and isolated as to be awkwardly strange, pathetically incongruous. The summons to the chivalry of a Gavin Stevens is imperative. That his response often is quixotic illustrates him as man of feeling and aristocrat of the moral world; it also contributes to the drama, since his most extreme actions are elicited by situations grotesque in themselves, tending to force respondents into similarly exaggerated postures and parries.

Herein may be found a crucial issue in the evaluation of Faulkner's achievement. That it abounds in the grotesque brooded upon until it deepens into a kind of Gothic darkness is undeniable. Characters as various as Mink and Linda, too severely beset and hurt, are twisted thereby into almost inhumanly strange attitudes, and in Flem the grotesque eclipses the human. When such evil is traced to its source, it seems to rise out of nature itself, grossly atavistic and unamenable, as in all the Snopeses, the life process at its most alarmingly mutative, until to judge the species by the sport would be to see man as Stevenson's "disease of the agglutinated dust." But Faulkner does not imply even any such momentary surrender to a sense of overwhelming corruption. While the Snopeses confirm Mrs. Moore's vision at Malabar of something "snub-nosed, incapable of generosity—the undying worm itself," many of Faulkner's commoners are sound and honorable, and for him the cosmos is still the stage of a running battle between darkness and light, neither of them illusory. Yet in such an evenly matched fight, there is much mutually impelled awkwardness. If Faulkner's wrongdoers are particularly distorted by their obsessions, those who resist them are forced to complementary extremes. The resultant grotesqueness in Faulkner's fiction can scarcely be read as mere expedient melodrama; it is rather the shadowing-forth of a realistic world-view, with a conviction integrated against prevalent vulgarities, indifference, inequities, and aggression.

Linda becomes the chief case in point. Widowed and deafened in Spain in the ideologically most crucial of modern wars, with her quacking voice and the tablet for Gavin to write on, living with Flem her not-father in his ill-gotten mansion, in a suspension of her womanly life that makes her seem a lady bewitched in an ogre's castle, where she herself turns avenger, she is certainly a figure shadowed and weird. Yet she has a basic reality, in her own fate and as to its sources. She is companion to other quite different Faulkner figures, all portrayed with similarly extreme strokes — to the poor-white, abused, laconically enduring Mrs. Armstid of *The Hamlet;* to Joanna Burden of *Light in August,* the racked victim of history, heredity, repression, and chance; and to Eula, Linda's mother, bartered to Flem in *The Hamlet* and caught in *The Town,* between an illicit passion and maternal love and driven to suicide. Strangeness in these women is the scar inflicted by external evil; similarly Linda, for all her grotesqueness, is universalized as victim. It is a tortuous path she follows from a Greenwich Village love affair through injurious war to soiling manual labor in a wartime shipyard and a return to loneliness in her nominal home, but in all that she is so vulnerable a woman as to make more basic the indictment against typically afflictive circumstance.

Seen in context, the darkly shaded grotesquerie in Faulkner's works is neither obscuration nor clap-trap, as impercipients have accused him of — sometimes in stubborn persistence, clinging to the end of a limb gone out on. Even at its most intense and extreme it is for thematic emphasis, by those main bold lines which as in caricature bound the concept at its limits and thereby starkly contain basic implication. Neither is Faulkner the calculating virtuoso of symbolism some loftier criticism alleges. In his hands the grotesque becomes means of a searching realism, corresponding vividly to the central fact that evil conduct born of obsessions distorts the natural and defeats the human potential, with the corollary that even at its best, in resisting evil, right intention can fall short, into the partial, the inadequate, the preposterous. As grotesqueness carries over into resistance of the exaggerated forms evil takes, the crusades of Faulkner's champions become a series of sallies afoot, and virtually barehanded, so to speak, but this too is realism. Where find the complete and proper champion, this side of romantic melodrama? It takes Gavin Stevens, V. K. Ratliff, and Charles Mallison as a vigilant committee, and even so they often fumble, Gavin most of all, since although most experienced he is also made susceptible by being most personally and sensitively concerned. Yet despite their inescapable human fallibility, how can such thinking-feeling men refuse to oppose the enemies of propriety and wholesomeness and to aid the victims of such enmity? And how close the mind against inquiry for the definition of principle and that means of grace, an ideal purpose? It is in these terms of civilized man's running battle with fate and his worse fellows, as a common and continuous ordeal, that Faulkner's spectator-interventionists have their being; consequently in them too eccentricity implies a center, as in all his characters aberration becomes the negative definition of the norm, in a whole creation which groans and travails.

A brooding over experience itself, turning around and about the event, has always been a main mode of Faulkner's art, being his mind's way and core of his temperament. It may seem to point toward a more particular question of extravagance. Not necessarily as to the action itself and its somber rendition, however; the recurrent nightmare aspect of life in Yoknapatawpha County is no more appalling than a present reality of which many are sufficiently conscious to have bad dreams about it, and to wake to find the fact of the matter more terrifying and more baffling than the dream. If Faulkner is extravagant, perhaps it is rather in endowing many different well-intentioned characters not only with percipience but with a flair for expressing it ironically. A reserved judgment seems called for. Just as it would take a sentimentalist wearing glasses of deepest rose to deny the reality of that distorting malevolence Faulkner has depicted in many guises, so it would be a bold cynic who would assert that people aren't as discerning and also calmly wry-voiced as Faulkner makes so many of them. Exaggeration or not, in its way it is the most hopeful thing Faulkner has said about the South, or about his larger subject, humanity.

Its epitome is Ratliff, the indigenous, ubiquitous, wily, and detached, manifesting undemonstratively his humane outlook, "quizzical, speculative, but not bemused." He stands at the center of a scale, with Mink Snopes at one end in his sharp sarcastic retorts to Houston, and at the other extreme Gavin Stevens, with his informed intelligence, his gallant disinterestedness, and what Ratliff terms a "simple natural normal anguish," comprehending everything from the materialistic flabbiness of American democracy to the pathos of adolescent girls flowering in a town and a world that will not sufficiently cherish them — and with Gavin himself summing up an aspect of modernity, the rational and impulsive being so mixed in him as to provoke his irony at the expense of his own unrest. Charles too has mastered this idiom of outlook and mood, though he speaks it with his own accent. So do minor characters, such as the Warden at Parchman. Such irony manifests a competence to deal with the multiple and the incongruous, and not to be utterly confused by it, much less disconcerted, and this peculiar wryness suggests an aplomb that without detracting from dramatic urgency keeps perspectives wide.

Yet the actors' irony, even as a servicable artifice and a pervasive tone making for aesthetic unity, is not all. The voices have their master, and they exist within his personal vision of the human condition, in an evoked climate more than county-

wide. Faulkner's creative dominance has been hitherto dis-
approved by some, but this perhaps comes of giving too much
weight to certain restrictive conventions in current fiction. In
a larger view one sees how in the arts magnitude always casts
its recognizable shadow, how unmistakable is the thumbprint,
the slant of the script (Faulkner's, like Mr. Compson's, "sloped
whimsical ironic hand out of Mississippi attenuated"), and
how mystically omnipresent a potent artist is in any world and
work of his own making. Hitherto the idiosyncratic stamp of
temperament upon major creations has not only been noted
but valued, *sui generis* — in Milton or Hopkins, Rembrandt or
Matisse, Beethoven or Delius, Shakespeare or Molière, Jane
Austen or Thomas Mann. Every name evokes a style, but
behind style a choice of matter, and behind that selection an
imperiously originative personality. Since the fictionist or dramatist bequeaths to the deserving children of his mind his
most precious holdings, his tastes and attitudes and even the
images of their formulation, it is not surprising if Faulkner is
detectable in Mink's perception of old Ike McCaslin's integrity: "He has done spent too much time in the woods with deer
and bears and panthers that either they are or they aint, right
quick and now and no shades between. He wont know how to
believe a lie even if I could tell him one." It is as plainly
Faulkner behind Gavin's diatribe: "That one already in Italy
and one a damned sight more dangerous in Germany because
all Mussolini has to work with are Italians while this other man
has Germans. And the one in Spain that all he needs is to be
let alone a little longer by the rest of us who still believe that if
we just keep our eyes closed long enough it will all go away."
This too will be allowed as fiction by anyone who has not
closed his eyes and hoped apprehensive men like Gavin Stevens
would go away; there indeed are those who are more acutely
conscious of our terrifying one world than of the local
weather, and the dramatization of their concern, the vocaliza-
tion of their anguish, is a function of realistic art.

More importantly, though, and beyond such occasional
emergence of abstractions, Faulkner's creation is per-

meated by the spirit in which he has seized upon his concepts, a concern so ardent that it impregnates the whole work
aesthetically and exists as an emanation from it. In *The
Mansion* such an atmosphere, as generated by a rare force of
imagination, and extending to the grotesque, is to be chiefly
felt as of the two disparate and differently realized figures,
Linda and Mink. Linda is seen from three main angles,
through Gavin, Ratliff, and Charles, and also in refractions
produced by their views of each other's views, sometimes in
dialogue, sometimes in their subjectively centered first-person
recapitulations. The resultant picture of her, a genuine grotesque, is a faceted, almost fractured representation, like a
Picasso multiple-profile face. Just as in the Picasso there is a
transcendence of the restriction to any one view, so in
Faulkner's study of Linda by three interlocutors there is no
diminishing reduction to an isolated aspect; rather she appears instantly in all the contiguous mortal dimensions of time
and her total conditionings by heredity and by past and
present circumstance. It is a remarkable execution so to have
suspended the sense of a whole life of one who could be said
scarcely to have had a moment to herself apart from her rôle
as victim. That what repeatedly victimizes Linda is aggression,
whether in personal, social, or ideological terms, makes her a
main figure in Faulkner's development of theme. That she is
preserved for the reader less by her own assertions (drastic as
some of them are) than through the individualized concern of
a trio of commentators (one of them also a devoted aide)
makes *The Mansion* a further expression of Faulkner's own
moral conviction through his faith in its presence in personalities as various as Gavin, Ratliff, and Charles. That the
grotesque, intensified by severally overlaid points of view, is
made to enhance the essence of an authentic and representative subject is a particular aesthetic triumph. That the
presentation of Linda is quite different from that of Mink, as
both differ from the setting-forth of Flem, shows not only
Faulkner's technical command but his faithfulness to the
variety of persons and events themselves, multiplied almost

infinitely by the ways they impinge and thus complicate situation and experience.

This complex reality is not abstracted or attenuated; it is dramatized in sharply illuminative scenes. Faulkner's fiction, like most great narrative and dramatic works, turns upon epiphanal moments, when crucial realization is precipitated out of the circumstantial flux. This may be an objective manifestation to the reader, as when Flem at the conclusion of *The Hamlet,* having glanced at his latest victim, the deceived and besotted Armstid digging for buried money at Frenchman's Bend, "spat over the wagon wheel" and "jerked the reins slightly," on his way to Jefferson out of the rural community he had thoroughly exploited. The epiphany may be subjective, an inclusive vision like Hightower's reverie in "the final copper light of afternoon." Scarcely anywhere, however, has Faulkner represented a character's more complicated and poignant experience than Gavin Stevens' final view of Linda and his connection with her, and never has Faulkner offered the reader a revelation with a more reticent yet richly implicative art, or a more subtle transmuting of the grotesque into the pathetic.

Gavin had not only defended young Linda's faith as well as he could; he had sought to preserve certain illusions of his own about her. As a man both worldly-wise and aware of faults in his own society, he is not shaken by her uncertified alliance with Kohl or her passing involvement with Communist politics, seeing all this as a youthful quest for the dream, and seeking only to protect Linda from local animosities. So when Linda asks that Mink's release be advanced two years by a pardon, Gavin tries to think of her as merely merciful, and to promote the understanding that Mink is to have his freedom and a quarterly remittance on condition that he leave Mississippi at once and stay away. Ratliff, while the pardon is being arranged and then after Mink, released, has disappeared, plagues Gavin with hints that Linda knows what Mink will do and wants it done. Then after Mink has shot Flem (and as the reader has seen, Linda has handed him the pistol he dropped and has directed him to the door for escape) Gavin discovers that Linda's order for the foreign car she leaves Jefferson in had been placed as soon as Mink's pardon was assured. Thus when Ratliff suggests Linda brought about Mink's release to avoid her mother's reproaches in heaven for not having seen vengeance done upon Flem, Gavin can say nothing, and his tears are indicated only by Ratliff's handing him a clean handkerchief, just as he had done earlier, in *The Town,* after Eula's burial.

The nature of Gavin's latest grief, undefined, is to be sensed from its sources in the trilogy. His is no mere conventional regret or shock that the cherished Linda has been accessory before the fact of a murder and has similarly involved him. It seems rather a lament for all that Linda has been through, and he with her, the loss and grief and ghastly wrongs endured with that fortitude which is also a numbing, perhaps a hardening, and above all a distortion; what Linda is driven to mirrors what it has been like for her to have been so driven. Thus the grotesque becomes the pathetic; the absurd is lifted to the level of the tragic by humane regret. *Sunt lacrimae rerum* — except as such Gavin Stevens' undescribed tears are indescribable, and as such they resemble those which Byron Bunch sees run like sweat down the cheeks of Hightower when he was burdened with the woes of Joe Christmas and his grandmother; Gavin's tears are like Dilsey's in the Negro church on Easter morning, sliding "down her fallen cheeks, in and out of the myriad coruscations of immolation and abnegation and time," and continuing unchecked as she walked back to her endless labors for decadent Compsons she chided and pampered; Gavin's tears are like those the retired French Quartermaster General, at the conclusion of *A Fable,* shed over the bloodied but invincible English veteran, also a devotee.

It is concerning Mink, however, that the Faulknerian tone emerges most familiarly, meticulously realistic and boldly intense, and with lingering resonance. All the chapters centered on Mink's struggle with Houston and Flem and impersonal

obstacle are conveyed within the limitations of that wretched
obsessed little man's consciousness, yet made striking by his
pathetically morbid purposefulness and by the grotesque
shadowing-forth of his animal endurance, stealth, and relent-
lessness. Then having seen him through all this with most vivid
narration, Faulkner carries him beyond it and into higher
levels, especially in those passages toward the end where Mink
becomes archetypal in his awareness of the pull of the ground
on a man, "to draw you back down into it," that "power and
drag of the earth" against which womenfolk must support the
infant, "the old patient biding unhurried earth" which even
the strong man napping upon it wakes to find "has already
taken that first light holt on you." This knowledge in Mink as
an old man, after he has murdered Flem and has escaped
westward, lets him feel community at last, knowing his
individual life will "creep, seep, flow easy as sleeping . . . down
and down into the ground already full of the folks that had the
trouble but were free now," and he, Mink (as Faulkner will
put it, pausing sometimes thus to name the individual in his
mysterious and moving uniqueness) to be "himself among
them, equal to any, good as any, brave as any, being inextricable from, anonymous with all of them."

With those polysyllables the narration has transcended
Mink's powers, and now the style rises in a characterization,
like a great crowded Renaissance painting, of "all of them" as
"the beautiful, the splendid, the proud and the brave, right on
up to the very top itself among the shining phantoms and
dreams which are the milestones of the long human recording
— Helen and the bishops, the kings and the unhomed angels,
the scornful and graceless seraphim." Those last two adjectives
(an imaging not unlike Fra Lippo Lippi's winged urchins),
with their enlarging touch of the grotesque, bring Faulkner's
whole subject into view, apprehending the ineffable within the
bounds of human imagination. Thus Faulkner may allow one
Snopes, little ignorant Mink, vengeful murderer by a primitive
code, to approach the fringe of such a glorious company, to be
judged with compassion under the common law of life as

ordeal, endured in representative human terms. Mink, though abandoned, exposed, and blind to much, is no Oedupus, setting out at last alone and august; he has been tricked and betrayed and retaliates according to his convictions, but he is no Hamlet, neither such a gentleman nor so much a doubter, being not only the lowliest of commoners but with no faithful friend, and certainly not destined to burial with honors. Neither is Mink the statistically monumental, ideologically glamorized common man ground down by villainous capitalism, though he has existed on the economic margin and in no little bitterness of heart about it. He too is simply and impressively one of those whom Hightower elegized, along with Joe Christmas, when he said, "Poor man. Poor mankind."

Mink of *The Mansion* will no doubt be generally recognized as one of Faulkner's major characterizations; the particular nature of the achievement deserves notice, as one facet of Faulkner's technique. It is something for Mink to have promoted himself into a sense of belonging, if only to the kingdom of the dead, by little but a long stretch of penal servitude bounded by two murders. The point is that just as it took him a lifetime to reach this moment of vision and identification, so by Faulkner's great skill Mink has been seen all along more and more clearly, cumulatively revealed, less in his own growth than growing upon the spectator, who is called to a role of insight and empathy. Conversely with the mature Linda of *The Mansion* a more complex character is nevertheless more promptly approximated, in the intuitions of the three who watch and aid, and who read her implicit fate in a web of circumstance stretching out from Jefferson to the fields of Spain. If with Flem's death she emancipates herself from mansion and town, it is into a world to which she is still deafened, so that she still exists in a tragic suspension, a woman prematurely superannuated by a society not good enough for the goodness she had seemed capable of. Mink, appearing more directly in immediate event and in his simple accommodations thereto, is discovered with a comprehension and a pathos gradually deepening. With him, the simple is found subtle; with Linda the complex is given salience. By diverse methods Faulkner rounds out the fictional composition, upon which he throws added lights from respective angles through a trio of ironic commentators who all play the representative human rôles of concern and response. It is a protean practice, but it is bound up in terms of two elements envisaged as universals—the ubiquity and persistence of evil, and the innate tendency in many men to resist it, often themselves skeptically and even grotesquely, but with a slight edge, so far, and no disposition yet to give over, though a complete congruity remains out of reach.

In the perspectives extended by the completion of Faulkner's trilogy, his achievement looms larger than ever as a triumph of realism, through an art drawing on traditional modes—epic concept, dramatic chorus, and fictional penetration of the subjective within a chronicle—yet also an art of unique intent and devices, sounding resonantly its personal tone, disclosing the actual through the grotesque, and authenticating the humanly representative by provincial instance acutely specified. Genuinely a Southern writer by breeding and commitment, Faulkner has nevertheless always been more than regionalist. It illuminates a range of literary and cultural history in America and also gives some measure of Faulkner's magnitude to note him uncontainable in anything like a New Englander's parochialism or a Westerner's camp too isolated in space and time, and to see how far he stands above other contemporary fictionists concerned with American society—the superficial and morbidly rancorous Sinclair Lewis, Dos Passos the thoughtful student but plodding documentarian, Steinbeck keenly observant but of unsteady conscience subject to anarchistic sentimentality. By Faulkner's masculine vitality and tremendous productivity and also by the range of each of his novels he is set above his two most excellent contemporaries in the sheer art of fiction, Katherine Anne Porter and Eudora Welty. One is turned back to *Huckleberry Finn* for something comparable as vision and performance, and in mirroring a regional society Mark Twain had the advantage of a simpler epoch, a picaresque procedure, and an easier containment in a juvenile point of view and in Huck's comparative detachment, reiterated at the end. (Contrast this with young Chick Mallison's involvement in *Intruder in the Dust,* where his dilemma and choice resemble Huck's but foreshadow Charles' permanent adult commitment — or with Bayard's lengthy progress, in *The Unvanquished,* from child's play to precocious violence to searing renunciation.) The broad stage of Yoknapatawpha County, the full cast of the novels *in toto,* the crucial conflicts in multiplied instances give an impressive sense of man in society, but without reduction to sociological thesis, and the characters, arrested as of that ghostly aspect Faulkner's art so tellingly captures, are yet seen in their habits as they lived and live, their idiosyncrasies aspects of a reality both personal and abstract, the grotesque an actuality born of stress, the absurd made not only credible but open to confrontation.

It all depends, however, upon immediacy, verisimilitude, singularity, and force of characterization. This, joined to a sustained sense of socio-ethical import and given wide narrative range, enables Faulkner to make a dramatic action of reaction and to represent tentative consciousness, deeply self-aware and even self-beset, as nevertheless primarily responsive to external event and moved to a part in it. In this response judicious reflection, ardent feeling, and active assertion are intricately reciprocal, and bound by a containing mood to represent temperament. With Faulkner's characters the formation of attitude as a process in itself is no mere preliminary to the real story, or something to be disposed of summarily. He does not follow that American naturalism which allows the narrowest social science to define man for it as a structure of conditioned reflexes and the creature of external determinants, reducing action to that of puppets or pawns, with no logic of motive and indeed no very clear glimpse of the mover's hand. Faulkner rises to a genuine realism which not only documents events and searches motives but celebrates the saving mystery of men's innate urge to postulate values and to react in terms of these evaluations, in resistance to devaluation and in successive corrections of their own eccentricities. If Snopesism is object, response to it is subject, and if besides the trio of chief respondents in *The Mansion* two Snopseses figure — Montgomery Ward the remorseful betrayer and Mink the intent avenger — it is so that evolution of attitude precedent to emerging action may be more widely traced, in a realization of man alive, by a scrutiny of "poor man" extended to embrace "poor mankind." Realism, for Faulkner, thus has its roots in what he speaks of as "the human heart and its dilemma."

If Faulkner does not make a set naturalistic pattern the measure for all mankind, neither does he pause too long in the back eddies of a self-examining stream of consciousness. Proceeding from "as a man thinketh, so is he" to the corollary "so acts he," the Faulkner narrative implies that concepts, bred between temperament and circumstance, have consequences, and it is out of the human heart that human behavior proceeds, to be echoed again in consciousness and so to issue realigned as further assertion. Not the least part of Faulkner's achievement is his aesthetic synthesis of motive rising our of reactive process to take overt form, with the effect moving to the pulse and breath of attitude deeply grounded and, above all, continuously reconstituted, ever tentative, usually partial and often even eccentric, but always operative. Here would seem to be a crux for Faulkner criticism — the adequate assessment of his presentation of this existential reality, this sustained sense of being in the process of becoming what it instantly is in terms of a response at once subjective and effective, yet never resting in itself or its result, since it is constituted in a continuum both psychological and external, from which it derives and to which it contributes, becoming the past to create a further present yet still to flow in upon it and be itself modified by modifying. Perhaps more than anything else it is this persuasively fictional representation of action rooted in reaction and returning upon it which makes Faulkner's many-faceted and massive realism so peculiarly impressive.

As a phase of Faulkner's conceptual and stylistic practice the grotesque, so conspicuously and powerfully employed, is therefore no fad or flourish but is made the special means of encompassing that perennial reality currently termed the existential absurd. Fictional tradition appears here too, and connections with Dickens may be remarked, as to a sociological focus, and with Conrad, in his ethical probings; in both of these writers grotesqueness, which a careless view might dismiss as exuberance if not affectation, may be seen as the studied aesthetic means of a serious art, responsible to interactive character and circumstance, and so too with Faulkner. A more immediate predecessor in the tradition was Sherwood Anderson, who had made the grotesque a book's theme and pictured in his Winesburg folk not only the distorting effects of obsession but some of its roots in societal and personal inadequacies. However, in Faulkner what lies deeper than any theme is temperament—his own almost pained sensitivity to the specter-shadows frequently cast by men's most determined efforts, so that the more explicit an intention (whether Flem's, Mink's, Linda's, or Gavin's, for instance) the greater its liability to exaggeration, until the comic discrepant swells into what may be the ominous or even the terrifying. Thus Faulkner's grotesquerie goes beyond caricature, which (as typified by the political cartoon wielding the well-ground ax) is seldom disinterestedly comprehensive and almost never compassionate. The element of pathos differentiates Faulkner's grotesques also from pure comedy with its surface satire and unemotive wit. Yet while the grotesque throughout Faulkner's work is with artistic propriety more a matter of dominant creative mood than formalized thesis, it must be recognized too upon its large conceptual grounds and not mistaken for expedient gimmick or self-indulgent mannerism. It is best seen as some aspect of the truth writ very large, like the magnified shadow of a common object, somewhat distorted but mainly a massive correspondence, gaining force by an immense looming simplification. (Again the aesthetic resemblance to some modern painting is evident.) Every leading character in the Snopes saga casts such a silhouette, and so does every main trend of intention, whether Flem's animal acquisitiveness or Gavin's quixotic intervention or whatever else between. Indeed Faulkner seldom brings even the most minor character into view without some touch of the grotesque, often to a humorous extreme, but not so much for nominal identification as to give an immediate sense of unique human entity, solitary in its concerned consciousness of self and externality and in its intent self-assertion as of the moment, prey to its own exaggerations and yet warily adaptive, no matter how quaint and even ludicrous its tactics.

In his great and indeed noble seriousness Faulkner can be funny too, and knows it, and thinks enough of it to have given Phil Stone credit for doing "half the laughing." This is no anomaly, since the comic as Faulkner sees it is a facet, not a separable detail, of the totality which includes the tragic. One plainly recurrent but always freshly manifested quality, Faulkner's very hallmark, is what might be called opalescence, that immediate conceptual merging and fluid aesthetic mingling of the diverse and even the antithetical, achieving in fiction a genuine, sustained tragicomic mode. (In the fourth part of *The Hamlet* is a clear example, the pages describing the sale of wild horses, stubborn Henry Armstid's brutality to his wife and his injury in the stampede, and Varner's coming to tend him with his veterinary's bag; there is the rich surrealistic imagery of the milling horses, the violent humor of mishap sobered by serious accident, the shadow of Flem as exploiter falling most sharply upon Mrs. Armstid, Ratliff's wryly amused consciousness of his own discomfiture, and Varner's rustic vulgarity under the moon that beautifully silvers the pear tree where the mockingbird sings, with the injured man's groan's eliciting Varner's folk-epigram — "Breathing is a sight-draft dated yesterday.") Such opalescence is found in *The Mansion* too, if anything more pervasive than in the trilogy's earlier sections, while also less marked, the method refined to a golden mean, the antithetical modes deeply interfused. With

Faulkner the comic is not a relaxing interlude to make way for a renewed tensing in pity and terror; it is rather the lighter side of the grotesque, almost a picturesqueness of the absurd, with humor the regulative medium of both judgment and compassion. Thus there are thematically relevant points to all the jests, recurrent irony frames event in the perspective of detachment, and even slapstick episode wears the aura of anarchic folly as its darker abstraction.

Thomas Mann (as William Van O'Connor recently pointed out) cited the grotesque, in its fusion of tragic and comic modes, as modern art's "most genuine style" and "the only guise in which the sublime may appear." Mann's further statement that "the comic-grotesque" has always been the "strong point" of Anglo-Saxon art prompts recognition that the grotesque embodies the tragic as well, and particularly with Faulkner. That herein is a profoundly right intention toward a more organic art, and an art more responsible to reality, should be evident. The formula that life is a comedy to those who think, a tragedy to those who feel, would be definitive if there were such human categories, but man both thinks and feels and his thoughts and feelings in their complications may be matters for either laughter or tears and sometimes both. This total reality, comprising extremes and antitheses, strains the individual in his striving for comprehension and admits the liability to distortion, so that the grotesque emerges in dark profile against the illuminating ideal. It becomes the fictionist's task and privilege to represent tragicomic reality as a whole, indivisible and irreducible without loss of essence.

Therefore it may become a function of realism to allow certain fictional characters an ironic perception comparable to the fictionist's own and to that presupposed in other men of good will and anxious mind. Irony thus employed in fiction can encompass the grotesque with a peculiar force, by mirroring the mode of the thing confronted, meeting the inordinate in its own terms yet without surrender. Thus Ratliff repeatedly will pinpoint the outrageous by an extreme understatement, and Gavin will suggest the scrupulousness of his evaluations by giving full play to exaggerated fancies, until their incredibility becomes a foil to the veracious. Irony can thus be an ideal regulative mode, implying a human competence without heroics, a conviction principled and ardent enough to coexist with tentativeness and even skepticism, and a reassuring detachment. By its acceptance of "the human heart's dilemma" irony rises to fortitude, equalizes judicious perspective and concerned involvement, and expresses the tragicomic through an organic work of art that does not minimize the inextricable tangle of life, nor on the other hand deny those configurations of meaning in vindication of values which men are capable of conceiving and partially enacting.

Such is Faulkner's vision of reality, and he has made his rhetoric ample for the aesthetic expression of it. That rhetoric, the total stylistic and narrative strategy, while rooted in conventions, is in the main even more original than the vision. In both is the free play of intuition, and the two interpermeate as immediate sensibility and conceptual power in an imagination meriting the supreme epithet, Shakespearian. Indeed, in one way Faulkner surpasses the Elizabethans and the fictionists who in their wake have also essayed the tragicomic. He has come closer to comprising the matter whole, tragicomedy unhyphenated. "This t., called life 1649" — thus the O.E.D. cites the term, and thus three centuries later Faulkner has glimpsed a present reality and reviewed it for the reader. Consequently the dense texture, the antithetical stresses, the progressive realignments of past and present, and the structural counterpoint. Hence the opalescent surface, its colors changed with shifting points of view, but its details never extracted from the total reality, its meanings never oversimplified by isolation from their constantly and multifariously qualifying context. To look into the mansion is to look out upon the town and back to the hamlet — and beyond. Moreover, the real presence of the past, its continuous refraction and reconstitution by event, the natural human glance forward and impetus into the future, and the continuum of a remembering, responsive consciousness stretched taut between extremes yet making its assertions—all this is what Faulkner renders.

The first marvel is the encompassing vision, the sheer conceptual containment. The second and not lesser marvel is its rendition, not by abstraction but by recreation of this reality as known to living breathing men going their ways wryly, with laughter and tears, but onward, under their author's announced belief that "living is motion" and his artistic sense that such motion should be rendered with something of its accumulated thrust, its immediate and transcendent complexity, and its inexorable effective continuation. Faulkner's creations form themselves under this aspect, which if not of eternity at least is of the ideal as Santayana defined it, as "a function of reality." His art moves to the pulses of time as a condition of human existence, but is also true to the mind's ranging powers and all that looking before and after which reaps hope and grief and man's acceptance of grief for the sake of hope.

12

Told with Gusto

THE REIVERS is an intricately plotted, pell-mell story, figuring the theft of an automobile and a horse and the fixing of a horse race, and displaying, besides its principals, such gamy items as a corrupt deputy sheriff, Memphis prostitutes, and an utterly delinquent juvenile from Arkansas; it is also, in the Faulknerian mode, a highly moral tale. Told retrospectively in first person with unabated natural human gusto for the outrageous, it expresses as well an awareness of consciousness and conscience in many sorts of persons, variously situated. In typical Faulknerian vein it adumbrates, behind elaborations of behavior, even more extreme complexities of motive and fluidity of mood. The novel abounds in sin and — being the work of a complete realist — in sentiment. Some, no doubt, will read one side of the coin and neglect or else condemn the other. But that has always been Faulkner's fate, which plainly he has surived.

What this book may encounter is a supercilious latter-day depreciation as the benign foolery of an elder citizen — whether Grandfather Priest, the reminiscent narrator, or Faulkner himself, grandfather and chief of American fiction. *The Reivers* merits recognition for a true virtuosity that combines exuberance, implicativeness, and commitment, as a narrative wherein humor and wit spring from judicious in-

This essay first appeared in *The Virginia Quarterly Review,* Autumn 1962, pp. 681-85.

sight, in a nice fusion of value judgments and hearty tolerant interest. The funniest stories are always the most pointed ones, and they most require a conceptually oriented perspective for their appreciation. Read with such acknowledgment, *The Reivers* may be found a substantial work, significant in the Faulkner canon.

Connections are not lacking. Some scenes are in Miss Reba's Memphis bordello, with a glimpse of the Mr. Binford lamented in *Sanctuary*. The anecdotal opening, which primarily introduces thematic elements in burlesque guise, shows Boon Hogganbeck of "The Bear," here too a main character, still an incredibly bad marksman. He is also an intensely passionate man, as enamored of his employer's automobile ("this was 1905") as he was devoted to the great dog Lion. More important than connections are parallels, especially with *Intruder in the Dust* as well as "The Bear," for *The Reivers* too tells of a boy's maturation, accelerated by acquaintance with a sagacious, self-possessed Negro.

Parallels with *Huckleberry Finn* are conspicuous, in a picaresque progress through eye-opening encounters with idiosyncratic folk. A basic difference is more significant; Huck is a well-scarred waif, of disreputable parentage, whereas well-fostered eleven-year-old Lucius Priest lapses from social status and family regimen, and while Huck lives by solitary empirical assertions, whether against his father or Mississippi valley society or Tom Sawyer, Lucius — after conniving in what Huck would have called borrowing his grandfather's automobile — faces up to the whorehouse and racetrack worlds by the code of a gentleman.

Indeed, the word recurs pointedly, though with no sense of caste or taint of snobbish pretense. It suggests the essence of the social, a mutual reckoning and regard, as in the tacit assumption between Lucius' father and the Negro hostler John Powell that John's prized pistol would be kept out of sight, mention, or use at the stable; and in such matters of conduct agreed and depended upon, John (as Grandfather recollects it) "was a gentleman." The rough, childish Boon recognizes a rule of reciprocal assent, letting the boy drive the automobile to "seduce" him into conspiracy, and thereby beating him "in fair battle, using, as a gentleman should and would, gloves." When the incorrigible Otis calls Ned nigger, Lucius remembers his grandfather's teaching that "no gentleman ever referred to anyone by his race or religion." Finally Lucius' grandfather, bringing the boy to judgment for his escapade, says, "A gentleman accepts the responsibility of his actions and bears the burden of their consequences," and adds more specifically that "A gentleman cries too, but he always washes his face."

Lucius' tears are not just the ready penance of a caught culprit but an overflow from the four-day adventure become ordeal, his "having to learn too much too fast, unassisted," especially of "non-virtue's" awful potency while the devotees of Virtue must depend besides on "luck." Yet the boy has acted, and not just in providing strategy for Boon's making away with the automobile, nor in winning the horse race under Ned's direction; enraged at Otis' vileness concerning the beset prostitute Corrie, he attacks the older boy, and his defense of her revives Corrie's self-esteem. Her reformation and marriage to Boon may be disparaged as facile sentimentality, but that implies denial of the way common vital people break through adverse circumstance into idealistic assertion, and thus "endure." It is to this basic human quality quite as much as to the concept of gentleman that the ethos of Faulkner's new novel is keyed.

This is most subtly shown (and strikingly too in dénouement) through Ned, the Priests' middle-aged coachman, a never-daunted, wily, wry-spoken Negro, stowaway in the back seat on the Memphis expedition. When he trades automobile for horse, it seems irresponsible caprice until a gentlemen's court of inquiry finds that Ned in his mysterious ways has performed wonders to extricate a young Jefferson-born Negro from a white blackmailer. Like his creator, Ned is a fantastic improviser with an unshakable sense of fact; a principled opportunist, determinedly aligned on the side of the angels, he gets here by the long way around, yet with full effect.

As Grandfather Lucius Priest's deliberate "reminiscence" concerning a too-crowded and crucial period in his twelfth year, *The Reivers* has qualities typical of recollection in old age, a sharpness of detail but under an abstracting light. Sometimes the tone is like Huck's in its boyish immediacy:

> Then there was all the spring darkness: the big bass-talking frogs from the sloughs, the sound that the woods makes, the big woods, the wilderness with the wild things: coons and rabbits and mink and mushrats and the big owls and the big snakes — moccasins and rattlers — and maybe even the trees breathing and the river itself breathing, not to mention the ghosts — the old Chicasaws who named the land before the white men ever saw it, and the white men afterward. . . .

Sometimes though not so often the old man, envisaging no less clearly but more impressionistically, voices the Old Master, as on pulling the automobile out of a mud-hole by mule-team:

> There was something dreamlike about it. Not nightmarish: just dreamlike — the peaceful, quiet, remote, sylvan, almost primeval setting of ooze and slime and jungle growth and heat in which the very mules themselves, peacefully swishing and stamping at the teeming infinitesmal invisible myriad life which was the actual air we moved and breathed in, were not only unalien but in fact curiously appropriate, being themselves biological dead ends and hence already obsolete before they were born; the automobile: the expensive useless mechanical toy rated in power and strength by the dozens of horses, yet held helpless and impotent in the almost infantile clutch of a few inches of the temporary confederation of two mild and pacific elements — earth and water. . . .

and so on. Yet it all enters fluently into composition. There is real antiphony between the recalled rush of action, with all the drive and quick elliptical talk of the unforgettable characters, and the prolonged musings, in the perspectives of a lifetime, over the essence of events once so keenly sensed and now so deeply reassessed. What the boy felt the old man now defines, chorus to his own drama. It is a not uncommon fictional procedure, but Faulkner has used it uncommonly well. The alternations are not interruptive but responsive and complementary, the two periods and levels of experience are made real, each in its kind, and the modulations between them are part of a spontaneous continuum of remembering as act revived.

It is thus that the grotesqueries of this tall tale can comprise raucousness, kindliness, vulgarity, gentility, brutality, manly honor, passion and poise, the impulsive and the meditative, comic exuberance and *lacrimae rerum,* while embracing it all is the felt sense of life, dynamic in all the characters, who whatever else they may be are never indifferent, never enervated, never wholly lost or beat—not even an eleven-year-old boy in a crude and tricky world he was unprepared for, not even an old man, recollecting the irrevocable and relishing its evocation even as he judges it and himself in it.